T0135175

IFIP Advances in Information and Communication Technology 659

Editor-in-Chief

Kai Rannenberg, Goethe University Frankfurt, Germany

Editorial Board Members

IFIP – The International Federation for Information Processing

IFIP was founded in 1960 under the auspices of UNESCO, following the first World Computer Congress held in Paris the previous year. A federation for societies working in information processing, IFIP's aim is two-fold: to support information processing in the countries of its members and to encourage technology transfer to developing nations. As its mission statement clearly states:

IFIP is the global non-profit federation of societies of ICT professionals that aims at achieving a worldwide professional and socially responsible development and application of information and communication technologies.

IFIP is a non-profit-making organization, run almost solely by 2500 volunteers. It operates through a number of technical committees and working groups, which organize events and publications. IFIP's events range from large international open conferences to working conferences and local seminars.

The flagship event is the IFIP World Computer Congress, at which both invited and contributed papers are presented. Contributed papers are rigorously refereed and the rejection rate is high.

As with the Congress, participation in the open conferences is open to all and papers may be invited or submitted. Again, submitted papers are stringently refereed.

The working conferences are structured differently. They are usually run by a working group and attendance is generally smaller and occasionally by invitation only. Their purpose is to create an atmosphere conducive to innovation and development. Refereeing is also rigorous and papers are subjected to extensive group discussion.

Publications arising from IFIP events vary. The papers presented at the IFIP World Computer Congress and at open conferences are published as conference proceedings, while the results of the working conferences are often published as collections of selected and edited papers.

IFIP distinguishes three types of institutional membership: Country Representative Members, Members at Large, and Associate Members. The type of organization that can apply for membership is a wide variety and includes national or international societies of individual computer scientists/ICT professionals, associations or federations of such societies, government institutions/government related organizations, national or international research institutes or consortia, universities, academies of sciences, companies, national or international associations or federations of companies.

More information about this series at https://link.springer.com/bookseries/6102

Zhongzhi Shi · Yaochu Jin ·
Xiangrong Zhang (Eds.)

Intelligence Science IV

5th IFIP TC 12 International Conference, ICIS 2022
Xi'an, China, October 28–31, 2022
Proceedings

 Springer

Editors
Zhongzhi Shi
Institute of Computing Technology
Chinese Academy of Sciences
Beijing, China

Yaochu Jin
Department of Computer Science
University of Surrey
Guildford, UK

Xiangrong Zhang
College of Artificial Intelligence
Xidian University
Xi'an, China

ISSN 1868-4238 ISSN 1868-422X (electronic)
IFIP Advances in Information and Communication Technology
ISBN 978-3-031-14905-4 ISBN 978-3-031-14903-0 (eBook)
https://doi.org/10.1007/978-3-031-14903-0

This Springer imprint is published by the registered company Springer Nature Switzerland AG
The registered company address is: Gewerbestrasse 11, 6330 Cham, Switzerland

Preface

This volume comprises the Fifth International Conference on Intelligence Science (ICIS). Artificial intelligence research has made substantial progress in some special areas so far. However, deeper understanding of the essence of intelligence is far from sufficient and, therefore, many state-of-the-art intelligent systems are still not able to compete with human intelligence. To advance the research in artificial intelligence, it is necessary to investigate intelligence, both artificial and natural, in an interdisciplinary context. The objective of this conference is to bring together researchers from brain science, cognitive science, and artificial intelligence to explore the essence of intelligence and the related technologies. The conference provides a platform for discussing some of the key issues that are related to intelligence science.

For ICIS 2022, we received more than 87 papers, of which 44 were included in the program as regular papers and five as short papers. All papers submitted were reviewed by three referees. We are grateful for the dedicated work of both the authors and the referees, and we hope these proceedings will continue to bear fruit over the years to come.

A conference such as this could not succeed without the help of many individuals, who contributed their valuable time and expertise. We want to express our sincere gratitude to the Program Committee members and referees, who invested many hours for reviews and deliberations. They provided detailed and constructive review reports that significantly improved the papers included in the program.

We are very grateful for the sponsorship of the following organizations: the Chinese Association for Artificial Intelligence (CAAI), IFIP TC12, and the China Chapter of the International Society for Studies of Information. ICIS 2022 was organized by Xidian University and the CAAI Intelligence Science Technical Committee, and supported by IFIP TC 12 and the Institute of Computing Technology of the Chinese Academy of Sciences. Thanks go to Biao Hou as chair of Local Organizing Committee. We specially thank Dan Zhang, Junpeng Zhang, Bo Ren, and Weitong Zhang for carefully preparing the proceedings.

Finally, we hope you find this volume inspiring and informative.

July 2022

Zhongzhi Shi
Yaochu Jin
Xiangrong Zhang

Organization

General Chairs

Yixin Zhong   Beijing University of Posts and Telecommunications, China
David B. Leake   Indiana University Bloomington, USA
Licheng Jiao   Xidian University, China

Program Chairs

Zhongzhi Shi   Institute of Computing Technology, CAS, China
Yaochu Jin   University of Surrey, UK
Xiangrong Zhang   Xidian University, China

Program Committee

Cungen Cao   Institute of Computing Technology, CAS, China
Mihir Chakraborty   Jadavpur University, India
Gong Cheng   Northwestern Polytechnical University, China
Wanyang Dai   Nanjing University, China
Sujit Das   NIT Warangal, India
Biao Hou   Xidian University, China
Xiangkui Jiang   Xi'an University of Posts and Telecommunications, China
Licheng Jiao   Xidian University, China
Yaochu Jin   University of Surrey, UK
David B. Leake   Indiana University Bloomington, USA
Chen Li   Xi'an Jiaotong University, China
Qingyong Li   Beijing Jiaotong University, China
Kai Liu   Bohai University, China
Tamás Mihálydeák   University of Debrecen, Hungary
Mikhail Moshkov   King Abdullah University of Science and Technology, Saudi Arabia
Rong Qu   University of Nottingham, UK
Andrzej Skowron   Polish Academy of Sciences and CNT at UKSW, Poland
Shusaku Tsumoto   Shimane University, Japan
Guoyin Wang   Chongqing University of Posts and Telecommunications, China
Pei Wang   Temple University, USA
Qi Wang   Northwestern Polytechnical University, China
Shi Wang   Institute of Computing Technology, CAS, China

Xiaofeng Wang	Shanghai Maritime University, China
Juyang Weng	Michigan State University, USA
Jingzhan Wu	Guangxi Medical University, China
Min Xie	City University of Hong Kong, China
Shuyuan Yang	Xidian University, China
Yiyu Yao	University of Regina, Canada
Hong Yu	Chongqing University of Posts and Telecommunications, China
Dan Zhang	Xidian University, China
Shanshan Zhang	Nanjing University of Science and Technology, China
Xiangrong Zhang	Xidian University, China
Yinsheng Zhang	Institute of Scientific and Technical Information of China, China
Chuan Zhao	Chengdu University of Technology, China
Yixin Zhong	Beijing University of Posts and Telecommunications, China
Huiyu Zhou	University of Leicester, UK
Zhiguo Zhou	University of Kansas Medical Center, USA
Xiaohui Zou	Sino-American Searle Research Center, China

Organization Committee

Chair

Biao Hou	Xidian University, China

Secretary General

Dan Zhang	Xidian University, China

Vice Secretary General

Shi Wang	Chinese Academy of Sciences, China

International Liaison

Sijing Huang	Xidian University, China

Sponsors

Chinese Association for Artificial Intelligence (CAAI)
China Chapter under International Society for Information Studies

Organizers

Xidian University, China
CAAI Intelligent Science Technical Committee (in preparation)

Support

IFIP Technical Committee 12
Institute of Computing Technology, Chinese Academy of Sciences (CAS)

Abstracts of Keynote and Invited Talks

Tactile Situations: A Basis for Manual Intelligence and Learning

Helge Ritter

Center of Cognitive Interaction Technology (CITEC) & Faculty of Technology,
Bielefeld University
helge@techfak.uni-bielefeld.de

Abstract. Intelligence as we see it in humans and some animals appears key to enable agents to cope with situations of high variability. This is still a challenge for AI systems which currently excel in focused domains for which abundant training data is available. To bring these methods to domains such as robotics, where physical interaction is a strong bottleneck for obtaining large data sets, is still a largely unsolved problem. Comparing artificial and natural cognitive agents reveals that the latter are much more capable of generalizing their skills to novel situations - a key capability to learn and act successfully when interaction data are costly and possibly even dangerous to obtain. Therefore, a key challenge for further progress is a better understanding of how a cognitive agent can represent situations with regard to relevance and generalizeability of interaction skills under conditions of data parsimony. While we begin to see encouraging progress on this question when the focus is on the visual modality, actions in the real world require to complement vision with the management of physical contact in order to move the body or even manipulate objects. We argue that this requires to understand how to sense and represent "tactile situations" and point out how these are crucial for shaping physical interactions with the environment and enabling agents to control their hands in a way that exhibits "manual intelligence". We take a look at the challenges that are involved, how representing "tactile situations" needs to cover a hierarchy from low level sensing to high level cognition, and how we can create the necessary touch sensing and processing capabilities for dextrous robot hands. We present examples and results on different situations of tactile learning and action control in robotics contexts and point out ideas about how we can bring together these elements for creating manual intelligence anchored in the combined control of touch and vision. We finally comment on how this research fits with ideas and recent insights about how situations may be represented in the brain, and how connections between robotics and brain science can foster our scientific understanding and help to create better cognitive interaction technology in the future.

Brain-like Perception and Cognition: Challenges and Thinking

Licheng Jiao

School of Artificial Intelligence, Xidian University
lchjiao@mail.xidian.edu.cn

Abstract. The intelligent interpretation of high-resolution remote sensing images is a technological high point that countries all over the world compete for. However, the high-resolution observation requirement brings difficulties to efficient target information acquisition, and the multi-scale singularity, complexity and diversity of targets greatly increase the difficulty of target modeling and target information learning and identification. Visual perception and brain cognition (sparseness, learning, selectivity and directionality) provide ideas for efficient and accurate high-resolution remote sensing image perception and interpretation. Drawing on the mechanism of biological visual cognition and perception, the acquisition (sense), interpretation (knowledge) and application (use) of high-resolution remote sensing information are studied.

Dealing with Concept Drifts in Data Streams

Xin Yao[1,2,3]

[1] Research Institute of Trustworthy Autonomous Systems (RITAS)
[2] Department of Computer Science and Engineering,
Southern University of Science and Technology (SUSTech), Shenzhen, China
[3] CERCIA, School of Computer Science,
University of Birmingham, Birmingham, UK
xiny@sustech.edu.cn

Abstract. One of the major challenges in machine learning is that future testing data are usually different from historical training data. What was learned from the historical data may or may not be appropriate for future data. In online learning of data streams, learned concepts may drift due to changes in underlying data distributions. How to detect and adapt to concept drifts have been an active research topic for many years. Such research has a wide range of real-world applications, e.g., in online fault diagnosis and condition monitoring. First, this talk introduces learning in the model space as an effective approach to deal with changes in data streams. Instead of trying to detect changes in a data stream directly, the approach first learns generative models of the data stream and then detect changes in such a model space. Second, this talk describes an ensemble learning approach, i.e., DDD (Diversity for Dealing with Drifts), to online learning with concept drift, where ensembles with different diversity levels are learned and adapted before and after a drift is detected. The impact of class imbalance is investigated in online learning with concept drift. Class evolution, i.e., class emergence and disappearance, in data streams will be discussed. An ensemble learning method, i.e., Diversity and Transfer-based Ensemble Learning (DTEL), that adapts selected base learners while maintaining ensemble diversity will be mentioned. Finally, the talk presents a Hierarchical Change Detection Test (HCDT) for concept drift detection in data streams. Finally, concluding remarks will be made at the end of the talk.

A Novel Bionic Imaging and Its Intelligent Processing

Guangming Shi

School of Artificial Intelligence, Xidian University
gmshi@xidian.edu.cn

Abstract. To overcome the inconvenience of undesirable imaging quality of traditional cameras under extreme lighting conditions and high-speed motion scenes, the bio-inspired imaging technology, which subverts the information acquisition mode and photoelectric conversion method of traditional imaging system, is researched with an increasingly quickening developing pace. The bionic vision sensor is independent of exposure time and frame rate, which offers attractive properties: high-speed imaging (in the order of μs), very high dynamic range (greater than 100dB), low power consumption. Hence, bionic imaging has a large potential for industrial intelligence manufacturing and intelligent transportation in challenging scenarios with high speed and high dynamic range. The photosensitive chip involved in the imaging technology and the back-end intelligent processing algorithm (e.g., Denoising, Recognition and Reconstruction) are developed by our research group, with a high degree of independent controllability.

Skill Learning in Dynamic Scene for Robot Operations

Fuchun Sun

Department of Computer Science and Technology, Tsinghua University
fcsun@mail.tsinghua.edu.cn

Abstract. The robot AI is dominated by physical interaction in closed-loop form. It not only emphasizes the perception and processing of simulated human brain information, but also emphasizes brain body cooperation to solve the dynamic, interactive and adaptive problems of behavior learning in dynamic scene. As the core of robot AI, skill learning for robot operations is a difficult and hot issue in current research. In view of the problems that the existing skill learning methods do not make use of the teaching samples efficiently and cannot achieve efficient strategy learning, and the imitation learning algorithm is sensitive to the teaching preference characteristics and the local operation space. This talk studies the skill learning for robot operations in the complex dynamic environment, and proposes skill learning framework based on human preference. By using the guidance of the existing poor teaching samples, this talk proposes an optimization method of reinforcement learning based on teaching imitation, which improves the sample utilization rate and strategy learning performance of skill learning in high-dimensional space. Finally, the future development of robot skill learning is prospected.

Emerging Artificial Intelligence Technologies in Healthcare

Huiyu Zhou

School of Computing and Mathematical Sciences, University of Leicester, UK

Abstract. Artificial intelligence has significantly influenced the health sector for years by delivering novel assistive technologies from robotic surgery to versatile biosensors that enable remote diagnosis and efficient treatment. While the COVID-19 pandemic is devastating, the uses of AI in the healthcare sector are dramatically increasing and it is a critical time to look at its impact in different aspects. In this talk, Prof. Zhou will introduce the application of new deep learning models in medical image understanding. Then, he will discuss Parkinson's disease (PD) whilst investigating the behaviour analysis of PD mice. He also presents the use of machine learning technologies in sentiment analysis, followed by the discussion on several challenges.

Memory Cognition

Zhongzhi Shi

Key Laboratory of Intelligent Information Processing, Institute of Computing
Technology, Chinese Academy of Sciences, Beijing 100190, China
shizz@ict.ac.cn

Abstract. Memory is the core cognitive function of human beings. It is one of the most concerned topics in the field of intelligence science and artificial intelligence. Memory is the basis of learning and intelligence. It is the bridge and link between human spiritual activities and intelligent system simulation. With the support of the national 973 projects, we carried out research on memory cognition and put forward mind model CAM, cognitive model on brain computer integration, etc. In this talk, I will focus on mind model CAM, memory classifications and the integration of memory and computing.

Contents

Data Intelligence

Language Cognition

Remote Sensing Images

Perceptual Intelligence

Wireless Sensor

Medical Artificial Intelligence

Brain Cognition

Mouse-Brain Topology Improved Evolutionary Neural Network for Efficient Reinforcement Learning

Xuan Han[1,2], Kebin Jia[1(✉)], and Tielin Zhang[2(✉)]

[1] Beijing University of Technology, Beijing 100124, China
kebinj@bjut.edu.cn
[2] Institute of Automation, Chinese Academy of Sciences, Beijing 100190, China
tielin.zhang@ia.ac.cn

Abstract. The brain structures are key indicators to represent the complexity of many cognitive functions, e.g., visual pathways and memory circuits. Inspired by the topology of the mouse brain provided by the Allen Brain Institute, whereby 213 brain regions are linked as a mesoscale connectome, we propose a mouse-brain topology improved evolutionary neural network (MT-ENN). The MT-ENN model incorporates parts of biologically plausible brain structures after hierarchical clustering, and then is tuned by the evolutionary learning algorithm. Two benchmark Open-AI Mujoco tasks were used to test the performance of the proposed algorithm, and the experimental results showed that the proposed MT-ENN was not only sparser (containing only 61% of all connections), but also performed better than other algorithms, including the ENN using a random network, standard long-short-term memory (LSTM), and multi-layer perception (MLP). We think the biologically plausible structures might contribute more to the further development of artificial neural networks.

Keywords: Evolutionary neural network · Reinforcement learning · Mouse-brain topology

1 Introduction

The mammalian brain has been studied deeply in the past decades. The brain structures are key indicators for representing the learned knowledge from millions of years of evolution in different animals. Like many genetic evolutionary algorithms in machine learning, the biological brain is the best evolutionary outcome in a natural organism. However, it is still an open question whether new network structures copied from natural brains could contribute to the development of artificial neural networks, whereby the design of structures is usually considered more important than neuronal types. At present, the whole mouse brain has been widely examined, which contains around 213 brain regions, and the sparseness of the entire brain is about 36% [5]. Many types of research have been given on the topology of the mouse brain, and one of the most important motivations is copying it to the conventional artificial neural networks (ANNs) for higher performance, or more energy efficiency [6].

Inspired by the biological networks and evolutionary algorithms, we propose a mouse-brain topology improved evolutionary neural network (MT-ENN), which incorporates biologically plausible brain structures and an evolutionary learning algorithm for efficient learning on two benchmark reinforcement learning (RL) tasks. The dynamic neurons contain 1st-order dynamics of membrane potentials supported by some additional key dynamic parameters. Then these neurons are connected by the copied topology from the biological brain and tuned by a global evolutionary algorithm. The two open-AI gym tasks, e.g., MountainCar-v2 and Half-cheetah-v2, are selected to verify the proposed MT-ENN. In addition, we also made a three-dimensional (3D) visual reconstruction of the entire network topology after network learning, which is convenient for identifying the connectome of different brain regions and might inspire back to the neuroscience researchers and answer the question that why some topology or brain regions are important for reinforcement learning.

2   Related Works

A new continuous-time differential learning was proposed for RL tasks containing continuous dynamics [1]. Then, a hybrid learning framework was proposed by extending this new learning rule with a multi-scale dynamic coding [9]. The topology-focused algorithm was proposed by using a sub-network to replace a previous global network and achieved comparable performance, named as the lottery ticket hypothesis. A biological network using C.elegans topology was proposed to achieve higher performance than algorithms using random networks [3], which showed the efficiency of the biological topology.

These algorithms all performed well on RL tasks. However, they seldom use complicated network topology. One of the main motivations of this paper is that the further incorporation of network topologies, especially from smarter animals than C.elegans, will strengthen intelligent algorithms on cognitive functions to handle RL tasks. In addition, we think reducing the size of fully connected networks for better interpretability is at least as important as performance, which will also be further discussed in the following sections.

3   Methods

3.1   The Allen Mouse Brain Atlas

The Allen Institute for Brain Science has provided the public with the whole mouse brain atlas, containing neuronal types and network topology from some standard mouse brains. The network topology contains the directional mapping of 213 brain regions, which are further visualized by Houdini software for a better understanding. The overall connectome of the mouse brain is shown in Fig. 1A, where the 213×213 matrix is the connectomes between 213 brain regions. The connectome is sparse, indicating that the bottom-up and top-down connections are hierarchical and highly related to cognitive functions.

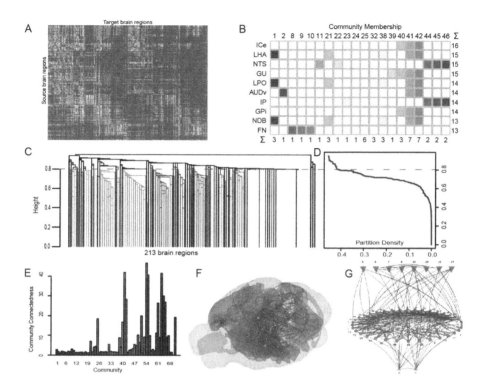

Fig. 1. The generation procedure of brain-inspired topology. (A) The mesoscale connectome of the Allen mouse brain atlas [5]. (B) An example of clustered topology from 213 brain regions. (C, D) The hierarchically clustered brain regions. The 213 mouse brain regions are split into 71 clusters at a cutting height of 0.8 (C) and the partition density (D). (E) The connectedness of different communities (clusters). (F) Schematic diagram of the connection of 46 brain regions in the 3D brain. (G) Schematic diagram of the connection of 46 brain regions in 2D visualization. (Color figure online)

3.2   The Clustered Hierarchical Circuits

The connectivity matrix of the mouse brain atlas was then clustered into sub-clusters for easier analysis. It is a general challenge to find a proper clustering algorithm that could filter out trivial branches but leave out the key functional topology. A special hierarchical clustering method, i.e., Tanimoto coefficient algorithm, is selected for this clustering. The algorithm could generate multiple clusters given a directional topology. The detailed procedure of the clustering algorithm could be concluded as the following equations:

$$S(e_{ik}, e_{jk}) = \frac{a_i \cdot a_j}{\mid a_i \mid^2 + \mid a_j \mid^2 - a_i \cdot a_j}, \tag{1}$$

We divide 213 regions of the mouse brain into 71 clusters at a cutting height of 0.8 (relative value designed by experience) based on the links or connections between each two brain regions in both directions as well as weights or intensities of projections (Fig. 1C, D).

3.3 The Neuron Model

Here, we briefly describe the neuron and synapse model to design neural circuit dynamics [2] by using the following equation.

$$\begin{cases} \dot{V}_i(t) = [I_L + \sum I_C(t)]/C_m \\ I_L(t) = \omega_L[E_L - V_{post}(t)] \\ I_C(t) = \omega_C[E_C - V_{post}(t)]g(t) \\ g(t) = 1/[1 + exp(-\sigma(V_{pre}(t) - \mu))] \end{cases}, \tag{2}$$

where C_m is the membrane capacitance of the neuron, I_C and I_L are the input currents of the chemical channel and leakage channel, respectively. E_C and E_L are the corresponding reversal potentials. $V_{post}(t)$ and $V_{pre}(t)$ are the membrane potentials of post-synapses and pre-synapses, respectively. $g(t)$ is the membrane conductance, defining whether a synapse is excitatory or inhibitory by E_C. ω_C and ω_L stand for the conductances of the chemical channel and leakage channel. These equations show that the algorithms have a strong ability to model the time series reaching any time step.

3.4 Coping the Biological Circuits to Artificial Ones

According to the definition of these 213 brain regions in the Allen mouse brain atlas, we reorganized them into sensation, hidden, and motor brain regions, according to structural projection and physiological function. We also annotate the biological functions of the brain regions at each level of the communities of interest, which makes it possible to compare the hierarchical composition and functional circuitry of the community or groups of interest with the combination of the atlas.

Hence, some different types of topology are selected for the next-step simulation, including the whole 213 brain regions (directly copied from the biological atlas) and some other sub-brain topology (selected from 31, 46, and 49 brain regions based on the hierarchical clustering), which will be further discussed in the experimental sections.

3.5 The Network Learning

In this paper, a simple search-based algorithm is selected for network reinforcement learning [3], whereby the agent learns to make decisions after observing the current state in an environment and then receives a timely or delayed reward.

A fitness function is designed to collect these rewards and guide the direction of the random search. At the beginning of learning, the agent makes random decisions for exploration, and a good decision for a lower fitness function will be kept by saving the current parameters and focusing more on the exploitation. The search-based algorithm ARS can train a network by repeating two training strategies until convergence. First, V_n values are obtained by calculating θ with fitness function f. Then the adaptive search algorithm calculates $\mathbb{E}(R_\theta)$ by the average value of the worst K samples among the V_n values.

In addition, two benchmark Mujoco RL tasks are used to test the performance of the proposed algorithm. One important motivation is that the RL tasks are more related to the biological agent's learning procedure, which makes decisions after observation by maximizing its predicted rewards.

4   Experiments

4.1   The Clustered Brain Regions

The 213 brain regions were clustered into multiple graphs, and parts of critical brain regions shared by different communities were recorded in Fig. 1B. It represents a sparse connection between different brain regions, congruent to the biological brain.

The community-61, community-65, and community-71 in 71 clusters were selected for subsequent experiments, given the cutting height of 0.8. It is impressive that the number of nodes in the largest connectedness in all clusters is less than 60 (Fig. 1E), indicating the network is very sparse. The community-61 contains 46 brain region nodes, which is called Circuit-46 (which means the clustering containing 46 brain regions). Similar to it, we give the names of community-65 and community-71 as Circuit-49 and Circuit-31, respectively. These circuits obtained after clustering will be used for the next-step RL experiments.

4.2   The Network Topology from Biological Mouse Brain

The Circuit-46 is visualized in a standard 3D mouse brain common coordinate framework (CCF) from the Allen Brain Institute (Fig. 1F), where each point represents a brain region, and each link represents excitatory (blue ones) or inhibitory (red ones) connections between different regions (the total is 819 connections). We set 657 excitatory, and 162 inhibitory connections for Circuit-46, inspired by the biological discovery [8]. The connectivity strength lower than 0.05 was omitted and only left for those larger than the threshold for the ease of visualization (i.e., only 207 excitatory connections and 60 inhibitory connections were left after filtering).

In addition, the sensory, hidden, and motor brain regions are visualized in a 2D figure, including 8 sensory areas (red inverted triangles), 36 hidden areas (blue circles), and 2 motor areas (yellow triangles), as shown that in Fig. 1G.

4.3   Results with Circuit-46 and Random Networks

We conducted an experiment where random connections were given to a MT-ENN with the same number of neurons and synapses as those in the Circuit-46. The synapses' initial polarity was set randomly (excitatory or inhibitory). Only feedforward connections were given from sensory to hidden neurons, same as those in the hidden to motor neurons. The random circuits were then trained on RL tasks whose performances are reported in Fig. 2A, D. We observed that the performance of MT-ENN using mouse brain topology was higher than that using random connections, and the performance would be more significant for a simple (e.g., MountainCar-v2) instead of hard (e.g., Half-cheetah-v2) tasks. This result on two benchmark RL tasks demonstrates the usefulness of the biological structures.

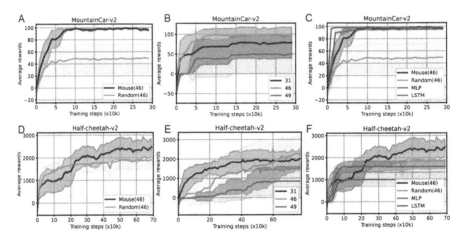

Fig. 2. Performance of different algorithms on reinforcement learning tasks. (A, D) Performance of the MT-ENN using Circuit-46 and random structures on the MountainCar-v2 and Half-cheetah-v2 tasks, respectively. (B, E) Same to those in (A, D) but for the MT-ENNs using Circuit-31, Circuit-46, and Circuit-49. (C, F) Same to those in (A, D) but for the MT-ENNs using Circuit-46, random connections, MLP, and LSTM.

4.4   Result Comparison with Different Algorithms

We conducted a series of experiments to test the influence of the number of brain regions, including MT-ENNs using Circuit-31, Circuit-46, and Circuit-49, respectively. As shown in Fig. 2B, E, the MT-ENN using Circuit-46 is better than those using the other two structures. This result confirmed our hypothesis that Circuit-46 could be a winning ticket, containing better performance and lower sparsity. Hence, we selected Circuit-46 as MT-ENN's main biological structure basis for the subsequent experiments.

We further tested the performance of our MT-ENN with other SOTA algorithms, including long short-term memory (LSTM) and multi-layer perception (MLP). We keep the comparisons fair by using the same number of neurons, linear mapping functions, and learning algorithms. Other key parameters were also kept learnable. We chose the same number of cells (neurons) for the LSTM and MLP networks, equal to the size of the MT-ENN. The LSTM and MLP networks are fully connected, and the MT-ENN achieves 61% network sparsity. The result is shown in Table 1 and Fig. 2C, F.

As shown in Table 1, for the MountainCar-v2 task, our MT-ENN reached the score (mean reward) of 99.14, higher than other algorithms tuned with backpropagation. Given a more complex task, e.g., the Half-cheetah-v2 task, our MT-ENN reached a much higher performance (2,468 scores) than the state-of-the-art MLP (1,601 scores) and LSTM (1,009 scores). These results showed the efficiency of the biologically plausible brain circuits.

Table 1. The performance comparisons of the proposed MT-ENN with other SOTA algorithms on MountainCar-v2 and Half-cheetah-v2 tasks.

Tasks	Architectures	Learning rules	Performance	Sparsity
MountainCar-v2	LSTM [4]	BPTT	98.98 ± 0.59	0%
	MLP [7]	PPO	95.5 ± 1.5	0%
	Random	Search	49.59 ± 49.59	61%
	MT-ENN (ours)	**Search**	**99.14 ± 0.12**	**61%**
Half-cheetah-v2	LTSM [4]	BPTT	1009.51 ± 641.95	0%
	MLP [7]	PPO	1601.05 ± 506.50	0%
	Random	Search	1917.40 ± 819.39	61%
	MT-ENN (ours)	**Search**	**2468.18 ± 962.36**	**61%**

5   Discussion

Selectively copying biological structures into artificial neural networks is a shortcut for efficiently designing neural networks. In this paper, 213 mouse brain regions were clustered and analyzed to generate some sub-graph topology for the network design of MT-ENN. The 3D morphology helps us learn more about the neuron types [11], sparseness, and connectome of different brain regions during analysis. The comparisons of different sub-graph topologies will be extended for further discussion [10]. Combined with the biological understandings, these clustered results will help us select more topology that satisfies biological plausibility and efficiency. The experimental results have verified our hypothesis that mouse brain topology can improve evolutionary neural networks for efficient RL. In this paper, the brain region structure obtained by the joint action of mouse brain clustering and biological trust is better than the commonly used LSTM and MLP in RL tasks. In addition, the mouse brain structure also showed advantages in terms of sparsity. In the future, more biologically credible principles can be borrowed from biological networks and applied to neural networks to achieve better integration of neuroscience and artificial intelligence and promote each other.

Acknowledgements. This work was supported in part by the Shanghai Municipal Science and Technology Major Project (2021SHZDZX), the Youth Innovation Promotion Association CAS, and the National Natural Science Foundation of China under Grants No. 82171992 and 81871394.

References

1. Doya, K.: Reinforcement learning in continuous time and space. Neural Comput. **12**(1), 219–245 (2000)
2. Hasani, R., Lechner, M., Amini, A., Rus, D., Grosu, R.: Liquid time-constant networks. arXiv preprint arXiv:2006.04439 (2020)
3. Hasani, R., Lechner, M., Amini, A., Rus, D., Grosu, R.: A natural lottery ticket winner: reinforcement learning with ordinary neural circuits. In: International Conference on Machine Learning, pp. 4082–4093. PMLR (2020)
4. Hochreiter, S., Schmidhuber, J.: Long short-term memory. Neural Comput. **9**(8), 1735–1780 (1997)
5. Oh, S.W., et al.: A mesoscale connectome of the mouse brain. Nature **508**(7495), 207–214 (2014)
6. Rubinov, M., Ypma, R.J., Watson, C., Bullmore, E.T.: Wiring cost and topological participation of the mouse brain connectome. Proc. Natl. Acad. Sci. **112**(32), 10032–10037 (2015)
7. Schulman, J., Wolski, F., Dhariwal, P., Radford, A., Klimov, O.: Proximal policy optimization algorithms. arXiv preprint arXiv:1707.06347 (2017)
8. Wildenberg, G.A., Rosen, M.R., Lundell, J., Paukner, D., Freedman, D.J., Kasthuri, N.: Primate neuronal connections are sparse in cortex as compared to mouse. Cell Rep. **36**(11), 109709 (2021)
9. Zhang, D., Zhang, T., Jia, S., Xu, B.: Multiscale dynamic coding improved spiking actor network for reinforcement learning. In: Thirty-Sixth AAAI Conference on Artificial Intelligence (2022)
10. Zhang, T., Zeng, Y., Xu, B.: A computational approach towards the microscale mouse brain connectome from the mesoscale. J. Integr. Neurosci. **16**(3), 291–306 (2017)
11. Zhang, T., et al.: Neuron type classification in rat brain based on integrative convolutional and tree-based recurrent neural networks. Sci. Rep. **11**(1), 7291 (2021)

DNM-SNN: Spiking Neural Network Based on Dual Network Model

Zhen Cao[(✉)], Hongwei Zhang, Qian Wang, and Chuanfeng Ma

School of Artificial Intelligence, Xidian University, Xi'an, Shaanxi, People's Republic of China
icaozhen@163.com

Abstract. In recent years, deep neural network (DNN) has shown excellent performance in many applications. However, the huge energy consumption leads to many problems. In order to solve this problem, spiking neural network (SNN) has attracted extensive research attention. SNN is the third-generation neural network that is used to process complex spatiotemporal data, and it has become a hot research topic due to its event-driven and low-power characteristics. However, the propagation function of spiking neurons is usually non-differentiable, which prevents back propagation and makes the training of SNN difficult. This paper proposes an efficient supervised learning algorithm framework based on dual-network-model spiking neural network (DNM-SNN), which is universal to various supervised learning algorithms of spiking neural networks and can effectively improve the prediction accuracy. DNM-SNN includes two key methods. Firstly, a dual model training method in training stage is proposed, which requires an additional auxiliary network same as the network used. Single model training is easy to fall into local optimal problems. By maintaining two networks, the same problem can be viewed from different perspectives, which solves the problem and improves the training effect. Second, we propose a multi-channel mix module inference method in the prediction stage. The prediction accuracy of the model is improved and the performance of the spiking neural network is optimized by multi-channel optimization of mix module. Experimental results show that the DNM-SNN outperforms the single-model algorithm on classification tasks, with a slight improvement on the MNIST dataset and a 3% improvement on the CIFAE-10 dataset.

Keywords: Spiking neural network · Dual model · Mix module · DNM-SNN

1 Introduction

The emergence of back-propagation algorithm [1] has significantly promoted the development of traditional artificial neural network (ANN), which can effectively solve many real-life problems, such as image recognition, control and prediction. With the advent of training algorithms for deep convolutional neural networks [2], deep neural networks were only understood in the fields of computer vision and machine learning and became

Z. Shi et al. (Eds.): ICIS 2022, IFIP AICT 659, pp. 11–19, 2022.
https://doi.org/10.1007/978-3-031-14903-0_2

the mainstream method for solving tasks such as image recognition and speech recognition. Research on spiking neural networks dating back to the 1950s has not received as much attention as ANNs, one of the main reasons being the lack of efficient deep spiking due to its replicated dynamics and non-differentiable operations Learning algorithms for neural networks. Many researchers have proposed some algorithm frameworks, such as the deep convolutional neural network based on STDP rules proposed by Kheradpisheh [3], which achieved an accuracy level of 98.4% on the MNIST dataset; Rueckauer et al. VGG-16 and GoogLeNet models; Hu et al. [4] used the deep structure of ResNet-50 to achieve 72.75% accuracy classification results. However, their algorithms are either only used for classification tasks on simple datasets, or the accuracy of the algorithms is not guaranteed and cannot achieve the same performance as ANN. In recent years, cao [5] and Sengupta [6], etc. proposed a new simple and effective algorithm, which imported the pre-trained parameters from DNN to SNN, and realized the conversion from DNN to SNN. In MNIST and CIFAR datasets Competitive results have been achieved. However, due to the existence of the temporal dimension, transforming SNNs on deep networks often suffers from the problem of vanishing gradients, and simple transplant transforms can also cause the problem of insufficient burst firing rate.

It can be seen that the spiking neural network lacks an efficient and stable supervised training algorithm, and it is a difficult task to train a spiking neural network well. There are three main reasons for the poor performance of the algorithm: a) The neural information is expressed in the form of a pulse sequence, which is essentially a discrete signal, and the state variables and error propagation functions inside the spiking neuron do not satisfy the continuous differentiability property, which makes the gradient descent learning method based on backpropagation cannot be directly applied to the spiking neural network. b) In the prediction stage, due to the low firing rate of spiking neurons, the output neurons of the last layer of the deep spiking neural network are prone to not firing pulses, resulting in serious deviations from the target pulse sequence. c) During the training process, due to the low firing rate of spiking neurons, the model cannot converge, and the single-network model is prone to fall into the local optimal solution.

To sum up, the main contribution of this paper is as follows:

Dual-model spiking network training method: In order to enhance the reliability of the algorithm, the dual networks jointly learn a problem, improve the convergence speed of training, and prevent the trouble of falling into local optimum.

Multi-channel mix module prediction method: multi-channel prediction, find the most suitable prediction channel, and effectively improve the prediction accuracy.

Dual model achieves better performance than single model: On the CIFAR-10 dataset, the dual-model Resnet11 is 3% higher than the single-model, and the dual-model Resnet20 is 1% to 3% higher than the state-of-the-art single-model Resnet20.

2   Methods

The traditional supervised learning algorithm of spiking neural network is to find a suitable synaptic weight matrix for the network for a given set of multiple input pulse sequences and a set of multiple target pulse sequences through a network model. The resulting matrix minimizes the error between the pulse sequence output by the network and the corresponding target pulse sequence. However, in classification tasks, traditional supervised learning algorithms often predict wrong classification results, and the performance of the algorithm is seriously degraded. In-depth analysis of its reasons, the possible explanations for this are:

(a)   The single-network model is often biased, and it is easy to fall into the local optimal solution, resulting in the degradation of the performance of the algorithm.
(b)   Unstable pulse firing rates lead to very severe biases in predictions.

In order to overcome these two problems, this paper proposes two methods: the dual-model spiking network supervised learning training method and the mix module prediction method. The overall framework is shown in Fig. 1.

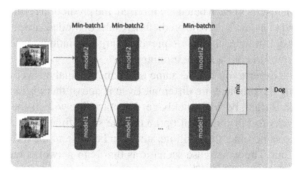

Fig. 1. The framework of the dual-model supervised learning algorithm is divided into four parts. The first part is the encoding operation of the data set, which encodes the data set into a pulse sequence. The second part is the training of dual models, where model1 and model2 are two identical models, and the output pulse sequences of each batch of the two models are exchanged with each other. The third part is the multi-channel mix prediction module, which can select the channel with the best accuracy to complete the classification task. The last part is the output of the classification result, and the selected mix channel outputs the classification result.

2.1   Traditional SNN Supervised Learning Algorithm Framework and Its Limitations

The training of the traditional spiking neural network supervised learning algorithm [7] is divided into three stages: first, the sample data is encoded into a spike sequence through a specific encoding method. Second, the pulse sequence is input into the neural network, and a certain simulation strategy is applied to run the same neural network to obtain the actual output pulse sequence. Then, according to the target pulse sequence, the synaptic weights of the current neural network are adjusted through the loss function and its learning rules. Finally, when the prediction error reaches a pre-specified value or the number of iterations is completed, the training is complete. Obviously, single-model training is very risky. Once there is a deviation, it is difficult to correct, because the data obtained is always the result predicted by its own network, so it is easy to fall into the trouble of local optimization. The traditional prediction method is to directly apply the trained weights to the current network, and the output result is the prediction result. However, due to the problem of low firing rate of the pulse, the final result has a large deviation from the actual target result. There may be cases where the category cannot be predicted or the classification effect is poor.

2.2 Proposed Dual-Model Spike Network Supervised Learning Algorithm

This paper proposes a more efficient SNN training algorithm, which we call a dual-model spiking network supervised learning training method. Our method is to establish two network models with the same structure, instead of one network model in the traditional method, as shown in Fig. 1, establish two identical networks model1 and model2, and input the encoded data sets into the two neural networks respectively. In the network, after the prediction results of each batch are inferred, the prediction results of model1 are respectively passed to model2, and the prediction results of model2 are passed to model1. The two networks constrain each other to prevent a large deviation in one network. Then repeat the above steps to complete the training.

This is like two experts solving the same problem, the final answer is the same, but the ideas of solving the problem are different. Even if one of them is in trouble, as long as the other person is right, he will quickly get out of trouble with his help. It is difficult for the two networks to fall into local optima at the same time. Even if they fall into local optima at the same time, they will iterate again because of the difference between the two local optima. The worst case scenario is that both networks fall into the same local optimum at the same time. This paper has not encountered this situation in the experiment. If this situation occurs, it is likely that the two selected network models are inappropriate.

2.3 Proposed Multi-channel Mix Module Prediction Method

The output of a spiking neural network is a binary sequence of spikes, and the differences between categories are enormous. Therefore, when the pulse firing rate is insufficient, all the classification results will be 0. In order to solve this problem, a multi-channel mix module prediction method is proposed, which can cooperate with the dual-model supervised learning algorithm to optimize the prediction results and improve the prediction accuracy. The specific algorithm is as follows:

Algorithm 1: Multi-Channel mix Module Prediction Method

```
1 class Mix:
    # Get the output of the dual model
2     def __init__(self,  model1output, model2output):
3         self.model1output = model1output
4         self.model2output = model2output
   #   maximum channel
5     def maxChannel(self):
6         newoutput = getMax(self.model1output, self.model2output)
7         return newoutput
   # Average channel
8     def averageChannel(self):
9         newoutput = getAverage(self.model1output, self.model2output)
10        return newoutput
   # Choose the channel best suited for the current task
11    def betterOutput(self):
12        flag = whichBetter(self.maxChannel(), self.averageChannel())
13        if flag:
14            return 1
15        else:
16            return 2
```

2.4 The Chosen Network Model

We choose Resnet [8] model as the dual model, which is of great significance to the study of deep spike neural network [9]. Here is our snn-resnet11 model:

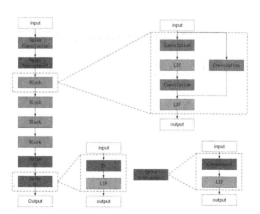

Fig. 2. SNN-Resnet11 single network architecture

2.5 Selection of Spiking Neurons

Figure 3 shows the difference in electrical properties between spiking and non-spiking neurons. Non-spiking neurons are memoryless, their current output is completely depen-dent on the current input, while spiking neurons have inherent memory, they all have a memory element [11].

Fig. 3. Spiking neuron (right) and non-spiking neuron (left) circuit primitives

As shown in Fig. 2, the Leaky Integrate-and-Fire (LIF) spiking neuron [12] is selected in this paper. Its working process is shown in Fig. 4.

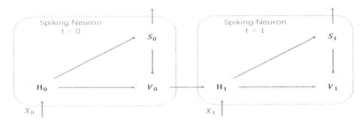

Fig. 4. LIF model working process

Figure 4 shows the working process of LIF neurons [13] and its dynamic model can be described by three discrete equations of charging, discharging and resetting.

The charging equation is:

$$H_t = f(V_{t-1}, X_t) \tag{1}$$

$$f(V_{t-1}, X_t) = V_t + \frac{1}{\tau_m}((-V_{t-1} - V_{reset}) + X_t) \tag{2}$$

Among them, X_t is the external input, which represents the input of the pulse sequence at time t, such as the increment of the voltage, H_t is the hidden state of the neuron, and is the membrane voltage of the neuron before the pulse at time t. τ_m is the time constant, V_t is the membrane voltage of the neuron at time t, and V_{reset} is the reset voltage.

The discharge equation is as follows:

$$S_t = \Theta(H_t - V_t) = \begin{cases} 1, & H_t \geq V_{th} \\ 0, & H_t < V_{th} \end{cases} \tag{3}$$

where V_{th} is the threshold voltage, is an $\Theta(H_t - V_t)$ step function, and S_t represents the neuron firing the pulse.

Its reset equation is as follows:

$$V_t = r(H_t, S_t) \tag{4}$$

$$r(H_t, S_t) = H_t \cdot (1 - S_t) + V_{reset} \cdot \leq S_t \tag{5}$$

3 Experimental Results

3.1 Single- and Dual-Model Resnet11 Performance on the CIFAR-10 Dataset

(See Table 1 and Fig. 5)

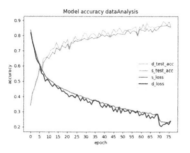

Fig. 5. Performance of the two models on the CIFAR-10 dataset

Table 1. Results for CIFAR-10 and MNIST dataset.

Model	Dataset	Test Acc
Resnet11 (single)	MNIST	98.27%
Resnet11 (Dual)	MNIST	99.11%
Resnet11 (single)	CIFAR-10	86.62%
Resnet11 (Dual)	CIFAR-10	**89.93%**

3.2 Related Work Comparison

(See Table 2)

Table 2. Comparison with other conversion methods on CIFAR-10.

Model	Author	Dataset	Test Acc
Resnet11 (single)	This work	CIFAR-10	86.62%
Resnet20	Abhronil Sengupta [6]	CIFAR-10	89.1%
Resnet20	Bing Han [14]	CIFAR-10	91.36%
Resnet20 (single)	This work	CIFAR-10	88.74%
Resnet20 (Dual)	This work	CIFAR-10	**92.33%**

4   Conclusion

In this paper, we introduce a dual-model spiking neural network supervised learning algorithm framework, and propose a dual-model training method and a multi-channel mix module prediction method corresponding to the algorithm. We successfully applied it to the SNN-Resnet11 single-network model and obtained a dual-model SNN-Resnet11. Experiments show that the dual-model structure achieves an accuracy improvement of about 3% over the single-network model on the CIFAR-10 dataset. We believe that this algorithm can be applied to a variety of network architectures to better facilitate the exploration of learning algorithms for spiking neural networks.

Acknowledgements. This work was supported in part by the China Postdoctoral Science Foundation under Grant 2019M663637, in part by the Natural Science Basic Research Program of Shaanxi under Program 2021JQ-201, and in part by the National Natural Science Foundation of China under Grant 62104176.

References

1. Rumelhart, D.E., Hinton, G.E., Williams, R.J.: Learning representations by back-propagating errors. Nature **323**(6088), 533–536 (1986)
2. Krizhevsky, A., Sutskever, I., Hinton, G.E.: ImageNet classification with deep convolutional neural networks. In: Advances in Neural Information Processing Systems, vol. 25 (2012)
3. Kheradpisheh, S.R., Ganjtabesh, M., Thorpe, S.J., et al.: STDP-based spiking deep convolutional neural networks for object recognition. Neural Netw. **99**, 56–67 (2018)
4. Rueckauer, B., Lungu, I.A., Hu, Y., et al.: Conversion of continuous-valued deep networks to efficient event-driven networks for image classification. Front. Neurosci. **11**, 682 (2017)
5. Cao, Y., Chen, Y., Khosla, D.: Spiking deep convolutional neural networks for energy-efficient object recognition. Int. J. Comput. Vis. **113**(1), 54–66 (2015)
6. Sengupta, A., Ye, Y., Wang, R., et al.: Going deeper in spiking neural networks: VGG and residual architectures. Front. Neurosci. **13**, 95 (2019)
7. Lin, X., Wang, X., Zhang, N., et al.: Supervised learning algorithms for spiking neural networks: a review. Acta Electonica Sinica **43**(3), 577 (2015)
8. He, K., Zhang, X., Ren, S., et al.: Deep residual learning for image recognition. In: Proceedings of the IEEE Conference on Computer Vision and Pattern Recognition, pp. 770–778 (2016)

9. Hu, Y., Tang, H., Pan, G.: Spiking deep residual networks. IEEE Trans. Neural Netw. Learn. Syst. (2018)
10. Zambrano, D., Nusselder, R., Scholte, H.S., et al.: Sparse computation in adaptive spiking neural networks. Front. Neurosci. **12**, 987 (2019)
11. Kim, S., Park, S., Na, B., et al.: Spiking-yolo: spiking neural network for energy-efficient object detection. In: Proceedings of the AAAI Conference on Artificial Intelligence, vol. 34, no. 07, pp. 11270–11277 (2020)
12. Lapique, L.: Recherches quantitatives sur l'excitation electrique des nerfs traitee comme une polarization. J. Physiol. Pathol. **9**, 620–635 (1907)
13. Dayan, P., Abbott, L.F.: Computational and Mathematical Modeling of Neural Systems. Theoretical Neuroscience. MIT Press (2001)
14. Han, B., Srinivasan, G., Roy, K.: RMP-SNN: residual membrane potential neuron for enabling deeper high-accuracy and low-latency spiking neural network. In: Proceedings of the IEEE/CVF Conference on Computer Vision and Pattern Recognition, pp. 13558–13567 (2020)

A Memetic Algorithm Based on Adaptive Simulated Annealing for Community Detection

Jie Yang[1], Yifei Sun[1(✉)], Shi Cheng[2], Kun Bian[1], Zhuo Liu[1], Xin Sun[1], and Yifei Cao[1]

[1] School of Physics and Information Technology, Shaanxi Normal University, Xi'an, China
{jieyang2021,Yifeis,Biankun,Zhuoliu,sunxin_,yifeic}@snnu.edu.cn
[2] School of Computer Science, Shaanxi Normal University, Xi'an 710119, China
cheng@snnu.edu.cn

Abstract. The application of community detection (community discovery) has been widely used in various fields for several years. To improve the algorithm accuracy, we proposed a memetic algorithm based on an adaptive simulated annealing local search (MA-ASA). Segmented label propagation (STLP) is used for initialization and variation operations. A hierarchical idea is adopted to form an initial cluster center during initialization, and random competition is used to select the next generation of solutions. Instead of using fixed probabilities in each crossover and variation operation, we used quality differences to switch to adaptive probabilities in simulated annealing (SA) for local search to accelerate convergence. The algorithm was extensively tested and experimented with 11 artificial and 4 real networks. Compared with other 10 algorithms, the results showed that MA-ASA performs well and is highly competitive.

Keywords: Community detection · Memetic algorithms · Dynamic probability · Simulated annealing

1 Introduction

Systems can be modeled as complex network for research, such as aviation networks, computer networks and social networks [1, 2]. Community structure is defined as one that is more tightly connected internally and more sparsely connected externally [3].

Many algorithms had been proposed in the past several decades. Newman and Girvan introduced modularity for community detection (GN) [4]. Newman proposed the FN algorithm based on GN [5]. Gong et al. [6] have introduced memetic algorithms (MAs) for community detection. It was optimized by modifying the local strategy [7]. Sun et al. [8] proposed the MAPL algorithm for community division. There are evolutionary algorithms [9, 10] which focus on optimizing multiple objective functions.

In this paper, we proposed a new memetic algorithm for community detection named MA-ASA. We primarily use label propagation to initialize the nodes. In each generation of selection and crossover, the poorly performing individuals are labeled for change

© IFIP International Federation for Information Processing 2022
Published by Springer Nature Switzerland AG 2022
Z. Shi et al. (Eds.): ICIS 2022, IFIP AICT 659, pp. 20–28, 2022.
https://doi.org/10.1007/978-3-031-14903-0_3

by comparing the modularity. Secondly, dynamic probability is used to select specific variation strategies in local search. We use MA-ASA to test 4 real world networks and 11 synthetic networks. The final results of the experiments demonstrated that MA-ASA is highly competitive.

The rest of this dissertation is organized as follows. Section 2 illustrates the complex networks and the common concepts of community detection. Section 3 presents the proposed algorithm. Section 4 provides the results and data analysis of the experiments. Section 5 summarizes the full paper and suggests possible follow-up studies.

2 Background

In graph theory, complex networks are usually described by a graph $G = (V, E)$, where V stands for the nodes in the network and E stands for the connection between nodes. If there is a connection between the node A and B, then $A_{ij} = 1$, otherwise 0.

2.1 Modularity

Modularity was proposed by Newman and Girvan to assess the quality of community division [4, 5]. The formula is as follows:

$$Q = \sum_{i=1}^{c} \left[\frac{l_i}{m} - (\frac{k_i}{2m})^2 \right] \tag{1}$$

where c denotes the number of communities partitioned, m is the total number of edges, l_i is the sum of edges contained in the ith community and k_i indicates the sum of the node degrees of the ith community.

2.2 Normalized Mutual Information

Normalized mutual information (NMI) was used to evaluate the quality of the generated solutions. The value of NMI ranges from 0 to 1. When it is equal to 1, the resulting solution is consistent with the actual division. The NMI is defined as follows:

$$NMI(A, B) = \frac{-2 \sum_{i=1}^{C_A} \sum_{j=1}^{C_B} C_{ij} log\left(\frac{C_{ij}N}{C_{i.}C_{.j}} \right)}{\sum_{i=1}^{C_A} C_{i.} log\left(\frac{C_{i.}}{N} \right) + \sum_{j=1}^{C_B} C_{.j} log\left(\frac{C_{.j}}{N} \right)} \tag{2}$$

where $C_A(C_B)$ is the number of communities divided into A(B), $C_{i.}(C_{.j})$ is the sum of the elements of the ith row (jth column) of the adjacency matrix and N denotes the number of network nodes.

3 Description of MA-ASA

3.1 Segmented Label Propagation

In this paper, we apply segmented label propagation (STLP) to network initialization. Assume that each node has a set of neighbors $\Omega(i) = \{x_1, x_2, \ldots, x_i\}$, and $L(i)$ is denoted as the label of the ith node. We initialize the node labels as $L(i) = i$, i.e., $L = \{1, 2, \ldots, i\}$. We stratify label propagation into potential community nodes and common nodes. In the first stage (STLP-1), the nodes are divided into two layers of strong and weak nodes; while the second stage (STLP-2) is used for variation.

We filter out the nodes which are much larger than average node degrees. Assume that they are more influential individuals and radiate their labels. And these identically labeled nodes are then highly likely to be a potential community respectively.

3.2 Selection and Crossover Operation

In MA-ASA, we use random competitive selection to preserve the better individual. Dynamic probabilities are used to improve the overall population quality. Figure 1 shows an example when the dynamic crossover probability equals to 50%. The inferior performing solution evolves into a new solution after crossover pairing.

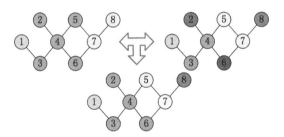

Fig. 1. The process of secondary solution updated to a new solution

3.3 Mutation Operation

We adopted three different strategies which selected by adaptive probability. The first two strategies we called STLP-2. The labels are mainly updated by (a) roulette selection and (b) equal probability selection. Meanwhile, to avoid local convergence, we set a small probability event (c) to do a random update for the labels. In Fig. 2, the green and orange circles are the division of node 5 neighbor set. When operation (a) is taken, the mutation probability is determined by neighbors. When operation (b) is adopted, the probability is changed to the ratio of the number of circles.

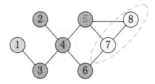

Fig. 2. Node 5 variation operation description diagram (Color figure online)

3.4 Improved Simulated Annealing

Conventional SA is based on the principle of thermodynamics. We set the temperature $T = 100$, the decay rate $\alpha = 0.98$ and the stopping condition $T < 0.1$. We improved the probability equation as follows:

$$P = exp(-\frac{G(Q_{old} - Q_{new})}{T}) \tag{3}$$

where G is the fitness gain coefficient, which is associated with the number of nodes. Q_{new} is the fitness of the newly obtained solution of the current population and Q_{old} means the historical optimal fitness of the current population.

Algorithm 1: Framework of Improved Simulated Annealing

Input: The population size: N_p; the temperature: T; the attenuation rate: α.
Output: Node labels for each population

    for $(i = 1:N_p)$
    $T \leftarrow ResetOperation$;
      while (T)
        $pop \leftarrow Mutation(pop)$;
        $pop \leftarrow EvaluateFitness(pop)$;
        $bestQ \leftarrow MetropolisRule(pop)$;
        $T \leftarrow AttenuationOperation(\alpha)$;
      end while
    end for

3.5 Framework of MA-ASA

The proposed MA-ASA algorithm in this article is composed of STLP for initialization, mutation, random competitive selection and improved simulated annealing. The algorithm framework is given in **Algorithm 2**.

Algorithm 2: Framework of MA-ASA

Input: The adjacency matrix: A; the population size: N_p; the maximum number of
        generations: G_{max}; the initial temperature: T; the attenuation rate: α.

Output: The partition of the network with the largest modularity: Q.

    $pop \leftarrow STLP\text{-}1(pop)$;

    $pop \leftarrow EvaluateFitness(pop)$;

    $bestQ \leftarrow SaveBest(pop)$;

    for $(i = 1: G_{max})$

      while (N_p)

        $pop \leftarrow$ Selection and Crossover operation;

      end while

      while (T)

        $pop \leftarrow LocalSearch(pop)$;

        $bestQ \leftarrow SaveBest(pop)$;

        $T \leftarrow AttenuationOperation(\alpha)$;

      end while

    end for

---

4   Experiments and Analysis

4.1   Experimental Settings

The algorithm was written in C and compiled by gcc version 5.4.0 with Ubuntu 16.04. The simulation was tested on a PC with Intel (R) Core (TM) i5-10210U CPU @ 1.60 GHz 2.11 GHz, 8 GB DDR4 RAM, Microsoft (R) Windows 10 Home OS. The population size is set to 100 and the number of iterations is 200.

Experimental Networks. The GN benchmark network [11] is a benchmark network. There exists a mixing parameter γ, which represents the percentage of each node within the community that is connected to other community nodes. In layman's terms, the larger γ is, the more difficult it is to delineate the correct partition. 11 GN networks were generated at 0.05 intervals in the range of γ from 0 to 0.5.

    Four real-world networks were selected to test the effectiveness of MA-ASA and to compare with other algorithms. These networks are Zachary's Karate Club network (Karate) [12], Bottlenose Dolphins network (Dolphins) [13], American College Football network (Football) [11], and Jazz musicians' network (Jazz) [14]. The details of these networks are listed in Table 1. V, E and $\bar{k}$ are the total number of nodes, the sum of edges and the average node degree of each network respectively.

Table 1. Topological characteristics of each real network.

Networks	V	E	$\bar{k}$
Karate	34	78	4.59
Dolphins	62	159	5.13
Football	115	613	10.66
Jazz	198	2742	27.70

4.2 Experimental Results and Analysis

In this paper we compared the result of real network by testing with MODPSO [15], MOGA-net [16], MOEA/D-net [17], MOCD [18], Meme-net [6], GA-net [19], GN [11], NIMA [20], Louvain [21] and CNM [22].

Table 2 shows the experimental results of the 4 real-world networks. Specifically, in the three networks, Karate, Dolphins, and Football, the proposed MA-ASA was able to find the clusters with the largest Q value in each run. MODPSO was able to find the best partition in Karate and Football, but was unstable. Although Louvain could find the maximum Q value in Football and Jazz as well, its results were also unstable. Both MA-ASA and MODPSO did not reach the maximum Q value in Jazz, but were more stable than Louvain. MA-ASA had better performance than MODPSO. Figure 3 shows the community partition of Jazz network, where the nodes are divided into four communities and painted with different colors.

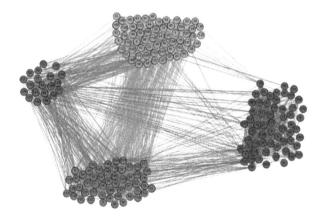

Fig. 3. Partition of Jazz network through MA-ASA

Table 2. Comparison results of modularity Q values in real-world networks for algorithms.

Networks	Indexes	MA-ASA	MODPSO	MOGA-net	Louvain
Karate	Q_{max}	**0.4198**	**0.4198**	0.4159	0.4188
	Q_{ave}	**0.4198**	0.4182	0.3945	0.4165
	Q_{std}	**0**	0.0079	0.0089	0.0077
Dolphins	Q_{max}	**0.5222**	0.5216	0.5034	0.5168
	Q_{ave}	**0.5222**	0.5208	0.4584	0.5160
	Q_{std}	**0**	0.0062	0.0163	0.0029
Football	Q_{max}	**0.6046**	**0.6046**	0.4325	**0.6046**
	Q_{ave}	**0.6046**	0.6038	0.3906	0.6043
	Q_{std}	**0**	0.0011	0.0179	0.0009
Jazz	Q_{max}	0.4450	0.4421	0.2952	**0.4451**
	Q_{ave}	0.4445	0.4419	0.2929	0.4443
	Q_{std}	**0.0001**	**0.0001**	0.0084	0.0023

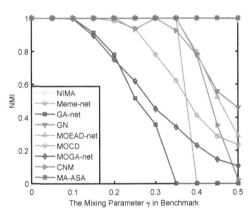

Fig. 4. Average NMI of different algorithms on GN benchmark networks

Figure 4 plots the comparison results of algorithms in 11 GN benchmark networks. On the graph, it can be seen that all algorithms can get the best partition when the mixing parameter $\gamma \leq 0.10$. With the increase of the mixing parameter, the average NMI value starts to decrease. NIMA also has a mean NMI value of 1 at $\gamma \leq 0.45$, but it drops to 0.9875 when the mixing parameter increases to 0.5. Even when the mixing parameter reaches 0.50, the MA-ASA can find the correct partition. To confirm the authenticity of the experiment, we increased the number of tests to 100 times. In 100 independent tests, when the mixing parameter reaches 0.50, its average NMI is 1, i.e., the probability of incorrect partitioning is less than 1%, which is the best performance among the various algorithms in the figure.

5   Conclusion

This article proposes an adaptive memetic algorithm MA-ASA to solve the community detection problem. The algorithm consists of segmented label propagation initialization, random-competition based selection and crossover, variation, and improved simulated annealing for local search. At the same time, dynamic probability is used to determine the chance of change according to its fitness. Numerous experiments show that MA-ASA is an effective method in community detection.

Although MA-ASA performs well in the experimental results, the algorithm will take long time. We should use the relevant properties to accelerate the convergence and shorten runtime. Meanwhile, we can extend MA-ASA to detect dynamic networks and use the properties of simulated annealing to avoid the premature convergence.

Acknowledgements. This work was supported by the National Natural Science Foundation of China (Grant No. 61703256, 61806119), Natural Science Basic Research Plan in Shaanxi Province of China (Program No. 2022JM-381, 2017JQ6070) and the Fundamental Research Funds for the Central Universities (Program No. GK201803020, GK201603014).

References

1. Latora, V., Nicosia, V., Russo, G.: Complex Networks: Principles, Methods and Applications, 1st edn. Cambridge University Press, UK (2017)
2. Wasserman, S., Faust, K.: Social Network Analysis, p. 825. Cambridge University Press (25 November 1994)
3. Li, Q., Zhong, J., Li, Q., Cao, Z., Wang, C.: Enhancing network embedding with implicit clustering. In: Li, G., Yang, J., Gama, J., Natwichai, J., Tong, Y. (eds.) Database Systems for Advanced Applications: 24th International Conference, DASFAA 2019, Chiang Mai, Thailand, April 22–25, 2019, Proceedings, Part I, pp. 452–467. Springer International Publishing, Cham (2019). https://doi.org/10.1007/978-3-030-18576-3_27
4. Newman, M.E.J., Girvan, M.: Finding and evaluating community structure in networks. Phys. Rev. E **69**(2), 026113 (2004)
5. Newman, M.E.J.: Fast algorithm for detecting community structure in networks. Phys. Rev. E **69**(6), 066133 (2004)
6. Gong, M., Fu, B., Jiao, L., Du, H.: Memetic algorithm for community detection in networks. Phys. Rev. E **84**, 056101 (2011)
7. Gong, M., Cai, Q., Li, Y., Ma, J.: An improved memetic algorithm for community detection in complex networks. In: 2012 IEEE Congress on Evolutionary Computation (CEC) (2012)
8. Sun, X., Sun, Y., Cheng, S., Bian, K., Liu, Z.: Population learning based memetic algorithm for community detection in complex networks. In: Tan, Y., Shi, Y., Zomaya, A., Yan, H., Cai, J. (eds.) DMBD 2021. CCIS, vol. 1454, pp. 275–288. Springer, Singapore (2021). https://doi.org/10.1007/978-981-16-7502-7_29
9. Bian, K., Sun, Y., Cheng, S., Liu, Z., Sun, X.: Adaptive methods of differential evolution multi-objective optimization algorithm based on decomposition. In: Zhang, H., Yang, Z., Zhang, Z., Wu, Z., Hao, T. (eds.) NCAA 2021. CCIS, vol. 1449, pp. 458–472. Springer, Singapore (2021). https://doi.org/10.1007/978-981-16-5188-5_33
10. Sun, Y., Bian, K., Liu, Z., Sun, X., Yao, R.: Adaptive strategies based on differential evolutionary algorithm for many-objective optimization. Discrete Dyn. Nat. Soc. **2021**, 1–17 (2021)

11. Girvan, M., Newman, M.E.J.: Community structure in social and biological networks. Proc. Natl. Acad. Sci. U.S.A. **99**(12), 7821–7826 (2002)
12. Zachary, W.W.: An information flow model for conflict and fission in small groups. J. Anthropol. Res. **33**(4), 452–473 (1977)
13. Lusseau, D., Schneider, K., Boisseau, O.J.: The bottlenose dolphin community of doubtful sound features a large proportion of long-lasting associations. Behav. Ecol. Sociobiol. **54**(4), 396–405 (2003)
14. Gleiser, P., Danon, L.: Community structure in jazz. Adv. Complex Syst. **6**(4), 565 (2003)
15. Gong, M., Cai, Q., Chen, X., Ma, L.: Complex network clustering by multiobjective discrete particle swarm optimization based on decomposition. IEEE Trans. Evol. Comput. **18**(1), 82–97 (2014)
16. Pizzuti, C.: A multiobjective genetic algorithm to find communities in complex networks. IEEE Trans. Evol. Comput. **16**(3), 418–430 (2012)
17. Gong, M., Ma, L., Zhang, Q., Jiao, L.: Community detection in networks by using multiobjective evolutionary algorithm with decomposition. Phys. A **391**(15), 4050–4060 (2012)
18. Shi, C., Yan, Z., Cai, Y., Wu, B.: Multi-objective community detection in complex networks. Appl. Soft Comput. **12**(2), 850–859 (2012)
19. Pizzuti, C.: GA-Net: a genetic algorithm for community detection in social networks. Proc. Parallel Probl. Solving Nat. **5199**, 1081–1090 (2008)
20. Liu, Z., Sun, Y., Cheng, S., Sun, X., Bian, K., Yao, R.: A node influence based memetic algorithm for community detection in complex networks. In: Pan, L., Cui, Z., Cai, J., Li, L. (eds.) Bio-inspired Computing: Theories and Applications, BIC-TA 2021. Communications in Computer and Information Science, vol. 1565. Springer, Singapore (2022). https://doi.org/10.1007/978-981-19-1256-6_16
21. Blondel, V.D., Guillaume, J.-L., Lambiotte, R., Lefebvre, E.: Fast unfolding of communities in large networks. J. Stat. Mech. Theor. Exp. **2008**(10), P10008 (2008)
22. Clauset, A., Newman, M.E.J., Moore, C.: Finding community structure in very large networks. Phys. Rev. E **70**(6), 066111 (2004)

The Model of an Explanation of Self and Self-awareness Based on Need Evolution

Bowen Sun and Xiaofeng Wang[✉]

College of Information Engineering, Shanghai Maritime University,
Shanghai 201306, China
xfwang@shmtu.edu.cn

Abstract. The nature of the self has always been an unsolved problem. This study combines a biological theory of the essential features of life with a review of views of the self in philosophy, brain science, mathematics and artificial intelligence. Combining the primary needs of living things with evolutionary theory, a new explanation of the fundamentals of life is provided. The primary needs of life are centred on energy and the transmission of information about oneself. These two intrinsic needs combine with the environment to form a new universal need and a necessary mechanism. And driven by the needs, the organism's perception of its own needs and state gives rise to self-awareness. Based on this new theory, an iterative model of the evolution of needs and an evolutionary model of the self are proposed. These models are alternative interpretations of the self and self-awareness, and offer improved directions for machine simulation of artificial intelligence.

Keywords: Self · Primary needs · Evolution of needs

1 Background and Significance

The nature of the self has long been an unsolved problem for human beings to contemplate, and has been investigated by philosophers. With the rapid development of brain science and life sciences such as neurobiology, many famous neurobiological and cognitive scientists have joined the research bandwagon and tried to study the self from the perspective of neural mechanisms. Mathematicians and experts in artificial intelligence and information technology have begun to explore the issue from the perspective of models and engineering applications, and have achieved some enlightening research results.

There are three main dimensions to the study of the self.

– Philosophy and psychology
  The study in the nature of the self and the mystery of life is mainly based on the relationship between human with society, environment, nature and the universe. In the field of philosophy and psychology, the most representative viewpoint is the philosopher Descartes "I think, therefore I am" [4].

© IFIP International Federation for Information Processing 2022
Published by Springer Nature Switzerland AG 2022
Z. Shi et al. (Eds.): ICIS 2022, IFIP AICT 659, pp. 29–36, 2022.
https://doi.org/10.1007/978-3-031-14903-0_4

- The Brain and Neurobiology

  Reflections from neurobiological experiments and cases exploring the brain and biology of the self. [2] explored the self and self-awareness in terms of evolution and brain evolution. A threefold self of autobiographical self; core self; proto self is proposed.

- Mathematics and Artificial Intelligence

  [10] described the personified entity-the 'self', through five attributes: identity, physical embodiment, mental states, experiences, and reflections on how others may think about oneself. To explain self-awareness, a brain inspired model of self-awareness is proposed.

Scientists in three fields (philosophy, brain science, mathematics and artificial intelligence) offer perspectives on the self from their own perspectives. We believe that if we describe life as matter and information, the most important parts of the self, apart from the physical organism of life (matter), are the two parts of needs and mechanisms (corresponding to the information part). All life has needs, and needs drive the evolution of life. All the activities of living beings are a continuous process of satisfying various needs. This paper proposes a model of the self based on the evolution of needs to explain the self and self-awareness from another perspective [9].

2   The Nature and Needs of Life

2.1   The Nature and Representation of the Self

We believe that the nature of the self should be the same as the nature of life. In terms of the relationship between the organism and its environment, the self, representing the organism, is the starting and origin of observation of the world. This starting stems from the birth of life. With the development of perception, it grows to become the observer and manager of life, the system that identifies and controls the relationship between the object and the environment on behalf of the living object. Only if these conditions are met can the self be characterised and self-awareness explained.

2.2   The Primary Needs and Principle of Life

The nature of life involves the structure and origin of life, and there is no universally accepted conclusion on the origin of life. However, there is a relatively unanimous consensus that life consists of both material and information [3,7,11].

Being alive is not only a primary needs of living beings, but also a goal to be pursued and a source of various needs. The primary needs of life are thus briefly summarised: energy and the transmission of information about oneself. Further, taking into account the history of the evolution of life, we have the following primary principles of life [8].

- All life has primary needs that are endogenous to the organism and live and die with it.

- In an open and changing environment, the needs of life change in response to changes in form and environment, but the primary needs remain the same.
- The primary needs inherent in all organisms are the fundamental driving force behind their evolution. And all life phenomena are the result of the internal needs of organisms acting on themselves and interacting with their external environment.

Briefly, the primary needs of life are centred on energy and the transmission of information about oneself. These two primary intrinsic needs, combined with the internal and external environment, drive and give rise to complex forms of life, giving rise to a multitude of new needs. Different stages of evolution and different types of life have different expressions of life forms and needs.

3   Evolution and Representation of the Needs of Life

On the basis of the previous arguments we can argue that:

- primary needs and life are essentially the same and unified. So this primary needs, which is endogenous to the organism, should be the central feature of the primitive self.
- As life evolving, needs evolving and expanding, the primordial self also evolves and develops.

3.1   Needs Representation and Original Self-evolution in Single-Celled and Complex Organisms

Pheromones in the Reproduction of Budding Plant Yeast. The budding yeast is a mononuclear fungus with two reproductive phenotypes [5], a and α, each secreting a and α factors, a peptide pheromone. A cells secrete an a factor that also expresses a GPCR as a receptor for another α factor. And α cells secrete an α factor that also expresses a GPCR as a receptor for another a factor. In order to reproduce and mate, the opposite cells secrete peptide pheromones that activate receptors. The opposing factor and its own receptor are internalised to activate the cellular pathway. Then the a and α cells grow towards each other's polarity and produce a cell fusion. More budding yeasts are then propagated (Fig. 1).

The example of budding yeast illustrates that cells have the ability to express their needs and sense information about their environment. Thus, in addition to its primary needs (such as replicating DNA and capturing glucose), a single-celled organism interacts with its environment, including exchanging energy and information. Environmental changes, as well as organismal experiences, also alter genetic information.

The needs of an organism, such as biological perception, emotional needs and social needs, are generated by the interaction of an intact individual organism with its environment and other organisms. Thus, the core features of the 'self' of a complex multi-system. From a simple primitive self, it evolves into a complex

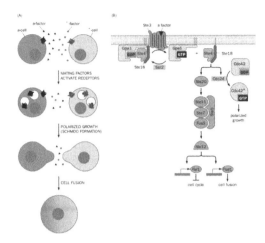

Fig. 1. Mating propagation of budding plant yeast [6].

'primary self'. This 'primary self' is characterised by a number of coding proteins, neurons and neural to impulse that encode the needs of the core characteristic of the 'self'.

From an evolutionary point of view, the move from a gene-cellular self to an organismal self integrated into a system is a breakthrough. The 'self' of each relatively independent functioning system brings together the 'selves' of many cells, and the 'self' of a complex multi-system organism brings together the self of many systems. The 'self' of a multi-system complex organism brings together the 'self' of multiple systems. A recursive nested pattern of selves is formed.

3.2   Representation Needs and Self-awareness of Human

What is most important in humans compared to other primates and mammals is that the brain has a well-developed neocortex. The neocortex, together with the hippocampus, provides a variety of specific neurological functions for the memory and sensory processing of information. The neocortical system includes several centres for the processing of sensory information such as language, vision, hearing, smell, touch, taste, movement and decision-making. Neural groups such as the hypothalamus and amygdala are responsible for primary needs perception and regulatory processing functions such as fear, hunger and thirst, sexual urges and emotions. The clusters of neurons form a distributed multicentre sensory processing system that works in concert with each other to process the various needs inherent in the organism [1].

The neocortex has the capacity for long-term memory, feature extraction and inductive deduction of needs and experiential information. This ability allows human needs to evolve from simple and clear primitive needs, rich and concrete primary needs, abstract and complex higher needs. It also allows the self to evolve into a complex system of abstract concepts.

4   Self-model Based on the Evolution of Needs

4.1   Iterative Model of Needs Evolution

In Sect. 3, the evolution of needs is discussed in terms of the evolution of life. By constantly exchanging energy and information with the environment, new needs and processing mechanisms evolve, and a new self evolves, in an interactive iterative process with reflexivity. This section further takes a formal approach to represent this self-referential reflexive interactive iterative process in a mapping to construct an iterative model of needs evolution.

X represents the space composed of all needs, and Y is the space of information and the energy of inside and outside the organism.

Mapping $F: X \rightarrow Y$ represents the needs x of the living organism, the effect of energy and information on the environment through action F as y, i.e. $y = F(x)$. Mapping $Q: Y \rightarrow X$. The energy and information of the environment is y, and the effect on (self) needs through the feeling process Q is x, i.e. $x = Q(y)$. $x \subseteq X$ is the needs corresponding to the self, and $y \subseteq Y$ is the environmental energy and information associated with the self.

Q and F mathematically represent mappings, which are actions and processes for the organism. $x' = Q[F(x)]$ represents the iterative evolution of self-needs as they interact with the environment. When $x \subseteq x'$, the needs is increasing with time.

This iterative evolution takes place in specific spatial. So it is important to consider the spatio-temporal aspects of the evolution of life. $x(t + 1) = Q[F(x(t))]$, t is time and represents the different stages in the evolution of life. For example, single-celled organisms, fish, reptiles, mammals, primates, humans, etc.

If t_0 is the primitive stage of life, then $x(t_0)$ is the primitive intrinsic primary needs of life (energy and information), which correspond to the primitive self. If t_1 represents the neuronal emergence stage, then $x(t1) = Q[F(x(t_0))]$ adds intercellular communication and simple integration to the primitive needs, similar to the ascidian model. If at the t_m stage life evolves a long-term memory nervous system, a well-established metabolic system, a simple language system, $x(tm)$ is a multi-layered, complex system of needss. The sum of all needs and the corresponding need-processing mechanisms form a 'primary self'. The primary self, with its predictive and simple reasoning capabilities.

When evolution reached the primate and human stages, the needs for social communication led to the evolution of a well-developed long-term memory system, complex language and abstract concepts. And primates and humans develop the ability to abstract, reasoning, thinking and comprehension. At some point during the $m + 1$ stage the brain's nervous system integrates and abstracts information about its various needs and states into a symbol and binds it to itself. The primary self evolves into the social self.

$x(t + 1) = Q[F(x(t))]$ indicates from the perspective of needs evolution that life increases in needs from simple to complex in its interaction with the environment as it evolves through time and space. The growth of energy and information in living organisms can also be observed in terms of $y(t+1) = F[Q(y(t))]$, indicating that the information memory and processing capacity of living organisms grows as life evolves, from genes, protein molecules, to neuronal cells and clusters of neuronal cells. In addition to natural biological memory, humans have invented new methods of memory storage such as paper, magnetic media and photoelectric media to meet the growing needs for complex information memory and processing.

This iterative process reveals that the mystery and meaning of life lies in the continuous transformation of energy into information. Life is a product of information and a processor of information, as well as a converter of energy to information.

Needs are the driving force behind the continuous evolution within the living organism. The evolution of needs facilitates the evolution of mechanisms for the representation of needs and the management of needs, forming the self and self-awareness. The self and the model of self evolution are further explored below.

4.2   Evolutionary Model of the Self

Self-awareness. Self-awareness is an organism's perception of its own needs and state, driven by the self (needs). The needs-centred self of single-celled organisms is still in its infancy. Mammals have long-term memory, and some ability to integrate abstraction, and a needs-integrated abstraction of the self begins to emerge. Some animals that live in packs and cooperate, such as wolves, have some language and have the need to express themselves and their self-perception, i.e. awareness. Needs is integrated and abstracted into a speech. The needs is integrated with the state of the self and map to the brain nervous system to gain attention. The sum of the needs of the biological individual is the connotation of the self. The organism's degree of self-awareness of this abstraction of needs constituting the self varies, depending on the ability to abstract and predict.

Embodied mapping is a process of abstract mapping of information about the organism's own self to its own brain. This is because the brain is already equipped with information about its own various needs and states (functional areas of the cerebral cortex). But it may not have integrated the abstraction into a concept. The establishment of the self is completed when the abstraction is mapped into a concept driven by needs.

The human brain has a highly developed neocortical layer. The neocortex is capable of integrating and abstracting the various needs and state information transmitted to the brain's nerves into a representation of the need bundled with symbols and with itself. The expression of this operation is the self. It is a process of embodied mapping of needs. This process is not just a symbol but also manipulates the biological individual with a representation of the highest level of need. This means that the mapping goes both ways, from the abstract ego which in turn affects needs and itself. This process constitutes the limit loop of the neural network system. Brain networks are distributed and dynamically connected, so the limit loops of this mapping may also be dynamically connected (Fig. 2).

The abstract mapping of neurological perceptions and information about the needs of the biological individual into its own brain becomes the self.

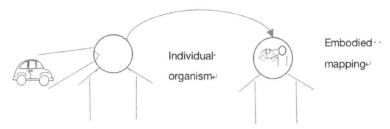

Fig. 2. The process of embodied mapping.

The Evolution Model of the Self. The cell is the simplest and independent living organism. The self is the general term for the sum of the organism and its needs and its management mechanisms. As the environment changes, needs and self, life object and management mechanisms evolve. It evolves from the primitive self to the primary self and the socialised self, etc. Depending on the evolution of the composition of the self and its connotative features, these different evolutionary stages of the self can be expressed in the following formalised model of the quintet or Seven-tuple.

The quintet represents $[O, N, C, M, E]$. O is organism. N represents primitive or complex needs. C is the control mechanisms and awareness. M is memory of based or long-term. E is different kind of environmental interaction.

The Seven-tuple represents $[O, N, C, M, E, Input, Output]$. Compared to a quintet, a Seven-tuple has more inputs and outputs.

Primitive self = (cellular organism, primitive needs, control mechanisms with primitive awareness, genetically based memory and language, primitive environmental interaction), molecular polarity and proteins and DNA as internal language for triadic communication and control, genes encode memory needs information, entity is the cell.

Primary self = (organism with neurological system, complex needs, control mechanisms with prediction and low-level awareness, long-term memory, complex environmental interactions).

Socialized self = (organism with developed nervous system, complex abstract needs, control mechanisms with higher consciousness, long-term memory, symbolic language, input, output).

5   Dicussion and Conclusion

The process of human development and growth reflects the evolution of the self and self-awareness.

Self-awareness is the perception of oneself and the establishment of a relationship with the surrounding environment. The human being is progressively refined, a process of knowing oneself. The newborn infant first perceives its own body, successively perceiving the temperature and pressure of the self, the skin, then the mouth, the sense of sight and hearing, the hands and limbs, the torso, etc. Perception of self in relation to needs, for example, the mouth can eat and satisfy the need to eat; vision can see the environment and satisfy a certain sense of security. Then comes the perception of one's own needs and the establishment of a sense of self. Needs are changing and the ego is constantly developing. Self-awareness builds gradually as language and abstraction skills develop. The needs-based model of self-evolution provides ideas for exploring the nature of life, and the direction for exploring the development of general-purpose intelligent robots.

References

1. Crick, F., Clark, J.: The astonishing hypothesis. J. Conscious. Stud. **1**(1), 10–16 (1994)
2. Damasio, A.R.: Self Comes to Mind: Constructing the Conscious Brain. Vintage, New York (2012)
3. Davies, P.: Does new physics lurk inside living matter? Phys. Today **73**(8), 34–41 (2020)
4. Descartes, R.: The Philosophical Works of Descartes, (2 volumes) (1955)
5. Foltman, M., Molist, I., Sanchez-Diaz, A.: Synchronization of the budding yeast *Saccharomyces cerevisiae*. In: Sanchez-Diaz, A., Perez, P. (eds.) Yeast Cytokinesis. MMB, vol. 1369, pp. 279–291. Springer, New York (2016). https://doi.org/10.1007/978-1-4939-3145-3_19
6. Futcher, B.: Cell cycle synchronization. Methods Cell Sci. **21**(2), 79–86 (1999)
7. Krakauer, D., Bertschinger, N., Olbrich, E., Flack, J.C., Ay, N.: The information theory of individuality. Theory Biosci. **139**(2), 209–223 (2020). https://doi.org/10.1007/s12064-020-00313-7
8. Levin, M., Dennett, D.C.: Cognition All the Way Down. Aeon Essays, Retrieved (2020)
9. Luo, L.: Principles of Neurobiology. Garland Science, New York (2020)
10. Subagdja, B., Tan, A.H.: Towards a brain inspired model of self-awareness for sociable agents. In: Thirty-First AAAI Conference on Artificial Intelligence (2017)
11. Wołos, A., et al.: Synthetic connectivity, emergence, and self-regeneration in the network of prebiotic chemistry. Science **369**(6511), eaaw1955 (2020)

Spiking Neuron Network Based on VTEAM Memristor and MOSFET-LIF Neuron

Jiahui Fu[1] , Shuiping Gou[1,2] , and Zhang Guo[2(✉)]

[1] Key Laboratory of Intelligent Perception and Image Understanding of Ministry of Education, School of Artificial Intelligence, Xidian University, Xi'an 710071, Shaanxi, China
shpgou@mail.xidian.edu.cn
[2] Academy of Advanced Interdisciplinary Research, Xidian University, Xi'an 710071, Shaanxi, China
guozhang@xidian.edu.cn

Abstract. Neuromorphic computing has been widely developed due to its low power consumption and powerful interpretability. LIF neurons, the general-purpose neurons in neuromorphic computing, are under constant research in hardware implementations of spiking neural networks. In this paper, we design a LIF circuit with MOSFET based on the mathematical model of the LIF neuron. The simulated circuit can be directly applied to the spiking neural network through the VTEAM memristor crossbar architecture. The effect of parameter changes in the circuit on the membrane potential is demonstrated. Finally, we validate feasibility of the process on the DVS128 gesture dataset using a generic spiking neural network architecture and obtain satisfactory performance.

Keywords: LIF neuron · Spiking neural network · Memristor

1 Introduction

Spiking neural networks [1] is a critical development in neuromorphic computing. For the trade-off between model reasonableness and computational feasibility, Leaky Integrate-and-Fire(LIF) neuron has been widely used in spiking neural networks [2]. Many improvements in the model structure are currently being made in the field of spiking neuron networks [3,4]. A Circuit Simulation tool, such as SPICE, allows LIF neurons to be used more efficiently in spiking neural networks.

This research was funded by the Natural Science Foundation of Shaanxi Province (Grant No. 2022JQ-661) and the Fundamental Research Funds for the Central Universities (Grant No. XJS222215).

Z. Shi et al. (Eds.): ICIS 2022, IFIP AICT 659, pp. 37–44, 2022.
https://doi.org/10.1007/978-3-031-14903-0_5

In this paper, we designed a LIF circuit based on the biological properties of LIF neurons. With this circuit, the values of the membrane time constant, threshold voltage and other indicators of the LIF neuron can be adjusted by the circuit properties [2]. The input to the model will be converted into voltage pulses. The crossbar structure [5] passes the input voltage pulses through a memristor node with a resistance value to generate the output voltage pulses. Next, we built a spiking neural network with layer-by-layer propagation. After steps such as integration processing on the DVS128 gesture dataset [6], the feasibility of the network for the action classification task on the DVS dataset is verified.

2   Proposed Method

In this section, we will briefly describe the structure of the LIF neuron model and analyse its modelling mechanisms. Next, the circuit designed to control the parametric characteristics of the LIF model is described, along with an analysis of its construction principles and component characteristics. Finally, the acquisition process and the processing of the adopted dataset will be presented.

2.1   Leaky Integrate-and-Fire Model

From a dynamical system perspective, the LIF model reduces the Hodgkin Huxley(HH) model's computational complexity while maintaining the HH model's [7,8] necessary properties and is now the more commonly used neuron for large-scale SNN simulations [9]. The LIF model can be summarised in the following equation:

$$C_m \frac{dV}{dt} = -G_L \left(V(t) - E_L \right) + I_{in} \tag{1}$$

assume that $\tau = RC_m$, then the above equation can be expressed as:

$$\tau \frac{dV}{dt} = E_L - V(t) + RI_{in} \tag{2}$$

where C_m represents the capacitance of the cell membrane surface, G_L represents the conductance of the leakage term, E_L represents the resting potential, I_{in} represents the incoming current, τ represents the time constant. When the external current input raises the accumulated potential to a certain threshold, a pulse will be generated. The membrane potential then returns to a reset potential V_{reset}. Since the model is a computationally tractable first-order differential equation, it is often used as a spiking neuron in large-scale spiking neural network construction.

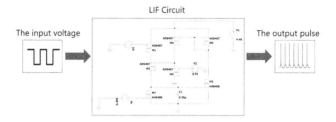

Fig. 1. Input and output of LIF circuit

2.2   Design of LIF Circuit

LIF neurons are classical neurons that are often applied to spiking neural networks. The LIF Circuit can be simulated by LTSpice, which is a general-purpose simulation software based on SPICE. The LTspice simulation circuit designed in this section can achieve the setting of the film time constant, pulse amplitude, and threshold voltage. This model uses a combination of PMOS and NMOS to design the circuit. The circuit can achieve the functional characteristics of the memristive devices. The circuit components used are shown in Fig. 1. A capacitor is used as a potential leakage element. The parameters of the MOSFET used are shown in Table 1.

Table 1. Parameters of MOSFET in LIF circuits

Parameter	Rg	Rd	Rs	Vto	Kp	Cgd(max)	Cgd(min)	Cgs	Cjo	Is	Rb	Vds	Ron	Qg
PMOS	3	14m	10m	−0.8	32	0.5n	0.07n	0.9n	0.26n	26p	17m	−20	34m	13n
NMOS	3	4.8m	3.6m	0.8	0.7	0.7n	0.25n	1n	0.36n	0.1u	6m	20	12m	18n

In Fig. 1, V1 is the voltage source that controls the threshold voltage for pulse issuance, V2 is the voltage source that controls the pulse amplitude, V3 is the voltage source that causes the membrane potential to rise, Vt is the voltage source that controls the membrane time constant, M1–M5 are PMOS of type AO6047, and M6–M7 are NMOS of type AO6408.

The crossbar structure is used in our designed spiking neural network testing process. There are many types of memristors. The device used here is one in which the voltage value does not vary in resistance between the V_{on} and V_{off}. Therefore it can be used as a fixed weight in the test process. Crossbar consists of a set of memristors, and the memristor model used is the VTEAM model [10]. It is a current threshold-based memristor model, i.e., the change in the memristor's resistance depends on the relationship between the current real-time value flowing through the memristor and the current elucidation value. The equations for the state variables of the model are as follows:

$$\frac{dx}{dt} = \begin{cases} k_{\text{off}} \cdot (v/V_{\text{off}} - 1)^{\alpha_{\text{off}}} \cdot f_{\text{off}}(x) & 0 < V_{\text{off}} < v \\ 0 & V_{\text{on}} < v < V_{\text{off}} \\ k_{\text{on}} \cdot (v/V_{\text{on}} - 1)^{\alpha_{\text{on}}} \cdot f_{\text{on}}(x) & v < V_{\text{on}} < 0 \end{cases} \qquad (3)$$

where $k_{off}, k_{on}, \alpha_{off}, \alpha_{on}$ are the fitted parameters of the model. V_{off}, V_{on} are the voltage thresholds of the model. f_{off}, f_{on} are the window functions of the model (Shahar).

v is the voltage across the memristor:

$$v = R_M(x) \cdot i \tag{4}$$

where R_M is the amnestic resistor resistance value:

$$R_M(x) = R_{\mathrm{on}} + \frac{x - x_{\mathrm{on}}}{x_{\mathrm{off}} - x_{\mathrm{on}}} (R_{\mathrm{off}} - R_{\mathrm{on}}) \tag{5}$$

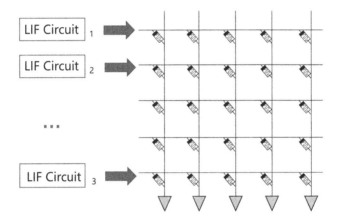

Fig. 2. Schematic of the output from the LIF circuit to the Crossbar structure.

With the pulse output from this circuit, it can be inserted into the crossbar structure [5]. The circuit corresponds to the neuron layer of the neural network. Afterwards, we can test the spiking neural network to arrive at the output of the pattern recognition problem. A schematic of the process is shown in Fig. 2.

2.3   Correspondence Between Network and Circuit

The Fig. 3 shows the correspondence of the parameters between the neural network and the LIF circuit. The input in the network is converted into a voltage input into the LIF circuit, and the weight of the network is converted into the conductance value of the memristor. The LIF model used is a simplified model built into SpikingJelly [11].

Upon inputting an RGB picture to the neural network, the values of the pixel points on the picture are first converted into voltage values and loaded on the input port of the neural network. Subsequently, the weights of the columns corresponding to this input voltage in the network are set, at which point the corresponding amnesia resistance of the crossbar in the circuit is also changed.

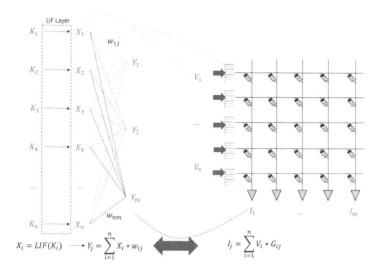

Fig. 3. Correspondence between spiking neural network and simulated circuit

2.4 Processing of the DVS128 Gesture Dataset

The DVS dataset is a neuromorphic dataset obtained from event camera shots. DVS128 gesture dataset contains 11 hand gestures from 29 subjects under 3 illumination conditions [6]. We integrate the original event stream into frame data and divide the data evenly by the number of events according to the set number size [4]. The resulting frame of the dataset after integration is shown in Fig. 4.

The image shown in Fig. 4 is a random selection of examples from the DVS 128 Gesture dataset after integrating the pulses. Subsequently, we intend to apply spiking neural networks to the obtained image frames for classification.

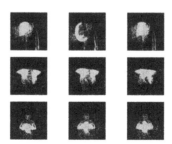

Fig. 4. Continuous frame of the DVS dataset after integration

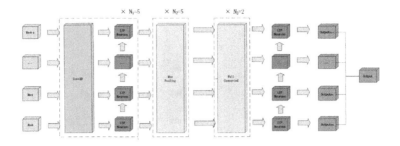

Fig. 5. Spiking neural network architecture diagram

2.5 Network Formulation

A generic spiking neural network is constructed here, as shown in Fig. 5 contains five 2D convolutional layers, five pooling layers, two fully connected layers and several spiking neuron layers [4]. There are about 27 million model parameters. The input image is expanded into a vector and fed into the network.

The vectors are encoded in the LIF layer in the first Conv2D layer. Finally, an 11-dimensional classification probability vector is output by a one-dimensional pooling operation. The one with the highest probability dimension is the predicted classification.

3 Performance Analysis and Discussion

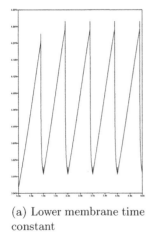

(a) Lower membrane time constant

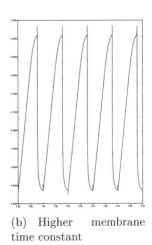

(b) Higher membrane time constant

Fig. 6. Performance of different film time constants

The LIF circuit design allows us to simulate the mathematics of some LIF neurons. This is shown below is the membrane potential curve obtained in the circuit by setting different values of the voltage source to control the membrane period. The membrane time constant is determined by the conductance and capacitance values of the circuit, and when the circuit is determined, the value is a definite term, and it can be seen that the time for the circuit to reach the threshold voltage in a cycle varies while the membrane time constant varies. A comparative plot of the effect of voltage adjustment on the membrane potential corresponding to the membrane time constant is shown in Fig. 6.

 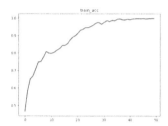

(a) Value of the loss function for train dataset

(b) Accuracy of the train dataset

Fig. 7. Loss and accuracy graph for training

This LIF circuit also adjusts the resetting potential of the LIF neuron. The circuit controls the return of the membrane potential to the resetting potential when the pulse release threshold potential is reached.

As shown in Fig. 7, this simple network performs well on the DVS128 gesture dataset, with an accuracy of about 90% on the test dataset. The performance of the test dataset is shown in Fig. 8.

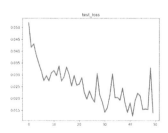 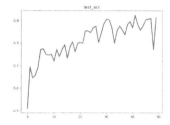

(a) Value of the loss function for test dataset

(b) Accuracy of the test dataset

Fig. 8. Loss and accuracy graph for test dataset

4   Conclusion

In this paper, we propose a LIF circuit that can simulate LIF neurons using different parameters controlled by the value of the supply voltage. We compare the effect of different parameter values obtained at various voltages on the membrane potential profile. Additionally, we propose a method in which the pulses generated by the circuit are directly incorporated into the neural network algorithm. The input voltage pulses can be used for pattern recognition after passing through the crossbar structure. Also, the DVS128 gesture dataset was processed, and a network was designed and tested using a spiking neural network based on LIF neurons. It can be seen that our training converges very fast and that the convergence of the model is very effective. In addition, a well performed result was obtained on the test dataset.

References

1. Maass, W.: Networks of spiking neurons: the third generation of neural network models. Neural Netw. **10**(9), 1659–1671 (1997)
2. Gerstner, W., et al.: Neuronal Dynamics: From Single Neurons to Networks and Models of Cognition. Cambridge University Press, Cambridge (2014)
3. Fang, W., et al.: Deep residual learning in spiking neural networks. In: Advances in Neural Information Processing Systems, vol. 34 (2021)
4. Fang, W., et al.: Incorporating learnable membrane time constant to enhance learning of spiking neural networks. In: Proceedings of the IEEE/CVF International Conference on Computer Vision (2021)
5. Yakopcic, C., Taha, T.M.: Energy efficient perceptron pattern recognition using segmented memristor crossbar arrays. In: The 2013 International Joint Conference on Neural Networks (IJCNN). IEEE (2013)
6. Amir, A., et al.: A low power, fully event-based gesture recognition system. In: Proceedings of the IEEE Conference on Computer Vision and Pattern Recognition (2017)
7. Hodgkin, A.L., Huxley, A.F.: A quantitative description of membrane current and its application to conduction and excitation in nerve. J. Physiol. **117**(4), 500 (1952)
8. Gupta, A., Long, L.N.: Hebbian learning with winner take all for spiking neural networks. In: 2009 International Joint Conference on Neural Networks. IEEE (2009)
9. Indiveri, G.: A low-power adaptive integrate-and-fire neuron circuit. In: Proceedings of the 2003 International Symposium on Circuits and Systems, 2003, ISCAS 2003, vol. 4. IEEE (2003)
10. Kvatinsky, S., et al.: VTEAM: a general model for voltage-controlled memristors. IEEE Trans. Circ. Syst. II Express Briefs **62**(8), 786–790 (2015)
11. Fang, W., et al.: SpikingJelly (2020). https://github.com/fangwei123456/spikingjelly

Machine Learning

A Deception Jamming Discrimination Method Based on Semi-supervised Learning with Generative Adversarial Networks

Hongliang Luo, Jieyi Liu[✉], Jingyao Liu, Yue Wu, and Yaru Yin

Xidian University, Xi'an 710071, China
jieyiliu@xidian.edu.cn

Abstract. For deception jamming countermeasures of multistatic radar systems, existing intelligent anti-jamming methods require sufficient training samples and a large amount of labelled data, but it is difficult to obtain abundant labelled radar echo data in realistic operational environments. A deception jamming discrimination method based on semi-supervised learning with generative adversarial networks is proposed to specifically handle the situation of inadequate labelled samples. In this way, a small amount of labelled data and a large amount of unlabelled data obtained from radar stations, together with pseudo-labelled data generated by the generator are used to train the discriminator to improve the performance of jamming discrimination and the robustness of the discrimination network by exploiting the game between the generator and the discriminator. Simulation results show that, the proposed method can achieve the same performance using less than 10% of the labelled data of existing algorithms. It reduces data requirements and enhances operational capabilities, which is better suited to real-world battlefield environments.

Keywords: Multistatic radar systems · Semi-supervised learning · Anti-jamming method · Signal processing

1 Introduction

The electromagnetic environment of modern warfare is becoming more and more complex [1, 2]. The information collected by the multistatic radar system is shared and fused in the fusion centre, which pushes for better identification and suppression of the interference and greatly improve the system's systematic capability [3, 4].

Existing intelligent anti-jamming methods have exploited deep neural networks to multistatic radar jamming countermeasures, Liu proposed an anti-jamming method based on convolutional neural network, which effectively reduces the impact of noise and pulse number. At the same time, the influence of radar distribution on jamming discrimination under non-ideal conditions is mitigated [5]. Luo proposed a semi-supervised deception jamming discrimination method based on convolutional deep belief network, which lowers data requirements and enhances operational capability [6]. All these methods use various deep neural networks to address the technical bottlenecks of the traditional echo signal processing process, such as insufficient feature extraction, single discrimination method, and information loss in the conversion process, in order to achieve effective discrimination of false targets.

However, the existing methods have common flaws that they all rely highly on big data volume and the performance is poor under non-ideal conditions. However, in the reality, it is difficult to collect the labelled data of the target and the interference discrimination cannot perform well when the SNR or sampling volume is low. To address the above issues, this paper focuses on constructing an end-to-end generative adversarial network and introduces a semi-supervised neural network training model from the perspective of learning the feature representation of the true distribution of the echo data. In this paper, a small amount of labelled data, a large amount of unlabelled data, and a large amount of pseudo-labelled data generated by the generator are used to train the discriminator. We borrow the idea from min-max game to help discriminate between the generator and the discriminator, the advantage of which is better performance of deceptive interference discrimination and robustness of the discrimination network, as well as less dependence of the network on the amount of data and improved effectiveness of small sample interference discrimination.

2 Signal Model

2.1 The Construction of a Multistatic Radar System Model

A multistatic radar system is composed with M transmitters and N receivers, and the transmitting signals of each transmitter are orthogonal to each other, as shown in Fig. 1. Supposing that the transmitting signal of the m-th transmitting station is $S_m(t, q)$, $m = 1, \ldots, M$, where t denotes the fast time domain, $0 \leq t \leq T$ (T stands for the length of time for a pulse repetition interval (PRI)), while q denotes the slow time domain, $q = 1, 2, \cdots, Q$ (Q equals the quantity of pulse repetition interval). Owing to the orthogonality of transmit signal, the target signal of a total of MN transmit-receive channel can be obtained by a matched filter set consisting of each transmit signal, where

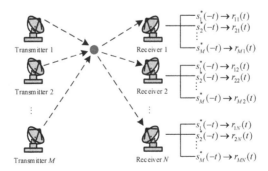

Fig. 1. Target detection channels of the multistatic radar system

the channel consisting of the m-th transmitter to the n-th receiver ($n = 1, \ldots, N$) is labelled as Channel-mn, the target echo signal of which is defined as $r_{mn}(t, q)$.

Before the joint process of echo signals from each radar station in a multistatic radar, time and phase should be synchronized. The method of time synchronization is based on the unified time with reference to the multistatic radar, while phase synchronization is based on grid search to capture the target echoes from different radar stations in the same spatial resolution cell (SRC) for correlation identification.

Assuming that the target is equipped with a self-defense jammer, the received signal at each receiver $r_n(t, q)$ is the superposition of the real target signal $S_m(t, q)$, the jamming signal $J_m(t, q)$ and the noise signal $N_m(t, q)$:

$$r_n(t, q) = \sum_{m=1}^{M} r_{mn}(t, q) = \sum_{m=1}^{M} \left[S_m(t, q) + J_m(t, q) + N_m(t, q) \right] \tag{1}$$

Assuming that the real target obeys Swerlling-II undulation, assume α_n^q is the complex amplitude of the real target echo in the q-th PRI of the n-th receiver station, where α_n^q is a Gaussian distribution random variable with mean 0 and variance σ_n^2. For jamming signal, complex amplitudes in different pulse repetition intervals obey the same distribution and are independent of each other. Determined by the modulation method of the jammer, path attenuation and other factors, assume β_n^q is the complex amplitude of the false target captured by the n-th receiver. The noise signal is mutually independent complex Gaussian white signal $N_n(t, q) \sim CN\left(0, \sigma_{nk}^2\right)$, where σ_{nk}^2 denotes the variance of n-th echo's noise power.

2.2 Generation of Echo Data

After pulse compression of the echo by each receiver, considering the amount of sample data obtained by a single sampling of one PRI is too low to accurately describe the target characteristics, the slow time domain is detected to get multiple consecutive PRIs in the corresponding distance unit of the target, and use them as the signal vector of each radar station.

For unknown target echo, the sample data of real target is a complex Gaussian random vector with complex amplitudes component independent of each other, $\boldsymbol{\xi}^n = \left[\alpha_n^1, \alpha_n^2, \ldots, \alpha_n^q, \ldots, \alpha_n^Q \right]^{\mathrm{T}}$, where $\boldsymbol{\xi}^n \sim CN\left(0, \sigma_k^2 \mathbf{I}_{Q \times Q}\right)$ and $[\bullet]^{\mathrm{T}}$ denotes matrix transposition operation. The sample data of the active false target is an unknown random vector $\boldsymbol{\xi}^n = \left[\beta_n^1, \beta_n^2, \ldots, \beta_n^q, \ldots, \beta_n^Q \right]^{\mathrm{T}}$, which is related to the amplitude modulation parameters of the interfering signal. With the noise existing, what can be obtained from the received signal is slow time complex envelope sequences mixed with noise sequence, where $\mathbf{N}^n \sim CN\left(0, \sigma_{nk}^2 \mathbf{I}_{Q \times Q}\right)$ is noise signal sequence.

Finally, the slow time complex envelope sequences detected by receivers are sent into the multi-hidden layer network model to obtain the fusion centre's multidimensional and essential feature differences among different receivers for discrimination between true and false targets.

3 The Discrimination Network Based on SGAN

The training process of existing intelligent jamming adversarial methods relies on a large amount of labelled data. However, in real battlefield environments, the labelled data available for network training is limited. Therefore, this paper considers the construction of a semi-supervised generative adversarial network for jamming discrimination to improve battlefield operational performance.

In this paper, a SGAN model is constructed to obtain the multidimensional features of the received signals thus completing the discrimination of false targets. In semi-supervised GAN, we propagate data positively from the input layer to the output layer, and adjust the network structure parameters according to the error between the output and the input by a certain cost function, so that the output signal gradually approaches the label signal.

The input data of SGAN is made up with a combination of labelled real echoes and unlabelled generated data. For true target echoes, the data from different radar stations are linked horizontally after pre-processing (slow time complex envelope sampling) to build a data block and use it as a labelled input. The number of receiving stations N is set to be 4. Considering each input data block consists of $N * Q$ complex amplitude data, to facilitate the training of the network under different PRI conditions, the data block is then repeatedly expanded to a 40 * 40 data block, which is sent for supervised training.

The SGAN network uses a large amount of unsupervised data generated by the generator to enhance the discriminator's performance, in order to meet the output dimension matching the real echoes of a 40 * 40 block of data. Deconvolution is an inverse process of convolution (conv), thus scaling up the input dimension, where the input data of the generator is 5 * 5 noisy data passing through 3 inverse convolution layers, as is shown in Table 1 and Fig. 2. The output dimension is a simulated target echo signal of 40 * 40. The generator generates echo data that is highly similar to the real data and uses the unlabelled data to assist in the training of the discriminator. At the same time, the discriminator improves the imitation capability of the generator, which in turn improves the SGAN echo discrimination performance.

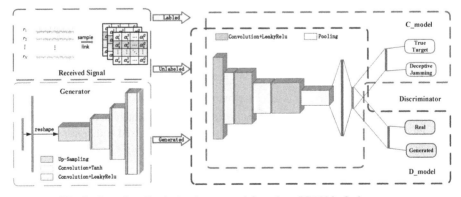

Fig. 2. Jamming discrimination network based on SGAN in fusion center

Table 1. The structure of SGAN

	Type	Number	Filter	Step
Generator	Conv 1	256	3 * 3	2
	Conv 2	128	3 * 3	2
	Conv 3	64	3 * 3	2
Discriminator	Deconv 1	64	4 * 4	2
	Deconv 2	128	4 * 4	2
	Deconv 3	256	4 * 4	2
	fc 1	Number	6400	
	fc 2	Number	2	
	C_Model	Activation function	softmax	
	D_Model	Activation function	sigmoid	

For the discriminator, two output layers are included, one for the unsupervised task and the other for the supervised task. They share the same feature extraction layer. The feature extraction layers constructed in this paper are 3 convolutional layers, the output of each convolutional layer containing a pooling operation with a step size of 2. The results of the convolutional part are passed into two fully connected layers and all outputs are normalized by batch processing. Ultimately, after 5 layers of operations, multidimensional essential features are extracted from the constructed block of data for echo discrimination. There are always two output predictions for each input data. One is a real/generated prediction, constructed as a C_model together with a feature extraction layer to predict whether the input data is true or false. A sigmoid activation function is used in the output layer and optimized using a binary cross entropy loss function. An output for supervised category prediction is constructed together with a feature extraction layer as D_model to predict the category of a given model. A softmax activation function is used in the output layer as well using the categorical cross entropy loss function for optimization. Although C_model and D_model have different output layers, they share all the feature extraction layers. This means that updates to one of the networks will affect both models [7, 8].

During training, the discriminator is trained on the network parameters by the unla-belled data generated by the generator together with the labelled data captured by the radar. The echo data are all simulated, set to a target noise ratio TNR range of −3 to 18 dB (TNR for real targets is the signal noise ratio SNR and TNR for fake targets is the interference noise ratio JNR) and PRI range of 4 to 24. Each TNR and PRI generates a large amount of training data for each of the target and interference respectively according to the same other parameters. 10% of the data is used for C_model network training, and the remaining 90% of the unlabelled data is used for D_model network training along with the pseudo-echo data generated by generators.

During testing, each TNR and PRI generates 1000 sets of training samples for each of the target and interference respectively according to the same other parameters. The test samples are fed into the trained SGAN model using a multi-dimensional essential feature vector for interference discrimination.

4 Simulation

4.1 Simulation Analysis

All methods are tested on the same computer, Intel(R) Xeon(R) Gold 5218 CPU @ 2.30 GHz 64-core, GeForce RTX 2080 TI. In contrast with the experiments in the references, the results and analysis are as follows.

Table 2. Discrimination probability of different algorithms

Methods	Traditional method	DNN	CNN	CDBN	SGAN
Discrimination probability	75.4%	98.9%	99.2%	91.3%	99.1%

When PRI is set to be 12 and SNR is set to be 6, the simulation result is listed in Table 2. The jamming discrimination effect based on SGAN with 10% labelled date, it is significantly better than the discrimination method using only single feature of manually extracted (the Traditional method [9]), indicating that SGAN network can extract the multi-dimensional essential features of signal data and jointly apply to the discrimination of real and false targets. Meanwhile, compared to DNNs [10] and CNNs [5] using 20,000 labelled data for training, SGAN's interference discrimination accuracy remains essentially the same, but with a 90% reduction in the number of labels required. Meanwhile, in contrast to semi-supervised CDBN's [6] 91.3% discrimination accuracy with the same labelled data, the SGAN interference discrimination algorithm's discrimination performance improves a lot.

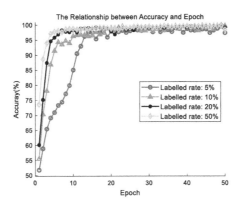

Fig. 3. Acc curves with different labeled data volumes

With the same parameter settings as above, Fig. 3 demonstrates the relationship between accuracy and epoch. SGAN algorithm improves the discrimination probability for different ratios of labeled data rapidly, as epoch increases eventually reaching over an accuracy higher than 98%. These experiments demonstrate the effectiveness of the proposed SGAN interference discrimination network. However, the increase in labelled rate leads to a faster increase in discrimination probability and ultimately a steadier result. A 5% label rate is less stable after multiple training rounds due to the small number of available labels. A label rate of 10% is able to guarantee a stable discrimination probability of greater than 99%, so this paper suggests using more than 10% of labels for the training of semi-supervised GAN interference discrimination networks to reduce the data dependency of the intelligent algorithm while ensuring the discrimination performance.

4.2   Simulation Results with Different PRI

Other parameters consistent with Sect. 4.1, by varying SNR and PRI, the simulation validates the effect of the number of pulses on the false target identification performance. The range of TNR is set between −3 dB and 18 dB, and obtaining the target identification probability through the constructed SGAN model at different number of pulses, where the number of PRI Q varies from 4 to 20 with a stride of 4.

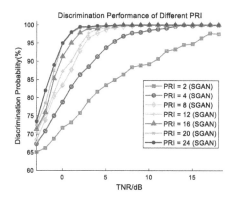

Fig. 4. The effect of the different TNR and PRI

As shown in Fig. 4, as the number of pulses PRI increases, the discrimination probability improves significantly for that the more samples used for interference discrimination in each group, the more information the deep neural network can use for reference, effectively improving the discrimination performance. When the amount of information satisfies the discrimination requirements, the discrimination probability tends to smooth out and no longer varies with PRI.

At the same time, as the TNR increases, the discrimination probability increases significantly, because the increase of TNR will reduce the influence of noise on the echo signal. The network can more easily obtain the essential characteristics of the real target or active deceptive interference, thus improving the performance of discrimination. Comparing with the literature [9], the above experiments demonstrate that the SGAN interference discrimination algorithm is able to guarantee interference discrimination performance under different PRI conditions.

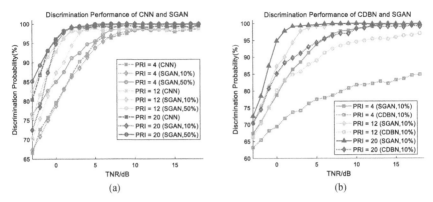

Fig. 5. The comparison of CNN, CDBN and SGAN. (a) The comparison of jamming discrimination effects between CNN and SGAN. (b) The comparison of jamming discrimination effects between CDBN and SGAN

4.3 The Comparison of Different Discrimination Methods

Compared with CNN jamming discrimination methods under the same condition, Fig. 5(a) simulation results reveals that the algorithm in this paper with 10% labelled data is slightly worse than CNN at low TNR. However, when TNR is greater than 0 dB, the discrimination probability of the two methods converges and are greater than 99% eventually. Also, when the proportion of labelled data is increased to 50%, the SGAN discrimination network can significantly outperform the fully supervised CNN discrimination network. The above comparison experiments are sufficient to demonstrate that the SGAN network is superior to existing CNN interference discrimination algorithms.

As shown in Fig. 5(b), the algorithm is able to guarantee a significant improvement in discrimination performance with the same label rate compared to the same semi-supervised CDBN interference discrimination algorithm. This experiment demonstrates that the SGAN network is a robust interference discrimination method that outperforms the CDBN semi-supervised interference discrimination network in different environments.

5   Conclusion

A semi-supervised GAN method for jamming discrimination of multi-base radar systems is put forward in this paper, specifically addressing the drawbacks of insufficient labelled samples on deceptive jamming discrimination network. The network uses a small amount of labelled data, a large amount of unlabelled data obtained from reality and pseudo-labelled data generated by generators to train the discriminator. The pseudo-labelled data reduces the dependence of the interference discrimination network on the amount of data, thus improving the robustness and universality of the discrimination performance under small sample conditions. Simulation results show that the method can achieve the same performance as CNN with 10% of the labelled data, much better than the performance of CDBN network with the same rate, compared with existing artificial intelligence interference identification methods that require tens of thousands of labelled data for network training. At the same time, this method significantly outperforms the original CNN interference discrimination method at 50% of the labelled data. The experiments demonstrate that this method lowers down data requirements, enhances the practicality of network construction, and is more suitable for real-world battlefield environments.

Acknowledgment. This work was funded by the National Natural Science Foundation of China under Grant No. 62106185 and the Fundamental Research Funds for the Central Universities under Grant No. JB210211.

References

1. Griffiths, H.: Multistatic, MIMO and networked radar: the future of radar sensors? In: The 7th European Radar Conference, pp. 81–84 (2010)
2. Godrich, H., Haimovich, A.M., Blum, R.S.: Target localization accuracy gain in MIMO radar-based systems. IEEE Trans. Inf. Theory **56**(6), 2783–2803 (2010)
3. Gao, Y., Li, H., Himed, B.: Knowledge-aided range-spread target detection for distributed MIMO radar in nonhomogeneous environments. IEEE Trans. Signal Process. **65**(3), 617–627 (2017)
4. Abdalla, A., Yuan, Z., Tang, B.: ECCM schemes in netted radar system based on temporal pulse diversity. J. Syst. Eng. Electron. **27**(5), 1001–1009 (2016)
5. Liu, J., Gong, M., Zhang, M., Li, H., Zhao, S.: An anti-jamming method in multistatic radar system based on convolutional neural network. IET Signal Process **16**, 220–231 (2021)
6. Luo, H., Liu, J., Wu, S., Nie, Z., Li, H., Wu, J.: A semi-supervised deception jamming discrimination method. In: 2021 IEEE 7th International Conference on Cloud Computing and Intelligent Systems (CCIS), pp. 428–432 (2021)
7. Prabhat, N., Vishwakarma, D.K.: Comparative analysis of deep convolutional generative adversarial network and conditional generative adversarial network using hand written digits. In 2020 4th International Conference on Intelligent Computing and Control Systems (ICICCS), pp. 1072–1075 (2020)
8. Goodfellow, I.J., et al.: Generative adversarial nets. In: Advances in Neural Information Processing Systems (NIPS 2014), vol. 27, pp. 2672–2680 (2014)
9. Zhao, S., Zhang, L., Zhou, Y., Liu, N., Liu, J.: Discrimination of active false targets in multistatic radar using spatial scattering properties. IET Radar Sonar Navig. **10**(5), 817–826 (2016)
10. Liu, J., Gong, M., Zhang, M., Zhan, T., Li, H., Zhang, M.: Method for discrimination of false targets in multistation radar systems based on the deep neural network. J. Xidian Univ. **48**(2), 133–138 (2021)

Fast Node Selection of Networked Radar Based on Transfer Reinforcement Learning

Yanjun Cao[1], Yuan Wang[2(✉)], Jingjing Guo[3], Li Han[1], Chao Zhang[1],
Jin Zhu[1], Tianyang Zhang[2], and Xiangrong Zhang[2]

[1] The 54th Research Institute of China Electronics Technology Group Corporation,
Beijing, China
[2] Key Laboratory of Intelligent Perception and Image Understanding of Ministry
of Education, Xidian University, Xian 710071, Shaanxi, China
963671029@qq.com
[3] National Laboratory of Radar Signal Processing, Xidian University, Xian 710071,
People's Republic of China

Abstract. The networked radar system can synthesize different echo signals received by various radars and realize the cooperative detection of multiple radars, becoming more and more critical for data fusion sharing and network collaboration. However, due to the large number and wide range of nodes in the networked radar system, there exists a redundancy problem in radar node assignment, which causes additional resource consumption and slows down the task execution speed of radar node selection. To solve the above problem, this paper proposes a fast radar node selection method based on transfer reinforcement learning to quickly select the optimal and minimum node resources. The proposed method devises a novel reward function for the Monte Carlo Tree and a different termination state of iteration to select the minimize the number of radar nodes. In order to further accelerate the selection of radar nodes, transfer reinforcement learning is presented to fully leverage the previous knowledge. Experimental results show that our proposed method can quickly select the optimal and minimum radar nodes in a brief period, significantly improving the speed of radar node selection in the networked radar.

Keywords: Reinforcement learning · Transfer learning · Monte Carlo Tree

1 Introduction

The nodes of the networked radar system can coordinate in different dimensions such as time, space, frequency, waveform, polarization and angle of view through the central node, which can better realize data fusion sharing and network coordination. However, due to the wide range of networked radar deployment and numerous nodes, there is a lot of redundancy for nodes assigned by a single

© IFIP International Federation for Information Processing 2022
Published by Springer Nature Switzerland AG 2022
Z. Shi et al. (Eds.): ICIS 2022, IFIP AICT 659, pp. 56–67, 2022.
https://doi.org/10.1007/978-3-031-14903-0_7

task, which seriously slows down the execution speed of the task and the timely response of the networked radar system.

Reinforcement learning has the ability to actively explore the environment, which can obtain feedback from the environment and make action decisions based on the feedback. This ability to continuously learn in a dynamic environment has given reinforcement learning a lot of attention. Silver et al. [13,14] learned the strategy of go game through reinforcement learning and achieved excellent results. Bello et al. [1] used reinforcement learning to train pointer networks to generate solutions for up to 100 nodes of the synthetic Travelling Salesman Problem (TSP) instances. In the networked radar system, different radar nodes may be unselectable when occupied by other tasks and the radar observation target usually moves fast, which leads to the rapid change in the search environment of the networked radar system. Therefore, reinforcement learning, as a learning method that interacts with the environment, is well suited for the radar node selection task in the networked radar system.

This paper presents a fast networked radar node selection method based on transfer [15] reinforcement learning. Specifically, we devise a novel reward function of the Monte Carlo Tree and redefine the termination state to select the least and optimal combination of nodes, which tackles the redundancy problem of single task radar node assignment. Besides, a large number of searches are required to reconstruct the Monte Carlo Tree for different tasks each time, seriously reducing the search efficiency and constraining the quick response of the networked radar systems. To further accelerate the search progress, this paper proposes transfer reinforcement learning to avoid random blind global searches, which highly reduces the node search time of networked radar system, and improves the quick response performance of networked radar system.

2 Related Work

2.1 Radar Node Selection

In the past few decades, radar node selection of MIMO array has attracted great attention in radar applications. Berenguer et al. [2] proposed a fast adaptive node selection method based on discrete random optimization, which uses active random approximation iteration to generate an estimated sequence of solutions. Mendezrial selected radar nodes through a compressed spatial sampling of received signals to reduce the complexity and power consumption of millimetre-wave MIMO systems. X. Wang et al. developed a series of deterministic based theory and optimization based methods for selecting radar node subsets and reconfiguring array structures to maximize the output SNR and improve the estimation of azimuth (DoA). In MIMO radar, most scholars mainly study node selection from target parameter estimation. Godrich [5] proposed an optimal radar node arrangement scheme to reduce the CRLB of aircraft speed estimates. Then he used combinatorial optimization to minimize the positioning error of multiple radar systems. Gorji [6] minimized its estimation error by calculating the target position estimation performance (CRLB) of MIMO radar node combinations. In MIMO radar sensor networks, joint antenna subset selection and optimal power distribution are realized by convex optimization.

Nevertheless, none of these methods can make feedback on changes in the environment. We use reinforcement learning to constantly interact with the environment to achieve efficient search in the rapidly changing environment of networked radar systems.

2.2 Reinforcement Learning

Reinforcement learning comprises Agent, Environment, State, Action, and Reward. After an agent acts, the environment will shift to a new state, for which the environment will give a reward signal (positive reward or negative reward). The agent then performs the new action according to specific strategies based on the reward of the new state and the environment feedback. The process described above is how an agent and the environment interact through states, actions, and rewards. Through reinforcement learning, an agent can know what state it is in and what actions it should take to get the maximum reward.

In the face of the complex networked radar system, it contains a lot of information and rules, which causes some difficulties in establishing the corresponding search environment. Monte Carlo search tree (MCTS) is an algorithm based on reinforcement learning, which does not require a given domain strategy or specific practical knowledge to make a reasonable decision. The ability to work effectively with no knowledge beyond the basic rules of selection scenarios means that MCTS can be widely used in many domains with only minor adjustments.

2.3 Transfer Learning

Transfer learning refers to acquiring knowledge from a source problem to solve a completely different but related new problem to achieve more efficient learning in a new task.

In transfer learning, there are two fundamental ideas: domain and task. The existing data is called the source domain, and the new knowledge to be learned is called the target domain. The data includes information data and model data. The specific task is to design the model to solve this problem. Generally, source domain data is migrated to solve the task of the target domain, that is, to build and design the ideal model of the target domain. This paper divides the transfer learning paradigm into three categories: inductive transfer, direct transfer learning, and unsupervised transfer learning. Among them, inductive transfer learning requires that the target task and source task are not the same but have a correlation, and so does unsupervised transfer learning. According to the content steps of transfer learning, transfer learning can be divided into four cases: transfer based on samples, transfer based on feature representation, transfer based on parameters, and transfer based on relative knowledge. Among them, the transfer from the sample to the sample refers to the transfer of source domain information to the target domain by assigning a certain weight to the target domain. The theory of feature transfer is to extract the main elements from the information contained in the source and target domains to make their distribution consistent. Relative data-based migration refers to mining the mapping of relative knowledge in the source domain and target domain.

The application of transfer learning can solve the drawbacks of information acquisition, that is, the absence of knowledge annotation or the utilization of historical source domain information, and generate valuable data for new tasks. In addition, individual users will be on the "shoulders of giants" when applying reinforcement learning and will be able to train their own tasks by using models placed on devices with superior computing power so as to improve the generalization ability of models. At the same time, a model with a high general degree is built on the basis of the individuation of other tasks. The model with better training results can flexibly cope with completely different environments and tasks, and the end-to-end requirements can meet the practical application.

Machine learning often relies on better training results: training and test data are crucial and must be distributed in the same domain. If the two data sets are very different, machine learning must spend more time accumulating new knowledge and models. Therefore, the study of transfer learning has begun to attract the attention of many researchers. Compared with machine learning in the past, transfer learning aims to extract high-quality training data by using the knowledge left by historical tasks to guide the rapid completion of recent tasks.

Reinforcement learning algorithm takes a long time to solve in the search process and is difficult to meet the requirements of real-time decision-making in a short time. The apparent advantage of transfer reinforcement learning lies in knowledge transfer ability. That is, every solving task is no longer independent and unrelated, and initial reconstruction is no longer required after inputting new tasks, so the acquired knowledge can be better utilized. Migration learning algorithm based on a large number of existing optimization of the effective extraction of knowledge, overcome classical mathematical calculation method relies on the building of mathematical model, to further speed up the optimization calculation of the traditional heuristic algorithm, effectively avoid the random global explore blindly, to guide the individual performs high accuracy of local search, optimization and improve efficiency and quality. Finally, it can give the minimum combination of nodes satisfying the requirements in more than a second among hundreds of millions of node combinations.

3   Methodology

3.1   Revisiting of Monte Carlo Tree

MCTS uses trees to store state, action and return data of Markov Decision Process(MDP), which simulates intelligent agent to generate data and calculate expectation to obtain the optimal strategy. The node attributes of the Monte Carlo Tree Search [4] include N, which represents the number of visits of the node during the training, with an initial value of 0. R, which is the reward of the current node and the initial value is 0. The larger the reward value is, the better the performance of the radar node will be for the target detection task executed. *Parent*, which is the parent node used for back propagation to traverse the entire tree up to the root node; *Children*, which is the set of the children in the current node; *State*, which is the node's state, each state corresponding to a node combination.

We employ Monte Carlo Tree to simulate a large number of radar node combinations and calculate their reward. The prefix tree records these node combinations and the calculation results. The final optimal node combinations are predicted by simulation results. In Sect. 3.2, we introduce the selection operation of our Monte Carlo Tree when simulating the generation of various combinations of radar nodes. For the original Monte Carlo tree, it can only carry out fixed radar node selection and cannot settle node redundancy. Therefore, we introduce a new reward function in Sect. 3.3 to realize the minimization of node numbers. In order to further accelerate the search, we introduce transfer reinforcement learning in Sect. 3.4.

3.2   The Lower Bound of Cramero ($CLRB$)

We use the lower bound of Cramero ($CLRB$) to evaluate the performance of the radar node selection scheme. The smaller CLRB is and the fewer radar nodes it contains, the better the selection of radar node combinations, resulting in the larger reward value.

$CLRB$ is the linear unbiased lower bound of the target location parameter estimation problem. We first simulate the multi-node echo signal according to the target location provided by the on-duty radar, then obtain the fisher information matrix by taking the second derivative of the target location parameters in the echo signal, and finally obtain the lower bound of the unbiased estimation corresponding to the target location. In this paper, we use the on-duty radar to provide the approximate location range of the target and select the node combination through the node selection algorithm to minimize the target's positioning error at this position and achieve accurate positioning of the target. The approximate calculation process is as follows:

1) Calculate the time delay based on the approximate target position provided by the on-duty radar.

$$
\begin{aligned}
\tau_{mn}\left(X_q\right) &= \frac{R\left(T_m, X_q\right) + R\left(R_n, X_q\right)}{c} \\
&= \frac{\sqrt{(x_m - x_q)^2 + (y_m - y_q)^2 + (z_m - z_q)^2} + \sqrt{(x_n - x_q)^2 + (y_n - y_q)^2 + (z_n - z_q)^2}}{c}
\end{aligned}
\tag{1}
$$

$R\left(T_m, X_q\right)$ and $R\left(R_n, X_q\right)$ are the approximate distances of the transmitting node T_m and the receiving node R_n to the target respectively. x_q, y_q, z_q is the approximate position of the aircraft detected by the watch radar. x_m, y_m, z_m is the coordinates of the transmitting node T_m. x_n, y_n, z_n is the coordinates of the receiving node R_n.

2) Time delay is used to calculate the echo signal of multiple nodes

$$rcp_n(t) = G_{R_n} \sum_{m=1}^{M} \sum_{q=1}^{Q} \delta_q a_{mn} \sqrt{P_m} G_{T_m} \exp\left(-j2\pi f_c \tau_{mn}(X_q)\right) s_m \left(t - \tau_{mn}(X')\right) + N_n(t)$$

$$\approx G_{R_n} \sum_{m=1}^{M} \delta_q a_{mn} \sqrt{P_m} G_{T_m} \exp\left(-j2\pi f_c \tau_{mn}(X_q)\right) s_m \left(t - \tau_{mn}(X')\right) + N_n(t)$$

$$(2)$$

G_{R_n}, G_{T_m} is array gain. δ_q is the reflectivity of each scattered point. $P_m(m = 1, 2, ..., M)$ is the transmitting power of the transmitting node T_m. S_m is the waveform. $N_n(t)$ is additive white Gaussian noise. $a_{mn}(m = 1, 2, ..., M, n = 1, 2, ..., N)$ is the direction vector of the transmitting or receiving node. f_c is the carrier frequency.

3) Using echo signal $rcp_n(t)$, spatial coherent processing, pulse compression and Angle measurement are used to predict target position parameters $\left(x, y, z, \delta^R, \delta^I\right)$.

4) Fisher information matrix is used to calculate the error of prediction target location parameters $\left(x, y, z, \delta^R, \delta^I\right)$, and then the lower bound of Cramero is:

$$CLRB_c = \sigma_{x_c CRB}^2 + \sigma_{y_c CRB}^2 + \sigma_{z_c CRB}^2 \qquad (3)$$

where, $\sigma_{x_c CRB}^2$, $\sigma_{y_c CRB}^2$, $\sigma_{z_c CRB}^2$ and are the errors of coordinates X, Y and Z respectively, which are obtained from time delay τ_{mn}, echo signal $rcp_n(t)$ and Fisher information matrix. The detailed calculation process is referred to [7].

3.3   Selection Flow

We start with the root node and then add new radar nodes in turn. For the node that has not reached the termination state, we randomly generate a child node of the current node as the new node or select the child node with the largest UCB value among the children nodes of the current node that have been visited as the new node. The selection stops for nodes that reach the terminal state, and an iteration ends. Where, the calculation formula of confidence value UCB is as follows:

$$UCB = \frac{r_i}{n_i} + C \times \sqrt{\frac{\ln F}{n_i}} \qquad (4)$$

where n_i is the access times of the node i, r_i is the reward value of the node i, and F is the total times that the parent node of the node i has been accessed. C is an adjustable hyperparameter (that is, an artificially set constant). In particular, we count the number of children to determine whether they are not accessed, partially accessed, or fully accessed.

3.4   Variable-Number Node Search

The Reward Function for the Number of Nodes. In reinforcement learning, the intelligent agent's goal is formalized as a particular signal, called return, which is transmitted through the environment and is calculated by the reward function. Monte Carlo Tree searches in the direction of maximizing return. In order to simultaneously search in the direction of minimizing the number of nodes, we introduce the number of nodes as a variable into the reward function r. Its specific calculation formula is as follows:

$$r = \begin{cases} (levels - len(move) + 1)/levels & 0 < CLRB \leq 10 \\ 0 & other \end{cases} \quad (5)$$

where $levels$ is the number of radar nodes that can observe a target, $moves$ is the combination of radar nodes, and $len(moves)$ is the number of nodes. We give the reward value referring to the number of radar nodes. The fewer the number of radar nodes, the greater the reward value.

Two Cases of Termination. After obtaining the reward function, we redefined the termination state of Monte Carlo Tree. The termination state is the symbol of the end of tree search, indicating that the node combination has met the requirements and there is no need to continue the search to add new radar nodes layer-by-layer. Since our goal is to find the minimum node combinations that satisfy the requirements, we don't have to search all the way to the leaf node. We set up two cases to reach the termination state, ensuring that each iteration outputs the minimum combination of nodes. One is to reach the leaf node of the tree (including all radar nodes); In another case, these selected radar nodes have met the performance requirements.

3.5   Transfer Reinforcement Learning

Transfer Reinforcement Learning. Transfer learning refers to acquiring knowledge from the source problem to solve another task or a new problem with different but related environment in order to achieve more efficient learning in the new task. The application of transfer learning can solve the drawbacks of information acquisition, that is, the absence of knowledge annotation or the utilization of historical source domain information, and generate valuable data for new tasks. Transfer learning and reinforcement learning are combined to extract high quality training data by using the knowledge left by historical tasks to guide the rapid completion of tasks in different environments.

The transfer reinforcement learning used in this paper achieves the fixed domain migration of the target task across multiple source tasks [8]. In this case, different source tasks share the same domain, and the migration algorithm will take the knowledge gathered from a set of source tasks as input and use it to improve performance in the target task [9]. The RL algorithm has a large number of parameters that define initialization and algorithm behavior [11]. Some migration methods change and adjust algorithm parameters based on the source task [16]. For example, if the action values in some state-action pairs are very similar across the source task, then the node parameters of the Monte Carlo tree of the target task can be initialized accordingly to speed up the learning process [10]. By doing this, we can accelerate the convergence of the model.

Training and Preservation. We repeatedly trained the same tree by inputting aircraft positions in different directions. And then node parameters(moves, reward, visits) are saved through breadth traversing the Monte Carlo Tree.

Rebuilding Tree. As the number of nodes increases layer by layer, we start to rebuild from the root node to find the combination of nodes whose prefix is the same as the parent node of this layer, and build new tree nodes. Ultimately, a trained Monte Carlo Tree is obtained by expanding layer by layer.

Fine Tuning. The search for node combination is carried out on the basis of the real-time aircraft coordinates. A bias item is introduced into the reward function to give more rewards to the combination of nodes that meet the requirements during fine-tuning to search for the direction of the optimal combination of nodes. Finally, according to the fine-tuning Monte Carlo Tree, the optimal node combination is picked out (Table 1).

Table 1. Radar node selection input parameters.

Parameters	Value
Number of nodes	145
K (Boltzmann's constant)	1.38e−23
T0	290
Noise factor	1e0.3
Radar loss	1e0.4
RCS	12.5
SNR	100
Number of large node lattice elements	256
Number of section lattice elements	16
B (Radar bandwidth)	1e6
Angle between radar plane and Z axis	$-\pi/4$

4   Experiments and Analysis

We employ 145 radar nodes, including five large nodes for transmitting and 140 small nodes for receiving, facing in all directions. Specific input parameters is as shown in Table 2. In the fine-tuning stage, the target's position is (667.65, 7631.29, 6427.87), which is $1e4\ m$ away from the origin of the coordinate system, and the number of iterations is 1000.

(1) Validation of minimum number of nodes

Based on the coordinate information of our radar nodes and the target, the minimum number of nodes our algorithm searched is four. So we search 50000 times randomly in the case of fixed three nodes and calculate CLRB. Since the baseline of CLRB is 10, as shown in Fig. 1, the subgraph is a local amplification of the ranges of 10, it can be seen that the CLRB of the 3-node combination cannot meet the requirement. Therefore, we can analyze that our Monte Carlo Tree can find the minimum number of nodes that meet the requirements, which can solve the problem of node redundancy distribution to improve the execution speed of tasks.

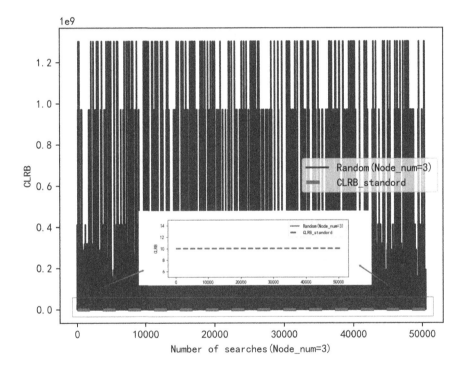

Fig. 1. 50,000 searches (number of nodes = 3).

Table 2. The average time of 50 times experiment.

Method	Time (s)
The original Monte Carlo Tree [4]	2.105
Ours	0.325
Genetic algorithm [12]	13.209
Simulated annealing algorithm [3]	6.300

(2) Comparison results

After obtaining the minimum number of nodes, we employ classical search methods to conduct comparative experiments. In order to ensure that each method can search for solutions that meet the conditions, we set the minimum number of iterations, respectively, among which the original Monte Carlo Tree and the simulated annealing algorithm is 1000. Ours is 10 and the genetic algorithm is 50. In the comparison of time performance in Fig. 2 and Table 2, when the number of fixed radar nodes is 4, our Monte Carlo Tree based on transfer learning is much faster. As shown in Fig. 3 and Table 3, the node combination searched by our algorithm is better than that of other search algorithms in most

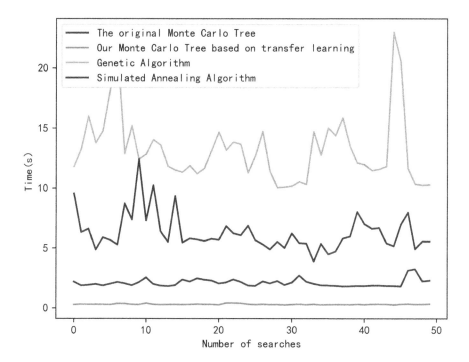

Fig. 2. Search time performance comparison(s).

Table 3. The average CLRB of 50 times experiment.

Method	CLRB (m)
The original Monte Carlo Tree [4]	2.098
Ours	1.239
Genetic algorithm [12]	2.406
Simulated annealing algorithm [3]	3.025

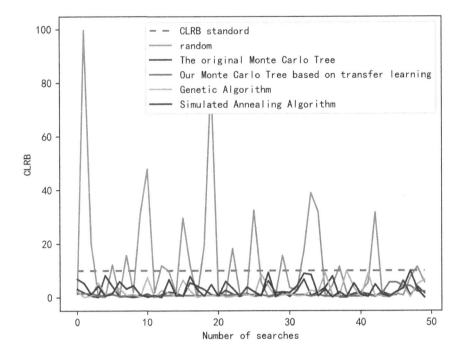

Fig. 3. Search results performance comparison(s).

cases. It can be seen that our algorithm is better able to find the optimal solution, which is conducive to improving the detection performance of the networked radar system.

5 Conclusion

In this paper, we propose a fast networked radar node selection method based on transfer reinforcement learning to tackle the redundancy problem in radar node assignment and accelerate the execution speed of radar node assignment in the networked radar system. Concretely, we devise a novel reward function and iterative termination state for the Monte Carlo tree to achieve the minimize and optimize radar nodes selection. To further speed up the radar node selection, we introduce transfer reinforcement learning to reuse the previous knowledge. Experimental results show that our proposed method can not only select the minimize and optimize radar node combination but also has a faster speed.

References

1. Bello, I., Pham, H., Le, Q.V., Norouzi, M., Bengio, S.: Neural combinatorial optimization with reinforcement learning. arXiv preprint arXiv:1611.09940 (2016)
2. Berenguer, I., Wang, X., Krishnamurthy, V.: Adaptive MIMO antenna selection. In: The Thrity-Seventh Asilomar Conference on Signals, Systems & Computers, vol. 1, pp. 21–26. IEEE (2003)
3. Bertsimas, D., Tsitsiklis, J.: Simulated annealing. Stat. Sci. **8**(1), 10–15 (1993)
4. Browne, C.B., et al.: A survey of Monte Carlo tree search methods. IEEE Trans. Comput. Intell. AI Games **4**(1), 1–43 (2012)
5. Godrich, H., Petropulu, A.P., Poor, H.V.: Sensor selection in distributed multiple-radar architectures for localization: a knapsack problem formulation. IEEE Trans. Signal Process. **60**(1), 247–260 (2011)
6. Gorji, A.A., Tharmarasa, R., Blair, W., Kirubarajan, T.: Multiple unresolved target localization and tracking using colocated MIMO radars. IEEE Trans. Aerosp. Electron. Syst. **48**(3), 2498–2517 (2012)
7. Guo, J., Tao, H.: Cramer-Rao lower bounds of target positioning estimate in netted radar system. Digital Signal Process. **118**, 103222 (2021)
8. Hou, Y., Ong, Y.S., Feng, L., Zurada, J.M.: An evolutionary transfer reinforcement learning framework for multiagent systems. IEEE Trans. Evol. Comput. **21**(4), 601–615 (2017)
9. Huang, B., Feng, F., Lu, C., Magliacane, S., Zhang, K.: AdaRL: what, where, and how to adapt in transfer reinforcement learning. arXiv preprint arXiv:2107.02729 (2021)
10. Konidaris, G., Barto, A.: Autonomous shaping: knowledge transfer in reinforcement learning. In: Proceedings of the 23rd International Conference on Machine Learning, pp. 489–496 (2006)
11. Lazaric, A.: Transfer in reinforcement learning: a framework and a survey. In: Reinforcement Learning, pp. 143–173. Springer, Cham (2012). https://doi.org/10.1007/978-3-642-27645-3_5
12. Mirjalili, S.: Genetic algorithm. In: Evolutionary Algorithms and Neural Networks. SCI, vol. 780, pp. 43–55. Springer, Cham (2019). https://doi.org/10.1007/978-3-319-93025-1_4
13. Silver, D., et al.: Mastering the game of Go with deep neural networks and tree search. Nature **529**(7587), 484–489 (2016)
14. Silver, D., et al.: Mastering the game of Go without human knowledge. Nature **550**(7676), 354–359 (2017)
15. Torrey, L., Shavlik, J.: Transfer learning. In: Handbook of Research on Machine Learning Applications and Trends: Algorithms, Methods, and Techniques, pp. 242–264. IGI global (2010)
16. Zhu, Z., Lin, K., Zhou, J.: Transfer learning in deep reinforcement learning: a survey. arXiv preprint arXiv:2009.07888 (2020)

Weakly Supervised Liver Tumor Segmentation Based on Anchor Box and Adversarial Complementary Learning

Mengyao Fan, Haofeng Liu, Zhenyu Zhu, Changzhe Jiao$^{(\boxtimes)}$, and Shuiping Gou

School of Artificial Intelligence, Xidian University, Xi'an 710071, Shaanxi, China
cjiao@xidian.edu.cn

Abstract. Segmentation of liver tumors plays an important role in the subsequent treatment of liver cancer. At present, the mainstream method is the fully supervised method based on deep learning, which requires medical experts to manually label a large number of pixel level labels for training, resulting in high time and labor cost. In this article, we focus on using bounding boxes as weak label to complete the segmentation task. It can be roughly divided into two steps. The first step is to use region mining technology to obtain pixel level labels from the bounding box. The second step uses pixel level labels to train the semantic segmentation network to obtain segmentation results. In the whole task, the quality of pixel level labels obtained from bounding boxes plays an important role in the performance of segmentation results. Therefore, our goal is to generate high-quality pixel level labels. Aiming at the problem that the current region mining method based on classification network is inaccurate and incomplete in object location, we use the Adversarial Complementary Learning module to make the network pay attention to more complete objects. We conduct analysis to validate the proposed method and show that our approach performs is comparable to that of the fully supervised method.

Keywords: Weakly supervised learning · Tumor segmentation · Bounding box annotation

1 Introduction

Liver cancer is one of the most common and highest mortality cancers in the world. According to the World Cancer Report 2020, liver cancer ranks fifth in incidence and second in mortality [1].

A liver tumor segmentation mask obtained from a medical image such as computed tomography (CT) provides important delineation information of liver tumor, which is of great significance for subsequent diagnosis and treatment.

Recently, semantic segmentation networks based on deep learning have achieved excellent performance in the field of medical image segmentation [2].

© IFIP International Federation for Information Processing 2022
Published by Springer Nature Switzerland AG 2022
Z. Shi et al. (Eds.): ICIS 2022, IFIP AICT 659, pp. 68–75, 2022.
https://doi.org/10.1007/978-3-031-14903-0_8

However, the fully supervised semantic segmentation network based on full pixel annotation needs a large number of pixel level labels to train, which leads to huge labor and time costs, especially in the field of medicine.

Therefore, Many scholars have focused on how to use weak label to complete the segmentation task. Figure 1 shows pixel level label and common weakly supervised label. In Fig. 1(a), (c), (d) and (e) are weakly typed annotations, while (b) is a complete pixel level annotation.

Image-level labels are the easiest to obtain. But it only indicates whether an object is present in the image, and provides no other information about the object's location or profile. Therefore, image-level labels make the problem very challenging and performance is limited.

Another common type of weakly label is the bounding box, which limits the object to a rectangular area and specifies the background area (outside the box). WSSL [3] first uses Dense Conditional Random Field (CRF) [4] to generate pixel-level labels and then carries out iterative training. Youngmin Oh et al., [5] proposed the background aware pooling method, which calculates the cosine similarity between the background features outside the box and the features inside the box, so as to obtain different weights for different positions inside the box and enhance the distinction between the background and the foreground inside the box. This process makes the generated label more accurate.

The region mining technique is usually based on the classification network to obtain the location and shape information of a specific class objects. At present, the mainstream region mining method for weakly supervised semantic segmentation is using Class Activation Map (CAM) [6] to obtain localization map, which is used to generate pixel level labels through refinement algorithms such as Dense CRF [4]. However, CAM often only highlights the salient area of the object, resulting in inaccurate generated pixel labels.

In this work, we focused on the segmentation of liver tumors using boxes. In order to make up for the shortcomings of CAM [6], we used an Adversarial Complementary Learning (ACoL) [7] module to mine the non-salient object regions.

The accuracy of classification and the completeness of acquisition object can be balanced by setting appropriate salient threshold. If the salient threshold is too high, only a very small part of the area will be shielded, which is not obvious to the mining of the remaining area of the object. If the salient threshold is too low, the background may be identified as the foreground.

   (a) image   (b) fully pixel   (c) box   (d) scribble   (e) point

Fig. 1. Examples of fully supervised mask annotation and weakly supervised box annotation

2　Approach

Our approach mainly consists of two stages. First, we trained a classification network based on Adversarial Complementary Learning [7] to obtain pixel level labels using box as positive and negative samples. The second is to train the semantic segmentation network with pixel level labels.

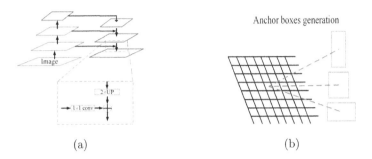

Anchor boxes generation

(a)　　　　　　　　　　　　　　(b)

Fig. 2. (a): Feature Pyramid Network. (b): Region Proposal Network anchor boxes generation process.

2.1　Anchor Boxes Generation

The first problem we need to solve is how to obtain Bounding boxes from the image. It is obvious that the positive samples are the Ground truth bounding boxes containing tumors labeled by us. For the generation of negative samples, our solution strategy is as follows. More specifically, we adopt the anchor generation process of Faster RCNN with Feature Pyramid Network (FPN) [8] structure, which collects the features of different scale boxes on different feature layers through feature fusion.

Figure 2 shows the generation process of anchor boxes and FPN.

2.2　Adversarial Complementary Learning

For mining complete tumor from bounding boxes, we use Adversarial Complementary Learning (ACoL) [7] strategy, which is a CAM-based variant.

It is necessary to review CAM [6], which is one of the most basic mining techniques. After the feature of the picture is extracted by the feature extractor, followed by a Global Average Pooling (GAP) and a fully connected layer with length C (number of the classes). It is assumed that the feature map of the last C channels is $S \in R^{W \times H \times C}$ and the weight of the fully connected layer is W. The localization map M_c of class c is calculated as follows:

$$M_c = \sum_k S_k \cdot W_k^c \tag{1}$$

where S_k is the $k-th$ channel of S and W_k^c is the weight of class c for the $k-th$ channel.

The main idea of ACoL [7] consists of two classification branches A and B, which mine different regions through a complementary operation. A and B have the same structure. Where, the input feature map of branch B is guided by the tumor localization map of A to shield the salient regions (see Fig. 3). The tumor localization map M_A of A is subjected to RELU operation and normalized by min-max to obtain $\overline{M}_A$. The erasing operation is performed by setting a salient threshold δ. Specifically, if $\overline{M}_A$ in the position (i, j) is greater than δ, multiply the feature at (i, j) by 0 and finally send the feature after erasing the salient area to B to mine the non-salient regions.

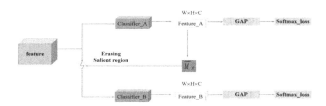

Fig. 3. ACoL architecture

2.3 Application

So far, the two main modules used to generate pixel-level labels from the bounding box have been introduced. Next, we use these two modules to build region mining model based anchor and ACoL [7], as shown in Fig. 4. Negative Bounding boxes are defined as anchors completely non-overlapping with Ground truth bounding boxes.

It should be noted that we do not use all anchors generated on all feature layers, because this may lead to the imbalance of positive and negative samples.

Therefore, The sampling strategy is to first calculate the Euclidean distance between the center point of each anchor and the center point of its closest Ground truth bounding box. According to the distance, give priority to the negative samples with short distance. We select the top 10% anchor boxes of each layer according to the distance, and then randomly select N anchor boxes from the selected anchor boxes. Each classifier consists of two convolution layers, in which the output channel of the first convolution layer is 512 and the second is 2 (foreground and background). RELU operation is performed between two convolution layers.

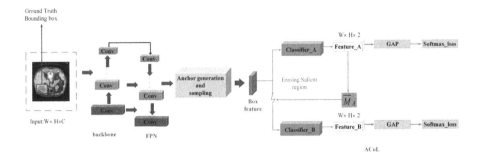

Fig. 4. The structure of regional mining method based on ACoL and anchor

2.4   Pseudo Mask Generation

In order to generate pseudo pixel level labels. For a Ground truth bounding box, the tumor localization map M_A of A and the tumor localization map M_B of B are generated according to the pipeline of CAM [6]. M_A and M_B are subjected to RELU operation and normalized by min-max to obtain $\overline{M}_A$ and $\overline{M}_B$.

The fused object localization map $\overline{M}_{fuse}$ is defined as the element-wise maximum result over $\overline{M}_A$ and $\overline{M}_B$. The $\overline{M}_{fuse}$ is adjusted to the size of the Ground truth bounding box through bilinear interpolation. The ACoL [7] fused tumor localization map and tumor localization map of CAM are shown in Fig. 5. We use Dense CRF [4] to estimate pixel level labels from bounding box localization maps. The unary term of Dense CRF for tumor class is set $\overline{M}_{fuse}$. The unary term of the background class is set $(1 - \overline{M}_{fuse})$.

Considering the influence of noise in the Ground truth bounding boxes, we adopt a method similar to [9], ignoring the background in the Ground truth bounding boxes (when training the segmentation model, the background area in the Ground truth bounding boxes will not be calculated in the loss).

3   Experiments

In this section, We will describe the experimental details and the environment. We use pytorch deep learning framework to build the proposed network model, and use NVIDIA 2080Ti GPU for training and verification.

3.1   Datasets and Evaluated Metric

In this paper, public dataset Liver Tumor Segmentation Challenge (LiTS-ISBI2017) is used as the research.

We use SGD optimizer with momentum of 0.9 and weight decay of 0.0005 train the region mining model based on classification network for 50 epochs, and the batch size was set to 8. The learning rate is initialized to 0.001.

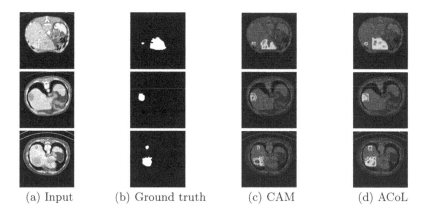

(a) Input   (b) Ground truth   (c) CAM   (d) ACoL

Fig. 5. Visualization of localization map generated by using CAM and ACoL

The image size is 512×512. We select 3762 images from LiTS-ISBI2017 as the training set and 1669 images as the test set. The Dice coefficient is used as an evaluation metric.

3.2 Classification Network and Hyperparameter Settings

ResNet50 is used as backbone. In ResNet [10], the layers with the same output feature size are classified into the same stage. The output of the last residual block of each stageC_i are used for features fusion and generate anchor.

The fusion results of $\{C_2, C_3, C_4, C_5\}$ according to FPN strategy are called $\{P_2, P_3, P_4, P_5\}$. Follow the settings of [8], the anchor area on P_2 is set to 32^2, P_3 to 64^2, P_4 to 128^2 and P_5 to 256^2 pixels, and use 3 aspect ratios $\{1{:}1, 1{:}2, 2{:}1\}$. For a feature map with size $W \times H$, a total of $W \times H \times 3$ anchors are generated.

The salient threshold δ mentioned in Sect. 2.2 is set to 0.6, and the number of negative samples N mentioned in Sect. 2.3 is set to 256. A box with height h and width w (on the input image) is assigned to P_k to obtain features, where k is calculated according to the following formula:

$$k = \lfloor 4 + \log_2^{(\sqrt{wh}/224)} \rfloor \tag{2}$$

3.3 Segmentation Network and Test Results

We use the pixel level labels to train the semantic segmentation network. For the segmentation model, we choose Deeplab-v3 [11] with ResNet-50 architecture as the backnone model, and use dice loss proposed in [12] for training. Dice loss can well solve the problem of imbalance between foreground and background in image segmentation. DeepLabV3 is trained for 50 epochs using the SGD optimizer with momentum of 0.9 and weight decay of 0.0001. Batch size is set to 6. The initial learning rate is 0.005. The learning rate adjustment strategy of DeepLabV3 is $(initial\_learning\_rate) \times (1 - \frac{iter}{max_{iter}})^{0.9}$.

The segmentation results on the test set are shown in Table 1. We define a naive baseline that treats all pixels in the boxes as foreground. The comparison of baseline, CAM and ACoL is shown in Table 2

Finally, in Fig. 6 we show some segmentation examples.

Table 1. Comparison of segmentation performance between based on ACoL method and fully supervised and weakly supervised methods on test set.

Methods	Annotation type	Dice
U-Net [13]	Pixel-level	0.702
DeepLab-V3 [11]	Pixel-level	0.711
SDI$_{box}$ [9]	Box-level	0.626
WSSL [3]	Box-level	0.632
Our	Box-level	0.658

Table 2. Comparison of baseline, CAM and ACoL segmentation results on test set.

Methods	Annotation type	Dice
Baseline	Box-level	0.563
CAM	Box-level	0.617
Our	Box-level	0.658

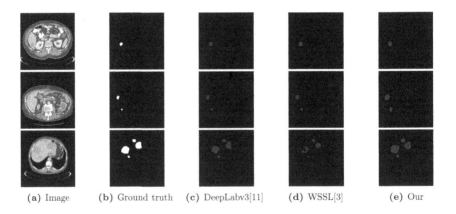

(a) Image   (b) Ground truth   (c) DeepLabv3[11]   (d) WSSL[3]   (e) Our

Fig. 6. Examples of predicted semantic masks

4   Conclusions

A weakly supervised liver tumor segmentation method based on box labeling is proposed with the help of ACoL [7] region mining strategy. The final results on the test set showed that the proposed method is comparable to the fully supervised method, which proved the effectiveness of the proposed method in liver tumor segmentation.

References

1. Wild, C., Weiderpass, E., Stewart, B.W.: World Cancer Report: Cancer Research for Cancer Prevention. IARC Press (2020)
2. Long, J., Shelhamer, E., Darrell, T.: Fully convolutional networks for semantic segmentation. In: Proceedings of the IEEE Conference on Computer Vision and Pattern Recognition, pp. 3431–3440 (2015)
3. Papandreou, G., Chen, L.-C., Murphy, K.P., Yuille, A.L.: Weakly-and semi-supervised learning of a deep convolutional network for semantic image segmentation. In: Proceedings of the IEEE International Conference on Computer Vision, pp. 1742–1750 (2015)
4. Krähenbühl, P., Koltun, V.: Efficient inference in fully connected CRFs with Gaussian edge potentials. In: Advances in Neural Information Processing Systems, vol. 24 (2011)
5. Oh, Y., Kim, B., Ham, B.: Background-aware pooling and noise-aware loss for weakly-supervised semantic segmentation. In: Proceedings of the IEEE/CVF Conference on Computer Vision and Pattern Recognition, pp. 6913–6922 (2021)
6. Zhou, B., Khosla, A., Lapedriza, A., Oliva, A., Torralba, A.: Learning deep features for discriminative localization. In: Proceedings of the IEEE Conference on Computer Vision and Pattern Recognition, pp. 2921–2929 (2016)
7. Zhang, X., Wei, Y., Feng, J., Yang, Y., Huang, T.S.: Adversarial complementary learning for weakly supervised object localization. In: Proceedings of the IEEE Conference on Computer Vision and Pattern Recognition, pp. 1325–1334 (2018)
8. Lin, T.-Y., Dollár, P., Girshick, R., He, K., Hariharan, B., Belongie, S.: Feature pyramid networks for object detection. In: Proceedings of the IEEE Conference on Computer Vision and Pattern Recognition, pp. 2117–2125 (2017)
9. Khoreva, A., Benenson, R., Hosang, J., Hein, M., Schiele, B.: Simple does it: weakly supervised instance and semantic segmentation. In: Proceedings of the IEEE Conference on Computer Vision and Pattern Recognition, pp. 876–885 (2017)
10. He, K., Zhang, X., Ren, S., Sun, J.: Deep residual learning for image recognition. In: Proceedings of the IEEE Conference on Computer Vision and Pattern Recognition, pp. 770–778 (2016)
11. Chen, L.-C., Papandreou, G., Schroff, F., Adam, H.: Rethinking atrous convolution for semantic image segmentation. In: Conference on Computer Vision and Pattern Recognition (CVPR). IEEE/CVF (2017)
12. Milletari, F., Navab, N., Ahmadi, S.-A.: V-Net: fully convolutional neural networks for volumetric medical image segmentation. In: 2016 4th International Conference on 3D Vision (3DV), pp. 565–571. IEEE (2016)
13. Ronneberger, O., Fischer, P., Brox, T.: U-Net: convolutional networks for biomedical image segmentation. In: Navab, N., Hornegger, J., Wells, W.M., Frangi, A.F. (eds.) MICCAI 2015. LNCS, vol. 9351, pp. 234–241. Springer, Cham (2015). https://doi.org/10.1007/978-3-319-24574-4_28

Weakly Supervised Whole Cardiac Segmentation via Attentional CNN

Erlei Zhang[1], Minghui Sima[2], Jun Wang[2], Jinye Peng[2(✉)], and Jinglei Li[3(✉)]

[1] Northwest A&F University, No. 22 Xinong Road, Yangling, Shaanxi, China
[2] Northwest University, No. 1, Xuefu Avenue, Xi'an, Shaanxi, China
pjy@nwu.edu.cn
[3] Department of Radiology, Guangdong Provincial People's Hospital, Guangdong Academy of Medical Sciences, Guangzhou, China
lijinglei80@126.com

Abstract. Whole-heart segmentation aims to delineate substructures of the heart, which plays an important role in the diagnosis and treatment of cardiovascular diseases. However, segmenting each substructure quickly and accurately is arduous due to traditional manual segmentation being extremely slow, the cost is high and the segmentation accuracy depends on experts' level. Inspired by deep learning, we propose a weakly supervised CNN method to effectively segment the substructure from CT cardiac images. First, we utilize the deformable image registration technology to generate pseudo masks with high confidence for whole heart datasets, which can provide rich feature information to distinguish foreground and background. Meanwhile, the ground truth is used to cut patches containing more heart substructures so that the network can obtain more information about heart substructures. Then, we developed a novel loss function based on the weighted cross-entropy to enforce CNN to pay more attention to the tricky voxels nearby the boundary of cardiac substructures during the training stage. The proposed method was evaluated on MICCAI2017 whole heart CT datasets, and the overall segmentation score of 91.30%.

Keywords: Whole-heart segmentation · Weakly supervised

1 Introduction

The whole heart segmentation is essential for the diagnosis of heart disease. However, the efficiency is limited due to both the annotation of experts and the subjective judgments of doctors. Meanwhile, the segmentation results can only be annotated by doctors and experts, which makes medical images available for research much less than other image datasets. In recent years, deep learning has achieved great success in computer vision and artificial intelligence, which enables the auto segmentation of the substructure of the heart from Computed Tomography (CT) [3]. U-net [9] and Fully Convolutional Network [7] have greatly improved medical image segmentation in terms of accuracy and execution speed, but there exist gradient vanishing and gradient explosion problems when the depth of the network increases. To tackle this problem, Lee et al. [10] added

The original version of this chapter was revised: For the author Jinye Peng a wrong affiliation had been assigned. This has now been corrected. The correction to this chapter is available at https://doi.org/10.1007/978-3-031-14903-0_50

Z. Shi et al. (Eds.): ICIS 2022, IFIP AICT 659, pp. 76–83, 2022.
https://doi.org/10.1007/978-3-031-14903-0_9

depth supervision mechanism into the network, effectively alleviate the problem caused by gradient. Yang et al. [1] applied a deep supervision mechanism to the whole heart segmentation, through integrating DICE loss and cross-entropy loss into the network, they obtained excellent segmentation results. Based on this work, Ye et al. [5] replaced the weighted cross-entropy loss function with the Focal loss function, which makes the model focus on the indistinguishable boundary and improves the Dice accuracy.

For medical images, they contain more background voxels than foreground voxels. Thus, it suffers from the problem of high misclassification. To overcome these limitations, some segmentation frameworks [6, 8] are put forward in recent years. These frameworks, known as cascade networks, are divided into two steps: (1) the first step is to locate the target and simplify the task; (2) the second step is segmentation. Among these frameworks, Payer et al. [8] performed this method on whole heart images and won first place in the MICCAI2017 Whole Heart Segmentation Challenge. However, these frameworks have the disadvantage of excessive or redundant use of parameters, such as repeated extraction of underlying features. Oktay et al. [11] proposed the plug-play Attention Gates (AGS) model, which makes the network automatically focus on relevant areas through training, effectively overcoming the shortcomings of CNNs to some extent. Wu et al. [4] have proposed a WSL (Weakly supervised learning)-based method for brain lesion segmentation. Through weak supervision learning, the network can automatically select the relevant region to suppress the irrelevant image information.

In this paper, we proposed a novel 3D CNN combining WSL learning for cardiac segmentation. We firstly used deformable image registration (DIR) [2] technology to generate pseudo masks of all the CT images for producing weakly supervised information. Then, we utilized that weakly supervised information to guide a novel 3D U-net learning. Furthermore, we developed a novel loss function based on the weighted cross-entropy to enforce CNN to pay more attention to the tricky voxels nearby the boundary of cardiac substructures during the training stage.

The main contributions of this paper are as follows:

(1) We applied traditional medical image registration technology to generate weakly supervised information as the prior knowledge for guiding deep network learning, which not only helps distinguish background and foreground organs but also can be as a data augmentation way avoiding overfitting problems.
(2) We developed an improved weighted cross-entropy loss for enforcing the deep network to pay attention to the missegmented voxels and alleviate the class imbalance problem.

2 Method

2.1 Pseudo Masks

The inputs of the network consist of two parts: one is the original CT image, while another is the pseudo masks that format the one-hot after the background is removed. For the generated pseudo masks, relevant image regions can be automatically selected. Although pseudo masks are not able to segment accurately, they can provide relevant positional features of background and foreground for the region, and effectively extract heart substructure from background. This paper utilized DIR (deformable image registration) [2] technology to generate pseudo masks for medical images. Set $\{(T_i)\}_{i=1}^N$ as N training samples, $\{(V_j)\}_{j=1}^M$ as M test samples. There are two training methods, called Model_N-1 and Model_1, as shown in Fig. 2. For a certain training sample T_i, the other N-1 training samples are respectively used as atlas to generate pseudo masks for T_i. In the Model_N-1, we concatenate T_i with its N-1 pseudo masks respectively and put them into deep network for training. In the Model_1, the N-1 pseudo masks of T_i are firstly majority voting to get a final pseudo mask, then we concatenate it with T_i and put them into deep network for training. Thus, similarly, there are two ways to generate test results, called IND and MV, as shown in Fig. 2. IND model is that each training sample is used as atlas to respectively generate pseudo mask for test sample V_j. At testing stage, we concatenate each of N pseudo masks with V_j and pass through the deep network. Then we can obtain N segmentation results for test sample V_j. Finally, we use majority voting method to generate the final segmentation result. MV model is that N pseudo masks of V_j are majority voting to obtain a final pseudo mask, the it is concatenated with V_j and put into the deep network for generating a segmentation result.

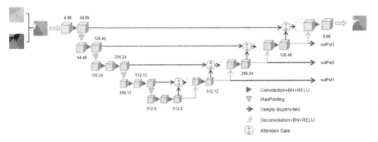

Fig. 1. The framework of the proposed Deep U-net network. In input layer, we concatenated the generated pseudo masks with the cropped patches and placed them into the network for training. The details of pseudo masks generation and patch cropping will be introduced in Sect. 2.1 and 2.2.

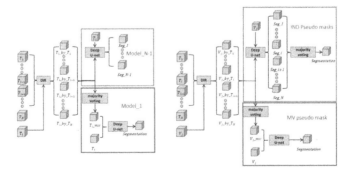

Fig. 2. Two training methods (left) of pseudo masks, two test methods (left) of pseudo masks.

2.2 Deep U-Net Network

In order to better train the deep network, we adopt the method of deep supervision, which increases the output path in different network layers and shortened the backpropagation path of gradient flow. In this paper, three deep supervised branches are introduced in the decoding stage. The output of each branch is the same as that of the main branch, in Fig. 1, out1, out2, and out3 are the three deep supervised branches, and the final total loss is the sum of the losses of each branch and the main branch.

2.3 Improved Weighted Cross-Entropy Loss

The commonly used weighted cross-entropy loss does not perform well for voxels that are difficult to segment. In this paper, we added predicted false negative (FN) and true positive (TP) voxels losses into the weighted cross-entropy to formula the total loss. As shown in Eq. (1).

$$L_{mw}Cross(x, y, z) = -\sum_c^C \sum_{i=1}^N w_c \left[\left(G_c^i + G_{cFN}^i \right) log P_c^i + P_{cTP}^i log \left(1 - P_c^i \right) \right] \quad (1)$$

where G_{cFN}^i is 0 or 1, where 1 indicates that the current voxel belongs to class c but is predicted to be of another class. P_{cTP}^i is 0 or 1, where 1 indicates that the current voxel is predicted to be class c, but is actually something else. $P_c^i (0.005 < P_c^i < 0.995)$ is the probability that the current voxel is class c, and the range is limited to prevent the excessive loss, which is not conducive to network convergence. w_c is the weight coefficient of class c, which can be used to alleviate class imbalance.

MDSC (Multi-Class Dice Similarity Coefficient) based loss function to balance the training for multiple classes [1]. This loss can be defined as:

$$L_{mDSC} = -\sum_{c=1}^C \frac{\frac{2}{N} \sum_{i=1}^N G_c^i P_c^i}{\sum_{i=1}^N G_c^i G_c^i + \sum_{i=1}^N P_c^i P_c^i} \quad (2)$$

where N is the number of voxels; G_c^i is a binary value, where 1 indicates the voxels belong to class c, 0 stands for other categories; P_c^i $(0 < P_c^i < 1)$ denotes the probability that the current voxels belong to class c.

After and are added into the network, the new loss function can be defined as follows:

$$L_{out\_x}(d, w) = 100 d L_{mDSC} + w L_{mw} Cross \quad (3)$$

where d and w are the weights of different branches, x represents the output of the deep supervised branch, the final loss function, called the Improved Weighted Cross-Entropy (IWCE), is:

$$L_{total} = L_{out\_1}(0.2, 0.3) + L_{out\_2}(0.4, 0.6) + L_{out\_3}(0.8, 0.9) + L_{out\_4}(1.0, 1.0) \quad (4)$$

3   Experimental and Results

3.1   Datasets and Implementation Details

We evaluated our approach with the MICCAI2017 whole-heart CT datasets, which contains 20 publicly available CT data [1]. We randomly selected 10 samples as training samples and the rest as test sets. These data were collected in the actual clinical environment, which was variable and contained some images of poor quality, so the robustness of the algorithm in this paper remains to be verified. Each sample is stacked with multiple 2D images of 512 * 512 size. All training data were normalized to zero mean and unit variance. Adam is used to optimize network parameters, the number of iterations was 35,000 epochs [5], the batch size was 2, and the initial learning rate was 0.001.

3.2   Patch Selection

Due to the particularity of heart medical images, and the 7 substructures voxels in whole heart CT image account for less. When the random cropped size is 96, the background occupied than half of the training data, which is not conducive to the better learning prospects of the network. To tackle this problem, we adopted an effective cropped method, which utilized ground truth to crop the patches with less background. For the randomly cropped patches, we calculated the proportion p of the background voxels in the whole patch. If the background proportion p is less than a ($a = 0.5$), this patch will be called the available patch and sent into the network for training, otherwise, the patch will be re-cropped.

3.3   Experimental Results

We took deeply-Supervised U-net [1] as the baseline network, Multi-Depth Fusion [5] is an improvement of the baseline network and Dice score as performance evaluation. In order to the efficiency of the proposed method in this paper, we conducted a series of ablation experiments.

The experimental results of cardiac substructure, pulmonary artery (PUA), ascending aorta (ASA), right ventricular blood chamber (RVBC), right atrial blood chamber (RABC), left ventricular blood chamber (LVBC), left atrial blood chamber (LABC), and myocardium of the left ventricle (MLV) were shown in Table 1. Except for the PUA (Dice score about 82%–86%), we can see that all the methods achieved relatively accurate substructures' segmentation for the whole heart. The reason could be that the shape and appearance of the PUA always has greater variability.

Compared with the baseline method, the proposed the four methods with the pseudo masks can produce better segmentation results in almost substructures of the whole heart. And all the proposed four methods have comparable performance with the advanced Multi-Depth Fusion method. Although, these regions of MLV (has the epicardial surface and the endocardial surface of the left ventricular) and RABC have much larger variation in terms of shapes and heterogeneous intensity of the myocardium and the blood. All the proposed methods outperform the two compared methods on the MLV and RABC. Particularly, "MV + Model_1" achieves the best results on MLV, RVBC, ASA, and PUA.

Table 1. Segmentation accuracy (%) of the state-of-the-art segmentation methods and the proposed four methods. "IND + Model_N-1" indicated that it used Model_N-1 at training stage and IND model at testing stage; "IND + Model_1" indicated that it used Model_1 at training stage and IND model at testing stage; "MV + Model_N-1" indicated that it used Model_N-1 at training stage and MV model at testing stage; "MV + Model_1" indicated that it used Model_1 at training stage and MV model at testing stage. The Bold Font in the proposed four methods means it outperform the Baseline and Multi-Depth Fusion methods. The values with underline mean that they are the best results in the six methods.

Method	MLV	LABC	LVBC	RABC	RVBC	ASA	PUA	Mean
Baseline	87.6	90.5	92.1	86.0	88.6	94.8	82.6	88.93
Multi-Depth Fusion	88.9	<u>91.6</u>	94.4	87.8	89.5	96.7	86.2	90.73
IND + Model_N-1	**89.9**	90.7	94.2	**89.6**	89.4	93.0	**<u>87.0</u>**	90.56
IND + Model_1	**<u>90.2</u>**	90.8	**<u>94.4</u>**	**89.6**	89.8	94.0	85.7	90.68
MV + Model_N-1	**89.5**	91.1	94.2	**<u>90.0</u>**	89.9	96.5	**86.3**	**91.14**
MV + Model_1	**89.8**	91.3	94.1	**89.9**	**<u>90.0</u>**	**<u>96.9</u>**	**86.9**	**<u>91.30</u>**

3.4 Ablation Experiments

We verify the effectiveness of the proposed IWCE LOSS, patch selection, and pseudo mask modules in the proposed model. We used the best model "MV + Model_1" as the basic model "Model". Then, we ablate or replace each proposed module, respectively. Other experimental conditions are the same as the Table 1.

Table 2 shows the experimental results. We can see that the segmentation results of six substructures become worse after the model without using the Patch Selection module. It proved that the Patch Selection module can select meaningful image patch conducive to the better learning prospects of the network. The third row is the best model using traditional Cross-Entropy loss without using the proposed IWCE loss. We can see that the segmentation results of the almost substructures are slightly worse than the best model. It proved that the proposed loss function takes the class imbalance problem into account and perform well for the voxels, like PUA, that are difficult to segment. The forth row is the model without using pseudo mask information for training, we can see that it achieved comparable performance on five substructures except ASA (reduce ~1%) and PUA (reduce ~3%). One reason is that the pseudo masks generated by simple DIR have lower quality which introduced very limit information for guiding deep network learning on some substructures that are easy to segment. Other reason is that the pseudo masks can provide some useful information, such as location information, for the PUA segmentation.

Table 2. Ablation experiment for the effect of the modules in the proposed MV + model_1 model. "PS" refers to Patch Selection modules; "IWCE" refers to the proposed mixing loss; "pseudo mask" refers to the proposed pseudo mask label modules. "↓" or "↑" denote the increase or decrease of the Dice score (%) compared with the values of "MV + Model_1" method.

Method	MLV	LABC	LVBC	RABC	RVBC	ASA	PUA	Mean
MV + Model_1	**89.8**	**91.3**	**94.1**	**89.9**	**90.0**	**96.9**	**86.9**	**91.30**
Model without PS	89.2↓	90.9↓	92.5↓	89.9	90.2↑	96.5↓	86.4↓	90.90↓
Model without IWCE	89.5↓	91.0↓	94.1	89.6↓	89.1↓	96.2↓	85.6↓	90.82↓
Model without pseudo mask	90.2↑	90.6↓	94.1	89.7↓	90.1↑	95.9↓	83.9↓	90.75↓

Table 3. Generality of the proposed modules. "Baseline" method is the deeply-Supervised U-net [1]; "Baseline PS" is the combination of the baseline method and Patch selection module; "Baseline IWCE" refers to the baseline method whose lose function is replaced for the IWCE loss function; "Baseline Pseudo mask" refers to the baseline method integrates the pseudo mask information during training stage. "↓" or "↑" denote the increase or decrease of the Dice score compared with the values of "Baseline" method.

Method	MLV	LABC	LVBC	RABC	RVBC	ASA	PUA	Mean
Baseline	87.6	90.5	92.1	86.0	88.6	94.8	82.6	88.93
Baseline PS	89.91↑	90.14↓	94.08↑	89.39↑	89.98↑	94.68↓	84.69↑	90.41↑
Baseline IWCE	88.70↑	89.89↓	93.66↑	88.86↑	89.99↑	96.57↑	85.74↑	90.49↑
Baseline Pseudo mask	89.29↑	90.48↓	93.16↑	89.71↑	89.64↑	96.57↑	86.63↑	90.78↑

3.5 Generality Experiments

In order to analysis and discuss the generality of the proposed modules including the Patch Selection, IWCE loss, and pseudo masks, we use the deeply-Supervised U-net [1] as the baseline segmentation network and combine it with proposed modules respectively. Table 3 shows the experimental results. We can see that the baseline method with each proposed module has a positive effective on most substructures except LABC. Especially, the performance of the baseline with pseudo mask method has significant improvement on PUA. It further proved that the pseudo masks can provide certain prior information which is useful for the hard to segment problem.

4 Conclusion

In this paper, a weakly supervised segmentation method based on CNN is proposed for whole-heart segmentation. We first generate pseudo masks using traditional deformable image registration methods, then perform them on whole-heart data for training. The information provided by pseudo masks is used to distinguish foreground and background. In order to obtain better experimental results, we improved the weighted cross-entropy loss function and mined the training samples to solve the problems of fuzzy boundary and class imbalance. We performed validation on the MICCAI 2017 whole-heart CT dataset, and the results demonstrate that our method can effectively improve the accuracy of heart segmentation.

Acknowledgements. Guangdong Basic and Applied Basic Research Foundation No. 2022A1515011650, the QinChuangyuan high-level innovation and entrepreneurship talent program of Shaanxi (2021QCYRC4-50). Supported by the International Science and Technology Cooperation Research Plan in Shaanxi Province of China (No. 2022KW-08).

References

1. Yang, X., Bian, C., Yu, L., Ni, D., Heng, P.-A.: Hybrid loss guided convolutional networks for whole heart parsing. In: Pop, M., et al. (eds.) STACOM 2017. LNCS, vol. 10663, pp. 215–223. Springer, Cham (2018). https://doi.org/10.1007/978-3-319-75541-0_23
2. Andrade, N., Faria, F.A., Cappabianco, F.A.M.: A practical review on medical image registration: from rigid to deep learning based approaches. In: 2018 31st SIBGRAPI Conference on Graphics, Patterns and Images, pp. 463–470. IEEE (2018)
3. Zhuang, X., et al.: Evaluation of algorithms for multi-modality whole heart segmentation: an open-access grand challenge. Med. Image Anal. **58**, 101537 (2019)
4. Wu, K., Du, B., Luo, M., Wen, H., Shen, Y., Feng, J.: Weakly supervised brain lesion segmentation via attentional representation learning. In: Shen, D., et al. (eds.) MICCAI 2019. LNCS, vol. 11766, pp. 211–219. Springer, Cham (2019). https://doi.org/10.1007/978-3-030-32248-9_24
5. Ye, C., Wang, W., Zhang, S., Wang, K.: Multi-depth fusion network for whole-heart CT image segmentation. IEEE Access **7**, 23421–23429 (2019)
6. Ammar, A., Bouattane, O., Youssfi, M.: Automatic cardiac cine MRI segmentation and heart disease classification. Comput. Med. Imaging Graph. **88**, 101864 (2021)
7. Long, J., Shelhamer, E., Darrell, T.: Fully convolutional networks for semantic segmentation. In: Proceedings of the IEEE Conference on Computer Vision and Pattern Recognition, pp. 3431–3440 (2015)
8. Payer, C., Štern, D., Bischof, H., Urschler, M.: Multi-label whole heart segmentation using CNNs and anatomical label configurations. In: Pop, M., et al. (eds.) STACOM 2017. LNCS, vol. 10663, pp. 190–198. Springer, Cham (2018). https://doi.org/10.1007/978-3-319-75541-0_20
9. Ronneberger, O., Fischer, P., Brox, T.: U-net: convolutional networks for biomedical image segmentation. In: Navab, N., Hornegger, J., Wells, W.M., Frangi, A.F. (eds.) Medical Image Computing and Computer-Assisted Intervention—MICCAI 2015. LNCS, vol. 9351, pp. 234–241. Springer, Cham (2015). https://doi.org/10.1007/978-3-319-24574-4_28
10. Lee, C. Y., Xie, S., Gallagher, P., Zhang, Z., Tu, Z.: Deeply-supervised nets. In: Artificial Intelligence and Statistics, pp. 562–570. PMLR (2015)
11. Oktay, O., et al.: Attention u-net: learning where to look for the pancreas. arXiv preprint arXiv:1804.03999 (2018)

Noisy Label Learning in Deep Learning

Xuefeng Liang$^{(\boxtimes)}$, Longshan Yao, and XingYu Liu

School of Artificial Intelligence, Xidian University, Xi'an, China
xliang@xidian.edu.cn

Abstract. Currently, the construction of a large-scale manual annotation databases is still a prerequisite for the success of DNN. Although there is no shortage of data, there is a lack of clean label data in many fields, because it takes a lot of time and huge labor costs to build such a database. As many studies have shown that noisy label will seriously affect the stability and performance of the DNN. Learning from noisy labels has become more and more important, and many methods have been proposed by scholars. The purpose of this paper is to systematically summarize the different ideas for solving the noisy label learning problem, analyze the problems with existing methods, and try to analyze how to solve these problems. First, we will describe the problem of learning with label noise from the perspective of supervised learning. And then we will summarize the existing methods from the perspective of dataset usage. Subsequently, we will analyze the problems with the data and existing methods. Finally we will give some possible solution ideas.

Keywords: DNN · Noisy label · Large-scale manual annotation dataset

1 Introduction

In recent years, the good performance of deep learning and its successful application in many fields greatly depend on the establishment of large-scale manual label databases, such as ImageNet [5], etc. However, the construction of large-scale databases is time consuming and labor-intensive. Therefore, there are still many fields that lack large-scale and reliable databases, which hinders the development and application of deep learning. In order to overcome the difficulty of large-scale database construction, scholars have proposed many low-cost alternatives in recent years. For example, we can collect a large amount of data from search engines or social media and then label the data based on surrounding text and tags, or using Amazon's Mechanical Turk and so on. The datasets obtained by these methods inevitably contain a large number of noisy labels. Recent studies have shown that deep neural networks will overfit with noisy label data [1,34], thereby affecting the generalization performance and stability of the network.

This work was supported by the Guangdong Provincial Key Research and Development Programme under Grant 2021B0101410002.

In addition, the data in some fields has strong ambiguity and is extremely difficult to be labeled. Thus, it's also inevitable to generate noisy labels, such as speech emotion, lip language, and facial aesthetics.

Noisy label learning has been one of the core areas of deep learning and scholars have proposed a large number of solutions to address this problem. Each of these methods has its own advantages and disadvantages as well as specific constraints. This paper hopes to systematically expatiate the different approaches to solve the problem of noisy label learning, discuss the problems that may be neglected, and try to give some ideas about solving the problems.

Firstly, we will explain the preliminary knowledge in Sect. 2; in Sect. 3, we will try to expatiate the various ideas and methods for solving the noisy label learning problem; in Sect. 4, the potential problems in the existing methods and possible solutions will be discussed; Sect. 5 for summary.

2 Preliminary Knowledge

In order to facilitate the reader's understanding, this section will introduce the relevant terms used in this paper and briefly clarify related issues.

2.1 Noisy Labels in Deep Learning

The goal of deep learning tasks under supervised learning is to learn a mapping function f from dataset $D = \{(x_i, y_i)|i = 1, 2, 3...n\}$, where the parameters of the mapping $f : x_i - y_i$ are expressed as θ, which can also be called the parameters of the neural network, f called the classifier. Look for the best classifier, by calculating the loss $L(f(x_i, \theta), y_i)$ of each sample data, and find the best mapping θ^* by optimizing the cost function.

$$R_D(f(\theta)) = \sum_{i=0}^{n} L(f(x_i, \theta), y_i) \tag{1}$$

when the dataset D contains noisy labels $(x_i, \widetilde{y}_i)$, $\widetilde{y}_i \neq y_i$, the sample loss $L(f(x_i, \theta), \widetilde{y}_i)$ cannot truly represent the loss of the sample. So the parameters $\widetilde{\theta}_i$ obtained by optimizing the cost function is not the best parameters, where $\widetilde{\theta}^* \neq \theta^*$.

2.2 Noisy Label Dataset and Noisy Label Types

Synthetic Dataset. The types of simulated noise label: Pair noise [7], Symmetric noise [27], Asymmetric noise [29], as Fig. 1. Applying the simulated noise type to the basic dataset, such as CIFAR-10, CIFAR-100, MNIST, etc., generates new dataset containing noisy label which called Synthetic dataset.

Pair Noisy Label Dataset [7]. Pair noise is the transfer of labels between two adjacent classes. As shown in the left of Fig. 1, Pair noise with a noise ratio of 45%, the first class of data retains 55% of the total, and the remaining 45% of the data is labeled as the second class, and so on. (The row represents the real category, and the column represents the label category.)

Symmetric Noisy Label Dataset [27]. Symmetric noise is to keep a certain proportion of the main class label unchanged, and the rest is uniform distributed to other classes. As shown in the mid of Fig. 1. The first class of data retains 50% of the whole, and the remaining 50% of data are equally divided into the remaining 4 classes, and so on.

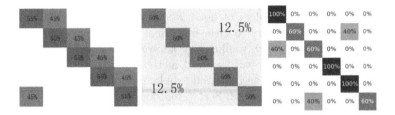

Fig. 1. Example of noise transfer matrix (From left to right are Pair noise, Symmetric noise, and Asymmetric noise.)

Asymmetric Noisy Label Dataset [29]. Asymmetric noise transfers the label according to the provided noise transfer matrix. As shown in the right of Fig. 1, the first class of data is not transferred to other classes; the sixth class of data is retained at 60% of the whole, and the remaining 50% of data is changed to the third class, and so on.

Actual Dataset. The datasets containing noisy labels collected in the real world are called Actual datasets: Clothing1M [30], Webvision [16], Food101 [4], etc.

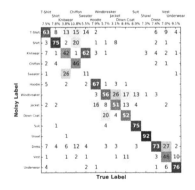

Fig. 2. Noise transfer matrix of Clothing1M.   **Fig. 3.** Example from Clothing1M.

Clothing1M [30]. The database builder used crawler technology to collect 14 categories of pictures on several shopping websites, gave them labels through the description text around the pictures. More than 1 million data is collected and the correct ratio of labels is about 61.54%. The noise transition matrix is shown in Fig. 2.

As shown in Fig. 2, the noisy label composition of Clothing1M is very complicated, and there are many categories similar to Pair noise type, such as Windbreaker, Chiffon and Shirt, etc. Noise similar to Symmetric noise type are Hoodie, T-Shirt, Dress And Vest. There are also three types of analogue noise that do not fall into the three categories at all, for example, almost 1% of the samples in each category are assigned to the other category. In addition, there are noise forms that deviate from normal values, such as Knitwear and Sweater.

Webvision [16]. There are two versions of Webvision, both of which are collected on the Flickr website and Google Image Search through crawler technology. The first version has 1000 categories and uses the same 1000 concepts as ILSVRC2012 for querying images, and the label is the keyword used in the query. The total number is 2.4 million. In the second version, the number of visual concepts was expanded from 1,000 to 5,000, and the total number of images in the training set reached 16 million. The first version is mostly used in existing papers.

The Webvision database is a typical long-tail dataset, where the amount of data for each category ranges from 300 to 10,000, as shown in Fig. 4. To explore the noise form of the data, the builders took 200,000 photos, 200 of each category, and posted the task on Amazon's Mechanical Turk (AMT). The user is required to tell the label of each image is correct or not. Each image is judged by three users. If more than two users find it is correct, it is the correct label data. Finally, statistics (Fig. 5) show that 20% of the data is real noise (0 votes), and 66% have the correct label (2 votes or 3 votes).

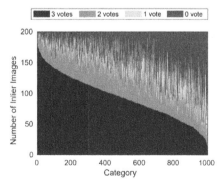

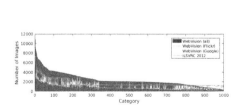

Fig. 4. Number of each class in Webvision

Fig. 5. The result of manual voting in Webvision. Samples with more than 2 votes are considered clean labels, with 0 votes are noise labels.

2.3   Analysis the Problems in Noisy Label Learning

Mathematical Representation: The theoretical performance of the neural network $f(\theta)$ with the parameter θ on the dataset D can achieve: $P_D = f(\theta, D)$.

The Theoretical Performance on Different Sub-dataset:

$$P_{D_{all}} \leq P_{D_{clean}} < P_{D_{clean}+D_{unlabel}} < P_{D_{all\_clean}} \tag{2}$$

where, $D_{all} = Shuffle\{D_{clean}, D_{noise}\}$, D_{clean} is the clean label data subset, D_{noise} is the noisy label data subset, $D_{unlabel}$ is the unlabeled data subset after D_{noise} deletes the label, and D_{all_clean} is the union of D_{all_clean} and D_{clean} after D_{noise} is given the true label.

3   Existing Methods of Noisy Label Learning

In this section, combined with the analysis of the problems with noisy label learning in Sect. 2.3, we summarize the existing methods into three categories from the perspective of how to use dataset: Full-equal-using method, Clean-based method and Full-differ-using method.

3.1   Full-Equal-Using Method

This type of methods do not divide the noisy label data and the clean label data during training, and treat all the data equally. Typical methods include estimating noise transfer matrix, designing noise robust loss function, etc.

Estimating the noise transfer matrix [18,23] is to correct the model prediction and adjust the loss function so that its gradient can descend in the right direction. A further method, Dual T [32], converts the estimating noise transfer matrix into two steps. First, it will estimate the transfer matrix from clean label to intermediate category label (network prediction label). Then, estimating the transfer matrix from intermediate category label to noisy label. It uses two consecutive matrices to simplify the problem. This kind of method generally requires a clean dataset to estimate the noise transfer matrix. In addition, the SIGUA [6] methods also attempt to solve the noise label learning problem from the perspective of correcting the gradient back propagation, which can adjust the gradient of the clean label data in each batch to reduce the learning rate of the noisy label data gradient.

The goal of designing robust loss function method is that the loss can be effectively calculated for the clean label data, and the influence of the loss of noisy label data can be controlled within a certain range. In the paper [36], the author finds that Mean Absolute Error (MAE) deals with equal weight to each category, while Cross Entropy (CE) only focuses on the current category, leading to preference for hard samples. Therefore, for noisy labels, the MAE is more robust than the CE, but the CE loss has higher accuracy and fitting speed than MAE. Based on the above analyses, the author proposes GCE loss by combining the advantages of MAE and CE. Different from the analysis of the adaptive characteristics of various loss functions, Symmetric loss [28] is proposed by focusing on the prediction results of different classes. The author found that DNN learning with CE can be **class-biased** on clean label data and **under learning** on noise label data. To balance this problem, the author puts forward the idea of symmetric Cross Entropy loss. 'Symmetric' means weighted sum of the Cross Entropy loss and inverse Cross Entropy loss (label and predicted value are interchanged). APL [19] divides the existing loss functions into 'Active' and 'Passive', and proposes the 'activate passive learning' method to use the advantages of different types loss functions at different training stages. Different from the distance-based loss function, L_DMI [31] based on information entropy is not only theoretically prove robust to instance-independent label noise, but also easily apply to any classification network.

Designing noise-robust network structure, adding a specific layer or branch to the network to deal with noisy labels has the advantage of very targeted, but the network is not extended well. CleanNet [13], in the training process, abstracts the paradigm of each category by clustering method according to clean data, which will be used as the similarity measurement calculating loss during training. MetaCleaner [35] divides the training process into two steps. The first step is to estimate the confidence of each data. The second step is to generate a clean abstract training sample by summarizing the confidence score of the data. By classifying noise types, ClothingNet [30] can calculate the posterior probability of the noise type after the noise type is learned. Self-learning [8] adds additional clustering modules to the network, maintains the abstract category features generated by the clustering module in the training process, and gives corresponding pseudo-labels through the similarity between the training data and the abstract category features.

3.2 Clean-Based Method

This type of method only uses clean label subset during training, and the key problem is to improve the classification accuracy between clean label data and noisy label data. Once the subset of cleanly labeled data is divided, the model can be trained according to the normal dataset, so that the influence of noisy labeled data can be avoided. The main directions of this type of method are: screening clean label data and adjusting the weight of samples. Currently, The methods used to identify noisy label and clean label data include: Small-Loss criterion, Gaussian mixture model (GMM), Bayesian mixture model (BMM), etc.

Small-Loss criterion: Data with a small training loss is considered clean data.

Decouple [20] first propose the idea of decoupling the problem of 'how to update' from 'when to update' in the training process, and give an update strategy based on network inconsistent information. This method first initializes two networks randomly, and in the subsequent training process, only when the two networks have a disagreement, the reverse update is performed. Co-teaching [7] is a representative method of dealing with noisy labels based on Co-training

[2] ideas. During the training, the two networks calculate the loss of the same batch data and make a ranking. Then, according to the Small-Loss Criterion, the samples with Small loss value are selected and regarded as clean label data, and then they are passed to each other for gradient update. Mandal et al. [21] adds the idea of self-supervision on the basis of Co-teaching to improve the accuracy of clean label recognition, and then increases the proportion of clean labels in each iteration and improves the model performance. Also on the basis of Co-teaching, Jo-CoR [29] introduces the idea of 'agreement' into two networks (under the same database, different models will reach agreement on most sample labels. In addition, different models trained on the same view are unlikely to reach agreement on incorrect labels [12,24]), which improves the accuracy of data screening. The author adds contrast loss (JS divergence) between the two networks to realize the 'agreement' of the two networks, and filters the clean label data according to the Small-Loss criterion. MentorNet [10] uses the idea of curriculum learning (referencing from human learning mode) to implement the sequential learning of the model from easy to difficult in data that contain noisy label through two networks (a teacher network and a student network).

3.3   Full-Differ-Using Method

This type of method can be regarded as a further extension of Clean-based method. There is another reason that when the noise ratio is higher than a certain threshold, the clean label data in the training data is not enough for the network to solve the problem, the noise label data should be considered.

The idea of correcting noisy labels comes from the theory that network has the possibility of self-correcting. Based on this idea, PENCIL [33] treats the pseudo-label (corrected label of the network) as an independent parameter and updates it during the training process as the network parameter, so as to obtain a correct pseudo-label. However, this method sets all the training data as correctable, leading to the fact that in the training process, the network often 'corrects' clean labels into false labels by mistake. With the similar idea, Joint-optimization [25] use a single network to realize the function of training and correcting noisy labels, and regularize the noise sample loss after correction to reduce the impact of errors.

As for the method of designing robust network structure, there are also some methods divide the clean label and noisy label data and then use them separately during training. For example, based on the idea of weakly supervised learning [9], a residual network branch is specially designed to process noisy label data and maintain noisy label and clean label subsets continuously to train the network. Mean Teacher [26] based on knowledge distillation method and Meta-learning based on meta learning method [15]. These methods are similar to Mentornet [10], which requires a teacher network to provide soft label which is the label for student network to learn. Differently, it will consider to divide clean label and noisy label data in the process and only correct the noisy label. Other methods, such as NLNL [11], enhance the use of noisy label data through 'negative learning'. Its core idea is that if the label of the sample is wrong, it can be sure that the sample does not belong to the labeled category. This information is also useful, which can assist network training and improve network performance.

The type of method based on semi-supervised learning treats the noisy label data as unlabeled data and uses the semi-supervised learning method to deal with it. Because there are many effective algorithms for semi-supervised learning, such methods usually only need to consider how to optimize the partitioning of training data. DivideMix [14] also refers to the ideas of the two models in Co-training, using Gaussian mixture model to select clean samples and noisy label samples, and treat the noisy label samples as unlabeled data, combined with the excellent algorithm MixMatch [3] in semi-supervised learning for training; ERL [17] found the characteristics of early learning of the network, and added regular means to prevent the network from remembering noisy labels.

4   Problems in Existing Methods

4.1   Difference Between Synthetic Dataset and the Actual Dataset

Difference in the Size: The basic dataset used in the Synthetic dataset only contains 60,000 on average, and the pixel size is within 32 * 32; in the contrast, the Actual dataset is generally more than 1 million, and the pixel size is more than 224 * 224.

Difference in Noise Type: Only have three types of synthetic noise, Pair noise [7], Symmetric noise [27], Asymmetric noise [29], and there are some regularities in them. AS for Actual datasets such as Clothing1M, it's noise transfer matrix (Fig. 2) is very complicated than synthetic noise dataset.

Differences in the Data Itself: The basic databases of Synthetic datasets such as CIFAR-10, CIFAR-100, MNIST always have single and prominent objects in the pictures, while the complexity of the data in the Actual dataset is far greater than the above three, such as shown in Fig. 3.

Difference in Frequency of Use: Through the statistics of the databsets used in the experiment of 47 related papers, the frequency of each databset is obtained, as shown in Table 2. We find that CIFAR-10 is used as the baseset to generate Synthetic datasets with a frequency of 75%, CIFAR-100 is used at 62%, and MNIST is used at 36%. According to statistics, the usage ratios of the three Actual datasets are 55% of Clothing1M, 12.7% for both Webvision and Food101 (Table 1).

Table 1. Dataset usage frequency statistics (Only shown used more than 2 times).

Dataset	CIFAR-10	CIFAR-100	minist	ILSVRC	News	F-minist	Clothing1M	Food101	Webvision
Time	35	29	17	6	3	6	26	6	6
Frequency	75%	62%	36%	13%	6%	13%	55%	13%	13%

4.2 Problems with Existing Methods

Due to space limitations, we only show some results of representative methods, as shown in Table 2. CE (Cross Entropy Loss) is a benchmark for comparison.

Table 2. Experimental results (Symmetrical noise sym., Asymmetric noise asym., %).

Noise ratio-Data set-Noise type	CE	F-correction [22]	Co-teaching [7]	PENCIL [33]	Meta-Learning [15]	DivideMix [14]	ELR [17]
20%- ciar10-sym.	86.80	86.80	89.50	92.40	92.90	96.10	94.60
50%- ciar10-sym.	79.40	79.80	85.70	89.10	89.30	94.60	93.80
80%- ciar10-sym.	62.90	63.30	67.40	77.50	77.40	93.20	91.10
20%- ciar100-sym.	62.00	61.50	65.60	69.40	68.50	77.30	77.50
50%- ciar100-sym.	46.70	46.60	51.80	57.50	59.20	74.60	72.40
80%- ciar100-sym.	19.90	19.90	27.90	31.10	42.40	60.20	58.20
40%-ciar10-asym.	83.20			88.50		93.40	92.70
40%-ciar100-asym.						72.10	76.50
Clothing1M	69.21	69.84			73.47	74.76	74.81
Webvision		61.12	63.58			77.32	77.78

It can be seen from Table 2 that the improvement of the current optimal method comparing to the benchmark method is as follows: on CIFAR-10 and CIFAR-100 with noise ratio of 20%, the improvement of 10% and 15% is achieved respectively, and the optimal results are 96.1% and 77.3%, respectively. With noise ratio of 50%, the improvement of 15% and 28% is achieved respectively, and the optimal results are 94.6% and 74.6%. With noise ratio of 80%, the improvement of 31% and 40% were obtained, respectively, and the optimal results were 93.6% and 60.2%, respectively. There is a 5% improvement on the Clothing1M comparing to the benchmark method, and the best result is 74.81%. The current optimal result on the Webvision dataset is 77.78%, and the noise label in the Webvision accounts for about 34%. Due to the lack of experimental results of the benchmark method on this dataset, we use the F-correction [22] method as the evaluation benchmark. Further statistics are made based on Table 2, as shown Table 3. Combining Tables 2 and 3, it is easy to find the problems existing in the current methods:

The performance improvement of existing methods on Actual datasets is much lower than on Synthetic datasets

Table 3. The improvement of the best results on each dataset compare to the benchmark.

Noisy label dataset	Noise ratio	Increase
CIFAR-10 sys.	20%	10%
	50%	15%
	80%	31%
CIFAR-100 sys.	20%	15%
	50%	28%
	80%	40%
CIFAR-10 asys.	40%	10%
Clothing1M	38%	5%
Webvision	34%	16%

Detailed Analysis: On the Synthetic dataset, when the noise rate is 20%, the results of the three type methods are similar. At this time, the clean label data still has a large proportion of the training data, and the three methods have no significant difference in the amount of available data. When the noise ratio continues to rise to 50%, the gap between the F-correction method and other methods gradually widens. This is because as the proportion of noisy label data increases, this method does not distinguish between clean and noisy labels, resulting in the network being gradually affected by noise. Although the performance of Co-teaching method is not much different from PENCIL and other methods, the gap between it and DivideMix and ELR methods is gradually increasing. This is because DivideMix and ELR consider the correction and use of noisy label data by MixMatch and other methods. Effective use of noisy label data, increased training data. This phenomenon also exists in the experimental results with the noise ratio of 80%.

Clothing1M is the most frequently used Actual dataset in paper, and its noise label accounts for about 38%. Through analysis, we can find that the performance of Meta-Learning, which has a quite gap with the optimal method on Synthetic dataset, is similar with the optimal method on Clothing1M. Combined with further analysis, we still found that the performance of Full-equal-using method (such as F-correction) on the Actual dataset is far worse than Clean-based method and Full-differ-using method, which is also in line with the findings on the Synthetic dataset. Compared with the benchmark results on the Clothing1M and Synthetic datasets, we found that the benchmark method result on the Webvision is 61.12%, which does not reach 66% (100% −34%). The reason for this phenomenon is probably because Webvision is a long-tailed dataset. Although the benchmark method has the ability to deal with noisy labels, it does not have the ability to deal with the imbalance of the data itself.

4.3 Possible Solutions

This section will put forward some feasible solutions for the series of method problems summarized above.

More Analysis of the Characteristics of Noise in Actual Datasets: Through the data analysis in Sect. 4.1, we can clearly know that the complexity of the noisy label in the Actual dataset is much higher than the Synthetic dataset in all dimensions. For example, Clothing1M include both Symmetric noise type and Pair noise type, while Synthetic datasets only have one type of noise. Webvision, the vote count of 0 is considered as noisy label, and the vote of 2 and 3 is clean label. For data with one vote, we should do more analysis instead of doing nothing. Therefore, to solve the problem of noisy labels, it is necessary to increase the analysis of the characteristics of different noisy labels in the dataset.

Adjust Accordingly with the Dataset: Because the actual data collected in the real world has a wide variety and inconsistent complexity. Even without considering the noisy label, the sample complexity in the Actual dataset is much higher than that in the Synthetic dataset. As shown in Fig. 3, in Actual datasets, even among samples of the same category, there are usually large differences. Webvision is a typical long-tail dataset. When dealing with this kind of noisy dataset, increasing the processing capacity for long-tail data will make the algorithm more effective.

Improve the Accuracy of Dividing Between Clean Labels and Noisy Labels: Comparing the results from perspective of data usage, we found that: Full-equal-using methods are very sensitive to the noise in training set. When the noise ratio is larger, it is difficult to exclude the influence of the noisy label on the model. The performance of the Clean-based methods greatly depend on the purity and quantity of the clean label data subset. It can be seen from the experimental results that the better of subset division, the better results can get. Full-differ-using method is the more stable and more effective method among the three methods. How to effectively use noisy label data greatly affects the final result.

At present, the commonly used distinguishing methods are: Small-loss, GMM, BMM, etc. These methods all rely on the calculated loss value, but the loss value is deviated from the actual loss value, so that the above methods cannot completely eliminate the influence of noise labels. Therefore, more attention should be paid to how to divide clean label and noisy label data.

Pay Attention to How to Use Noisy Labels Data: Comparing the experimental results in Sect. 4.2, we can see that in the case of using the same basic method, due to the different ways of using noisy label data, the performance of each method on the Actual datasets appears to be quite different, such as PENCIL and DivideMix.

Increase Training Epoch: Through the analysis of all the papers using Actual datasets, we found that the average epoch of network training is not less than 200 in experiment of Synthetic datasets. And in the experiment of the Actual dataset, the training time is much longer than the Synthetic dataset due to the huge amount of data, the average epoch of training is only about 20. Due to the greatly reduced training epochs, the test results obtained may be incorrect.

5   Conclusion

This paper summarizes the current methods form the perspective of how to use data, analyzing the existing problems, and giving some potential solutions. At present, due to the efforts of many scholars, the noise label learning methods have been able to achieve satisfactory results on three types of Synthetic datasets. However, these methods still have some deficiencies in Actual datasets, which need to be further studied.

References

1. Arpit, D., et al.: A closer look at memorization in deep networks. In: International Conference on Machine Learning, pp. 233–242. PMLR (2017)
2. Balcan, M.F., Blum, A., Yang, K.: Co-training and expansion: towards bridging theory and practice. Adv. Neural. Inf. Process. Syst. **17**, 89–96 (2005)
3. Berthelot, D., Carlini, N., Goodfellow, I., Papernot, N., Oliver, A., Raffel, C.: MixMatch: a holistic approach to semi-supervised learning. arXiv preprint arXiv:1905.02249 (2019)
4. Bossard, L., Guillaumin, M., Van Gool, L.: Food-101 – mining discriminative components with random forests. In: Fleet, D., Pajdla, T., Schiele, B., Tuytelaars, T. (eds.) ECCV 2014. LNCS, vol. 8694, pp. 446–461. Springer, Cham (2014). https://doi.org/10.1007/978-3-319-10599-4_29
5. Deng, J., Dong, W., Socher, R., Li, L.J., Li, K., Fei-Fei, L.: ImageNet: a large-scale hierarchical image database. In: 2009 IEEE Conference on Computer Vision and Pattern Recognition, pp. 248–255. IEEE (2009)
6. Han, B., et al.: SIGUA: forgetting may make learning with noisy labels more robust. In: International Conference on Machine Learning, pp. 4006–4016. PMLR (2020)
7. Han, B., et al.: Co-teaching: robust training of deep neural networks with extremely noisy labels. arXiv preprint arXiv:1804.06872 (2018)
8. Han, J., Luo, P., Wang, X.: Deep self-learning from noisy labels. In: Proceedings of the IEEE/CVF International Conference on Computer Vision, pp. 5138–5147 (2019)
9. Hu, M., Han, H., Shan, S., Chen, X.: Weakly supervised image classification through noise regularization. In: Proceedings of the IEEE/CVF Conference on Computer Vision and Pattern Recognition, pp. 11517–11525 (2019)
10. Jiang, L., Zhou, Z., Leung, T., Li, L.J., Fei-Fei, L.: MentorNet: learning data-driven curriculum for very deep neural networks on corrupted labels. In: International Conference on Machine Learning, pp. 2304–2313. PMLR (2018)
11. Kim, Y., Yim, J., Yun, J., Kim, J.: NLNL: negative learning for noisy labels. In: Proceedings of the IEEE/CVF International Conference on Computer Vision, pp. 101–110 (2019)

12. Kumar, A., Saha, A., Daume, H.: Co-regularization based semi-supervised domain adaptation. Adv. Neural. Inf. Process. Syst. **23**, 478–486 (2010)
13. Lee, K.H., He, X., Zhang, L., Yang, L.: CleanNet: transfer learning for scalable image classifier training with label noise. In: Proceedings of the IEEE Conference on Computer Vision and Pattern Recognition, pp. 5447–5456 (2018)
14. Li, J., Socher, R., Hoi, S.C.: DivideMix: learning with noisy labels as semi-supervised learning. arXiv preprint arXiv:2002.07394 (2020)
15. Li, J., Wong, Y., Zhao, Q., Kankanhalli, M.S.: Learning to learn from noisy labeled data. In: Proceedings of the IEEE/CVF Conference on Computer Vision and Pattern Recognition, pp. 5051–5059 (2019)
16. Li, W., Wang, L., Li, W., Agustsson, E., Van Gool, L.: Webvision database: visual learning and understanding from web data. arXiv preprint arXiv:1708.02862 (2017)
17. Liu, S., Niles-Weed, J., Razavian, N., Fernandez-Granda, C.: Early-learning regularization prevents memorization of noisy labels. In: Advances in Neural Information Processing Systems, vol. 33 (2020)
18. Liu, T., Tao, D.: Classification with noisy labels by importance reweighting. IEEE Trans. Pattern Anal. Mach. Intell. **38**(3), 447–461 (2015)
19. Ma, X., Huang, H., Wang, Y., Romano, S., Erfani, S., Bailey, J.: Normalized loss functions for deep learning with noisy labels. In: International Conference on Machine Learning, pp. 6543–6553. PMLR (2020)
20. Malach, E., Shalev-Shwartz, S.: Decoupling "when to update" from "how to update". arXiv preprint arXiv:1706.02613 (2017)
21. Mandal, D., Bharadwaj, S., Biswas, S.: A novel self-supervised re-labeling approach for training with noisy labels. In: Proceedings of the IEEE/CVF Winter Conference on Applications of Computer Vision, pp. 1381–1390 (2020)
22. Patrini, G., Rozza, A., Krishna Menon, A., Nock, R., Qu, L.: Making deep neural networks robust to label noise: a loss correction approach. In: Proceedings of the IEEE Conference on Computer Vision and Pattern Recognition, pp. 1944–1952 (2017)
23. Ren, M., Zeng, W., Yang, B., Urtasun, R.: Learning to reweight examples for robust deep learning. In: International Conference on Machine Learning, pp. 4334–4343. PMLR (2018)
24. Sindhwani, V., Niyogi, P., Belkin, M.: A co-regularization approach to semi-supervised learning with multiple views. In: Proceedings of ICML Workshop on Learning with Multiple Views, vol. 2005, pp. 74–79. Citeseer (2005)
25. Tanaka, D., Ikami, D., Yamasaki, T., Aizawa, K.: Joint optimization framework for learning with noisy labels. In: Proceedings of the IEEE Conference on Computer Vision and Pattern Recognition, pp. 5552–5560 (2018)
26. Tarvainen, A., Valpola, H.: Mean teachers are better role models: weight-averaged consistency targets improve semi-supervised deep learning results. arXiv preprint arXiv:1703.01780 (2017)
27. Van Rooyen, B., Menon, A.K., Williamson, R.C.: Learning with symmetric label noise: the importance of being unhinged. arXiv preprint arXiv:1505.07634 (2015)
28. Wang, Y., Ma, X., Chen, Z., Luo, Y., Yi, J., Bailey, J.: Symmetric cross entropy for robust learning with noisy labels. In: Proceedings of the IEEE/CVF International Conference on Computer Vision, pp. 322–330 (2019)
29. Wei, H., Feng, L., Chen, X., An, B.: Combating noisy labels by agreement: a joint training method with co-regularization. In: Proceedings of the IEEE/CVF Conference on Computer Vision and Pattern Recognition, pp. 13726–13735 (2020)

30. Xiao, T., Xia, T., Yang, Y., Huang, C., Wang, X.: Learning from massive noisy labeled data for image classification. In: Proceedings of the IEEE Conference on Computer Vision and Pattern Recognition, pp. 2691–2699 (2015)
31. Xu, Y., Cao, P., Kong, Y., Wang, Y.: L_DMI: a novel information-theoretic loss function for training deep nets robust to label noise. In: NeurIPS, pp. 6222–6233 (2019)
32. Yao, Y., et al.: Dual T: reducing estimation error for transition matrix in label-noise learning. arXiv preprint arXiv:2006.07805 (2020)
33. Yi, K., Wu, J.: Probabilistic end-to-end noise correction for learning with noisy labels. In: Proceedings of the IEEE/CVF Conference on Computer Vision and Pattern Recognition, pp. 7017–7025 (2019)
34. Zhang, C., Bengio, S., Hardt, M., Recht, B., Vinyals, O.: Understanding deep learning requires rethinking generalization. arXiv preprint arXiv:1611.03530 (2016)
35. Zhang, W., Wang, Y., Qiao, Y.: MetaCleaner: learning to hallucinate clean representations for noisy-labeled visual recognition. In: Proceedings of the IEEE/CVF Conference on Computer Vision and Pattern Recognition, pp. 7373–7382 (2019)
36. Zhang, Z., Sabuncu, M.R.: Generalized cross entropy loss for training deep neural networks with noisy labels. arXiv preprint arXiv:1805.07836 (2018)

Accelerating Deep Convolutional Neural Network Inference Based on OpenCL

Yong Wu[1], Huming Zhu[2(✉)], Lingyun Zhang[2], Biao Hou[2], and Licheng Jiao[2]

[1] Xidian-Wuhu Research Institute, Wuhu, China
[2] Key Laboratory of Intelligent Perception and Image Understanding, Ministry of Education,
Xidian University, Xi'an 710071, China
zhuhum@mail.xidian.edu.cn

Abstract. In recent years, in order to facilitate the efficient application of deep convolutional neural networks, it has become increasingly important to accelerate the inference stage of deep convolutional neural networks. But with the development of numerous heterogeneous computing devices, today's popular deep learning inference tools only support specific devices, so they cannot effectively utilize different GPU devices to accelerate DNN inference. To address this issue, we propose an OpenCL-based parallel deep convolutional neural network inference algorithms. Firstly, we design and implement parallel kernel code using OpenCL to accelerate depthwise separable convolution, and implement parallel matrix multiplication combined with clBLAS to accelerate traditional convolution. Meanwhile, we design OpenCL parallel kernel codes for other operations in the inference stage of deep convolutional neural networks. Secondly, we further improve the inference performance by means of kernel fusion and increasing the workload per core. Finally, MobileNet v1 network and the 21-layer residual network based on OpenCL are run on AMD Radeon Vega Frontier GPU and Nvidia GeForce GTX 1070 GPU. Compared to the Caffe implementation, 40.16x, 1.67x speedups are achieved on the AMD GPU and 14.95x, 1.11x speedups are achieved on the Nvidia GPU.

Keywords: OpenCL · Deep convolutional neural network · Inference · GPU

1 Introduction

In recent years, deep neural networks have been widely used in image analysis [1], speech recognition, object detection [2], semantic segmentation, face recognition, and autonomous driving because of their excellent performance.

GPUs have been used to accelerate the training and inference of various neural network models due to their powerful parallel computing capabilities [3, 4]. However, with the development of numerous heterogeneous computing devices, the manufacturers and models of GPUs have become increasingly complex and diverse. The programming environment for different GPUs also tends to be different. Therefore, it is of great value to study parallel algorithms with portability to adapt to different GPUs.

© IFIP International Federation for Information Processing 2022
Published by Springer Nature Switzerland AG 2022
Z. Shi et al. (Eds.): ICIS 2022, IFIP AICT 659, pp. 98–108, 2022.
https://doi.org/10.1007/978-3-031-14903-0_11

OpenCL is a cross-platform parallel programming standard, and it provides APIs with parallel programming. It not only can be applied on FPGA, but also can on CPU, GPU and DSP (Digital Signal Processors). By using OpenCL implement the inference of deep convolutional networks [5, 6], we can deploy the networks on different devices, which extend the scope of application.

Accelerating deep neural networks usually involves two stages. The first stage is training a model on a large dataset. In this stage, the commonly used parallel methods are data parallelism and model parallelism. For single-node data parallelism, by using parallel programming technology, independent computation is distributed to multiple computing cores of a single hardware device. Model parallelism decomposes the network model, distributes the convolution operation located in the same layer to different computing devices for calculation, and the output results are synchronized and transmitted to the next layer through communication between devices. The second stage is deep neural network inference stage. In this stage, we need to deploy the trained model on a device for image classification or object detection [7]. And there are many tools have been proposed to accelerate different deep neural network models on parallel computation device. Such as Intel OpenVINO [8] and NVIDIA TensorRT [9]. These inference tools both only support one manufacturer's GPU, which limited the scope of application.

Our main contributions of this work are summarized as follows:

Compared with related works, we firstly design OpenCL kernel code to accelerate depthwise separable convolution. We test the performance of MobileNet v1 network and the 21-layer residual net-work based on OpenCL on AMD Radeon Vega Frontier and Nvidia Ge-Force GTX 1070 GPU. By using kernel fusion and batch image processing, we further improve the performance of parallel acceleration without decreasing the accuracy.

2 Related Work

At present, there have been some researches on accelerating the inference stage of neural networks, for example, Akshay Dua et al. [10] presents Systolic-CNN, an OpenCL-defined scalable, run-time-flexible FPGA accelerator architecture, optimized for accelerating the inference of various convolutional neural networks (CNNs)in multi-tenancy cloud/edge computing. Dian-Lun Lin et al. [11] introduce SNIG, an efficient inference engine for large sparse DNNs. SNIG develops highly optimized inference kernels and leverages the power of CUDA Graphs to enable efficient decomposition of model and data parallelisms, thereby accelerating large sparse neural network inference in parallel. Shengyu He et al. [12] propose PhoneBit, a GPU-accelerated BNN inference engine for mobile devices that fully exploits the computing power of BNNs on mobile GPUs. Jiale Chen et al. [13] presents a model split framework, namely, splitCNN, in order to run a large CNN on a collection of concurrent IoT sensors. The splitCNN achieves significant reduction in the model size and inference time while maintaining similar accuracy. Although these studies have made significant progress in inference acceleration, there are still some limitations to the current work; most of these studies are based on a particular device, cannot effectively use different GPUs to accelerate inference, and the cross-platform problem remains unresolved.

3 Design, Implementation and Optimization of CNN on OpenCL

3.1 Parallel Strategy for Convolution Layer

Traditional parallel computing of convolution usually uses the method of converting convolution to matrix multiplication. This kind of method is called im2col. MobileNet [14] uses deep separable convolution to replace the traditional convolution operations, which greatly reduces the number of mathematical operations and parameters. It uses depth wise convolution (DWC) and point wise convolution (PWC) to replace traditional convolution. We use OpenCL to design a kernel function to accelerate depth wise convolution of deep separable convolution and use matrix multiplication method to accelerate point wise convolution of deep separable convolution.

In order to achieve cross-platform performance portability, we use OpenCL to implement im2col operation and combine the matrix multiplication API provided by clBLAS library to speed up traditional convolution in parallel.

When using the clBLASCgemm function in clBLAS to speed up batch convolution operations, im2col needs to first convert the four-dimensional input data (NCWH) into a two-dimensional matrix, and then the clBLASCgemm function is called to complete the multiplication of input matrix and convolution core weight matrix. The output matrix is stored in the form of CNWH, so the data need to be rearranged into the storage in the form of NCWH. At the same time, the final output of clBLAS only completes the convolution operation without bias, so it is necessary to start another kernel function to complete the operation of adding bias.

Therefore, in order to realize the clBLAS accelerated convolution operation, it is necessary to use OpenCL to implement three kernels, As shown in the left picture of Fig. 1, to perform im2col, data conversion and adding bias respectively.

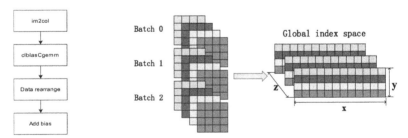

Fig. 1. Convolution process by suing clBLAS(left picture) and mapping relationship of OpenCL global index space for deep convolution(right picture)

The process of depth separable convolution operation on the output feature map is equivalent to a vector point product. The calculation process of different pixels is independent and can be carried out in parallel. In the structure of convolution neural network, the size of convolution filter is generally small, if using parallel reduction, the cost of synchronization may outweigh the benefits of parallelism, so the result of different filter's pixels are added serially. Therefore, the parallel scheme of deep convolution calculation designed by OpenCL is as follows: the size of the global index space corresponds to the number of pixels in the output feature map, that is, each work item is responsible for calculating a pixel in the output feature map, and a certain number of work items are formed into a working group. The global index space is set to three dimensions: x, y and z. The x dimension corresponds to the pixels of the same channel in the output feature map, the y dimension corresponds to the number of channels in the output feature map, and the z dimension corresponds to the batch size of the output feature map. The pixel points that each thread is responsible for is determined by obtaining the global index value. The mapping relationship is shown in the right figure of Fig. 1.

For the depth convolution operation, the input data addresses to be accessed by consecutive pixels located in the same channel feature map are consecutive, and the weight addresses are the same. Therefore, in order to achieve memory coalescing, consecutive index values in the global index space should correspond to two consecutive output feature map pixel points. The point-by-point convolution is the same as the traditional convolution method, except that the size of the convolution kernel becomes 1×1, so we use the matrix multiplicative convolution implemented in Sect. 3.1 to accelerate the point-by-point convolution.

3.2 Parallel Strategy for Other Layers

In order to achieve the parallel acceleration of the deep convolution neural network inference stage in OpenCL, other operations in the inference stage need to be implemented in parallel, such as global average pooling, shortcut operation, batch normalization, activation function and full connection operation.

Global mean pooling directly calculates the global mean of the input feature map. The Shortcut operation is equivalent to a matrix addition operation. Batch normalization is to calculate each pixel in the input feature map according to the calculation process of formula (2) and activation function is to calculate the activation function for each pixel in the input feature map, and the fully connected layer can be regarded as a dot product operation of two vectors. Similar to convolution operations, these operations output a set of feature maps. The computation of pixels in the feature map is independent. Therefore, we use the same parallel approach as convolution to design the kernel function. Finally, the overall inference process of the OpenCL-based parallel deep convolutional neural network is shown in Fig. 2.

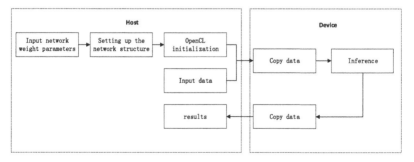

Fig. 2. Inference flow of parallel deep convolution neural network based on OpenCL

3.3 Kernel Fusion and Increasing Global Task

Since the start of the kernel takes extra time, as the number of network layers increases, using kernel frequently would increase more extra consumption. We can use kernel fusion method to reduce the consumption. As Fig. 3 shown, we combine the two operations of BN and Relu, as well as the operations of shortcut and Relu.

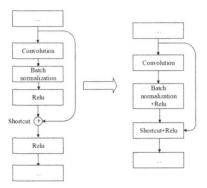

Fig. 3. Schematic diagram of the kernel fusion method

For the kernel fusion of batch normalization and convolution, we can implement it by using the following formula. First, the convolution formula shown as (1).

$$X_{conv} = x \times W + b \tag{1}$$

X_{conv} represents output, x represents input, W represents weights, b represents bias. And the formula of batch normalization shown as (2).

$$X_{bn} = \gamma \times \frac{(x-E[x])}{\sqrt{Var[x]+\varepsilon}} + \beta \tag{2}$$

γ, β are learnable parameters, $E[x]$ represents the mean of x, $Var[x]$ represents the variance of x. ε is a minimal positive number to prevent denominator from becoming zero. We can combine formula (1) and formula (2):

$$X_{bn} = x \times \frac{\gamma W}{\sqrt{Var[x]+\varepsilon}} + \frac{\gamma(b-E[x])}{\sqrt{Var[x]+\varepsilon}} + \beta \tag{3}$$

And then we can use the follows formulas to obtain new weights and bias to replace old ones.

$$W_{new} = \frac{\gamma W}{\sqrt{Var[x]+\varepsilon}} \quad b_{new} = \frac{\gamma(b-E[x])}{\sqrt{Var[x]+\varepsilon}} + \beta \tag{4}$$

When we obtain new weights and bias and replace old values, we can use them to compute formula (1) directly, and obtain the same results as using old values to compute formula (1) and formula (2). So the batch normalization operation is omitted and has no effect on the results.

In addition to kernel fusion, it can further improve performance by increasing batch size to increase the workload per core and occupy more GPU resources. Compared to inputting only one image, inputting multiple images at a time can reduce the number of OpenCL kernel functions to start, which will reduce the extra time consumption.

4 Experiment and Evaluations

4.1 Experimental Environment

In order to verify the inference performance of the OpenCL accelerating convolution neural network proposed in this paper, we implemented a deeply separable convolutional neural network and a residual neural network using OpenCL as shown in Table 1. We run the proposed method on NVIDIA and AMD GPU to verify portability. The hardware information is shown in Table 2.

Table 1. The networks used in experiments

CNNs	Convolution layers	Dataset	Accuracy
MobileNet v1 [14]	27	ImageNet	70.81%
ResNet [15]	21	Cifar 10	91.7%

Table 2. The platforms used in experiments

GPU	Single precision peak performance	Cores	Memory
AMD Radeon Vega Frontier	13.1TFLOPS	4096 cores 1600 MHz	16 GB 483 GB/s
NVIDIA GTX 1070	6.5TFLOPS	1920 cores 1506 MHz	8 GB 256 GB/s

As shown in Table 1, the depth separable neural network is MobileNet v1, which is used to classify the Imagenet dataset. There are 27 convolution layers and one full connection layer. The residual neural network we used has 21 convolution layers. And the network is used to classify cifar10 dataset. In addition, the host side of the NVIDIA platform is an AMD FX-8300 processor with a frequency of 3.3 GHz, the host side of the AMD platform is an AMD A10-7870K Radeeon R7 processor with a frequency of 3.9 GHz, and the host operating system is Ubuntu16.04. The Caffe version is the Hip version, which is an accelerated Caffe GPU version based on ROCm. ROCm is AMD's general-purpose GPU programming framework. This paper adopts ROCm 2.0. The compiler uses g++ 5.4.0. OpenCL uses OpenCL 1.2.

4.2 Performance Comparison of Depthwise Convolution Operations

Firstly, we compare our proposed method that accelerates depth convolution with Caffe and Diagonal method proposed in [16]. We extract depth convolution from MobileNet v1, and divide them into 9 different layers according to the size of input feature map and convolution parameters. The results for batchsize = 1 are shown in Table 3.

Table 3. Time comparison of different depth convolution parallel methods

	OpenCL (ms)	Caffe (ms)	Diagonal (ms)
Conv2_1dw	0.1488	1.7928	0.2915
Conv2_2dw	0.1461	2.8236	0.3024
Conv3_1dw	0.1531	4.2580	0.6749
Conv3_2dw	0.1005	5.1743	0.4954
Conv4_1dw	0.1420	9.3704	1.0614
Conv4_2dw	0.0991	13.2270	0.7529
Conv5dw	0.0985	27.2045	1.6190
Conv5_6dw	0.0895	28.0888	1.7314
Conv6dw	0.0879	51.3935	4.0700

From the result data in the Table 3, we can see that the proposed method is obviously better than the other two. Caffe's depth convolution performance is the worst, and with the increase of the number of input channels, the serial execution between multiple channels results in low parallel efficiency. Especially in several layers of conv4_1dw to conv6d, the input feature maps become relatively small, result in the matrices converted by im2col become small, too. So it can't use more GPU computing resources. The diagonal method avoids serial execution and directly converts the convolution filters and input data into two large matrices for parallel acceleration. Although it avoids the overhead of serial execution and increases the utilization of GPU hardware resources, it also increases the computational complexity and runtime due to its conversion of deep convolution into traditional convolution.

4.3   Comparison of Parallel DCNN Inference Performance

After the implementation of OpenCL inference to accelerate MobileNet V1 and residual neural network for performance comparison with Caffe. First, we run the forward propagation of MobileNet V1 network and residual neural network on the same GPU through Caffe. The inference time of MobileNet V1 network and residual neural network are shown in Table 4.

Table 4. Parallel acceleration time of MobileNet V1 and ResNet neural network inference

	Caffe (ms)	OpenCL (ms)	Speedup
MobileNet v1	45.9460	7.4873	7.2275
ResNet	8.1670	4.4939	1.8174

According to Table 4, the parallel inference time of MobileNet V1 is 7.4873 ms, which is 7.2275 times faster than that of Caffe GPU, thanks to the acceleration of deep convolution. The parallel inference time of residual neural network is 4.4939 ms, which is 1.8174 times faster than that of Caffe. In order to further optimize the acceleration, we use the method of kernel fusion to eliminate the time proportion of batch normalization and activation function.

We using kernel fusion combine the kernels of convolution and batch normalization, after this, we continue to combine the kernels of convolution and activation. Finally, the result shown in Table 5 We can see that, after kernel fusion. The performance of MobileNet v1 improves 22.26%, and the performance of ResNet improves 30.95%.

Table 5. Process time before and after kernel fusion

	Before (ms)	After (ms)	Reduced time percentage (%)
MobileNet v1	7.48729	5.8145	22.26
ResNet	4.4939	3.1031	30.95

After kernel fusion, we can increase the batch size to improve global task load, and to occupy more hardware resources. Compared to classifying only one image at a time, increasing batch size can reduce the overhead of OpenCL kernels when classify the same number images.

Table 6. Inference time of MobileNet V1 and ResNet in different batch size

Bitch size	OpenCL GPU		Caffe GPU		Diagonal GPU
	MobileNet V1	ResNet	MobileNet V1	ResNet	MobileNet V1
1	5.8145 ms	3.1031 ms	45.9460 ms	8.1670 ms	16.5178 ms
5	2.1951 ms	0.7953 ms	40.0650 ms	1.6890 ms	6.1303 ms
10	1.7568 ms	0.4330 ms	39.6705 ms	0.9090 ms	5.3144 ms
20	1.7178 ms	0.2543 ms	40.7603 ms	0.4940 ms	6.0869 ms
30	1.6190 ms	0.1928 ms	40.1693 ms	0.3510 ms	5.8368 ms
40	1.5480 ms	0.1652 ms	47.8613 ms	0.2820 ms	5.4615 ms
50	1.4891 ms	0.1434 ms	46.6712 ms	0.2500 ms	5.1117 ms
60	1.4108 ms	0.1385 ms	45.4217 ms	0.2230 ms	4.8595 ms
70	1.2815 ms	0.1273 ms	50.3016 ms	0.2130 ms	3.8701 ms
80	1.2642 ms	0.1597 ms	48.8303 ms	0.1960 ms	3.8503 ms
90	1.2024 ms	0.1373 ms	48.2878 ms	0.1900 ms	3.8516 ms
100	1.2370 ms	0.1494 ms	52.8464 ms	0.1840 ms	3.7961 ms

As shown in Table 6, first, with the increase of batch size, the time of inference single image decreases gradually. But when the batch size is above 90, even if the batch size increases, the time for a single image will not decrease any more. Therefore, the MobileNet V1 network performs best when the batch size is 90, It shows that when the batch size is 90, the number of work items can make full use of the hardware computing resources of GPU. At this time, the inference time of an image is 1.2024 ms. Residual network has the best performance when the batch size is 70. The inference time of an image is 0.1273 ms, which improves the performance by 79.32% and 95.90% respectively compared with that before increasing the global task load.

4.4 Performance Comparison of Different Hardware Environments

To verify OpenCL code's portability, we test the performance of parallel deep convolutional neural networks on NVIDIA GeForce GTX 1070. The results are shown in Table 7.

Table 7. Inference time of MobileNet V1 and ResNet on NVIDIA GeForce GTX 1070

Bitch size	OpenCL implementation		Caffe implementation	
	MobileNet V1	ResNet	MobileNet V1	ResNet
1	3.9697 ms	3.0494 ms	31.3674 ms	7.8862 ms
5	2.7944 ms	0.9113 ms	25.2806 ms	1.7380 ms
10	2.4275 ms	0.6165 ms	26.2420 ms	0.8253 ms
20	1.9580 ms	0.3997 ms	24.7225 ms	0.4764 ms
30	1.9634 ms	0.2786 ms	25.3207 ms	0.3343 ms
40	1.7546 ms	0.2670 ms	25.4780 ms	0.2991 ms
50	1.7213 ms	0.2498 ms	25.6426 ms	0.2583 ms
60	1.6903 ms	0.2188 ms	25.2632 ms	0.2440 ms

As shown in Table 7, the method also shows good acceleration effect on NVIDIA GPU, combining with the performance of this method on AMD GPU, the OpenCL accelerated deep convolution neural network inference algorithm proposed in this paper has achieved good performance on both AMD GPU and NVIDIA GPU hardware platforms. Compared to Caffe implementation, the performance of MobileNet V1 network has been improved by 40.16 and 14.95 times, respectively. And residual neural network has been improved by 1.67 and 1.11 times, respectively. The OpenCL accelerated deep convolutional neural network inference algorithm proposed in this paper is more effective in accelerating MobileNet v1, and some performance portability on NVIDIA and AMD GPUs.

5   Conclusions

In this paper, we propose an OpenCL-based parallel deep convolutional neural network inference algorithm with kernel fusion to further improve the performance and increase the global task load without affecting the accuracy of the algorithm. The problem of not being able to efficiently utilize different GPU devices to accelerate DNN inference is addressed.

In the future, we will consider optimizing our approach for more hardware, and combine it with kernel auto-tuning methods for automatic parameter tuning.

Funding. This work is funded in part by the Key Research and Development Program of Shaanxi (Program No. 2022ZDLGY01-09), GHfund A (No. 202107014474) GHfund C (No. 202202036165), Wuhu and Xidian University special fund for industry-university-research cooperation (Project No. XWYCXY-012021013), and Cloud Computing Key Laboratory of Gansu Province.

References

1. Guo P.: Multi-institutional collaborations for improving deep learning-based magnetic resonance image reconstruction using federated learning. In: Proceedings of the IEEE Conference on Computer Vision and Pattern Recognition, pp. 2423–2432. IEEE, Piscataway, NJ (2021)
2. Wang J.: End-to-end object detection with fully convolutional network. In: Proceedings of the IEEE Conference on Computer Vision and Pattern Recognition, pp. 15849–15858. IEEE, Piscataway, NJ (2021)
3. Das A.: Enabling on-device smartphone GPU based training: lessons learned. In: 2022 IEEE International Conference on Pervasive Computing and Communications Workshops and other Affiliated Events (PerCom Workshops), pp. 533–538. IEEE, Piscataway, NJ (2022)
4. Kim, S.: Performance evaluation of INT8 quantized inference on mobile GPUs. IEEE Access **9**, 164245–164255 (2021)
5. Wai, Y.J.: Fixed point implementation of Tiny-Yolo-v2 using OpenCL on FPGA. Int. J. Adv. Comput. Sci. Appl. **9**(10), 506–512 (2018)
6. Mu, J.: Optimizing Opencl-Based CNN design on FPGA with comprehensive design space exploration and collaborative performance modeling. ACM Trans. Reconfigurable Technol. Syst. (TRETS) **13**(3), 1–28 (2020)
7. Koo, Y., Kim, S., Ha, Y.-G.: OpenCL-Darknet: implementation and optimization of OpenCL-based deep learning object detection framework. World Wide Web **24**(4), 1299–1319 (2020). https://doi.org/10.1007/s11280-020-00778-y
8. Dagli, R., Eken, S.: Deploying a smart queuing system on edge with Intel OpenVINO toolkit. Soft. Comput. **25**(15), 10103–10115 (2021). https://doi.org/10.1007/s00500-021-05891-2
9. Marco, V.S.: Optimizing deep learning inference on embedded systems through adaptive model selection. ACM Trans. Embed. Comput. Syst. **19**(1), 1–28 (2020)
10. Dua A.: Systolic-CNN: an OpenCL-defined scalable run-time-flexible FPGA accelerator architecture for accelerating convolutional neural network inference in cloud/edge computing. In: Annual International Symposium on Field-Programmable Custom Computing Machines (FCCM), p. 231. IEEE, Piscataway, NJ (2020)
11. Lin, D.L.: Accelerating large sparse neural network inference using GPU task graph parallelism. IEEE Trans. Parallel Distrib. Syst. **33**(11), 3041–3052 (2021)
12. He, S.: An efficient GPU-accelerated inference engine for binary neural network on mobile phones. J. Syst. Architect. **117**, 102156 (2021)
13. Chen, J.: Split convolutional neural networks for distributed inference on concurrent IoT sensors. In: International Conference on Parallel and Distributed Systems (ICPADS), pp. 66–73. IEEE, Piscataway, NJ (2021)

14. Howard A.G.: MobileNets: efficient convolutional neural networks for mobile vision applications. arXiv preprint arXiv:1704.04861 (2017)
15. He, K.: Deep residual learning for image recognition. In: Proceedings of the IEEE Conference on Computer Vision and Pattern Recognition, pp. 770–778. IEEE, Piscataway, NJ (2016)
16. Qin Z.: Diagonal wise refactorization: an efficient training method for depthwise convolutions. In: 2018 International Joint Conference on Neural Networks (IJCNN), pp. 770–778. IEEE, Piscataway, NJ (2016)

A Simple Approach to the Multiple Source Identification of Information Diffusion

Xiaojie Li[1,2], Xin Yu[1,2(✉)], Chubing Guo[1,2], Yuxin Wang[1,2], and Jianshe Wu[1,2]

[1] Xidian University, Xi'an, China
Yx_yuxin@hotmail.com
[2] The 20th Research Institute of China Electronics Technology Group Corporation,
Joint Laboratory of Artificial Intelligence, Xidian University, Xi'an, China

Abstract. This paper studies the problem of identifying multiple information sources in networks. Assuming that the information diffusion follows a Susceptible-Infected (SI) model which allowing all nodes in the network are in the susceptible state or infected state. The number of information sources is known, we propose a simple method to identify multiple diffusion sources. After the diffusion started, any node can be infected very quickly, for an arbitrary node, it is infected by its closest source in terms of spreading time. Therefore, to identify multiple diffusion sources, we partition the information diffusion network and minimize the sum of all partition propagation times. Then in each partition we can find a node which has the minimum spreading time as diffusion source. Furthermore, we also give a new method to estimate the spreading time which can improve the proposed multiple sources identification algorithm. Simulation results show that the proposed method has distinct advantages in identifying multiple sources in various real-world networks.

Keywords: Complex networks · Information diffusion · Multiple sources identification · SI model

1 Introduction

Interconnection in networks brings us many conveniences, but it also makes us vulnerable to various network risks. For instance, disease or epidemic spread in the human society [1, 2], rumors spread incredibly fast in online social networks such as WeChat, Facebook, and Twitter [3], etc. To contain these network risks, we need to identify the source of the propagation accurately [4]. By accurately identifying the sources, we can predict its further spread and develop timely mitigation strategies.

In the past few years, some methods are designed to work on tree-like networks whose propagation follows the classical Susceptible-Infected (SI) model [5–9]. Some other methods to identify diffusion sources in tree-like networks but with different epidemic

Z. Shi et al. (Eds.): ICIS 2022, IFIP AICT 659, pp. 109–117, 2022.
https://doi.org/10.1007/978-3-031-14903-0_12

models, such as the Susceptible-Infected- Recovery (SIR) model and the Susceptible-Infected-Susceptible (SIS) model [10–12]. These methods mainly aim at the identification of a single diffusion source. It is shown that even in tree networks the source identification problem is NP-complete [5]. Recently, some heuristic methods are designed to relax the constraints from tree-like topologies to general networks [13–16].

Usually there is not a single source in the initial stage of the diffusion, such as infection disease can start from multiple locations. However, only a few of existing methods are designed to identifying multiple diffusion sources, such as the multi-rumor-center method [12], dynamic age method [17] and K-Center method [18]. In this paper, we adopt the SI model and propose a simple method named KST method to identify multiple diffusion sources in general networks. In general, a node is infected by its closest source in terms of spreading time, so we can identify diffusion sources by minimize the sum of all partition propagation times. At first we partition the diffusion network into several parts, then we find a node for each partition which has the minimum spreading time as the diffusion sources. We evaluate the KST method in the North American Power Grid and the Yeast protein-protein interaction network. Experiments show that our method outperforms the other competing methods.

2   Related Works and Motivations

We briefly introduce several state-of-the-art methods about multiple diffusion sources identification.

2.1   Related Methods

Dynamic Age. Fioriti *et al.* propose a method to identify multiple diffusion sources under the SI model [17]. The method only requires the topology of an undirected network and the infected network. However, due to the high complexity $O(N^3)$, the dynamic age method is not suitable in large-scale networks.

Multiple Rumor Center. Shah and Zaman introduce a rumor centrality method for single source identification in tree-like networks [5, 7]. The rumor centrality is defined as the number of distinct propagation paths originating from the source. The node with the maximum rumor centrality is called rumor center. For regular trees, the rumor center is considered as the propagation origin. Based on the definition of rumor centrality for a single node, Luo *et al.* extend the rumor centrality to a set of nodes [8], which is defined as the number of distinct propagation paths originating from the node set.

The computational complexity of this method is $O(n^k)$, where n is the number of infected nodes and k is the number of sources. Similar as the dynamic age, the method does not consider the propagation probabilities.

K-Center. Jiang *et al.* propose the K-Center method on the SI model to identify multiple diffusion sources in general networks [18]. They adopt a measure named as effective distance proposed in [13] to transform propagation probability to distance. The effective distance is defined as

$$e(i, j) = 1 - \log(\eta_{ij}) \tag{1}$$

where η_{ij} is the propagation probability from v_i to v_j. The concept of effective distance reflects the idea that a small propagation probability is equivalent to a large distance between them, and vice versa.

Based on the altered network, they derive an objective function for the multiple source identification:

$$\min f = \sum_{i=1}^{k} \sum_{v_j \in C_i} d\left(v_j, s_i\right) \tag{2}$$

where v_j is the infection node associated with source s_i, and $d\left(v_j, s_i\right)$ is the shortest path distance in terms of effective distance between v_j and s_i. By using the effective distance, the problem is simplified and K-Center has higher accuracy.

2.2 Motivations

Motivation 1. Existing source identification methods only take the probability of propagation into consideration and not consider the propagation time. In this paper, we take the propagation time into consideration and define an objection function for the multiple source identification problems by minimizing the sum of all partition propagation times.

Motivation 2. The multiple rumor center methods introduced above has computational complexity $O\left(n^k\right)$, and the complexity of Dynamic Age method is also $O\left(n^3\right)$. In most cases, identifying propagation sources quickly is of great significance in the real world.

3 Preliminaries and Problem Formulation

3.1 Susceptible-Infected (SI) Model

In the SI model, the nodes in a network have two possible states: susceptible (S) and infected (I). All the nodes are in the susceptible state initially except the diffusion sources. Infected nodes are those nodes that possess the infection and will remain infected throughout. Susceptible nodes are uninfected nodes, but may receive the infection from their infected neighbors and become infected.

Suppose the diffusion start at time $T = 0$, and we use $P_S(i, t)$ and $P_I(i, t)$ to denote the probability of node v_i being susceptible and infected at time $T = t$ respectively. At time $T = 0$, all infected nodes, namely the diffusion sources have the initial state of $P_S(i, t) = 0$ and $P_I(i, t) = 1$. Similarly all susceptible nodes have the initial state of $P_S(i, 0) = 1$ and $P_I(i, t) = 0$. Then using following formulas, we can obtain the probability of each node in various states at an arbitrary time.

$$P_S(i, t) = \left[1 - Inf(i, t)\right] \cdot P_S(i, t - 1) \tag{3}$$

$$P_I(i, t) = Inf(i, t) \cdot P_S(i, t - 1) + P_I(i, t - 1) \tag{4}$$

where $Inf(i, t)$ denotes the probability of node v_i to be infected by its neighbors at time $T = t$, which can be computed by

$$Inf(i, t) = 1 - \prod_{j \in N_i} \left[1 - \eta_{ji} \cdot P_I(j, t - 1)\right] \tag{5}$$

where the η_{ji} denotes the propagation probability from node v_j to its neighboring node v_i, and N_i denotes the set of neighbors of node v_i.

3.2 Problem Formulation

Suppose there are $k (k \geq 1)$ sources: $S^* = \{s_1, s_2, \ldots s_k\}$, and these sources start diffusion simultaneously at time $T = 0$. After the diffusion sustains for several time ticks, there are N nodes infected. These nodes form a connected networks $G(V, E)$, which we call the infection network.

Given an infection network G and the propagation probability between any two connected nodes, the problem is to identify a set of diffusion sources S^*.

4 KST Method

Suppose the diffusion source number k is known, we propose KST method to identify multiple diffusion sources in general networks. We firstly analyze the problem formulation for the KST method. Then we introduce the KST method for detail including two variables that need to be calculated in advance and the specific iterative process of KST method.

4.1 Analysis

According to the previous introduction, the diffusion sources start diffusion simultaneously, and for each source s_i, it has its infection region $C_i(\subseteq V)$. In other words, the infected network is composed of k regions, $C^* = \{C_1, C_2, \ldots C_k\}$, supposing $C^* = \bigcup_{i=1}^{k} C_i$ and $C_i \cap C_j = \emptyset$ for $i \neq j$. In each region, there is only one source and the infection of other nodes in the region can be traced back to the corresponding source.

To identify the multiple diffusion sources S^*, we suppose the time of infection process is very short, therefore for an arbitrary infected node v_j in V we consider it is infected by the closest source in terms of spreading time. According to previous analysis, we can divide the infection network G into k partitions, so that each infected node belonging to the partition has the shortest spreading time to the corresponding sources. Then we get a partition of G and we think each partition is similar to the real region of infection network. The source node should be the node from which the diffusion takes the shortest spreading time to cover all the partition.

From the above analysis, we define an objective function as follow, which aims to find a partition of the infection network minimizing the sum of all partition propagation times as much as possible.

$$\min_{C^*} f = \sum_{i=1}^{k} t_i \tag{6}$$

where t_i is the spreading time of partition C_i, which is computed by

$$t_i = \max\{h(s_i, v_j)|v_j \in C_i\} \tag{7}$$

where node v_j belongs to partition C_i associated with source s_i and $h(s_i, v_j)$ is the minimum number of hops between s_i and v_j. The formula suggests that we can find a partition which can minimize the sum of spreading time of each partition, then for each partition the node with the minimum spreading time is the diffusion source.

4.2 KST Method

We first introduce two elementary knowledge including hop-based spreading time and propagation probability. These two variables need to be obtained in advance. Secondly, from a set of initial nodes in the infection network, an iterative approach is proposed to locate the diffusion sources.

4.2.1 Hops-Based Spreading Time

In SI model, it at least takes one time tick for the diffusion from one node to its neighbor, which means the spreading time can be estimated by the minimum number of hops [18]. Given an infection network $G(V, E)$, where $V = \{v_1, v_2, \ldots, v_n\}$ and $E = \{e_{ij}\}, i, j \in \{1, \ldots, n\}$, are the sets of nodes and edges, respectively. Suppose the network has one information source s, for an arbitrary node v_i, let $h(s, v_i)$ denote the minimum number of hops between s and v_i, which can be simply considered as the spreading time between s and v_i. Then, the spreading time is

$$t = \max\{h(s, v_i)|v_i \in V\} \tag{8}$$

The hops number of shortest path between node v_i and node v_j is regard as the spreading time between node v_i and node v_j.

4.2.2 Propagation Probability

For the infection network $G(V, E)$, there exists a propagation probability η_{ij} between any pair of neighbor nodes v_i and v_j. For any pair of unconnected nodes, the propagation probability is computed by the shortest path based method. That is to say, we assume that the propagation of information between any two nodes in the network is along the shortest path, and the propagation probability of the shortest path is the propagation probability between these nodes. In general, the shortest path has the highest propagation probability compared to other paths.

In order to calculate the propagation probability between any two nodes in the network, we first make the following conversion on each edge in the network:

$$q(i, j) = -\log(\eta_{ij}) \tag{9}$$

where η_{ij} is the probability of propagation on the edge. Using $q(i, j)$ as the weight of the edge, we can find the shortest path between by using a shortest path algorithm, e.g. the Dijkstra algorithm used in this paper. Then convert $q(i, j)$ to the probability of propagation between v_i and v_j by Eq. (10):

$$p(i, j) = e^{-q(i,j)} \tag{10}$$

4.2.3 Initialize Sources Set

First of all, we need to select k nodes as initial sources. Here, we choose them with the maximum distance because these nodes most likely are associated with different sources. We say an infected node v is associated with source s if the infection of v is traced back to source s. To select the initial sources, we first select a pair of infected nodes with the maximum distance, then we select other $k - 2$ nodes greedily. The detail is shown in Algorithm 1.

4.2.4 Network Partition with Multiple Sources

Given an infection network G_n and a set of sources $S^* = \{s_1, s_2, \ldots s_k\}$, we should partition G_n into k partitions. According to our previous analysis, each node $v_j \in G_n$ should be classified into partition C_i associated with source s_i, such that

$$t(v_j, s_i) = \min_{s_l \in S} t(v_j, s_l) \tag{11}$$

The detail is presented in Algorithm 2. For each node v_j, we find the minimum spreading time from v_j to these sources. When there is only one source, denoted s_i, which satisfies above condition, we classify the node v_j into partition C_i associated with source s_i. If there are equal or greater than two sources which satisfy the condition, we further compare the propagation probability from v_j to these sources and classify the v_j to the source which has the maximum propagation probability between itself and v_j.

4.2.5 Identifying Diffusion Sources

The complete process of KST is presented in this subsection. We first use Algorithm 1 to select an initial set of sources, then partition the infection network into k partitions by Algorithm 2. The partition algorithm can find a local optimal solution for (6). In order to further minimize the objective function, our method selects a new source for each partition which has the minimum spreading time in each partition. We call the method as K Shortest spreading Time nodes (KST). The detailed process of the KST is shown in Algorithm 3. The main computation is the calculation of the shortest path between node pairs. In the simulations, the Dijkstra algorithm is used to calculate the shortest path, whose computational complexity is $O(n^2)$. Therefore, the computational complexity of the KST is $O(n^2)$.

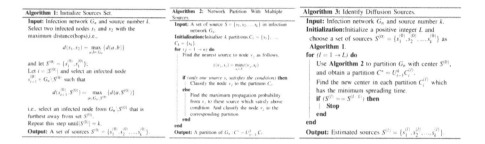

5   KST-Improved Method

In KST, the shortest path is used to estimate the spreading time between two nodes, without considering the influences of propagation probability. In this subsection, propagation probability is used to estimate the spreading time between two nodes, which is defined as follows:

$$et(i,j) = -\log(p_{ij}) \qquad (12)$$

where p_{ij} is the propagation probability between v_i and v_j, refer to Subsect. 4.2 for the calculation method. We call the new spreading time as the effective spreading time.

Then we partition the infection network G_n into k partitions according to the effective spreading time. For $v_j \in G_n$, it should be classified into partition C_i associated with source s_i, such that

$$et(v_j, s_i) = \min_{s_l \in S} et(v_j, s_l) \qquad (13)$$

We denote the improved KST method as KST-Improved. Experiments show that the effective propagation time can improve accuracy of multiple source identification.

6   Evaluation

6.1   Experiments Settings

The North American Power Grid network and the Yeast protein-protein interaction network are used. Table 1 gives the basic statics of the networks. Previous works [19] show that the accuracy of the SI model cannot be affected by the distribution of propagation probability on each edge, therefore we set the propagation probability on each edge, η_{ij}, uniformly distributed in $(0, 1)$. We set the number of infection source k to be 2 to 5 and perform 100 simulation runs for each k. In each simulation, we randomly select k nodes from network as the initial source and simulate the propagation process using the SI model. Each simulation terminates when the number of infected node is greater than a number such as 100 or the spreading time is equal a number such as 5.

6.2 Accuracy of Identifying Sources

We match the estimated sources with the real sources so that the sum of the error distances is minimized [8]. The average error distance is given by

$$\Delta = \frac{1}{|S^*|} \sum_{i=1}^{|S^*|} h(s_i, \hat{s}_i) \qquad (14)$$

where $s_i \in S^* = \{s_1, s_2, \ldots s_k\}$, and $\hat{s}_i$ is the estimated sources corresponding to s_i.

The simulation result is given in Table 2, which show than KST and KST-Improved have the smaller average error distances. KST-Improved is better than KST method, which proves that the effective spreading time is more precise than hop-based spreading time.

Table 1. Statistics of data collected in the experiments

Dataset	Power grid	Yeast
Number of nodes	4941	2361
Number of edges	13188	13554
Average degree	2.67	5.74
Maximum degree	19	64

Table 2. Average error distance of three methods

Experiment settings		Average error distance			
Network	k	KST	KST-improved	K-Center	Dynamic age
Power grid	2	1.39	1.31	1.78	2.593
	3	1.67	1.687	2.152	3.434
	4	1.775	1.6	2.373	3.957
	5	1.893	1.741	2.725	4.467
Yeast	2	0.925	0.91	1.721	3.057
	3	0.98	0.936	2.222	3.823
	4	1.15	1.099	2.383	3.7
	5	1.226	1.158	3.04	4.133

7 Conclusion

We provided a simple method for general network to detect multiple information sources, its computational complexity is $O(n^2)$, which is much less than other methods. We propose a new measure to estimate the spreading time between nodes from the propagation probability, which improves the accuracy of source identification.

References

1. Neumann, G., Noda, T., Kawaoka, Y.: Emergence and pandemic potential of swine-origin H1N1 influenza virus. Nature **459**(7249), 931–939 (2009)
2. Hvistendahl, M., Normile, D., Cohen, J.: Influenza. Despite large research effort, H7N9 continues to baffle. Science **340**(6131), 414 (2013)
3. Doerr, B., Fouz, M., Friedrich, T.: Why rumors spread so quickly in social networks. Commun. ACM **55**(6), 70–75 (2012)
4. Jiang, J., Wen, S., Yu, S., Xiang, Y., Zhou, W.: Identifying propagation sources in networks: state-of-the-art and comparative studies. IEEE Commun. Surv. Tut. **19**, 465–481 (2017)
5. Shah, D., Zaman, T.: Rumors in a network: who's the culprit? IEEE Trans. Inf. Theor. **57**, 5163–5181 (2011)
6. Karamchandani, N., Franceschetti, M.: Rumor source detection under probabilistic sampling. In: 2013 IEEE International Symposium on Information Theory Proceedings (ISIT), pp. 2184–2188 (2013)
7. Shah, D., Zaman, T.: Rumor centrality: a universal source detector. SIGMETRICS Perform. Eval. Rev. **40**(1), 199–210 (2012)
8. Luo, W., Tay, W.P., Leng, M.: Identifying infection sources and regions in large networks. IEEE Trans. Sig. Process. **61**(11), 2850–2865 (2013)
9. Milling, C., Caramanis, C., Mannor, S., Shakkottai, S.: On identifying the causative network of an epidemic. In: 2012 50th Annual Allerton Conference on Communication, Control, and Computing, Allerton, pp. 909–914. IEEE (2012)
10. Zhu, K., Ying, L.: Information source detection in the sir model: a sample path based approach. In: Information Theory and ApplicationsWorkshop (ITA), pp. 1–9 (2013)
11. Zhu, K., Ying, L.: A robust information source estimator with sparse observations. arXiv preprint arXiv:1309.4846 (2013)
12. Luo, W., Tay, W.P.: Finding an infection source under the sis model. In: 2013 IEEE International Conference on Acoustics, Speech and Signal Processing (ICASSP), pp. 2930–2934 (2013)
13. Brockmann, D., Helbing, D.: The hidden geometry of complex, network-driven contagion phenomena. Science **342**(6164), 1337–1342 (2013)
14. Altarelli, F., Braunstein, A., DallAsta, L., Lage-Castellanos, A., Zecchina, R.: Bayesian inference of epidemics on networks via belief propagation. Phys. Rev. Lett. **112**(11), 118701 (2014)
15. Chen, Z., Zhu, K., Ying, L.: Detecting multiple information sources in networks under the sir model. In: 2014 48th Annual Conference on Information Sciences and Systems (CISS), pp. 1–4. IEEE (2014)
16. Luo, W., Tay, W.P.: Identifying multiple infection sources in a network. In: 2012 Conference Record of the 46th Asilomar Conference on Signals, Systems and Computers (ASILOMAR), pp. 1483–1489. IEEE (2012)
17. Fioriti, V., Chinnici, M., Palomo, J.: Predicting the sources of an outbreak with a spectral technique. Appl. Math. Sci. **8**(135), 6775–6782 (2014)
18. Jiang, J., Wen, S., Yu, S., Xiang, Y., Zhou, W.L.: K-center: an approach on the multi-source identification of information diffusion. IEEE Trans. Inf. Forensics Secur. **10**(12), 2616–2626 (2015)
19. Wen, S., Zhou, W., Zhang, J., Xiang, Y., Zhou, W., Jia, W.: Modeling propagation dynamics of social network worms. IEEE Trans. Parallel Distrib. Syst. **24**(8), 1633–1643 (2013)

Data Intelligence

A Directed Search Many Objective Optimization Algorithm Embodied with Kernel Clustering Strategy

Michael Aggrey Okoth, Ronghua Shang$^{(\boxtimes)}$, Weitong Zhang, and Licheng Jiao

Key Laboratory of Intelligent Perception and Image Understanding
of Ministry of Education, School of Artificial Intelligence, Xidian University,
Xi'an 710071, Shaanxi, China
{rhshang,lchjiao}@mail.xidian.edu.cn, wtzhang_1@xidian.edu.cn

Abstract. With the vast existence of multi-objective optimization problems to the scientific research and engineering applications, Many-objective Evolutionary Algorithms (MaOEAs) demand to systematically perpetuate population diversity and convergence distributions in the objective space with high dimensionality. To fulfill the balance in the relationship between convergence, distributions, and diversity, this paper proposes a directed search many-objective optimization algorithm embodied with kernel clustering strategy (DSMOA-KCS) in decision space where some mechanisms such as adaptive environmental selection which efficiently assimilates design for control of diversity and convergence in the distribution of the solutions in the decision scopes. DSMOA-KCS is a stochastic, multi-start algorithm using clustering to increase efficiency. DSMOA-KCS finds the starting point in the regions of interest. Then, it improves them by the directed search method. DSMOA-KCS is compared with several existing state-of-the-art algorithms (NSGA-III, RSEA, and MOEADPas) on many-objective problems with 5 to 30 objective functions using the Inverted Generational Distance (IGD) performance metric. DSMOA-KCS evaluation results illustrate that it is competitive and promising, performing better with some problems. Then, even distribution, convergence, and diversity are maintained.

Keywords: Many-objective optimization · Kernel cluster · Diversity and convergence · Evolutionary algorithm

1 Introduction

Evolutionary Many-objective optimization has become a popular and influential research field in recent years. Its application to real-world problems has significantly been shown. That is to say, many practical problems can be defined as Many objective problems (MaOPs), such as time series learning [4] and engineering design [3]. Moreover, many optimization problems refer to multi-objective setbacks with more than three objectives.

© IFIP International Federation for Information Processing 2022
Published by Springer Nature Switzerland AG 2022
Z. Shi et al. (Eds.): ICIS 2022, IFIP AICT 659, pp. 121–129, 2022.
https://doi.org/10.1007/978-3-031-14903-0_13

$$Minimize \quad f(x) = (f_1(x), f_2(x), \cdots, f_M(x))^T$$
$$Subject \quad to \quad x \in \Omega \tag{1}$$

where $x = (x_1, x_2, \ldots, x_n)^T$ is the n-dimensional decision vector in the decision space Ω, $M > 3$ the number of objectives, and $f(x)$ is the M-dimensional objective vector. While solving MaOPs with many Objective Evolutionary Algorithms, there is an incomparability of solutions that is caused due to the proportion of non-dominated solutions increasing significantly [2,7]. This makes optimization using only the dominance relationship infeasible and challenging to maintain population diversity in a high-dimensional objective space.

Researchers presented many solutions, most of which fall into three categories. First, Pareto dominance-based MaOEAs use modified Pareto mechanisms to identify non-dominated solutions. 2-dominance and fuzzy dominance modify dominance definitions to sustain selection pressure. Divergent distance computations improve Pareto-based MaOEAs [9]. Zhang et al. used a knee-point-based selection approach [11]. Li et al. suggested a shift-based density estimation technique for many-objective optimization [8]. Indicator-based MaOEAs evaluate solutions and steer search processes. IGD is a popular indicator. Hyper Volume (HV) and R2 are also noteworthy. Decomposition-based MaOEAs decompose a MOP into SOPs or simple MOPs to be solved collectively. Certain MOEAs, such as RVEA [1] and MOEA/D [10], decompose a MOP into SOPs. NSGA-III [5], and SPEA, based on reference direction [6], decompose a MOP into multiple simpler MOPs by subdividing the objective space.

2   The Proposed Method

The DSMOA-KCS evolutionary process is restarted when the best solution is reached; if not after a specific number of generations, it is denoted by parame-

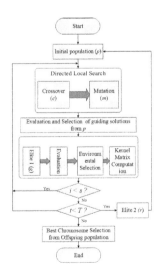

Fig. 1. Flowchart of the proposed DSMOA-KCS

ters. Each evolution of DSMOA-KCS starts from a different initial population. Figure 1 shows how the number of leading chromosomes r changes over time.

Figure 1 's I parameter indicates the number of generations in which the best solutions are found and improved. Current and provided computing times are t and T. Every evolution involves chromosomal transmission. g indicates the number of chromosomes. Population size (p), crossover rate (c), mutation (m), elite count 1 (g), elite count 2 (r), and adaptive restarting condition (s) are methodically tweaked to improve directed sampling search outcomes. The crossover rate (c) is improved using local directed search, mutation, and environmental selection. A mating pool P' is formed by selecting the union P (Population size) and CSA (Corner Solution Archive) in Algorithm 2. It specifies the convergence of solutions by randomly selecting two solutions from P' each time results are needed.

2.1 Directed Search Sampling and Guiding Solutions

Firstly this paper takes into consideration unconstrained Many objective problems.

$$Min \quad F(x)$$
$$x \in \mathbb{R}^n \tag{2}$$

where F is defined as the vector of objective functions $F : \mathbb{R}^n \to \mathbb{R}^k$, $F(x) = (f_1(x), \dots, f_k(x))^T$, and each objective $f_i : \mathbb{R}^n \to \mathbb{R}$ is smooth. The optimality of MaOEAs is defined by the dominance of a vector $y \in \mathbb{R}^n$ dominated by vector $x \in \mathbb{R}^n (x \prec y)$ with respect to MaOP if $f_i(x) < f_i(y)$ or else y is dominated by x. Point $x \in \mathbb{R}^k$ is a Pareto point if there exists no $y \in \mathbb{R}^n$ that dominates x. The set of all Pareto optimal solutions is symbolized by P. The $F(p)$ is the Pareto front. Using the Jacobian of F at point x is illustrated by

$$J(x) = \begin{pmatrix} \nabla f_i(x)^T \\ \vdots \\ \nabla f_k(x)^T \end{pmatrix} \in \mathbb{R}^{k \times n} \tag{3}$$

where $\nabla f_i(x)$ symbolizes the gradient of the objective f_i. If the MaOEAs are differentiable then this necessitates condition for Pareto optimality of unconstrained MaOPs. Assumption point $x_0 \in \mathbb{R}^n$ with rank $(j(x_0)) = k$ is given and vector $d \in \mathbb{R}^k$ showing the desired search direction in objective space. Then the search direction $v \in \mathbb{R}^n$ in the decision space is sought such that for $y_0 := x_0 + hv$, where $h \in \mathbb{R}_+$ is the step size that represents the movement from x_0 in the direction v and as shown in Eq. 4 below with y_0 representing the movement from x_0 in direction of V:

$$\lim_{h \searrow 0} \frac{f_i(y_0) - f_i(x_0)}{h} = \{\nabla f_i(x_0), v\} = d_i, i = 1, \cdots, k, if \|v\| = 1 \tag{4}$$

In this research paper $|.|$ represents the 2-norm. F in Eq. 4 is stated as matrix vector notations as

$$J(x_0)v = d \tag{5}$$

Solving linear equations yields the search direction v. Considering the number of decision variables is substantially higher than the number of objectives for a particular MaOP, $n >> k$ is uncertain, implying the solution is not unique; hence, the algorithm chooses

$$v_+ := J(x_0)^+ d \tag{6}$$

where $J(x_0)^+ \in \mathbb{R}^{k \times n}$ symbolizes the pseudo inverse of $J(x_0)$ with candidate solution of x_0 obtaining a new solution by $x_1 = x_0 + hv$ where $v \in \mathbb{R}^n$ is the vector satisfying Eq. 5. v_+ is the solution of Eq. 5 with the nominal Euclidean norm. With h, progress in direction d is expected to be significant in the objective space. Guiding solutions are aimed to help MaOEAs accelerate convergence. DSMOA-KCS divides search space using w'. Identify the solutions closest to the ideal point of the objective space, then draw a line from the lower upper bound points to the solution in the choice space. DSMOA-KCS ends with a calculation. Encoding, crossover, mutation, and evaluation are not included because they are problem-dependent. As directed search sampling implies, this study selects elite individuals, elite count 1 (g) and elite count 2 (r), to integrate and strengthen the exploration and exploitation capabilities of the suggested algorithm to assess individual quality. DSMOA-KCS generates possible solutions by sampling a problem space. Local searches from good sample points can provide local optima. Points lead to unknown, potentially better local optima. Algorithm 1 shows the algorithm's highest level of abstraction after we have examined its inspiration and ideas.

Algorithm 1: Framework of proposed DSMOA-KCS

    Input: $F : \mathbb{R}^n \rightarrow \mathcal{R}$.
    $a, b \in \mathbb{R}^n$: bottom, and upper bounds
1 **return** Value $opt \in \mathbb{R}^n$: global minimum candidate
2 $i \leftarrow 1, N \leftarrow 126, \lambda \leftarrow 0.5, opt \leftarrow \infty$
3 new, unclustered, reduced, clustered $\leftarrow \{\}$
4 **while** *stopping criteria is false* **do**
5   new $\leftarrow$ new $\cup$ generate N sample from $[a, b]$ distributed uniformly
6   merged $\leftarrow$ sort clustered $\cup$ new by ascending order regarding F
7   last $\leftarrow i \cdot N \cdot \lambda$
8   reduced $\leftarrow$ select $[0, \dots, last]$ element from merged
9      $x^* \leftarrow$ select $[0]$ element from reduced
10     $opt \leftarrow minimum$ of $\{opt, x^*\}$
11   clustered, unclustered $\leftarrow$ cluster reduced
12   new $\leftarrow \{\}$
13   **while** *size of unclustered* > 0 **do**
14        $x \leftarrow$ pop from unclustered
15        $x^* \leftarrow$ local search over F from x within $[a, b]$
16        $opt \leftarrow minimum$ of $\{opt, x^*\}$
17   cluster x^*
18   **if** x^* *is not clustered* **then**
19   create cluster from $\{x^*, x\}$
20   **end**
21   **end**
22     $i \leftarrow i + 1$
23 **end**
24 **return** opt.

2.2   Environmental Selection

Algorithm 2 outlines environmental selection. The reproduction by corner solution Archive uses guiding solutions to speed up and balance convergence and variety. P and E are unioned to find non-dominated solutions. N is greater than the stated number of non-dominated answers. Each individual of the parent population P will execute a crossover with randomly selected guiding solutions, generating $|P|$ candidate solutions. A mutation is conducted on solutions to get an intermediate offspring population, joined with a guiding solution set to form a combined population. The environmental selection algorithm 2 uses kernel matrix calculation.

Algorithm 2: Environmental selection process

> **Input:** P (population), E (Expectant Population), N (population size), CSA (Corner
> Solution Archive), z^* (*idealpoint*), z^{nad} (nadir point)
> 1 $P \leftarrow$ Non-dominated $P \cup E$
> 2 **if** $|P| > N$ **then**
> 3 $\quad$ Normalization (CSA, Z^*, Z^{nad})
> 4 $\quad$ Normalization (P, Z^*, Z^{nad})
> 5 $\quad$ $L \leftarrow$ Kernel Matrix calculation (P, CSA)
> 6 $\quad$ $A \leftarrow$ Mutation/crossover operation (L, N)
> 7 $\quad$ $P \leftarrow P(A)$
> 8 **end**
> **Output:** P.

Matrix L incorporates convergence and population diversity. CSA (Corner Solution Archive) differentiates inside and outside Pareto space, finds corner solutions of objective functions, and sorts solutions in levitating order of objective space. First, environmental selection produces offspring after union selection with the original population. Pareto dominance, crowding distance, and normalized solutions are combined. If $(|P| > N)$, the non-dominated front is measured as a critical front, and solutions are picked from the Corner Solution Archive (CSA). The kernel matrix L illustrates population convergence and diversity. Equation 7 is used to calculate L_{xy}.

$$L_{xy} = q(x)s(x,y)q(y) \tag{7}$$

where $x, y \in P, q(x)$ shows the solution x quality and $S(x, y)$ is the similarity between x and y defined by Eq. 8 below

$$S(x,y) = exp(-cos(x,y)) \tag{8}$$

where $cos(x, y)$ is cosine of angles between solutions x and y. The quality of $q(x)$ of solution x is calculated basing on its convergence, as illustrated in Eqs. 9 and 10.

$$q(x) = \begin{cases} con_1(x)x \in \text{outside space} \\ 2^* \max_{p \in P}(con_1(P))x \in \text{inside space} \end{cases} \tag{9}$$

$$con_1(x) = \frac{con(x)}{\max_{p \in P}(con(P))} \tag{10}$$

where con_1 is the normalized convergence. Outside space and inside space describe the different areas of the objective space. If $\sqrt{\sum_{i=1}^{M} f_i(x)^2} \leq t$ the solution x belongs to the inside space or otherwise to the outside space. The threshold

t is set to $t = \max \left\{ \sqrt{\sum_{i=1}^{M} f_i(x)^2} \middle| x \in CSA \right\}$. Corner Solution Archive (CSA) differentiates the outside space and inside space. This paper uses the approximation method to initiate the CSA regarding the value of k, leading in two situations. $k = 1$: to find the corner solutions of objective $i = 1, 2, \ldots, M$ proposed algorithm classifies the solutions in ascending order of objective value f_i so we get sorted lists and add the first $\lceil \frac{N}{3M} \rceil$ solutions of each list into the CSA. $1 < K < M$: With consideration of $k = M - 1$ an approximation method to attain CSA is used. with any objective $i = 1, 2, \ldots, M$, solutions are sorted in ascending criteria of $\sqrt{\sum_{j=1, k \neq i}^{M} (f_j(x))^2}$ and attain M sorted lists. The initial solutions of each list is selected in the CSA. With the above two situations, $|CSA| = \lceil \frac{N}{3M} \rceil \times M + \lceil \frac{2N}{3M} \rceil \times M \approx N$ is obtained. Calculating the Kernel matrix is done after calculating the cosine of the angle between every two solutions in the population and the quality $q(x)$ of each solution x. Row vector q then accommodates the qualities of all solutions, after which a quality matrix Q is generated as the product of q^T and q. Decisively, Q is multiplied with L in an element-wise manner to revise and output L.

3   Experimental Results and Analysis

The proposed algorithm is compared to state-of-the-art algorithms NSGA-III, RSEA, and MOEADPas on a set of benchmark problems with 5, 10, 13, and 15 objective functions.

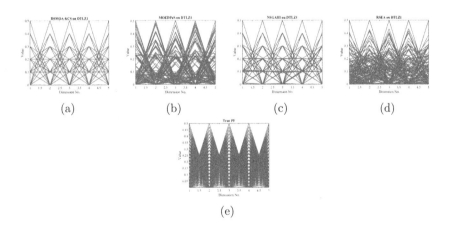

(a)   (b)   (c)   (d)

(e)

Fig. 2. Pareto front distributions of optimal solutions comparisons of DTLZ1

Figure 2 shows the parallel coordinate plots and regular Pareto fronts of (a) DSMOA-KCS, (b) MOEADPaS, (c) NSGA-III, (d) RSEA, and (e) as DTLZ1's True Pareto Front. The $x - axis$ symbolizes the objective numbers, and the $y - axis$ represents the objective values. It can also be seen intuitively in Fig. 2

that the convergence value ranges from 1–2 for the algorithms DSMOA-KCS, RSEA, and NSGA-III with corresponding consistent values of the True Pareto Front.

Table 1. IGD Values obtained by MOEADPaS, NSGA-III, RSEA, and DSMOA-KCS

Problem	M	MOEADPaS	NSGA-III	RSEA	DSMOA-KCS
DTLZ1	5	5.1984e+0 (7.83e+0) -	6.3430e-2 (1.63e-4) -	6.3430e-2 (1.63e-4) -	**6.3395e-2 (1.28e-4)**
DTLZ1	10	1.6379e+1 (1.10e+1) -	1.3664e-1 (1.28e-2) -	1.4493e-1 (2.49e-2) =	**1.1553e-1 (1.62e-2)**
DTLZ1	13	2.5126e+1 (6.74e+0) -	1.4782e-1 (3.77e-2) -	1.9635e-1 (4.02e-2) -	**1.3470e-1 (7.78e-3)**
DTLZ1	15	2.3236e+1 (1.04e+1) -	1.5283e-1 (3.52e-2) =	1.9237e-1 (2.04e-2) -	**1.4904e-1 (2.87e-2)**
DTLZ2	5	3.0698e-1 (9.93e-2) -	1.9489e-1 (1.94e-5) =	2.4765e-1 (1.88e-2) -	**1.9489e-1 (1.69e-5)**
DTLZ2	10	1.1756e+0 (1.51e-1) -	4.6852e-1 (3.22e-2) -	5.1935e-1 (2.09e-2) -	**4.6908e-1 (3.10e-2)**
DTLZ2	13	1.2822e+0 (1.62e-7) -	5.4978e-1 (4.02e-2) -	6.1536e-1 (2.74e-2) -	**5.4591e-1 (3.56e-2)**
DTLZ2	15	1.2896e+0 (6.47e-8) -	5.7042e-1 (3.26e-2) -	6.6712e-1 (2.07e-2) -	**5.6608e-1 (3.43e-2)**
DTLZ4	5	3.3055e-1 (5.13e-2) -	2.6457e-1 (1.08e-1) =	2.6000e-1 (2.68e-2) -	**2.3413e-1 (8.92e-2)**
DTLZ4	10	5.3467e-1 (1.91e-2) -	4.7282e-1 (3.63e-2) -	5.3787e-1 (1.03e-2) -	**4.7219e-1 (3.58e-2)**
DTLZ4	13	6.1679e-1 (1.94e-2) -	5.5299e-1 (4.00e-2) -	6.0308e-1 (1.02e-2) -	**5.4235e-1 (3.75e-2)**
DTLZ4	15	6.3863e-1 (1.10e-2) -	5.5156e-1 (3.51e-2) -	6.5844e-1 (1.29e-2) -	**5.4496e-1 (3.70e-2)**
DTLZ6	5	1.4736e+0 (6.78e-16) -	**9.9562e-1 (1.03e-1) +**	1.1655e+0 (6.88e-2) -	1.0009e+0 (1.38e-1)
DTLZ6	10	6.5482e+0 (1.38e+0) -	1.6124e+0 (1.93e-1) -	2.0422e+0 (1.43e-1) -	**1.5907e+0 (1.87e-1)**
DTLZ6	13	1.0572e+1 (9.99e-3) -	1.9119e+0 (3.98e-1) -	2.2510e+0 (1.45e-1) -	**1.8563e+0 (3.96e-1)**
DTLZ6	15	1.0674e+1 (2.93e-3) -	1.7980e+0 (3.46e-1) =	2.3528e+0 (1.66e-1) -	**1.7410e+0 (2.30e-1)**
WFG1	5	9.3854e-1 (1.16e-1) -	4.3655e-1 (3.98e-3) -	4.6716e-1 (1.08e-2) -	**4.3487e-1 (3.46e-3)**
WFG1	10	2.4955e+0 (1.31e-1) -	1.1086e+0 (8.50e-2) -	1.0764e+0 (3.13e-2) -	**1.066e+0 (3.14e-2)**
WFG1	13	2.9502e+0 (1.55e-1) -	1.6082e+0 (6.93e-2) =	1.6072e+0 (3.02e-2) -	**1.5841e+0 (5.43e-2)**
WFG1	15	2.7066e+0 (2.19e-1) -	1.6281e+0 (9.06e-2) -	1.6015e+0 (3.69e-2) -	**1.5543e+0 (1.09e-1)**
WFG2	5	1.0322e+0 (2.11e-1) -	4.7210e-1 (1.77e-3) -	4.9358e-1 (1.27e-2) -	**4.7062e-1 (2.13e-3)**
WFG2	10	1.4558e+1 (4.97e+0) -	1.2569e+0 (1.15e-1) -	1.1006e+0 (3.73e-2) -	**1.0876e+0 (1.48e-1)**
WFG2	13	2.3162e+1 (4.45e+0) -	1.7446e+0 (1.20e-1) -	1.6880e+0 (1.19e-1) -	**1.59795e+0 (1.28e-2)**
WFG2	15	2.4836e+1 (5.73e+0) -	1.5650e+0 (9.09e-2) =	2.0002e+0 (3.05e-1) -	**1.5585e+0 (8.52e-2)**
WFG6	5	1.6458e+0 (4.56e-1) -	1.1632e+0 (1.95e-3) +	1.3021e+0 (3.55e-2) -	**1.1630e+0 (1.84e-3)**
WFG6	10	1.5090e+1 (3.58e+0) -	4.7755e+0 (1.22e-2) -	4.9503e+0 (1.02e-1) -	**4.7755e+0 (1.24e-2)**
WFG6	13	2.1633e+1 (3.87e+0) -	7.6367e+0 (3.49e-1) -	**7.4523e+0 (1.93e-1) +**	7.7059e+0 (3.93e-1)
WFG6	15	2.6594e+1 (4.04e+0) -	8.4332e+0 (6.92e-1) -	9.3531e+0 (3.07e-1) -	**8.4029e+0 (5.08e-1)**
WFG7	5	1.7394e+0 (1.78e-1) -	1.1770e+0 (5.14e-4) -	1.3236e+0 (3.93e-2) -	**1.16822e+0 (5.15e-4)**
WFG7	10	1.8234e+1 (1.81e+0) -	4.7855e+0 (1.72e-2) -	4.9491e+0 (1.05e-1) -	**4.7788e+0 (5.82e-2)**
WFG7	13	2.5556e+1 (1.68e+0) -	7.2118e+0 (1.72e-1) -	7.3819e+0 (1.97e-1) -	**7.2083e+0 (1.63e-1)**
WFG7	15	2.9696e+1 (1.63e+0) -	**8.1386e+0 (1.04e-1) +**	9.4909e+0 (3.05e-1) -	8.2267e+0 (1.83e-1)
+/-/=		0/32/0	2/26/6	1/30/1	29/3/0

As shown in Fig. 2, DSMOA-KCS shows a uniform and better distribution, not forgetting diversity compared to the other algorithms regarding the DTLZ True Pareto Front. As can be seen in Table 1, IGD results show that DSMOA-KCS attains the best IGD values of 29 out of 32 benchmark instances of DTLZ1, DTLZ2, DTLZ4, & DTLZ6 and WFG1, 2, 6, & 7 all with 5, 10, 13, and 15 objectives, respectively. MOEADPaS attains the least results, NSGA-III on 2 and RSEA on 1. DSMOA-KCS is suitable for resolving problems that are not time-critical but sufficiently tricky.

4 Conclusion

In order to solve the problem of equity between convergence and diversity, this paper proposes a directed search sampling method and Environmental selection procedures to act as guiding solutions for the execution of crossover together with parent solutions and seconded to reproduce guiding solutions for the execution of the offspring. While also taking into consideration the improvement of the offspring. A modified single cluster linkage is constructed to handle multiple MaOPs, and DSMOA-KCS is compared with recent algorithms on the WFG and DTLZ benchmarks, with the number of objectives ranging from 5 to 15. The results reveal that the proposed DSMOA-KCS significantly outperforms other algorithms in certain problem instances; however not better in all the problem instances than other algorithms.

Acknowledgments. This work was partially supported by the National Natural Science Foundation of China under Grants Nos. 62176200, 61773304, and 61871306, the Natural Science Basic Research Program of Shaanxi under Grant No.2022JC-45, 2022JQ-616 and the Open Research Projects of Zhejiang Lab under Grant 2021KG0AB03, the 111 Project, the National Key R&D Program of China, the Guangdong Provincial Key Laboratory under Grant No. 2020B121201001 and the GuangDong Basic and Applied Basic Research Foundation under Grant No. 2021A1515110686.

References

1. Cheng, R., Jin, Y., Olhofer, M., Sendhoff, B.: A reference vector guided evolutionary algorithm for many-objective optimization. IEEE Trans. Evol. Comput. **20**(5), 773–791 (2016)
2. Fonseca, C.M., Fleming, P.J.: Multiobjective optimization and multiple constraint handling with evolutionary algorithms. i. unified formulation. IEEE Trans. Syst. Man Cybern. Part A: Syst. Humans **28**(1), 26–37 (1998)
3. Purshouse, R.C., Fleming, P.J.: An adaptive divide-and-conquer methodology for evolutionary multi-criterion optimisation. In: Fonseca, C.M., Fleming, P.J., Zitzler, E., Thiele, L., Deb, K. (eds.) EMO 2003. LNCS, vol. 2632, pp. 133–147. Springer, Heidelberg (2003). https://doi.org/10.1007/3-540-36970-8_10
4. Gong, Z., Chen, H., Yuan, B., Yao, X.: Multiobjective learning in the model space for time series classification. IEEE Trans. Cybern. **49**(3), 918–932 (2018)
5. Jain, H., Deb, K.: An evolutionary many-objective optimization algorithm using reference-point based nondominated sorting approach, part ii: Handling constraints and extending to an adaptive approach. IEEE Trans. Evol. Comput. **18**(4), 602–622 (2013)
6. Jiang, S., Yang, S.: A strength pareto evolutionary algorithm based on reference direction for multiobjective and many-objective optimization. IEEE Trans. Evol. Comput. **21**(3), 329–346 (2017)
7. Li, B., Li, J., Tang, K., Yao, X.: Many-objective evolutionary algorithms: a survey. ACM Comput. Surv. (CSUR) **48**(1), 1–35 (2015)
8. Li, H., Deng, J., Zhang, Q., Sun, J.: Adaptive epsilon dominance in decomposition-based multiobjective evolutionary algorithm. Swarm Evol. Comput. **45**, 52–67 (2019)

9. Singh, H.K., Bhattacharjee, K.S., Ray, T.: Distance-based subset selection for benchmarking in evolutionary multi/many-objective optimization. IEEE Trans. Evol. Comput. **23**(5), 904–912 (2018)
10. Zhang, Q., Li, H.: Moea/d: A multiobjective evolutionary algorithm based on decomposition. IEEE Trans. Evol. Comput. **11**(6), 712–731 (2007)
11. Zhang, X., Tian, Y., Jin, Y.: A knee point-driven evolutionary algorithm for many-objective optimization. IEEE Trans. Evol. Comput. **19**(6), 761–776 (2014)

A Two-Branch Neural Network Based on Superpixel Segmentation and Auxiliary Samples

Zhidong Dong[1], Caihong Mu[1]([✉]) [iD], Haikun Yu[1], and Yi Liu[2]([✉])

[1] Key Laboratory of Intelligent Perception and Image Understanding of Ministry of Education, School of Artificial Intelligence, Xidian University, Xi'an 710071, China
mucaihongxd@foxmail.com
[2] School of Electronic Engineering, Xidian University, Xi'an 710071, China
yiliuxd@foxmail.com

Abstract. Existing hyperspectral image (HSI) classification methods generally use the information in the neighborhood of the samples but seldom utilize the regional homogeneity of the ground objects. We propose a two-branch neural network based on superpixel segmentation and auxiliary samples (TBN-SPAS) for HSI classification. TBN-SPAS uses superpixel segmentation to find samples within the superpixel, which have high spatial correlation with the sample to be classified. Then TBN-SPAS further selects samples from the samples within the superpixel as auxiliary samples, which have high spectral similarities with the sample to be classified. Finally, the neighborhood patch of the preprocessed HSI and the corresponding sorted auxiliary samples are input into a two-branch neural network for feature extraction and classification. TBN-SPAS achieves significantly better classification results compared with several state-of-the-art methods.

Keywords: Hyperspectral image classification · Superpixel segmentation · Two-branch neural network

1 Introduction

Hyperspectral images (HSIs) have rich spatial and spectral information and can be used for the detection or identification of ground objects, so they have been widely used in military target identification, geological resource detection, agricultural crop monitoring, archaeological relics restoration and other fields [1, 2].

In recent years, deep learning techniques have been applied to HSI classification, such as stacked autoencoders [3], deep belief networks [4], and convolutional neural networks (CNNs) [5, 6], etc., among which CNN-based HSI classification methods have been the most widely used. The CNN-based methods use the neighborhood block of the samples as input, and perform feature extraction through two-dimensional (2D) convolution and three-dimensional (3D) convolution. They can extract spatial features,

© IFIP International Federation for Information Processing 2022
Published by Springer Nature Switzerland AG 2022
Z. Shi et al. (Eds.): ICIS 2022, IFIP AICT 659, pp. 130–137, 2022.
https://doi.org/10.1007/978-3-031-14903-0_14

spectral features or combined spatial-spectral features from the neighborhood patch, which greatly improves the classification accuracy of HSIs.

Hamida et al. [7] studied the classification effects of different 3D convolutional networks on hyperspectral images, and designed a network consisting of 4 layers of 3D convolution and 1 fully connected layer (3DCNN) for feature extraction. The model achieved high classification accuracy. Zhong et al. [8] proposed the spectral-spatial residual network (SSRN). Referring to the residual structure, they designed a spatial feature extraction module and a spectral feature extraction module with multiple 3D convolutional layers, which also achieved high classification accuracy. Roy et al. [9] proposed the hybrid spectral convolutional neural network (HybridSN), which first extracted spatial spectral features to obtain feature maps by using multiple 3D convolutional layers, and then extracted spatial features from the obtained feature maps by using 2D convolutional layers, reducing the complexity of the model.

The above methods achieved good classification results, however, they made more use of the spectral features of HSIs and extract spatial-spectral joint features from the neighborhood patch of the input samples for classification. In reality, the distribution of ground objects is spatially continuous. Especially in HSI images with high spatial resolution, ground objects tend to be distributed in a large area with irregular shapes, the size of which generally exceeds the range of neighborhood patch. When the classifier uses the neighborhood patch as the input, it can only obtain the information within the neighborhood, and the distribution information of the objects beyond the neighborhood is not used. Therefore, some researchers proposed HSI classification methods that utilized a wider range of spatial information, such as introducing a wider range of spatial information through superpixel segmentation.

Superpixel segmentation is a commonly used unsupervised image segmentation method that divides adjacent pixels in an image into multiple disjoint regions, called superpixels [10]. Pixels belonging to the same superpixel in an image often have similar features such as texture, brightness, and color [11]. The purpose of superpixel segmentation is to achieve the following two effects: each superpixel contains only one class of objects; the set of superpixel boundaries is a superset of the object boundaries [12].

Jiang et al. [13] proposed a superpixel-based principal component analysis (PCA) method (SuperPCA) for HSI classification. This method first performed superpixel segmentation on the first principal component of the HSI at different scales, and applied PCA method to samples inside the obtained superpixels to reduce the data dimension. Then the classifier was trained on the data of each scale, and the final classification result was obtained through decision fusion. This method achieved high classification accuracy even with limited samples. However, the utilization of neither the superpixel segmentation results nor the regional homogeneity of the ground objects was sufficient. Samples belonging to the same superpixel have higher distribution consistency in space and are more likely to belong to the same class. This fact can provide more auxiliary information for HSI classification. Therefore, we propose a two-branch neural network based on superpixel segmentation and auxiliary samples (TBN-SPAS) for HSI classification. TBN-SPAS makes full use of superpixel segmentation and spectral similarities to obtain the auxiliary samples that have high spatial correlation and spectral similarities with the sample to be classified, and then uses a two-branch neural network for feature extraction and classification. Experimental results on two HSI datasets demonstrate that TBN-SPAS achieves better classification results compared with several state-of-the-art methods.

2 Proposed Method

2.1 Selection of Auxiliary Samples

We first reduce the dimension of the HSI by PCA, and obtain the first principal component (FPC) of the HSI. Suppose x_i is the sample to be classified. We perform the entropy rate superpixel segmentation (ERS) [12] on the FPC, and find samples around x_i within the obtained superpixels, which can ensure that these samples have high spatial correlation with x_i. Since the spatial distribution of ground objects in the HSI may be large, the obtained superpixels may contain many samples. To ensure the computational efficiency and avoid introducing too much redundant information, we further select some samples within the superpixel as the final auxiliary samples by measuring the spectral similarities between these samples and x_i.

We use the cosine distance to measure the spectral similarities of the samples. For other samples in the superpixel where x_i is located, we sort them in ascending order according to the cosine distances between their spectral vectors and the spectral vector of x_i, and select a certain number (denoted as m) of samples at the top of the ranking list as auxiliary samples, which will be introduced into the process of classification.

2.2 The Structure of TBN-SPAS

We design a two-branch neural network called TBN-SPAS. The main branch takes the preprocessed neighborhood patch of x_i as input. The input of the auxiliary branch is the 2D data composed of m sorted auxiliary samples. The sorted auxiliary samples have sequential features that can be learned by the network.

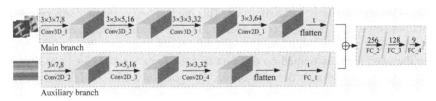

Fig. 1. The structure of the two-branch neural network based on superpixel segmentation and auxiliary samples (TBN-SPAS)

The structure of TBN-SPAS is shown in Fig. 1. The main branch includes three cascaded 3D convolutional layers and one 2D convolutional layer, namely Conv3D_1, Conv3D_2, Conv3D_3 and Conv2D_1. The auxiliary branch includes three 2D convolutional layers and one fully connected layer, namely Conv2D_2, Conv2D_3, Conv2D_4 and FC_1. Three fully connected layers (FC_2, FC_3, and FC_4) are used to perform feature fusion on the outputs of the main branch and the auxiliary branch. The network layers Conv3D_1, Conv3D_2, Conv3D_3, Conv2D_1, Conv2D_2, Conv2D_3, Conv2D_4 and FC_1 are all followed by a BatchNorm layer and a rectified linear unit (ReLU) activation layer. The network layers FC_2 and FC_3 are followed by a ReLU activation layer and a Dropout layer with a dropout rate of 0.4. The network layer FC_4 is followed by a Softmax function to map the network output to a vector of the probability that the sample x_i belongs to each class. In the main branch, t represents the length of the flattened output of Conv2D_1. The number of output neurons of FC_1 in the auxiliary branch is set to t. The hyper-parameters in the network are shown in Fig. 1.

3   Implementation Process of TBN-MERS

The overall process of the TBN-SPAS method is as follows.

An HSI is denoted as $X \in \mathbb{R}^{w \times h \times b}$ and the corresponding label map is denoted as $Y \in \mathbb{R}^{w \times h}$, where w, h are the width and height of the HSI, respectively, and b is the number of spectral bands of the HSI. The value of each position y_{ij} in the label map Y is among the set $\{0, 1, 2, ..., c\}$, in which c represents the total number of object classes.

PCA is applied to X to extract the FPC $X_{pca1} \in \mathbb{R}^{w \times h}$, and the values of X_{pca1} are scaled to the interval $[0, 255]$. Then ERS is applied to X_{pca1} to obtain the corresponding 2D segmentation map S_{pca1}.

We standardize the data of each band of X, and denote the preprocessed HSI as X'. Each sample x_i consists of two parts of data: (1) the neighborhood patch $p_i^A \in \mathbb{R}^{p \times p \times b}$ taken from X', where p is the length or width of the neighborhood patch, and b is the number of bands of the hyperspectral image; (2) 2D data $p_i^B \in \mathbb{R}^{m \times b}$ composed of auxiliary samples extracted from superpixels, where m is the number of auxiliary samples.

We randomly select a certain number of samples from each class to form the training set, and draw an equal number of samples from the remaining samples of each class to form the validation set. The remaining samples are used as the test set.

We feed the two parts p_i^A and p_i^B of each sample x_i into the two branches of TBN-SPAS, and train the network. The model is tested on the verification set every epoch. When the classification accuracy of the model on the validation set no longer rises, the training is completed. The best model on the validation set is used to predict the classes of the samples in test set.

The network is trained with the cross-entropy loss function:

$$L = -\frac{1}{N} \sum_i^N \sum_j^c y_{ij} \log(p_{ij}) \tag{1}$$

where N is the number of training samples, c is the number of classes, and p_{ij} is the probability predicted by the model that the sample x_i belongs to the class j. If sample x_i belongs to the class j, the value of y_{ij} is 1; otherwise, it is 0.

4 Experiment and Analysis

4.1 Experimental Settings

To explore the role of auxiliary branch in TBN-SPAS and verify the performance of the proposed TBN-SPAS, we design the following experiments: (1) verification of the role of auxiliary branch; (2) comparison with other existing methods. The comparison methods used include: 3DCNN [7], SSRN [8], HybridSN [9] and SuperPCA [13]. Indian Pines (IP) and Pavia University (PU) datasets [9] are used for the experiments. Overall classification accuracy (OA), Average classification accuracy (AA) and Kappa coefficient (Kappa) [9] are used to measure the performance of these methods.

In TBN-SPAS, the number of target superpixels in ERS is set to 800, α (a parameter in ERS) is set to 0.5, and the number of auxiliary samples m is set to 8. We randomly select 50 samples from each class (10 samples for the class with less than 50 samples) to form the training set. We randomly select the same number of samples for each dataset as the validation set, and the remaining samples as the test set. The batch size in the experiment is set to 32. We use the Stochastic Gradient Descent (SGD) optimizer, and set the learning rate to 0.0005. In 3DCNN, SSRN, HybridSN, and TBN-SPAS, the patch size of input samples is set to 25 × 25. The experimental parameters and SuperPCA are consistent with those described in the original paper. All experimental data in this paper are the average of five runs of each method on the RTX TITAN.

4.2 The Role of Auxiliary Branch

We design comparative experiments to verify the effect of auxiliary branch. The comparative experiments include: (1) a single-branch network without auxiliary branches (marked as SBN-XAB), where only the main branch and the classification part in TBN-SPAS are used to form a model and the auxiliary branch is deleted; (2) a two-branch model with the main and the auxiliary branches, that is, TBN-SPAS. The other hyperparameters in the comparative experiments are the same. Table 1 shows the classification results of the comparative experiments.

Table 1. Results of SBN-XAB and TBN-SPAS

Dataset	Metrics	SBN-XAB	TBN-SPAS
IP	OA (%)	93.77	**96.56**
	AA (%)	97.01	**98.34**
	Kappa (×100)	92.88	**96.05**
PU	OA (%)	95.54	**98.96**
	AA (%)	95.21	**99.21**
	Kappa (×100)	94.09	**98.63**

It can be seen in Table 1 that on the IP dataset, compared with the classification results of SBN-XAB, TBN-SPAS achieves an OA with 96.56% that is increased by 2.79%, an AA with 98.34% that is increased by 1.33%, and a Kappa with 0.9605 that is increased by 0.0317. On the PU dataset, compared with the classification results of SBN-XAB, TBN-SPAS achieves the values of OA, AA and Kappa with 98.96%, 99.21% and 0.9863, which are increased by 3.42%, 4.00%, and 0.0454, respectively. Such significant improvement demonstrates that the information of auxiliary samples is very effective in improving the HSI classification effect.

4.3 Comparison with Existing Methods

We compare TBN-SPAS with four existing methods: 3DCNN [7], SSRN [8], HybridSN [9] and SuperPCA [13].

The experimental results and analysis of the five different methods on the IP and PU dataset are as follows. In the following tables, the best values are marked in bold. The numbers in parentheses are the standard deviations.

Table 2. Experimental results of different methods on IP dataset

Metrics	3DCNN	SSRN	HybridSN	SuperPCA	TBN-SPAS
OA (%)	82.16	88.38	93.77	95.06	**96.56**
	(1.47)	(1.58)	(1.22)	(1.24)	(0.58)
AA (%)	84.47	75.06	97.01	96.70	**98.34**
	(1.58)	(1.07)	(0.55)	(1.00)	(0.26)
Kappa	79.72	86.73	92.88	94.32	**96.05**
($\times 100$)	(1.65)	(1.79)	(1.38)	(1.42)	(0.67)

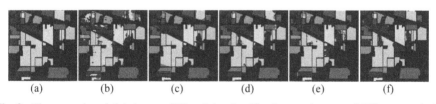

| (a) | (b) | (c) | (d) | (e) | (f) |

Fig. 2. The ground-truth label map of IP and the classification result maps of different methods (a) Ground-truth (b) 3DCNN (c) SSRN (d) HybridSN (e) SuperPCA (f) TBN-SPAS

(1) Results and analyses of IP: Table 2 shows the three metrics of the five methods on IP. From Table 2, it can be seen that TBN-SPAS achieves an OA of 96.56%, which is increased by 14.40%, 8.18%, 2.79%, 1.50% over 3DCNN, SSRN, HybridSN and SuperPCA, respectively. TBN-SPAS achieves an AA of 98.34%, which is increased by 13.87%, 23.28%, 1.33%, 1.64% over 3DCNN, SSRN, HybridSN and SuperPCA, respectively. A higher AA indicates that TBN-SPAS is good at classifying difficult

classes on IP datasets, and also indicates that TBN-SPAS has better generalization. TBN-SPAS also achieves the best results in terms of Kappa. The standard deviation of each metric is low, indicating that TBN-SPAS has better robustness on the IP dataset. Figure 2 shows the ground-truth label map of IP and the classification results of different methods, demonstrating the effectiveness of TBN-SPAS.

(2) Results and analyses of PU: Table 3 shows the OA, AA, and Kappa of the five different methods on PU. From Table 3, it can be seen that TBN-SPAS achieves an OA of 98.96%, an AA of 99.21% and a Kappa of 98.63%. Compared with other comparison methods, TBN-SPAS has achieved a great improvement of more than 3% in OA and AA, which shows that the introduction of auxiliary samples and the use of two branch network are effective. Figure 3 shows the ground-truth label map of PU and the classification results of different methods, which also demonstrates the effectiveness of TBN-SPAS.

Table 3. Experimental results of different methods on PU dataset

Metrics	3DCNN	SSRN	HybridSN	SuperPCA	TBN-SPAS
OA (%)	88.38	95.08	95.54	93.24	**98.96**
	(0.99)	(1.27)	(0.71)	(0.67)	(0.73)
AA (%)	85.32	91.51	95.21	94.42	**99.21**
	(0.94)	(1.00)	(0.70)	(0.37)	(0.18)
Kappa (×100)	84.69	93.47	94.09	91.10	**98.63**
	(1.25)	(1.66)	(0.94)	(0.85)	(0.96)

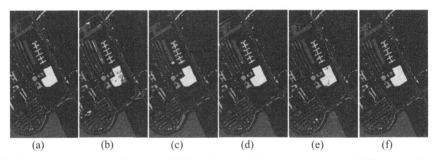

(a)   (b)   (c)   (d)   (e)   (f)

Fig. 3. The ground-truth label map of PU and the classification result maps of different methods (a) Ground-truth (b) 3DCNN (c) SSRN (d) HybridSN (e) SuperPCA (f) TBN-SPAS

5   Conclusions

We design a two-branch neural network based on superpixel segmentation and auxiliary samples (TBN-SPAS) for HSI classification. TBN-SPAS obtains the auxiliary samples that have high spatial correlation and spectral similarities with the sample to be classified by fully utilizing superpixel segmentation and spectral similarities, which are sorted and then input together with the neighborhood patch of the preprocessed HSI into a two-branch neural network for further feature extraction and classification. Experimental results demonstrate that TBN-SPAS achieves significantly better classification results compared with several state-of-the-art methods, indicating that the idea of selecting auxiliary samples through superpixel segmentation and spectral similarities is effective. In the future, we will study more effective way of making use of superpixel segmentation.

Acknowledgements. This work was supported by the National Natural Science Foundation of China (Nos. 62077038 and 61672405).

References

1. Li, S., Song, W., Fang, L., et al.: Deep learning for hyperspectral image classification: an overview. IEEE Trans. Geosci. Remote Sens. **57**(9), 6690–6709 (2019)
2. Camps-Valls, G., Tuia, D., Bruzzone, L., et al.: Advances in hyperspectral image classification: earth monitoring with statistical learning methods. IEEE Signal Process. Mag. **31**(1), 45–54 (2013)
3. Chen, Y., Lin, Z., Zhao, X., et al.: Deep learning-based classification of hyperspectral data. IEEE J. Sel. Top. Appl. Earth Observ. Remote Sens. **7**(6), 2094–2107 (2014)
4. Chen, Y., Zhao, X., Jia, X.: Spectral–spatial classification of hyperspectral data based on deep belief network. IEEE J. Sel. Top. Appl. Earth Observ. Remote Sens. **8**(6), 2381–2392 (2015)
5. Hu, W., Huang, Y., Wei, L., et al.: Deep convolutional neural networks for hyperspectral image classification. J. Sens. **2015** (2015)
6. Cao, X., Zhou, F., Xu, L., et al.: Hyperspectral image classification with Markov random fields and a convolutional neural network. IEEE Trans. Image Process. **27**(5), 2354–2367 (2018)
7. Hamida, A.B., Benoit, A., Lambert, P., et al.: 3-D deep learning approach for remote sensing image classification. IEEE Trans. Geosci. Remote Sens. **56**(8), 4420–4434 (2018)
8. Zhong, Z., Li, J., Luo, Z., et al.: Spectral–spatial residual network for hyperspectral image classification: a 3-D deep learning framework. IEEE Trans. Geosci. Remote Sens. **56**(2), 847–858 (2017)
9. Roy, S.K., Krishna, G., Dubey, S.R., et al.: HybridSN: exploring 3-D-2-D CNN feature hierarchy for hyperspectral image classification. IEEE Geosci. Remote Sens. Lett. **17**(2), 277–281 (2019)
10. Ren, X., Malik, J.: Learning a classification model for segmentation. In: Computer Vision IEEE International Conference, p. 10. IEEE Computer Society (2003)
11. Achanta, R., Shaji, A., Smith, K., et al.: SLIC superpixels compared to state-of-the-art superpixel methods. IEEE Trans. Pattern Anal. Mach. Intell. **34**(11), 2274–2282 (2012)
12. Liu, M., Tuzel, O., Ramalingam, S., et al.: Entropy rate superpixel segmentation. In: IEEE Conference on Computer Vision and Pattern Recognition, pp. 2097–2104, IEEE (2011)
13. Jiang, J., Ma, J., Chen, C., et al.: SuperPCA: a superpixelwise PCA approach for unsupervised feature extraction of hyperspectral imagery. IEEE Trans. Geosci. Remote Sens. **56**(8), 4581–4593 (2018)

Augmentation Based Synthetic Sampling and Ensemble Techniques for Imbalanced Data Classification

Wakjira Mulugeta Asefaw, Ronghua Shang[✉], Michael Aggrey Okoth, and Licheng Jiao

Key Laboratory of Intelligent Perception and Image Understanding of Ministry of Education, School of Artificial Intelligence, Xidian University, Xi'an, Shaanxi 710071, China
wakjira@stu.xidian.edu.cn, {rhshang,lchjiao}@mail.xidian.edu.cn

Abstract. The imbalance data problem appears in data mining fields and has recently attracted the attention of researchers. In order to solve this problem, scholars proposed various approaches such as undersampling majority class, oversampling minority class, synthetic Minority Oversampling (SMOTE) technique, Proximity Weighted Random Affine Shadowsampling (ProWRAS), etc. However, this work proposes a new method called Augmentation Based Synthetic Sampling (ABS) for imbalanced data classification that concatenates data to predict features with imbalance problems. The proposed study integrates sampling and concatenated features to generate synthetic data. This study shows the ability of the proposed method and the average of the AUC (area under the curve) to generate good data samples while experimenting compared to the previous study. In addition, this study merged the proposed method with the boosting to create a technique known as ABSBoost. Therefore, the experimental outcomes show that the proposed ABS method and ABSBoost are effective on the given datasets.

Keywords: Data augmentation · Imbalanced data · Concatenated data · Oversampling · Undersampling

1 Introduction

In the field of data mining, imbalanced data are a common problem when the data is made up of minority and majority classes [16]. It is challenging to balance between the majority and minority classes. To overcome the imbalanced data, many researchers used different techniques such as Synthetic Minority Oversampling (SMOTE) technique [3], Proximity Weighted Random Affine Shadowsampling (ProWRAS) [1], Evidential Combination of Classifiers (ECC) [10], Deep Density Hybrid Sampling (DDHS) [8], Distributed SMOTE (D SMOTE) and Modified Biogeography-Based Optimization (M BBO) [6], Spatial Distribution-based UnderSampling (SDUS) [14], etc.

The existing classification methods mainly focus on the majority class accuracy and classification of sample categories into the majority class, but there is no fair division of minority class [15]. Synthetic Minority Oversampling (SMOTE) is a technique that works and relies on a random oversampling algorithm and adds new sample values

ⓒ IFIP International Federation for Information Processing 2022
Published by Springer Nature Switzerland AG 2022
Z. Shi et al. (Eds.): ICIS 2022, IFIP AICT 659, pp. 138–146, 2022.
https://doi.org/10.1007/978-3-031-14903-0_15

between minority samples of data of the neighbours to produce new minority samples and insert them into the dataset [3,4,15]. Data augmentation helps to enlarge the training of datasets and increase the performance accuracy of the model [2]. The Formula that generates synthetic data samples:

$$y_{new} = y_i + (y_i' - y_i) * z \tag{1}$$

where y_i is the minority class of data samples, y_i' is the chosen neighbor for y_i, and z is a random number distributed uniformly from 0 until 1. According to SMOTE formula in equation (1), y_{new} relies on the random number z, which identifies the location of synthetic data in linear interpolation between y_i and y_i'. Given that z is near 0, the synthetic data samples will be near y_i. In contrast, the synthetic sample will be near y_i' as z approaches 1.

Today, many organizations have large amounts of data, but the data is not balanced. However, we propose an augmentation based synthetic sampling method to overcome this challenge. This proposed method works by concatenating features with other features. This paper achieves state-of-the-art performance for imbalanced data on several public large-scale datasets. Experiments also indicate that the proposed method can be easily integrated into various backbones with significant performance improvements. The main structure of this work is organized as follows. Section 2 introduces the principles and execution process of the proposed method in detail. In Sect. 3, an explanation of the experimental setting and the experimental result is displayed and analyzed. In Sect. 4, draft the Conclusions.

2   Augmentation Based Synthetic Sampling Method

This part introduces the proposed method, including Data Augmentation (DA), notation, and proposed method.

2.1   Data Augmentation (DA)

Data Augmentation (DA) is a process of enlarging the feature size [5,12]. The extra features are generated synthetically by applying simple transformations to existing data. Its purpose may differ based on the particular use case and challenge. However, according to the existing applications, DA has two main benefits [7]: On one hand, it improves the generalization ability of a model by adding a piece of useful information to the training data, and on the other hand, it enhances the robustness of a model against the input perturbations. Data augmentation (DA) can enlarge the training features of the input dataset.

2.2   Notations

In this part, the notations used in the following part are introduced. Each data object $y^{(a)}$ is represented as a feature vector of length p i.e., $y^{(a)} = [y_1^{(a)}, y_2^{(a)}, ..., y_p^{(a)}]$. y_{-b} is introduced to represent all the features of data y except feature b. The data collection is represented by $M = [y_1^{(1)}, y_2^{(2)}, ..., y_p^{(q)}]$, indicating that the number of data objects is q and $y^{(a)} \in \mathbb{R}^p$. To simplify the explanation, we focus on binary classification, but the proposed work could be expanded to multi-class problems. The focus of this study is imbalanced data; therefore, data could be separated into two classes, namely, the minority class and the majority class. We use M^c to denote the minority class samples and use M^d to represent majority class samples. Thus, the entire data set can be divided into two divisions, namely, $M = M^c \cup \mathbf{M}^d$. Using the sampling feature, we generate temporary synthetic data, so we further introduce the value set $W = [w_1, w_2, ..., w_p]$ for all the possible feature values of the minority class, so that $\forall y^{(a)} \in M^c, y_1^{(a)} \in w_1, y_2^{(a)} \in w_2, ..., y_p^{(a)} \in w_p$.

2.3 Proposed Method

The proposed method aims to concatenate data to generate synthetic data and balance data as original features. In this study, the proposed method involves three parts. The first part concatenates input data with sample feature and training feature models. The second part selects the sample feature to generate temporary sampling data randomly. The third part is concatenated minority data with temporary data to generate final synthetic data. The previous study used to generate synthetic data by training features without concatenated input data with trained features. The main objective of this proposed algorithm is to concatenate features with other features and keep the originality of the given data. [9]. Therefore, concatenated data is helpful to enhance and enlarge the minority class.

Concatenate Input Data with Sample Feature and Training Feature Models. In order to concatenate the input data with trained features and find the relationship between the features, we proposed an augmentation-based synthetic sampling method. This work concatenates various features so that features characterize each data sample.

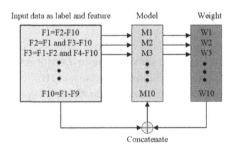

Fig. 1. The list of feature weights.

In the given data sample $y^{(a)}$, we use one of the features, say $y_b^{(a)}$, as a label, but the other remaining is as a feature, $y_{-b}^{(a)}$, train using model b after training the feature we concatenate both the first trained feature y_{-b} as a feature, y_b as a label with an output of trained feature.

As shown in Fig. 1, first, we calculate $F1$ as a label and the remaining $F2 - F10$ as a feature using model $M1$ to obtain the trained feature as weight. Next, concatenate the weight $W1$ with the feature $F2 - F10$, then train using model $M1$ to gain the final trained feature as weight. The main target of this step is to create a relationship with various features and augment the feature to increase the performance of the algorithms.

Randomly Select the Sample Feature to Generate Temporary Sampling Data. To generate the initial synthetic data, we used a sampling technique with a replacement (1/7) formula that calculates the number of sample possibility values from the given feature domains $W = [w_1, w_2, ..., w_p]$ for all features in the minority class from the training samples data. Given the value set $W_1 = [w_{11}, w_{12}, ..., w_{1q}]$, the first step is to sample a value from the set $w1$ with replacement, and the sampled one is the value of the first feature, namely $y_1^{(a)}$, for the temporary synthetic data sample $y^{(a)}$. The second step is to implement the sampling process to get the next sample feature value for the temporary synthetic data value until the bth sample feature value.

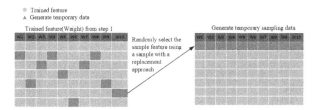

Fig. 2. Model of the sampling feature.

Continuing from step 1, using the final trained feature as weight, use a sample with a replacement approach to generate temporary sample data, as shown in Fig. 2.

Concatenate Minority Data with Temporary Data to Generate Final Synthetic Data. In order to predict synthetic data, we concatenate the minority data with temporary data using model b. This last step goals to make the synthetic data reproduce the feature relationships with real observations. Given an initial synthetic data sample $y^{(a)}$ obtained from the previous step, one can predict y_b, the feature of the final synthetic data sample, with the trained model b and the input y_{-b}. $F1 - F10$ are represented as minority data, as shown in Fig. 3. Continuing from step 2, concatenate generated temporary sampling data $W1 - W10$ with minority data $F1 - F10$, as shown in Fig. 3, to predict final synthetic data $S1 - S10$.

As proposed algorithm 1 indicates, the input data include the minority data M^c, over-sampling rate R, the feature sample value set W, and the number of iterations for repeating the generation process L. In the first step, the temporary sampling data set T, and the synthetic data set Z are initialized as empty matrices of size $p * q^{sy}$ as shown in Algorithm 1. In the next step, we train p feature models for the p features, in which model b $(1 \leq b \leq p)$ is trained with y_b as the label concatenates y_{-b} as

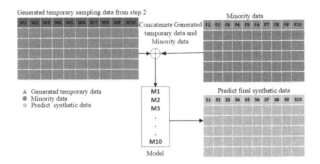

Fig. 3. Model of the synthetic prediction feature.

Algorithm 1: Augmentation based synthetic sampling for imbalanced data classification.

Input: M^c: minority data, R: Oversampling rate. $W = [w_1, w_2, \cdots, w_p]$: possible feature values of minority dataset, L: total iteration for repeating generation process.

Output: Z Generate synthetic data.

$q^c \leftarrow$ The number of minority data samples

$p \leftarrow$ The number of features

$q^{sy} \leftarrow q^c * R$ (The size of a synthetic data sample)

$T \leftarrow \emptyset$ (temporary data with p columns and q^{sy} rows)

$Z \leftarrow \emptyset$ (synthetic data with p columns and q^{sy} rows)

1 **for** $b \leftarrow 1$ *to* p **do**
2 | Train model b with y_b as label, concatenate y_{-b} as a feature with y_b as label
3 **end**
4 **for** $a \leftarrow 1$ *to* q^{sy} **do**
5 | **for** $b \leftarrow 1$ *to* p **do**
6 | | $T_{ab} \leftarrow$ randomly sample a value from w_b with replacement
7 | **end**
8 **end**
9 **for** $l \leftarrow 1$ *to* L **do**
10 | **for** $b \leftarrow 1$ *to* p **do**
11 | | $Z_b \leftarrow$ predict feature b by model b and concatenate T with minority data.
12 | | $T = Z$ (update the temporary dataset for predicting by predicted dataset Z)
13 | **end**
14 **end**
15 **return** Z.

---

the features, y_b as the label with train feature. The second step, generate temporary data randomly using a sample with a replacement technique on the features using the proposed method. The final step, generate synthetic data samples, which Z_b denotes the bth feature of the synthetic data sample and is obtained from the prediction of the model b by concatenating temporary data T with minority data as the input.

3 Experiment Settings and Result Analysis

3.1 Datasets

In order to evaluate the performance of the proposed method and other existing methods, thirteen datasets were used in the experiments conducted. All of the data used in the experiments are publicly available datasets from Kaggle and UCI machine learning repository:https://www.kaggle.com/ and https://archive.ics.uci.edu/ml, which are used the same dataset in [9].

3.2 Evaluation Metric

Classification is the task that calculates the probability's performance and accuracy. However, the restriction performance measure of imbalanced dataset accuracy had built immediately, and receiver operating characteristic (ROC) curves soon appeared as a well-known possibility, with the true positive rate (TPR) is on the y-axis and the false positive rate (FPR) is the x-axis. Therefore, as an alternative method of evaluating the accuracy performance of the classifier, we use the area under the curve (AUC) as the evaluation metric.

3.3 Experimental Results

We apply the proposed method to the twelve datasets and use AUC as the performance metric. We have a baseline method called original in the experiments, which trains the model using original data without a sampling method.

Table 1. Average of AUC results for proposed and different existing methods.

Dataset	Original	Over	Under	CBO	SBC	Smote	ADASYN	ProWRAS	MBS	**ABS**
Pima	0.8329	0.8320	0.8308	0.8125	0.8257	0.8323	0.8311	0.5979	0.8322	**0.8734**
Haberman	0.6699	0.6680	0.6685	0.5512	0.6514	0.6671	0.6657	0.7396	0.6791	**0.7549**
Satimage	0.7638	0.7627	0.7626	0.7446	0.7438	0.7639	0.7543	0.5797	0.7663	**0.8265**
Ecoli	0.9066	0.9042	0.9022	0.8880	0.8886	0.9074	0.9039	0.6256	0.9178	**0.9678**
Ionosphere	0.8270	0.8145	0.7847	0.8005	0.7799	0.8371	0.8309	0.8063	0.8275	**0.9759**
Vehicle	0.9829	0.9828	0.9728	0.9850	0.9663	0.9900	0.9931	0.8297	0.9838	**0.9989**
Credit	0.6993	0.7010	0.7004	0.6968	0.7072	0.7001	0.7008	0.6267	0.7173	**0.7343**
Diabetes	0.6302	0.6303	0.6304	0.5455	0.6017	0.6293	0.6280	0.5019	0.6317	**0.6990**
Hmeq	0.7909	0.7914	0.7916	0.6754	0.7818	0.7911	0.7907	0.7393	0.7913	**0.8563**
Promotion	0.6481	0.6483	0.6480	0.6444	0.6423	0.6485	0.6488	0.6245	0.6486	**0.6885**
Bank	0.8577	0.8593	0.8590	0.7592	0.8425	0.8591	0.8606	0.5187	0.8608	**0.9052**
Spambase	0.9683	0.9681	0.9653	0.9341	0.8539	0.9657	0.9677	0.8780	0.9685	**0.9993**
Average	0.7981	0.7969	0.7930	0.7531	0.7738	0.7993	0.7980	0.6723	0.8021	**0.8567**

We used "ABS_method" to represent our proposed method. We used different existing methods to compare with our works: "Over" and "Under" to denote random oversampling and random undersampling, respectively; "CBO" and "SBC" to represent the cluster-based oversampling method and undersampling method, respectively. This paper has also compared: "ProWRAS" [1] with the proposed method on 12 datasets. In addition, we also compare: "Smote"; "MBS" which represent the linear feature model and "ADASYN" [9]. We used the R programming language, an open-source programming language and a free software environment in this experiment. The experimental results, including the average AUCs for all methods, are presented in Table 1. The experimental results show that the proposed method consistently outperforms the given datasets as the number of iterations increases. Table 1 shows that we used 12 different datasets with different existing methods, and the ABS method outperforms all other methods based on AUC results.

4   Integration of Augmentation Based Synthetic Sampling Method and Ensemble Techniques

The bagging method is a bootstrap ensemble method that can improve model stability. Boosting is a machine learning technique to improve the performance of a classifier. The most well known boosting algorithm is Adaboost, or Adaptive Boosting [13]. Using the ensemble learning approach to deal with imbalance problems is popular, so we further combined the proposed ABS with the boosting technique to devise a method called ABSBoost, which is an integration of AdaBoost.M2 [11] and ABS. ABS was performed to increase minority samples at each iteration of model training so that each weak classifier could be trained on a relatively balanced subset.

Table 2. Average AUC results for different ensemble-based methods.

Dataset	**ABSBoost**	RUSBoost	UnderBagging
Pima	**0.8473**	0.8168	0.8273
Haberman	**0.7107**	0.6600	0.6835
Satimage	**0.9719**	0.9512	0.9385
Ecoli	**0.9465**	0.9249	0.9312
Ionosphere	**0.9895**	0.9558	0.9410
Vehicle	**0.9998**	0.9879	0.9757
Credit	**0.7842**	0.7168	0.7473
Diabetes	**0.6310**	0.5627	0.6035
Hmeq	**0.9872**	0.9265	0.9113
Promotion	**0.6246**	0.5916	0.5166
Bank	**0.8863**	0.8746	0.8557
Spambase	**0.9967**	0.9763	0.9690
Average	**0.8646**	0.8288	0.8251

We compare ABSBoost with state of the art ensemble-based methods, including RUSBoost and UnderBagging. The experimental results are presented in Table 2, indicating that ABSBoost is effective and better than the existing method.

5   Conclusion

In data mining, imbalanced data is a prevalent problem in the world. In order to overcome the challenge that some standard imbalanced data techniques cannot accurately balance majority and minority classes, Augmentation Based Synthetic Sampling (ABS) for imbalanced data classification is proposed. ABS method concatenates the features and increases the number of samples from existing samples to generate synthetic data. This study conducted experiments on 12 datasets and compared the proposed method with existing methods. In addition, this study combines the proposed method with the boosting technique to devise a method called ABSBoost and compare the performance of the combination with two states of the art ensemble-based methods. The experimental outcomes show that the proposed method and ABSBoost are effective and better than other existing methods on the given datasets. In future work, this paper will focus on other datasets by keeping the original data and balancing data such as primary and minority classes to further improve the algorithm's accuracy. At the same time, this paper will apply reinforcement learning with different methods to improve the execution efficiency of the algorithm.

Acknowledgements. This work was partially supported by the National Natural Science Foundation of China under Grants Nos. 62176200, 61773304, and 61871306, the Natural Science Basic Research Program of Shaanxi under Grant No.2022JC-45, 2022JQ-616 and the Open Research Projects of Zhejiang Lab under Grant 2021KG0AB03, the 111 Project, the National Key R&D Program of China, the Guangdong Provincial Key Laboratory under Grant No. 2020B121201001 and the GuangDong Basic and Applied Basic Research Foundation under Grant No. 2021A1515110686.

References

1. Bej, S., Schulz, K., Srivastava, P., Wolfien, M., Wolkenhauer, O.: A multi schematic classifier independent oversampling approach for imbalanced datasets. IEEE Access **9**, 123358–123374 (2021)
2. Frid-Adar, M., Klang, E., Amitai, M., Goldberger, J., Greenspan, H.: Synthetic data augmentation using gan for improved liver lesion classification. In: 2018 IEEE 15th international symposium on biomedical imaging (ISBI 2018), pp. 289–293. IEEE (2018)
3. Gameng, H.A., Gerardo, B.B., Medina, R.P.: Modified adaptive synthetic smote to improve classification performance in imbalanced datasets. In: 2019 IEEE 6th International Conference on Engineering Technologies and Applied Sciences (ICETAS), pp. 1–5. IEEE (2019)
4. He, H., Garcia, E.A.: Learning from imbalanced data. IEEE Trans. Knowl. Data Eng. **21**(9), 1263–1284 (2009)
5. Jiang, X., Ge, Z.: Data augmentation classifier for imbalanced fault classification. IEEE Trans. Autom. Sci. Eng. **18**(3), 1206–1217 (2020)
6. Khurana, A., Verma, O.P.: Optimal feature selection for imbalanced text classification. IEEE Trans. Artifi. Intell. (2022)
7. Laermann, J., Samek, W., Strodthoff, N.: Achieving generalizable robustness of deep neural networks by stability training. In: Fink, G.A., Frintrop, S., Jiang, X. (eds.) DAGM GCPR 2019. LNCS, vol. 11824, pp. 360–373. Springer, Cham (2019). https://doi.org/10.1007/978-3-030-33676-9_25

8. Liu, C.L., Chang, Y.H.: Learning from imbalanced data with deep density hybrid sampling. IEEE Trans. Syst. Man Cybern. Syst. (2022)
9. Liu, C.L., Hsieh, P.Y.: Model-based synthetic sampling for imbalanced data. IEEE Trans. Knowl. Data Eng. 32(8), 1543–1556 (2019)
10. Niu, J., Liu, Z., Lu, Y., Wen, Z.: Evidential combination of classifiers for imbalanced data. IEEE Trans. Syst. Man Cybern. Syst. (2022)
11. Schapire, R.E., Singer, Y.: Improved boosting algorithms using confidence rated predictions. Mach. Learn. 37(3), 297–336 (1999)
12. Taylor, L., Nitschke, G.: Improving deep learning with generic data augmentation. In: 2018 IEEE Symposium Series on Computational Intelligence (SSCI), pp. 1542–1547. IEEE (2018)
13. Wah, Y.B., Rahman, H.A.A., He, H., Bulgiba, A.: Handling imbalanced dataset using svm and knn approach. In: AIP Conference Proceedings, vol. 1750, p. 020023. AIP Publishing LLC (2016)
14. Yan, Y., Zhu, Y., Liu, R., Zhang, Y., Zhang, Y., Zhang, L.: Spatial distribution-based imbalanced undersampling. IEEE Trans. Knowl. Data Eng. (2022)
15. Yuan, Z., Zhao, P.: An improved ensemble learning for imbalanced data classification. In: 2019 IEEE 8th Joint International Information Technology and Artificial Intelligence Conference (ITAIC), pp. 408–411. IEEE (2019)
16. Yusof, R., Kasmiran, K.A., Mustapha, A., Mustapha, N., MOHD ZIN, N.A.: Techniques for handling imbalanced datasets when producing classifier models. J Theor. Appli. Inf. Technol. 95(7) (2017)

Language Cognition

BA-GAN: Bidirectional Attention Generation Adversarial Network for Text-to-Image Synthesis

Ting Yang, Xiaolin Tian$^{(\boxtimes)}$, Nan Jia, Yuan Gao, and Licheng Jiao

School of Artificial Intelligence, Xidian University, Xi'an 710071, China
{xltian,lchjiao}@mail.xidian.edu.cn,
{20171213676,ygao_5}@stu.xidian.edu.cn

Abstract. It is difficult for the generated image to maintain semantic consistency with the text descriptions of natural language, which is a challenge of text-to-image generation. A bidirectional attention generation adversarial network (BA-GAN) is proposed in this paper. The network achieves bidirectional attention multi-modal similarity model, which establishes the one-to-one correspondence between text and image through mutual learning. The mutual learning involves the relationship between sentences and images, and between words in the sentences and sub-regions in images. Meanwhile, a deep attention fusion structure is constructed to generate a more real and reliable image. The structure uses multi branch to obtain the fused deep features and improves the generator's ability to extract text semantic features. A large number of experiments show that the performance of our model has been significantly improved.

Keywords: Text-to-image generation · BA-GAN · Mutual learning

1 Introduction

In recent years, text-to-image synthesis is a hot research topic. It covers two major areas, Natural Language Processing [13] and Computer Vision [1], which can be used in the interaction of art generation and entertainment.

At present, the research of text-to-image synthesis based on GAN [2] has become the mainstream trend. The research shows that the adversarial training of generator and discriminator in GAN can promote the matching relationship between the generated image and the text semantics.

Attention mechanism has also been applied to text - to - image synthesis in previous studies. AttnGAN [14] introduced the attention mechanism for the first time. The mechanism guides the generator to focus on the words in the sentence related to the different sub regions of the image. But AttnGAN only considers

The work is supported by the National Natural Science Foundation of China (No. 61977052).

the context vector of sub-regions base on sentences. And this ignores some fine-grained information between two modalities and leads to inaccuracy of text-image matching. Aiming at this problem, this paper proposes a bi-directional attention multimodal similarity model (BAMSM).

The quality of the generated image is still not satisfactory in the initial stage although it has made great progress to use multi-stage GAN for text-to-image synthesis. In this paper, the deep attention fusion structure is proposed to improve the feature extraction ability of generator and get more high-quality initial image.

The main contribution of this paper as follows:

We propose BAMSM, a bidirectional attention multimodal similarity model, which calculates the cross-modal similarity through mutual learning.

A deep attention fusion structure (DAFS) is proposed to improve the feature extraction capability of the generator and integrate more information to achieve the generation of high-quality images.

The channel perception adjustment module (CPAM) is proposed to promote the generation of high-quality initial images by extracting multi-level features.

2   Related Work

It is a basic challenge for text-to-image synthesis to determine high semantic consistency between text and image in the field of computer vision.

In recent years, a variety of generation models based on GAN have appeared successively with the development of deep learning. The original GAN-INT-CLS [9] generated images with a resolution of only 64 * 64 and low matching degree with text. GAWWN [10] is proposed to get the generated images with a resolution of 128 * 128. StackGAN [15] uses two stages as basic network architecture to generate images that meet the requirements. In the first stage, rough images similar to the texture, color and content of text description are generated. Then in the second stage, the initial image is refined continuously to synthesize the final image. StackGAN++ [16] is an improvement of the end-to-end model that generates higher quality images. However, the above methods always use global sentence vectors when selecting conditional constraints, resulting in the omission of word information in sentences in the process of image generation. Furthermore, some details of text semantics are lost.

AttnGAN [14] is proposed to solve this problem. It can find the word that is most relevant to the image sub-region by considering the context vector of sub-regions base on sentences, and then calculates the similarity between image and text. A text-image-text circular structure is proposed by MirrorGAN [8], which transformed the generated image into text through encoding, and then compared it with the given text description. Obj-GAN [6] proposed a new object-driven attentional image generator and a target recognizer based on Faster RCNN. Compared with the above methods, the BAMSM proposed in this paper has its advantages. It mainly points at the mutual learning between the word features of the text and the sub region features of the image, so as to improve the semantic consistency between the generated image and the input text.

3   Our Model

In this paper, we propose a bidirectional attention generation adversarial network for text-to-image synthesis. The network is always used to extract information from text and generate corresponding image. The network structure is shown in Fig. 1.

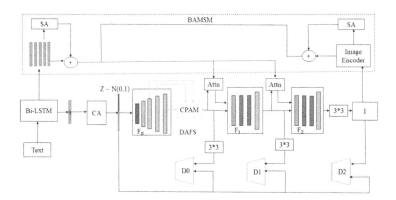

Fig. 1. The architecture of the proposed BA-GAN. I indicates the generated image.

3.1   Text Encoder and Image Encoder

Text Encoder. Bi-LSTM [4] is used as a text encoder to encode the input sentences. The output of the encoder is the word feature matrix e^{D*T}, where D is the dimension of the word vector and T is the number of words in the sentence. In addition, the last hidden state of Bi-LSTM is taken as the global vector of the sentence, representing $\bar{e} \in R^D$, which is used for similarity comparison with the global feature of the image.

Image Encoder. Inspired by previous studies, we use the pretrained network Inception-v3 [11] to extract image features. Firstly, we scale the image to $299 * 299$ resolution and input into the encoder. Then local feature $f \in R^{768*N}$ is extracted from the "$mixed\_6e$" layer in Inception-v3, where 768 is the dimension of local feature vector, N is the number of image sub-regions. Meanwhile, global features $\bar{f} \in R^{2048}$ are extracted from the last layer of Inception-v3. Finally, image features are mapped to the same semantic space of text features, and two new feature vectors $v \in R^{D*N}$ and $\bar{v} \in R^{2048}$ are obtained.

Bidirectional Attention Multi-Modality Similarity Model. The principle of BAMSM is to calculate the similarity between the words and the sub-regions through mutual learning. The first, we input e and v into the self-attention module, and extract the self-attention weights w_e and w_v respectively. The main purpose of this operation is to find the context weight inside the modality. Then the context proportion between text and image is calculated by bidirectional attention. Finally, we calculate the image-text matching score.

We multiply weights with the vector itself to obtain the weighted word vector and image vector respectively, we compute them with:

$$e' = e + e * SA(e) \tag{1}$$

where SA represents the self-attention extraction module. e' is the weighted word vector. We define the Formula (1) as $v' = v + v * SA(v)$ to obtain the weighted sub-region vector. Then we calculate the similarity matrix s between the word vector and the sub-region vector :

$$s = e'^T v' \tag{2}$$

where $s \in R^{T*N}$, $s_{i,j}$ represents the similarity between the i-th word and the j-th subregion. We take $w = s^T$, and then normalize the s and w matrices respectively, they are computed by:

$$\overline{s}_{i,j} = \frac{\exp(s_{i,j})}{\sum_{k=0}^{T-1} \exp(s_{k,j})}, \quad \overline{w}_{j,i} = \frac{\exp(w_{j,i})}{\sum_{k=0}^{N-1} \exp(s_{j,k})} \tag{3}$$

where $w_{j,i}$ is similarity between the j-th sub-region and the i-th word. Then, the bidirectional attention mechanism is used to get the word context vector and sub-region context vector. They are calculated respectively as follows:

$$c_i = \sum_{j=0}^{N-1} \alpha_j v_j', \quad c_j = \sum_{i=0}^{T-1} \alpha_i e_i', \tag{4}$$

where $\alpha_i = \frac{\exp(\gamma \overline{w}_{j,i})}{\sum_{k=0}^{T-1} \exp(\gamma \overline{w}_{j,k})}$, $\alpha_j = \frac{\exp(\gamma \overline{s}_{i,j})}{\sum_{k=0}^{N-1} \exp(\gamma \overline{s}_{i,k})}$, γ is a hyperparameter.

Finally, we calculate the matching score of text vector and image vector using cosine similarity theorem. Inspired by the minimum classification error formulation [5], the match score of text and image based on bidirectional attention mechanism is computed as follows:

$$R(Q, D) = \log \left(\sum \exp(\gamma_0 R(c_i, e_i'))\right)^{\frac{1}{\gamma_0}} \tag{5}$$

$$R(D, Q) = \log \left(\sum \exp(\gamma_0 R(c_j, v_j'))\right)^{\frac{1}{\gamma_0}} \tag{6}$$

where $R(c_i, e_i') = \frac{c_i e_i'}{\|c_i\| \|e_i'\|}$, $R(c_j, v_j') = \frac{c_j v_j'}{\|c_j\| \|v_j'\|}$. D is the text and Q is the image corresponding to the text. γ_0 is a hyperparameter.

Loss Function. Text and image encoder aims to make text and image learn from each other and achieve better image-text matching. The calculation process of text-image matching score is different from DAMSM.

$$L_{BAMSM} = L_1{}^w + L_2{}^w + L_1{}^s + L_2{}^s \tag{7}$$

where, $L_1{}^w$ and $L_1{}^s$ indicates the word loss and sentence loss when the image matches with the given text, and $L_2{}^w$ and $L_2{}^s$ represents the word loss and sentence loss when the text matches with the given image.

$$L_1{}^w = -\sum_{i=1}^{M} \log P\left(D_i|Q_i\right), \; L_2{}^w = -\sum_{i=1}^{M} \log P\left(Q_i|D_i\right) \tag{8}$$

where $P\left(D_i|Q_i\right) = \frac{\exp(\gamma_1 R(Q_i,D_i))}{\sum_{j=1}^{M} \exp(\gamma_1 R(Q_j,D_i))}$, and it is the probability that the generated image can correspond to the text description; $P\left(Q_i|D_i\right) = \frac{\exp(\gamma_1 R(D_i,Q_i))}{\sum_{j=1}^{M} \exp(\gamma_1 R(D_j,Q_i))}$, and it denotes the probability of text corresponding to image. In addition, M refers to the batch size at the time of training. γ_1 is a hyperparameter.

L_s is similar to L_w. We just define formula (5) as $R\left(Q, D\right) = \frac{\bar{v}^T \bar{e}}{\|\bar{v}\|\|\bar{e}\|}$, and then substitute it into formula (8) to get the sentence loss in the process of text-image matching.

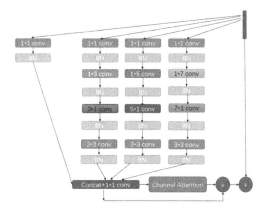

Fig. 2. The architecture of the proposed CPAM.

3.2   Multi-stage Generative Adversarial Networks

Basic Framework. Three-stage GAN is adopt to synthesize realistic and high-dimensional images in our model. We feed the acquired sentence vector $\bar{e}$ into the initial stage of GAN. The process of generating the final image I is as follows:

$$f_0 = F_0(z, (\bar{e})^{CA}), \; f_i = F_i(f_{i-1}, Attn\left(f_{i-1}, e'\right)), \; I = G_i(f_i) \tag{9}$$

in which z is a random noise vector satisfying normal distribution. $(\bar{e})^{CA}$ represents global sentence features augmented by conditions, F_0, F_i, G_i are neural network model. $Attn$ indicates attention model.

The illustration of the proposed DAFS is shown in Fig. 1. There are five layers in F_0. Since the shallow layer has little influence on the performance, the last three layers are cascaded. And then the multi-level and multi-scale features with different information are extracted by utilizing the proposed CPAM.

Channel Perception Adjustment Module. Inspired by RFB network [7], this module can obtain features of different depths by using multi-branch structure. Figure 2 depicts the structure of CPAM. There are five branches in this structure. Four of which are mainly for extracting multi-level and multi-scale features from the input feature graph. 1 * 1 convolution is to fuse multi-channel information from the input characteristic graph.

Loss Function. In order to generate a more realistic and clearer image, we define the generator loss function as:

$$L = L_G + \alpha L_{BAMSM}, \; L_G = \sum L_{G_i} \tag{10}$$

where $L_{G_i} = -\frac{1}{2} E_{\widehat{I}_i \sim P_{G_i}} \left[\log D_i(\widehat{I}_i) \right] - \frac{1}{2} E_{\widehat{I}_i \sim P_{G_i}} \left[\log D_i(\widehat{I}_i, \overline{e}) \right]$. α is the hyperparameter, which is used to indicate the importance of BAMSM. The generator and discriminator carry on adversarial training in the GAN network. The loss function of the discriminator is computed as:

$$L_{D_i} = -\frac{1}{2} E_{I_i \sim P_{real_i}} \left[\log D_i(I_i) \right] - \frac{1}{2} E_{\widehat{I}_i \sim P_{G_i}} \left[\log(1 - D_i\left(\widehat{I}_i\right)) \right]$$
$$-\frac{1}{2} E_{I_i \sim P_{real_i}} \left[\log D_i(I_i, \overline{e}) \right] - \frac{1}{2} E_{\widehat{I}_i \sim P_{G_i}} \left[\log(1 - D_i\left(\widehat{I}_i, \overline{e}\right)) \right] \tag{11}$$

where I_i is real image from sampling the distribution P_{real_i} of stage i, $\widehat{I}_i$ is the generate image from sampling the distribution P_{G_i} of stage i.

4   Experiments

Dataset and Evaluation Metrics. As in previous studies on text-to-image synthesis, we evaluated the model on the CUB and COCO datasets. In order to evaluate the performance of the model and measure whether the generated image is true or false, Inception score(IS) [12], R-precision [14] and Fréchet inception distance(FID) [3] are used for evaluation. In addition, we use some generated images as examples to specify the practical effects of the models as shown in Fig. 3.

Fig. 3. Comparison of images generated by AttnGAN and our model.

Ablation Studies. In order to study the effect of each part of the proposed method on the quality of generated image in CUB dataset, we conducted some ablation experiments. The baseline model of this paper is AttnGAN. The experimental results are described in Table 1. Effective experiment based on data set on baseline network, we set the hyperparameters as: $\gamma = 5$, $\gamma_0 = 5$, $\alpha = 5$, $\gamma_1 = 10$.

We mainly evaluate the validity of BAMSM and DAFS. The experimental results are described in Table 1. It can be seen the proposed module can improve network performance significantly compared with baseline model.

Table 1. Performance of ablation study both in IS and FID on CUB dataset

Model	IS ↑	FID ↓
Baseline	4.36	23.98
Baseline + BAMSM	4.80	21.84
Baseline + DAFS(F_0)	4.73	23.82
Baseline + DAFS(F_0, F_1, F_2)	4.74	23.72
Baseline + BAMSM + DAFS(F_0)	4.88	20.82
Baseline + BAMSM + DAFS(F_0, F_1, F_2)	4.68	23.04

Function of the Proposed BAMSM. BAMSM is mainly proposed to better learn the semantic correspondence between texts and images. Text-image matching is realized by considering the relationship within the text and semantic relevance between text and image. In addition, the self-attention mechanism is used to extract the self-attention weights of word vectors and local features of images. The context relations within modes are represented by the weights.

Function of the Proposed DAFS. DAFS is proposed to generate high quality initial images in the initial stage of the network. It is applied to obtain multichannel and multi-level information. Then images containing more semantic information are generated by fusing them. In additon, the proposed CPAM plays a important role in this module. The experimental results show that DAFS is effective.

Comparative Experiment. We compared our method with the existing text-to-image synthesis method on CUB and COCO datasets, and the results are shown in Table 2.

Table 2. IS, R-precision and FID scores by existing method and our BA-GAN on CUB and COCO testsets.

Dataset	CUB			COCO		
Method	IS ↑	R-precision ↑	FID ↓	IS↑	R-precision ↑	FID↓
GAN-INT-CLS	2.88	–	68.79	7.88	–	60.62
GAWWN	3.62	–	53.51	–	–	–
stackGAN	3.70	–	35.11	8.45	–	33.88
stackGAN++	4.04	–	25.99	8.30	–	–
AttnGAN	4.36	53.82	23.98	25.89	82.98	35.49
MirrorGAN	4.56	57.51	18.34	26.47	82.44	34.71
Our model	4.88	58.64	20.82	27.79	83.21	31.08

5   Conclusion

In this paper, we propose a generative adversarial network based on bidirectional attention for text-to-image synthesis, abbreviated BA-GAN. Firstly, we build a bidirectional attention multi-modality similarity model to learn the semantic corresponding relationship between text and image. The text encoder containing the image information is obtained through the model. Secondly, we propose a deep attention fusion structure to generate high-quality initial image. Deeper feature and multi-channel information are extracted through multi branch structure to generate clearer initial image. A large number of experiments show the effectiveness of our proposed BA-GAN in the text-to-image synthesis.

References

1. Bissoto, A., Valle, E., Avila, S.: The six fronts of the generative adversarial networks. arXiv preprint arXiv:1910.13076 (2019)
2. Goodfellow, I., et al.: Generative adversarial nets. In: Advances in Neural Information Processing Systems, vol. 27 (2014)

3. Heusel, M., Ramsauer, H., Unterthiner, T., Nessler, B., Hochreiter, S.: Gans trained by a two time-scale update rule converge to a local nash equilibrium. In: Advances in Neural Information Processing Systems, vol. 30 (2017)

4. Hochreiter, S., Schmidhuber, J.: Long short-term memory. Neural Comput. **9**(8), 1735–1780 (1997)

5. Juang, B.H., Hou, W., Lee, C.H.: Minimum classification error rate methods for speech recognition. IEEE Trans. Speech Audio Process. **5**(3), 257–265 (1997)

6. Li, W., et al.: Object-driven text-to-image synthesis via adversarial training. In: Proceedings of the IEEE/CVF Conference on Computer Vision and Pattern Recognition, pp. 12174–12182 (2019)

7. Liu, S., Huang, D., Wang, Y.: Receptive field block net for accurate and fast object detection. In: Ferrari, V., Hebert, M., Sminchisescu, C., Weiss, Y. (eds.) ECCV 2018. LNCS, vol. 11215, pp. 404–419. Springer, Cham (2018). https://doi.org/10.1007/978-3-030-01252-6_24

8. Qiao, T., Zhang, J., Xu, D., Tao, D.: Mirrorgan: learning text-to-image generation by redescription. In: Proceedings of the IEEE/CVF Conference on Computer Vision and Pattern Recognition, pp. 1505–1514 (2019)

9. Reed, S., Akata, Z., Yan, X., Logeswaran, L., Schiele, B., Lee, H.: Generative adversarial text to image synthesis. In: International Conference on Machine Learning, pp. 1060–1069. PMLR (2016)

10. Reed, S.E., Akata, Z., Mohan, S., Tenka, S., Schiele, B., Lee, H.: Learning what and where to draw. In: Advances in Neural Information Processing Systems, vol. 29 (2016)

11. Russakovsky, O., et al.: Imagenet large scale visual recognition challenge. Int. J. Comput. Vision **115**(3), 211–252 (2015)

12. Salimans, T., Goodfellow, I., Zaremba, W., Cheung, V., Radford, A., Chen, X.: Improved techniques for training gans. In: Advances in Neural Information Processing Systems, vol. 29 (2016)

13. Sutskever, I., Vinyals, O., Le, Q.V.: Sequence to sequence learning with neural networks. In: Advances in Neural Information Processing Systems, vol. 27 (2014)

14. Xu, T., et al.: Attngan: fine-grained text to image generation with attentional generative adversarial networks. In: Proceedings of the IEEE Conference on Computer Vision and Pattern Recognition, pp. 1316–1324 (2018)

15. Zhang, H., et al.: Stackgan: text to photo-realistic image synthesis with stacked generative adversarial networks. In: Proceedings of the IEEE International Conference on Computer Vision, pp. 5907–5915 (2017)

16. Zhang, H., et al.: Stackgan++: realistic image synthesis with stacked generative adversarial networks. IEEE Trans. Pattern Anal. Mach. Intell. **41**(8), 1947–1962 (2018)

Personalized Recommendation Using Extreme Individual Guided and Adaptive Strategies

Yifei Cao[1], Yifei Sun[1(⊠)], Shi Cheng[2], Kun Bian[1], Zhuo Liu[1], Xin Sun[1], and Jie Yang[1]

[1] School of Physics and Information Technology, Shaanxi Normal University, Xi'an, China
{yifeic,yifeis,biankun,zhuoliu,sunxin_,jieyang2021}@snnu.edu.cn
[2] School of Computer Science, Shaanxi Normal University, Xi'an, China
cheng@snnu.edu.cn

Abstract. In the era of information explosion, recommender systems have been widely used to reduce information load nowadays. However, mainly traditional recommendation techniques only paid attention on improving recommendation accuracy without considering additional criteria such as diversity, novelty. Moreover, such traditional recommendation algorithms were also struggled with matthew effect, that is, the gap between the popularity of popular and non-popular items grows. Therefore, a multi-objective recommendation model with extreme individual guided and mutation adaptation based on multi-objective evolutionary algorithms (MOEA-EIMA) is proposed in this paper. It maximizes two conflicting performance metrics termed as precision and novelty. In MOEA-EIMA, the iteration of population is guided by extreme individuals, and the adaptive mutation operator is designed for saving the better individuals. The algorithm is tested in several sparse datasets. The experiment results demonstrate the proposed algorithm can achieve a good trade-off between accuracy and novelty.

Keywords: Recommender systems · Multi-objective evolutionary optimization · Matthew effect · Accuracy · Novelty

1 Introduction

Recommendation systems are not only an important tool in our daily life, but also a key component of commercial enterprise [1, 2]. The great commercial value and practical significance of recommendation system make it one of the hottest research projects nowadays [3]. The traditional recommendation algorithms can be divided into three types: content-based, collaborative and hybrid filtering [4–6].

Since some other additional criteria are as important as accuracy, more and more personalized algorithms based on multi-objective evolution are proposed [7–10]. Zang and Hurley [11] modeled the recommendation problem as a quadratic programming problem. Zhuo [12] introduced a hybrid algorithm which used HeatS to improve diversity and Probs to increase the accuracy. Zuo et al. [13] proposed a multi-objective recommendation algorithm combining MOEA and ProbS to improve the diversity with high

© IFIP International Federation for Information Processing 2022
Published by Springer Nature Switzerland AG 2022
Z. Shi et al. (Eds.): ICIS 2022, IFIP AICT 659, pp. 158–165, 2022.
https://doi.org/10.1007/978-3-031-14903-0_17

accuracy. Wei et al. [14] proposed a hybrid probabilistic multi-objective evolutionary algorithm to optimizes the profit and diversity. However, the Matthew effect, which is the growing gap between the popularity of popular and non-popular items, has not been well addressed. This will lead to the long tail problem.

In this paper, a multi-objective recommendation model with extreme individual guided and mutation adaptation called MOEA-EIMA are proposed to improve the accuracy and the novelty. In MOEA-EIMA, the top-n maximum points on the two objectives of each user are used for constitute the extreme individuals. In addition, during the process of iteration, adaptive operators make it possible to retain elites and conduct better global searches. Experimental results show that the proposed method has a good performance in improving the degree of novelty without reducing the accuracy.

The rest of this paper is organized as follows. In Sect. 2, the definition of the recommendation and some preliminaries of multi-objective optimization are introduced. The details of this work are given in Sect. 3. Section 4 presents the performances of our algorithm. Finally, we conclude our work in Sect. 5.

2   Background

2.1 Definition of Recommendation Problem

Let the set *Users* contains all the users and the set *Items* contains all the recommended items in the system. $R(i, \alpha)$ means the preference of a user i to an item α. As only a few numbers of products are rated by each user, recommender system should predict the preference of user for unknown products through a certain recommendation method first. Then, a recommendation list is generated based on the predicted rating i.e.,

$$\forall i \in C, \alpha = argmaxR \tag{1}$$

2.2 Multi-objective Optimization Problem

A multi-objective optimization problem is defined as follows [15]:

$$minF(x) = (f_1(x), f_2(x), \ldots, f_m(x),)^T \tag{2}$$

where $x = [x_1, x_2, \ldots, x_d] \in \Omega$ is the decision vector, and Ω is the D-dimensional decision space.

The goal of a MOP is to find out a set of non-dominated to approximating the true Pareto front. The definition of Pareto set and Pareto front are shown in Eq. (3) and Eq. (4), respectively.

$$PS = \left\{ x \in \Omega | \neg \exists x^* \in \Omega, x^* \succ x \right\} \tag{3}$$

$$PF = \{F(x)|x \in PS\} \tag{4}$$

2.3 Probs

The Probs [16] is a suitable method for the recommendation systems without explicit ratings. The specific operation is that the initial resource placed on each item is equally distributed to all neighboring users, and then redistributed back to those users' neighboring items in the same way. The transition matrix can be computed by (5), where M represents the total number of users, k_i is the degree of the item node i. The element $\omega_{\alpha\beta}$ in this matrix denotes the fraction of the initial resource of β transferred to α.

$$\omega_{\alpha\beta} = \frac{1}{k_\beta} \sum_{i=1}^{M} \frac{r_{i\alpha} r_{i\beta}}{k_i} \tag{5}$$

3 Proposed Algorithm

3.1 Framework of MOEA-EIMA

The process of a MOEA-EIMA is divided into two stages: project scoring evaluation and multi-objective optimization. In the project evaluation stage, according to the historical user-project evaluation matrix, some project evaluation algorithms predict the unknown evaluation of the project of each input user. In the multi-objective optimization phase, the initial solution and parameters of the multi-objective optimization algorithm are initialized as a loop process. During the loop, the fitness value, which is calculated by the objective function, is calculated first. New solutions are then generated by crossover and mutation manipulation of the original solution, and the next generation solution is updated by comparing the old and new solutions. This looping process repeats until the termination condition is met. The final solution is to output the recommendation results.

3.2 Individual Encoding and Initialization

Generally, all the items recommended to a user will be encoding to the chromosome with their item number as a matrix. For L items will be recommended to K users separately, we build a $K * L$ matrix as the Table 1 shows, where rows represent users and columns represent items. It should be taken a note that one item will not be recommended to a user twice and the rated item can't be recommended. This means duplicate numbers do not appear on the same line.

Since the extreme points in the prediction matrix have a positive effect on extend the Pareto-optimal front [17]. In this paper, all selectable items under each target value for each user are ranked. The top-n points on each objective are selected into the initialized individuals of the population as extreme value points in the initialization process. These extreme individuals will guide the algorithm during the evolutionary process.

Table 1. Illustration of chromosome encoding.

	Item 1	Item 2	...	Item L
User 1	3	6		15
User 2	1	29		9
...		...		
User K	17	26		10

3.3 The Two Objectives

Since the scoring matrix is generally a sparse matrix, predicted rating should be calculated based on Probs first just as Sect. 2.3 said. Each item rated or unrated will have its own predictive rating which equal to f_α'. We measured the accuracy as following formula for each user:

$$PR = \frac{\sum_{U \in S} \sum_{i=1}^{N} f_{\alpha u,i}'}{P * L} \tag{6}$$

where S is the user number, N is the number of items to be recommended, $f_{\alpha u,i}'$ is the predicted rating for item i given by user u, P denotes the population size, L means the length of recommendation list.

Recommend popular products all the time will maintain the high accuracy of the recommendation system. Novelty is a measure of a recommender's ability to recommend non-hot form items to users, so high novelty can often lead to lower accuracy. The novelty of the recommended list is calculated from the item's self-information. The self-information of item i can be calculated as:

$$SI_i = \log_2(\frac{M}{k_i}) \tag{7}$$

where k_i is the degree of the item i.

The mean value of the sum of all items' self-information given by the computing system to all users is the novelty of the recommended result.

$$Nov(N) = \frac{1}{SN} \sum_{u=1}^{S} \sum_{i \in O_L^u} SI_i \tag{8}$$

where O_L^u is the list recommended to user u.

3.4 Genetic Operators

The uniform crossover is more applicable to our work. Since it is not possible to recommend an item twice to a user at the same time, we need to add a judgment to the crossover to avoid generating invalid solutions. This judgment identifies elements that are identical in both parents and passes them directly to the offspring. The other elements follow the following operation. A random number is generated in [0, 1], and if

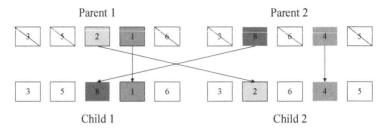

Fig. 1. Illustration of crossover operator. Only the positions without slash perform crossover. Two generated random numbers are 0.2 and 0.6, respectively

this number is greater than 0.5, child 1 will get the corresponding allele from parent 1. Otherwise the allele will be obtained from parent 2. The graphical representation of the crossover operator is shown in Fig. 1.

In the mutation operation, the following formula is used to adjust the individual mutation rate so that it changes smoothly:

$$p_m^i = \begin{cases} \frac{0.5}{1+e^{-\alpha_1(i-N_s)}}, i < N_s \\ \frac{0.5}{1+e^{-\alpha_2(i-N_s)}}, i \geq N_s \end{cases} \qquad (9)$$

where the parameters α_1, α_2 and N_s are set to 0.2, 0.1, 0.4, respectively.

4 Experiments and Analysis

4.1 Experiment Settings

The performance of the algorithm is evaluated on the datasets from MovieLens. This data set can be downloaded from the web of GroupLens Research (http://www.groupl ens.org/). This data set contains 943 users and 1682 movies. Since the Probs algorithm is applied to the 0–1 rating system, an item will be rated as 1 if its score is equal or greater than 3, and otherwise, it will be rated as 0.

As for the partition of the data set, we divided the whole data set into five disjoint parts. Then we randomly select 80% of the data as the training set, and 20% of the data set constitutes the test set. The sparsity, which is defined as the number of links divided by the total number of user-object pairs, of all training data sets is 5.94×10^{-3}. A sparse data set indicates that only a few items are rated by users. This means the recommendation systems may face the cold-start problem. The parameter setting is shown in Table 2.

Precision is widely used to measure the accuracy of recommendations [18]. For a given user i, precision $P_i(L)$ is defined as

$$P_i(L) = \frac{d_i(L)}{L} \qquad (10)$$

where $d_i(L)$ is the number of relevant items, which are in the recommendation list and also preferred by user i in the probe set. The obtained mean precision of all users can reveal recommendation accuracy of RSs.

Besides, the hypervolume [19] is adopted as the performance metrics.

Table 2. Parameter settings of the algorithm.

Algorithms	Parameters settings
User-based-CF	*L = 10*
MF	*L = 10*
MOEA-Probs	*Pc = 0.8, Pm = 1/L, L = 10, Gen = 3000*
MOEA-EIMA	*Pc = 0.8, L = 10, Gen = 3000*

4.2 Experimental Results

In this section, we compare MOEA-EGMA with four existing algorithms (i.e., MOEA-EPG, MOEA-Probs, and User-based-CF). To study the effectiveness of MOEA-EIGA, the final *PF* with the highest hypervolume for every data set are shown in Fig. 2. The mean hypervolume values of the non-dominated solutions form 30 independent runs are shown in Table 3.

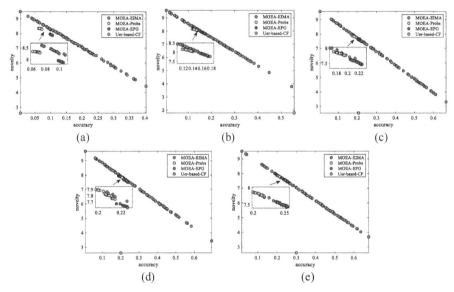

Fig. 2. Final recommendation results for (a) Movielens 1, (b) Movielens 2, (c) Movielens 3, (d) Movielens 4, (e) Movielens 5

In Fig. 2, Experimental results show that MOEA-EIGA can obtain better novelty at the same accuracy under sparse matrices than User-based-CF. MOEA-EPG have a better performance for the accuracy. For the novelty, MOEA-Probs performs better. Adaptive operators give higher-ranked individuals a lower probability of variation, while lower-ranked individuals have a higher probability of variation. This makes MOEA-EIGA a great improvement in both accuracy and novelty. The guidance of the extremum individual ensures the MOEA-EIMA can always get a longer Pareto front than others. The highest mean hypervolume indicate that the MOEA-EIMA performs more steadily than MOEA-Probs and MOEA-EPG. Since the two objectives are non-negative obviously, the reference point for computing hypervolume is set to the origin.

Table 3. HV comparison results

Data set	MOEA-EIMA	MOEA-EPG	MOEA-ProbS
Movielens 1	**2.7890**	0.8395	0.6035
Movielens 2	**3.5887**	1.3691	1.1346
Movielens 3	**4.2556**	1.7183	1.5424
Movielens 4	**4.4805**	1.8332	1.7055
Movielens 5	**4.4639**	1.9265	1.7193

5   Conclusions

In this article, the accuracy and novelty are used as indicators to build multi-objective models to try to solve the Matthew effect in the recommendation system. In the initialization phase we added two extreme individuals on accuracy and novelty to enhance the local search. Adaptive variation operators are added to the cross-variation phase to make sure the top-ranking individuals have a lower mutation probability. Experimental results show that the algorithm is effective and efficient to find a set of trade-off solutions between recommending popular items and non-hot items.

Although the algorithm has increased the novelty of the recommendation system, the value of non-popular goods is far higher than imagined, that is, the long tail problem has not been better solved. Our future work will focus on how to better extract the value of non-popular commodities and apply it to large-scale data sets.

Acknowledgement. This work was supported by the National Natural Science Foundation of China (Grant No. 61703256, 61806119), Natural Science Basic Research Plan in Shaanxi Province of China (Program No. 2022JM-381, 2017JQ6070) and the Fundamental Research Funds for the Central Universities (Program No. GK201803020, GK201603014).

References

1. Resnick, P., Varian, H.R.: Recommender systems. Commun. ACM **40**(3), 56–58 (1997)
2. Bobadilla, J., Ortega, F., Hernando, A., Gutiérrez, A.: Recommender systems survey. Knowl.-Based Syst. **46**, 109–132 (2013)
3. Shi, X., Fang, W., Zhang, G.: A personalized recommendation algorithm based on MOEA-ProbS. In: Tan, Y., Shi, Y., Tang, Q. (eds.) ICSI 2018. LNCS, vol. 10941, pp. 572–579. Springer, Cham (2018). https://doi.org/10.1007/978-3-319-93815-8_54

4. Adomavicius, G., Tuzhilin, A.: Toward the next generation of recommender systems: a survey of the state-of-the-art and possible extensions. IEEE Trans. Knowl. Data Eng. **17**(6), 734–749 (2005)
5. Pazzani, M.J., Billsus, D.: Content-based recommendation systems. In: Brusilovsky, P., Kobsa, A., Nejdl, W. (eds.) The Adaptive Web. LNCS, vol. 4321, pp. 325–341. Springer, Heidelberg (2007). https://doi.org/10.1007/978-3-540-72079-9_10
6. Yang, Z., Lin, X., Cai, Z.: Collaborative filtering recommender systems. Found. Trends® Hum. Comput. Interact. **4**(2), 81–173 (2007)
7. Wang, J., Liu, Y., Sun, J., Jiang, Y., Sun, C.: Diversified recommendation incorporating item content information based on MOEA/D. In: 2016 49th Hawaii International Conference on System Sciences (HICSS), pp. 688–696 (2016)
8. Mcnee, S.M., Riedl, J., Konstan, J.A.: Being accurate is not enough: how accuracy metrics have hurt recommender systems. Extended Abstracts Proceedings of the 2006 Conference on Human Factors in Computing Systems, CHI 2006, Montréal, Québec, Canada, April 2006
9. Hurley, N., Zhang, M.: Novelty and diversity in top-n recommendation – analysis and evaluation. ACM Trans. Internet Technol. **10**(4), 14 (2011)
10. Castells, P., Vargas, S., Wang, J.: Novelty and diversity metrics for recommender systems: choice, discovery and relevance. In: Proceedings of International Workshop on Diversity in Document Retrieval (2011)
11. Zhang, M., Hurley, N.: Avoiding monotony: improving the diversity of recommendation lists. In: Proceedings of the ACM Conference on Recommender Systems, New York, pp. 123–130 (2008)
12. Zhou, T., Kuscsik, Z., Liu, J.G., Medo, M., Wakeling, J.R., Zhang, Y.C.: Solving the apparent diversity-accuracy dilemma of recommender systems. Proc. Natl. Acad. Sci. **107**(10), 4511–4515 (2010)
13. Zuo, Y., Gong, M., Zeng, J., et al.: Personalized recommendation based on evolutionary multi-objective optimization. IEEE Comput. Intell. Mag. **10**(1), 52–62 (2015)
14. Wei, G., Wu, Q., Zhou, M.C.: A hybrid probabilistic multiobjective evolutionary algorithm for commercial recommendation systems. IEEE Trans. Comput. Soc. Syst. **8**, 589–598 (2021)
15. Adomavicius, G., Manouselis, N., Kwon, Y.: Multi-criteria recommender systems. In: Ricci, F., Rokach, L., Shapira, B., Kantor, P.B. (eds.) Recommender Systems Handbook, pp. 769–803. Springer, Boston (2011). https://doi.org/10.1007/978-0-387-85820-3_24
16. Zhou, T., Ren, J., Medo, M., Zhang, Y.: Bipartite network projection and personal recommendation. Phys. Rev. E Stat. Nonlinear Soft Matter Phys. **76**(4 Pt. 2), 046115-1-046115-7-0 (2007)
17. Lin, Q., Wang, X., Hu, B., Ma, L., Chen, F., Li, J.: Multiobjective personalized recommendation algorithm using extreme point guided evolutionary computation. Complexity **2018**, 18, 1716352 (2018). https://doi.org/10.1155/2018/1716352
18. Beume, N., Naujoks, B., Emmerich, M.: SMS-EMOA: multiobjective selection based on dominated hypervolume. Eur. J. Oper. Res. **181**(3), 1653–1669 (2007)
19. Sun, Y., Bian, K., Liu, Z., Sun, X., Yao, R.: Adaptive strategies based on differential evolutionary algorithm for many-objective optimization. Discrete Dyn. Nat. Soc. **2021**, 17, 2491796 (2021). https://doi.org/10.1155/2021/2491796

Improved Transformer-Based Implicit Latent GAN with Multi-headed Self-attention for Unconditional Text Generation

Fuji Ren[1(✉)], Ziyun Jiao[2], and Xin Kang[2]

[1] University of Electronic Science and Technology of China, Chengdu, China
renfuji@uestc.edu.cn
[2] Tokushima University, Tokushima, Japan
c501947010@tokushima-u.ac.jp, kang-xin@is.tokushima-u.ac.jp

Abstract. Generative Adversarial Network (GAN) is widely used in computer vision, such as image generation and other tasks. In recent years, GAN has also been developed in the field of unconditional text generation. In this work, we improve TILGAN for unconditional text generation by refactoring the generator. In short, we use Multi-headed Self-attention to replace the Linear layer and BN layer to endow the generator with better text generation capabilities. Our model consists of three components: a transformer autoencoder, a Multi-headed Self attention based generator and a linear based discriminator. The encoder in transformer autoencoder is used to generate the distribution of real samples, and the decoder is used to decode real or generated sentence vector into text. The loss functions for autoencoder and GAN are cross entropy and KL divergence, respectively. On the MS COCO dataset, the proposed model has achieved a better BLEU score than TILGAN. Our ablation experiments also proved the effectiveness of the proposed generator network for unconditional text generation.

Keywords: TILGAN · Self-attention · GAN · Unconditional text generation

1 Introduction

1.1 Generative Adversarial Network (GAN) for Unconditional Text Generation

A generative adversarial network (GAN) [1] can be leaned in an unsupervised way by letting two neural networks play against each other. GAN includes a Generator and a Discriminator, where the goal of the generator is to generate fake samples that can fool the discriminator, and the goal of the discriminator to distinguish between the real and fake samples. In the end, the Generator and the Discriminator reach a Nash equilibrium in the process of playing against each other. In this way, learning GAN models can essentially be thought of as a minimax game, with the objective function given by:

$$\min_{G} \max_{D} V(D, G) = \mathbb{E}_{x \sim P_{data}(x)}[\log D(x)] + \mathbb{E}_{z \sim P_{z(z)}}[\log(1 - D(G(x)))] \quad (1)$$

© IFIP International Federation for Information Processing 2022
Published by Springer Nature Switzerland AG 2022
Z. Shi et al. (Eds.): ICIS 2022, IFIP AICT 659, pp. 166–173, 2022.
https://doi.org/10.1007/978-3-031-14903-0_18

where x represents the real sample and, z represents the random noise. The goal of the Generator is:

$$\arg maxP(D(G(z))) \qquad (2)$$

and the goal of the Discriminator is:

$$\arg maxP(D(x)) - P(D(G(z))) \qquad (3)$$

In the field of computer vision, GANs rapidly become the hotspot in recent years due to its superior performance. There are some problems when extending the idea of GAN to text generation. In Eq. (2), $G(z)$ generates samples through the 'arg max' (this process also calls sampling). Because this operation in text generation is non-derivable process, gradients cannot transfer properly between the generator and the discriminator, which prohibits the normal gradient based training.

For the above problems, text GANs have proposed some effective solutions, such as reinforcement learning (RL) for sequence generation, Gumbel–Softmax relaxation [2], and Wasserstein Distance [3].

At present, GANs for text generation have been able to generate fluent text. GANs are often used in unconditional text generation. In some tasks that need to control the generation direction, such as machine translation, dialogue generation, text summarization, etc., gaps remain between GANs and Seq2seq architecture. Therefore, this work only involves unconditional text generation. And most of the evaluation datasets used for unconstrained text generation include the COCO Captions, EMNLP2017 WMT, Chinese Poems, etc.

1.2 Research Objective and Content

In this work, we propose a new generator architecture based on Multi-headed Self-attention and linear layer. The overall structure of GAN is improved from TILGAN [4], We rebuilt the generator architecture with Multi-headed Self-attention to make the generator obtain better text generation capabilities. Our model consists of a transformer autoencoder, a generator with Multi-headed Self-attention and a linear-based discriminator. We use the Wasserstein distance or Kullback-Leibler (KL) divergence as the GAN's loss functions. The encoder in transformer autoencoder is used to generate the distribution of real samples, and the decoder is used to decode real sample encoding or generated sample encoding into text. The loss function of autoencoder is cross entropy. The detailed model structure and parameters can be found in Sect. 3. We experiment on the MS COCO dataset. On the MS COCO dataset, the proposed model has achieved a better BLEU score than TILGAN. Through the ablation experiments, we prove that the proposed generator has better ability for unconditional text generation. And the details can be found in Sect. 4. Section 5 presents a discussion of the results and the conclusions at last.

2   Related Works

For the above problems to text GANs, researchers have proposed many excellent models in recent years, which can be divided into the following categories:

(1) Using REINFORCE algorithm. This method focuses on dealing with non-differentiable problems caused by discrete data by considering RL methods or reformulating problems in continuous space [5].

A typical representative model using this method is SeqGAN [6]. For the problem that the generator is difficult to transfer gradients, authors regard the entire GAN as a reinforcement learning system and use the Policy Gradient algorithm to update the parameters of the Generator. For the problem that it is difficult for discriminator to evaluate non-complete sequences, the authors draw on the idea of Monte Carlo tree search (MCTS), so that the discriminator can evaluate incomplete sequences at any time.

The LeakGAN [7], which is improved on SeqGAN, also uses the REINFORCE algorithm for training. Different from SeqGAN, the author additionally "leaks" some high-level information of the discriminator to the generator to help the generator to complete the generation task. Specifically, in addition to the reward given by the discriminator, the generator can additionally obtain the high-level feature representation of the discriminator at each moment. In this way, the generation of long texts will be more accurate and varied.

(2) Using Gumbel–Softmax relaxation. Gumbel-Softmax relaxation was first proposed for reparameterization of categories. The improvement goal applied to GAN can be considered to design a more "powerful" softmax, which can replace the sampling operation in the original GAN.

The typical representative network is RelGAN [5]. For the problem that the generator is difficult to transfer gradients, RelGAN utilizes Gumbel-Softmax relaxation to simplify the model, thus replacing reinforcement learning heuristics. At the same time, RelGAN uses relational memory on the generator, which makes it have stronger expression ability and better generation ability on long text. And RelGAN uses multi-layer word vector representation on the discriminator to make the generated text more diverse. Experiments show that RelGAN achieves very good results in the quality and diversity of the generated text.

(3) Using Wasserstein Distance or KL divergence.

The typical representative network is Wasserstein GAN (WGAN). For the problem that the generator is difficult to transfer gradients, Wasserstein Distance can directly calculate the distance between the real and the generated sample distribution, so there is no non-derivable problem. WGAN completely solves the problem of unstable GAN training, and no longer needs to carefully balance the training degree of the generator and the discriminator. It is worth noting that the proposal of WGAN is not aimed at solving the problems faced by GAN in text generation.

Benefit from the idea of WGAN and the extensive use of Transformer auto-encoder, the idea of GAN in text generation can be slightly changed, that is, the output of the generator is not necessarily a sentence, but also a sentence vector in the latent space. Correspondingly, the task of the discriminator has also changed, that is, from judging whether the current sentence is true, to judging whether the current sentence vector is true. Therefore, TILGAN is proposed. Before TILGAN training, the author trains a Transformer-based auto-encoder on the real corpus. After the training, the sentence vectors in the real corpus through the encoder of the auto-encoder will be used as real data, while the generated sentence vectors will be used as fake data.

In addition to the above three categories, there are some other excellent models, such as RankGAN [8], MaskGAN [9], CatGAN [10], etc., which will not be repeated here.

3 Model Architecture

3.1 Overall Framework

The overall framework of our model is shown in Fig. 1. The model receives a random noise ε under a Gaussian distribution and takes in real text samples from a corpus X. Through the generator network G_θ, random noise ε is transformed into the generated sentence vector $\hat{Z}$. Through the Transformer Encoder, the real text sample is transformed into Z. $\hat{X}$ and $\tilde{X}$ represent the sentences obtained by $\hat{Z}$ and Z through the Transformer Decoder, respectively.

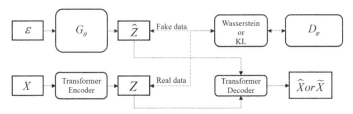

Fig. 1. The overall framework

The proposed GAN framework can be divided into three parts: the Transformer auto-encoder, the Generator and the Discriminator.

The Transformer Encoder is used to generate the distribution of real samples, and the Decoder is used to decode sentence vector into text. The loss function of autoencoder is cross entropy. The task of Transformer is to minimize the gap between X and $\tilde{X}$ to ensure the accuracy of the real sentence vector distributions.

The Discriminator consists of three linear layers and two BN layers, with the ReLU activation function for each layer. The loss function of GAN is Wasserstein distance or KL divergence. The goal of the generator is to minimize the distance between the generated sentence vector and the sentence vector of the real sample. On the other hand, the discriminator tries to maximize the distance between the real data and the fake data.

3.2 Multi-headed Self Attention Based Generator

Different from the stacking of linear layers and BN layers of the TILGAN generator, we use multi-head self-attention to build the generator. The proposed generator framework is shown in Fig. 2, where $\otimes$ means the dot product, and the two linear layers are used for reshaping.

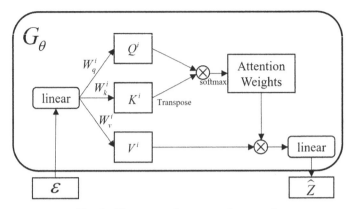

Fig. 2. The proposed generator framework

Formally, we employ $L(\varepsilon)$ to represent the processed noise ε through the linear layer. By setting the number of attention heads to I, we can get I sets of queries, keys and values. For each attention head, we have:

$$\begin{cases} Q^i = L(\varepsilon)W_q^i \\ K^i = L(\varepsilon)W_k^i \\ V^i = L(\varepsilon)W_v^i \end{cases} \tag{4}$$

Accordingly, we can get the sentence vector $\hat{Z}$ by:

$$\hat{Z} = L'(\sigma(\frac{Q^i(K^i)^T}{\sqrt{d_k}})V^i) \tag{5}$$

where σ is the softmax function and, d_k is the column dimension of the keys.

3.3 Training Details

Limited by hardware equipment, we set the batch size to 64. We used the Adam [11] optimizer, the learning rate of the GAN is 1×10^{-4}. And the learning rate of auto-encoder is 0.12. The current loss function is KL divergence, in the future work, we may change the loss function.

4 Experiments

4.1 Evaluation Metrics

In this work, we use two metrics to evaluate the models. The first metric is bilingual evaluation understudy(BLEU-test) [12]. This score indicates how similar the candidate text is to the reference text. The BLEU-test value is in the range of [0, 1], and a larger BLEU-test value indicates a better generation result. In general, the BLEU score could provide an overall assessment of model quality.

The second metric is Self-BLEU [13]. Self-BLEU is a diversity metric, by calculating the similarity between one generated sentence and the whole remaining generation. A lower the Self-BLEU score is, indicates a higher diversity we can obtain in the generated texts [4].

4.2 Microsoft COCO: Common Objects in Context

In order to test our model, we firstly conduct experiments on MSCOCO [14]. All the preprocessing steps are same as Chen et al. (2018) [15]. The details of the dataset are shown in Table 1.

Table 1. The details of MS COCO

Dataset	MS COCO
Vocab_Size	27842
Average_len	10.4
Train sentence Num	120K
Test sentence Num	10K

Similar with TILGAN, we set the Transformer autoencoder with 2 layers, 4 heads, and 512 hidden dimensions. In addition, we set the generator with 4 heads, 256 head size, 32 hidden dimensions. All the sentences will be padded to the maximum length during training. Then the BLEU scores on MSCOCO dataset are shown in Table 2. The proposed model has achieved significantly better performance compared to the existing models in BLEU-2, 3 and 4 and Self-BLEU-2 and 3, The results suggest that our text generation model is generally more effective on the MSCOCO dataset than the existing models.

Table 2. The BLEU scores on MSCOCO. For BLEU-test, the higher the better. For Self-BLEU, the lower the better.

Method	BLEU-test				Self-BLEU		
	B2%	B3%	B4%	B5%	B2%	B3%	B4%
SEQGAN [6]	82.0	60.4	36.1	21.1	80.7	57.7	27.8
RANKGAN [8]	85.2	63.7	38.9	24.8	82.2	59.2	28.8
LEAKGAN [7]	92.2	79.7	60.2	41.6	91.2	82.5	68.9
GSGAN [16]	81.0	56.6	33.5	19.7	78.5	52.2	23.0
WGAN [3]	73.0	53.8	34.2	12.5	90.4	80.9	69.0
TILGAN [4]	96.7	90.3	77.2	**53.2**	61.6	35.6	**9.9**
Our model	**98.6**	**92.8**	**79.9**	42.0	**54.8**	**27.0**	12.1

4.3 Ablation Experiment

To indicate that our changes to the generator are effective, we also conduct ablation experiment on MSCOCO. We keep all model parameters the same with TILGAN except the generator (including learning rate, model structure, number of autoencoder layers, number of hidden layers, etc.). The only difference is the generator. The BLEU-3 curve is shown in Fig. 3. The overfitting part is not shown in the figure.

Through the curves, we find that our generator converges much faster than TILGAN. The results show that our generator has better text generation ability. Compared with the original generator, our model can achieve better results on large datasets as well as for long text generation.

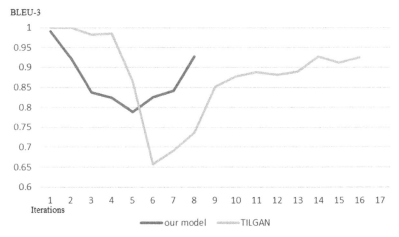

Fig. 3. Ablation experiment

5 Conclusion and Future Work

This paper proposes an improved model for text generation, we use Multi-headed Self-attention to replace the Linear layer and BN layer to make the generator obtain better text generation capabilities. Compared with the existing models, our model has higher evaluation scores and diverse sample on MSCOCO dataset. In the future work, we will continue to conduct experiments on other datasets, while looking for the best model parameters to obtain better performance.

Acknowledgments. This research has been supported by JSPS KAKENHI Grant Number 19K20345.

References

1. Goodfellow, I., et al.: Generative adversarial networks. Commun. ACM **63**, 139–144 (2020)

2. Kusner, M.J., Hernández-Lobato, J.M.: GANs for sequences of discrete elements with the gumbel-softmax distribution. arXiv arXiv:1611.04051 (2016)
3. Arjovsky, M., Chintala, S., Bottou, L.: Wasserstein GAN. arXiv arXiv:1701.07875 (2017)
4. Diao, S., Shen, X., Shum, K., et al.: TILGAN: transformer-based implicit latent GAN for diverse and coherent text generation. In: Findings of the Association for Computational Linguistics: ACL-IJCNLP 2021, pp. 4844–4858 (2021)
5. Nie, W., Narodytska, N., Patel, A.: RelGAN: relational generative adversarial networks for text generation. In: Proceedings of the International Conference on Learning Representations, Vancouver, BC, Canada, 30 April–3 May 2018
6. Yu, L., Zhang, W., Wang, J., Yu, Y.: SeqGAN: sequence generative adversarial nets with policy gradient. In: Proceedings of the Thirty-First AAAI Conference on Artificial Intelligence, San Francisco, CA, USA, 4–9 February 2017
7. Guo, J., Lu, S., Cai, H., Zhang, W., Yu, Y., Wang, J.: Long text generation via adversarial training with leaked information. arXiv arXiv:1709.08624 (2017)
8. Juefei-Xu, F., Dey, R., Boddeti, V.N., Savvides, M.: RankGAN: a maximum margin ranking GAN for generating faces. In: Jawahar, C.V., Li, H., Mori, G., Schindler, K. (eds.) ACCV 2018. LNCS, vol. 11363, pp. 3–18. Springer, Cham (2019). https://doi.org/10.1007/978-3-030-20893-6_1
9. Fedus, W., Goodfellow, I., Dai, A.M.: MaskGAN: better text generation via filling in the ____. arXiv arXiv:1801.07736 (2018)
10. Liu, Z., Wang, J., Liang, Z.: CatGAN: category-aware generative adversarial networks with hierarchical evolutionary learning for category text generation. In: Proceedings of the AAAI Conference on Artificial Intelligence, vol. 34, no. 05, pp. 8425–8432 (2020)
11. Kingma, D.P., Ba, J.: Adam: a method for stochastic optimization. arXiv arXiv:1412.6980 (2014)
12. Papineni, K., Roukos, S., Ward, T., Zhu, W.J.: BLEU: a method for automatic evaluation of machine translation. In: Proceedings of the 40th Annual Meeting on Association for Computational Linguistics, Philadelphia, PA, USA, 7–12 July 2002
13. Zhu, Y., et al.: Texygen: a benchmarking platform for text generation models. In: The 41st International ACM SIGIR Conference on Research & Development in Information Retrieval, pp. 1097–1100 (2018)
14. Lin, T.-Y., et al.: Microsoft COCO: common objects in context. In: Fleet, D., Pajdla, T., Schiele, B., Tuytelaars, T. (eds.) ECCV 2014. LNCS, vol. 8693, pp. 740–755. Springer, Cham (2014). https://doi.org/10.1007/978-3-319-10602-1_48
15. Chen, L., et al.: Adversarial text generation via feature mover's distance. In: Advances in Neural Information Processing Systems, pp. 4666–4677 (2018)
16. Wu, H.Y., Chen, Y.L.: Graph sparsification with generative adversarial network. In: 2020 IEEE International Conference on Data Mining (ICDM), pp. 1328–1333. IEEE (2020)

Learning a Typhoon Bayesian Network Structure from Natural Language Reports

Zhangrui Yao[1], Junhan Chen[1], Yinghui Pan[2(✉)], Yifeng Zeng[3(✉)],
Biyang Ma[4], and Zhong Ming[2]

[1] Department of Automation and Xiamen, Key Laboratory of Big Data Intelligent
Analysis and Decision-Making, Xiamen University, Xiamen, China
[2] College of Computer Science and Software Engineering, Shenzhen University,
Shenzhen, China
panyinghui@szu.edu.cn
[3] Department of Computer and Information Sciences, Northumbria University,
Newcastle upon Tyne, UK
yifeng.zeng@northumbria.ac.uk
[4] School of Computer Science and Engineering, Minnan Normal University,
Zhangzhou, China

Abstract. Given the huge toll caused by natural disasters, it is critically important to develop an effective disaster management and emergency response technique. In this article, we investigate relationships between typhoon-related variables and emergency response from natural language (NL) reports. A major challenge is to exploit typhoon state information for typhoon contingency plan generation, especially from unstructured text data based on NL input. To tackle this issue, we propose a novel framework for learning typhoon Bayesian network structures (FLTB), which can extract typhoon state information from unstructured NL, mine inter-information causal relationships and then generate Bayesian networks. We first extract information about typhoon states through NL processing (NLP) techniques, and then analyze typhoon reports by designing heuristic rules to identify causal relationships between states. We leverage these features to improve the learned structures and provide user-interaction mechanisms to finalize Bayesian networks. We evaluate the performance of our framework on real-world typhoon datasets and develop the Bayesian networks based typhoon emergency response systems.

Keywords: Causal structure learning · Bayesian networks · Typhoon emergency plan

1 Introduction

Intelligent decision models have shown significant application values in the prediction of natural disaster events [4]. An effective decision-making model can be

---

Supported by NSF: 62176225 and 61836005.

built by analyzing how natural disasters occur and what they are leading to. The analysis is often accompanied with a large amount of text, such as news reports and real-time microblogs.

In many cases, emergency response systems often need to interact with users lacking professional knowledge. Hence, probabilistic graphical models (PGMs) are an ideal tool for developing decision models in emergency response systems [8]. In this paper, we construct Bayesian network as the typhoon decision model. Due to its high interpretability, Bayesian networks have become a reliable decision-making tool in many application fields.

There have been many studies on Bayesian network structure learning [2], but existing techniques rarely focus on unstructured data. In addition, the information in the text is highly fragmented, the text features are sparse, and the available open annotated corpus is scarce. Consequently, it is rather difficult to directly generate a Bayesian network from the text.

Under this setting, we propose a Bayesian network structure learning scheme based on natural language inputs, namely FLTP. We adopt Bert model to extract the state pairs of typhoons in which its bidirectional encoder can extract feature factors of each word. Then we employ domain knowledge to normalize the state of the variables. We design a rule template to find causal relationships between states and build the Bayesian network. We also provide a knowledge-based approach to pruning Bayesian networks. The resulting Bayesian networks can be compiled by a general PGM tool, e.g. GeNIe[1] or HUGIN[2] application. In addition, we design an interactive component so that users can provide useful knowledge and optimize the final output of the Bayesian networks.

The rest of the article is organised as follows. Section 2 reviews related works. Section 3 presents our novel techniques that learn Bayesian network structures in a typhoon contingency plan. Experiments are conducted in Sect. 4. Section 5 concludes our work and discusses directions of future research.

2   Related Works

An intelligent decision model has many application precedents in the field of disaster response [8]. Most of the existing typhoon emergency decision-making research is based on statistical methods, and the data affecting emergency decision-making is obtained through demographic characteristics such as questionnaires [11]. However, these statistics-based models also have many limitations, such as slow data collection process and analysis process. Although learning Bayesian networks from data has been extensively studied in various fields [1], learning network structure from text input remains a challenge. Learning Bayesian network structure can be divided into two steps - states and their relations extraction.

There are few studies on extracting node status directly from text, and most of them are extracted by rules. For example, Trovati et al. [10] extracted and populate BN fragments based on grammar and lexical properties. In recent years, many studies have applied natural language processing technology in the fields

---

[1] https://www.bayesfusion.com/genie/.

[2] https://www.hugin.com/.

of disaster prevention [3]. However, most of the current works only identify and analyze disaster events without extracting their relations.

The most noteworthy information in the text is the causal relationship, which contains a lot of knowledge and resources in the form of causal relationship. Understanding possible causal relationships between pairs of events is of great significance in Event Prediction and Decision Processing [7]. The methods of causal extraction can be divided into rule-based methods [9], machine learning-based methods[12], and deep learning-based methods [5]. In this article, we adapt the machine learning based methods with additional rule-based knowledge model to discover causal relations in Bayesian networks.

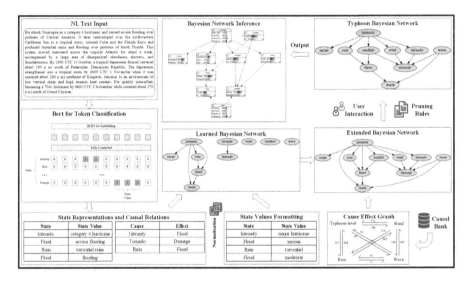

Fig. 1. A framework of learning typhoon Bayesian network structures (FLTB) contains five main parts from learning typhoon information from NL text to construct a Bayesian network.

3   The Framework of Learning Typhoon Bayesian Network Structures

FLTB focuses on the identification of states and relations, and then learn the network structure. As shown in Fig. 1, FLTB contains five parts. ① State extraction. ② State values Normalization. ③ Causal relationship extraction. ④ Bayesian network Generation ⑤ Network output and inference.

3.1   State Extraction Model

The goal of state extraction is to identify all possible (state, state value) pairs in a sentence. We adapt BERT(Bidirectional Encoder Representations from Transformers) for token classification in the FLTB. In general, for a given data set D

with utterance x_j and state pair label $T_j = (s, v)$, we aim to maximize the probabilistic likelihood in the data set D: $p_\theta(s, v|x) = \prod_{j=1}^{|D|} [\prod_{(s,v) \in T_j} p((s, v)|x_j)] = \prod_{j=1}^{|D|} [\prod_{s \in T_j} p(v|x_j)]$.

The state value tagger optimizes the following likelihood function to identify the span of value v given a sentence representation x: $p_{\theta s}(v|x) = \prod_{i=1}^{L} (p_i^s)^{I\{y_i^s=1\}} (1 - p_i^s)^{I\{y_i^s=0\}}$, where L is the length of the sentence. $I\{z\} = 1$ if z is true and 0 otherwise. y_i^s is the binary tag of state for the ith token in x.

3.2 Standardize State Information

Due to the diversity and complexity of NL expressions and the characteristics of the extraction model, the state we capture may have different representations. Thus, we need to merge and unify the extracted state information.

We create a normalization base to standardize the states we extract. Specifically, we screen out representative statements from typhoon news on the Internet, and summarize their representative feature representations. We develop a uniform representation of state values. For example, we filter out some representative expressions of *rainfall* from typhoon news: *widespread heavy rain, local heavy rain, general heavy rain*, etc. Then we unify all these expressions into the state value of *heavy rain* in the state *rain*. Second, for the numerical status value attributes obtained in the news, we design rules to classify them into levels. After this process, we get the normalized state values.

3.3 Causal Relationship Extraction

We Identify causality by checking whether a sentence contains causal patterns. Then we use a Bayesian classifier to filter out noisy pairs.

3.3.1 Identify Causal Patterns

To represent the syntactic structure of the causal relationship in the sentence, we define some lexical syntactic patterns based [9].

- Using causal links to link two phrases or sentences. (e.g. therefore, because)
- Using a single verb that expresses cause and effect. (e.g. cause, produce)
- Using causal verbs in the passive voice. (e.g. cause by, triggered by)
- Using a single preposition to connect cause and effect (e.g. after, from)

To make the causal patterns more general, we expand the list by adding common phrases that contain those words. For example, the *cause* in the cause and effect list can be extended to include phrases such as *the main causes of, the leading cause of*.

For each causal pattern, a corresponding regular expression is defined to identify sentences containing this pattern, e.g. the regular expression $(.*) < produce|cause|triggers|... > (.*)$ can match the type of causative verbs. Then we define a series of rules to confirm cause and effect.

3.3.2   Causality Extraction Rules

The rules for detecting causality are based on syntactic structures. We divide the causal words into forward causal words (e.g. cause, therefore) and reverse causal words (e.g. resulted by, caused by), and then determine which part is the cause and which the effect based on the position of the state and the trigger words in the text. The main rule is:

$$((C, P^+) \cup (P^-, C)) \cap ((E, P^-) \cup (P^+, E)) \rightarrow cRel(C, E) \tag{1}$$

where P^+ and P^- are forward causal and reverse causal respectively, and (C, P^+) means that the state C is in the front of P^+.

In order to deal with multiple causal relationships in the same sentence, we also study causal chain relationships in a sentence. For example, a sentence contains a sequence of causal events, event e_1 causes another event e_2 to occur, which in turn causes event e_3 to occur. In this case, e_2 would be marked as an *effect* for $e1$ and a *cause* for e_3.

Table 1. Main notations used in this paper.

x	State
X_T	The state set of typhoon information
X_M	The state set of meteorology information
X_S	The state set of secondary disaster
X_D	The state set of disaster information
(a, b)	a and b form a causal relationship, with a as the cause and b as the effect
$X_h > X_l$	X_h has a higher priority than X_l

Using the above rules, we create a causal rule base. We use a dependency parser to segment each input sentence into words. Once any causal marker words are identified in the sentence, we apply the above rules to them, thereby extracting causal relationships between states.

3.3.3   Candidate Pair Filtering

The relationships we extracted using the above rules may be noisy, there are some pairs (C, E) that do not have a causal relationship. To address this, we create a causal database of 8392 sentences from the collected sentences (among them, 1541 are marked as causality), and then obtain prior knowledge from the causal database and use a Naive Bayes classifier to remove false causal pairs.

$$P(c_i|r) = P(r|c_i) * P(c_i)/P(r) \tag{2}$$

where, with $i = 0$ or 1, c_1 is causal and c_0 is non-causal, and r is candidate causal pair, $P(c_1)=1541/8392$, $P(c_0)=6851/8392$. $P(r|c_i)$ refers to the number of r in c_i. According to the Bayesian classification rule, the relation is classified as causal if $P(c_1|r) > P(c_0|r)$.

3.4   Generate Typhoon Bayesian Network

3.4.1   Generate Backbone Network

Firstly, we consider aspects of the impact caused by typhoons, and classify states into four categories based on catastrophology [13]: ① Typhoon information: The properties of the typhoon itself, like *intensity, landfall...* ②Meteorological information: Typhoon would bring some meteorological impacts, like *rain, wind, surge...* ③ Secondary disasters: Typhoons would cause a series of secondary hazards, like *tornado, flood...* ④ Disaster information: The impact of the typhoon and the measures taken by the government, including *damage, death, warn...* We define the main notations in Table 1.

3.4.2   Prior Knowledge-Based Bayesian Network Extension

We construct a prior causal knowledge base through the causal bank [6]. Then the Bayesian network is extended through this prior knowledge base and typhoon domain rules we develop below.

Rule 1: We collect the information of typhoon disaster chain and combine it with the knowledge of disaster science [14]. We assume the following priority of the four categories: $X_T > X_M > X_S > X_D$. The lower ranked states can not be used as the cause of the higher states.

Rule 2: We find that issuing the wrong level of warning would lead to more severe disasters. So we assume that the *warn* status only can be the reason for the others in disaster information status.

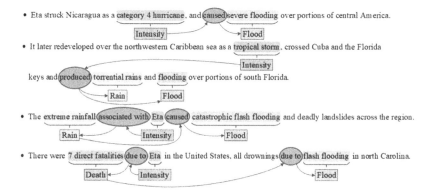

Fig. 2. Results of extracting the S1–S4 sentences.

Rule 3: Since the subject of our study is typhoon, the secondary disaster should be caused by typhoon. Therefore we assume that states of the secondary disaster must have at least one cause node.

Thus, for isolated nodes in the backbone network, we extend the network through selecting the node with the highest frequency in the prior knowledge base to form causal relationships.

3.4.3   Bayesian Network Pruning

Based on the nature of the network structure and the pattern of typhoon event development, we develop the following rules for pruning a network structure.

Rule 1: We assume that there is causal transitivity between the four typhoon categories. In other words, The states between four levels follow the head-to-tail, i.e., $A \rightarrow B \rightarrow C$. A and C are independent given B.

Rule 2: We find when there are multiple weather states pointing to the same secondary disaster information, the relationship between them is irrelevant and can be pruned.

Rule 3: We assume that the secondary hazards are all caused by typhoons. No causal relationship will be formed between the secondary hazards, i.e., secondary disaster states can not form a causal relationship with each other.

In addition, we introduce user interaction in practical applications so that users can define specific causal relationships according to the actual situation.

3.4.4   Bayesian Network Output and Inference

In the last step, we create a Bayesian network using states and causal relationships obtained by FLTB. Then we use PGM software (e.g. GeNIe) to inference the network. Having a Bayesian network can enhance many downstream applications, including question answering and inference.

4   Experimental Results

We collected 169 influential hurricane reports from the U.S. National Hurricane Center that occurred between 2011 and 2021. We create the training data from given sentences for extracting states, and then test FLTB on learning Bayesian network from news of the typhoon Eta, in order to illustrate that our FLTB is effective and automatic in unstructured data.

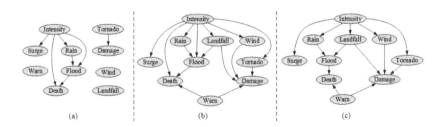

Fig. 3. Results of the step of generating a typhoon Bayesian network through FLTB. (*a*) The basic Bayesian network (*b*) The extended Bayesian network, and (*c*) The final output Bayesian network.

We have built the FLTB based typhoon BN learning engine and developed the demo as shown in the link[3].

Table 2. The states obtained from sentences S1-4 by our FLTB.

Sentence	States and State Values	States Normalization	Causal Relationships
S1	(Intensity , category 4 hurricane) (Flood , severe flooding)	(intensity , major hurricane) (flood , serious)	(intensity , flood)
S2	(intensity , tropical storm) (rain , torrential rains) (flood , flooding)	(intensity , tropical storm) (rain , torrential) (flood , moderate)	(intensity , rain) (intensity , flood)
S3	(rain , extreme rainfall) (flood , catastrophic flash flooding) (intensity , eta)	(rain , torrential) (flood , serious) (intensity , eta)	(intensity , rain) (rain , flood)
S4	(flood , flash flooding) (death , 7 direct fatalities) (intensity , eta)	(flood , serious) (death , serious) (intensity , eta)	(intensity , death) (flood , death)

Taking the four input sentences as an example, Fig. 2 illustrates the extracting results of sentences S1, S2, S3 and S4, respectively.

After an automatic process on the dataset, the sets of states, state values and causal relationships, corresponding nodes, random variables and directed edges are shown in Table 2. As shown in Fig. 3 (a), FLTB can construct a basic Bayesian network based on the extracted information. Then we clearly see that the backbone network is incomplete with lots of isolated nodes. We add rule constraints to extend isolated nodes based on the external database and the causal bank.

From the new network in Fig. 3 (*b*), we can see that the network is obviously complex and redundant. Hence we simplify the network according to the constrains formulated in Sect. 3.5. The result in Fig. 3 (*c*) illustrates the automation and rationality of FLTB.

5   Discussions and Conclusions

We develop a novel framework, namely FLTB, to automate the structure learning in a Bayesian network from the inputs of NL text. This is also the first attempt at extracting typhoon states for constructing Bayesian network by using the NLP technique. The new method can see the benefit of generating Bayesian networks for small unstructured text data as shown in our empirical study.

As we are deploying this framework in a practical application of generating typhoon contingency plans, there is a need to further reduce the user interaction and develop a more automatic process. In addition, we may consider adopting disaster news reports from multiple disasters as input to gradually establish a larger network, and build more accurate plans.

---

[3] https://github.com/lamingic/LBfT.

References

1. Behjati, S.: An order-based algorithm for learning structure of bayesian networks. In: International Conference on Probabilistic Graphical Models, 11–14 September 2018 (2018)
2. Constantinou, A.C.: Learning bayesian networks with the saiyan algorithm. ACM Trans. Knowl. Discov. Data (TKDD) **14**(4), 1–21 (2020)
3. Domala, J., et al.: Automated identification of disaster news for crisis management using machine learning and natural language processing. In: 2020 International Conference on Electronics and Sustainable Communication Systems (ICESC), pp. 503–508. IEEE (2020)
4. Huo, Y., Tang, J., Pan, Y., Zeng, Y., Cao, L.: Learning a planning domain model from natural language process manuals. IEEE Access **8**, 143219–143232 (2020)
5. Li, Z., Li, Q., Zou, X., Ren, J.: Causality extraction based on self-attentive bilstm-crf with transferred embeddings. Neurocomputing **423**, 207–219 (2021)
6. Li, Z., Ding, X., Liu, T., Hu, J.E., Van Durme, B.: Guided generation of cause and effect (2021). arXiv preprint arXiv:2107.09846
7. Miranda Ackerman, E.J.: Extracting a causal network of news topics. In: Herrero, P., Panetto, H., Meersman, R., Dillon, T. (eds.) OTM 2012. LNCS, vol. 7567, pp. 33–42. Springer, Heidelberg (2012). https://doi.org/10.1007/978-3-642-33618-8_5
8. Sankar, A.R., Doshi, P., Goodie, A.: Evacuate or not? a pomdp model of the decision making of individuals in hurricane evacuation zones. In: Uncertainty in Artificial Intelligence, pp. 669–678. PMLR (2020)
9. Sorgente, A., Vettigli, G., Mele, F.: Automatic extraction of cause-effect relations in natural language text. In: DART@ AI* IA 2013, pp. 37–48 (2013)
10. Trovati, M., Hayes, J., Palmieri, F., Bessis, N.: Automated extraction of fragments of bayesian networks from textual sources. Appli. Soft Comput. **60**, 508–519 (2017)
11. Yongsatianchot, N., Marsella, S.: Modeling human decision-making during hurricanes: from model to data collection to prediction. In: AAMAS Conference Proceedings (2019)
12. Zhao, S., Liu, T., Zhao, S., Chen, Y., Nie, J.Y.: Event causality extraction based on connectives analysis. Neurocomputing **173**, 1943–1950 (2016)
13. Zheng, L., Wang, F., Zheng, X., Liu, B.: A distinct approach for discovering the relationship of disasters using big scholar datasets. In: Yuan, H., Geng, J., Liu, C., Bian, F., Surapunt, T. (eds.) GSKI 2017. CCIS, vol. 848, pp. 271–279. Springer, Singapore (2018). https://doi.org/10.1007/978-981-13-0893-2_28
14. Zheng, L., Wang, F., Zheng, X., Liu, B.: Discovering the relationship of disasters from big scholar and social media news datasets. Int. J. Digital Earth **12**(11), 1341–1363 (2019)

What Is Information? An Interpretation Based on the Theory of Modern Complexity Science

Zhikang Wang[✉]

Sun Yat-Sen University, Guangzhou, People's Republic of China
zdwangzk@126.com

Abstract. This study seeks to answer the question "information is information, not matter or energy" asked by Norbert Wiener, focuses on the relationship between the material system and information, and makes the two concepts of information and information entity clear based on the theory of modern complexity science. Information is understood or defined as the form of interactions between different layers of matter systems, which not only broadens the knowledge of interactions and causality in nature but also enables AI.

Keywords: Information · Hierarchical interactions · Informatization · Information causality · Information entities

1 Introduction

The progress of Information and Artificial Intelligence Science since the 20th century, in a sense, has benefited from the proposal of the information concept and the formation of information entity, but both are not very clear in science and philosophy. They need to be explained through hermeneutics.

Norbert Wiener said, "Information is information, not matter or energy. No materialism which does not admit this can survive at the present day" [6, p. 182]. What is information, then? This is still a question for science and philosophy.

Before we dive deep in what information is, the word information is used only in the sense of human culture and its transmission, so it is one kind of abstract description about "message" and "thought". As existence of the objective world, information begins after scientists learning about the special way of biological heredity and the communication mode of machines and animals. Although the concept of information has not been clear, but its importance has been increased for science and philosophy to the point that neither scientists nor philosophers can ignore its position in the objective world. Norbert Wiener's question promoted positive thinking in the sense of information ontology, yet there was no obvious progress before the viewpoint of world changed from simplicity to complexity, namely before the birth of complexity science. Obviously, the answer to the question is very important to us because it involves the human artificial intervention in biological information and communication, and the realization of artificial intelligence.

© IFIP International Federation for Information Processing 2022
Published by Springer Nature Switzerland AG 2022
Z. Shi et al. (Eds.): ICIS 2022, IFIP AICT 659, pp. 183–190, 2022.
https://doi.org/10.1007/978-3-031-14903-0_20

The rest of the article is going to explain and define information from a new perspective. I will explain how information can be understood or defined as "a form of interaction between different layers of material complexity systems", how it is realized, and I will demonstrate it based on the biological systems and communication systems by the theory of modern complexity systems. Information is considered as the entity (so-called "Relationship entity" by Aristoteles [1, pp. 156–157]) that maintains itself in transformations with different carriers of material layers, so it answered Norbert Wiener's question about the relationship between matter, energy, and information. This paper tries hard to clarify the essence of information, and reveal the essence of artificial intelligence which is a new information mutual relationship established at different layers of the material system.

2 Material Hierarchies and Complexity Systems

Everything in the world, no matter how huge and small, is the unity of "multiple" and "single", which is the concrete manifestation of the unification of material diversity; as such, everything can be called a material system. When we begin to chart a variety of things presented before us in the relationship and order their qualities (see Fig. 1(A)), we find a hierarchical relationship between the various specific forms of matter [2, pp. 1–8] [7]. This is a reality manifestation of the unification of diversity in the material world. The things at the same material layer are called "simple diversity", they can be easily distinguished through the conceptual methods of general formal logic, but the things at different material layers are called "complex diversity", to distinguish these things we usually cannot find the logic or other theoretical criteria. In further research, we can also find that the chart reveals the two most basic situations of the unified diversity of things: one is at the same layer, and the other is across different layers. For the reasons above, the system composed of the unified diversity of substances within the same layer is called the "simplicity system", while the system composed of the unified diversity of substances across different layers is called the "complexity system". From their parent,

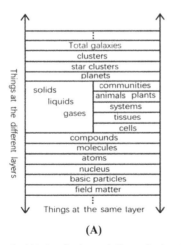
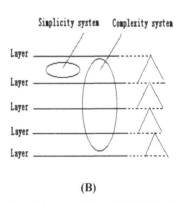

Fig. 1. (**A**) Continuity and discontinuity, diversity and unity of the material world. (**B**) Simplicity system and the complexity system.

the matter hierarchy, we can see the fundamental difference between simplicity systems and complexity systems (see Fig. 2(B)), and the secret of the complexity of the world [5, pp. 109–112].

3   How Information Comes into the View of Scientists

From the brief description above, it is not difficult to find the dilemma of traditional scientific theory dominated by reduction. There are many layers inside and outside complexity system, the existence of layers blocks the direct causal link from the local to the whole and generally presents the characteristics of emergence and mutation, so the overall nature of a complexity system cannot be segmented and cannot be reduced to its local properties by analytical approaches. This situation is prominent in studying biological systems and mechanical machine communication systems. Scientists first explain the genetic mechanisms of life in ways such as messaging and symbolic recording in human culture. The introduction and use of the concept of "gene" (basic reason) marks the beginning of people's understanding of the world into the information field, in which, the objective existence of information is accepted, that is, there is real existence on the objective world that can only be found through the human spirit, and be explained by the human spirit. The cognitive focus of the world extends from physical interaction to information interaction, and physical reduction to information reduction. Let's see the process of this transformation in the following chapters.

3.1   The Reduction of Three Types of Determinism

The Reduction of Mechanical Determinism. There are three types of determinism, they are used to deal with interrelationships between the layers of systems. First is the reduction of mechanical determinism which claims that any high-layer law can be recovered by complex calculations into low-layer laws, which is the mechanical laws of a single or a small number of particles, and that the material hierarchy is irrelevant.

The Reduction of Statistical Determinism. The scientists trying to make such efforts believe that the relationship between various things and material layers can only be attributed to the laws of statistics, and that all material movements can be described by pure statistical methods between the two layers. This view claims that non-statistical features between hierarchies are just unknowable and any further exploration is meaningless.

The Reduction of Cryptodeterminism. A famous theoretical physicist, one of the founders of molecular biology, Erwin Schrödinger was the first to point out that neither of the reduction forms of determinism, mentioned above, is possible in a biological genetic system. Erwin then put forward the theory of genetic cryptography [3, p. 23], arguing that the high and low layers of organisms cannot be restored through the traditional scientific theories we know, that there are many cryptographic relations between them, and only through translation can they become physical and chemical laws we know. The proposal and establishment of cryptodeterminism is a major thought revolution in scientific epistemology and methodology. It marks a new stage in human research on complex things, including humanity itself (cryptodeterminism is also known as information- determinism).

3.2 Interpretation of Information on Biological Genetics

1953 James D. Watson and Francis Crick discovered DNA double helix structure and a special relationship between nucleotides forming DNA molecules and amino acids of protein molecules, this relationship cannot be explained by traditional physicochemical interactions. Scientists explain this particular interrelationship in "natural language" by using the characteristics of human cultural transmission, and it is interpreted as a similar text communication coding relationship (see Fig. 2). A set of cryptobooks used by the whole organic world was then discovered, thus, the theory of biological genetic information was finally established.

In this way, the scientific vision really moves into the information world starting with the biological system: a world with special interactions.

Fig. 2. Nucleotide program and corresponding proteins of the mRNA molecule of phage R17 (part). The bioinformation interpretation based on human cultural information model. The genetic characteristics of organisms are recorded in encoding form, similar to a string of characters in human culture, it is material and also informational.

3.3 Information and Communication Connections Are Established between Different and Across Layers of the Organism

The living system should obtain time, so that the various parts of it are coordinated and unified, and the spatial and temporal relationship between the parts at each layer can be adjusted at any time. So, how does one layer change its state of time and space according to the change of another layer? Therefore, there must be a set of communication connections between the high and low layers in organisms, in addition to the "native" and "evolutionary" connections determined by the cipher book, which occurs not only between the various relatively separate parts of the same material layer, but more importantly, between the various parts of the different material layers.

The best way to establish communication connections is to send messengers to each other at different layers, as in the human social system. Take humans as an example, it has been found that the three messengers delivering life information between the layers of human body are: hormone, prostaglandin, and adenosine cyclic phosphate (cAMP), they work together to complete the task of delivering life-sustaining information in a relay way, and it is really similar to human communication [5, pp. 123–124].

Figure 3 illustrates vividly the information interactions (communication) that occur between the two systems. It shows that the information transfer between the same layers must be accomplished by a direct physical interaction at another layer. Norbert Wiener emphasizes that communication between machines, animals, and humans has the same mechanisms [6].

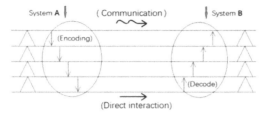

Fig. 3. Information interactions between different systems. Information transfer at the same layer is achieved through direct interactions at different layers.

4 The Interaction between Layers in Complexity System and Its Informatization

Now, let us come back to the main question of this paper, how to understand the presence of information. To explain the changes in the overall properties of complex systems, many new concepts for causal analysis are created, such as: downward causal, bidirectional causal, causal feedback, causal cycle, causal network and causal map etc., which all face the problem of the causal chain fracture between different and crossed layers in complex systems. Don't the interactions between the whole and parts or layers in a complex system like an organism follow the laws of physical causality?

4.1 The Change of Causal Ideas

The interactions between different and crossed layers lead to complex causal relations inside and outside the system (see Fig. 4). However, the traditional concept of causality (once questioned by David Hume) is a view of causality focusing only on inevitable connections, which attributes accidental connections to the defects of the cognitive ability of human being. In this way, the traditional view of causality cannot explain the complex causal relations of the hierarchy in complexity systems. The basic tenet of traditional determinism is to ensure the smooth flow of necessity and causal chain, it is to set the existence of the universal physical mechanism of "cause" and "result". However, life phenomena violate and do not exactly follow such a determinism. The mutual relationship between different layers and crossed layers inside and outside organisms appears in the form of coding. The same information content can have different material carriers, and the inevitable and accidental results of the interactions between layers can be transformed into information forms. Life exists as an "information entity", transforming and moving between different layers. In complexity systems like biological system, the interpretation of information causality is far greater than the traditional mechanical and statistical determinism, and the traditional view of causality yield to the view of information causality.

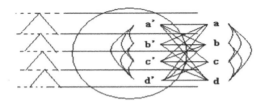

Fig. 4. Layers and complexity.

Information Causality. The existence of the material system hierarchy indicates that there are not only quantitative points of inflection, but also qualitative points of inflection between layers, which have relations of containing and being contained. The attributes of things having sudden or emergent characteristics in different layers cannot be normalized or restored, therefore, the unfolding form of causal relation of things between hierarchies is not traditional, eternal or universal. Based on mechanical and statistical decisions, the interactions between the layers develop special coding relations, representing the information causal connection, and the interaction turns to the "information causal form".

Causation Encoded and Information Causality Analysis. The causal connection (inevitable and accidental) of all layers and elements of material system is written into an encrypted form and stored in the carrier at various layers. The interactions of crossed layers are the initiator. A large number of accidental and inevitable connections can collide and intersect: The accidental connection at the same layer is transformed into the inevitable connection between different layers, which in turn restricts the accidental connection of the same layer, and the accidental connection between different layers can also be transformed into the inevitable connection of the same layer, so that any changes happened at all layers within the system are mutations or protrusions relative to the other layers and system as a whole. We are unable to find the direct (physical) cause for the results at another layer, and it is the locking of action by hierarchical interactions on randomness. The originally complex causal connection transforms into simple information connection (from certain point of view, information is a mapping of complex hierarchical relationships of matter systems). Complex causal relation of different and crossed-layer translates into "information causal relations" with coded form, and different hierarchies and attributes are the performance of information entities. This explains why the structure and attributes of different layers cannot be reduced and reducible between the layers, but can be unified through the transcription, translation and decoding of the information entity, then achieve the overall attributes of the system. The causal analysis of the complexity system is thus transformed into the "information causal analysis".

4.2 Information Entity

Information entity is the "model" of the overall attributes of the system, hidden in the intercommunication of different layers, existed according to the carriers, but independent of the carriers.

Information Entities Flow in the Material System. The information that encodes overall attributes of the material system is stored in various hierarchies, it is converted between different layers through interaction, layer by layer or across layers, by bottom up or top down. During the conversion process, the information carrier experiences different material forms.

The relationship between different layers in the material system is no longer a pure physical connection, but an information connection that encodes the material form. The phase transition (leap) between matter hierarchies has limited kinds of possibilities, it does not depend on mere mechanical decisions or the regulation of continuous functions, or mere the law of statistics, it also depends on the law of information. The transformation of matter forms at different layers depends on mutual complex connections. Erwin Schrödinger once pointed out that "genetics shows that there are many small, incredible atomic clusters, they are so small that are not enough to represent accurate statistical laws, but they definitely have dominant impact on the order and regular events within living organisms" [3, pp. 20–21], and predicted that there is an information entity in the activity.

Information Entities Remain Their Immutability in the Information Flow. Information entity that represents the overall attributes of the system (subsystem) has a certain autonomy or intrinsic regulation. No matter what the information carrier is, how it transforms, the information entity moving in different layers of the system through the hierarchical interaction must always maintain their own immutability, and the information content will not be easily changed, so that the system keeps the structure and the overall attributes stable to a certain extent. Information entities can be considered, in a sense, as attractors for the complex interactions of the components at various layers of the material system.

4.3   The Role of the Hierarchical Interactions

Over time, many inevitable and accidental interactions occur inside and outside the system. In this case, the change of various layers of the system must occur accordingly, which are usually locked by the hierarchy of the system, and the interaction between layers appears as the behavior of the information. A complex physical system is also an information-generating system, in which each layer can act as an information carrier, an information intermediary, an information generator and receiver, and a messenger, and the interaction between the layers plays the role of information encoding, communication, overcoming the change, loss or tampering, and error correction of the content in the process of information carrier conversion, thus ensuring the integrity of the information entity and the overall attributes of the system. The following Fig. 5 (see Fig. 5) shows how physical interactions between layers in complexity systems become information interactions, and why we say that information is a special form of interaction locked by the system hierarchy relationship.

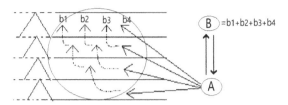

Fig. 5. Physical interactions are encoded by the hierarchical construction of the system.

5 Short Conclusion

There is no independent information in nature, and information is not pure objective reality. Information is the product of our human interpretation of a special form of interaction that occurs between different and crossed layers of complexity systems in nature. Information and the other related concepts and terms describe only a form of interaction in nature that can (or can only) be understood and operated by the spirit. The existence of information is inseparable from our deep understanding to the human cultural signaling and complexity systems. A causal interpretation of information on interactions between layers of complexity systems not only broadens traditional causal beliefs, but also makes AI possible.

Plato's Epinomis thinks hermeneutics as a guess of the will of God from symbolic symbols. Then, information as a form of interaction between the layers of material complex systems is a successful guess by scientists.

References

1. Aristoteles: Metaphysics, Chinese Version, Translation by Litian Miao, pp.156–157. China People's Press, Beijing (2003)
2. Pattersson, M.: Complexity and Evolution, pp. 1–8. Cambridge university Press, Cambridge (1996)
3. Schrodinger, E.: What Is Life? The Physical Aspect of the Living Cell, Chinese version, Translation by Shanghai Foreign Natural Science Philosophy Works Compilation and Group, pp. 20–21; p. 23. Shanghai People's Press, Shanghai (1973)
4. Wang, Z.: Cognitive complexity and the 'supports' of modeling. In: Magnani, L. (ed.) Texts in Logic Volume 2: Model Based Reasoning in Science and Engineering, pp. 249–263. King's College Publications, London, UK (2006)
5. Wang, Z.: Mutation and Evolution, pp. 109–112; 123–124. Guangdong Higher Education Publishing House, Guangzhou (1993)
6. Wiener, N.: Cybernetics or Control and Communication in the Animal and the Machine, 2nd edn., p. 182. The MIT Press, Cambridge (2019)
7. Wimsatt, W.C.: Complexity and organization. In: Grene, M., Mendelsohn, E. (eds.) Topics in the Philosophy of Biology. Reidel, Dordrecht-Boston (1976)

Remote Sensing Images

Deep Siamese Network with Contextual Transformer for Remote Sensing Images Change Detection

Mengxuan Zhang[1], Zhao Liu[1], Jie Feng[1], Licheng Jiao[1], and Long Liu[2(✉)]

[1] Key Laboratory of Intelligent Perception and Image Understanding of Ministry of Education, School of Artificial Intelligence, Xidian University, Xi'an 710071, Shaanxi, China
[2] School of Electronic Engineering, Xidian University, Xi'an 710071, Shaanxi, China
lunar_xdun@163.com

Abstract. Change detection is one of the most important and challenging tasks in remote sensing images processing. Deep learning has gradually become one of the most popular technologies in remote sensing image change detection. Recently, the success of self-attention mechanism in computer vision provides new ideas for change detection task. In this paper, a new method based on deep siamese network with self-attention mechanism for bi-temporal remote sensing image change detection is proposed. In order to obtain more powerful image features, the contextual transformer module is added into the feature extractor. In order to make full use of the low-level and the high-level features from the feature extractor, the multi-scale fusion strategies are applied to integrate features. Furthermore, the obtained image features are input into the transformer to get more refined pixel-level features. The proposed model is testified on CCD dataset, and the results demonstrate its effectiveness.

Keywords: Change detection · Contextual transformer · Siamese network · Transformer

1 Introduction

With the development of remote sensing technology, remote sensing images have become a common data source for monitoring the Earth's surface [1]. Change detection is an effective task to observe changes in the Earth's surface, which aims to compare the surface differences in the same area at different times. It is widely used in the fields of land cover survey, natural disaster monitoring, resource exploration, environmental detection, and urban expansion [2].

This work was supported in part by the Natural Science Basic Research Program of Shaanxi (No. 2022JM-336), the Fundamental Research Funds for the Central Universities (No. XJS211906 and No. XJS210205), the Postdoctoral Science Foundation of China (No. 2018M633467).

© IFIP International Federation for Information Processing 2022
Published by Springer Nature Switzerland AG 2022
Z. Shi et al. (Eds.): ICIS 2022, IFIP AICT 659, pp. 193–200, 2022.
https://doi.org/10.1007/978-3-031-14903-0_21

Over the past few decades, the researchers have proposed various approaches to deal with the change detection task. The traditional change detection methods can be divided into three categories: the image arithmetic-based method, the image transformation-based method and the post-classification method. The image arithmetic-based methods generate the image change maps by comparing the pixel values directly and apply the thresholds to classify pixels into changing and invariant classes. Since the image arithmetic-based method is affected by radiation and noise easily, it is difficult to select an appropriate threshold. In the image transformation-based methods, the image spectral combination is converted into a specific feature space to distinguish the changed pixels. The post-classification is a supervised method which uses a trained classifier to classify two-phase images and compares the resulting feature maps pixel-by-pixel to obtain the change maps.

In recent years, the deep learning techniques have achieved a great success. With its powerful generalization ability, deep learning breaks the limitations of traditional algorithms. Therefore, many deep learning-based methods have been proposed in the field of remote sensing images change detection. Daudt et al. [3] proposed three U-Net-based Siamese networks, FC-EF, FC-Siam-Conc and FC-Siam-Diff. The FC-EF connects the bi-temporal images as a single input to the fully convolutional network. The FC-Siam-Conc contains two skip connections, which are concatenated in the decoding part for later fusion. The FC-Siam-Diff concatenates the absolute value of the difference of two skip connections. Liu et al. [4] proposed LGPNet with a local and global pyramid-structured feature extractor. The local and global feature pyramid module capture buildings of different scales from multiple perspectives and avoid to miss the buildings of different scales and shapes. Peng et al. [5] proposed an improved U-Net++ model. A deep supervised module is applied to capture subtle changes in challenging scenes. Chen et al. [6] proposed a spatial-temporal attention neural network with two kinds of self-attention modules, a basic spatial-temporal attention module and a pyramid spatial-temporal attention module. Zhang et al. [7] proposed IFN. The VGG-16 is utilized to extract bi-temporal image features, then the channel and spatial attention modules are used in the decoder to concatenate image features. Furthermore, the intermediate layers of the IFN are trained with deep supervision. Fang et al. [8] proposed SNUNet, which is composed of the Siamese network and the NestedUNet. The channel attention module is utilized to refine the features in each level of the decoder.

Although the deep learning methods have made outstanding contributions to the development of change detection, there still exist some problem. To improve the performance of change detection, many existing change detection methods introduce an attention mechanism into the final prediction stage and the decoder. Unlike above methods, the self-attention module is added into the feature extractor to get refined feature representations in this paper. A deep Siamese network with contextual transformer (DSNCoT) for bi-temporal image change detection is proposed. In order to get more obvious and distinguishable features, the contextual transformer (CoT) [9] is integrated into the network to improve the ability of feature extraction. A transformer module [10] is adopted to add more useful spatial and semantic information so as to enhance the pixel-level features of the image.

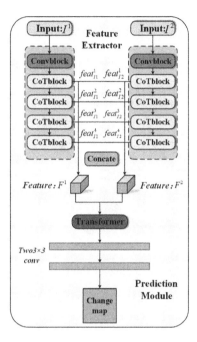

Fig. 1. The architecture of DSNCoT.

2   Methodology

As shown in Fig. 1, the proposed DSNCoT is a Siamese-based network, which contains three parts: Firstly, a weights-shared feature extractor to extract multi-scale features from bi-temporal images. Secondly, a transformer module excavates image pixel-level features, which is helpful to identify the change of interest and exclude irrelevant changes. Thirdly, a prediction module generates the final change map.

2.1   Feature Extractor

Given a set of bi-temporal images, a weight-sharing feature extractor is utilized to obtain the different levels of the features for each image. The feature extractor is designed on the basis of ResNet-50. The feature extractor consists of five stages. The first stage utilizes a convolutional layer with the kernel size 7×7 to extract the low-level features from the input image. Then, a 2×2 max-pooling layer with stride 2 is applied to resize the feature map to half the size of the input

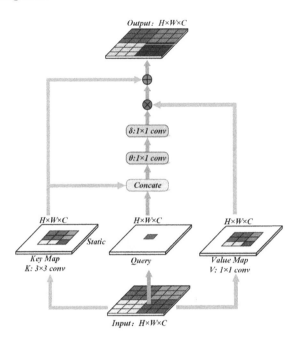

Fig. 2. The details of the CoT module.

image. Four bottleneck blocks constitute the remaining four stages. As shown in Fig. 2, all the 3×3 convolutional layers are replaced by the CoT [9] module in ResNet-50 which aims to improve the capability of feature extractor. The CoT module consists of two parts. The static contextual features are obtained by 3×3 convolution. Then, a new designed self-attention mechanism is used to integrate the static and the dynamic contextual features. Finally, the static and the dynamic contextual information are combined together. In order to make full use of the sufficient spatial information of the low-level features and semantic information of the high-level features, the nonlinear interpolation is utilized to integrate the features obtained at each stage.

2.2   Transformer Module

In order to get more obvious feature pairs, as shown in Fig. 3, the transformer [10] is introduced to make the feature pairs distinguish easily. The characteristics of the original pixel space are enhanced by using the relationship between each pixel and the semantic tokenizer. Firstly, the Siamese semantic tokenizer is utilized to extract compact semantic tokens from the feature map. Similar to the tokenizer of NLP, it splits the input sentence into several elements and represents each element with a token vector. The Siamese semantic tokenizer splits the feature maps from the feature extractor into a few visual words, and each word corresponds to one token vector. Then, the token vectors are transformed

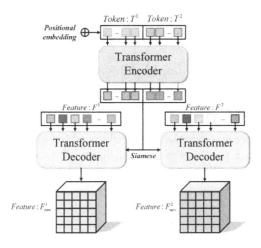

Fig. 3. The transformer module.

into sets of features in the spatial space, which are named as the token sets. Secondly, these token sets are input into a transformer encoder to model the context between each token so as to generate more context-rich token representations. Finally, the token representation output by the transformer encoder is input into the transformer decoder to obtain pixel space-level features.

2.3 Prediction Module

In this paper, a very shallow FCN is used for change discrimination. The FCN consists of two 3×3 convolutional layers with BatchNorm, and the output channels of each convolution are "32,2". We put the bi-temporal upsampling feature map $F_{new}^1, F_{new}^2 \in R^{H \times W \times C}$ obtained by DSNCoT into FCN to get the change map $P \in R^{H \times W \times 2}$, where H and W represents the height and width of the original image respectively. The formula can be written as follow:

$$P = \delta(f(D)) = \delta(f(F_{new}^1, F_{new}^2)) \tag{1}$$

where $D \in R^{H \times W \times C}$ is the absolute value of the element subtraction of the bi-temporal feature map. $f(\cdot)$ is the change classifier, where the number of output channels changes from C to 2. $\delta(\cdot)$ represents a softmax operation on the classifier output.

2.4 Details of Loss Function

Given a set of training image pairs and corresponding ground truth maps, the objective function is optimized to obtain accurate predictions. In change detection, the number of unchanged pixels is always much more than the number of changed pixels. In order to alleviate the influence of sample imbalance, the objective function is defined on two different loss functions in this paper.

In the training stage, we combine two loss functions to optimize the parameters of the entire network. The overall loss function is defined as follow:

$$L(X,Y) = L_{CE}(X,Y) + \lambda L_{DICE}(X,Y) \tag{2}$$

where X is the prediction map and Y is the ground truth map. L is the overall loss, L_{CE} is the cross-entropy loss and L_{DICE} is the dice loss. λ is the weight coefficient of dice loss which is set to 0.1.

The cross-entropy loss function is usually used for image classification. The change detection task can be viewed as a binary classification for partitioning the observed image into the changed and unchanged regions. The dice loss can alleviate the problem of sample imbalance. The above two loss function formulas are written as:

$$L_{CE}(X,Y) = \frac{1}{H \times W} \sum_{h=1,w=1}^{H,W} l(X_{hw}, Y_{hw}) \tag{3}$$

$$L_{DICE}(X,Y) = 1 - \frac{2\,|X \cap Y|}{|X| + |Y|} = 1 - \frac{1}{W} \sum_{w=1}^{W} \frac{2 \sum_{h=1}^{H} X_{h,w} Y_{h,w}}{\sum_{h=1}^{H} X_{h,w} + \sum_{h=1}^{H} Y_{h,w}} \tag{4}$$

where X_{hw} and Y_{hw} are the prediction map and the label map for the pixel at location (h, w) respectively. H and W are the height and width of the original image, respectively.

3   Experiment

3.1   Dataset

The CCD [11] dataset contains two types of image pairs, the artificially synthesized images and the remote sensing images. The remote sensing images are observed in our experiments. These real season-varying remote sensing images are obtained through the Google Earth API. The CCD dataset contains 16,000 remote sensing image pairs. The training set contains 10,000 pairs. The validation set and test set contain 3,000 pairs. The size of each image is 256×256, and the spatial resolution is 0.03–1 m/pixel.

3.2   Implementations

All of the experiments are completed by the PyTorch framework and a work station with GeForce RTX 3090 and 24 G memory. The stochastic gradient descent with momentum is used to optimize the model. The values of the momentum, the weight decay and the learning rate are set to 0.99, 0.0005 and 0.01 respectively. The entire model is trained for 200 epochs until it converges. To verify the effectiveness of the proposed model, five typical metrics are applied: precision (Pre), recall (Rec), F1-score (F1), intersection over union (IoU) and overall accuracy (OA).

Table 1. The numerical results on CCD dataset.

Method	Pre (%)	Rec (%)	F1 (%)	IoU (%)	OA (%)
FC-EF [3]	60.91	58.31	59.20	64.81	91.47
FC-EF-Conc [3]	70.92	60.32	63.71	66.46	92.52
FC-EF-Diff [3]	76.26	57.37	65.33	68.72	93.15
SNUNet [8]	92.07	84.64	88.20	78.69	97.33
IFN [7]	**97.46**	86.96	91.91	85.03	98.19
DSNCoT	96.88	**95.81**	**96.34**	**92.94**	**99.14**

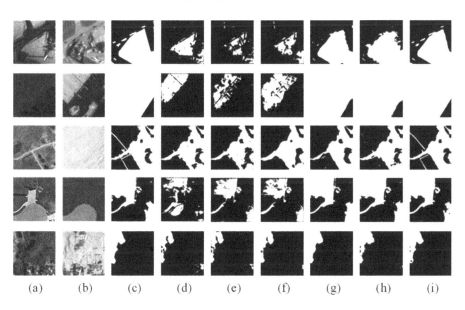

(a)   (b)   (c)   (d)   (e)   (f)   (g)   (h)   (i)

Fig. 4. Visualization results on CDD dataset: (a) the images at time1, (b) the images at time2, (c) the ground truth, (d) the results of FC-EF, (e) the results of FC-Siam-Conc, (f) the results of FC-Siam-Diff, (g) the result of IFN, (h) the results of SNUNet, (i) the results of the proposed model.

3.3   Results and Analyses

To show the effectiveness of our proposed DSNCoT, we compare it with five change detection methods, including the FC-EF [3], the FC-Siam-conc [3] and the FC-Siam-diff [3], the IFN [7] and the SNUNet [8]. All the numerical results are given in Table 1. It can be observed that the proposed DSNCoT model outperforms other five methods with higher values of Rec, F1, IoU and OA. The visualization results on the CCD dataset are shown in Fig. 4. FC-EF, FC-EF-diff and FC-EF-conc can capture the large-sized changing regions, but they neglect some small changes in the observed images. The IFN can get better change maps on the most change areas of large targets, but its ability to catch small targets is not good enough. Although the SNUNet can get the complete change regions in most cases, it is not sensitive to some edges in the change regions. The proposed DSNCoT can obtain both the complete large-scaled changing areas and the small changing areas, which include cars, roads, villages and new urban buildings.

4   Conclusion

In this paper, we propose a new deep learning method based on deep siamese network with self-attention mechanism for change detection of bi-temporal remote sensing images. The CoT module is introduced into the feature extractor to obtain bi-temporal image features with refined representations. The transformer module is added to model the bi-temporal image features at the pixel level, in order to obtain more refined bi-temporal image features. Compared with other five change detection methods, DSNCoT can detect more detailed changes and show better performance on the CCD dataset.

References

1. Hong, D., et al.: More diverse means better: multimodal deep learning meets remote-sensing imagery classification. IEEE Trans. Geosci. Remote Sens. **59**(5), 4340–4354 (2021)
2. Xiao, J., et al.: Evaluating urban expansion and land use change in Shijiazhuang, China, by using GIS and remote sensing. Landsc. Urban Plan. **75**(1), 69–80 (2006)
3. Daudt, C., et al.: Fully convolutional siamese networks for change detection. In: 2018 25th IEEE International Conference on Image Processing (ICIP), pp. 4063–4067 (2018)
4. Liu, T., et al.: Building change detection for VHR remote sensing images via local-global pyramid network and cross-task transfer learning strategy. IEEE Trans. Geosci. Remote Sens. **60**, 1–17 (2022)
5. Peng, D., et al.: End-to-end change detection for high resolution satellite images using improved UNet++. Remote Sens. **11**(11), 1382 (2019)
6. Chen, H., et al.: A spatial-temporal attention-based method and a new dataset for remote sensing image change detection. Remote Sens. **12**(10), 1662 (2020)
7. Zhang, C., et al.: A deeply supervised image fusion network for change detection in high resolution bi-temporal remote sensing images. ISPRS J. Photogramm. Remote. Sens. **166**, 183–200 (2020)
8. Fang, S., et al.: SNUNet-CD: a densely connected siamese network for change detection of VHR images. IEEE Geosci. Remote Sens. Lett. **19**, 1–5 (2022)
9. Li, Y., et al.: Contextual transformer networks for visual recognition. IEEE Trans. Pattern Anal. Mach. Intell. (2022). https://doi.org/10.1109/TPAMI.2022.3164083
10. Chen, H., et al.: Remote sensing image change detection with transformers. IEEE Trans. Geosci. Remote Sens. **60**, 1–14 (2022)
11. Lebedev, M., et al.: Change detection in remote sensing image using conditional adversarial networks, vol. 42, no. 2, pp. 565–571 (2018)

GSoP Based Siamese Feature Fusion Network for Remote Sensing Image Change Detection

Puhua Chen[✉] and Lu Wang

The Key Laboratory of Intelligent Perception and Image Understanding of Ministry of Education, School of Artificial Intelligence, Xidian University, Xi'an 710071, China
phchen@xidian.edu.cn

Abstract. Change detection is an important research direction for remote sensing image application. Finding the change location automatically is the goal, which could provide useful information for disaster evaluation, disaster evaluation or urban development planning etc. In this paper, a Siamese feature fusion network is designed for change detection, which applies GSoP, a kind of attentional mechanism, to fuse the information of two feature extraction branches. The feature fusion strategy could build an information bridge which could also ensure the uniqueness of each branch, but also realize the information interaction of them to give more attention to important features during feature learning procedure. In the experimental section, many experiments were designed on many public datasets with some related methods. The results were shown that the proposed Siamese fusion network was efficient for change detection and had obvious advantage than some related methods.

Keywords: Change detection · Siamese network · Attentional mechanism · Remote sensing image

1 Introduction

Chang detection is one typical research direction of remote sensing, which have so many application scenes, such as environmental monitoring, marine pollution monitor, urban development, disaster analysis and battle damage assessment etc. [1]. Although there are many decades of research on this topic, there still exist some problems appearing real application processing are not solved faultlessly. Firstly, remote sensing images used for change detection almost obtained from different sensors in different times, which could bring in many additional discrepancies to effect the change detection performance. Next, the difference of weather and season also may cause inaccurate change detection results. In addition, recently, many researchers focus into the change detection using different kinds of remote sensing sensors, such as optical sensor and SAR sensor. The difference of imaging mechanism may improve the difficulty of change detection. Therefore, to deal those problem for real applications of remote sensing technique, change detection still is a research topic of great research value.

© IFIP International Federation for Information Processing 2022
Published by Springer Nature Switzerland AG 2022
Z. Shi et al. (Eds.): ICIS 2022, IFIP AICT 659, pp. 201–213, 2022.
https://doi.org/10.1007/978-3-031-14903-0_22

Difference map generation and difference map segmentation are the key processing of typical change detection methods. Difference map could be obtained by many simple methods such as ratio method, similarity measurement methods [2] or feature transformation methods [3] etc. Difference map segmentation also could be realized by many methods such as threshold methods, clustering methods and Markov methods [4] etc. With the advent of deep learning, change detection also emerge a deep learning boom. Many change detection methods based on deep learning are proposed, which are clearly analyzed and classified in review papers [5]. The advantage of deep learning on feature learning also brings high change detection results.

Although many advanced deep learning methods like contrast learning or self-learning, end-to-end pattern also is the most famous learning pattern of deep learning. Under this pattern, based on labeled data, deep learning methods could obtain features with high discrimination ability. It's similar to the requirement of change detection to find better feature space for distinguishing changed pixels with unchanged pixels. For change detection, there are at least two temporal images and one classification output. So, the information of different image must be fused in the network. Siamese network is commonly network for change detection recently. Two temporal image are inputted into feature learning branches with same structure and then combine high level feature together for the following classification layer.

In this paper, we proposed a change detection method based on Siamese network, which denoted as GSoP based Siamese Feature Fusion Network. The purpose of this work was to enhance the information interaction/fusion of two feature learning branches. Global Second-order Pooling (GSoP) is one typical attention module, which were use to built the information bridge of them. Based on GSoP fusion model, important feature channel could obtain much more attention during feature learning process, of which the importance weights were computed from two feature maps together. In experimental section, comparing with Siamese ResNet-32 based method and ResNet-32 based method, the experimental results verified the feasibility of the proposed methods. The efficiency of it was also proved by comparing with related deep learning methods. We also analyzed the effect of fusion location in GSoP module for final performance.

2   Methodology

2.1   GSoP Module

In [6], GSoP module was proposed to learn the attention factor for each channel, which could obtain better performance than Global Average Pooling in many visual tasks. The structure of GSoP module is shown in Fig. 1. In this module, the core is 2nd-Order pool. Firstly, the input feature maps denoted as $I \in R^{h' \times w' \times c'}$ is transformed to $F \in R^{h' \times w' \times c}$ through convolution with 1×1 kernel. In this step, each channel of feature map F is treated as one random variable with $M = h' \times w'$ random independent samplings. Therefore, feature maps $F \in R^{h' \times w' \times c}$ can be represented as Eq. 1.

Fig. 1. The schematic diagram of GSoP.

$$F = \begin{bmatrix} F_{1,1} & F_{1,2} & \cdots & F_{1,c} \\ F_{2,1} & F_{2,2} & \cdots & F_{2,c} \\ \vdots & \vdots & \vdots & \vdots \\ F_{M,1} & F_{M,2} & \cdots & F_{M,c} \end{bmatrix} = [c_1, c_2, \cdots, c_c] \tag{1}$$

Then, the covariance matrix of F can be computed through Eq. 2, where I is a $M \times M$ matrix, of which whole elements are 1 and E is a $M \times M$ diagonal matrix.

$$CovMatrix = F^T \left[-\frac{1}{M \times M} I + \frac{1}{M} E \right] F \tag{2}$$

The covariance matrix contains the relevant information among c feature channels, which is better than average value to present the importance of channels. After that, considering the intrinsic structure information, covariance matrix is operated by row-wise convolution which is realized by group convolution with c group. The combination of row-wise convolution with 1×1 convolution is equivalent to depthwise separable convolution. Through the active layer with S function, the weight vector c × 1 is outputted to multiply with original feature map I. Through above options, feature learning process could give more attention to more important feature channels.

2.2 Information Fusion Based on GSoP

Here, three different information fusion models based on GSoP are proposed. The first fusion model is shown in Fig. 2. Feature maps of two branches are spliced on channel dimension and inputted into GSoP block. The final attention weights are computed on

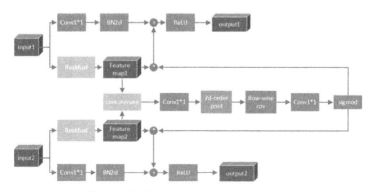

Fig. 2. The first information fusion model.

these feature maps through those operators in GSoP block, and then they are superposed into the original feature maps through channel weighting, which reflect the importance of each channel. Based on the weighting processing, feature learning processing could pay much attention on those more important feature channels. In this block, this attention computation can be treated as information fusion of two feature learning branches.

The first fusion model is shown in Fig. 3. In this model, the feature maps of two branches are changed the channel number through 1×1 convolution respectively and reshaped as same as GSoP module mentioned above. Then, these reshaped feature maps are concatenated together to computed the important weight and jointed into the original feature maps of two branches.

The third fusion model is shown in Fig. 4. Feature maps of two branches are concatenated after 1×1 convolution, reshaping and second-order pooling operators to compute the important weight.

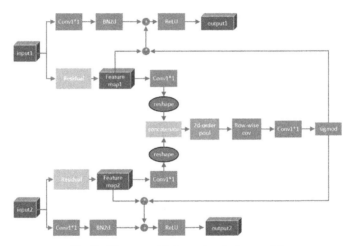

Fig. 3. The second information fusion model.

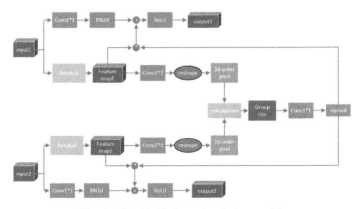

Fig. 4. The third information fusion model.

In above contents, three information fusion model were introduced, which could fuse different information from different images of same scene. The information fusion was mainly realized by the attention weight computation based on GSoP. The difference of those three models is the concatenation of two branch information is operated in different stages of GSoP. In the experimental section, some experiments were designed to evaluate the performance of them.

2.3 Siamese Feature Fusion Network with GSoP for Change Detection

In this work, ResNet-32 [7] was chosen as the basic network framework, which have three Layers one of which contains 5 residual blocks with two convolution operators respectively. Here, aiming to verify the performance of information fusion for change detection, original change detection framework based on ResNet-32 and Siamese ResNet-32 are also discussed, which are shown in Fig. 5 and Fig. 6. In Fig. 5, there is just a data fusion, where two different images are treated as different data channel and learn features synthetically. In Fig. 6, two different images have their own feature learning network and finally learned features are fused together for the next classification.

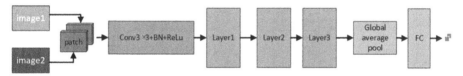

Fig. 5. The schematic diagram of ResNet-32 for change detection.

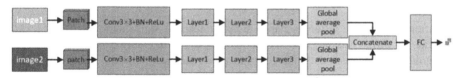

Fig. 6. The schematic diagram of Siamese ResNet-32 for change detection.

Although the method based on Siamese ResNet-32 have two feature learning branches for two different images, there is not any information interaction or information fusion among the feature learning processing. In this paper, a Siamese Feature Fusion Network based on GSoP is proposed for change detection, of which the schematic diagram is shown in Fig. 7. Different from the above methods, the Layers of two branches are not independently, they are connected with each other by using GSoP moduel. Because of this procedure, two advantage could be obtained. First, attention mechanism is involved into feature learning, which could promote the performance. Second, it builds the information bridge of two feature learning branches and could enhance information fusion degree to obtain better results.

In the proposed Siamese fusion network for change detection, GSoP fusion model described in above subsection is applied in each Layer shown in Fig. 8. Just the last residual blocks are replaced by GSoP fusion model of each Layer.

For change detection, Siamese fusion network shown in Fig. 7 are firstly trained on training data of which each data/pixel are labeled as unchanged/0 or changed/1. The rest pixels are testing data. For testing data, the classification probability could be obtained from trained Siamese fusion network. Commonly, the change probability map is treated as difference map.

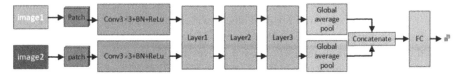

Fig. 7. The schematic diagram of Siamese fusion network based on ResNet-32 for change detection.

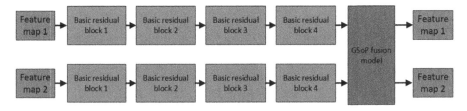

Fig. 8. The schematic diagram of each Layer in Siamese fusion network.

After obtained the different map, a simple threshold segmentation method is used to divide the difference map into two data sets. Pixels with higher difference value than threshold are distinguished as changed pixels and pixels with lower difference value are distinguished as unchanged pixels.

3 Experiments and Analysis

In this section, aiming to verify the performance of the proposed Siamese fusion network based on GSoP, three public datasets are chosen and DNN based change detection method [8], CNN-LSTM based method [9], ResNet-32 based method and Siamese ResNet-32 based method are also involved in experiments as comparing methods.

3.1 Dataset Introduction and Experiments Setting

There were many public datasets for change detection. In this paper, Tiszadob-3 Dataset, Szada-2 Dataset, QuickBird-1 Dataset and Shuguang Village Dataset were chosen as experimental datasets, which are usually used to verify performance in related works.

Tiszadob-3 Dataset and Szada-2 Dataset were selected from SZTAKI AirChange Bench-mark [10], of which the spatial resolution was 1.5 m. Tiszadob-3 Dataset displayed the areas changing from one kind of vegetation to another vege-tation, which is obvious in two images. However, Szada/2 only labeled areas changing from vegetation to human-made ones, such as roads, buildings and places. QuickBird-1 Dataset was provided by the Data Innovation Competition of Guangdong Government, which was captured in 2015 and 2017. Shuguang Village Dataset is a heterogeneous data which involves two images captured in different time by different imaging sensors. Original images obtained in different times and the ground truthing of those three datasets were shown in Fig. 9, Fig. 10, Fig. 11 and Fig. 12 respectively.

In experiments, 400 changed samples and 1600 unchanged samples were chosen randomly for network training. The size of image patch was set to be 10×10. The preliminary learning rate was set to be 0.001 and reduced into 0.1 percentage of original value per 80 iterations. The maximum iteration number was 200. The whole network was built on The PyTorch framework and running in the computer with NVIDA GeForce RTX2060.

For well evaluating the performance of those methods, five numerical indexes were utilized in experiments. It contains Precision rate (Pre), Recall rate (Rec), Accuracy rate (Acc), Kappa coefficient (Kappa) and F1 coefficient. Those numerical indexes could verify the performance of each method across-the-board.

(a)   (b)   (c)

Fig. 9. Tiszadob-3 dataset. (a) is the image obtained in time 1; (b) is the image obtained in time 2; (c) is the ground truthing.

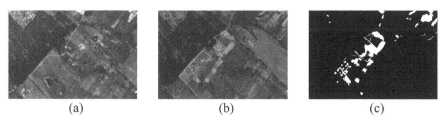

(a)   (b)   (c)

Fig. 10. Szada-2 dataset. (a) is the image obtained in time 1; (b) is the image obtained in time 2; (c) is the ground truthing.

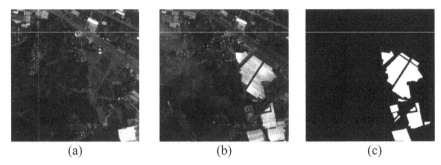

(a)   (b)   (c)

Fig. 11. QuickBird-1 dataset. (a) is the image obtained in time 1; (b) is the image obtained in time 2; (c) is the ground truthing.

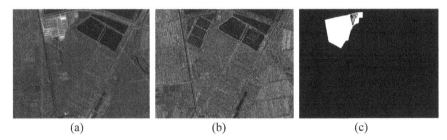

(a)   (b)   (c)

Fig. 12. Shuguang Village dataset. (a) is the image obtained in time 1 by optical sensor; (b) is the image obtained in time 2 by SAR sensor; (c) is the ground truthing.

3.2   Experimental Results and Analysis

In this subsection, experimental results on above three datasets were shown and analyzed. For Tiszadob-3 dataset, the change detection maps obtained by different methods were shown in Fig. 13. Model-1, Model-2 and Model-3 were the proposed Siamese fusion network with different fusion models described in Subsect. 2.2. Most of changes shown in ground truthing were detected by those methods. However, each method had more or less false detection or leak detection. For clearly analyzing the results, Table 1 gave the numerical index results. By analyzing these results, the proposed fusion models could obtain better results because of the advantage shown on Most indicators such as Rec, Acc, Kappa and F1.

Results on Szada-2 dataset were shown in Fig. 14 and Table 2. Comparing these change detection maps in Fig. 14, less unchanged pixels were detected as changed pixels about these proposed methods (Model-1, Model-2 and Model-3) than other threes comparing methods. In addition, the leak detection of changed pixels also was lower of these proposed methods. The proposed methods with feature fusion strategy could obtain better performance than others, which also was verified by those numerical results shown in Table 2.

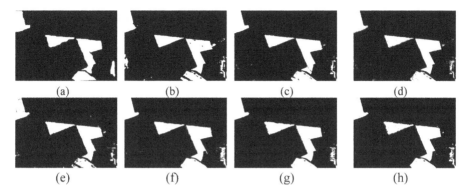

Fig. 13. Experimental results on Tiszadob-3 dataset. (a) ground trothing, (b) DNN, (c) CNN-LSTM, (d) ResNet-32, (e) Siam-ResNet-32, (f) Model-1, (g) Model-2, (h) Model-3.

Table 1. Numerical index results on Tiszadob-3 dataset.

Methods	Pre	Rec	Acc	Kappa	F1
DNN	0.606	0.624	0.955	0.615	0.591
CNN-LSTM	0.930	0.939	0.981	0.935	0.923
Resnet-32	**0.931**	0.919	0.978	0.925	0.912
Siam-ResNet-32	0.914	0.914	0.975	0.914	0.899
Model-1	0.913	**0.971**	0.982	0.941	0.931
Model-2	0.922	0.967	**0.983**	**0.944**	**0.934**
Model-3	0.927	0.955	0.982	0.941	0.930

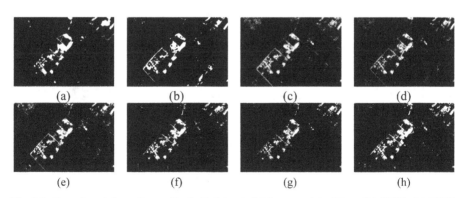

Fig. 14. Experimental results on Szada-2 dataset. (a) is ground trothing, (b) DNN, (c) CNN-LSTM, (d) ResNet-32, (e) Siam-ResNet-32, (f) Model-1, (g) Model-2, (h) Model-3.

Table 2. Numerical index results on Szada-2 dataset.

Methods	Pre	Rec	Acc	Kappa	F1
DNN	0.606	0.624	0.955	0.615	0.591
CNN-LSTM	0.532	0.690	0.947	0.601	0.573
ResNet-32	0.639	0.623	0.958	0.631	0.609
Siam-ResNet-32	0.550	0.693	0.950	0.613	0.587
Model-1	**0.726**	0.731	**0.969**	**0.728**	**0.712**
Model-2	0.682	**0.758**	0.966	0.718	0.700
Model-3	0.708	0.707	0.966	0.707	0.690

Results on QuickBird-1 dataset were given in Fig. 15 and Table 3. In this dataset, the ground trothing showed the changes from soil to building, which was obvious in original images. In those change detection maps of DNN, LSTM Resnet32 and Siam-Resnet, there were many false detection pixels in the left part. But, in the changed area, more changed pixels were not accurately detected. In numerical index results, just Siam-Resnet obtained the better results than proposed methods only on Rec. On other numerical indexes, proposed methods had obvious advantage performance than others.

Shuguang Village Dataset contains two heterogeneous images obtained by different sensors. The difference of imaging mechanism enhanced the difference of images, which would make change detection more difficult than homologous images. The change detection results on Shuguang Village Dataset were given in Fig. 16 and Table 4. Because the results of DNN was too bad than other methods, we ignored it on this dataset. Observed from change detection maps in Fig. 16, the detection results of CNN-LSTM, ResNet-32

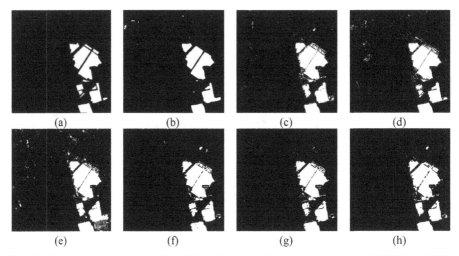

Fig. 15. Experimental results on QuickBird-1 Dataset. (a) is ground trothing, (b) DNN, (c) CNN-LSTM, (d) ResNet-32, (e) Siam-ResNet-32, (f) Model-1, (g) Model-2, (h) Model-3.

and Siam-ResNet-32 were better in the outside of the changed area. However, in the inside of the change area, there were some unchanged pixels, which were not detected by them. However, those proposed methods could still detect them. Observed form those numerical results shown in Table 4, those proposed methods had obvious advantages on Pre, Rec, Kappa and F1.

Table 3. Numerical index results on QuickBird-1 dataset.

Methods	Pre	Rec	Acc	Kappa	F1
DNN	0.606	0.624	0.955	0.615	0.591
CNN-LSTM	0.835	0.906	0.972	0.869	0.853
ResNet-32	0.819	0.894	0.968	0.855	0.837
Siam-ResNet-32	0.745	**0.917**	0.959	0.822	0.799
Model-1	0.869	0.887	0.974	0.878	0.863
Model-2	**0.877**	0.883	**0.975**	0.880	0.866
Model-3	0.865	0.901	**0.975**	**0.883**	**0.869**

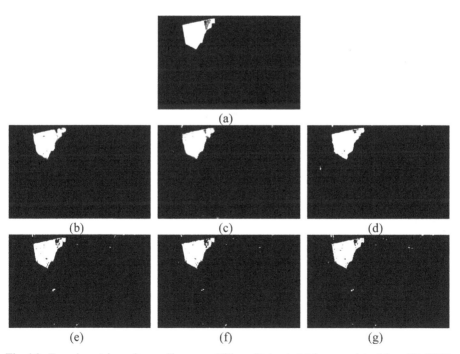

Fig. 16. Experimental results on Shuguang Village Dataset. (a) is ground trothing, (b) CNN-LSTM, (c) ResNet-32, (d) Siam-ResNet-32, (e) Model-1, (f) Model-2, (g) Model-3.

From these results shown in Table 1, Table 2, Table 3 and Table 4, we found that the proposed three different fusion models had obtained better results than those comparing methods. Especially, the comparison with ResNet-32 and Siam-ResNet-32 had shown that the information fusion between two feature learning branches could promote the performance of change detection. However, we also found that the performance difference of Model-1, Model-2 and Model-3 was not very remarkable. Therefore, we considered that the information fusion based on GSoP was efficient but the stages where fusion operated were not important for the final performance.

Table 4. Numerical index results on Shuguang Village Dataset.

Methods	Pre	Rec	Acc	Kappa	F1
CNN-LSTM	0.893	0.899	0.992	0.896	0.892
ResNet-32	0.884	0.822	0.988	0.852	0.846
Siam-ResNet-32	**0.954**	0.869	0.993	0.909	0.906
Model-1	0.941	**0.957**	**0.996**	**0.949**	**0.947**
Model-2	0.953	0.936	**0.996**	0.944	0.942
Model-3	0.930	0.958	0.995	0.943	0.941

4 Conclusion

In this work, considering the importance of information fusion of feature extraction for change detection, a Siamese fusion network for change detection was proposed, which utilized GSoP to construct the information fusion model. Experimental results verified the efficient of information fusion compared with related methods. However, the performance relied on labeled samples which involved high labor cost. In the future, self-supervised learning combined with fewer human guidance for changed detection would be valuable to be researched deeply.

References

1. Ban, Y., Yousif, O.: Change detection techniques: a review. In: Ban, Y. (ed.) Multitemporal Remote Sensing. RSDIP, vol. 20, pp. 19–43. Springer, Cham (2016). https://doi.org/10.1007/978-3-319-47037-5_2
2. An, L., Li, M., Zhang, P., et al.: Multicontextual mutual information data for SAR image change detection. IEEE Geosci. Remote Sens. Lett. **12**(9), 1863–1867 (2015)
3. Seto, K.C., Woodcock, C.E., Song, C., et al.: Monitoring land-use change in the pearl river delta using Landsat TM. Int. J. Remote Sens. **23**(10), 1985–2004 (2020)
4. Yusif, O., Ban, Y.: Improving SAR-based urban change detection by combining MAP-MRF classifier and nonlocal means similarity weights. IEEE J. Sel. Top. Appl. Earth Observ. Remote Sens. **7**(10), 4288–4300 (2014)

5. Khelifi, L., Mignotte, M.: Deep learning for change detection in remote sensing images: comprehensive review and meta-analysis. IEEE Access **8**, 126385–126400 (2020)
6. Gao, Z., Xie, J., Wang, Q., et al.: Global second-order pooling convolutional networks. In: 2019 IEEE/CVF Conference on Computer Vision and Pattern Recognition (2019)
7. He, K., Zhang, X., Ren, S., et al.: Deep residual learning for image recognition. In: Proceedings of the IEEE Conference on Computer Vision and Pattern Recognition (2016)
8. Gong, M., Zhao, J., Liu, J., et al.: Change detection in synthetic aperture radar images based on deep neural networks. IEEE Trans. Neural Netw. Learn. Syst. **27**(1), 125–138 (2017)
9. Mou, L., Bruzzone, L., Zhu, X.X.: Learning spectral-spatial-temporal features via a recurrent convolutional neural network for change detection in multispectral imagery. IEEE Trans. Geosci. Remote Sens. **57**(2), 924–935 (2018)
10. SZTAKI AirChange Benchmark. http://web.eee.sztaki.hu/remotesensing/airchange_benchmark.html

PolSF: PolSAR Image Datasets on San Francisco

Xu Liu(⊠), Licheng Jiao, Fang Liu, Dan Zhang, and Xu Tang

Xidian University, Xi'an, Shannxi, China
xuliu361@163.com

Abstract. Polarimetric SAR data has the characteristics of all-weather, all-time and so on, which is widely used in many fields. However, the data of annotation is relatively small, which is not conducive to our research. In this paper, we have collected five open polarimetric SAR images, which are images of the San Francisco area. These five images come from different satellites at different times, and has great scientific research value. We annotate the collected images at the pixel level for image classification and segmentation. For the convenience of researchers, the annotated data is open source https://github.com/liuxuvip/PolSF.

Keywords: PolSAR image · Classification · Segmentation

1 Introduction

With the development of sensors, studying their differences and characteristics are significative research topics [1]. Different sensors produce different characteristics of data and images. That is to say, each kind of data has its own characteristics and advantages. Making full use of these data is significative and challenging.

In the literature, polarimetric SAR image classification is a hot topic [2–8]. polarimetric SAR image classification is also a pixel level remote sensing image

Supported in part by the Key Scientific Technological Innovation Research Project by Ministry of Education, the National Natural Science Foundation of China Innovation Research Group Fund (61621005), the State Key Program and the Foundation for Innovative Research Groups of the National Natural Science Foundation of China (61836009), the Major Research Plan of the National Natural Science Foundation of China (91438201, 91438103, and 91838303), the National Natural Science Foundation of China (U1701267, 62076192, 62006177, 61902298, 61573267, and 61906150), the Fund for Foreign Scholars in University Research and Teaching Program's 111 Project (B07048), the Program for Cheung Kong Scholars and Innovative Research Team in University (IRT 15R53), the ST Innovation Project from the Chinese Ministry of Education, the Key Research and Development Program in Shaanxi Province of China (2019ZDLGY03-06), the National Science Basic Research Plan in Shaanxi Province of China (2019JQ-659, 2022JQ-607).

Z. Shi et al. (Eds.): ICIS 2022, IFIP AICT 659, pp. 214–219, 2022.
https://doi.org/10.1007/978-3-031-14903-0_23

interpretation task, which has the characteristics of fine recognition and need to determine the category of each pixel.

Polarimetric SAR image classification tasks can be divided into unsupervised classification, semi-supervised classification and supervised classification according to the label of training data. According to the quality of the label, it can be divided into strong supervised learning and weak supervised learning, the latter includes incomplete supervised learning, inexact supervised learning and inaccurate supervised learning [9]. Therefore, it can adopt different learning methods and ideas to deal with polarimetric SAR image classification problems. However, there are very few labeled data that can be used in practical research.

In this paper, we introduced the data and gave our labeled ground truth. To meet the needs of researchers. First, we download the original data from the website [10]. Second, we use the ESA PolSARpro v6.0 (Biomass Edition) software [11, 12] read the original data files and get the PauliRGB images. Third, we get the high-resolution Google map of the same period, mark the image with its information by the labelme software [13]. Finally, the marked color map is remapped and encoded to get the mark file. In the following chapters, dataset details will be introduced (Fig.1).

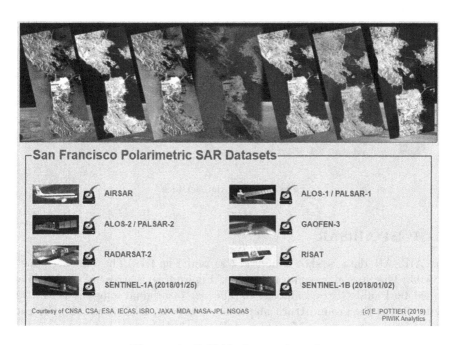

Fig. 1. The PolSAR data in the web.

2   PolSF

In this section, the PolSAR dataset *PolSF* is presented [See Fig. 4]. The original PolSAR data is downloaded the IETR website [See Fig. 4] [10]. We select five the PolSAR data of five satellites for the San Francisco area, cut and mark the adjacent area. Figure 2 show different raw data packages, these data are uploaded in August 9th, 2019. In addition, we can see from Fig. 3 that the data formats of different satellite imaging are different. Table 1 also give the details of the satellites.

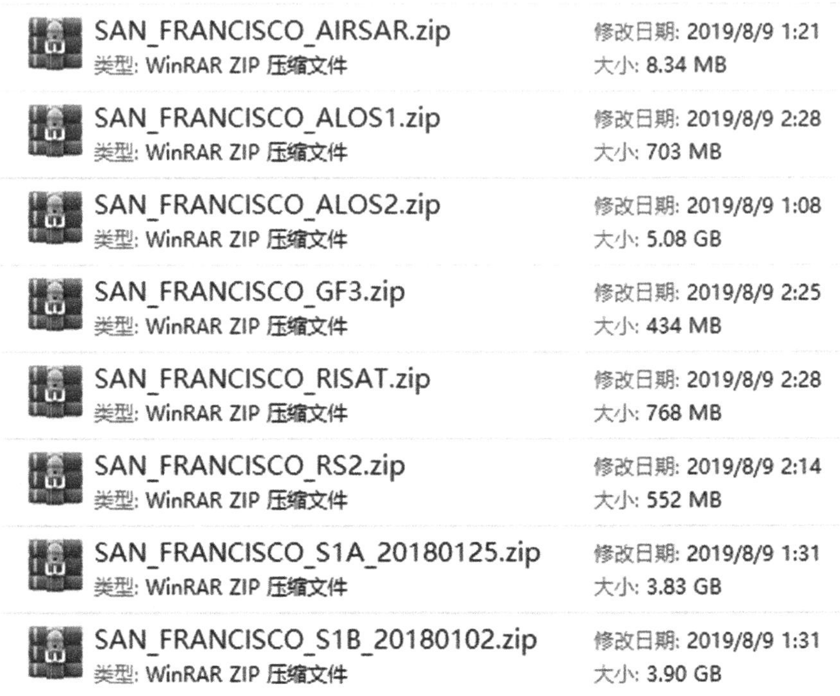

SAN_FRANCISCO_AIRSAR.zip   修改日期: 2019/8/9 1:21
类型: WinRAR ZIP 压缩文件   大小: 8.34 MB

SAN_FRANCISCO_ALOS1.zip   修改日期: 2019/8/9 2:28
类型: WinRAR ZIP 压缩文件   大小: 703 MB

SAN_FRANCISCO_ALOS2.zip   修改日期: 2019/8/9 1:08
类型: WinRAR ZIP 压缩文件   大小: 5.08 GB

SAN_FRANCISCO_GF3.zip   修改日期: 2019/8/9 2:25
类型: WinRAR ZIP 压缩文件   大小: 434 MB

SAN_FRANCISCO_RISAT.zip   修改日期: 2019/8/9 2:28
类型: WinRAR ZIP 压缩文件   大小: 768 MB

SAN_FRANCISCO_RS2.zip   修改日期: 2019/8/9 2:14
类型: WinRAR ZIP 压缩文件   大小: 552 MB

SAN_FRANCISCO_S1A_20180125.zip   修改日期: 2019/8/9 1:31
类型: WinRAR ZIP 压缩文件   大小: 3.83 GB

SAN_FRANCISCO_S1B_20180102.zip   修改日期: 2019/8/9 1:31
类型: WinRAR ZIP 压缩文件   大小: 3.90 GB

Fig. 2. PolSF dataset files.

2.1 PolSF-AIRSAR

The AIRSAR data is shown in Fig. 4(a) and Fig. 4(f). The imaging time is 1989.08. The spatial resolution is 10 m. Figure 4(a) is a pseudo color image formed by PauliRGB decomposition. The size of original image is 1024×900. Figure 4(b) is the ground truth marked by our team IPIU, there are five categories of objectives. i.e. 1, Mountain, 2, Water, 3, Urban, 4, Vegetation, 5, Bare soil.

2.2 PolSF-ALOS2

The ALOS2 data is shown in Fig. 4(b) and Fig. 4(g). The imaging time is 2015.03. The spatial resolution is 18 m. The size of original image is 8080×22608, the coordinates of cut region is (x1:736, y1:2832, x2:3520, y2:7888), which is the coordinates of the upper left corner and the lower right corner. Figure 4(a) is a pseudo color image formed by PauliRGB decomposition. Figure 4(b) is the ground truth marked by our team IPIU, there are six categories of objectives. i.e. 1, Mountain, 2, Water, 3, Vegetation, 4, High-Density Urban, 5, Low-Density Urban, 6, Developed.

Fig. 3. The data format in each satellite.

2.3   PolSF-GF3

The GF3 data is shown in Fig. 4(c) and Fig. 4(h). The imaging time is 2018.08. The spatial resolution is 8 m. The size of original image is 5829 × 7173, the coordinates of cut region is (1144, 3464, 3448, 6376). Figure 4(a) is a pseudo color image formed by PauliRGB decomposition. Figure 4. (b) is the ground truth marked by our team IPIU, there are six categories of objectives. i.e. 1, Mountain, 2, Water, 3, Vegetation, 4, High-Density Urban, 5, Low-Density Urban, 6, Developed.

2.4   PolSF-RISAT

For this image, the size of original image is 8719 × 13843, the coordinates of cut region is (2486, 4257, 7414, 10648). The RISAT data is shown in Fig. 4(d) and Fig. 4(i). The imaging time is 2016.08. The spatial resolution is 2.33 m. Figure 4(a) is a pseudo color image formed by PauliRGB decomposition. Figure 4(b) is the ground truth marked by our team IPIU, there are six categories of objectives. i.e. 1, Mountain, 2, Water, 3, Vegetation, 4, High-Density Urban, 5, Low-Density Urban, 6, Developed.

2.5   PolSF-RS2

The RS2 data is shown in Fig. 4(e) and Fig. 4(j). The size of original image is 2823 × 14416, the coordinates of cut region is (7326,661,9125,2040). The imaging

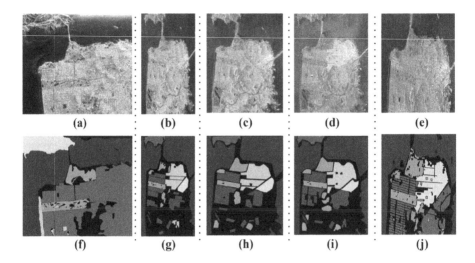

Fig. 4. PolSF Dataset visualization and annotation. (a)–(e), PauliRGB image of SF-AIRSAR, SF-ALOS2, SF-GF3, SF-RISAT and SF-RS2. (f)–(j), Color ground truth of SF-AIRSAR, SF-ALOS2, SF-GF3, SF-RISAT and SF-RS2.

time is 2008.04. The spatial resolution is 8 m. Figure 4(a) is a pseudo color image formed by PauliRGB decomposition. Figure 4(b) is the ground truth, there are five categories of objectives. i.e. 1, Water, 2, Vegetation, 3, High-Density Urban, 4, Low-Density Urban, 5, Developed.

Table 1. The details of each image.

Sensors	Time	Resolution	Dimensions	Class	PolarType
SF-AIRSAR	1989.08	10m	1024*900	5	full
SF-ALOS2	2015.03	18m	2784*5056	6	full
SF-GF3	2018.08	8m	2304*2912	6	full
SF-RISAT	2016.08	2.33m	4928*6391	6	ppl
SF-RS2	2008.04	8m	1380*1800	5	full

3   Conclusions

In this paper, we have published five image marker maps. These five images come from different satellites and have different data characteristics. There are similarities in the changes. They are suitable for further scientific research, such as single source image pixel level classification, multi-source image pixel level fusion classification, etc.

Acknowledgments. The authors would like to thank IETR provide the PolSAR data.

References

1. Chen, B., Huang, B., Bing, X.: Multi-source remotely sensed data fusion for improving land cover classification. ISPRS J. Photogramm. Remote. Sens. **124**, 27–39 (2017)
2. Liu, X., Licheng Jiao, X., Tang, Q.S., Zhang, D.: Polarimetric convolutional network for PolSAR image classification. IEEE Trans. Geosci. Remote Sens. **57**(5), 3040–3054 (2019)
3. Zhang, Z., Wang, H., Feng, X., Jin, Y.-Q.: Complex-valued convolutional neural network and its application in polarimetric SAR image classification. IEEE Trans. Geosci. Remote Sens. **55**(12), 7177–7188 (2017)
4. Guo, Y., Jiao, L., Wang, S., Wang, S., Liu, F., Hua, W.: Fuzzy superpixels for polarimetric SAR images classification. IEEE Trans. Fuzzy Syst. **26**(5), 2846–2860 (2018)
5. Bi, H., Sun, J., Xu, Z.: Unsupervised PolSAR image classification using discriminative clustering. IEEE Trans. Geosci. Remote Sens. **55**(6), 3531–3544 (2017)
6. Chen, S., Tao, C.: PolSAR image classification using polarimetric-feature-driven deep convolutional neural network. IEEE Geosci. Remote Sens. Lett. **15**(4), 627–631 (2018)
7. Liu, F., Jiao, L., Hou, B., Yang, S.: Pol-SAR image classification based on Wishart DBN and local spatial information. IEEE Trans. Geosci. Remote Sens. **54**(6), 3292–3308 (2016)
8. Yin, Q., Hong, W., Zhang, F., Pottier, E.: Optimal combination of polarimetric features for vegetation classification in PolSAR image. IEEE J. Sel. Top. Appl. Earth Obs. Remote Sens. **12**(10), 3919–3931 (2019)
9. Zhou, Z.-H.: A brief introduction to weakly supervised learning. Natl. Sci. Rev. **5**(1), 44–53 (2017)
10. San Francisco Polarimetric SAR Datasets. https://www.ietr.fr/polsarpro-bio/san-francisco/
11. Pottier, E., Sarti, F., Fitrzyk, M., Patruno, J.: PolSARpro-biomass edition: the new ESA polarimetric SAR data processing and educational toolbox for the future ESA & third party fully polarimetric SAR missions (2019)
12. The ESA PolSARpro v6.0 (Biomass Edition) Software. https://www.ietr.fr/polsarpro-bio/
13. LabelMe: the open annotation tool. http://labelme.csail.mit.edu/Release3.0/

RSMatch: Semi-supervised Learning with Adaptive Category-Related Pseudo Labeling for Remote Sensing Scene Classification

Weiquan Lin$^{(\boxtimes)}$, Jingjing Ma, Xu Tang, Xiangrong Zhang, and Licheng Jiao

School of Artificial Intelligence, Xidian University, Shaanxi 710071, China
3518076613@qq.com

Abstract. Remote sensing scene classification (RSSC) has become a hot and challenging research topic in recent years due to its wide applications. Due to the development of convolutional neural networks (CNN), the data-driven CNN-based methods have achieved expressive performance in RSSC. However, the lack of labeled remote sensing scene images in real applications make it difficult to further improve their performance of classification. To address this issue, we propose a novel adaptive category-related pseudo labeling (ACPL) strategy for semi-supervised scene classification. Specifically, ACPL flexibly adjusts thresholds for different classes at each time step to let pass informative unlabeled data and their pseudo labels according to the model's learning status. Meanwhile, our proposed ACPL dose not introduce additional parameters or computation. We apply ACPL to FixMatch and construct our model RSMatch. Experimental results on UCM data set have indicated that our proposed semi-supervised method RSMatch is superior to its several counterparts for RSSC.

Keywords: Remote sensing scene classification (RSSC) · Adaptive category-related pseudo labeling (ACPL) · Semi-supervised method

1 Introduction

Remote sensing image scene classification (RSSC) plays an important role in a wide range of applications, such as scene classification, ship detection and change detection [1–3]. As a basic image understanding work, it has attracted increasing attention. RSSC aims at automatically assign high-level semantic labels to local areas of remote sensing images for achieving scene-level classification. Therefore, the core of RSSC lies in obtaining the discriminative features of high-resolution remote sensing scenes.

This work was funded in part by the National Natural Science Foundation of China (No. 62171332) and the Fundamental Research Funds for the Central Universities and the Innovation Fund of Xidian University.

© IFIP International Federation for Information Processing 2022
Published by Springer Nature Switzerland AG 2022
Z. Shi et al. (Eds.): ICIS 2022, IFIP AICT 659, pp. 220–227, 2022.
https://doi.org/10.1007/978-3-031-14903-0_24

Along with the development of deep learning [10], CNNs, trained on a large number of labeled data, show powerful feature learning ability. In RSSC community, CNNs-based methods gradually occupy the mainstream [4–6]. However, in real applications, it is hard and time-consuming to collect and annotate enough samples of unseen categories for our learning system to retrain while limited labeled samples and abundant unlabeled samples are relatively easy to obtain. Thus, a new machine learning technology, semi-supervised learning (SSL) [11], has been a hot research topic in the last decade. SSL algorithms provide a way to explore the latent patterns from unlabeled examples and thus improve the learning performance given a small number of labeled samples.

According to loss function and model design, SSL can be divided into generative methods, consistency regularization methods, graph-based methods, pseudo-labeling methods and hybrid methods. In RS community, for generative methods, Guo et al. [7] propose SAGGAN. A gating unit, a SAG module, and an Inception V3 branch are introduced into the discriminative network to enhance the discriminant capability for facilitating semi-supervised classification. For pseudo-labeling methods, Zhang et al. [8] introduced the center loss into a semi-supervised network (SSCL) by using the unlabeled samples to update centers. For hybrid methods, a pseudo labeling combined with consistency regularization is proposed [9] based on EfficientNet [12] (MSMatch) to achieve semi-supervised classification.

In this paper, based on the recent work, FixMatch [13], we upgrade it by replacing the fix threshold with an adaptive category-related strategy to obtain pseudo labels for unlabeled samples for semi-supervised RSSC. This operation is called ACPL, which takes the learning difficulties of different classes into account and thus achieves promising classification performance.

The rest of this paper is organized as follows, Sect. 2 introduces our proposed network in detail, Sect. 3 exhibits the experimental configurations and results, and conclusion are summarized in Sect. 4.

2   Proposed Method

2.1   Preliminary Knowledge

Consistency regularization is a simple but effective technique in SSL [11]. With the introduction of pseudo labeling techniques, the consistency regularization is converted from ℓ-2 loss [14] to an entropy minimization process [15], which is more suitable for the classification task. The improved consistency loss with pseudo labeling can be formulated as:

$$\frac{1}{\mu B} \sum_{i=1}^{\mu B} \mathbb{1}\left(\max\left(p\left(y\left|\alpha\left(u_i\right)\right)\right)\right) > \tau\right) H\left(\widehat{p}\left(y\left|\alpha\left(u_i\right)\right)\right), p\left(y\left|\alpha\left(u_1\right)\right)\right)\right), \quad (1)$$

where $\mathbb{1}\left(\cdot\right)$ is the indicator function, B is the batch size of labeled data, μ is the ratio of unlabeled data to labeled data, α is a random data augmentation, u_i denotes a batch of unlabeled data in an iteration, p represents the output probability of the model, H is cross-entropy, $\widehat{p}(y|\alpha(u_i))$ is the pseudo label and τ is the pre-defined threshold, which is used to mask out noisy unlabeled data that have low prediction confidence.

In FixMatch [13], weak augmentation operates on unlabeled data to generate artificial labels, which are then used as the target of strongly-augmented data. The unsupervised loss term based on consistency regularization between weakly-augmented and strongly-augmented data can be formulated as:

$$\frac{1}{\mu B}\sum_{i=1}^{\mu B}\mathbb{1}\left(\max\left(p\left(y|\alpha\left(u_i\right)\right)\right)>\tau\right)H\left(\widehat{p}\left(y|\alpha\left(u_i\right)\right),p\left(y|v\left(u_i\right)\right)\right), \tag{2}$$

where v is a strong augmentation function compared with weak augmentation α.

2.2   Adaptive Class-Related Pseudo Labeling

The framework of our proposed RSMatch is exhibited in Fig. 1. The main idea of our method is to use ACPL algorithm to upgrade the fixed threshold in FixMatch to adaptive category-related one and thus learns the scenes in RS data set that are difficult to be recognized better.

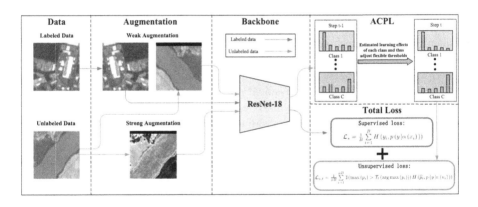

Fig. 1. Framework of our proposed RSMatch.

The threshold τ in Eq. 2 is a pre-defined scale, which implicitly forces Fix-Match treat the learning difficulty of each category in data set as same. However, different scenes always contain various volume of semantic information for model to learn. For example, in UCM data set[1], "dense residential", "medium residential", and "sparse residential" are difficult for model to recognize them because of the latent content in these scene images are similar.

To solve the limitation of FixMatch, we propose an adaptive class-related pseudo labeling strategy (ACPL) to adjust the thresholds according to the

---

[1] http://vision.ucmerced.edu/datasets/landuse.html.

model's learning status of each class. This operation allows the model to assign the pseudo labels to different classes at different time steps. Nevertheless, it does not introduce additional parameters.

Specifically, based on the assumption [13] that when the threshold is high, the learning effect of a class can be reflected by the number of samples whose predictions fall into this class and above the threshold, we can dynamically adjust the threshold according to the learning status estimated on learning effect, which can be formulated as:

$$\sigma_t(c) = \sum_{i=1}^{N} \mathbb{1}(\max(p_t(y \mid u_i)) > \tau) \cdot \mathbb{1}(\arg\max(p_t(y \mid u_i) = c)), \qquad (3)$$

where $\sigma_t(c)$ reflects the learning effect of class c at time step t. $p_t(y \mid u_i)$ is the model's prediction for unlabeled data u_i at time step t, and N is the total number of unlabeled data. After normalizing $\sigma_t(c)$ to make its range between 0 to 1, it can be used to scale the fixed threshold τ:

$$\beta_t(c) = \frac{\sigma_t(c)}{\max_c \sigma_t}, \qquad (4)$$

$$\mathcal{T}_t(c) = \beta_t(c) \cdot \tau, \qquad (5)$$

where $\mathcal{T}_t(c)$ is the flexible threshold for class c at time step t.

Note that because of the confirmation bias caused by the parameter initialization, the model may predict most unlabeled samples into a certain class mistakenly at this stage. Therefore, a warm-up operation is introduced to Eq. 5 as:

$$\beta_t(c) = \frac{\sigma_t(c)}{\max\left\{\max_c \sigma_t, N - \sum_{c=1}^{C} \sigma_t(c)\right\}}, \qquad (6)$$

where C is the number of categories per iteration. $N - \sum_{c=1}^{C} \sigma_t(c)$ can be regarded as the number of unlabeled data that have not been used. This ensures that at the beginning of the training, all estimated learning effects gradually rise from 0 until most unlabeled data participate in model training.

In addition to the issue we discussed above that will affect the performance of the model, another problem may contribute to an unstable model. In Eq. 5, the flexible threshold depends on the normalized estimated learning effects via a linear mapping. However, in the real training process, this linear mapping will sensitive to the change of $\beta_t(c)$ in the early stage when the predictions of the model are still unstable, and only make small fluctuations after the class is well-learned in mid and late training stage. Therefore, it is preferable if the flexible thresholds can be more sensitive when $\beta_t(c)$ is large and vice versa.

By rewriting the Eq. 5, a non-linear mapping function is used to enable the threshold to have a non-linear increasing curve when $\beta_t(c)$ ranges uniformly from 0 to 1 as:

$$\mathcal{T}_t(c) = \frac{\beta_t(c)}{2 - \beta_t(c)} \cdot \tau \qquad (7)$$

This non-linear mapping strategy ensures the threshold grows slowly when $\beta_t(c)$ is small, and becomes more sensitive as $\beta_t(c)$ gets larger.

After obtaining the category-related threshold, APCL can be achieve by calculating the unsupervised loss, which can be formulated as:

$$\mathcal{L}_{u,t} = \frac{1}{\mu B} \sum_{i=1}^{\mu B} \mathbb{1}(\max(p_i) > \mathcal{T}_t(\arg\max(p_i))) H(\widehat{p}_i, p(y|v(u_i))), \quad (8)$$

where $p_i = p(y|\alpha(u_i))$. The category-related flexible thresholds are updated at each iteration. Finally, the total loss $\mathcal{L}_t$ of APCL as the weight combination of supervised ans unsupervised loss by a pre-defined scale λ can be formulated as:

$$\mathcal{L}_t = \mathcal{L}_s + \lambda \mathcal{L}_{u,t}, \quad (9)$$

where $\mathcal{L}_s$ is the supervised loss on labeled data:

$$\mathcal{L}_s = \frac{1}{B} \sum_{i=1}^{B} H(y_i, p(y|\alpha(x_i))). \quad (10)$$

From the above discussion, ACPL is a cost-free method. Practically, once the prediction confidence of unlabeled data u_i is above the fixed threshold τ, the data and its predicted label are marked and will be used for calculating $\beta_t(c)$ at the next step. Such simply marking action force the model pay more attention to those scenes that difficult to be recognized. Moreover, ACPL can easily cooperate with other pseudo labeling semi-supervised methods to improve their performance and do not introduce new parameters.

3   Experiments

3.1   Experimental Settings

To verify the effectiveness of our RSMatch, we select the UC Merced Land Use (UCM) data set. There are 2100 high-resolution aerial images with a pixel resolution of 1 foot. UCM contains 21 semantic categories, each of which has 100 images. The size of images is 256×256

All of the experiments are implemented by the Pytorch platform using a workstation with two Amax GeForce RTX 3090 GPUs. For a fair comparison, the optimizer for all experiments is stochastic gradient descent (SGD) with a momentum of 0.9 [16]. We use an initial learning rate of 0.03 with a cosine learning rate schedule [17] as $\eta = \eta_0 \cos\left(\frac{7\pi k}{16K}\right)$, where η_0 is the initial learning rate, k is the current training step and K is the total training step that is set to 2^{17}. An exponential moving average with the momentum of 0.999 are also utilized. The batch size of labeled data is 32. μ is set to 7, which means the batch size of unlabeled data is 32 * 7 for RSMatch and its compared methods. τ is set to 0.95 for FixMatch and our RSMatch. The strong augmentation function used in our experiments is RandAugment [18] while the weak augmentation is a standard flip-and-shift augmentation strategy. We use ResNet-18 [19] as our backbone.

3.2   Classification Results

To evaluate the effectiveness of our model, we conduct the classification experiments and compare our method with several semi-supervised algorithms proposed in recent years, including FixMatch [13], MSMatch [9], and SSCL [8]. UCM data set is split into 20% for validation, 20% for test, and 60% for training. Among them, all training samples are further divided into 10% labeled training data and 50% unlabeled training data. We train all the methods with 5 label samples, 8 label samples and 10 label samples per class, respectively. Following the common training definition in semi-supervised methods [13,14], we use the label amount to define these three classification tasks as 105 lables, 168 labels and 210 labels, respectively. The classification results are exhibited in Table 1. What's more, we pose the confusion matrix of RSMtach of three semi-supervised classification scenarios in Fig. 2. Form the observation of the results, we can find RSMatch achieves the best performance than others. The promising results illustrate our method is effective for semi-supervised RSSC task.

Table 1. Classification accuracy (%) on UCM data set.

Method	UCM		
	105 labels	168 labels	210 labels
MSMatch	78.36 ± 0.77	86.48 ± 1.01	88.43 ± 0.56
SSCL	78.43 ± 0.67	87.10 ± 0.44	90.26 ± 0.68
FixMatch	77.08 ± 0.27	86.33 ± 0.56	88.42 ± 0.18
RSMatch (ours)	$\mathbf{78.64 \pm 0.32}$	$\mathbf{87.56 \pm 0.17}$	$\mathbf{90.75 \pm 0.24}$

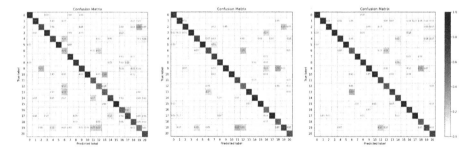

Fig. 2. Confusion matrix of UCM data set. The scene numbers and names are summarized as follows. 1-Agricultural, 2-Airplane, 3-Baseball Diamond, 4-Beach, 5-Buildings, 6-Chaparral, 7-Dense Residential, 8-Forest, 9-Freeway, 10-Golf Course, 11-Harbor, 12-Intersection, 13-Medium Density Residential, 14-Mobile Home Park, 15-Overpass, 16-Parking Lot, 17-River, 18-Runway, 19-Sparse Residential, 20-Storage Tanks, and 21-Tennis Courts

4 Conclusion

In this paper, RSMatch, which utilizes adaptive category-related pseudo labeling (ACPL) strategy, is adopted for remote sensing scene classification based on limited labeled samples and enough unlabeled samples to learn discriminative feature representation according to the learning effects of each class in data set and the learning status of the model. The positive experimental results have demonstrated our proposed RSMatch outperforms the several comparison semi-supervised methods.

References

1. Tang, X., Ma, Q., Zhang, X., Liu, F., Ma, J., Jiao, L.: Attention consistent network for remote sensing scene classification. IEEE J. Sel. Top. Appl. Earth Obs. Remote Sens. **14**, 2030–2045 (2021). https://doi.org/10.1109/JSTARS.2021.3051569
2. Yang, Y., et al.: AR2Det: an accurate and real-time rotational one-stage ship detector in remote sensing images. IEEE Trans. Geosci. Remote Sens. **60**, 1–14 (2022). Art no. 5605414. https://doi.org/10.1109/TGRS.2021.3092433
3. Tang, X., et al.: An unsupervised remote sensing change detection method based on multiscale graph convolutional network and metric learning. IEEE Trans. Geosci. Remote Sens. **60**, 1–15 (2022). Art no. 5609715. https://doi.org/10.1109/TGRS.2021.3106381
4. Cheng, G., Yang, C., Yao, X., Guo, L., Han, J.: When deep learning meets metric learning: remote sensing image scene classification via learning discriminative CNNs. IEEE Trans. Geosci. Remote Sens. **56**(5), 2811–2821 (2018). https://doi.org/10.1109/TGRS.2017.2783902
5. Wang, Q., Liu, S., Chanussot, J., Li, X.: Scene classification with recurrent attention of VHR remote sensing images. IEEE Trans. Geosci. Remote Sens. **57**(2), 1155–1167 (2019). https://doi.org/10.1109/TGRS.2018.2864987
6. Liu, X., Zhou, Y., Zhao, J., Yao, R., Liu, B., Zheng, Y.: Siamese convolutional neural networks for remote sensing scene classification. IEEE Geosci. Remote Sens. Lett. **16**(8), 1200–1204 (2019). https://doi.org/10.1109/LGRS.2019.2894399
7. Guo, D., Xia, Y., Luo, X.: GAN-based semisupervised scene classification of remote sensing image. IEEE Geosci. Remote Sens. Lett. **18**(12), 2067–2071 (2021). https://doi.org/10.1109/LGRS.2020.3014108
8. Zhang, J., Zhang, M., Pan, B., Shi, Z.: Semisupervised center loss for remote sensing image scene classification. IEEE J. Sel. Top. Appl. Earth Obs. Remote Sens. **13**, 1362–1373 (2020). https://doi.org/10.1109/JSTARS.2020.2978864
9. Gomez, P., Meoni, G.: MSMatch: semisupervised multispectral scene classification with few labels. IEEE J. Sel. Top. Appl. Earth Obs. Remote Sens. **14**, 11643–11654 (2021). https://doi.org/10.1109/JSTARS.2021.3126082
10. Li, Y., Zhang, H., Xue, X., et al.: Deep learning for remote sensing image classification: a survey. Wiley Interdisc. Rev. Data Min. Knowl. Disc. **8**(6), e1264 (2018)
11. Yang, X., Song, Z., King, I., et al.: A survey on deep semi-supervised learning. arXiv preprint arXiv:2103.00550 (2021)
12. Tan, M., Le, Q.: EfficientNet: rethinking model scaling for convolutional neural networks. In: International Conference on Machine Learning, pp. 6105–6114. PMLR (2019)

13. Sohn, K., Berthelot, D., Carlini, N., et al.: FixMatch: simplifying semi-supervised learning with consistency and confidence. Adv. Neural. Inf. Process. Syst. **33**, 596–608 (2020)
14. Tarvainen, A., Valpola, H.: Mean teachers are better role models: Weight-averaged consistency targets improve semi-supervised deep learning results. In: Advances in Neural Information Processing Systems, vol. 30 (2017)
15. Grandvalet, Y., Bengio, Y.: Semi-supervised learning by entropy minimization. In: Advances in Neural Information Processing Systems, vol. 17 (2004)
16. Sutskever, I., Martens, J., Dahl, G., et al.: On the importance of initialization and momentum in deep learning. In: International Conference on Machine Learning, pp. 1139–1147. PMLR (2013)
17. Loshchilov, I., Hutter, F.: SGDR: stochastic gradient descent with warm restarts. arXiv preprint arXiv:1608.03983 (2016)
18. Cubuk, E.D., Zoph, B., Shlens, J., et al.: RandAugment: practical automated data augmentation with a reduced search space. In: Proceedings of the IEEE/CVF Conference on Computer Vision and Pattern Recognition Workshops, pp. 702–703 (2020)
19. He, K., Zhang, X., Ren, S., et al.: Deep residual learning for image recognition. In: Proceedings of the IEEE Conference on Computer Vision and Pattern Recognition, pp. 770–778 (2016)

Visual Question Answering of Remote Sensing Image Based on Attention Mechanism

Shihuai Zhang[1], Qiang Wei[1], Yangyang Li[1(✉)], Yanqiao Chen[2],
and Licheng Jiao[1]

[1] The Key Laboratory of Intelligent Perception and Image Understanding
of Ministry of Education, International Research Center for Intelligent Perception
and Computation, Joint International Research Laboratory of Intelligent Perception
and Computation, Collaborative Innovation Center of Quantum Information
of Shaanxi Province, School of Artificial Intelligence, Xidian University,
Xi'an 710071, China
yyli@xidian.edu.cn

[2] The Key Laboratory of Aerospace Information Applications,
The 54th Research Institute of China Electronics Technology Group Corporation,
Shijiazhuang 050081, China

Abstract. In recent years, the research of attention mechanism has made significant progress in the field of computer vision. In the processing of visual problems of remote sensing images, the attention mechanism can make the computer focus on important image areas and improve the accuracy of question answering. Our research focuses on the role of synergistic attention mechanisms in the interaction of question representations and visual representations. On the basis of Modular Collaborative Attention (MCA), according to the complementary characteristics of global features and local features, the hybrid connection strategy is used to perceive global features at the same time without weakening the attention distribution of local features. The impact of attention mechanisms on various types of visual question answering questions has been evaluated:(i) scene classification (ii)object comparison (iii) quantitative statistics (iv) relational judgment. By fusing the global features and local features of different modalities, the model can obtain more information between modalities. Model performance evaluation under the RSVQA-LR dataset. Experimental results show, the method in this paper improves the global accuracy by 9.81% than RSVQA.

Keywords: Co-attention · VQA · Feature fusion

1 Introduction

Visual Question Answering (VQA) is an emerging task in computer vision, Simply put, it is given a question about the content of the image, and the computer

© IFIP International Federation for Information Processing 2022
Published by Springer Nature Switzerland AG 2022
Z. Shi et al. (Eds.): ICIS 2022, IFIP AICT 659, pp. 228–238, 2022.
https://doi.org/10.1007/978-3-031-14903-0_25

gives an appropriate answer based on the text question and the input image. The problem can be split into sub-problems in computer vision, such as:

- Image classification - what area is this?
- Object comparison - is the farmland on the left larger or the farmland on the right larger?
- Quantity statistics - how many buildings are there?
- Relationship Judgment - Is there a small river next to the residential area?

Not only these, the VQA task also contains complex questions. Answering these questions requires certain thinking logic. The questions contain the spatial relationship between the targets, such as (how many villas are around this beach?). And some about behavioral reasoning, such as (Why is this boy running?). These complex problems require the VQA model to have a certain reasoning ability like a human.

In real life, VQA is useful for a wide range of application scenarios. As an open question answering system, it can obtain the specific information in the image in many aspects. For the blind, VQA can describe the content of the image in detail and realize the interaction between virtual and reality. It can also complete text-to-image retrieval through its analysis of image attributes. Usually, the information contained in the label of an image cannot cope with all scenarios. For example, to find a summer landscape of the Gold Coast, just ask the question (is there a coast, sand, hot sun?) instead of looking for answers from irrelevant tags. Therefore, VQA can improve the experience of human-computer interaction without relying on image labels.

Remote sensing image data is widely used in our daily life. Whether land detection, environmental protection, resource exploration, and urban monitoring require the direct or indirect participation of remote sensing images. For these applications, professional processing of remote sensing images is required, and effective information cannot be obtained directly from images. Conventional remote sensing image processing tasks only start from a single task (such as classification, detection, segmentation), Only a small number of experts can directly process this information. A VQA task for remote sensing images can directly obtain answers to questions related to remote sensing images, which greatly reduces the threshold for using remote sensing images in other fields.

Deep neural networks models learn a relational representation to generate a mapping from input to output, While the answer to the VQA task is open-ended (e.g. what's next to the beach? The answer can be a villa, a crowd, a car, etc.), This means that more attention needs to be paid to the potential connections in the question sentence, which is a difficult problem for the network model to learn. On the contrary, as long as we pay attention to the questions given in the VQA task, we can focus on the two key words of beach and beside, reducing the interference of other unnecessary information in the sentence. This paper adopts the strategy of stacking attention units and text features to guide visual features, and uses the category information in the question features to focus on relevant regions in the image.

For the VQA task of natural images, it is necessary to extract features and eliminate redundant information in the visual channel. Natural images cover a small range of realistic scales, generally ranging from a few meters to hundreds of meters. However, for remote sensing images, the scene information contained in them covers far more ground objects than natural images, and the number of targets in a scene is several times that of natural images. In answering visual questions about remote sensing images, there are both macroscopic global problems and microscopic details. Therefore, it is necessary to focus on both local features and global perception. This paper adopts the strategy of cross-modal feature fusion, which combines global information with local information, makes full use of the complementarity of information between modalities, and solves the shortcomings of insufficient global perception of attention-based visual question answering models.

To this end, we propose a model for the remote sensing image VQA task and complete the performance evaluation on the RSVQA-LR dataset. In Sect. 3, HMCAN (Hybrid Moudlar Co-attention Network) is introduced in detail. In Sect. 4, HMCAN is evaluated and discussed on the RSVQA-LR dataset. The contributions of this paper are as follows:

- A Modular Collaborative Attention Mechanism with Hybrid Connections
- Cross-modal global feature and local feature fusion strategy

2   Related Work

With the development of deep neural networks, the visual question answering task also adopts the method of stacking deep network models to obtain deep features. Relying on the powerful feature extraction ability of deep networks, only using global features alone can achieve a good effect. However, this model blurs the task-related areas of the input information, and the model with attention mechanism can effectively overcome this shortcoming, these models have achieved great success in natural language processing (NLP) and other computer vision tasks, Such as object recognition [1], subtitle generation [13] and machine translation [2,10].

There are two main implementation methods for the spatial attention mechanism in the VQA problem. The first method uses a convolutional neural network (CNN) to generate a grid with local image features at each image location, flatten the grid, and determine the correlation of grids at different locations by the problem. The second method is to use the encoding to generate regional proposal boxes for the image, and the correlation of each box is generated by the proposal box and the question.

I. Ilievski [5] et al. proposed FDA. In this paper, the bounding box with object labels is obtained through ResNet, using word2vec [11] to calculate the similarity between the words in the question and the bounding box, and the region proposal boxes relevant to the question are generated. In [14], to emphasize the global image representation, the authors propose a stackable attention layer, using Softmax with CNN to compute the attention distribution across image locations in a single layer by weighting and focusing on spatially important locations. C. Xiong [12] et al. added a dynamic memory network DMN [6] to the VQA task, the text is fed into the recurrent neural network to generate "fact" features, and the CNN image features of each region are regarded as the words in the sentence and sequentially sent to the recurrent neural network to generate visual "fact" features. Finally, the answer is predicted from the text and image "facts".

In recent years, the neural network model based on the transformer structure has been widely used in the field of computer vision, and many scholars [3,7] introduced the transformer into the VQA task. In [9], the authors add a cross attention layer and a collaborative attention layer based on a two-way transformer to fully learn the context content and achieve efficient exchange of information between modalities. This paper mainly studies the attention distribution method that uses text features to generate image features, and uses text representations to guide the learning of image features.

2.1   Co-attention

Scaled Dot-Product Attention. The scaled dot-product attention on the left side of Fig. 1 is a normalized dot product attention, where Q, K and V represent *query, key* and *value*, respectively.

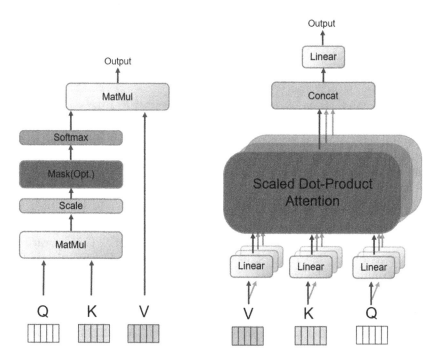

Fig. 1. The scaled dot-product attention model on the left, and the multi-head attention model on the right consists of several parallel attention layers.

Assuming that the input *query* and *key* dimensions are d_k, and the *value* dimension is d_v, first calculate the dot product of the query, and each *key* and divide by $\sqrt{d_k}$, and then apply the *softmax* function to calculate the weight.

$$\text{Attention}\,(Q, K_i, V_i) = \text{softmax}\left(\frac{Q^T K_i}{\sqrt{d_k}}\right) V_i \tag{1}$$

In the actual operation, each *query*, *key* and *value* are processed into Q, K and V matrices respectively.

$$\text{Attention}\,(Q, K, V) = \text{softmax}\left(\frac{QK^T}{\sqrt{d_k}}\right) V \tag{2}$$

where $Q \in \mathbb{R}^{m \times d_k}, K \in \mathbb{R}^{m \times d_k}, V \in \mathbb{R}^{m \times d_v}$, the dimension of the output matrix is $R^{m \times d_v}$.

Multi-head-attention. In the scaled dot-product attention, only one weight operation is performed on Q, K and V, which is obviously not sufficient. Therefore, Multi-head-attention adopts the method of parallel splicing of multiple attention layers to strengthen the attention generation of global features. First perform linear mapping on the Q, K and V matrices, and convert the input dimension from d_{model} to $Q \in \mathbb{R}^{m \times d_k}, K \in \mathbb{R}^{m \times d_k}, V \in \mathbb{R}^{m \times d_v}$. hen the mapping is sent into the attention in parallel, the formula is as follows:

$$\text{MultiHead}\,(Q, K, V) = \text{Concat}\,(\text{head}_1, \ldots, \text{head}_h)\,W^0 \tag{3}$$

$$\text{head}_i = \text{Attention}\left(QW_i^Q, KW_i^K, VW_i^V\right) \tag{4}$$

Among them, the weight matrix $W_i^Q \in \mathbb{R}^{d_{\text{model}} \times d_k}, W_i^K \in \mathbb{R}^{d_{\text{model}} \times d_k}, W^O \in \mathbb{R}^{hd_v \times d_{\text{model}}}, W_i^V \in \mathbb{R}^{d_{\text{model}} \times d_v}$. In this part, h represents the number of parallel attention layers, so the conversion relationship of the input dimension is: $d_k = d_v = d_{\text{model}}/h$, and finally a splicing operation is performed at the end, so that the input and output dimensions are consistent.

Self-attention and Guided-Attention. Self-attention (SA) is based on Multi-head attention, adding residual connections between outputs, adding a normalization layer and a fully connected forward network. This forward network consists of two linear layers, in which the activation The function is Relu, and the formula is as follows:

$$FFN(x) = \max\,(0, xW_1 + b_1)\,W_2 + b_2 \tag{5}$$

W_1, W_1 adjust the input and output dimensions to $d_{\text{model}} = 2224$, and the input feature of the middle layer is $d_{\text{ff}} = 2048$.

As shown in Fig. 2 (right), Guide-attention (GA) introduces another input, Y and X correspond to text input and image input, respectively, where $X \in \mathbb{R}^{m \times d_x}$, $Y = [y_1; \ldots; y_n] \in \mathbb{R}^{n \times d_y}$. The method of obtaining attention distribution by SA is used here, and the extraction of image features is guided by the input queryand keyof the text, and then the GA model is established according to the feature correlation of $<x_i, y_j>$. On the basis of the original, the interaction between modalities has been increased.

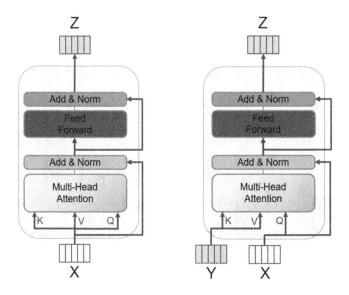

Fig. 2. The left side is the self-attention with multi-head attention as the main structure, and the right side is the guide-attention that introduces the dual modalities of text and images.

Moudlar Co-attention Network. The modular collaborative attention network (MCAN) in Fig. 4 (left) is composed of multiple modular collaborative attention layers $(MCA^{(1)}, MCA^{(2)})$ stacked. Each MCA layer is composed of one SA unit in the text branch and one SA and GA unit in the image branch. Suppose that the input $Y^{(0)}, X^{(0)}$ correspond to text features, image features Y, X, respectively, then the single-layer output is as follows:

$$\left[X^{(l)}, Y^{(l)} \right] = MCA^{(l)} \left(\left[X^{(l-1)}, Y^{(l-1)} \right] \right) \qquad (6)$$

The input of each layer of MCA is the output of the upper layer of MCA (Fig. 3).

3   Methods

We propose a novel structure for visual question answering for remote sensing data using a hybrid-connected Modular Collaborative Attention (HMCA) component, which is outlined in Fig. 4. The model takes question representation and image representation as input, uses a cross-layer attention-guided strategy to guide image representation with question representation, and finally implements visual question answering through a multi-layer perceptron (MLP). The detailed description of the components is expanded next (Fig. 4).

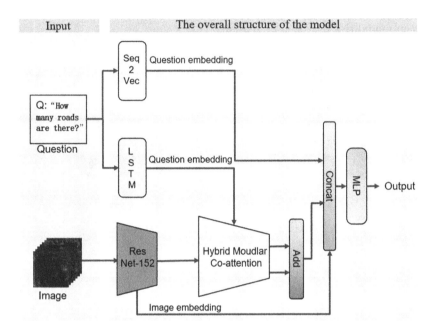

Fig. 3. The overall structure of the model.

3.1   Hybrid Moudlar Co-attention

In the MCA unit, the output of the last SA block of the Y branch is used as the input of the GA block of the X branch $\left[X^{(0)}, X^{(1)} \ldots X^{(L)} \right]$. On the whole, the text features with deep attention distribution can guide the image features effectively, making the network pay more attention to the text-related regions in the image, which is a good strategy. But at the same time, this approach will ignore some global information in the text features. In HMCA, the Y and X branches in MCA are replaced by the question representation Q and the visual representation V, where the number of stacking layers of attention layers is four, Using the parallel connection method in the first two layers, in $MCA^{(1)}$, $Q^{(1)}$ is used as the guide of $V^{(0)}$ to obtain $V^{(1)}$. The formula is as follows:

$$\left[V^{(l)}, Q^{(l)} \right] = MCA^{(l)} \left(\left[V^{(l-1)}, Q^{(l-1)} \right] \right) \tag{7}$$

In the first two layers of CMCA, the problem-based shallow attention distribution is used to guide the visual representation, which ensures that the visual

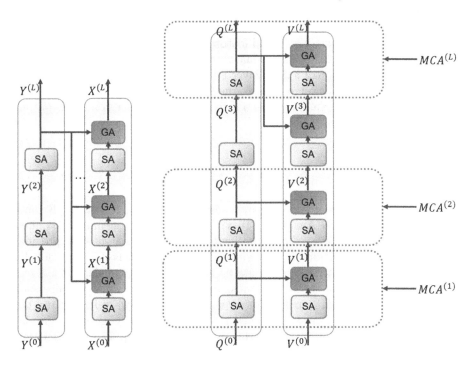

Fig. 4. The left figure shows MCA and the right figure shows hmca with hybrid connection strategy.

features have a global perception of the problem category, and the extreme distribution of the attention area will not occur due to the attention distribution. In the last two layers, the method of MCA is used:

$$\left[V^{(i)}, Q^{(i)}\right] = MCA^{(i)}\left(\left[V^{(i-1)}, Q^{(l)}\right]\right) \tag{8}$$

3.2 Cross-Modal Fusion of Global and Local Information

It is found that after adopting the CMAC component, the overall effect has been significantly improved, but it has a negative impact on specific problem categories, and has a good performance in such problems as quantity calculation, area estimation, and target comparison. However, the accuracy of the global scene judgment problem (is the area to the left of the forest urban or rural?) has declined. Due to the highly concentrated attention distribution obtained by the CMAC component, part of the global information is ignored, and the global features have not received due attention in large scene problems. Therefore, a cross-modal fusion strategy that combines global information with local information is deliberately adopted. In the question feature extraction stage, LSTM and Seq2Vec are used as two-way branches to extract the embedding vector of the question, respectively. The output of the LSTM branch is sent to CMCA as a guide, and the other branch that retains the global problem information is spliced and fused with shallow visual features and deep visual features.

Finally we map the 2224-dimensional vector to the answer space using a single hidden layer MLP with 512 hidden layer units. In the answer output stage, the open-ended question answer is transformed into a classification question, and each possible answer is classified into a category, so the dimension of the output is related to the question.

4   Experiments

4.1   Dataset

The dataset used in the experiments is RSVQA (Real Dataset for Remote Sensing Visual Question Answering Task), which is based on images acquired by Sentinel-2 satellite over the Netherlands. The Sentinel-2 satellite provides imagery at 10-m resolution (for the visible band used in this dataset) globally and is updated frequently (approximately 5 days). The RSVQA dataset is a real remote sensing image of the Netherlands, which includes complex terrains such as mountains, hills, rivers, coasts, towns, rural areas, and wasteland. Since the dataset covers most geographical scenes, the richness of its geographic information is conducive to the migration of this method to other application scenarios.

4.2   Experimental Setup and Hyperparameters

Our experimental setup and model hyperparameter details are as follows: Using pretrained Resnet-152 [4] for the image channel, Using pretrained Seq2Vec in one branch of the problem channel, the other branch needs to be trained by itself. Adam is used as the optimizer in the experiment, the learning rate is 0.0001, and the number of iterations is 20 epochs. Overall classification accuracy (OA), average classification accuracy (AA), and various classification accuracies are used in performance evaluation.

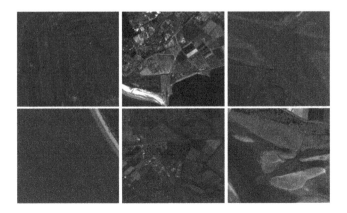

Fig. 5. RSVQA datasets.

4.3 Experimental Results and Analysis

Table 1. Comparison of the performance of the two models on the RSVQA-LR dataset using RSVQA as the baseline.

TypeModel	RSVQA [8]	HMCAN	Improvement
Count	67.01%	71.80%	↑ 4.79%
Presence	87.46%	91.45%	↑ 3.99%
Comparison	81.50%	93.01%	↑ 11.51%
Rural/Urban	90.00%	91.00%	↑ 1.00%
AA	81.49%	86.81%	↑ 5.32%
OA	79.08%	88.89%	↑ 9.81%

In Table 1, the performance of our method is presented. On this problem category based on comparison, our method achieves a significant improvement, which is 11.51% higher than the baseline. Due to the use of a pretrained network, 20 epochs ran for four hours on an NVIDIA 1080 configuration. On the overall accuracy OA, it is 9.81% higher than the benchmark.

5 Conclusion

In this work, we propose a hybrid connection unit based on a modular collaborative attention mechanism, employing different connection strategies at different positions of the stacked attention layers. In feature fusion, we adopt a cross-modal feature fusion strategy to obtain global and local information between modalities. For the remote sensing visual question answering task, our model outperforms previous models on the RSVQA-LR dataset. In the future, the attention mechanism should have more room for development. The performance of a model largely depends on the quality of the data. The next step is to apply the attention mechanism to remote sensing images with high noise, and compress the network as much as possible to realize a lightweight and highly portable remote sensing visual question answering model.

Acknowledgements. This work was supported in part by the National Natural Science Foundation of China under Grant 61772399 and Grant 62101517, in part by the Key Research and Development Program in Shaanxi Province of China under Grant 2019ZDLGY09-05, and in part by the Fund for Foreign Scholars in University Research and Teaching Programs (the 111 Project).

References

1. Ba, J., Mnih, V., Kavukcuoglu, K.: Multiple object recognition with visual attention. arXiv preprint arXiv:1412.7755 (2014)

2. Bahdanau, D., Cho, K., Bengio, Y.: Neural machine translation by jointly learning to align and translate. arXiv preprint arXiv:1409.0473 (2014)

3. Chen, Y.-C., et al.: UNITER: UNiversal Image-TExt Representation learning. In: Vedaldi, A., Bischof, H., Brox, T., Frahm, J.-M. (eds.) ECCV 2020. LNCS, vol. 12375, pp. 104–120. Springer, Cham (2020). https://doi.org/10.1007/978-3-030-58577-8_7

4. He, K., Zhang, X., Ren, S., Sun, J.: Deep residual learning for image recognition. In: Proceedings of the IEEE Conference on Computer Vision and Pattern Recognition, pp. 770–778 (2016)

5. Ilievski, I., Yan, S., Feng, J.: A focused dynamic attention model for visual question answering. arXiv preprint arXiv:1604.01485 (2016)

6. Kumar, A., et al.: Ask me anything: Dynamic memory networks for natural language processing. In: International Conference on Machine Learning, pp. 1378–1387. PMLR (2016)

7. Li, X., et al.: OSCAR: object-semantics aligned pre-training for vision-language tasks. In: Vedaldi, A., Bischof, H., Brox, T., Frahm, J.-M. (eds.) ECCV 2020. LNCS, vol. 12375, pp. 121–137. Springer, Cham (2020). https://doi.org/10.1007/978-3-030-58577-8_8

8. Lobry, S., Marcos, D., Murray, J., Tuia, D.: RSVQA: visual question answering for remote sensing data. IEEE Trans. Geosci. Remote Sens. 58(12), 8555–8566 (2020)

9. Lu, J., Batra, D., Parikh, D., Lee, S.: ViLBERT: pretraining task-agnostic visiolinguistic representations for vision-and-language tasks. In: Advances in Neural Information Processing Systems, vol. 32 (2019)

10. Luong, M.T., Pham, H., Manning, C.D.: Effective approaches to attention-based neural machine translation. arXiv preprint arXiv:1508.04025 (2015)

11. Mikolov, T., Sutskever, I., Chen, K., Corrado, G.S., Dean, J.: Distributed representations of words and phrases and their compositionality. In: Advances in Neural Information Processing Systems, vol. 26 (2013)

12. Xiong, C., Merity, S., Socher, R.: Dynamic memory networks for visual and textual question answering. In: International Conference on Machine Learning. pp. 2397–2406. PMLR (2016)

13. Xu, K., et al.: Show, attend and tell: neural image caption generation with visual attention. In: International Conference on Machine Learning, pp. 2048–2057. PMLR (2015)

14. Yang, Z., He, X., Gao, J., Deng, L., Smola, A.: Stacked attention networks for image question answering. In: Proceedings of the IEEE Conference on Computer Vision and Pattern Recognition, pp. 21–29 (2016)

Multi-scale Spatial Aggregation Network for Remote Sensing Image Segmentation

Xinkai Sun, Jing Gu[✉], Jie Feng, Shuyuan Yang, and Licheng Jiao

School of Artificial Intelligence, Xidian University, Xian, China
xuer6126@126.com

Abstract. Semantic segmentation of remote sensing images is of great significance to the interpretation of remote sensing images. Recently, convolutional neural networks have been increasingly used in this task since it can effectively learn the features in the image. In this paper, an end-to-end semantic segmentation framework, Multi-scale Spatial Aggregation Network (MSAN), is proposed for the remote sensing image segmentation. At first, a classical SegNet is employed as the backbone of the network because its simple structure is suitable for the remote sensing images that have a small quantity of samples. Then several skip connections and a densely connected block are utilized to enhance the usage of the low-level feature and reduce the loss of the detail information in the original image. Moreover, multi-scale spatial information fusion module and a spatial path are added between the encoder and decoder of SegNet, which can effectively extract the features of objects with different sizes in the remote sensing images. Finally, a smoothing algorithm is presented to improve the blocking effect of the remote sensing image segmentation results. The proposed MSAN is tested on the ISPRS Vaihingen dataset and the dataset of a city in southern China, which obtains the satisfactory results.

Keywords: Image segmentation · Remote sensing · Feature aggregation

1 Introduction

Remote sensing image is captured by the imaging equipment carried on the aircraft or space shuttle, which has the advantage of all-time imaging. Semantic segmentation [1, 2] is an important basis in the field of remote sensing image processing [3]. Its purpose is to distinguish different types of land covers in remote sensing image, and then provide useful information for many fields, such as geography [4], surveying [5] and mapping, military [6], and so on. However, the remote sensing images have the characteristics of the large scale scene, many objects with the small size, the blurred boundaries between different categories, and being easily interfered by factors such as seasons and shadows, which bring certain difficulties to the image segmentation. In recent years, more and more scholars are beginning to utilize the deep learning to achieve the image semantic segmentation [7, 8], especially the Convolutional Neural Network (CNN), because it

© IFIP International Federation for Information Processing 2022
Published by Springer Nature Switzerland AG 2022
Z. Shi et al. (Eds.): ICIS 2022, IFIP AICT 659, pp. 239–251, 2022.
https://doi.org/10.1007/978-3-031-14903-0_26

can learn the high-level feature representation and train the network model from a large number of data by an end-to-end way. At present, the mainstream semantic segmentation methods [9] can be divided into two categories: the region based semantic segmentation method [10, 11] and the full convolution network semantic segmentation method. The region based semantic segmentation method first divided the original image into numerous free-form regions, and then classified these regions by the extracted features of regions. Typical methods include EPLS [12], SPMK [13]. However, the extracted feature in this kind of method did not contain global spatial information, so the region based semantic segmentation method cannot accurately generate the boundary, which will affect the final segmentation effect greatly. On the other hand, the full convolution network based semantic segmentation methods [14, 15] replace the full connection layer with the convolution layer to realize the prediction of the input image with any size. Since FCN can perform end-to-end training on the entire input image and accurately restore the image through upsampling, the FCN based semantic segmentation methods have attracted the attention of many scholars. In this paper, the FCN is adopted as the basic frame work for the semantic segmentation.

In this paper, a novel multi-scale spatial aggregation network (MSAN) is proposed for remote sensing image segmentation. Considering that there is a small quantity of the labeled samples for the remote sensing images, MSAN employs a shallow network SegNet [16] as the backbone network, which includes an encoder and a decoder. A dense connection block [17] is added to the encoder; meanwhile several skip connections [18], multi-scale spatial information fusion module and a spatial path [19] are utilized to connect the features with the same scales in the encoding and decoding modules to enhance the performance of MSAN. Specifically, the contributions of this paper are described in detail as following.

1. We propose a Multi-scale Spatial Aggregation Network (MSAN) for the remote sensing image segmentation, which adopts skip connection structure and dense connection block to take full advantage of the low-level feature, thus reducing the loss of effective information in the downsampling process without increasing extra computational cost. Meanwhile, multi-scale spatial information fusion module and spatial path are utilized to aggregate the features with different receptive fields that can comprehensively describe the targets with different scales in the remote sensing image, thus improving the recognition performance of different land covers.
2. In order to avoid losing the semantic information of boundary, a smoothing algorithm is proposed in this paper, which alleviates the block effect of segmentation results effectively.

2   Related Work

The earlier semantic segmentation networks are often proposed and applied in the natural scene images, since a large number of the natural scene labeled images can more easily be obtained than the remote sensing. On this basis, some semantic segmentation methods of the remote sensing image are proposed. The two kinds of approaches will be explained in detail below.

2.1   Semantic Segmentation of Natural Scene Image

At present, many semantic segmentation methods have been presented to segment the natural scene image. First of all, Long et al. [14] replaced the fully connected layer in the VGG16 [20] network with a convolutional layer, and successfully applied a convolutional neural network to the natural image semantic segmentation. Subsequently, a SegNet was proposed, which used a pooling operation with locations to avoid the loss of spatial information in the down-sampling process. Then, an innovative encoder-decoder network structure was designed and named as U-Net, which could effectively restore the size of the original feature map and has been used widely. Furthermore, a multi-scale information fusion method, atrous spatial pyramid pooling (ASPP) [21], was proposed by Chen et al. in DeepLab v3+ [22], which used an atrous convolution in the spatial dimension. The ASPP module can take parallel sampling with different sampling rates for a given input by the atrous convolution [23]. Similarly, Zhao et al. introduced a pyramid pooling module (PPM) in PSPNet [24], which could obtain a set of feature maps with different receiving field sizes by performing the pooling operations on the feature maps with different proportions. In addition, a brand-new Efficient Spatial Pyramid (ESP) module [25] was proposed to replace the original convolution module, which has obvious advantages in speed, reaching 112 frames per second. Zhang et al. [26] focused on the network's comprehensive understanding of contextual information, and proposed a context encoding module, which greatly improved the effect of semantic segmentation at the expense of increasing a small amount of calculation. Since ASPP and PPM can effectively extract the features of image in various scales, they are introduced into a simple framework SegNet to reserve the low-resolution features of the deep network in this paper, thus increasing the accuracy of the segmentation results.

2.2   Semantic Segmentation of Remote Sensing Image

In recent years, more and more semantic segmentation methods [27, 28] have been applied in the remote sensing field [29], such as DST_2 [30], ONE_7, CVEO, CAS_Y1, CASIA. A multi-core convolutional layer was introduced to extract the image features by aggregating the convolutions of different scales. Chen et al. [31] were inspired by a residual module in ResNet and proposed a shortcut block to replace the conventional convolution operation, which ensures the rapid and direct transmission of the gradient information. At the same time, considering that it is difficult for the network to train the entire remote sensing image, an image cropping strategy [32] was proposed. Yu et al. [33] combined the PPM module in PSPNet with ResNet and proposed a brand new network. Liu et al. [34] replaced the original concatenation operation on all context information with fusing step by step in pairs and continuously corrected the image feature details to realize the image feature fusion. In most of the existing semantic segmentation methods, did not take advantage of the low-level features the detail and spatial information of the image were easily lost with the deepening network. The proposed MSAN takes full advantage of the low-level features and spatial information to optimize the network.

3 Proposed Method

In this paper, a novel MSAN is proposed for the semantic segmentation of the remote sensing image. Since the remote sensing image has large scale and constantly changing land covers with the change of the season, the labeled remote sensing image samples are difficult to be obtained. The deeper network will cause over-fitting in the case of a small amount of samples. Therefore, as a simple and effective shallow semantic segmentation network, SegNet is selected as the backbone network of MSAN. Meanwhile, the location-based pooling method in SegNet can accurately restore the position information lost during the downsampling process, which is crucial for the remote sensing image with the blurred boundaries and complex gradients. Moreover, the skip connection and densely connected block are employed to decrease the lost detail information. In order to make full use of the effective features in different levels and enhance the recognition ability of different scale targets, multi-scale information fusion module and spatial path are added to the proposed model. The overall framework of MSAN and the structure of every module will be elaborated as following.

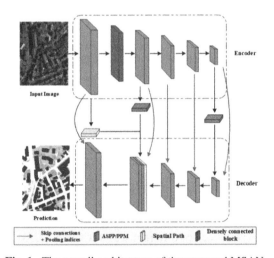

Fig. 1. The overall architecture of the proposed MSAN.

3.1 The Architecture of MSAN

The overall architecture of MSAN is shown in Fig. 1, which includes an encoder and a decoder. In the encoding part, the down-sampling network is composed of an encoding sub-network and a spatial path branch network to extract the high-level and low-level information of the image respectively. The encoding sub-network is composed of five convolutional layers and a densely connected block, where each convolutional layer has a corresponding pooling operation and a skip connection structure. The densely connection block is added between the first layer and the second layer of the encoding sub-network to enhance the fusion among the features. Furthermore, two spatial information fusion modules are added between the encoder and decoder to fuse middle-level and high-level features. Additionally, the output of the spatial path branch is cascaded with the fourth upsampling feature.

The decoder of MSAN mainly consists of five up-sampling layers corresponding to the encoded convolutional layers, where each layer is cascaded with the output of the corresponding skip connection, and the channel is compressed through convolution. The prediction of the image is completed by restoring the size of the original input image layer by layer.

3.2 Densely Connected Structure

Inspired by ResNet and Inception network, the dense connection structure was proposed in DenseNet by Huang et al., which is different from the previous network towards a deeper and wider direction, but starts from the characteristics. The features of all layers are connected to ensure the maximum transmission of effective information between the layers. In short, the input of each layer comes from the output of all previous layers, as shown in Fig. 2. The densely connected block consists of four layers, and each layer includes a convolution (Conv), batch normalization (BN), and nonlinear transformation based on ReLU function (Conv_BN_ReLU). This connection method achieves better effect and fewer parameters, which can also avoid the gradient disappearance and strengthen the transfer between the features. The above advantages make us add it to the proposed method to improve the performance of the network.

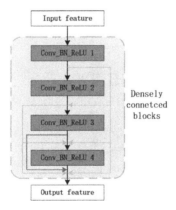

Fig. 2. Schematic diagram of densely connected blocks structure.

3.3 Multi-scale Information Fusion Module

The researches show that the performance of the semantic segmentation network can be greatly improved by combining the deep and shallow features of images, because it can get more global information and increase the ability of network to grasp the overall image at macro level. Along this idea, many scholars have made many meaningful attempts, where ASPP and PPM of PSPNet have been verified to have favorable performance. ASPP is composed of four atrous convolutions of different scales and a global average pool operation to obtain the feature maps with different receptive fields, and then they are integrated to obtain the fusion results concluding different scale spatial information. In PPM of PSPNet, four pooling operations with different sizes are used to explore the context information of different sizes. Then, the channel is compressed by convolution, and the original feature graph size is recovered by bilinear interpolation. Finally, the obtained features are cascaded to the input features, thus achieving the spatial information fusion.

3.4 Spatial Path

Practice has proved that the rich spatial information is essential to improve the accuracy of semantic segmentation networks, which is more prominent in the field of remote sensing image. At present, some mainstream semantic segmentation frameworks often encoded the input images through the deeper networks to obtain the feature maps with the higher resolution, or used the pyramid pooling modules to perform information fusion on feature maps of different sizes. However, a deeper network will increase the computational cost. At the same time, experimental data shows that the excessive compression of feature maps will bring about the loss of spatial information. Therefore, a too deep network is not suitable for remote sensing images with rich semantic information. Yu et al. creatively proposed a spatial path module, which is composed of three convolutional layers with a step size of 2. Each convolutional layer is followed by batch normalization [35] and ReLU [36], so the output of this module is 1/8 of the original input image size. This module can retain rich spatial features and has small computation complexity, which inspired us to apply it to the proposed method. Figure 3 shows the overall structure of the spatial path.

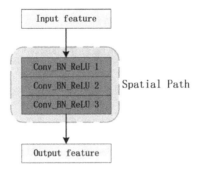

Fig. 3. The overall structure of the spatial path.

3.5 Smoothing Algorithm

It is well known that the size of remote sensing images is large. Therefore, it is difficult for the network to train the entire image. The original image needs to be cropped into small image blocks, and then these cropped image blocks are fed to the network. Finally, the network's prediction results are stitched into a complete image. The traditional cropping method generally crops the original image into some non-overlapping image blocks according to a prescribed step. In this process, the clipping operation will cause the loss of the semantic information of the boundary of the small image blocks, which makes the spliced image produce block effect and causes a sense of visual incoherence. In order to solve this problem, a smoothing algorithm is proposed in this paper. Specifically, the cropping interval is set to 1/2 of the required size so that the boundary in the large remote sensing images is repeated in different cropped image blocks to avoid losing the semantic information of the boundary. During the splicing process, the majority voting method is adopted for the overlapping part, and the voting result is used as the final prediction result. The presented smoothing method alleviates the block effect of the segmentation results effectively.

4 Experimental Results and Analysis

The performance of the proposed MSAN is verified by a series of the experiments. At first, the test dataset and the experiment setting are described respectively. Moreover, the experimental results of MSAN and other typical methods are shown and analyzed, where two common metrics overall accuracy (OA) and mean intersection over union (mIoU) are used to evaluate the performance of these semantic segmentation methods. Finally, several ablation experiments are carried out to demonstrate the effectiveness of the proposed network.

4.1 Dataset

The proposed MSAN is test on the ISPRS Vaihingen dataset [37] and the remote sensing image dataset of a city in southern China. The Vaihingen dataset shows a small town in Germany, which is composed of 33 pieces of different sizes cropped from a remote sensing image, where each image has its corresponding ground truth and digital surface model (DSM). The data set is manually divided into six different categories, including the impervious surfaces, building, low vegetation, tree, car, and clutter/background. There are five remote sensing images in the remote sensing image dataset of a city in southern China, showing scenes of rural and urban areas. All ground truths are manually marked, including the vegetation, buildings, water bodies, roads, and background.

4.2 Experimental Setting

On the ISPRS Vaihingen dataset, all the results of this dataset are fairly compared by using the conventional ground truth. Among them, 16 pictures are used as the training set and the rest are used as the test set, and the input size of the network is 256×256. At the same time, in order to overcome the overfitting of the data, all input images are randomly flipped. Multiple pooling sizes in PPM are set to 1×1, 2×2, 4×4, 8×8 pooling respectively. The sampling rates of the atrous convolution in ASPP are set to 6, 12, and 18 respectively.

The proposed method was compared with the mainstream semantic segmentation networks SegNet, U-Net, PSPNet and DeepLab v3+, and the segmentation results will be evaluated in terms of the running speed and segmentation accuracy. The experiment platform is Intel Core i7 9700K, 64 GB RAM and Nvidia GeForce GTX2080 Ti (11264 MB memory). The deep learning framework is Python 3.6, Tensorflow 1.4.0 and Keras 2.1.3.

4.3 Experimental Results

In order to verify the performance of the proposed MSAN, the prediction results of different remote sensing image semantic segmentation methods on a test image (ID 27) of the Vaihingen dataset are shown in Table 1. As shown in the Table 1, the accuracy of DST_2 has reached 86.1, but the amount of parameters is as high as 184 M. The parameter quantity of ONE_7 is the most competitive, and the accuracy is relatively higher. By contrast, the performance of CVEO and CAS_Y1 is relatively poor. MSAN is similar with CASIA in the segmentation accuracy and better than other methods, but the amount of the parameters in MSAN is much smaller than CASIA, which shows that the propose method balances the segmentation accuracy and the running speed greatly.

Table 1. Overall accuracy and the number of parameters of different methods on the Vaihingen dataset (ID 27).

Method	DST_2	ONE_7	CVEO	CAS_Y1	CASIA	MSAN
OA	86.1	86.9	85.5	84.7	87.5	87.3
Parameters	184 M	24 M	52 M	85 M	151 M	37 M

Figure 4 shows the comparison between the proposed method and mainstream semantic segmentation methods. Figure 4(a) and (b) shows an optical remote sensing image (ID 4) of a city in southern China and its corresponding ground truth. The results of SegNet and U-Net are shown in Fig. 4(c) and (d). As we can see, in Fig. 4(c) and (d), some dense buildings are not recognized due to without the information fusion module. Compared with Fig. 4(e) and (f) respectively corresponding to the results of PSPNet and DeepLab v3+, MSAN has better regional consistency, as shown in Fig. 4(g). Table 2 shows the OA and mIoU of the mentioned methods on 4 test images. Since the test images 3 and 4 contain many dense targets, the OA obtained by various methods is lower than the first two images. In general, the segmentation accuracy of MSAN is highest in Table 2.

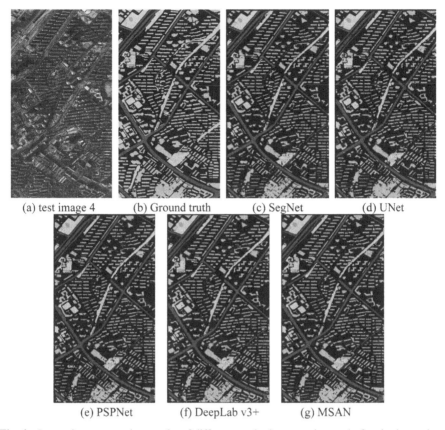

(a) test image 4   (b) Ground truth   (c) SegNet   (d) UNet

(e) PSPNet   (f) DeepLab v3+   (g) MSAN

Fig. 4. Semantic segmentation results of different methods on test image 4 of a city in southern China.

Table 2. OA and mIoU of the results of different methods on test images of a city in southern China.

Method	Test image 1		Test image 2		Test image 3		Test image 4	
	OA (%)	mIoU (%)	OA	mIoU	OA	mIoU	OA	mIoU
SegNet	85.3	72.5	85.8	72.5	73.3	49.9	74.3	50.0
U-Net	88.1	73.4	86.8	73.4	71.5	50.5	76.2	52.1
PSPNet	89.6	73.8	88.8	76.2	77.4	52.5	78.8	55.5
DeepLab v3+	90.1	74.0	87.4	77.0	77.6	53.8	78.2	55.3
MSAN	93.1	79.2	92.6	80.2	80.8	58.3	79.8	56.9

4.4 Ablation Experiments

In order to prove the effectiveness of the added modules, the segmentation results of adding different modules is shown in Fig. 5. Figure 5(a) and (b) shows a test image (ID 35) of the Vaihingen dataset and its corresponding ground truth, and Fig. 5(c) shows the prediction results of the basic backbone network SegNet. Figure 5(d) and (e) shows the prediction results of adding ASPP and PPM to SegNet respectively. Figure 5(f) and (g) shows the final prediction results under different spatial fusion modules. It can be seen that the spatial regional consistency has been significantly improved in the final prediction results.

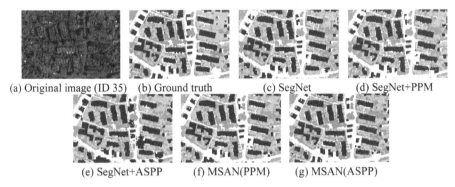

(a) Original image (ID 35)   (b) Ground truth   (c) SegNet   (d) SegNet+PPM

    (e) SegNet+ASPP   (f) MSAN(PPM)   (g) MSAN(ASPP)

Fig. 5. Semantic segmentation results of different network structures.

Table 3. OA and mIoU of the results of different network structures.

Method	OA	mIoU
SegNet	75.4	49.7
SegNet + PPM	77.1	50.2
SegNet + ASPP	77.9	50.4
MSAN(PPM)	83.2	56.9
MSAN(ASPP)	83.9	57.8

Table 3 shows the OA and mIoU of different methods. It can be seen from Table 3 that the recognition accuracy of targets with different scales is enhanced gradually with the increase of the modules, which shows that the adding modules are effective.

5   Conclusions

In this paper, a novel Multi-scale Spatial Aggregation Network (MSAN) is proposed for the semantic segmentation of the remote sensing images. First of all, MSAN adopts SegNet as the backbone network. Then, the skip connections and dense connection block are aggregated into the backbone network to reduce the loss of the detail information in the downsampling process. Moreover, in response to the large gap between different target sizes in the remote sensing images, multi-scale information fusion modules and spatial path are employed. Finally, a smoothing algorithm is given to improve blocking effect and increase the accuracy of the final image segmentation result.

References

1. Gupta, S., Arbelaez, P., Malik, J.: Perceptual organization and recognition of indoor scenes from rgb-d images. In: Proceedings of the IEEE Conference on Computer Vision and Pattern Recognition, pp. 564–571 (2013)
2. Silberman, N., Hoiem, D., Kohli, P., Fergus, R.: Indoor segmentation and support inference from RGBD images. In: Fitzgibbon, A., Lazebnik, S., Perona, P., Sato, Y., Schmid, C. (eds.) ECCV 2012. LNCS, vol. 7576, pp. 746–760. Springer, Heidelberg (2012). https://doi.org/10.1007/978-3-642-33715-4_54
3. Yu, C., Wang, J., Gao, C., Yu, G., Shen, C., Sang, N.: Context prior for scene segmentation. In: Proceedings of the IEEE Conference on Computer Vision and Pattern Recognition (2020)
4. Lin, G., Milan, A., Shen, C., Reid, I.: Refinenet: multi-path refinement networks with identity mappings for high-resolution semantic segmentation. In: Proceedings of the IEEE Conference on Computer Vision and Pattern Recognition (2017)
5. Fu, J., Liu, J., Tian, H., Fang, Z., Lu, H.: Dual attention network for scene segmentation. In Proceedings of the IEEE Conference on Computer Vision and Pattern Recognition (2019)
6. Silva-Rodríguez, J., Colomer, A., Naranjo, V.: WeGleNet: a weakly-supervised convolutional neural network for the semantic segmentation of gleason grades in prostate histology images. Computeriz. Med. Imag. Graph. **88**, 101846 (2021). https://doi.org/10.1016/j.compmedimag.2020.101846
7. Zhang, Z., Huang, J., Jiang, T., et al.: Semantic segmentation of very high-resolution remote sensing image based on multiple band combinations and patchwise scene analysis. J. Appl. Remote Sens. **14**(1), 1 (2020)
8. Ren, X., Bo, L., Fox, D.: Rgb-(d) scene labeling: features and algorithms. In: 2012 IEEE Conference on Computer Vision and Pattern Recognition, vol. 1, pp. 2759–2766. IEEE (2012)
9. Yu, C., Wang, J., Peng, C., Gao, C., Yu, G., Sang, N.: Learning a discriminative feature network for semantic segmentation. In. Proceedings of the IEEE Conference on Computer Vision and Pattern Recognition (2018)
10. Badrinarayanan, V., Kendall, A., Cipolla, R.: SegNet: a deep convolutional encoder-decoder architecture for image segmentation. IEEE Trans. Pattern Anal. Mach. Intell. **39**(12), 2481–2495 (2017)
11. Paszke, A., Chaurasia, A., Kim, S., Culurciello, E.: Enet: A deep neural network architecture for real-time semantic segmentation. (2016)
12. Liu, J., Geng, Y., Zhao, J., et al.: Image semantic segmentation use multiple-threshold probabilistic R-CNN with feature fusion. Symmetry **13**(2), 207 (2021)
13. Bergum, S., Saad, A., Stahl, A.: Automatic in-situ instance and semantic segmentation of planktonic organisms using Mask R-CNN[C]. In: IEEE Oceanic Engineering Society & Marine Technology Society. IEEE (2020)
14. Long, J., Shelhamer, E., Darrell, T.: Fully convolutional networks for semantic segmentation. IEEE Trans. Pattern Anal. Mach. Int. **39**(4), 640–651 (2014)
15. Chen, G., Zhang, X., Wang, Q.: Symmetrical dense-shortcut deep fully convolutional networks for semantic segmentation of very-high-resolution remote sensing images. IEEE J. Sel. Top. Appl. Earth Observ. Remote Sens. **11**(5), 1633–1644 (2018)

16. Badrinarayanan, V., Kendall, A., Cipolla, R.: Segnet: a deep convolutional encoder-decoder architecture for image segmentation. IEEE Trans. Pattern Anal. Mach. Int. **39**(12), 2481–2495 (2017)
17. Huang, G., Liu, Z., Laurens, V.D.M., et al.: Densely connected convolutional networks. In: Proceedings of the IEEE Conference on Computer Vision and Pattern Recognition (2017)
18. Ronneberger, O., Fischer, P., Brox, T.: U-net: convolutional networks for biomedical image segmentation. In: Navab, N., Hornegger, J., Wells, W.M., Frangi, A.F. (eds.) MICCAI 2015. LNCS, vol. 9351, pp. 234–241. Springer, Cham (2015). https://doi.org/10.1007/978-3-319-24574-4_28
19. Yu, C., Wang, J., Peng, C., Gao, C., Yu, G., Sang, N.: BiSeNet: bilateral segmentation network for real-time semantic segmentation. In: Ferrari, V., Hebert, M., Sminchisescu, C., Weiss, Y. (eds.) ECCV 2018. LNCS, vol. 11217, pp. 334–349. Springer, Cham (2018). https://doi.org/10.1007/978-3-030-01261-8_20
20. Simonyan, K., Zisserman, A.: Very deep convolutional networks for large-scale image recognition. In: Proceedings of the International Conference on Learning Representation (2014)
21. Chen, L.C., Papandreou, G., Kokkinos, I.: DeepLab: semantic image segmentation with deep convolutional nets, atrous convolution, and fully connected CRFs. IEEE Trans. Pattern Anal. Mach. Int. **40**(4), 834–848 (2018)
22. Chen, L.C.: Rethinking atrous convolution for semantic image segmentation. In: Proceedings of the International Conference on Computer Vision and Pattern Recognition (2017)
23. Chen, L.-C., Zhu, Y., Papandreou, G., Schroff, F., Adam, H.: Encoder-decoder with atrous separable convolution for semantic image segmentation. In: Ferrari, V., Hebert, M., Sminchisescu, C., Weiss, Y. (eds.) ECCV 2018. LNCS, vol. 11211, pp. 833–851. Springer, Cham (2018). https://doi.org/10.1007/978-3-030-01234-2_49
24. Zhao, H., Shi, J., Qi, X., Wang, X., Jia, J.: Pyramid scene parsing network. In: Proceedings of the IEEE Conference Computer Vision and Pattern Recognition, pp. 6230–6239 (2017)
25. Mehta, S., Rastegari, M., Caspi, A., Shapiro, L., Hajishirzi, H.: Espnet: efficient spatial pyramid of dilated convolutions for semantic segmentation. In: Ferrari, V., Hebert, M., Sminchisescu, C., Weiss, Y. (eds.) ECCV 2018. LNCS, vol. 11214, pp. 561–580. Springer, Cham (2018). https://doi.org/10.1007/978-3-030-01249-6_34
26. Zhang, H., et al.: Context encoding for semantic segmentation. In: Proceedings of the IEEE Conference on Computer Vision and Pattern Recognition, pp. 7151–7160 (2018)
27. Li, X., Liu, Z., Luo, P., Loy, C.C., Tang, X.: Not all pixels are equal: difficulty-aware semantic segmentation via deep layer cascade. In: Proceedings of the IEEE Conference on Computer Vision and Pattern Recognition (2017)
28. Mehta, S., Rastegari, M., Shapiro, L.G., Hajishirzi, H.: Espnetv2: a light-weight, power efficient, and general purpose convolutional neural network. In: Proceedings of the IEEE Conference on Computer Vision and Pattern Recognition (2019)
29. Audebert, N., Le Saux, B., Lefèvre, S.: Semantic segmentation of earth observation data using multimodal and multi-scale deep networks. In: Lai, S.-H., Lepetit, V., Nishino, K., Sato, Y. (eds.) ACCV 2016. LNCS, vol. 10111, pp. 180–196. Springer, Cham (2017). https://doi.org/10.1007/978-3-319-54181-5_12
30. He, Y., Dong, X., Kang, G., et al.: Asymptotic soft filter pruning for deep convolutional neural networks. IEEE Trans. Cybern. **50**(8), 3594–3604 (2020)
31. Chen, G., Zhang, X., Wang, Q.: Symmetrical dense-shortcut deep fully convolutional networks for semantic segmentation of very-high-resolution remote sensing images. IEEE J. Sel. Topics Appl. Earth Observ. Remote Sens. **11**(5), 1633–1644 (2018)
32. He, K., Zhang, X., Ren, S., Sun, J.: Deep residual learning for image recognition. In: Proceedings of the International Conference on Computer Vision and Pattern Recognition (2016)

33. Bo, Y., Lu, Y., Fang, C.: Semantic segmentation for high spatial resolution remote sensing images based on convolution neural network and pyramid pooling module. IEEE J. Sel. Topics Appl. Earth Observ. Remote Sens. 1–10 (2018)

34. Liu, Y., Fan, B., Wang, L.: Semantic labeling in very high resolution images via a self-cascaded convolutional neural network. ISPRS J. Photogramm. Remote. Sens. **145**, 78–95 (2018)

35. Ioffe, S., Szegedy, C.: Batch normalization: accelerating deep network training by reducing internal covariate shift. In: Proceedings of the International Conference on Machine Learning, ICML, pp. 448–456 (2015)

36. Nair, V., Hinton, G.E.: Rectified linear units improve restricted Boltzmann machines. In: Proceedings of the 27th International Conference on Machine Learning (2010)

37. Everingham, M., Eslami, S.A., Van Gool, L., Williams, C.K., Winn, J., Zisserman, A.: The pascal visual object classes challenge: a retrospective. Proc. Int. J. Comput. Vis. **111**(1), 98–136 (2015)

Deep Complex Convolutional Neural Networks for Remote Sensing Image Classification

Lingling Li, Yukai Sun, Fuhai Ma, Jingjing Ma[✉], Licheng Jiao, and Fang Liu

School of Artificial Intelligent, Xidian University, Xi'an 710071,
People's Republic of China
llli@xidian.edu.cn

Abstract. At present, the neural network is often based on the real field of operation, research shows that, compared with the real field, the complex has incomparable advantages in the field of image processing, such as the complex represents more information, such as the phase information and modulus value, which play a great role in some fields. To take full advantage of complex data, This paper mainly studies CNN network, and through complex value processing, and get Complex Convolutional Neural Networks(CCN), complete the construction of complex convolution neural network. In order to study complex neural network, we start from two aspects, one is convolution operation, the other is network construction. In this paper, we use ENet as the basic structure of the model, replace the convolutional structure, pooling structure, and BatchNorm structure with the complex form, use it in the Flevoland dataset, and get a good test results.

Keywords: Polarimetric SAR · Complex convolution neural network · Image classification

1 Introduction

In recent years, polarimetric synthetic aperture radar (PolSAR) is one of the most important research directions in the field of remote sensing. PolSAR image classification is a basic and effective way to interpret PolSAR images, and has extensive research and application value [1,2,14].

Based on the convolutional neural network, this paper studies the operation mode of the real number in the neural network, summarizes and analyzes the data of the convolutional neural network which is widely used at present. Further introduce the application of complex numbers in neural networks, the advantages

This work was supported in part by the National Natural Science Foundation of China (Nos. 61906150, 62076192), the State Key Program of National Natural Science of China (No. 61836009), the Major Research Plan of the National Natural Science Foundation of China (Nos. 91438201, 91438103).

Z. Shi et al. (Eds.): ICIS 2022, IFIP AICT 659, pp. 252–259, 2022.
https://doi.org/10.1007/978-3-031-14903-0_27

of complex numbers in processing polarimetric SAR data, and whether they can be implemented in neural networks based on complex number domains. Take lessons from the popular CNN networks and improve them. This paper introduces the convolutional neural network which changes the input from the real number domain to the complex number domain. The main research contents of this paper are summarized as the following three points:

1. Research on complex number-based convolutional neural networks It mainly studies how to perform convolution operations on complex numbers, how to input complex numbers, and how to train. In this part, we simulate the convolution operation of the real part and the imaginary part of the complex number to complete.
2. Research on deep convolutional neural networks based on complex numbers In this part, we refer to the ENet network, because the real part, imaginary part, and modulus value of complex numbers in the ENet network can be used as input for convolution operations, and the ENet network has a significant effect on image segmentation.
3. Analysis of experimental results based on real number field and complex number field

2 Related Work

2.1 Convolutional Neural Network

Over the past few years major computer vision research efforts have focused on convolutional neural networks, commonly referred to as ConvNets or CNNs. These efforts have resulted in new state-of-the-art performance on a wide range of classification [3,4] and regression [9,10] tasks.

Convolutional Neural Networks (CNNs) are a class of neural networks that are particularly suitable for computer vision applications because of their ability to abstract representations hierarchically using local operations. There are two key design ideas that drive the success of convolutional architectures in computer vision. First, CNNs exploit the 2D structure of images and pixels within adjacent regions are often highly correlated. Therefore, instead of using one-to-one connections between all pixel units (as most neural networks do), CNNs can use grouped local connections. Second, the CNN architecture relies on feature sharing, so each channel (i.e., the output feature map) is generated by convolution with the same filter at all locations as depicted in Fig. 1.

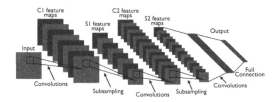

Fig. 1. Illustration of the structure of a standard convolutional network. Figure reproduced from [6]

2.2   ENet

ENet is an extension of the CNN network. It has been very popular in the field of image segmentation in recent years. It is an encoding and decoding network. Convolutional Neural Networks are designed to perform classification encoders. A decoder formed by an upsampling network that segments the original image [7].

Each block in ENet contains three convolutional layers like Fig. 2: a 1×1 map, the main convolutional layer, and a 1×1 dilation. Interspersed with BN layers and PReLU layers, this structural combination is defined as a bottleneck model. If bottleneck is downsampling, a max pooling layer is added to the main branch. At the same time, the first 1×1 mapping in bollteneck is replaced by a convolution of size 2×2 and stride of 2. The types are ordinary convolution, hole Convolutions, and transposed convolutions, etc., are sometimes replaced with 1×5 or 5×1 asymmetric convolutions.

The advantages of ENet are as follow: The ENet network structure is asymmetric and consists of a large encoding layer and a small decoding network. And The model replaces the convolutional layer in bottleneck with atrous convolution and concatenates it, which increases the receptive field and improves the IOU of segmentation [8]. Then, the paper replaces all ReLUs with PReLUs, adding an extra parameter for each featuremap.

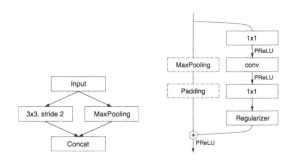

Fig. 2. The structure of ENet

3   Methodology

3.1   Complex Convolution Network

The method we use here is to simulate the convolution of two real numbers by the real and imaginary parts of complex numbers to realize the convolution operation of complex numbers. First, we define the complex filter parameters as $\overrightarrow{W} = \overrightarrow{A} + i\overrightarrow{B}$, the complex input information is $\overrightarrow{h} = \overrightarrow{x} + i\overrightarrow{y}$, through the deep network in the real number domain to simulate the value operation of complex numbers (where A and B are real numbers matrix, $\overrightarrow{x}$ and $\overrightarrow{y}$ are real vectors), the complex number is expressed in the form of convolution output, as shown in the Formula 3.1; And the real and imaginary parts of the operation are $\mathcal{R}(W \times \overrightarrow{h})$ and $\mathfrak{J}(W \times \overrightarrow{h})$.

$$W \times \overrightarrow{h} = (A \times \overrightarrow{x} - B \times \overrightarrow{y}) + i(B \times \overrightarrow{x} + A \times \overrightarrow{y}) \qquad (3.1)$$

$$\begin{bmatrix} \mathcal{R}(W \times \overrightarrow{h}) \\ \mathfrak{J}(W \times \overrightarrow{h}) \end{bmatrix} = \begin{bmatrix} A & -B \\ A & A \end{bmatrix} \times \begin{bmatrix} \overrightarrow{x} \\ \overrightarrow{y} \end{bmatrix} \qquad (3.2)$$

The above formula tells us that it can be used not only as a complex convolutional network, but also as a fully connected layer. The operations of the complex convolutional neural network are actually convolution operations and matrix product operations. Next, we try to build complex network structures: complex convolutional networks (CCN) and complex fully connected layers (CFC).

The input of the complex number field is that h with dimension $T_{in}/2$ consists of real part $\overrightarrow{x}$ and imaginary part $\overrightarrow{y}$ with dimensions $T_{in}/2$. The 3D tensor in the complex domain is the mapping to the input features required in the convolutional layer in the 2D complex domain. Where $W, H, T_{in}/2$ is the input signal, $i \times i$ is the size of the convolution kernel, and the parameter quantity of the four-dimensional complex weight tensor W of the output feature map is $T_{out}/2 \times T_{in}/2 \times i \times i$.

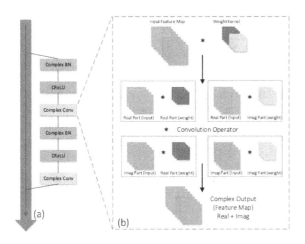

Fig. 3. Basic block of CCN

As shown in Fig. 3, the convolution kernel and feature map are the objects of convolution in the complex domain. We simulate the convolution operation using the real and imaginary parts of complex numbers as complex feature maps and complex convolution kernels, perform multiplication and accumulation operations, and obtain the convolution result.

3.2   Network Parameters Analysis

Compared with the CNN, CCN require a larger amount of parameters and operations. Set the input of the CNN and the complex number convolutional neural network as a three-dimensional tensor similar to $W \times H \times T_{in}$, and the size of the convolution kernel of size $i \times i$, T_{out} as the output channel of the convolutional layer. For real network input, the number of input channels is T_{in} The dimension of the weight tensor required by the model is $i \times i \times T_{in} \times T_{out}$.

For the complex convolutional neural network, the input feature of the channel number T_{in} represents the $T_{in}/2$-dimensional complex feature, and the number of channels the model needs to generate is a complex number of $T_{out}/2$ output features. At this time, each channel needs a complex convolution kernel of size $i \times i$. Then $i \times i$ is the number of parameters of the real and imaginary parts of the convolution kernel, so the number of parameters of a convolution kernel required by CCN is $2 \times i \times i$, and the required dimension of the complex convolutional neural network at this time is $i \times i \times T_{in} \times T_{out}/2$.

Table 1. Parameters for CNN and CCN

	Input	Kernel size	Output	Parameters
CNN	T_{in}	$i \times i$	T_{out}	$i \times i \times T_{in} \times T_{out}$
CCN	$T_{in}/2$	$2 \times i \times i$	$T_{out}/2$	$i \times i \times T_{in} \times Tv_{out}/2$

3.3   Complex Batch Norm

The covariance matrix V of the complex input is given by the Formula 3.3:

$$V = \begin{pmatrix} V_{rr} & V_{ri} \\ V_{ir} & V_{ii} \end{pmatrix} = \begin{pmatrix} Conv(R(x), R(x)) & Conv(R(x), i(x)) \\ Conv(i(x), R(x)) & Conv(i(x), i(x)) \end{pmatrix} \tag{3.3}$$

To scale the complex data x, the complex data needs to be centered and multiplied by the reciprocal of the quadratic root of a covariance matrix of size 2×2. The expression for x obtained after complex normalization is as follows:

$$\tilde{x} = (V)^{(-\frac{1}{2})}(x - E[x]) \tag{3.4}$$

Analogous to real numbers, in the complex domain β^c is the complex shift parameter and γ^c is the scaling parameter equivalent to the covariance matrix V.

$$\gamma^c = \begin{pmatrix} \gamma_{rr}^c & \gamma_{ri}^c \\ \gamma_{ir}^c & \gamma_{ii}^c \end{pmatrix} \tag{3.5}$$

Therefore, the mathematical formula for complex BN is as follows:

$$BN(\tilde{x}) = \gamma^c \tilde{x} + \beta^c \tag{3.6}$$

3.4 Complex Activate Function

The expression of the activation function ReLU function used in the convolutional neural network is show in Formula 3.7

$$\text{ReLU}(h) = \begin{cases} h & if \quad h \geq 0 \\ 0 & \text{otherwise} \end{cases} \tag{3.7}$$

The Formula 3.7 is the activation function of the real number domain. However, when we consider the calculation method of complex numbers, when h is a complex number variable [13], the size of the real part and the imaginary part is uncertain, and the relationship with 0 is also uncertain. Therefore, the ReLU function is in the complex number domain. cannot be used in complex arithmetic, and needs to be adjusted accordingly.

Here we use the phase of the complex domain as the inflection point of the relu function:

$$\text{ZReLU}(h) = \begin{cases} h & if \quad \theta_h \in [0, \frac{\pi}{2}] \\ 0 & \text{otherwise} \end{cases} \tag{3.8}$$

4 Experiment

The cropland dataset in the Flevoland region of the Netherlands is the L-band image data of the Flevoland region of the Netherlands acquired by TASA/JPL ARISAR. This is a four-view full-polarization image with a size of 750×1024 and a resolution of $12\,m \times 5\,m$, including 15 different types of ground objects (without background), namely potatoes, dried beans, rapeseed, sugar beets, alfalfa, and barley, grass, three kinds of wheat, peas, bare land, forest, water, built-up area. Unmarked areas are marked in white on the real class plot. After removing the background class, the total number of 15 different features is 157712 [12].

We use the AUG function for data enhancement, using point-by-point segmentation and random segmentation methods to separate 30 points in height and width, generate 30 points in height and 30 points in width, and obtain 900 random interpolations. The data is reshaped, and then pickled and persisted with the Numpy library to form a dataset that can be read by Pytorch. The labels come from BMP images to identify specific pixels. Then 1200 pieces of data of size 100 * 100 were formed, 1100 for training and 100 for testing.

According to the Fig. 4, it is obvious that the accuracy rate is still relatively low in the 30 epochs, the difference between the predicted image and the original image is still very large, and only two color blocks are distinguished, the accuracy is only 82.41%; after the 90 epochs, it can be seen that the same as the original image The difference is no longer large, and the classification effect has been significantly improved, the accuracy is increase to 89.19%. After 300 epochs, the accuracy rate can be maintained at 97.45%, and the training loss is maintained at a low level, achieving optimal classification results.

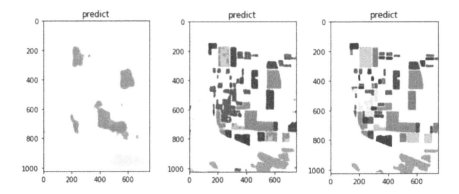

Fig. 4. Visualization of test results at epochs 30, 90 and 300

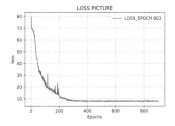

Fig. 5. Train loss

Table 2. Parameters for CNN and CCN

Epochs	30	90	120	300
Accuracy	82.4%	89.2%	93.1%	97.4%

Table 2 is a table of the output accuracy. From the table, it can be intuitively seen that our highest accuracy is maintained at 97.5%, and its position is exactly between 200–300. The subsequent test accuracy remained stable at about 96%, and the accuracy results were better.

Through the adjustment of experimental parameters, a loss map is output. Corresponding to the loss graph 5 and the test accuracy Table 1, it can be seen that when the loss value is at a high position, the test results are relatively poor. When the value of loss is close to stable, the model converges and the optimal result is obtained.

5   Conclusion

This paper mainly studies and analyzes deep complex neural network and complex residual neural network, summarizes and analyzes from the two, and finally realizes the task of remote sensing image classification based on deep complex convolutional neural network. The differences in the number of parameters and network depth between the real-domain convolutional network and the complex-domain convolutional network are compared, and it is found that the complex-domain convolutional neural network has advantages in parameters and network depth. In order to realize the complex domain data processing based on the deep residual network, how to combine the ENet network to construct the convolution layer, pooling layer and activation layer of the complex domain is analyzed in detail. The four modules are organized according to the network organization form of the real number domain, and finally the complex convolutional network of this paper is formed. In the follow-up research, we need to simulate the method of real number neural network to analyze the complex convolutional neural network, and explore the potential of more complex convolutional networks, which can be applied to different scenarios.

References

1. Harris, R.A.: Envisat: ASAR science and applications (1998)
2. Ulaby, F.T., Elachi, C.: Radar polarimetry for geoscience applications. **5**(3), 38 (1990)
3. Khan, A., Sohail, A., Zahoora, U., et al.: A survey of the recent architectures of deep convolutional neural networks. Artif. Intell. Rev. (2020)
4. Tran, D., Bourdev, L., Fergus, R., et al.: Learning spatiotemporal features with 3D convolutional networks (2014)
5. Liu, F., Shen, C., Lin, G.: Deep convolutional neural fields for depth estimation from a single image. IEEE (2014)
6. Lecun, Y., Kavukcuoglu, K., Farabet, C.: Convolutional networks and applications in vision. In: Proceedings of 2010 IEEE International Symposium on Circuits and Systems. IEEE (2010)
7. Paszke, A., Chaurasia, A., Kim, S., et al.: ENet: a deep neural network architecture for real-time semantic segmentation (2016)
8. Yu, F., Koltun, V.: Multi-scale context aggregation by dilated convolutions (2016)
9. Eigen, D., Fergus, R.: Predicting depth, surface normals and semantic labels with a common multi-scale convolutional architecture. In: 2015 IEEE International Conference on Computer Vision (ICCV) (2014)
10. Liu, F., Shen, C., Lin, G.: Deep convolutional neural fields for depth estimation from a single image. IEEE (2014)
11. Hadji, I., Wildes, R.P.: What do we understand about convolutional networks? (2018)
12. Zhou, Y., Wang, H., Xu, F., et al.: Polarimetric SAR image classification using deep convolutional neural networks. IEEE Geosci. Remote Sens. Lett. **13**(12), 1935–1939 (2017)
13. Trabelsi, C., Bilaniuk, O., Zhang, Y., et al.: Deep complex networks (2017)
14. Liu, F., Jiao, L., Tang, X.: Task-oriented GAN for PolSAR image classification and clustering. IEEE Trans. Neural Netw. Learn. Syst. 1–13 (2019)

Perceptual Intelligence

Dual Siamese Channel Attention Networks for Visual Object Tracking

Wenxing Gao, Xiaolin Tian$^{(\boxtimes)}$, Yifan Zhang, Nan Jia, Ting Yang, and Licheng Jiao

School of Artificial Intelligence, Xidian University, Xi'an 710071, China
{xltian,lchjiao}@mail.xidian.edu.cn,20171213676@stu.xidian.edu.cn

Abstract. Siamese network based trackers have achieved remarkable performance on visual object tracking. The target position is determined by the similarity map produced via cross-correlation over features generated from template branch and search branch. The interaction between the template and search branches is essential for achieving high-performance object tracking task, which is neglected in previous works as features of the two branches are computed separately. In this paper, we propose Dual Siamese Channel Attentions Networks, referred as SiamDCA, which exploits the channel attentions to further improve tracking robustness. Firstly, a convolutional version of Squeeze and Excitation Networks (CSENet) is embedded in backbone to explicitly formulate interdependencies between channels to recalibrate channel-wise feature responses adaptively. Meanwhile, we propose a novel Global Channel Enhancement (GCE) module, which is capable of capturing attention weights of each channel in template branch, so as to normalize the channel characteristics in search branch. We experiment on benchmark OTB2015, VOT2016 and UAV123 where our algorithm demonstrates competitive performance versus other state-of-the-art trackers.

Keywords: Siamese network · Visual object tracking · Channel attentions

1 Introduction

Visual object tracking is a fundamental but challenging task in computer vision, which has a wide range of applications, such as visual surveillance [22], human-computer interactions [15], automatic driving, robot sensing, etc. Given an arbitrary target location in the initial frame, the tracker needs to infer the location of the target in each subsequent frame. Although visual object tracking has received extensive attention over the last decades, it still faces challenges due

Supported by the National Natural Science Foundation of China (No. 61977052).

© IFIP International Federation for Information Processing 2022
Published by Springer Nature Switzerland AG 2022
Z. Shi et al. (Eds.): ICIS 2022, IFIP AICT 659, pp. 263–272, 2022.
https://doi.org/10.1007/978-3-031-14903-0_28

to numerous factors such as occlusion, scale variation, background clutters, fast motion, appearance variations.

The Siamese based trackers [1, 24] are trained completely offline by using massive frame pairs collected from videos. Both the features of template branch and search branch are extracted through the backbone independently. In addition, as observed in [11], each channel map of the high-level convolutional features usually responses for a specific object class. There is no information interaction between the template branch and the search branch, which limits the potential performance of Siamese architecture. SiamAttn [23] introduce a new Siamese attention mechanism which computes deformable self-attention and cross-attention jointly to improve discriminability, however, it imposes a heavy computational burden.

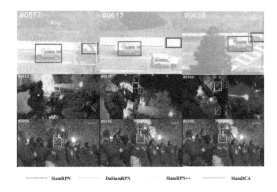

Fig. 1. Tracking results of our SiamDCA with three state-of-the-art trackers. Our results are more accurate, and are robust to appearance changes, complex background and close distractors with occlusions.

In this work, we first introduce the convolutional version of Squeeze and Excitation Networks (CSENet) [9] in the backbone to adaptively recalibrate channel-wise feature responses by explicitly modeling interdependencies between channels in template branch and search branch. Besides, we propose a Global Channel Enhancement (GCE) Module, which can capture rich global context information in each channel of template features, so as to enhance the obtained information and standardize the search feature of corresponding channel in the meanwhile. Extensive experiments on OTB2015, VOT2016 and UAV123 have illustrated the SiamDCA has effectively improved robustness of visual object tracking in scenes such as fast motion, background clutters, as illustrated in Fig. 1.

2   Related Work

2.1   Siamese Based Trackers

Siamese based trackers [1,11] has dominated tracking performance in recent years. A Siamese network takes an image pair as input, comprising a template branch and a search branch. SiamFC [1] first introduces correlation operators between the template branch and the search branch and highly improves the performance of trackers. Inspired by the Region Proposal Network (RPN) that is first proposed in Faster R-CNN [18], SiamRPN [12] performs the RPN extraction after the Siamese backbone to generate anchor boxes, which avoids the trouble of multi-scale testing in SiamFC. SiamRPN++ [11] uses ResNet [8] instead of AlexNet [10] in SiamRPN, so that the backbone can extract richer features. In addition, SiamRPN++ introduces depthwise separable convolution to reduce the amount of parameters in SiamRPN and further improves the performance of Siamese architecture.

2.2 Attention Mechanism

Recently, with the attention mechanism, many tasks in the field of computer vision and natural language processing have achieved better performance.

SENet [9] is an effective, lightweight attention mechanism that can self-recalibrate the feature map via channel-wise importance. It can effectively improve the representative quality of the network by explicitly modeling the interdependence between channels. As stated in SiamRPN++ [11], each channel map of the high-level convolutional features usually responses for a specific object class. Therefore, we focus on improving the robustness of tracker from the perspective of channel attention. Extensive experiments have proved that our framework can improve the visual object tracking performance.

In Non-local [20], for each point on the feature map, it needs to dot product with all other points to obtain the spatial attention vector. This attention mechanism has recently been used in many fields such as instance segmentation and visual object tracking, which have achieved excellent performance. GCNet [2] is a simplified version of Non-Local, which calculates the spatial attention that is common to all points on the feature map, hence this attention only needs to be calculated once.

3 Method

Overview. We apply a ResNet50 embedded with the proposed CSENet as our backbone network of Siamese construction. On the one hand, as the layers become deeper, it computes increasingly high level features. On the other hand, under the influence of CSENet, high level features of the last three stages of the two branches will be transformed into features with channel attention. Then features with channel attention of template branch are enhanced by the proposed GCE module, generating weights of importance on each channel. Meanwhile, these weights are applied to the corresponding channel of the search branch to normalize the characteristics of the search branch. Finally, three Siamese RPN blocks described in [11] were feed the last three features with channel attention of template branch and the last three normalized features of search branch, generating dense response maps, which are further processed by a classification head and a bounding box regression head to predict the location of the target.

3.1 Siamese-Based Trackers

The Siamese network based trackers formulate the visual object tracking as a similarity matching problem. There are two branches in Siamese construction, the template branch and the search branch. They pass through a backbone with shared parameters, obtaining the target's feature (Z) and the search area (X) in a common embedding space. A cross-correlation operation between template features and search features is performed in the embedding space, generating a similarity map. Hence, this tracking process can be expressed as,

$$f_i(Z, X) = \phi(Z) \star \phi(X), i \in \{cls, reg\}. \tag{1}$$

where $\star$ denotes the cross-correlation operation, $\phi(\cdot)$ indicates the backbone of siamese network for feature extraction and i denotes the subtasks, where "cls" represents the classification head, "reg" represents the bounding box regression head.

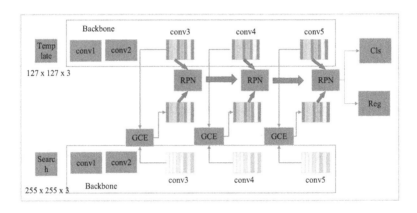

Fig. 2. An overview of the Dual Siamese Channel Attention Network (SiamDCA).

3.2 Convolutional SE Networks in Backbone

As observed in SiamRPN++ [11], each channel map of the high-level convolutional features usually responses for a specific object class. Therefore, improving the correlation between the channels in the two branch features can greatly improve the accuracy and robustness of visual object tracking. Inspired by SENet [9], we embed the SE module into the last four blocks of backbone to perform dynamic channel-wise feature recalibration. In the meanwhile, in order to reduce the computation, we apply two convolution layers with 1×1 kernels instead of FC layers after squeeze operation, referred as CSENet, as illustrated in Fig. 3. Consequently, the features of the search branch and the template branch are channel dependent.

In this work, we continue to follow the idea of the multi-level features in SiamRPN++ [11]. Features extracted from the last three residual blocks are used for the input of the subsequent network module. We refer these outputs as $F_3(z)$, $F_4(z)$ and $F_5(z)$, respectively. As shown in Fig. 2, these three outputs are fed into three GCE modules and RPN module individually.

3.3   Global Channel Enhancement Module

As we all know, in Siamese architecture, features of the template branch and search branch are computed independently. However, different from the template branch, features in search branch is not sensitive to target. In order to distinguish the target from background, we use the template branch to guide the other branch.

As shown in Fig. 4, the GCE block module contains two submodules, the first module is to strengthen the channel related features of the template branch. While the other module is to make use of enhanced channel-wise representation in the first module, then fully capture dependencies in channel level.

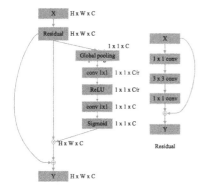

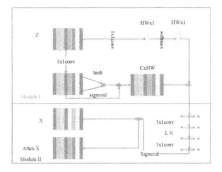

Fig. 3. Convolutional SE block used in last blocks of backbone, Residual is normal residual block in ResNet.

Fig. 4. An overview of the proposed Global Channel Enhancement (GCE) Module.

Specifically, in the first module, suppose the input features are $\mathbf{Z} \in \mathbf{R}^{C \times H \times W}$ in every block, we first apply two separate convolution with 1×1 kernels on $\mathbf{Z}$ to generate global features $\mathbf{G}$ and key features $\mathbf{K}$ respectively, where $\mathbf{G} \in \mathbf{R}^{C \times H \times W}$ and $\mathbf{K} \in \mathbf{R}^{1 \times H \times W}$. Then the $\mathbf{G}$ is filtered to $\widetilde{\mathbf{G}}$ that contains the crucial global information through the tanh and the sigmoid. Moreover, the significant information is added to the original information element-wise to ensure features are enhanced without losing the original feature information. This formula used for filtering as,

$$\widetilde{\mathbf{G}} = tanh(\mathbf{G}) \cdot sigmoid(\mathbf{G}) + \mathbf{G}. \tag{2}$$

Then the enhanced feature $\widetilde{\mathbf{G}}$ is reshaped to $\hat{\mathbf{G}} \in \mathbf{R}^{C \times N}$ where $N = H \times W$. Meanwhile, the $\mathbf{K}$ is reshaped to $\overline{\mathbf{K}} \in \mathbf{R}^{1 \times N}$ where $N = H \times W$, then we generate a filtered feature $\hat{K}$ via column-wise softmax operations. Finally we calculate the enhanced channel-related feature $\mathbf{O} \in \mathbf{R}^{C \times 1}$ as,

$$\mathbf{O} = \hat{\mathbf{G}} \hat{K} \in \mathbf{R}^{C \times 1}. \tag{3}$$

Then we reshape $\mathbf{O}$ to $\overline{\mathbf{O}} \in \mathbf{R}^{C \times 1 \times 1}$ and use $\overline{\mathbf{O}}$ as input for the next module.

There are two inputs in the second module, the first one is the output of the module $\overline{\mathbf{O}}$, while the other is the feature $\mathbf{X}$ of search branch. First of all, we apply a convolution layer with 1×1 kernels on $\overline{\mathbf{O}}$ to reduce the channels of $\overline{\mathbf{O}}$ to $\frac{C}{r}$ (we set r as 16). Besides, we add layer normalization to increase the convergence speed, as well as to benefit generalization ability. Finally we apply a convolution layer with 1×1 kernels to restore the channels of the strengthen feature, and use the feature to multiply $\mathbf{X}$ channel-wise to achieve the normalization of search branch features.

With our GCE module, the adjusted search features is sensitive to the target and objects are more discriminative against distractors and background.

4   Experiments

4.1   Implementation Details

The networks are trained on COCO [14], ImageNet DET [6], ImageNet VID [6], and YouTube-BoundingBoxes Dataset [17]. Our model is trained for 20 epochs, using a warmup learning rate in the first 5 epochs and a learning rate exponentially decayed in the last 15 epochs. Only the first layer of the weights of backbone are frozen, for the first 10 epochs, then the whole networks are trained end-to-end for the last 10 epochs.

During inference, the regression network branch will predict more than one box. As [11], in order to get more accurate tracking results, we use scale change penalty to suppress large changes in target size and cosine window to suppress large displacements. These two penalties will eventually affect the classification score. We will re-rank the constrained score, and finally select the box corresponding to the maximum value of the classification score as the tracking result, this result is more accurate.

4.2   Comparisons with the State-of-the-Art

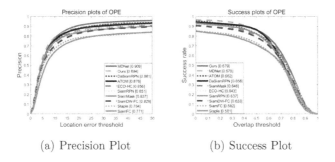

(a) Precision Plot   (b) Success Plot

Fig. 5. Comparisons on OTB2015.

We compare our SiamDCA tracker with the state-of-the-art trackers on three tracking benchmarks databases: OTB2015 [21], UAV123 [16], VOT2016 [7]. We tracker achieves state-of-the-art results and runs at 25 frames per second (fps).

OTB2015 [21]. OTB2015 is a commonly used benchmark, containing 100 sequences. It has two evaluation metrics, a precision score and an area under curve (AUC) of success plot respectively. As show in Fig. 5, Our SiamDCA tracker is compared with numerous state-of-the art trackers include ATOM [3], ECO [4], DaSiamRPN [24] et al. In the process of comparison, our method ranks amount top-2 in the accuracy and success score.

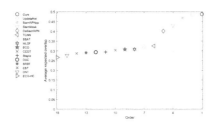

Fig. 6. Expected averaged overlap performance on VOT2016.

VOT2016 [7]. VOT2016 is a widely-used benchmarks for visual object tracking. It has three evaluation metrics, accuracy (A), robustness (R), and expected average overlap (EAO). We compare our SiamDCA tracker with the state-of-the-art trackers. As illustrated in Fig. 6, our SiamDCA tracker achieves 0.485 EAO. Compared with recent SiamRPN++ (SiamRPNpp) [11] and SiamMask [19], our methods increases 2.1% and 4.3% on EAO respectively.

Table 1. Result on UAV123. Red, blue represent 1st, 2nd respectively.

Tracker	AUC	Pr
SAMF [13]	0.395	0.592
SRDCF [5]	0.464	0.676
ECO [4]	0.525	0.741
SiamRPN [12]	0.527	0.748
DaSiamRPN [24]	0.586	0.796
SiamRPN++ [11]	0.613	0.807
ATOM [3]	0.644	–
Ours	0.630	0.822

Table 2. Ablation study on UAV123.

Method	AUC	Pr
Baseline	0.613	0.807
+CSE	0.614	0.814
+GCE (ours)	0.630	0.822

UAV123 [16]. UAV123 is a new aerial video benchmark which includes 123 sequences. It has two evaluation metrics, the same with OTB2015. Table 1 illustrates the precision and success plots of the compared trackers. Specifically, our SiamDCA tracker achieves a success score of 0.630, which outperforms SiamRPN++ (0.613), DaSiamRPN (0.586), SiamRPN (0.527), ECO (0.525) and SRDCF (0.464). In addition, our tracker achieves a precision score of 0.822, and improvements of 1.5%, 2.6%, 7.4%, 8.1% and 14.6%, compared with SiamRPN++, DaSiamRPN, SiamRPN, ECO and SRDCF.

4.3 Ablation Study

We study the impact of individual components in SiamDCA on UAV123 to illustrate the role of each part. We use SiamRPN++ [11] as baseline. As illustrated in Table 2, By adding convolutional SE block to backbone of SiamRPN++, the precision score can be imported to 0.614. And the success plot score can further imported to 0.814. By adding GCE Module, the precision can be imported to 0.630, and the success score can further increased by +1.5%. Therefore, this result also proves the effectiveness of our method. With the CSE and the GCE, the SiamDCA achieve a more accurate tracking effect.

5 Conclusion

We have presented a new Dual Siamese Channel Attention Networks for visual object tracking. We introduce CSENet to backbone to extract features with channel relationship in template branch and search branch. In addition, we proposed GCE module to enhanced the channel-related features in template branch, then make use of dependencies of enhanced features in channel level to standardize the features of the search branch. Finally the robustness of tracking is improved effectively. Extensive experiments on three visual tracking benchmarks demonstrate that SiamDCA achieves state-of-the-art performance.

References

1. Bertinetto, L., Valmadre, J., Henriques, J.F., Vedaldi, A., Torr, P.H.S.: Fully-convolutional Siamese networks for object tracking. In: Hua, G., Jégou, H. (eds.) ECCV 2016. LNCS, vol. 9914, pp. 850–865. Springer, Cham (2016). https://doi.org/10.1007/978-3-319-48881-3_56

2. Cao, Y., Xu, J., Lin, S., Wei, F.: GCNet: non-local networks meet squeeze-excitation networks and beyond. In: Proceedings of the IEEE/CVF International Conference on Computer Vision (ICCV) Workshops, October 2019

3. Danelljan, M., Bhat, G., Khan, F.S., Felsberg, M.: ATOM: accurate tracking by overlap maximization. In: CVPR, pp. 4660–4669, June 2019

4. Danelljan, M., Bhat, G., Shahbaz Khan, F., Felsberg, M.: ECO: efficient convolution operators for tracking. In: CVPR, pp. 6638–6646, July 2017

5. Danelljan, M., Hager, G., Shahbaz Khan, F., Felsberg, M.: Learning spatially regularized correlation filters for visual tracking. In: Proceedings of the IEEE International Conference on Computer Vision (ICCV), pp. 4310–4318, December 2015

6. Russakovsky, O., et al.: ImageNet large scale visual recognition challenge. Int. J. Comput. Vis. **115**(3), 211–252 (2015). https://doi.org/10.1007/s11263-015-0816-y

7. Hadfield, S., Bowden, R., Lebeda, K.: The visual object tracking VOT2016 challenge results. In: ECCV Workshops, vol. 9914, pp. 777–823, October 2016

8. He, K., Zhang, X., Ren, S., Sun, J.: Deep residual learning for image recognition. In: CVPR, pp. 770–778, June 2016

9. Hu, J., Shen, L., Albanie, S., Sun, G., Wu, E.: Squeeze-and-excitation networks. IEEE Trans. Pattern Anal. Mach. Intell. **99**, 7132–7141 (2017)

10. Krizhevsky, A., Sutskever, I., Hinton, G.E.: ImageNet classification with deep convolutional neural networks. Commun. ACM **60**(6), 84–90 (2017)

11. Li, B., Wu, W., Wang, Q., Zhang, F., Xing, J., Yan, J.: SiamRPN++: evolution of Siamese visual tracking with very deep networks. In: CVPR, pp. 4282–4291 (2019)

12. Li, B., Yan, J., Wu, W., Zhu, Z., Hu, X.: High performance visual tracking with Siamese region proposal network. In: CVPR, pp. 8971–8980, June 2018

13. Li, Y., Zhu, J.: A scale adaptive kernel correlation filter tracker with feature integration. In: Agapito, L., Bronstein, M.M., Rother, C. (eds.) ECCV 2014. LNCS, vol. 8926, pp. 254–265. Springer, Cham (2015). https://doi.org/10.1007/978-3-319-16181-5_18

14. Lin, T.Y., Maire, M., Belongie, S., Hays, J., Perona, P.: Microsoft COCO: common objects in context. In: ECCV, pp. 740–755 (2014)

15. Liu, L., Xing, J., Ai, H., Ruan, X.: Hand posture recognition using finger geometric feature. In: ICPR, pp. 565–568 (2013)

16. Mueller, M., Smith, N., Ghanem, B.: A benchmark and simulator for UAV tracking. In: Leibe, B., Matas, J., Sebe, N., Welling, M. (eds.) ECCV 2016. LNCS, vol. 9905, pp. 445–461. Springer, Cham (2016). https://doi.org/10.1007/978-3-319-46448-0_27

17. Real, E., Shlens, J., Mazzocchi, S., Pan, X., Vanhoucke, V.: YouTube-BoundingBoxes: a large high-precision human-annotated data set for object detection in video. In: CVPR, pp. 5296–5305, July 2017

18. Ren, S., He, K., Girshick, R., Sun, J.: Faster R-CNN: towards real-time object detection with region proposal networks. IEEE Trans. Pattern Anal. Mach. Intell. **39**(6), 1137–1149 (2017)

19. Wang, Q., Zhang, L., Bertinetto, L., Hu, W., Torr, P.H.: Fast online object tracking and segmentation: a unifying approach. In: CVPR, pp. 1328–1338, June 2019

20. Wang, X., Girshick, R., Gupta, A., He, K.: Non-local neural networks. In: CVPR, pp. 7794–7803, June 2018
21. Wu, Y., Lim, J., Yang, M.H.: Object tracking benchmark. TPAMI **37**(9), 1834–1848 (2015)
22. Xing, J., Ai, H., Lao, S.: Multiple human tracking based on multi-view upper-body detection and discriminative learning. In: ICPR, pp. 1698–1701 (2010)
23. Yu, Y., Xiong, Y., Huang, W., Scott, M.R.: Deformable Siamese attention networks for visual object tracking. In: CVPR, pp. 6728–6737, June 2020
24. Zhu, Z., Wang, Q., Li, B., Wu, W., Yan, J., Hu, W.: Distractor-aware Siamese networks for visual object tracking. In: ECCV, pp. 103–119 (2018)

Motion-Aligned and Hardness-Aware Dynamic Update Network for Weakly-Supervised Vehicle Detection in Satellite Videos

Quanpeng Jiang, Jie Feng[✉], Yuping Liang, Ziyu Zhou, Xiangrong Zhang, and Licheng Jiao

Key Laboratory of Intelligent Perception and Image Understanding of Ministry of Education, Xidian University, Xi'an 710071, Shaanxi, China
`jiefeng0109@163.com`

Abstract. Though the deep learning methods have achieved effective moving vehicle detection in satellite videos, there is a non-negligible premise that these methods require lots of object-level annotations for hundreds of small and blurry vehicles in the vast observation scene. These annotations can be quite labor-intensive and time-consuming. To address this problem, this paper is committed to realizing the vehicle detection based on point-level annotations, and a motion-aligned and hardness-aware dynamic update network is proposed, which consists of the basic detector, motion-aligned initialization method and online pseudo label update scheme. Specifically, the high-quality pseudo bounding boxes are initialized by revising the Gaussian mixture model to fully exploit the motion information in the video sequence and the location information from the point annotations. Then, the pseudo bounding boxes are utilized as the supervision for the basic detector. During the training phase, an online label refinement scheme is designed to refine the pseudo bounding box continuously, and the confidence-aware loss function is defined to adjust the example weight dynamically according to its learning hardness. Extensive experiments on the Jilin-1 and SkySat satellite video datasets show that our method achieves the comparative performance compared with fully-supervised learning methods.

Keywords: Weakly-supervised vehicle detection · Satellite video · Point-level annotations

1 Introduction

With the continuous improvement of remote sensing technology and satellite imaging technology, high quality remote sensing images and videos with analytical values are

This work was supported in part by the National Natural Science Foundation of China under Grant 61871306, Grant 61836009, Grant 62172600, Grant 62077038, by the Innovation Capability Support Program of Shaanxi (Program No. 2021KJXX-08), by the Natural Science Basic Research Program of Shaanxi under Grant No. 2022JC-45 and 2022GY-065, and by the Fundamental Research Funds for the Central Universities under Grant JB211901.

becoming easier to obtain. Remote sensing videos obtained by optical sensors of video satellites staring at a specific area contain richer temporal information and a larger range of observation than natural images. They have been widely used in dynamic traffic detection, agriculture, forestry, water conservancy, mining, land management, ocean observation, atmospheric observation and other fields [1].

In recent years, the vehicle detection has become a research hotspot of satellite video processing and analysis. Specifically, computer vision combining with satellite remote sensing technology has broad application prospects in the field of intelligent transportation. Compared with the traditional traffic target monitoring equipment, the vehicle detection methods based on satellite remote sensing videos have many advantages, such as one-time investment and lasting application, no damage to road surface, no impact on ground traffic, large coverage area, rich traffic information acquisition, and so on, which provides new data and method source for traffic management and traffic flow dynamic monitoring [2, 22, 23].

To handle vehicle detection tasks, traditional methods consider it as a segmentation problem of background and foreground. They are divided into three categories: optical flow, background subtraction and frame difference. The Optical flow methods [4] find the corresponding relationship between the last frame and the current frame by using the changes of pixels in the time domain and the correlation between adjacent frames in the image sequence, so as to calculate the motion information of objects between adjacent frames [5]. The basic principle of background subtraction [6] is to subtract the current frame and the background image determined by the model, and calculate regions whose pixels difference with the background exceeds a certain threshold as the moving region, so as to acquire the position, contour and size of the moving object. The frame difference [9] methods detect moving objects by looking for pixels that differ in adjacent frames. Unfortunately, most background subtraction are susceptible to moving backgrounds and changes in brightness and contrast, which are commonly present in satellite videos.

With the rise of deep learning and its powerful feature representation ability, object detection based on deep learning becomes a better choice. In the previous work, the classical object detectors can be divided into two categories: anchor-based methods and anchor-free methods. Based on anchor-based methods [10, 12], these detectors usually design a large number of anchor boxes with pre-defined size and aspect ratio, and then classify and regression them to get the bounding box. Compared to the anchor-based approach, anchor-free detectors [11, 14, 15] no longer need to preset anchor boxes, but they can still achieve comparable performance with the former method.

However, both anchor-based and anchor-free methods have a premise that annotation boundary box is needed, which brings a strong demand for data annotation. Collecting bounding box-level annotations [16] is very expensive and laborious, especially for remote sensing images containing hundreds of objects. Specifically, in the vehicle detection task, there are usually 150–200 vehicles in a remote sensing image, and the edge of each vehicle is very fuzzy, even if manual annotation, it is difficult to accurately annotate a bounding box. Compared to bounding box-level annotations, point-level annotations have been widely used in object detection or segmentation, greatly reduces annotation time. Specifically, it takes about 12 s to annotate a bounding box-level instance and only 4 s to annotate a point-level instance. It means we can save twice as much time on the same remote sensing image. For example, if we need to annotate 100 remote sensing images with an average number of 150 vehicles, the bounding box-level annotation takes 50 h, while the same point-level annotation takes less than 17 h. In order to solve the problem of object detection under fully-supervised network, a large number of bounding box annotations are labeled on the image firstly, which requires a lot of manpower and time, especially for satellite images containing hundreds of vehicles [18, 20]. While, weakly-supervised object detection network based on point-level annotations needs to operate a small amount of weakly labeled training data to learn the model, which reduces a large amount of human labor in labeling training samples [17].

In this paper, a motion-aligned and hardness-aware dynamic update network is proposed for moving vehicle detection in the satellite images based on CenterNet. First, combining unsupervised object detection algorithm GMM, some low-quality pseudo label boxes are generated. The motion-aligned initialization method which bases on the multi corresponding relation-ship between pseudo-label boxes and points generates higher quality pseudo label boxes. And then, the size of the pseudo-label boxes with higher confidence is constantly updated during the training process through the online pseudo label update mechanism designed. Finally, a newly-designed confidence-aware loss function is proposed to assist fully-supervised networks to better mine hard training samples for learning.

According to what have been argued above, the main contributions of this paper can be summarized as follows:

1. A motion-aligned and hardness-aware dynamic update network (MHDUN) based on only point annotations is proposed to reduce the manual labeling time and achieve performance comparable to the fully-supervised method.
2. An accurate motion-aligned initialization method is designed to initialize the pseudo-label box precisely, taking full advantage of the point annotations to mine the size information and combining with the motion information in the videos.
3. An online pseudo label update scheme is proposed, which contains a novel confidence-aware loss function by adjusting the training example weight to further improve the quality of the size of the pseudo label box during training and ensure the stability of the entire training process.

The rest of this paper is organized as follows. In Sect. 2, the overall structure and details of MHDUN are described. In Sect. 3, the detailed experimental results and analysis are discussed to verify the effectiveness of the proposed network. Finally, the conclusions and some suggestions for future work are given in Sect. 4.

2 Proposed Method

2.1 Overview

In this section, the proposed method is introduced in detail. Figure 1 shows the overall structure of MHDUN, which is capable of training an object detector only with point-level annotations for vehicle detection. Specifically, the network is based on an anchor-free object detector, CenterNet. Firstly, the motion-aligned initialization (MAI) method is proposed to generate the relatively accurate initial pseudo size for every vehicle. Furthermore, an online pseudo label update scheme (OPLU Scheme) is proposed to refine the pseudo sizes in every training epoch. Besides, a novel confidence-aware loss function contained in the OPLU Scheme is designed to pay more attention to hard training samples by adding a bigger weight in vehicle's size regression.

2.2 Motion-Aligned Initialization

In order to be able to train a fully supervised network later, we need to first initialize the pseudo label bounding box from the point annotations. The closer a natural image is taken, the larger the object is, and vice versa [20]. However, the size of objects in remote sensing images is not affected by this, and the size difference of object is not obvious. Therefore, based on this discovery, we propose a novel motion-aligned initialization method combined with the GMM to initialize the size of the object.

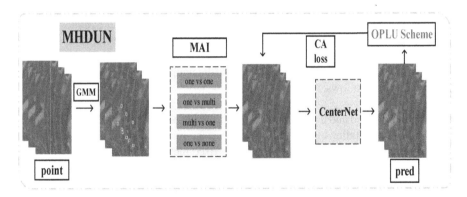

Fig. 1. Overview of motion-aligned and hardness-aware dynamic update network (MHDUN) for moving vehicle detection in the satellite videos. It consists of the basic detector, motion-aligned initialization method and online pseudo label update scheme.

2.3 Motion-Aligned Initialization

In order to be able to train a fully supervised network later, we need to first initialize the pseudo label bounding box from the point annotations. The closer a natural image is taken, the larger the object is, and vice versa [20]. However, the size of objects in remote sensing images is not affected by this, and the size difference of object is not obvious. Therefore, based on this discovery, we propose a novel motion-aligned initialization method combined with the GMM to initialize the size of the object.

First, as for how to generate a pseudo label bounding box, our strategy is to use the GMM, which can obtain a relatively accurate initial pseudo label bounding box for us.

Then, the different position inclusion relationship of the points and boxes need to be judged, there are four corresponding relationships between the pseudo label bounding box generated by GMM and the real point annotation as can be seen from Fig. 2. Specifically, 1) one vs. one (one point corresponds to one box): the box predicted by GMM is used as the pseudo label bounding box of the real point. 2) One vs. multi (one point corresponds to multi boxes): It means that there is only one real object here in the image, but GMM predicts multiple boxes. Therefore, in order to maintain the uniqueness and accuracy of the initial pseudo label box, the distance between the center point of each prediction box and the real point mark is calculated, and then the prediction box corresponding to the smallest distance is taken as the corresponding pseudo label bounding box of the point finally. 3) Multi vs. one (multi points corresponds to one box): The situation shows that GMM prediction is not accurate enough. Therefore, in order to avoid vehicle missing detection in subsequent fully-supervised training as much as possible, a fairly reasonable generation method of multiple pseudo-label boxes is proposed. First of all, the vertical distance from each point to predict box of four sides are calculated. Then, the minimum distance between each point and both sides of the predict box in the horizontal and vertical directions is calculated. Finally, we consider the real point as the center point, and take the minimum distance to the vertical boundary and horizontal boundary as its height and width to generate the corresponding pseudo label box of each point. 4) One vs. none (one point corresponds to no box): In order to make up for the deficiency of the traditional algorithm, a pseudo label box is generated for each point without corresponding box. To be specific, the mean and variance of the size of the pseudo label box generated in the first three cases are calculated. According to this, a three-sigma rule is adopted to random generate the size of the pseudo label box.

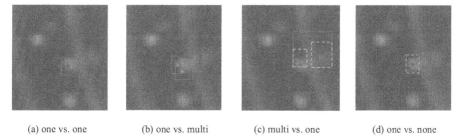

(a) one vs. one   (b) one vs. multi   (c) multi vs. one   (d) one vs. none

Fig. 2. Motion-aligned initialization. (a) is the GT point denoted in red point and pseudo label box predicted by the GMM denoted in green solid box, (b) is the center point of the pseudo label box denoted in blue point, (c) is new pseudo label boxes denoted in yellow dashed boxes, (d) is the pseudo label box generated by three-sigma rule denoted in light green dashed box. (Color figure online)

2.4 Online Pseudo Label Update Scheme

Due to the existence of inaccurate initial pseudo-label boxes, inputting such boxes will lead to the instability of target detection network training or convergence to local optimum. In order to train a reliable and stable object detection network, we propose an online pseudo label updating mechanism iteratively updating and refining pseudo label boxes in every epoch. We set an initial confidence value for each initial pseudo-label box. In the training process, the size of the pseudo-label box will be updated only when the predicted corresponding box in next epoch is greater than the initial confidence. At the same time, the initial confidence level will be replaced with a higher confidence level, which ensures that the fully supervised detection network trains with increasingly confident training samples.

Besides, a new-designed confidence-aware loss function is designed to focus on hard training samples by adding a bigger weight in vehicle's size regression to perfect and supplement online updating refinement scheme. Specifically, we can get the score of each prediction box and instinctively believe that the positive box with higher score is an easy sample while the positive box with lower score is a difficult one. Thus, we define the weights for each of these prediction bounding boxes:

$$w_i = 1/sigmoid(s_i) \tag{1}$$

where w_i denotes the weight of the i-th bounding box and s_i denotes the score of the i-th bounding box. Then, we apply to multiplied with the heatmap loss to get confidence-aware loss (CA Loss):

$$CA\ Loss = \frac{-1}{N} \sum_{xyc} \begin{cases} (1-\hat{Y}_{xyc})^\alpha \log(\hat{Y}_{xyc})w_i & if\ \hat{Y}_{xyc} = 1 \\ (1-Y_{xyc})^\beta (\hat{Y}_{xyc})^\alpha \log(1-\hat{Y}_{xyc})(1-w_i) & otherwise \end{cases} \tag{2}$$

which replace the original heatmap loss, where α and β are hyper-parameters of the focal loss and N is the number of keypoints in the image just same to CenterNet. The keypoint heatmap predicted by the network is $\hat{Y}_{xyc}$ and Y_{xyc} represents the ground truth keypoint heatmap, x and y represent the position on the heatmap and c represents the category. $\alpha = 2$ and $\beta = 4$ are used in our experiments.

3 Experimental Results and Analysis

3.1 Datasets

In this paper, Dubai and San Diego datasets captured by Jilin-1 satellite and the Las Vagas dataset captured by SkySat satellite are used to validate the effectiveness of the proposed network, as shown in Fig. 3. Dubai dataset is captured over Dubai, UAE, on November 9, 2018. AOIs 1–3 (areas of interests) come from the dataset and the size of the three frames are 1000 × 1000 pixels. AOIs 1, 2 are used for training, AOIs 3 is used for testing. San Diego dataset is captured over San Diego, USA, on May 23, 2017. AOIs 4–6 come from the dataset and the size of AOIs 5, 6 are 1000 × 1000 pixels, while the size of AOI 4 is 1500 × 700 pixels. AOIs 4, 5 are used for training, AOIs 6 is used for testing. Las Vagas dataset is captured over Las Vagas, USA on March 25, 2014. Video 001, 002 come from the dataset and the size of Video 001 is 400 × 400 pixels, while the size of Video 002 is 600 × 400 pixels. Video 002 is used for training and Video 001 is used for testing.

3.2 Experimental Setups

We implemented MHDUN in PyTorch 1.10.0 without pretrained parameters, and initialized by PyTorch default setting. The networks are trained on the Windows server 2019 system with a single RTX 3090 GPU and AMD Ryzen 9 5950X CPU. The benchmark

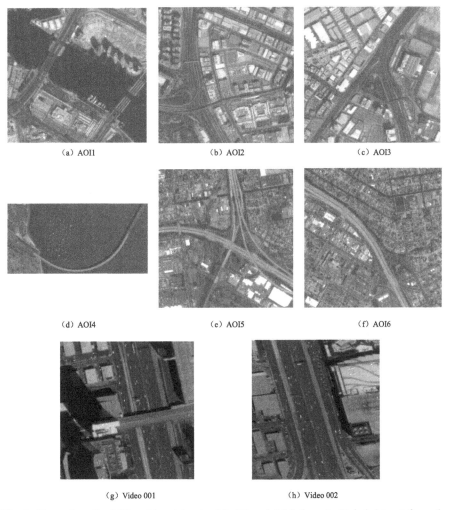

(a) AOI1   (b) AOI2   (c) AOI3

(d) AOI4   (e) AOI5   (f) AOI6

(g) Video 001   (h) Video 002

Fig. 3. Examples of satellite video datasets. (a), (b) and (c) belong to Dubai dataset from the Jilin-1 satellite, (d), (e) and (f) are from San Diego dataset from the Jilin-1 satellite, (g) and (h) are from Las Vegas dataset from the SkySat satellite.

network used in the experiment is CenterNet, and the backbone is Hourglass-104 [21]. Specifically, the network is trained with a batch size of 4 and learning rate 0.32e−4 with the Adam optimizer for 20 epochs. We use random cropping, and color jittering as data augmentation for the training data, and no any data augmentation for the testing data.

3.3 Detection Results of Different Methods

To verify the effectiveness of motion-aligned initialization and hardness-aware based dynamic update network, some representative traditional methods, FastMCD [13], ViBe [3], GMM [7], and deep learning methods, Faster R-CNN [10], YOLO v4 [16], CenterNet [11], CornerNet [14], and CentripetalNet [15], are selected for comparison. For a fair comparison, Faster R-CNN, YOLO v4, Cor-nerNet, CenterNet and CentripetalNet take three stacked frames as the input to exploit the temporal information but these models are based on bounding box annotations, not point annotations. The common evaluation of Precision, Recall and F1 score are used for all experiments. GMM algorithm has a relatively good performance in the traditional algorithm and thus it is selected to generate initial pseudo-label boxes in our network. It is not difficult to find that deep learning methods obtain better detection perfor-mance compared with traditional methods. At the same time, the most important thing is that motion-aligned initialization and hardness-aware based dynamic update network is based on point annotations, obtaining similar results with deep learning methods based on box annotations, which further illustrates the effec-tiveness of the network.

As shown in Fig. 4, most of the vehicles are detected rightly, and there is little difference in size. Besides, there is only some false detection for blurry objects and a little missing detection. In all, the overall detection effect is relatively good and the network can achieve similar performance to fully-supervision network (Table 1).

Table 1. Detection results of different methods in satellite videos.

	Las Vegas (SkySat)			Dubai (JiLin-1)			San Diego (JiLin-1)		
	Prec↑	Rec↑	F1↑	Prec↑	Rec↑	F1↑	Prec↑	Rec↑	F1↑
Traditional methods	(%)								
FastMCD	72.46	71.74	72.10	90.01	63.21	74.27	87.33	49.96	63.56
ViBe	53.24	78.43	63.43	47.00	66.85	55.20	61.17	61.07	61.12
GMM	55.63	72.56	62.98	82.92	71.48	76.78	88.46	62.38	73.16
Deep learning methods	(%)								
Faster R-CNN	86.13	87.27	86.70	88.47	84.28	86.32	85.14	80.81	82.92
YOLOv4	88.98	87.48	88.22	88.93	86.97	87.94	87.71	82.47	85.01
CenterNet	85.48	72.55	78.49	84.25	75.63	79.71	86.57	65.92	74.85
CornerNet	87.54	84.48	85.98	87.08	83.48	85.24	86.93	58.99	68.19
CentripetalNet	87.69	88.13	87.91	87.87	88.69	88.28	82.58	85.32	83.93
MHDUN(Our)	82.87	78.31	80.53	88.24	85.63	86.39	83.24	79.26	81.20

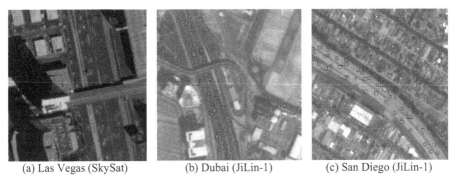

(a) Las Vegas (SkySat)   (b) Dubai (JiLin-1)   (c) San Diego (JiLin-1)

Fig. 4. Detection results in the Las Vegas, Dubai and San Diego satellite video datasets. The detection box is represented in blue, the ground truth box is represented in red. (Color figure online)

3.4 Ablation Experiments

The ablation experiments are implemented to investigate the effectiveness of MAI, OPLU Scheme and CA Loss on the San Diego Datasets. From the comparison between GMM and MAI, we can find that Prec., Rec. and F1 increase by 6.27%, 14.45% and 10.73% respectively, which indicates that OPLU Scheme has a strong ability to correct the pseudo-label box generated by GMM algorithm. From the comparison between GMM and OPLU Scheme, we can observe that Prec., Rec. and F1 increase by 2.92%, 4.18% and 4.31% respectively, which indicates that OPLU Scheme has the ability to update the pseudo-label box generated by GMM algorithm during the training. Comparing the results of the first three lines in the table above, we can draw a conclusion that MAI is more effective than OPLU Scheme in correcting the size of the pseudo-label box. Also, CA Loss can further improve the results which achieves a respectable performance compared to fully-supervised methods of 83.24% Prec., 79.26% Rec. and 81.20% F1 (Table 2).

Table 2. Ablation experiments on the San Diego Datasets.

	Prec (%) ↑	Rec (%) ↑	F1 (%) ↑
CenterNet w/GMM	73.46	63.38	68.04
CenterNet w/MAI	79.73	77.83	78.77
CenterNet w/GMM + OPLU scheme	76.38	67.56	72.35
CenterNet w/MAI + OPLU scheme	81.57	78.92	80.22
CenterNet w/MAI + OPLU scheme + CA loss	**83.24**	**79.26**	**81.20**

4 Conclusion

In this paper, a novel motion-aligned initialization and hardness-aware based dynamic update network is proposed for moving vehicle detection in satellite videos. Motion-aligned initialization method can accurately initialize the pseudo-label box of each object by combining GMM algorithm with the different correspondence between boxes and points. Online pseudo label update scheme can iteratively update and refine the size of pseudo label boxes every epoch to ensure stability of training. Besides, CA Loss even can further mine difficult training samples to guide the pseudo label box regression. These innovations presented in this paper are likely to be universal under the weakly supervised learning framework. In the future, it is not difficult to find that there are some defects in using the traditional background difference algorithm GMM to assist the generation of pseudo label boxes. Therefore, in the future, there is an attempt to adopt other different traditional algorithms, such as Vibe algorithm, or integrate multiple traditional models to achieve more accurate initialization of pseudo-label boxes.

References

1. Ao, W., Fu, Y., Hou, X., Xu, F.: Needles in a haystack: tracking city-scale moving vehicles from continuously moving satellite. IEEE Trans. Image Process. **29**, 1944–1957 (2020)
2. Ahmadi, S.A., Ghorbanian, A., Mohammadzadeh, A.: Moving vehicle detection, tracking and traffic parameter estimation from a satellite video: a perspective on a smarter city. Int. J. Remote Sens. **40**, 8379–8394 (2019)
3. Barnich, O., Van Droogenbroeck, M.: ViBe: a universal background subtraction algorithm for video sequences. IEEE Trans. Image Process. **20**, 1709–1724 (2011)
4. Roy, S.D., Bhowmik, M.K.: A comprehensive survey on computer vision based approaches for moving object detection. In: 2020 IEEE Region 10 Symposium (TENSYMP), pp. 1531–1534 (2020)
5. Ranjan, A., Black, M.J.: Optical flow estimation using a spatial pyramid network. In: 2017 IEEE Conference on Computer Vision and Pattern Recognition (CVPR), pp. 2720–2729 (2017)
6. Dale, M.A., et al.: Background differences in baseline and stimulated MMP levels influence abdominal aortic aneurysm susceptibility. Atherosclerosis **243**(2), 621–629 (2015)
7. Stauffer, C., Grimson, W.E.L.: Adaptive background mixture models for real-time tracking. In: Proceedings. 1999 IEEE Computer Society Conference on Computer Vision and Pattern Recognition (Cat. No. PR00149), vol. 2, pp. 246–252 (1999)
8. Sheather, S.J., Jones, M.C.: A reliable data-based bandwidth selection method for kernel density estimation. J. R. Stat. Soc. Ser. B-Methodol. **53**, 683–690 (1991)
9. Zhang, C., Du, X., Xu, S., Song, Z., Luo, M.: An improved moving object detection algorithm based on frame difference and edge detection. In: Fourth International Conference on Image and Graphics (ICIG 2007), pp. 519–523 (2007)
10. Ren, S., He, K., Girshick, R.B., Sun, J.: Faster R-CNN: towards real-time object detection with region proposal networks. IEEE Trans. Pattern Anal. Mach. Intell. **39**, 1137–1149 (2015)
11. Zhou, X., Wang, D., Krähenbühl, P.: Objects as points. ArXiv arXiv:1904.07850 (2019)
12. Bochkovskiy, A., Wang, C.Y., Liao, H.Y.M.: YOLOv4: optimal speed and accuracy of object detection. ArXiv arXiv:2004.10934 (2020)
13. Rousseeuw, P.J., van Driessen, K.: A fast algorithm for the minimum covariance determinant estimator. Technometrics **41**, 212–223 (1999)

14. Law, H., Deng, J.: CornerNet: detecting objects as paired keypoints. In: Ferrari, V., Hebert, M., Sminchisescu, C., Weiss, Y. (eds.) Computer Vision – ECCV 2018. LNCS, vol. 11218, pp. 765–781. Springer, Cham (2018). https://doi.org/10.1007/978-3-030-01264-9_45

15. Dong, Z., Li, G., Liao, Y., Wang, F., Ren, P., Qian, C.: CentripetalNet: pursuing high-quality keypoint pairs for object detection. In: 2020 IEEE/CVF Conference on Computer Vision and Pattern Recognition (CVPR), pp. 10516–10525 (2020)

16. Lin, T.-Y., et al.: Microsoft COCO: common objects in context. In: Fleet, D., Pajdla, T., Schiele, B., Tuytelaars, T. (eds.) ECCV 2014. LNCS, vol. 8693, pp. 740–755. Springer, Cham (2014). https://doi.org/10.1007/978-3-319-10602-1_48

17. Branson, S., Perona, P., Belongie, S.J.: Strong supervision from weak annotation: interactive training of deformable part models. In: 2011 International Conference on Computer Vision, pp. 1832–1839 (2011)

18. Yao, X., Feng, X., Han, J., Cheng, G., Guo, L.: Automatic weakly supervised object detection from high spatial resolution remote sensing images via dynamic curriculum learning. IEEE Trans. Geosci. Remote. Sens. **59**, 675–685 (2021)

19. Liu, Y., Shi, M., Zhao, Q., Wang, X.: Point in, box out: beyond counting persons in crowds. In: 2019 IEEE/CVF Conference on Computer Vision and Pattern Recognition (CVPR), pp. 6462–6471 (2019)

20. Li, Y., He, B., Melgani, F., Long, T.: Point-based weakly supervised learning for object detection in high spatial resolution remote sensing images. IEEE J. Sel. Top. Appl. Earth Observ. Remote Sens. **14**, 5361–5371 (2021)

21. Newell, A., Yang, K., Deng, J.: Stacked hourglass networks for human pose estimation. In: Leibe, B., Matas, J., Sebe, N., Welling, M. (eds.) ECCV 2016. LNCS, vol. 9912, pp. 483–499. Springer, Cham (2016). https://doi.org/10.1007/978-3-319-46484-8_29

22. Casagli, N., et al.: Spaceborne, UAV and ground-based remote sensing techniques for landslide mapping, monitoring and early warning. Geoenviron. Disasters **4**(1), 1–23 (2017). https://doi.org/10.1186/s40677-017-0073-1

23. Yang, T., et al.: Small moving vehicle detection in a satellite video of an urban area. Sensors (Basel, Switzerland) **16**, 1528 (2016)

A Multi-level Mixed Perception Network for Hyperspectral Image Classification

Huai Wang, Qinghua He, and Miaomiao Liang[✉]

School of Information Engineering, Jiangxi University of Science and Technology,
Ganzhou 341000, China
{6920190632,hqh}@mail.jxust.edu.cn, liangmiaom@jxust.edu.cn

Abstract. Objects in hyperspectral images (HSI) exist many subtle information differences, thus multi-level spectral-spatial perception will be beneficial to discriminative feature learning for HSI. We propose a multi-level mixed perception network (MMPN) for HSI classification, which is composed of three perceptrons: compact global and partition spectral perceptron (CSeP), pixel-wise spectral-partition perceptron (PSeP), and local spatial perceptron (LSaP). Specifically, we partition the object-centered block from HSI into non-overlapping spectral patches equidistantly. CSeP is designed on the squeezed feature to model spectral dependencies from overall and intra patches, respectively. The outputs are embedded together into the original patches for spectral information calibration. Then, PSeP is followed to avoid subtle spectra confusion, and LSaP is concurrently followed for multiscale spatial feature extraction. The learned features from each patch are used for label prediction respectively, and finally soft voting the classification result. Experimental results across two HSI datasets indicate that MMPN achieves expect performance in object classification when compared with the state-of-the-art methods.

Keywords: Hyperspectral image classification · Spectral partition · Multilayer perceptron · Feature fusion

1 Introduction

Hyperspectral images (HSI) contain abundant spectral and spatial information of ground objects and have aroused great concern in various fields, including environmental monitoring, urban planning, and mineral exploration [1,16,20], etc. HSI provides more abundant information for recognition of the target with a slight difference. However, it also presents new challenges for building models with a strong ability in capturing detailed information, which is subtler and easily overlooked in feature representation.

Deep learning (DL) has achieved great success in feature learning, such as multilayer perceptrons (MLP) and convolutional neural networks (CNN). Stacked autoencoders (SAEs) [15], deep belief networks (DBNs) [22], recursive

© IFIP International Federation for Information Processing 2022
Published by Springer Nature Switzerland AG 2022
Z. Shi et al. (Eds.): ICIS 2022, IFIP AICT 659, pp. 284–293, 2022.
https://doi.org/10.1007/978-3-031-14903-0_30

autoencoders (RAEs) [21], and other modified MLP forms are introduced to extract spectral-spatial information. Subsequently, CNN gradually becomes a standard with the benefits of local feature learning by weight sharing, of which the parameter steep decline compared to MLP, especially face to deep models [7,10,13]. However, inefficient long-range interaction gives rise to limited performance in scale adaptive contextual sensing. Some recent works design self-attention mechanisms to enhance long-range dependence [4,18,19]. Such as vision transformer (ViT) [4] divides an image into equal patches, and passes them through a series of multi-head attention layers for the transformer encoder. The attention block could excellently weigh the important region in the entire image while getting local perception on image patches.

Recently, researchers try to clarify why a transformer works so well. They proposed a series of pure MLP structured networks to demonstrate that MLP with no transformer performs the same well on ImageNet. Ding et al. [3] proposed a re-parameters multi-layer perceptron (RepMLP), where feature extraction is achieved in three levels: global perception, local perception, and partition perception. In addition, they introduced a parameter reconstruction approach to insert the convolutional parameters into the FC layer for more efficient inference. Luke et al. [9] replace the attention layer with a feed-forward layer and attempt to reveal the reason for transformer with good performance. Hugo et al. [3] designed a residual multi-layer perceptron (ResMLP), where affine transformation is used to achieve a similar effect as layer normalization and translation invariance. Furthermore, ResMLP uses two residual modules for feature extraction, one for linear interaction between patches, and the other for local feature learning in each patch. Ilya et al. [17] proposed a "mixing" multi-layer perceptron (MLP-Mixer), which uses two "mixing" strategies: channel-mixing that can be regarded as convolution with a kernel of size $N \times N$ and token-mixing do as a convolution with a kernel of size 1×1.

As mentioned above, all the methods divide the input image into patches in the spatial dimension, and then use MLP for feature extraction and object classification. HSI classification is a pixel-level object recognition task and usually takes a patch surrounded center pixel as the input of a network for feature learning. The neighborhood pixels usually act as assistant information for the central object identification and usually with a much small size, while the hundreds of spectrums in HSI provide a lot more cues for the physical properties of the object. Many subtle differences exist in the spectral response, while most recent deep models pay less attention to its local and meanwhile global perception. Therefore, we aim to build a multi-level spectral-spatial perception network for discriminative feature learning and classification of HSI.

Inspired by RepMLP [3], we design a lightweight network with MLP and CNN operation for HSI classification in this work. The input HSI is divided into equal blocks in spectral dimension, and then a multi-level mixed perception network is built with fully connected layers on squeezed features for information interaction in global and partition spectrum, with 3D convolution layers on each partition for pixel-wise spectral partition perception, and with multi-scale 2D convolution layers for multi-level spatial contextual extraction. Compared with other state-of-the-art methods, our proposed MMPN achieves good classification performance on two real HSI data sets, with fewer parameters and faster inference speed.

The remainder of this paper is organized as follows. Section 2 introduces the proposed method in detail. Section 3 shows the experimental results and analysis. Section 4 gives the conclusion of this paper.

2   Methodology

The backbone of our proposed MMPN is mainly divided into four parts: compact global and partition spectral perceptron (CSeP-g and CSeP-p), pixel-wise specatral-partition perceptron (PSeP), local spatial perceptron (LSaP), and the final classification module.

As shown in Fig. 1(a), block $\mathbf{M} \in \mathbb{R}^{C \times H \times W}$ that spitted from the original HSI is divided into $\frac{C}{b}$ patches in the spectral dimension, where C, H, W denote respectively the channel number, the height and width of the block, and b is the band number of each partition patch. Then, the input is in size of $(\frac{C}{b}, b, H, W)$ and is defined as $\mathbf{M}^{(\text{in})}$. In Fig. 1(c), global average pooling (GAP) is used to squeeze the spatial information, and the output is of size $(\frac{C}{b}, b, 1, 1)$.

$$\mathbf{M}^{(\text{GAP1})} = \text{GAP}(\mathbf{M}^{(\text{in})}, (\frac{C}{b}, b, 1, 1)), \tag{1}$$

Then, CSeP-g and the CSeP-p modules are set to achieve global and intra-patches dependencies. For CSeP-g, we reshape (RS) the $\mathbf{M}^{(\text{GAP1})}$ as the size of $(1, C)$, and feed them into FC layers to learn global spectral dependencies, which can be denoted as,

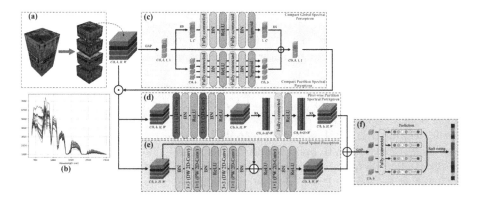

Fig. 1. The framework of MMPN for HSI classification. (a) Input from the original HSI is partitioned into non-overlapping patches in spectral dimension; (b) Spectral curves from some different ground objects; (c) CSeP module; (d) Pixel-wise spectral-partition perceptron; (e) Local spatial perceptron; (f) Classification with multiple group predictions.

$$\mathbf{M}_{\text{in}}^{(\text{CSeP}-\text{g})} = \text{RS}\left(\mathbf{M}^{(\text{GAP1})}, (1, C)\right),$$
$$\mathbf{M}_{\text{out}}^{(\text{CSeP}-\text{g})} = \text{MLP1}\left(\mathbf{M}_{\text{in}}^{(\text{CSeP}-\text{g})}, \mathbf{F}_1\right). \tag{2}$$

where the MLP1 contains two FC layers, two batch normalization layers, one ReLU activation function, and one Sigmoid function, as illustrated in Fig. 1. $\mathbf{F}_1$ is the corresponding weight matrix. The CSeP-p module is built the same as CSeP-g but performs on each partition, which means,

$$\mathbf{M}_{\text{out},i}^{(\text{CSeP}-\text{p})} = \text{MLP1}\left(\mathbf{M}_i^{(\text{GAP1})}, \mathbf{F}_{2,i}\right), \quad i = 1, 2, \cdots \frac{C}{b}. \tag{3}$$

Finally, we sum up the two outputs together to calibrate the spectral bands, the compact weighting matrix $\mathbf{W}$ and the output of CSeP module is defined as,

$$\mathbf{W} = \text{RS}\left(\mathbf{M}_{\text{out}}^{(\text{CSeP}-\text{g})}, \left(\frac{C}{b}, b, 1, 1\right)\right) + \mathbf{M}_{\text{out}}^{(\text{CSeP}-\text{p})},$$
$$\mathbf{M}_{\text{out}}^{(\text{CSeP})} = \mathbf{M}^{(\text{in})} \odot \mathbf{W}. \tag{4}$$

In PSeP module, we focus on intra-patches dependencies, which means each band partition is considered as an independent sample during feature learning. Figure 1 (d) gives the sketch of PSeP module that follows behind $\mathbf{M}_{\text{out}}^{(\text{CSeP})}$. Here, we design two sub-modules for pixel-wise spectral feature learning. One is built by two 3D convolutional layers with respectively one filter kernel, which is to overcome the defect of spectral confusion caused by spatial squeeze and thus worse performance in key spectral perception. The other sub-module is built by one FC layer when the inputs are reshaped to size of $\left(\frac{C}{b}, b \times H \times W\right)$, a design for overall partition spectral perception from all the neighborhood. It should be noted that all partitions share the same filter weights to avoid parameter increases. the operation can be written as follows,

$$\mathbf{M}_{\text{out},i}^{(\text{Conv3D})} = \text{Conv3D}\left(\mathbf{M}_{\text{out},i}^{(\text{CSeP})}, \mathbf{W}_1\right),$$
$$\mathbf{M}_{\text{out},i}^{(\text{MLP2})} = \text{MLP2}\left(\text{RS}\left(\mathbf{M}_{\text{out},i}^{(\text{Conv3D})}, \left(\frac{C}{b}, b \times H \times W\right)\right), \mathbf{F}_3\right). \tag{5}$$

where $\mathbf{W}_1$ is the 3D filter parameter of size $5 \times 1 \times 1$, and $\mathbf{F}_3$ is the weights of FC layer with size of (bHW, bHW). Here, MLP2 contains only one FC layer and one activation Layer by ReLU function. Finally, we shape $\mathbf{M}_{\text{out},i}^{(\text{MLP2})}$ back to $\left(\frac{C}{b}, b, H, W\right)$ and obtain the output $\mathbf{M}_{\text{out},i}^{(\text{PSeP})}$ of PSeP module for further feature fusion,

$$\mathbf{M}_{\text{out},i}^{(\text{PSeP})} = \text{RS}(\mathbf{M}_{\text{out},i}^{(\text{MLP2})}, (\frac{C}{b}, b, H, W)). \tag{6}$$

Many studies have shown that local spatial perception has great benefits in effective HSI classification [5,6]. The pure FC layer is suitable for learning large-range dependencies and location information but is poor in capturing local spatial features. In Fig. 1(e), we employ depth-wise separable convolution to extract local spatial features in LSaP module which is parallel with PSeP part.

This part can be defined as,

$$
\begin{aligned}
\mathbf{M}_{out,i}^{(DSConv)} &= DSConv\left(\mathbf{M}_{out,i}^{(CSeP)}, \mathbf{W}_2\right) + \mathbf{M}_{out,i}^{(CSeP)}, \\
\mathbf{M}_{out,i}^{(LSaP)} &= PConv\left(\mathbf{M}_{out,i}^{(DSConv)}, \mathbf{W}_3\right),
\end{aligned}
\tag{7}
$$

where $DSConv(\cdot,\cdot)$ contains two depthwise separable convolution layers with kernel of size 3×3 in depth-wise layers and $PConv(\cdot,\cdot)$ contains one point-wise convolution layer for further feature recombination. Besides, skip connection is used here for smooth flow of information.

Finally, features from PSeP and LSaP modules are fused together for object classification. Here, we perform class prediction separately on each patch and obtain the final results by soft voting. As shown in Fig. 1(f), each classifier consists of a mean statistics description of each feature map by a GAP layer and linear class prediction by an FC layer. The classification module can be represented as,

$$
\begin{aligned}
\mathbf{M}_i^{(GAP2)} &= GAP\left(\mathbf{M}_{out,i}^{(PSeP)} + \mathbf{M}_{out,i}^{(LSaP)}, (1, b, 1, 1)\right), \\
\mathbf{L} &= \frac{b}{C}\sum_{i=1}^{C/b} FC\left(\mathbf{M}_i^{(GAP2)}, \mathbf{F}_{4,i}\right),
\end{aligned}
\tag{8}
$$

where $\mathbf{F}_{4,i} \in {}^{b \times L}$ and L is the class number. $\mathbf{L}$ is the probability that a sample belongs to each class.

3   Experiments Results and Analysis

We evaluate our proposed MMPN model from parameter analysis, ablation study, and comparison with some state-of-the-art methods on two real HSI data sets. Indian Pines (IN) dataset contains 145×145 pixels with a spatial resolution of 20 m per pixel, and 200 spectral bands after some noisy bands are removed. There are 16 classes of ground objects in the ground truth. The Pavia University (UP) dataset contains 610×340 pixels and 103 bands after some noisy bands are removed. 9 classes of urban area ground objects are labeled in the ground truth. Figures 3 and 4 shows the false-color images and the ground truth of the two datasets.

All experiments in this work are implemented on the platform with Intel Xeon W-2133 CPU and NVIDIA GeForce RTX 2080 Ti GPU. The software environment is Python 3.8.3, PyTorch 1.7.0, and CUDA 11.0. We randomly select 10% and 3% samples from the labeled IN and UP dataset for model training, and the rest for testing. SGD optimizer is used to update the network parameters, the batch size is set respectively to 16 and 32, the learning rate is set to 0.01, weight decay is set to 0.0001, and momentum is set to 0.9. Overall accuracy (OA) is used to measure classification performance.

3.1   Parameters Analysis and Ablation Study

In MMPN, the band number b in each partition is a critical parameter that affects the classification performance of HSI. Thus, we verify the OAs as the b ranging from 10 to 200 for the IN dataset, and from 10 to 100 for the UP dataset when the last 3 spectra are removed for equal division. Here, '10' means that we divide the IN data into 20 patches from spectral dimension and '200' means there is no partition in feature learning, the same situation for the UP data. As the results in Fig. 2, we can observe that it does not look well to partition too coarse patches, or too finer. The best partition is $d = 50$ for both two experimental datasets.

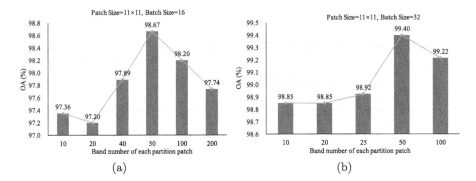

Fig. 2. Classification OAs (%) on the (a) IN and (b) UP data sets as the band number b of each partition ranging from 10 to all.

Table 1. Ablation study of each component in MMPN. ✓ denotes the corresponding module present in MMPN.

Components				IN			UP		
CSeP-g	CSeP-p	PSeP	LSaP	OA	AA	Kappa	OA	AA	Kappa
	✓	✓	✓	98.33	96.72	98.10	99.32	98.83	99.10
✓		✓	✓	98.28	96.74	98.04	99.17	98.68	98.90
		✓	✓	97.14	95.19	96.75	99.18	98.58	98.92
✓	✓		✓	98.65	97.22	98.47	99.35	98.78	99.11
✓	✓	✓		95.70	92.71	95.10	97.05	96.09	96.13
✓	✓	✓	✓	**98.67**	**97.30**	**98.48**	**99.40**	**98.88**	**99.21**

Besides, three main components are designed for discriminative feature learning, which are CSeP for compact spectral calibration, PSeP for pixel-wise partition perception, and LSaP for local spatial filtering. In this part, we discuss the importance of those components in MMPN through several sets of ablation studies. As the results reported in Table 1, the classification accuracy decreases more or less when any of the components are absent in MMPN. Specifically, CSeP achieves a 1–2% accuracy increase in the IN dataset, but the advantage is not obvious in the UP dataset. This indicates that CSeP contributes more to distinguishing the ground objects with a highly similar spectrum (such as IN dataset) but is not beneficial to the recognition of objects with a large spectral difference. LSaP is crucial for both of the datasets, boosting the accuracy increase by 2 to 3 points. PSeP is a less elegant solution for accuracy increase but will be beneficial for finer boundary location.

3.2 Comparison with State-of-the-Art Methods

We further compare our proposed MMPN model with seven deep learning-based methods, including one RNN-based model (RNN [11]), two spectral-spatial

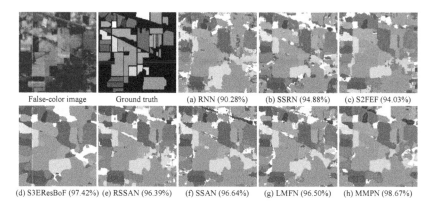

Fig. 3. Comparison of the classification maps with the state-of-the-art methods on IN data set.

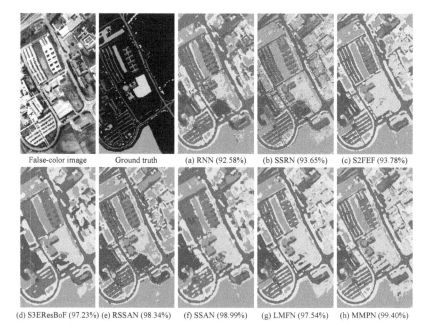

Fig. 4. Comparison of the classification maps with the state-of-the-art methods on UP data set.

convolution networks (SSRN [23] and S2FEF [2]), and four attention mechanism related models (S3EResBoF [12], RSSAN [24], SSAN [14], LMFN [8]). The parameter settings of the above deep models are set according to the original paper. We exhibit the best classification maps and report the OAs from all the comparing methods in Fig. 3 and Fig. 4, respectively. From the results, we can conclude that our method is superior in classification accuracy, meanwhile giving more clear and clean boundary positioning.

To demonstrate the stability of our model to the number of training samples, we further show the classification accuracies when 1% to 15% labeled samples in each class are randomly sampled for model training, and all the results are reported as the mean of ten runs. The results in Fig. 5 show that our method achieves the best classification accuracy, except for a slightly lower OA on IN dataset with 1% samples per class for model training.

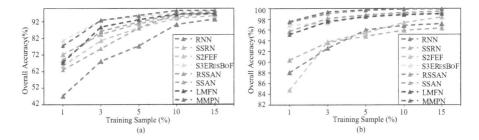

Fig. 5. Classification performance OA (%) on the IN (a) and UP (b) data sets with the number of training samples per class ranging from 1% to 15%.

4   Conclusion

In this paper, we introduce a multi-level mixed perception network for HSI classification. With the characteristics of the fully connected network and convolution network, MMPN divides the HSI into patches from the spectral dimension and builds three perceptrons: compact global and partition spectral perceptron, pixel-wise spectral-partition perceptron, and local spatial perceptron, to extract multi-scale spectral-spatial information from multiple perspectives. Besides, soft voting from each patch is designed at the end of the network to achieve the final class prediction. This multi-view feature extraction re-examines the importance of spectral information in HSI classification. Experimental results on two hyperspectral data sets show that MMPN presents some advantages in classification accuracy, including robustness and generalization.

In the future, we will pay close attention to automatic spectral partition and self-supervised learning of the potential rules or manifold.

Acknowledgements. This research was funded by the National Natural Science Foundation of China (Nos. 61901198, 62066018); the Natural Science Basic Research Plan in Shaanxi Province of China (No. 2022JQ-704); and the Program of Qingjiang Excellent Young Talents, Jiangxi University of Science and Technology (No. JXUSTQJYX2020019)).

References

1. Bioucas-Dias, J.M., Plaza, A., Camps-Valls, G., Scheunders, P., Nasrabadi, N., Chanussot, J.: Hyperspectral remote sensing data analysis and future challenges. IEEE Geosci. Remote Sens. Mag. **1**(2), 6–36 (2013). https://doi.org/10.1109/MGRS.2013.2244672
2. Chen, L., Wei, Z., Xu, Y.: A lightweight spectral-spatial feature extraction and fusion network for hyperspectral image classification. Remote Sens. **12**(9), 1395 (2020)
3. Ding, X., Zhang, X., Han, J., Ding, G.: RepMLP: re-parameterizing convolutions into fully-connected layers for image recognition (2021)
4. Dosovitskiy, A., et al.: An image is worth 16x16 words: transformers for image recognition at scale (2021)
5. Ghamisi, P., et al.: New frontiers in spectral-spatial hyperspectral image classification: the latest advances based on mathematical morphology, Markov random fields, segmentation, sparse representation, and deep learning. IEEE Geosci. Remote Sens. Mag. **6**(3), 10–43 (2018). https://doi.org/10.1109/MGRS.2018.2854840
6. He, L., Li, J., Liu, C., Li, S.: Recent advances on spectral-spatial hyperspectral image classification: an overview and new guidelines. IEEE Trans. Geosci. Remote Sens. **56**(3), 1579–1597 (2018). https://doi.org/10.1109/TGRS.2017.2765364
7. Lee, H., Kwon, H.: Going deeper with contextual CNN for hyperspectral image classification. IEEE Trans. Image Process. **26**(10), 4843–4855 (2017). https://doi.org/10.1109/TIP.2017.2725580
8. Liang, M., Wang, H., Yu, X., Meng, Z., Yi, J., Jiao, L.: Lightweight multilevel feature fusion network for hyperspectral image classification. Remote Sens. **14**(1), 79 (2021)
9. Melas-Kyriazi, L.: Do you even need attention? A stack of feed-forward layers does surprisingly well on ImageNet (2021)
10. Meng, Z., Li, L., Jiao, L., Feng, Z., Tang, X., Liang, M.: Fully dense multiscale fusion network for hyperspectral image classification. Remote Sens. **11**(22), 2718 (2019)
11. Mou, L., Ghamisi, P., Zhu, X.X.: Deep recurrent neural networks for hyperspectral image classification. IEEE Trans. Geosci. Remote Sens. **55**(7), 3639–3655 (2017)
12. Roy, S.K., Chatterjee, S., Bhattacharyya, S., Chaudhuri, B.B., Platoš, J.: Lightweight spectral-spatial squeeze-and-excitation residual bag-of-features learning for hyperspectral classification. IEEE Trans. Geosci. Remote Sens. **58**(8), 5277–5290 (2020)
13. Song, W., Li, S., Fang, L., Lu, T.: Hyperspectral image classification with deep feature fusion network. IEEE Trans. Geosci. Remote Sens. **56**(6), 3173–3184 (2018). https://doi.org/10.1109/TGRS.2018.2794326
14. Sun, H., Zheng, X., Lu, X., Wu, S.: Spectral-spatial attention network for hyperspectral image classification. IEEE Trans. Geosci. Remote Sens. **58**(5), 3232–3245 (2020)

15. Tao, C., Pan, H., Li, Y., Zou, Z.: Unsupervised spectral-spatial feature learning with stacked sparse autoencoder for hyperspectral imagery classification. IEEE Geosci. Remote Sens. Lett. **12**(12), 2438–2442 (2015). https://doi.org/10.1109/LGRS.2015.2482520

16. Tian, A., Fu, C., Yau, H.T., Su, X.Y., Xiong, H.: A new methodology of soil salinization degree classification by probability neural network model based on centroid of fractional Lorenz chaos self-synchronization error dynamics. IEEE Trans. Geosci. Remote Sens. **58**(2), 799–810 (2020). https://doi.org/10.1109/TGRS.2019.2940592

17. Tolstikhin, I., et al.: MLP-mixer: an all-MLP architecture for vision (2021)

18. Vaswani, A., et al.: Attention is all you need. In: Advances in Neural Information Processing Systems, pp. 5998–6008 (2017)

19. Wang, X., Girshick, R., Gupta, A., He, K.: Non-local neural networks. In: Proceedings of the IEEE Conference on Computer Vision and Pattern Recognition (CVPR), June 2018

20. Yokoya, N., Chan, J.C.W., Segl, K.: Potential of resolution-enhanced hyperspectral data for mineral mapping using simulated EnMAP and Sentinel-2 images. Remote Sens. **8**(3) (2016). https://doi.org/10.3390/rs8030172, https://www.mdpi.com/2072-4292/8/3/172

21. Zhang, X., Liang, Y., Li, C., Huyan, N., Jiao, L., Zhou, H.: Recursive autoencoders-based unsupervised feature learning for hyperspectral image classification. IEEE Geosci. Remote Sens. Lett. **14**(11), 1928–1932 (2017). https://doi.org/10.1109/LGRS.2017.2737823

22. Zhong, P., Gong, Z., Li, S., Schönlieb, C.B.: Learning to diversify deep belief networks for hyperspectral image classification. IEEE Trans. Geosci. Remote Sens. **55**(6), 3516–3530 (2017)

23. Zhong, Z., Li, J., Luo, Z., Chapman, M.: Spectral-spatial residual network for hyperspectral image classification: a 3-D deep learning framework. IEEE Trans. Geosci. Remote Sens. **56**(2), 847–858 (2018)

24. Zhu, M., Jiao, L., Liu, F., Yang, S., Wang, J.: Residual spectral-spatial attention network for hyperspectral image classification. IEEE Trans. Geosci. Remote Sens. **59**(1), 449–462 (2020)

A Lightweight SAR Ship Detection Network Based on Superpixel Statistical Modeling

Zhengxi Guo$^{(\boxtimes)}$, Biao Hou, and Bo Ren

Xidian University, Xi'an 710071, China
`XiDianGZX@stu.xidian.edu.cn`

Abstract. Deep learning technology has been widely used in SAR ship detection tasks. However, complex sea level backgrounds, such as sea clutter and shorelines, greatly interfere with the accuracy of the detection of ship targets. In addition, embedded devices need to deploy multiple detection models, such as FPGA, so model size and detection speed are also important indicators in practical applications. In order to solve these problems, we developed a method combining traditional detection methods with deep learning. In this paper, SAR image clutter distribution model is used to suppress SAR image clutter, and then the processed image is sent to the network for learning. Based on this idea, we have established a superpixel composite Gamma distribution model, which can obtain more accurate fitting results than pixel scale Gamma distribution and suppress background clutter more effectively. We also propose the YOLO-SX lightweight detection network, which significantly reduces model size, detection time, calculation parameters, and memory consumption. Its overall performance is superior to other detection methods.

Keywords: SAR ship detection · Lightweight deep learning · Superpixel statistical modeling · Gamma distribution

1 Introduction

Synthetic aperture radar (SAR) is an active sensor. Compared with optical and infrared sensors, SAR has the characteristics of all-weather, all-day and penetration capability [1]. Due to these advantages, SAR technology has been widely used in military and civilian fields. With the development of SAR technology, SAR image interpretation faces many opportunities and challenges.

The field of SAR ship detection is broadly divided into two development stages: traditional methods and deep learning methods. Before the advent of deep learning, CFAR (Constant False Alarm Rate) algorithm was widely used in the detection of ground and marine targets in SAR images. It is a common adaptive algorithm for radar systems to detect target echoes in noisy, cluttered and interfering backgrounds [2]. It detects ship targets by modeling the statistical distribution of background clutter, but it is often difficult to model the

© IFIP International Federation for Information Processing 2022
Published by Springer Nature Switzerland AG 2022
Z. Shi et al. (Eds.): ICIS 2022, IFIP AICT 659, pp. 294–301, 2022.
https://doi.org/10.1007/978-3-031-14903-0_31

clutter in a complex background with an appropriate probability density function [3]. Therefore, many previous researches have been devoted to the variation, combination, and adjustment of parameter models to meet the desired accuracy of statistical modeling of clutter to determine detection thresholds [4]. However, in practical applications, the processing speed of the algorithm can not meet the requirements. Since AlexNet won the ImageNet image classification challenge in 2012, deep neural networks have shown very high accuracy and reliability in image detection. Traditional feature extraction methods are gradually replaced by convolutional neural networks [5].

The purpose of this paper is to combine SAR image statistical modeling with deep learning, and propose a SAR ship detection method based on SAR image statistical distribution and YOLOV5. Different from the traditional statistical modeling, we establish the clutter distribution model in the superpixel domain of the image, and send the processed image into the lightweight deep network for learning, so as to improve the detection speed without losing accuracy and improve the ship detection ability under complex backgrounds. In this paper, Sect. 2 introduces the method based on superpixel statistical modeling, Sect. 3 describes the construction of the lightweight detection network, Section 4 introduces the experiments and Sect. 5 is the conclusion.

2 Superpixel-Based Composite Gamma Distribution Modeling

2.1 Superpixel

We define a block of pixels consisting of adjacent pixels with similar texture, color and grayscale value in an image as a superpixel region [6]. Most of these regions retain the effective information for further image processing, and generally do not destroy the boundary information of objects in the image. Few superpixels are used to express image features instead of a large number of pixels to reduce the complexity of subsequent image processing. The segmentation effect as shown in Fig. 1(a).

2.2 Composite Gamma Distribution Based on Superpixel

First, we calculate two key parameters based on the divided superpixels: 1) the number of pixels contained in each superpixel, called the superpixel domain; 2) the average gray value of the pixels contained in each superpixel, called the superpixel reflectivity [7].

Then we calculate the distribution law of each superpixel domain according to Eq. (1), that is, the proportion of the number of pixels in each superpixel do-main to the number of pixels in the whole image.

$$P(n) = \frac{N(n)}{\sum_{i=1}^{S} N(i)} \tag{1}$$

where n is the index of the superpixel domain, S is the number of superpixel domains of this image, and $N(i)$ denotes the number of pixels in the i-th superpixel domain.

Then calculate the probability density function of superpixel reflectivity as in (2).

$$f(Z) = \sum_{n=\min}^{\max} f_{z|n}(z \mid n)p(n) = \sum_{n=\min}^{\max} \frac{z^{\varphi_n-1}e^{-z/\sigma_n}}{\sigma_n^{\varphi_n}\Gamma(\varphi_n)}p(n) \qquad (2)$$

where $p(n)$ denotes the distribution law of the superpixel domain, φ_n and σ_n the Gamma parameters of the superpixel reflectance, min denotes the minimum superpixel domain, and max denotes the maximum superpixel domain.

Then calculate the threshold value T as (3).

$$P_{fa} = \int_T^\infty f(z)dz \qquad (3)$$

where P_{fa} is the preset constant false alarm rate and $f(z)$ is the probability density function of the superpixel reflectivity.

Finally, we perform clutter suppression on the image based on the threshold values calculated in the above steps, setting the pixel values smaller than the threshold T to 0 and keeping the pixel values larger than the threshold T. The result as shown in Fig. 1(b).

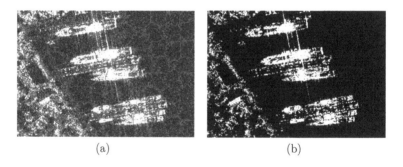

(a)   (b)

Fig. 1. (a) Superpixel segmentation result. (b) The result of clutter suppression.

3   Lightweight Ship Detection Network

3.1   ShuffleNeck Module

To achieve the lightweight effect, we constructed a ShuffleNeck module (see Fig. 2) to replace the BottleNeck module in the YOLOV5 backbone network.

It is constructed by depth separable convolution (DWConv), channel shuffle and residual edges [8]. Firstly, the feature map is divided into two feature maps T1 and T2 with the same number of channels (half of the original number of channels) by a channel split operation. The first feature map T1 is passed through

1×1 convolution layer, 3×3 DWConv, and 1×1 convolution layer to obtain a deep feature map T3 containing a part of the original feature map. Then, the second feature map T2 is spliced with T3 obtained by the first branch without any operation. Finally, the channel shuffle operation is used to obtain the deep feature maps with the same size and number of channels as the original feature maps.

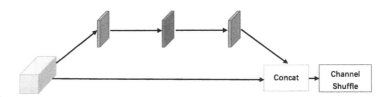

Fig. 2. The structure of ShuffleNeck module. In the figure, the orange cube represents 1×1 normal convolution and the blue cube represents 3×3 DWConv. (Color figure online)

3.2   Shuffle-X(SX) Module

Unlike ShuffleNet, the SX module (see Fig. 3) processes the feature maps in two branches [9]. The first branch is a 1×1 DWConv. The second branch is a 1×1 DWConv and a ShuffleNeck module. Finally, the feature maps of the two branches are channel stitched to obtain the final deep features.

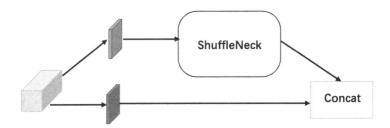

Fig. 3. The structure of SX module. In the figure, the orange cube represents 1×1 normal convolution and the blue cube represents 1×1 DWConv. (Color figure online)

3.3   YOLO-SX Algorithm Description

In this paper, we use the proposed SX module to replace the C3 modules in YOLOV5. Specifically, our lightweight backbone network consists of DWConv and SX modules, which greatly reduces the number of parameters in the network. In the network, all four convolutional layers from P1–P4 have a step size of 2 and are used for down-sampling. The first SX module is used to quickly extract shallow features. The second and third SX modules are used to extract medium-scale feature maps. The last SX module is used to extract large scale features.

In addition, our method makes extensive use of channel shuffle and residual edges. This allows our network to retain enough shallow features for multi-scale detection tasks. The network structure as shown in Fig. 4.

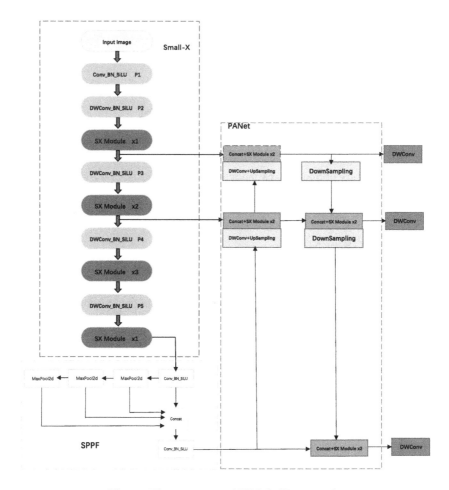

Fig. 4. The structure of YOLO-SX network.

4   Experiment

In this section, we will discuss the experimental dataset, process and results.

4.1   Experiment Dataset and Details

The experiment uses the SSDD (SAR-Ship Detection Dataset) which is publicly available and widely used for SAR ship detection algorithm performance measurement. The dataset has 1160 images with 2456 ships, and the average number of ships per image is 2.12. The dataset has small ships with insignificant features, ships densely parallel moored in ports, large ships, severe ships under speckle noise and in complex background. Four polarization modes HH, HV, VV and VH, are also included [10].

We first perform clutter suppression in the superpixel domain for all images in the dataset, and then divide the training set, validation set and test set in the ratio of 7:2:1. The GPU used for the experiments is a 24G GeForce GTX3090. And the experimental platform is Ubuntu 16.04, using the Pytorch deep learning framework, implemented in python language.

4.2 Ablation Experiment

To verify the effectiveness of the clutter suppression method in this paper, we conducted ablation experiments using complex background and nearshore target data in SSDD. The images processed with clutter suppression and the images without processing are detected respectively. The results as shown in Fig. 5. We can clearly see that the missed detection rate of the images without clutter suppression is higher than the processed images, and the confidence level is also relatively lower.

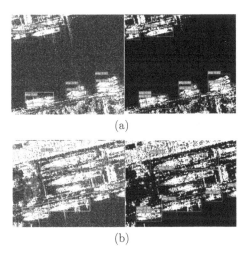

(a)

(b)

Fig. 5. The left side of (a) and (b) shows the ship images with complex backgrounds and near-shore targets without clutter suppression processing, and the right side shows the processed image. The red box is the detection result, and the yellow box is the missed ship target. (Color figure online)

We also conducted experiments on the tiny target data on the sea surface to verify the effectiveness of our method, and the results as shown in Fig. 6. Obviously, the unprocessed detection results in missed detection of small targets with lower confidence than the images processed with clutter suppression.

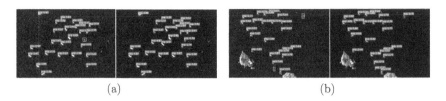

(a)   (b)

Fig. 6. The left side of (a) and (b) shows the image of tiny small targets on the sea surface without clutter suppression processing, and the right side shows the processed image. The red box is the detection result, and the yellow box is the missed ship target. (Color figure online)

In summary, our method not only performs excellently in detecting ship targets with complex backgrounds, but is also applicable to cross-scale detection tasks.

4.3   Comparison Experiment

To evaluate the performance of the model, we use mAP (average accuracy), FPS (frames per second) and model size as evaluation metrics for ship detection. mAP is the average of the average accuracy for detecting each category. Since we have only ship targets in our experiments, mAP is equal to the average accuracy (AP).

We compare the performance of YOLOV4-tiny, YOLOV5x, SSD, Faster R-CNN and YOLO-SX by evaluating their performance in the above three aspects. The results as shown in Table 1. It is obvious that SSD and Faster R-CNN, which are two-stage detection networks, perform worse than YOLO. And although YOLOV5x achieves the best performance in terms of mAP, our method is much superior to YOLOV5x and other models in terms of FPS and model size.

Table 1. Comparison of different methods in mAP, FPS and model size

Model	mAP	FPS	Model size (MB)
YOLOV4-Tiny	93.2%	43	22.4
YOLOV5x	**98.8%**	37	165.2
SSD	85.4%	36	93.2
Faster R-CNN	88.7%	27	527.8
YOLOV-SX	97.1%	**50**	**1.4**

5   Conclusion

This paper introduces a traditional SAR image statistical modeling method combined with deep learning. The method divides the image into several superpixel regions composed of adjacent pixels with similar texture, color, and grayscale values. These superpixels are then statistically modeled and clutter suppression using composite Gamma distributions. The experiments were conducted on SSDD, a widely accepted dataset that is superior in accuracy and speed to existing algorithms, both for small ship targets in large areas of the ocean and for ship targets in complex settings. At the same time, a lightweight backbone was introduced to replace the existing backbone based on YOLOV5, significantly reducing the model's size and number of parameters and improving detection speed. It also facilitates the deployment of the model in embedded devices and is suitable for real-time tasks. It is hoped that this paper can provide a solution idea for future deep learning lightweight work and SAR image ship detection work.

Acknowledgements. The authors would like to thank the Chinese Academy of Sciences for providing the SSDD dataset.

References

1. Leng, X., Ji, K., Yang, K., Zou, H.: A bilateral CFAR algorithm for ship detection in SAR images. IEEE Geosci. Remote Sens. Lett. **12**, 1536–1540 (2015)
2. Liu, W., et al.: SSD: single shot MultiBox detector. In: Proceedings of the European Conference on Computer Vision (ECCV), Amsterdam, The Netherlands, 8–16 October 2016, pp. 21–37 (2016)
3. Liao, M., Wang, C., Wang, Y., Jiang, L.: Using SAR images to detect ships from sea clutter. IEEE Geosci. Remote Sens. Lett. **5**, 194–198 (2008)
4. Zhou, X., Liu, X., Chen, Q., Zhang, Z.: Power transmission tower CFAR detection algorithm based on integrated superpixel window and adaptive statistical model. In: Proceedings of IGARSS - IEEE International Geoscience and Remote Sensing Symposium, pp. 2326–2329, July 2019
5. Krizhevsky, A., Sutskever, I., Hinton, G.: ImageNet classification with deep convolutional neural networks. In: Advances in Neural Information Processing Systems, pp. 1097–1105. ACM, New York (2012)
6. Girshick, R., Donahue, J., Darrell, T., Malik, J.: Rich feature hierarchies for accurate object detection and semantic segmentation. In: Proceedings of the 2014 IEEE Conference on Computer Vision and Pattern Recognition (CVPR), Columbus, OH, USA, 23–28 June 2014, pp. 580–587 (2014)
7. Li, M., Wen, G., Huang, X., Li, K., Lin, S.: A lightweight detection model for SAR air-craft in a complex environment. Remote Sens. **13**(24), 5020 (2021). https://doi.org/10.3390/rs13245020
8. Ren, S., He, K., Girshick, R., Sun, J.: Faster R-CNN: towards real-time object detection with region proposal networks. In: Advances in Neural Information Processing Systems, pp. 91–99. IEEE, New York (2015)
9. Chen, Z., Gao, X.: An improved algorithm for ship target detection in SAR images based on faster R-CNN. In: Proceedings of the 2018 Ninth International Conference on Intelligent Control and Information Processing (ICICIP), Wanzhou, China, 9–11 November 2018, pp. 39–43 (2018)
10. Jiang, K.J., Fu, X., Qin, R., Wang, X., Ma, Z.: High-speed lightweight ship detection algorithm based on YOLO-V4 for three-channels RGB SAR image. Remote Sens. **13**(10), 1909 (2021). https://doi.org/10.3390/rs13101909

Background Augmentation
with Transformer-Based Autoencoder
for Hyperspectral Anomaly Detection

Jianing Wang$^{(\boxtimes)}$, Yichen Liu, and Linhao Li

Xidian University, Xi'an, China
jnwang@xidian.edu.cn, lhli_7@stu.xidian.edu.cn

Abstract. Aiming at handling the problem caused by the lack of prior spectral knowledge of anomalous pixels for hyperspectral anomaly detection (HAD). In this paper, we propose a background augmentation with transformer-based autoencoder for hyperspectral remote sensing image anomaly detection. The representative background pixels are selected based on sparse representation for obtaining typical background pixels as training samples of the transformer-based autoencoder. The selected typical background pixels can be used for training the transformer-based autoencoder to realize background pixel reconstruction. Thereafter, the pseudo background samples can be reconstructed from the transformer-based autoencoder, which is used to subtract the original image to obtain the residual image. Finally, Reed-Xiaoli (RX) is used to detect the anomalous pixels from residual image. Experiments results demonstrate that the proposed transformer-based autoencoder which can present competitive hyperspectral image anomaly detection results than other traditional algorithms.

Keywords: Hyperspectral remote sensing · Transformer-based autoencoder · Anomaly detection · Reed-Xiaoli

1 Introduction

Hyperspectral images collect rich information from the scene by hundreds of spectral bands. The rich spectral information offers a unique diagnostic identification ability for targets of interest. As a branch of hyperspectral target location, anomaly detection has been studied since the advent of hyperspectral technology [1]. A lot of hyperspectral anomaly detection methods has been proposed in recent years.

HAD based on statistical theory are the most classical methods. As an important milestone of anomaly detection, Reed-Xiaoli (RX) algorithm is proposed by Reed and Yu [2], which characterizes the background as a multivariate Gaussian distribution and assigns anomaly scores according to the Mahalanobis distance. Among that, the local RX (LRX) detector [3] is a typically evolved version of

© IFIP International Federation for Information Processing 2022
Published by Springer Nature Switzerland AG 2022
Z. Shi et al. (Eds.): ICIS 2022, IFIP AICT 659, pp. 302–309, 2022.
https://doi.org/10.1007/978-3-031-14903-0_32

RX, which estimates background (BKG) by utilizing local statistics. But Gaussian distribution assumption of BKG in these methods is not fully reasonable due to the complexity of hyperspectral images. To address this issue, a collaborative representation-based detector (CRD) [4] is proposed, which can approximately represent each pixel in BKG by its spatial neighborhoods. Subsequently, the priority-based tensor approximation (PTA) [5] is proposed by introducing tensors into low-rank and sparse priors for achieving better detection performance. Recently, deep learning (DL)-based algorithms have been widely utilized in HAD area. There are mainly supervised and unsupervised two mainstreams for DL-based HAD task. As for supervised DL-based HAD, a convolutional neural network (CNN) is proposed to fully exploit the spatial correlation [6]. In [7], a deep belief network (DBN) is exploited for the feature representation and reconstruction of background samples. As for unsupervised methods, autoencoder (AE) and its similar variant structures have been applied for HAD, the residuals between the reconstructed background image and the original image are utilized to detect anomalies [8]. Thereafter, the generative adversarial networks (GAN) have also been proposed and applied in HAD task. In [9], the generator-based and discriminator-based detectors are exploited for realizing better reconstruction performance of background samples in HAD task.

According to the capability of efficient local and global feature extraction, transformer [10] has been successfully applied in natural language processing (NLP). Recently, researchers have gradually applied transformer in computer vision (CV) area. Vision transformer (ViT) [11] has achieved the state-of-the-art performance on multiple image recognition benchmarks. Meanwhile, in [12], transformer encoder-decoder architecture is proposed and explored for object detection. Therefore, in this paper, in order to mitigate the problem caused by the lack of prior spectral knowledge of anomalous pixels for HAD, we proposed a background augmentation with transformer-based autoencoder structure, which can realize better reconstruction performance by exploiting local and global attention in the spectral perspective. The pseudo background samples can be reconstructed from the transformer-based autoencoder, then the highlight anomaly pixels can be easily detected by the RX algorithm. We implement our proposed algorithm on several HAD data sets, the experiment results demonstrate the competitive performance and results than other traditional algorithms.

The rest of the paper is organized as follows. Section 2 presents the detailed process and principles of the algorithm in this paper. Section 3 performs experiments on real hyperspectral data sets. Section 4 draws some conclusions and provides hints at plausible future research lines.

2 Methodology

The overall procedure of our detection process is shown in Fig. 1. The main structure mainly composed of three main parts. The typical background samples selection, transformer-based autoencoder and RX detection. The hybrid pixel selection strategy based on sparse representation is exploited to select typical

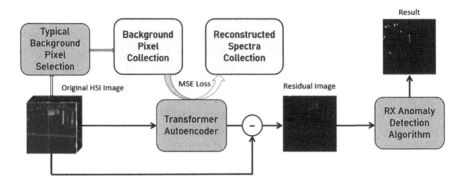

Fig. 1. Background augmentation with transformer-based autoencoder for hyperspectral anomaly detection process.

background samples, the selected samples would be fed into the transformer-based autoencoder for training and automatically reconstructing the pseudo background samples. Then, the residual image is obtained by subtracting the reconstructed hyperspectral image from the original hyperspectral image as

$$\mathbf{r} = \mathbf{s} - \mathbf{s}' \tag{1}$$

where $\mathbf{s}$ is the original hyperspectral image, $\mathbf{s}'$ is the reconstructed hyperspectral image and $\mathbf{r}$ is the residual image. Therefore, the backgrounds are augmented by suppressing the residual of background pixels in the residual image $\mathbf{r}$, since the RX algorithm can be utilized to realize more efficient anomaly detection performance.

2.1 Typical Background Samples Selection

The high-quality and representative background sample plays a key role for DL-based training procedure. Therefore, a hybrid pixel selection strategy based on sparse representation was presented. The given hyperspectral image $X \in \mathbb{R}^{H \times W \times C}$ is transformed into $X_{PCA} \in \mathbb{R}^{H \times W \times 3}$ by Principal Component Analysis (PCA) [13]. X_{PCA} aggregates into m clusters by the K-means algorithm, and each cluster consists of m_s pixels

$$\mathbf{E}^i = \left\{ \mathbf{e}_1^i, \mathbf{e}_2^i, \ldots, \mathbf{e}_{m_s}^i \right\}, 1 \leqslant i \leqslant m \tag{2}$$

Inspired by sparse representation, each pixel $\mathbf{e}_s^i$, $(1 \leq s \leq m_s)$ in the ith cluster can be approximately represented as a linear combination of pixels $\bar{E}_i$ in that cluster

$$\mathbf{e}_s^i = \overline{\mathbf{E}}_s^i \mathbf{a}_s^i, \quad 1 \leq i \leq m, 1 \leq s \leq m_s$$
$$\text{s.t. } \overline{\mathbf{E}}_s^i = \left\{ \mathbf{e}_1^i, \mathbf{e}_2^i, \ldots, \mathbf{e}_{s-1}^i, \mathbf{e}_{s+1}^i, \ldots, \mathbf{e}_{m_s}^i \right\} \tag{3}$$

where $\mathbf{e}_{m_s}^i$ can be sparsely represented by the sparse vector $\mathbf{a}_s^i$ and the dictionary $\bar{E}_s^i$. Orthogonal Matching Pursuit (OMP) [14] is applied to access each $\mathbf{a}_i$. The sparsity of each pixel is indicated by the magnitude of $\mathbf{a}_i$ L1 normalization value. The greater the value and the less sparsity of the pixel. The less sparsity of a pixel can be more easily linearly represented by lots of other pixels so as to select lower sparse samples in each cluster as typical background pixels.

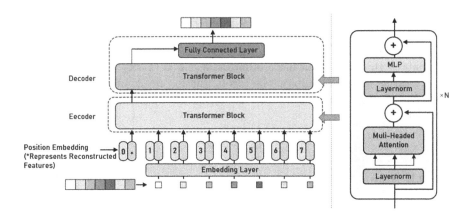

Fig. 2. Schematic diagram of transformer-based autoencoder.

2.2 Transformer-Based Autoencoder

The overview model of our proposed transformer-based autoencoder as shown in Fig. 2, which mainly consists of an encoder and a decoder with N transformer blocks and D dimensions latent vector in all layers. The spectral sequence of background pixel in a hyperspectral image with C bands can be represented as $\mathbf{x} = [x_1, x_2, \cdots, x_C] \in \mathbb{R}^C$, the input of multilayer perceptron $\mathbf{x}$ is mapped to D dimension, which can be concatenated with the position encoding information of each channel to form the embedded feature $\mathbf{z}_0$. Embedded features are sequentially fed into the encoder, decoder and fully connected layers to obtain the reconstructed spectral sequence $\mathbf{x}' \in \mathbb{R}^C$.

Similar to ViT [11], we add a learnable reconstruction feature $\mathbf{z}_0^0 = \mathbf{z}_{rebuild}$ at the head position of feature $\mathbf{z}_0$, which would fully interacts with features in other locations. Embedding vector generation and feature operations in transformer-based autoencoder is shown in the following formula as

$$
\begin{aligned}
\mathbf{z}_0 &= [\mathbf{z}_{rebuild}; x_1\mathbf{E}; x_2\mathbf{E}; \cdots; x_C\mathbf{E}] + \mathbf{E}_{pos}, \mathbf{E} \in \mathbb{R}^{1 \times D}, \mathbf{E}_{pos} \in \mathbb{R}^{(C+1) \times D} \\
\mathbf{z}'_n &= \mathrm{MSA}(\mathrm{LN}(\mathbf{z}_{n-1})) + \mathbf{z}_{n-1}, n = 1, 2, \cdots, 2N \\
\mathbf{z}_n &= \mathrm{MLP}(\mathrm{LN}(\mathbf{z}'_n)) + \mathbf{z}'_{n-1}, n = 1, 2, \cdots, 2N \\
\mathbf{x}' &= \mathrm{MLP}(\mathrm{LN}(\mathbf{z}_{rebuild}))
\end{aligned}
\tag{4}
$$

where $\mathbf{E}$ represents the weight of the encoded fully connected layer, $\mathbf{E}_{pos}$ is the position encoding matrix, $\mathbf{z}_n$ represents the output of the nth transformer block, and $\mathbf{z}'_n$ is an intermediate variable. $\mathbf{x}'$ represents the reconstructed spectral sequence. MSA means multiple self-attention mechanism in transformer, the MLP and LN distributions represent multilayer perceptrons and layer normalization layers. The activation function used by each layer of MLP is a Gaussian Error Linear Unit (GELU), which can be formulated as

$$GELU(a) = a\Phi(a) \approx 0.5a(1 + \tanh[\sqrt{2/\pi}(a + 0.044715a^3)]) \tag{5}$$

where $\Phi(a)$ is the standard Gaussian distribution function.

Assuming that the set of background pixels $X = [\mathbf{x}_1, \mathbf{x}_2, \cdots, \mathbf{x}_M] \in \mathbb{R}^{M \times C}$ can be used as training samples, the reconstruction result of background pixel $\mathbf{x}_i$ by the transformer-based autoencoder is $\mathbf{x}'_i$, the MSE loss function can be expressed as

$$loss_{mse} = \frac{1}{M} \sum_{i=1}^{M} (\mathbf{x}_i - \mathbf{x}'_i)^2 \tag{6}$$

2.3 RX Anomaly Detection Algorithm

The RX anomaly detection algorithm [2] performs anomaly detection by calculating the characteristics of the background and abnormal pixels, which assumes that the abnormal pixels and background pixels obey the same Gaussian distribution as

$$\begin{aligned} H_0 &: \mathbf{x}_0 \sim N(\mu, \sigma) \\ H_1 &: \mathbf{x}_1 \sim N(\mu, \sigma) \end{aligned} \tag{7}$$

where $\mathbf{x}_0$ is the background pixel, $\mathbf{x}_1$ is the abnormal pixel.

The hyperspectral image can be expressed as $\mathbf{X} \in \mathbb{R}^{H \times W \times C}$, H and W correspond to rows and columns of the hyperspectral image, the number C is the bands of hyperspectral image. While the three-dimensional matrix can be converted into a two-dimensional matrix of $\mathbb{R}^{(H \times W) \times C}$. Let $M = H \times W$, the mean and variance can be calculated as

$$\begin{aligned} \mu_b &= \frac{1}{M} \sum_{i=1}^{M} \mathbf{x}_i \\ C_b &= \frac{1}{M} \sum_{i=1}^{M} (\mathbf{x}_i - \mu_b)(\mathbf{x}_i - \mu_b)^T \end{aligned} \tag{8}$$

The value of $RX(\mathbf{x})$ can be calculated as

$$RX(\mathbf{x}) = (\mathbf{x} - \mu_b)^T C_b^{-1} (r - \mu_b) \tag{9}$$

The larger the value $RX(\mathbf{x})$ means the higher abnormal probability of the pixel.

3   Experiments and Results

3.1   Datasets and Implementation

Six different hyperspectral images obtained from the AVIRIS sensor are selected for anomaly detection test (Texas Coast, Los Angeles-1, Los Angeles-2, Cat Island, San Diego, Bay Champagne). We select 1000 background pixels as training and the number of transformer blocks is set to $N = 8$, while the dimension of transformer latent vector is set to $D = 64$. During the training process, the Adam optimization algorithm was selected as the optimizer, and the learning rate was set to 0.00001. In order to quantitatively evaluate the effect of object detection, AUC was used as evaluation metrics.

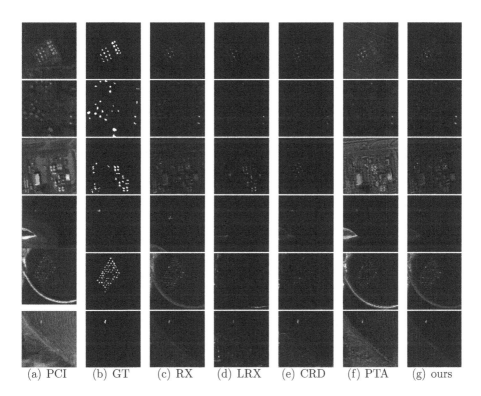

(a) PCI   (b) GT   (c) RX   (d) LRX   (e) CRD   (f) PTA   (g) ours

Fig. 3. Detection maps of each method. PCI indicates pseudo-color maps, GT means ground truth. The six datasets in order from top to bottom are: Texas Coast, Los Angeles-1, Los Angeles-2, Cat Island, San Diego, Bay Champagne.

3.2   Experimental Results

In this section, we mainly evaluate the proposed method with four related traditional anomaly detection algorithms: RX [2], LRX [3], CRD [4], PTA [5]. The AUC values of the detection results on the six datasets are shown in Table 1, respectively.

Table 1. AUC values of different methods on six HAD datasets.

HSIs	RX	LRX	CRD	PTA	Ours
Texas Coast	0.9945	0.9370	0.8805	0.9769	**0.9949**
Los Angeles-1	0.9887	0.9489	0.9408	0.8257	**0.9893**
Los Angeles-2	0.9694	0.8883	0.9371	0.8257	**0.9696**
Cat Island	0.9660	0.9543	**0.9853**	0.9183	0.9815
San Diego	0.9103	0.8801	0.9040	0.8298	**0.9117**
Bay Champagne	0.9997	0.9394	0.9941	0.9202	**0.9998**

The experimental results demonstrate that our proposed method achieves the better performance, the transformer-based autoencoder proposed in this paper presents more stable effect in improving the anomaly detection, and strikes a satisfactory balance between high detection rate and low false positive rate. For all datasets, our method can detect most anomalies while preserving the overall object shape, the detection maps for each method are shown in Fig. 3.

4   Conclusion

In this paper, a background augmentation with transformer-based autoencoder architecture is proposed to improve the effect of anomaly detection by efficiently enlarging the difference between background and abnormal pixels. Experiments demonstrate that our proposed method can be effectively applied in the field of hyperspectral remote sensing image interpretation and presents competitive anomaly detection results on several real hyperspectral datasets.

Acknowledgements. Manuscript received May 10, 2022, accepted June 1, 2022. This work was supported in part by the National Natural Science Foundation of China (No. 61801353), in part by The Project Supported by the China Postdoctoral Science Foundation funded project (No. 2018M633474), in part by GHfund under grant number 202107020822 and 202202022633.

References

1. Su, H., Wu, Z., Zhang, H., et al.: Hyperspectral anomaly detection: a survey. IEEE Geosci. Remote Sens. Mag. **10**(1), 64–90 (2021)

2. Reed, I.S., Yu, X.: Adaptive multiple-band CFAR detection of an optical pattern with unknown spectral distribution. IEEE Trans. Acoust. Speech Signal Process. **38**(10), 1760–1770 (1990)
3. Matteoli, S., Veracini, T., Diani, M., et al.: A locally adaptive background density estimator: an evolution for RX-based anomaly detectors. IEEE Geosci. Remote Sens. Lett. **11**(1), 323–327 (2013)
4. Li, W., Du, Q.: Collaborative representation for hyperspectral anomaly detection. IEEE Trans. Geosci. Remote Sens. **53**(3), 1463–1474 (2014)
5. Li, L., Li, W., Qu, Y., et al.: Prior-based tensor approximation for anomaly detection in hyperspectral imagery. IEEE Trans. Neural Netw. Learn. Syst. (2020)
6. Fu, X., Jia, S., Zhuang, L., et al.: Hyperspectral anomaly detection via deep plug-and-play denoising CNN regularization. IEEE Trans. Geosci. Remote Sens. **59**(11), 9553–9568 (2021)
7. Ma, N., Peng, Y., Wang, S., et al.: An unsupervised deep hyperspectral anomaly detector. Sensors **18**(3), 693 (2018)
8. Lu, X., Zhang, W., Huang, J.: Exploiting embedding manifold of autoencoders for hyperspectral anomaly detection. IEEE Trans. Geosci. Remote Sens. **58**(3), 1527–1537 (2019)
9. Jiang, T., Li, Y., Xie, W., et al.: Discriminative reconstruction constrained generative adversarial network for hyperspectral anomaly detection. IEEE Trans. Geosci. Remote Sens. **58**(7), 4666–4679 (2020)
10. Vaswani, A., Shazeer, N., Parmar, N., et al.: Attention is all you need. In: Advances in Neural Information Processing Systems, vol. 30 (2017)
11. Dosovitskiy, A., Beyer, L., Kolesnikov, A., et al.: An image is worth 16x16 words: transformers for image recognition at scale. arXiv preprint arXiv:2010.11929 (2020)
12. Fang, Y., Liao, B., Wang, X., et al.: You only look at one sequence: rethinking transformer in vision through object detection. In: Advances in Neural Information Processing Systems, vol. 34, pp. 26183–26197 (2021)
13. Abdi, H., Williams, L.J.: Principal component analysis. Wiley Interdiscip. Rev. Comput. Stat. **2**(4), 433–459 (2010)
14. Tropp, J.A., Gilbert, A.C.: Signal recovery from random measurements via orthogonal matching pursuit. IEEE Trans. Inf. Theory **53**(12), 4655–4666 (2007)

Point Cloud Registration Based on Global and Local Feature Fusion

Wenping Ma[1], Mingyu Yue[1], Yongzhe Yuan[2], Yue Wu[2(✉)], Hao zhu[1], and Licheng Jiao[1]

[1] School of Artificial Intelligence, Xidian University, Xi'an, China
{wpma,lchjiao}@mail.xidian.edu.cn, myyue@stu.xidian.edu.cn,
haozhu@xidian.edu.cn
[2] School of Computer Science and Technology, Xidian University, Xi'an, China
ywu@xidian.edu.cn

Abstract. Global feature extraction and rigid body transformation estimation are two key steps in correspondences-free point cloud registration methods. Previous approaches only utilize the global information while the local information is ignored. Moreover, global and local information may play different roles on multiple point clouds. In this paper, we verify the sensitivity of different types of point clouds to global and local information. We conducted extensive experiments on the ModelNet40 dataset by the SGLF-DQNet. Through the experimental results, we summarize the point cloud structure of the sensitivity to global and local features in the correspondence-free point cloud registration task.

Keywords: Point cloud registration · Feature extraction · Correspondence-free methods

1 Introduction

As the most primitive three-dimensional data, the 3D point cloud [2] can accurately reflect the real size and shape structure of objects and gradually become a data form that visual perception [3,4] depends on. Point cloud registration aims at finding a rigid transformation to align one point cloud to another. The most common algorithm for it is the Iterative Closest Point (ICP) [5].

Numerous deep learning registration methods [6–8] have been proposed to provide accurate alignments which improve the defects of traditional methods [9]. The baseline of correspondence-free methods is to extract the global features to regress the motion parameters of rigid transformation [10]. Early deep-learning methods usually utilize voxel-based [11] or pointcnn-based [12] feature extractors. PointNet [13] was firstly proposed for classification [14] and segmentation tasks, many correspondence-free registration architectures are utilize it for feature extraction Our previous work has proposed a network called GLF-DQNet [15], which fuse the global and local information and improve the defects of the PointNet.

© IFIP International Federation for Information Processing 2022
Published by Springer Nature Switzerland AG 2022
Z. Shi et al. (Eds.): ICIS 2022, IFIP AICT 659, pp. 310–317, 2022.
https://doi.org/10.1007/978-3-031-14903-0_33

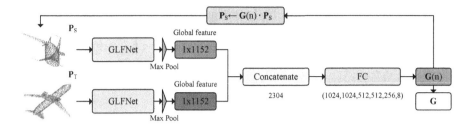

Fig. 1. GLF-DQNet architecture

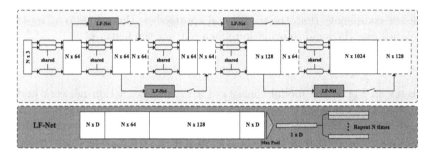

Fig. 2. SGLFNet architecture

However, various samples may have different sensitivity to global and local features. We want to analyse the impact of global and local characteristics on correspondences-free registration tasks. To test this idea, based on GLF-DQNet, we add switches to the feature extractor to separate global and local features and do experiments on ModelNet40 dataset. Experiments show that for different types of samples, global features and local features play different leading roles.

Contributions: Our main contributions can be summarized as follows:

- We propose a new feature extraction network SGLFNet, which can make up for the deficiency of local features and separate local features and global features at the same time.
- We verify the sensitivity of different categories of point clouds to global and local features.
- We summarize the structure characteristics of global feature high sensitivity point cloud and local feature high sensitivity point cloud respectively.

2   Related Work

2.1   Traditional Registration Method

ICP is considered as the most standard algorithm to solve point cloud registration. ICP iteratively extracts the closest source point to each template point, and refine the transformation by least-squares optimization. The variants of ICP improve the defects and enhances the registration accuracy. However, these methods are sensitive to the initial point cloud and hard to integrate these models into the end-to-end deep-learning pipelines.

2.2 Deep-Learning Registration Method

PointNet is emerged as a milestone which is apply deep-learning to point cloud directly and solve the unordered arrangement problems. Amount of models utilize PointNet as the global feature extractor such as PointNetLK, PCRNet and CorsNet, etc. These learning-based methods all achieve higher accuracy and lower complexity than the traditional approaches. However, PointNet-based techniques loss the local information when extract the feature.

2.3 GLF-DQNet

As shown in Fig. 1, the model consists of a feature extraction network and the pose estimation using the dual quaternion. The source and template point clouds through the GLFNet and max-pooling to obtain the global feature with local information. The rigid transformation is calculated by using the dual quaternion [16]. In GLFNet, features obtained from sharing MLP are entered into LF unit. In each layer, the output of the MLP and LF unit are connected and used as input in the next shared MLP.

3 Method

3.1 Problem Statement

The input of network are two unsorted 3D point pairs $\mathbf{P_s}$ and $\mathbf{P_t}$. The aim of registration is to calculate the best linear transformation $\mathbf{G} \in SE(3)$ to align the source $\mathbf{P_s}$ to the template $\mathbf{P_t}$ as follows:

$$\mathbf{P}_T = \mathbf{G} \cdot \mathbf{P}_S. \tag{1}$$

The transformation $\mathbf{G}$ consisting of two parts: rotation matrix $R \in SO(3)$ and translation vector $t \in R^3$. In correspondences-free methods, the predicted rigid transformation $\mathbf{G}_{est}$ is usually generated as:

$$\mathbf{G}_{est} = \begin{pmatrix} \mathbf{R}_{est} & \mathbf{t}_{est} \\ \mathbf{0} & 1 \end{pmatrix} \tag{2}$$

$\mathbf{G}_{est}$ and $\mathbf{t}_{est}$ are the predicted rotation matrix and translation vector

3.2 SGLFNet Network

On the basis of GLFNet, we add switches in the network. It can be seen from Fig. 2, there are switches behind each LF unit. When the switch is turned on, the network only extracts global features. But when the switch is turned off, the local information will be taken into account at the same time. In experiments, we can directly decide whether to extract local features by controling the switch.

Table 1. GLFNet verification experiments

Method	RMSE (R)	RMSE (R)	RMSE (t)	RMSE (t)
DirectNet	19.4791	5.0934 ($\downarrow$14.3857)	0.0122	0.0660 ($\uparrow$0.0538)
CorsNet	16.2356	12.7044 ($\downarrow$3.5312)	0.0070	0.9608 ($\uparrow$0.9538)
PCRNet	3.8837	2.7966 ($\downarrow$0.2709)	0.0064	0.0029 ($\downarrow$0.0035)

3.3 Loss Function

$\mathcal{L}_1$ is used to minimize the distance between the corresponding points in the source and the template point cloud. $\mathcal{L}_2$ is used to reduce the difference between estimated and ground truth transformation matrices. $\mathcal{L}_3$ combined two of them.

$$\mathcal{L}_1 = \frac{1}{N} \sum_{p_s \in \mathbf{P}_S} \min_{p_t \in \mathbf{P}_T} \|p_s - p_t\|_2 + \frac{1}{N} \sum_{p_t \in \mathbf{P}_T} \min_{p_s \in \mathbf{P}_S} \|p_s - p_t\|_2 \tag{3}$$

$$\mathcal{L}_2 = \|(\mathbf{G}_{est})^{-1}\mathbf{G}_{gt} - \mathbf{I}_4\|_F \tag{4}$$

$$\mathcal{L}_3 = \mathcal{L}_1 + 0.007\mathcal{L}_2. \tag{5}$$

4 Experiments

4.1 Experiments on GLFNet

In order to verify the effectiveness of local information for the correspondences-free registration task, we replace the feature extractors of DirectNet, CorsNet and PCRNet with GLFNet for experiments. From Table 1, when GLFNet is used as the feature extractor, the registration effect of these methods has been significantly improved after fusing local features.

4.2 Experiments on Local Registration

In order to verify the sensitivity of different categories to global and local features, we do experiments on 40 categories in ModelNet40 dataset respectively. By analyzing the point data of these categories, we find that point clouds which are more sensitive to global features usually include several special categories:

(a) Symmetry structure: As shown in Fig. 3, *chair* and *toilet* are classical symmetrical structure. When extracting local information, it usually causes confusion of symmetrical part information, resulting in deviation.
(b) Repetitive structure: It can be seen in Fig. 3, *bookshelf* and *dresser* are been as the repetitive structure. For such samples, the existence of repeated structure will make the local information extracted from multiple points very similar, so it will cause confusion of information in different parts.

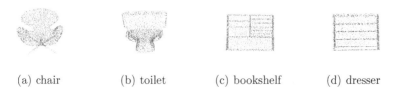

(a) chair   (b) toilet   (c) bookshelf   (d) dresser

Fig. 3. Visualization of symmetry structure and repetitive structure.

(c) Uniform distribution structure: Uniform distribution structure can be divided into compact structure and sparse structure. Compact structure like *airplane* and *curtain* in Fig. 4. When local information is incorporated, each point is equivalent to splicing the information of all points, resulting in the redundancy of individual point information. Sparse structure like *glass_ box* and *sink* in Fig. 4. When extracting local information from the same number of points, the local features extracted from sparse point clouds often contain only one-sided information.

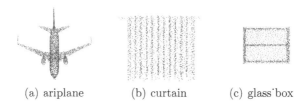

(a) ariplane   (b) curtain   (c) glass˙box

Fig. 4. Visualization of uniform distribution structure.

4.3   Experiments on Global Registration

To verify the sensitivity of different categories to global and local features, we do experiments on 40 different categories respectively. The training set includes 40 categories, and the testing set only contains individual categories each time.

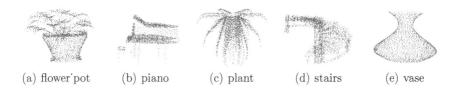

(a) flower˙pot   (b) piano   (c) plant   (d) stairs   (e) vase

Fig. 5. Visualization of five special categories.

Global Feature Registration. In this experiment, we turn on all the switches in the feature extractor. The GLFNet can only extract the global information. The results are presented in Table 2, in ModelNet40 dataset, for 25 categories, the

RMSE of rotation and translation can reach the optimal value at the same time when only extract the global features. For these categories, local features may become redundant information, thus reducing the registration results. There are five special types which are very poor when only global features are extracted, and will not be improved when local information is integrated. From the Fig. 5, it is clearly to see the structure of them is very irregular and the distribution of them is very uneven.

Table 2. Global feature experiments

Label	Global RMSE(R)	Global RMSE(t)
Airplane	1.4680	0.0025
Bathtub	1.1102	0.0021
Bed	0.8038	0.0019
Bench	1.8115	0.0015
Bookshelf	1.2594	0.0033
Car	1.2865	0.0018
Chair	1.4376	0.0020
Curtain	1.6539	0.0030
Desk	1.6202	0.0025
Dresser	0.9293	0.0020
Door	0.9933	0.0018
Flower_pot	4.2845	0.0027
Glass_box	1.7052	0.0018
Laptop	1.6977	0.0014
Mantel	1.2350	0.0031
Monitor	1.6495	0.0019
Piano	2.8199	0.0023
Plant	4.5942	0.0022
Range_hood	1.7030	0.0026
Sink	1.7412	0.0018
Sofa	1.1124	0.0016
Stairs	4.5999	0.0025
Toilet	1.4200	0.0027
Vase	4.5887	0.0025
Wardrobe	1.1882	0.0018

Global Feature with Local Feature Registration. In order to observe the influence of local features on different types of point clouds, we turn off all the switches to extract the global features and local features together. We found that there are 15 categories will improve the effect after incorporating the local features. Table 3 lists the results of only extracting global features and fusing local features and global features.

We believe that global information and local information have various effects on different kinds of point clouds. Therefore, we adjust the same weight of the original global module and local module to the model adaptive weight. Through training, the weight that best matches the registration task is obtained, so as to obtain higher accuracy. The registration result is displayed in Table 3.

Table 3. The 1st and 2nd column means the result for global registration. The 3rd and 4th column means the decreasing value for global fusing local feature registration. The 5th and 6th column means the decreasing value after giving appropriate weights.

Label	RMSE (R)	RMSE (t)	RMSE (R) ↓	RMSE (t) ↓	RMSE (R) ↓	RMSE (t) ↓
bottle	4.9081	0.0031	0.3457	0.0015	0.4158	0.0007
bowl	4.9378	0.0033	0.2084	0.0010	1.9012	0.0011
cone	4.6873	0.0024	0.2200	0.0002	0.7047	0.0003
cup	4.7784	0.0023	0.2529	0.0001	0.6875	0.0001
guitar	3.3302	0.0034	1.1238	0.0013	1.1550	0.0015
keyboard	1.7053	0.0027	0.4463	0.0010	0.5886	0.0010
lamp	5.0006	0.0028	0.2366	0.0002	0.7944	0.0009
night_stand	2.4431	0.0021	0.1482	0.0006	1.0880	−0.0014
person	3.7108	0.0025	0.6800	0.0000	0.7742	0.0003
radio	2.9787	0.0033	0.3884	0.0007	1.0192	0.0015
stool	4.1324	0.0025	0.1730	0.0012	0.2453	0.0000
table	1.2904	0.0022	·0.1755	0.0001	0.3507	−0.0005
tent	2.6244	0.0038	0.3316	0.0011	0.8698	0.0015
tv_stand	2.6446	0.0028	0.5681	0.0005	0.8877	0.0005
xbox	2.3177	0.0027	0.4837	0.0005	0.6106	0.0005

5   Conclusion

In this paper, we summarize the point cloud structure with better global feature effect and better local feature fusion effect. We carried out experiments by SGLF-DQNet, which can separate global information and local information. Through experiments, we found that near rotation or reflection symmetry structure, repetitive structure and uniform distribution structure are more sensitive to the global feature. Local uniform distribution is more sensitive to the global feature fusing the local information.

References

1. Jost, T., Hugli, H.: A multi-resolution scheme ICP algorithm for fast shape registration. In: International Symposium on 3D Data Processing Visualization & Transmission (2008)

2. Wang, Q., Kim, M.-K.: Applications of 3D point cloud data in the construction industry: a fifteen-year review from 2004 to 2018. Adv. Eng. Inform. **39**, 306–319 (2019)
3. Wu, Y., et al.: Computational intelligence in remote sensing image registration: a survey. Int. J. Autom. Comput. **18**(1), 17 (2021)
4. Ma, W., et al.: Feature split-merge-enhancement network for remote sensing object detection. IEEE Trans. Geosci. Remote Sens. **60**, 1–17 (2022)
5. Segal, A., Haehnel, D., Thrun, S.: Generalized-ICP. In: Robotics: Science and Systems (2009)
6. Rusu, R.B., Blodow, N., Beetz, M.: Fast point feature histograms (FPFH) for 3D registration. In: Proceedings of IEEE International Conference on Robotics and Automation, pp. 3212–3217 (2009)
7. Wang, Y., Solomon, J.M.: PRNet: self-supervised learning for partial-to-partial registration (2019)
8. Yew, Z.J., Lee, G.H.: 3DFeat-Net: weakly supervised local 3D features for point cloud registration. In: Ferrari, V., Hebert, M., Sminchisescu, C., Weiss, Y. (eds.) ECCV 2018. LNCS, vol. 11219, pp. 630–646. Springer, Cham (2018). https://doi.org/10.1007/978-3-030-01267-0_37
9. Bouaziz, S., Tagliasacchi, A., Pauly, M.: Sparse iterative closest point. In: Computer Graphics Forum, pp. 113–123 (2013)
10. Pöppelbaum, J., Schwung, A.: Predicting rigid body dynamics using dual quaternion recurrent neural networks with quaternion attention. arXiv preprint arXiv:2011.08734 (2020)
11. Nikhil, G.N., Meraz, M., Javed, M.: Automatic on-road object detection in LiDAR-point cloud data using modified VoxelNet architecture. In: Singh, S.K., Roy, P., Raman, B., Nagabhushan, P. (eds.) CVIP 2020. CCIS, vol. 1378, pp. 201–213. Springer, Singapore (2021). https://doi.org/10.1007/978-981-16-1103-2_18
12. Li, Y., Bu, R., Sun, M., Chen, B.: PointCNN (2018)
13. Sarode, V., et al.: One framework to register them all: PointNet encoding for point cloud alignment. arXiv preprint arXiv:1912.05766 (2019)
14. Ma, W., et al.: A collaborative correlation-matching network for multimodality remote sensing image classification. IEEE Trans. Geosci. Remote Sens. **60**, 1–18 (2022)
15. Wu, Y., et al.: Feature mining method of multi-dimensional information fusion in point cloud registration. J. Comput. Res. Dev. (59) (2022)
16. Kenwright, B.: A beginners guide to dual-quaternions: what they are, how they work, and how to use them for 3D character hierarchies. In: Proceedings of International Conference on Computer Graphics, Visualization and Computer Vision, pp. 1–13 (2012)

Gaussian Balanced Sampling for End-to-End Pedestrian Detector

Yang Yang[✉], Jun Li, Biao Hou[iD], Bo Ren, Xiaoming Jiang, Jinkai Cheng, and Licheng Jiao[iD]

Xidian University, No. 2 South Taibai Road, Xi'an, Shaanxi, China
525983640@qq.com

Abstract. Recently, NMS-free detector has become a research hotspot to eliminate negative influences, while NMS-based detector mis-suppress objects in crowd scene. However, NMS-free may face the problem of sample imbalance that affects convergence. In this paper, Gaussian distribution is adopted to fit the distribution of the targets so that samples can be chosen according to it. And we propose Gaussian Balance Sampling strategy to balance positive and negative samples actively. Besides, a simple loss function, PDLoss, is proposed to eliminate duplicated matches on the label assignment procedure and increase training speed. In addition, by a novel Non-target Response Suppression method, the designed network can focus more on hard samples and improve model performance. With these techniques, the model achieved a competitive performance on the CrowdHuman dataset.

Keywords: Gaussian balanced sampling · End-to-end · NMS-free · Pedestrian detection · PDLoss

1 Introduction

In the one-to-one NMS-free network, each target has only one positive sample. These positive samples need to be the most representative points for targets as Wang explored in [14]. In addition, too many negative samples will make the model difficult to focus on positive samples because negative samples will contribute more to gradient backpropagation. Therefore, it is necessary to select an appropriate number of negative samples. For the selection of negative samples, OneNet [12] and DeFCN [14] directly select all the points as negative except the positive ones. Most of the areas that belong to the background will bring too many easy negative samples.

Another noteworthy problem is that when two targets are highly overlapped, they could match the same sample point simultaneously. However, the sample points can only keep one target generally. For the one-to-one assignment model, the situation gets worse due to the other target getting discarded straightly because each target has only one positive sample. Some works like DeFCN [14], adopt Hungarian matching to eliminate duplicated matching. But the some of the positive samples may be non-optimal and the matching algorithm cost lots of time.

© IFIP International Federation for Information Processing 2022
Published by Springer Nature Switzerland AG 2022
Z. Shi et al. (Eds.): ICIS 2022, IFIP AICT 659, pp. 318–325, 2022.
https://doi.org/10.1007/978-3-031-14903-0_34

To solve these problems, we propose a sample selection method and duplicated matching elimination strategy. And our method has achieved excellent performance on the CrowdHuman [10] dataset.

Fig. 1. The mapping of the extracted features onto the original image. The mapping is somewhat smooth. The response value is larger near the target and smaller far away.

2 Approach

2.1 Gaussian Negative Sampling

We found in previous work that in the inference results of the one-to-one matching model, the confidence score is centered on the positive sample point with the highest score, and approximately decays with a Gaussian distribution. Therefore, we assume that the representative strength of the target feature also conforms to this distribution. The feature response of targets gets high in the keypoint and gradually decreases to the outward. Therefore, a two-dimensional Gaussian model is employed to represent the distribution of features:

$$f(x) = \lambda e^{[-\frac{1}{2(1-\rho^2)}(\frac{(x-\mu_1)^2}{\sigma_1^2} - \frac{2\rho(x-\mu_1)(y-\mu_2)}{\sigma_1\sigma_2} + \frac{(y-\mu_2)^2}{\sigma_2^2})]} \tag{1}$$

$$\lambda = \frac{1}{2\pi\sigma_1\sigma_2\sqrt{1-\rho^2}}$$

where x, y are the coordinate positions. For simplicity, we regard x and y as independent of each other. Then the formula can be simplified to:

$$f(x) = \lambda e^{[-\frac{1}{2}(\frac{(x-\mu_1)^2}{\sigma_1^2} + \frac{(y-\mu_2)^2}{\sigma_2^2})]} \tag{2}$$

The mean values μ_1, μ_2 of Gaussian distribution are the coordinates of positive sample points x_p, y_p. And the variance values σ_1, σ_2 of Gaussian distribution are set as half the length h and half the width w of the bounding box. We fit the distribution for each target and stack them. Thus, the response of features on the original input image I can be described.

We introduce an additional factor to normalize the values of gaussian distribution for different density of targets.So we set λ to $1/N_o^i$. N_o^i is the number of boxes that are overlapped with the box i.

Since the response graph with all targets is obtained, the positive samples can be chosen as positions with high distribution response. For the selection of negative samples, samples can be directly selected as the area with the response larger than a certain threshold.

(a)   (b)   (c)   (d)

Fig. 2. The matching result of positive sample points and the final detection.

2.2 PD Loss

In the process of label assignment, there is a case that two different targets match the same sample point simultaneously. Each sample point can only match one target, so repeated matching will lead to lose one of the targets. After our verification, in OneNet [12], it actually has the circumstance that two targets match the same sample at the same time, and one of them is discarded directly. This possibility may be relatively small since we only select one positive sample and there are more other samples to choose from, we have no reason to discard it. When the target becomes denser and denser, this risk will further expand, and we cannot ignore it at this time. In addition, we find that the overlapping of sample points will also lead to confusion when learning target features, which will affect the convergence speed.

DeFCN [14] utilizes Hungarian algorithm [5] to eliminate duplication, but its training convergence speed is too slow, which greatly increases the cost. Therefore, we hope to find a more elegant and effiecnt method. Inspired by Repulsion loss [15], we design a loss function to prevent duplication, called PDLoss:

$$\mathcal{L}_p = \lambda_p \sum_i^n \sum_j^n \hat{dist} \tag{3}$$

where $\hat{dist}$ is the inverse distance between match points:

$$\hat{dist} = \frac{1}{k} \times \frac{Sigmoid(\mu - |x_i - x_j|)^{|x_i - x_j|}}{|x_i - x_j| + \epsilon} \tag{4}$$

where $|x_i - x_j|$ represents the pixel distance between two matching points. k is a constant set to 0.5. When two targets overlap, the distance is 0, so we need to limit them to $1/k$ to prevent overflow. Without duplicated matching, the loss still exists in a certain range μ. This will make the distance between the close matching sample points as far as possible so as to obtain more discriminative features.ϵ set to prevent formulas from causing calculation errors if the denominator is 0. With a simple loss function, we achieve Hungarian matching with almost no increase in training time. At the same time, the samples of different targets are kept as far away as possible to avoid false detection caused by the similarity of close-range features.

2.3   Non-target Response Suppression

The non-target response suppression mainly includes two parts, one is about the loss function in training, the other is about the score weighting in inference. In front, we select the sample points according to the Gaussian distribution. Among these sample points, the one near the center is more representative. The negative samples close to the positive sample points are difficult to distinguish and should receive more attention; while the samples that are far away maybe belong to the background and relatively easy to distinguish, so we can pay less attention to them. Therefore, we use Gaussian distribution matrix to weigh the loss of each sample point:

$$\mathcal{L}_w = \hat{f}(x_s)\mathcal{L}_{reg}, \quad x_s \in S \tag{5}$$

where S is all the selected samples. This method is very similar to the attention mechanism.

3   Experiments

Our experiments are implemented by PyTorch on a server with 8 NVIDIA Tesla V100 and 32 G memory. Given that NMS-free's approach is more competitive in dense scenarios, we perform experiments on crowd scene benchmarks to verify the generality of our methods. We trained every model for 30K iterations on Detectron2 [16] with 2 images per GPU, which is consistent with the experimental setting of the baseline. For the model, we use ResNet50 [4] as our backbone and the initialized weights are pre-trained on ImageNet [2]. The learning rate is initially set to 0.01 and then decreased by 10 at the 20K and 25K iterations. We use SGD to optimize all the models with a weight decay of 0.0001 and a momentum of 0.9.

3.1   Performance on CrowdHuman Dataset

Because the NMS-free network is more competitive in dense scenarios, we verify our model on the CrowdHuman [10] dataset. Under the same experimental conditions and ImageNet [2] pre-trained backbone, we compare the performance of our method with the other two NMS-free networks and the traditional methods on the dataset. All the models are trained with the same setting: batch size of 16.

From the Table 1, we can see that our model can achieve a higher recall than the traditional models. In addition, our method is superior to other one-to-one networks due to its excellent sampling ratio. To be mentioned, OneNet only experiments on the COCO dataset in its paper and this result is obtained by our transfer training on the CrowdHuman dataset. In our experiment, the batch size of OneNet is set to 16, which is different from its reported 64 batch size. The worse performance of OneNet may be caused by this.

Table 1. The performance of different model on CrowdHuman dataset.

Method	AP	mMR	Recall
RetinaNet [6]	81.7	57.6	88.6
Faster RCNN [8]	84.95	50.49	90.24
Adaptive NMS [7]	84.71	49.73	91.27
PS-RCNN [3]	86.05	–	93.77
FCOS [13]	86.1	55.2	94.3
ATSS [17]	87.1	50.1	94.0
IterDet [9]	88.1	**42.2**	**95.8**
CrowdDet [1]	**90.3**	49.4	–
OneNet [12]	22.7	–	–
DeFCN-POTO [14]	**88.7**	52.0	96.6
Ours	**89.3**	**50.3**	**97.3**

3.2   Ablation Study

Selection of Sampling Threshold. Because we modeled the distribution of features with Gaussian distribution, we can judge the intensity of features according to the Gaussian response value. In Table 2, the region with Gaussian response value $v > \delta_h$ has strong characteristics, which are hard samples. The areas with response value v below δ_l are mainly the background areas because they are outside the box and have low response value. According to our experiment, we also tried to select segmented samples. The area with δ_h of 0.6 and the area with $v < \delta_l$ are selected. In this way, our samples include not only a certain number of hard samples but also a certain number of easy samples (background). When $\delta_l = 0$, the segmented sampling degenerates into the whole sampling.

We find it necessary to provide a certain number of easy samples for the model because only learning to distinguish the hard samples will lead to unexpected false detection in the easily divided samples. For the segmented sampling method, although its performance is lower than that of the whole sampling method. But we found that it can achieve the highest accuracy in earlier iterations.

Selection of Gaussian Radius. Different Gaussian radius can construct different distributions. Therefore, we explored which radius is the best. As shown in Table 2, the radius of Gaussian distribution should be as small as possible, but not less than half of the length and width. Because the distribution value is concentrated on the target due to a small Gaussian radius, so it is unable to sample some parts of the background. And for a large radius, it pays too much attention to the background. In this case, we can solve this problem by changing the sampling threshold.

PDLoss. For our PDLoss, we evaluated its speed relative to the Hungarian match. PDLoss can save up to a tenth of time during training. At the same time, positions of

Table 2. The influence of different sampling range thresholds in Gaussian balanced sampling. Where $1/r$ is the reciprocal of radius and δ_b is the threshold for selecting the background region ($<\delta_l$), δ_h is the threshold for selecting the foreground region ($>\delta_f$). Where "−" means 0. All the results are relative to the difference between our optimal results in the last line.

Norm	$1/r$	δ_l	δ_h	AP	mMR	Recall
w/o	4	–	0.9	−3.4	+6.3	−1.8
w/o	4	–	0.64	−2.2	+3.8	+0.1
w/o	4	–	0.62	−1.8	+3.0	−0.2
w/o	2	–	1.1	−3.9	+5.9	−1.5
w/o	2	–	0.7	−0.1	+0.5	−1.3
w/o	2	0.2	1.4	−1.0	+1.4	−0
w/o	2	0.1	1.4	−2.5	+4.2	−2.3
w/o	2	0.2	1.2	−0.6	+0.2	−0.6
w	2	–	0.4	−3.6	+6.4	−0.3
w	2	–	0.2	−1.7	+1.7	−0.1
w	2	–	0.1	**89.3**	**50.3**	**97.3**

the matched sample points are compared. As shown in Fig. 2, the simple maximum matching will dominate the loss of targets. Moreover, compared with Hungary matching, PD loss makes the selected sample points far away from each other, which helps the model better distinguish different targets. But we also need to limit it, it is easy to make the matching sample points too biased because the feature has a large offset. Predicting localization on biased features is no doubt unfriendly for the model. So we add distance clips to limit the effect of loss, and the results are shown in Table 3. Within a certain range, the loss function works and pushes them as far away as possible.

Table 3. The influence of Non-target Response Suppression. In this experiment, we set $\delta_l = 0$ and $\delta_h = 0.1$. Where "w" and "w/o" means using with and without. All the results are relative to the difference between our optimal results.

Dist-Clip	μ	AP	mMR	Recall
w/o	–	−3.9	+6.2	−0.2
w	10	−1.7	+1.7	+0.2
w	20	89.3	50.3	97.3

As shown in Fig. 2, (a) is the directly maximum matching method without Hungarian matching or our PDLoss. Compared with other methods, it has more missed detection, although there is no duplicated matching in our example. In fact, it does not distinguish overlapping targets sufficiently because of repetition. That's why it missed some targets. (b) is the method adopted Hungarian matching. The sample points matched by some targets may be close to each other. This makes the features of the matching points closer, resulting in insufficient discrimination. (c) is our PDLoss method which can make the matching points far away from each other than before, and the distance loss needs to be limited since the points are too biased shown in (d).

Non-target Response Suppression. For the suppression of non-target areas, our main purpose is using it to eliminate false detection. However, to our surprise, it played a crucial role instead. When the non-target area suppression is removed, the AP is greatly reduced as shown in Table 4. This is because the background is easier to distinguish than the target. Weighted loss makes the network pay more attention to positive samples and hard samples. This is also consistent with the consensus that more attention should be paid to hard samples in the traditional one to many methods [11]. In addition, it should be noted that the distribution values we use to weight need to be normalized, otherwise gradient explosion will appear soon.

Table 4. The influence of Non-target Response Suppression (NRS). In this experiment, we set $\delta_l = 0$ and $\delta_h = 0.1$. Where μ_l is the clipped low thresh and non-Norm means do not normalize Gaussian distribution by density. "w" and "w/o" means using NRS or not. All the results are relative to the difference between our optimal results.

NRS	Method μ_l		AP	mMR	Recall
w	Softmax		−1.4	+0.5	−1.3
w	Non-Norm		–	–	–
w/o	Clip	–	−15.2	+18.0	−0.9
w		0.5	−3.1	+4	−0.5
w		0.1	89.3	50.3	97.3

Since our sampling range δ_h is set to 0.1. Therefore, that we set μ_l to 0 means no lower limit for weight in essence. In addition, in order to prevent the gradient explosion, we also try to use Softmax to normalize the weight. After normalization, the original high response area will still have a higher value than the low response area. The only difference between them is that the loss gets smaller after doing softmax. Finally, if we do not normalize the Gaussian distribution by density and directly multiply it on the loss, the model will face a great risk of gradient explosion.

4   Conclusion

This paper proposes a balanced sampling method based on Gaussian prior distribution and the Non-target Response Suppression method, which effectively solves the problem of positive and negative sample imbalance, and makes the model pay more attention to hard samples. At the same time, PDLoss can effectively avoid the overlapping and dropping of target samples. Our end-to-end framework achieves excellent performance for many of the most advanced NMS detectors and existing NMS-free detectors on the CrowdHuman dataset.

References

1. Chu, X., Zheng, A., Zhang, X., Sun, J.: Detection in crowded scenes: one proposal, multiple predictions. In: Proceedings of the IEEE/CVF Conference on Computer Vision and Pattern Recognition, pp. 12214–12223 (2020)
2. Deng, J., Dong, W., Socher, R., Li, L.-J., Li, K., Li, F.-F.: Imagenet: a large-scale hierarchical image database. In: 2009 IEEE Conference on Computer Vision and Pattern Recognition, pp. 248–255. IEEE (2009)
3. Ge, Z., Jie, Z., Huang, X., Xu, R., Yoshie, O.: PS-RCNN: detecting secondary human instances in a crowd via primary object suppression. In: 2020 IEEE International Conference on Multimedia and Expo (ICME), pp. 1–6. IEEE (2020)
4. He, K., Zhang, X., Ren, S., Sun, J.: Deep residual learning for image recognition. In: Proceedings of the IEEE Conference on Computer Vision and Pattern Recognition, pp. 770–778 (2016)
5. Jonker, R., Volgenant, T.: Improving the Hungarian assignment algorithm. Oper. Res. Lett. 5(4), 171–175 (1986)
6. Lin, T.-Y., Goyal, P., He, K., Dollár, P.: Focal Loss for Dense Object Detection. Ross Girshick (2018)
7. Liu, S., Huang, D., Wang, Y.: Adaptive NMS: refining pedestrian detection in a crowd. In: Proceedings of the IEEE/CVF Conference on Computer Vision and Pattern Recognition, pp. 6459–6468 (2019)
8. Ren, S., He, K., Girshick, R., Sun, J.: Towards real-time object detection with region proposal networks. Faster R-CNN (2016)
9. Rukhovich, D., Sofiiuk, K., Galeev, D., Barinova, O., Konushin, A.: Iterdet: iterative scheme for object detection in crowded environments. arXiv preprint arXiv:2005.05708 (2020)
10. Shao, S., et al.: Crowdhuman: a benchmark for detecting human in a crowd. arXiv preprint arXiv:1805.00123 (2018)
11. Shrivastava, A., Gupta, A., Girshick, R.: Training region-based object detectors with online hard example mining. In: Proceedings of the IEEE Conference on Computer Vision and Pattern Recognition, pp. 761–769 (2016)
12. Sun, P., Jiang, Y., Xie, E., Yuan, Z., Wang, C., Luo, P.: Onenet: towards end-to-end one-stage object detection. arXiv preprint arXiv:2012.05780 (2020)
13. Tian, Z., Shen, C., Chen, H., He, T.: Fully convolutional one-stage object detection. FCOS (2019)
14. Wang, J., Song, L., Li, Z., Sun, H., Sun, J., Zheng, N.: End-to-end object detection with fully convolutional network. arXiv preprint arXiv:2012.03544 (2020)
15. Wang, X., Xiao, T., Jiang, Y., Shao, S., Sun, J., Shen, C.: Repulsion loss: detecting pedestrians in a crowd. In: Proceedings of the IEEE Conference on Computer Vision and Pattern Recognition, pp. 7774–7783 (2018)
16. Wu, Y., Kirillov, A., Massa, F., Lo, W.-Y., Girshick, R.: Detectron2. https://github.com/facebookresearch/detectron2 (2019)
17. Zhang, S., Chi, C., Yao, Y., Lei, Z., Li, S.Z.: Bridging the gap between anchor-based and anchor-free detection via adaptive training sample selection. In: Proceedings of the IEEE/CVF Conference on Computer Vision and Pattern Recognition, pp. 9759–9768 (2020)

Combining Spatial-Spectral Features for Hyperspectral Image Few-Shot Classification

Yonghao Zhou[1,2], Qiong Ran[1(✉)], and Li Ni[2]

[1] College of Information Science and Technology, Beijing University of Chemical Technology, Beijing 100029, China
{2020210532,ranqiong}@mail.buct.edu.cn
[2] Key Laboratory of Computational Optical Imaging Technology,
Aerospace Information Research Institute, Chinese Academy of Sciences,
Beijing 100094, China
nili@aircas.ac.cn

Abstract. Recently, deep learning has achieved considerable results in hyperspectral image (HSI) classification. However, when training image classification models, existing deep networks require sufficient samples, which is expensive and inefficient in practical tasks. In this article, a novel Combining Spatial-spectral Features for Hyperspectral Image Few-shot Classification (CSFF) framework is proposed, attempting to accomplish the fine-grained classification with only a few labeled samples and train it with meta-learning ideas. Specifically, firstly, the spatial attention (SPA) and spectral query (SPQ) modules are introduced to overcome the constraint of the convolution kernel and consider the information between long-distance location (non-local) samples to reduce the uncertainty of classes. Secondly, the framework is trained by episodes to learn a metric space, and the task-based few-shot learning (FSL) strategy allows the model to continuously enhance the learning capability. In addition, the designed network not only discovers transferable knowledge in the source domain (SD) but also extracts the discriminative embedding features of the target domain (TD) classes. The proposed method can obtain satisfactory results with a small number of labeled samples. Extensive experimental results on public datasets demonstrate the versatility of CSFF over other state-of-the-art methods.

Keywords: Hyperspectral image classification · Spatial-spectral · Few-shot learning · Domain adaption · Meta learning

1 Introduction

Hyperspectral image (HSI) contains rich spatial-spectral information and provides the possibility of accurate classification of complex features. As a result, it

This work was supported by the National Natural Science Foundation of China under Grant 62161160336 and Grant 42030111.

has been widely used in environmental monitoring and military defense, etc. Currently, it urgently requires accurate classification of HSI with the development toward big data, which demands sufficient labeled samples [8]. However, it is extremely difficult to obtain thousands of labeled samples without great human and material resources. In earlier years, Melgai et al. [13] used the support vector machine (SVM) to explore an optimal hyperplane for classification, which slightly alleviated the "hughes" phenomenon. It only calculated the spectral information of HSI without considering spatial features. Chen et al. [2] designed a deep network to extract deep invariant features. Moreover, some strategies, such as L2 regularization and dropout were investigated to avoid overfitting during training. In contrast, humans can combine empirical knowledge and thus quickly complete new classification tasks with only a few samples.

In recent years, FSL has become popular because of its ability to perform new classification tasks with only a few labeled samples. For example, Chen et al. [1] introduced classifier baselines and FSL baselines and proposed to pre-train the classification model through a meta-learning paradigm. Lately, Gao et al. [3] designed a relation network (RN-FSC) to classify HSI, which fine-tuned the SD training model by using a few shot datasets of the TD. A deep feature extraction FSL method (DFSL) with an attached classifier was proposed in [11]. Moreover, Li et al. [10] designed a supervised deep cross-domain FSL network (DCFSL), which adopted residual 3D-CNN networks to extract local information and ignored the significance of non-local spatial features. Although the above FSL-based networks utilized convolution kernels to extract spatial-spectral features, the information is rarely obtained from long-distance location samples [5]. Secondly, due to the frequent occurrence of spectral shifts, Various discrepancies in data distribution may occur between SD and TD [15]. Therefore, it is necessary to consider the non-local relationships between samples to reduce the negative effects of domain shifts.

To overcome the above two limitations, a Combining Spatial-spectral Features for Hyperspectral Image Few-shot Classification (CSFF) framework is proposed, which is based on the mechanism of combining domain adaptation and FSL. Firstly, the episodic learning pattern of FSL is implemented on the SD and TD, which is to build a meta-task (i.e., support set and query set). Then, the spatial-spectral information is extracted by SPA and SPQ units. Moreover, the similarity between the support set S and query set Q is calculated using a metric function. Finally, a domain adaptation strategy is adopted to overcome domain shifts and achieve the accurate classification of HSI. The main contributions of this paper can be summarized as follows.

1) Unlike most existing deep networks, the proposed CSFF is learning a metric space through the episodic and task-based learning strategy, which can obtain promising HSI classifications with only a few labeled samples.

2) The SPA and the SPQ modules introduced through transformers are designed to overcome the constraint of the convolution kernel, consider the relationship between long-distance location samples, and enable the network to better extract high-level features to reduce the uncertainty of the class.

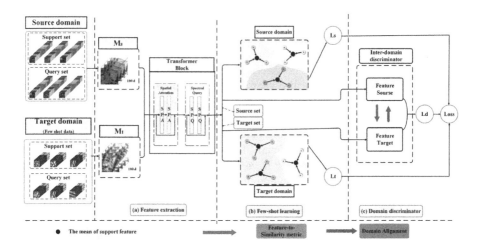

Fig. 1. Framework of the proposed CSFF, including feature extraction, few-shot learning and domain alignment.

3) Rather than focusing on a specific classification task, the proposed approach is to learn a deep nonlinear and transferable metric space, where the similarity metric is implemented by comparison. Meanwhile, to reduce the distribution difference between the SD and TD, we adopt a domain adaptation strategy to achieve distribution alignment of the data, which can help improve the generalization power of the model.

The remaining of the paper is arranged as follows. Section 2 introduces relevant concepts of the proposed approach CSFF. Experimental results and analyses are presented in Sect. 3. Finally, Sect. 4 draws comprehensive conclusions of this work.

2   Proposed Approach

The framework of the proposed CSFF is shown in Fig. 1, which contains three parts, i.e., feature extraction, few-shot learning, and domain alignment. During feature extraction, SPA and SPQ blocks are designed to overcome the limitations of fixed convolution kernel size. Also, an inter-domain discriminator (IDD) is used to alleviate the problem of domain shift caused by different sensors. Assuming that C_s, C_t represent the number of categories of $X_s \in \mathbb{R}^{d_s}$ and $X_t \in \mathbb{R}^{d_t}$, which denote d_s and d_t dimensional features from SD and TD. Note that TD is separated into training data $\mathcal{T}_f$ with a few labeled samples and testing data $\mathcal{T}_t$ with unlabeled samples.

2.1   Feature Extraction

Generally, HSI usually requires pre-processing with high dimensions. The mapping layers, $\mathbf{M}_s\,(\bullet)$ and $\mathbf{M}_t\,(\bullet)$ are used to map SD and TD to the same dimension d_map (d_map is set to 100 in this work). The transformer block f_{net} (•), including SPA and SPQ blocks, is employed to extract the spatial-spectral features of the HSI.

Most neural networks extract features from the local space but ignore the significance of the relationship between non-local space samples [7]. However, the purpose of the spatial attention mechanism is to explore the interactions between samples at different positions. Motivated by [4,6,14], we design the transformer's SPA blocks to calculate query, key, and value tensors as follows.

$$\mathbf{Q} = \mathcal{F}(X, W_q) \in \mathbb{R}^{c' \times h \times w} \tag{1}$$

$$\mathbf{K} = \mathcal{F}(X, W_k) \in \mathbb{R}^{c' \times h \times w} \tag{2}$$

$$\mathbf{V} = \mathcal{F}(X, W_v) \in \mathbb{R}^{c \times h \times w} \tag{3}$$

where: W_q, W_k, W_v denote the training parameters of the query, key, and value tensor, respectively, c, h, w are the channel size, height, and width of the input features X, respectively, $\mathcal{F}$ (•) denotes the 2D convolution operation. Thus, the output of the SPA block can be calculated as follows:

$$SPA_{out} = \mathbf{V} \cdot softmax\left(\mathbf{Q}^\mathsf{T} \cdot \mathbf{K}\right) \in \mathbb{R}^{c \times h \times w} \tag{4}$$

where SPA_{out} is the output of each position on the feature map. Now, the SPA module establishes the interactions between samples at different locations but ignores the abundant spectral information of HSI. Consequently, we design another SPQ block to extract spectral features and take masks to fuse the spatial information. Specifically, the kernel and output of the SPQ block can be formulated as follows:

$$\Psi = softmax\left(\mathcal{H}(X, W_\Psi)\right) \in \mathbb{R}^{hw \times k} \tag{5}$$

$$SPQ = \Psi^\mathsf{T} \cdot X^\mathsf{T} = (X \cdot \Psi)^\mathsf{T} \in \mathbb{R}^{k \times c} \tag{6}$$

$$SPQ_{out} = SPQ^\mathsf{T} \cdot \Psi^\mathsf{T} = (\Psi \cdot SPQ)^\mathsf{T} \in \mathbb{R}^{c \times h \times w} \tag{7}$$

where $\mathcal{H}$ (•) denotes 3D convolution operation to produce a tensor of size $k \times h \times w$. Finally, we use the generated mask W_Ψ to integrate it with the SPA_{out} of the input X, generating a spectral query kernel SPQ of size $k \times c$. So far, the SPQ block has established correlations between spatial locations and corresponding spectral features.

2.2   Source and Target Few-Shot Learning

FSL is executed simultaneously in source and target classes in each episode. Taking SD as an example, SD is divided into support set $\mathcal{S}_s$ and query set $\mathcal{Q}_s$, where $\mathcal{S}_s$ is the training set. Then, the features f_{S_s} and f_{Q_s} are extracted by network f_{net}. In each episode, FSL calculates the similarity between f_{Q_s} and each class prototype and minimizes the predicted loss. The predicted probability of the query sample is performed as follows:

$$P\left(\hat{y}|\mathbf{x}_i\right) = softmax\left(-E\left(\mathbf{x_i}, \mathbf{x_s^{c_i}}\right)\right) \tag{8}$$

where $E\left(\bullet\right)$ denotes an Euclidean distance function, $\mathbf{x}_s^{c_i}$ is the c_i-th class prototype of f_{S_s}, $c_i \in C_s$. The FSL loss of a query sample in SD is calculated by cross-entropy loss.

$$\mathcal{L}_S\left(P\left(\hat{y}|\mathbf{x}_i\right), y_i\right) = -\sum_{Q_s,i=1}^{C_s} y_i \log P\left(\hat{y}|\mathbf{x}_i\right) \tag{9}$$

Equivalently, the loss $\mathcal{L}_T$ of the TD is formulated in the same way as above.

2.3   Domain Alignment

Given the effect of domain shift on classification performance in FSL episodic training, domain alignment is one of the effective measures. Inspired by [12], we design an IDD block to analyze and adjust the data distributions $P_s\left(x\right)$ and $P_t\left(x\right)$ of the SD and TD. In particular, we denote $h = \left(f, g\right)$ to represent the joint distribution of the feature $f = F\left(x\right)$ and the classifier prediction $g = G\left(x\right)$. Following this, we formulate the domain alignment network as a minimax optimization problem with a loss error term:

$$\begin{aligned}\mathcal{L}_d \leftarrow \mathcal{E}\left(\mathbf{D}, \mathbf{G}\right) = &-\mathbb{E}_{x_i^s \sim P_s(x)} \log\left[D\left(f_i^s, g_i^s\right)\right] \\ &-\mathbb{E}_{x_j^t \sim P_t(x)} \log\left[1 - D\left(f_j^t, g_j^t\right)\right]\end{aligned} \tag{10}$$

where $D\left(\bullet, \bullet\right)$ and $1 - D\left(\bullet, \bullet\right)$ denote the probability that IDD predicts SD and TD samples x, $\mathcal{E}\left(\mathbf{D}, \mathbf{G}\right)$ can be considered as the loss metric of the IDD block, which is minimized over IDD but maximized over $F\left(x\right)$ and $G\left(x\right)$. By combining $h = \left(f, g\right)$, we condition IDD on g with the multilinear map as follows.

$$\mathbf{T}_\otimes\left(f, g\right) = f \otimes g \in \mathbb{R}^{d_f \times d_g} \tag{11}$$

where $\left(f \otimes g\right)$ defined as the outer product of multiple d_f and d_g dimensions random vectors. However, with the increasing number of training iterations, the dimension $d_f \times d_g$ of the multilinear map will become too high to be embedded the deep framework without causing parameter explosion. Luckily, according to the theoretical proof in [12], the dimension d of the randomized multilinear map($\mathbf{T}_\odot\left(f, g\right)$) is much smaller than $d_f \times d_g$. In other words, $\mathbf{T}_\odot$ is an approximate calculation of $\mathbf{T}_\otimes$, where $\odot$ is element-wise produc. If the dimension of $\mathbf{T}_\otimes$ is too large, we will adopt another strategy $\mathbf{T}_\odot$. Finally, the total objective function loss (together with Eq. 9) is shown as following,

$$\mathcal{L}_{oss} = \mathcal{L}_S + \mathcal{L}_T + \mathcal{L}_d \tag{12}$$

In this paper, we utilize multi-layer perceptrons in the IDD block. Furthermore, $\mathcal{T}_f$ is regarded as the support set and $\mathcal{T}_t$ as the query set in the testing stage.

Table 1. Classification results (%) on the UP data set with different methods (5 labeled samples from TD).

Class	Samples	Classification algorithms						
		SVM	3D-CNN	DFSL+NN	DFSL+SVM	RN-FSC	DCFSL	CSFF
Asphalt	6631	60.00	73.22	73.27	75.33	73.98	83.53	92.68±4.11
Meadows	18549	49.21	73.25	78.20	86.03	88.80	86.20	84.55±9.93
Gravel	2099	57.19	32.53	51.94	51.33	52.07	67.72	71.60±9.83
Trees	3064	79.49	86.30	85.95	90.91	90.64	94.26	91.28±2.72
Sheets	1345	90.74	95.35	99.37	97.64	98.94	98.85	99.58±0.43
Bare soil	5029	62.93	38.16	61.70	55.62	51.70	70.88	72.00±13.18
Bitumen	1330	80.96	43.82	69.75	71.09	71.86	79.92	82.61±9.81
Bricks	3682	62.55	49.24	53.34	55.46	58.62	65.92	85.66±3.57
Shadow	947	99.71	94.22	97.13	91.74	98.90	98.60	93.08±5.91
OA		59.60	62.50	73.44	76.84	77.89	82.39	**84.88±3.33**
AA		71.42	65.12	74.52	75.02	76.17	82.88	**85.89±2.10**
Kappa		50.77	52.67	65.77	69.61	70.83	77.06	**80.40±3.88**

3 Experimental Results

To prove the validity of the proposed framework CSFF, two publicly available HSI data sets were collected. The details of the two data sets are listed as following. Several state-of-the-art classification methods are adopted for comparison algorithms, SVM, 3D-CNN [9], DFSL+NN [11], DFSL+SVM [11], relation network (RN-FSC) [3], and DCFSL [10].

Source domain: the Chikusei data contains 19 classes and has 128 bands in the spectral range from 363 nm to 1018 nm nm. It has 2517×2335 pixels and a spatial resolution of 2.5m. Target domain: the University of Pavia data(UP) has 9 classes and 103 spectral bands in the spectral range from 430 nm to 860nm. The size of the image is 610×340 pixels with a spatial resolution is 1.3m per pixel.

3.1 Experimental Setting and Performance

In CSFF, 9×9 neighborhoods are selected as the spatial size of the input data. The learning rate is set to 0.001 and the number of training iterations is 10000 with being trained via Adam optimizer. For each meta-task of C-way K-shot in episodic training, C is set to the same number of classes as in TD. K for SD FSL and TD FSL is set to 1 in FSL-based experiments. In addition, the number of the query samples in $\mathcal{Q}$ is set to 19 to evaluate the learned classifier. Note that SVM and 3D-CNN only utilize the few-shot data set from the TD can to train a classifier. Furthermore, 5 labeled samples are randomly selected from each class of TD for FSL, and the data $\mathcal{T}_f$ is augmented by adding random Gaussian noise to the current known samples.

Table 1 reports the performance of all methods with overall accuracy (OA%), average accuracy (AA%), and kappa coefficients (Kappa%) in TD. Compared with SVM and 3D-CNN [9], several other FSL-based methods, including the proposed CSFF, provide over 9% improvement in both OA and AA. It indicates that FSL methods trained with meta-learning ideas in SD can better address the problem of few labeled samples in TD. Compared with DFSL+NN(SVM) [11] and RN-FSC [3] methods (without domain adaptation), DCFSL [10] and CSFF increased Kappa by 6.23% to 14.63%, which demonstrates that domain adaptation is essential. Furthermore, compared with the DCFSL [10] that only focuses on local features, the classification accuracy of CSFF is slightly lower than that of DCFSL for a few classes (i.e., Meadows, Trees and Shadow), which may be explained by the fact that the experimental UP HSI was taken during a period of lush green vegetation, in which some of the trees and pasture are similar in visual color. At the same time, some trees, shadows, and meadows overlap each other in the spatial distribution. Both of them can trigger serious spectral confusion. However, due to the transformer block can integrate non-local sample information, CSFF performs significantly better than DCFSL on non-vegetation classes. In particular, spectral shifts are significantly mitigated in some classes to enhance the classification performance, such as the 3-th class (Gravel), 6-th class (Bare soil), and 8-th class (Bricks) in the UP.

4   Conclusions

In this article, Combining Spatial-spectral Features for Hyperspectral Image Few-shot Classification (CSFF) has been proposed to address the issues of HSI classification with only a few labeled samples. It attempts to overcome the geometric constraints of the convolution kernel and reduce the negative effect of domain shift on FSL. Specifically, the spatial attention and spectral query modules are designed to extract and aggregate information from non-local samples in SD and TD. In addition, the framework is trained by episodes to learn a metric space, and a conditional domain adaptation strategy is utilized to achieve domain distribution alignment. The experimental results demonstrate that the proposed method has presented significant improvements over the state-of-the-art models. In the future, we will consider integrating local and non-local information (e.g., topological structure) and designing a multi-constrained domain distribution discrepancy metric to further reduce the data distribution differences. Meanwhile, a deep combined domain adaptation network will be constructed to achieve accurate classification of cross-domain hyperspectral images with a few labeled instances.

References

1. Chen, Y., Liu, Z., Xu, H., Darrell, T., Wang, X.: Meta-baseline: exploring simple meta-learning for few-shot learning. In: 2021 IEEE/CVF International Conference on Computer Vision (ICCV), pp. 9042–9051 (2021). https://doi.org/10.1109/ICCV48922.2021.00893

2. Chen, Y., Jiang, H., Li, C., Jia, X., Ghamisi, P.: Deep feature extraction and classification of hyperspectral images based on convolutional neural networks. IEEE Trans. Geosci. Remote Sens. **54**(10), 6232–6251 (2016). https://doi.org/10.1109/TGRS.2016.2584107

3. Gao, K., Liu, B., Yu, X., Qin, J., Zhang, P., Tan, X.: Deep relation network for hyperspectral image few-shot classification. Remote Sens. **12**(6) (2020). https://doi.org/10.3390/rs12060923

4. He, J., Zhao, L., Yang, H., Zhang, M., Li, W.: Hsi-bert: hyperspectral image classification using the bidirectional encoder representation from transformers. IEEE Trans. Geosci. Remote Sens. **58**(1), 165–178 (2020). https://doi.org/10.1109/TGRS.2019.2934760

5. Hong, D., Gao, L., Yao, J., Zhang, B., Plaza, A., Chanussot, J.: Graph convolutional networks for hyperspectral image classification. IEEE Trans. Geosci. Remote Sens. **59**(7), 5966–5978 (2021). https://doi.org/10.1109/TGRS.2020.3015157

6. Hong, D., et al.: More diverse means better: multimodal deep learning meets remote-sensing imagery classification. IEEE Trans. Geosci. Remote Sens. **59**(5), 4340–4354 (2021). https://doi.org/10.1109/TGRS.2020.3016820

7. Hong, D., et al.: Spectralformer: rethinking hyperspectral image classification with transformers. IEEE Trans. Geosci. Remote Sens. **60**, 1–15 (2022). https://doi.org/10.1109/TGRS.2021.3130716

8. Li, S., Song, W., Fang, L., Chen, Y., Ghamisi, P., Benediktsson, J.A.: Deep learning for hyperspectral image classification: an overview. IEEE Trans. Geosci. Remote Sens. **57**(9), 6690–6709 (2019). https://doi.org/10.1109/TGRS.2019.2907932

9. Li, Y., Zhang, H., Shen, Q.: Spectral-spatial classification of hyperspectral imagery with 3D convolutional neural network. Remote Sens. **9**(1) (2017). https://doi.org/10.3390/rs9010067

10. Li, Z., Liu, M., Chen, Y., Xu, Y., Li, W., Du, Q.: Deep cross-domain few-shot learning for hyperspectral image classification. IEEE Trans. Geosci. Remote Sens. **60**, 1–18 (2022). https://doi.org/10.1109/TGRS.2021.3057066

11. Liu, B., Yu, X., Yu, A., Zhang, P., Wan, G., Wang, R.: Deep few-shot learning for hyperspectral image classification. IEEE Trans. Geosci. Remote Sens. **57**(4), 2290–2304 (2019). https://doi.org/10.1109/TGRS.2018.2872830

12. Long, M., Cao, Z., Wang, J., Jordan, M.I.: Domain adaptation with randomized multilinear adversarial networks. arXiv preprint arXiv:1705.10667 (2017)

13. Melgani, F., Bruzzone, L.: Support vector machines for classification of hyperspectral remote-sensing images. In: IEEE International Geoscience and Remote Sensing Symposium, vol. 1, pp. 506–508 (2002). https://doi.org/10.1109/IGARSS.2002.1025088

14. Sun, H., Zheng, X., Lu, X., Wu, S.: Spectral-spatial attention network for hyperspectral image classification. IEEE Trans. Geosci. Remote Sens. **58**(5), 3232–3245 (2020). https://doi.org/10.1109/TGRS.2019.2951160

15. Tuia, D., Persello, C., Bruzzone, L.: Domain adaptation for the classification of remote sensing data: an overview of recent advances. IEEE Geosci. Remote Sens. Magaz. **4**(2), 41–57 (2016). https://doi.org/10.1109/MGRS.2016.2548504

SAR Scene Classification Based on Self-supervised Jigsaw Puzzles

Zhongle Ren[✉], Yiming Lu, Hanxiao Wang, Yu Zhang, and Biao Hou

Key Laboratory of Intelligent Perception and Image Understanding of Ministry of Education of China, Xidian University, Xi'an 710071, People's Republic of China
zlren@xidian.edu.cn

Abstract. Scene classification is a hot issue in the field of SAR image interpretation. Many SAR image interpretation tasks can be promoted with the development of highly credible scene classification methods. But the fussy steps of traditional methods and the imperious demands of labeled samples in deep learning-based methods restrict the effective feature learning in SAR scene classification. Hence, a self-supervised learning method based on Jigsaw puzzles is proposed to address the problems. Concretely, the Jigsaw puzzle reassembly of the SAR image block is firstly taken as the upstream task without manual labels. Once the correct spatial arrangement is obtained from it, the learned high-level feature from the upstream task is used as the pre-training model for the downstream task, which is then fine-tuned with only a few labeled samples to enhance the performance of the SAR scene classification task. Experimental results on 25-class real SAR scenes confirm the proposed method can greatly improve the scene classification performance than directly training the network with the same number of labeled samples used in the downstream task.

Keywords: SAR · Self-supervised learning · Jigsaw puzzles · Scene classification

1 Introduction

Synthetic Aperture Radar (SAR), is a system for observing the surface of the earth, which does not gets affected by sunlight, cloud cover and weather conditions. It is very important to interpret SAR images correctly and effectively, for instance, the SAR image classification, which is the most rudimentary issue in interpreting SAR images. SAR image classification has been proved to play a great role in agricultural detection [1], fuel pollution [2] and terrain surface classification [3].

The traditional classification method is cumbersome. For instance, the methods based on SVM (Support Vector Machine) [4] or random forest classifier [5] need to manually extract features and bring them into the classifier, which requires a high cost in manual experience. With the development of technology, many methods based on deep learning have emerged. Zhao et al. [6] proposed a SAR image classification method based on the

© IFIP International Federation for Information Processing 2022
Published by Springer Nature Switzerland AG 2022
Z. Shi et al. (Eds.): ICIS 2022, IFIP AICT 659, pp. 334–343, 2022.
https://doi.org/10.1007/978-3-031-14903-0_36

multi-scale local Fisher pattern, which uses the implicit generation and discrimination information of each Fisher vector to classify. Zhang et al. [7] used both the deep features learned from the convolutional neural network and the spatial constraints between super-pixels to achieve classification, but this method requires many samples to extract the deep features. To relieve the demand for the data, Li et al. [8] combined the convolutional neural network with metric learning, but the computational cost of this method is high. Many deep learning methods are inseparable from a large number of samples. However, due to insufficient open-source data for SAR images, these deep learning methods cannot obtain human enough labeled data for experiments, thus limiting the performance.

The datasets are not enough in many fields, and the cost of manually labeled data is also very high, which consumes a lot of human and financial resources. Hence, a new method is produced, which is called self-supervised learning. Self-supervised learning mainly uses upstream tasks to excavate its supervision information from large-scale unlabeled data, then gets a pre-trained model. Only a small number of labeled samples are used to fine-tune the parameters in the downstream task. This learning strategy is the latest variant of unsupervised learning topics, which can take advantage of tags provided by data "for free".

In this paper, an algorithm for self-supervised SAR image scene classification is proposed, using Jigsaw puzzles [9, 10] as the upstream task. The algorithm is to complete the Jigsaw puzzles problem in the upstream task and migrate the learned features to the downstream classification task. The remainder of this article is arranged as follows. Section 2 describes the background knowledge and the proposed method. Section 3 introduces the experimental details and results in upstream and downstream tasks. Finally, the conclusion and future work are drawn in Sect. 4.

2 Methodology

2.1 Jigsaw Puzzle Problem

Jigsaw puzzles have always been closely related to learning. By solving Jigsaw puzzles, we can learn the relationship between various blocks and understand their internal characteristics. It is also indicated by psychological research that Jigsaw puzzles can be used to evaluate human visual spatial processing [11]. Our work is to use the convolution neural network to learn the characteristics of images in the process of solving Jigsaw puzzles. The direct method of solving Jigsaw puzzles is to stack the blocks of the puzzle along the channel, then increase the filter depth of the first convolution layer in the convolution neural network accordingly. The problem with the solution is that the network will learn the correlation between low-level texture information among the blocks, which is one-sided for understanding the overall structure, and it may not be conducive to solving the downstream tasks of self-supervised learning. Hence, a network is proposed, which can calculate characteristics according to each block pixel, and find the permutation of the puzzle through the whole connection layer by using these characteristics. In this way, the network can learn representative and distinguishing characteristics without using any label.

2.2 Network Structure

A convolution neural network is built to complete Jigsaw puzzles. We make changes to the AlexNet [12] convolutional layer to obtain a network structure with a smaller number of parameters and design the fully connected layer (as shown in Fig. 1). The change index and parameter quantity are shown in Table 1 and Table 2, the network shares weights between the convolutional layer part and the first fully connected layer. The output of fc6 in the first layer of all full connection layers is connected as the output of fc7. After a full connection layer and softmax classifier, the final output value is obtained. The overall network structure is called the context-free network.

Table 1. Number of convolution cores.

	Conv1	Conv2	Conv3	Conv4	Conv5
AlexNet	96	256	384	384	256
Ours	**64**	**192**	**384**	**256**	**256**

At the beginning of the experiment, the size of the input image is adjusted to 255 × 255 and divided into 3 × 3 image blocks, each size of which is 85 × 85. Then a 64 × 64 pixel image block is randomly selected from each 85 × 85 image block. To make the input conform to the structure of the network, we resize it to 75 × 75. The nine image blocks are reordered by randomly selected permutations in the predefined permutation set and sent to the network. Our ultimate aim is to predict the index of the selected permutation.

Table 2. Number of parameters.

	Conv	Fc6
AlexNet	3.7M	37.7M
Ours	**2.4M**	**2.3M**

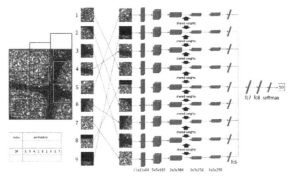

Fig. 1. Flowchart of proposed methods. The sample is cropped into blocks (red grid), and the pixel value is set to 255 for the part beyond the sample. This cutting method is more conducive in practice. 64 × 64 regions are randomly cut from the nine blocks respectively and resized to 75 × 75. After that, they are fed into the network, and the index value of the selected permutation is predicted accordingly. The stride of the first convolution layer in the upstream task is set to 2 to adapt to the size of the input samples. The network structure in the downstream task is consistent with this flowchart before the layer of fc6.

2.3 Network Training

For the 3 × 3 puzzle, there are 9! = 362880 possible permutations in total. The selection of permutation set also has a certain impact on the performance of the experiments, which will be explained in Sect. 2.4. An index is assigned to a predefined permutation set. Then one permutation is randomly selected to be sent to the network. It is also required to return a vector containing the probability value of each index.

The output of network can be regarded as the conditional probability density function of object space permutation

$$p(S|A_1, A_2, \ldots, A_9) = p(S|F_1, F_2, \ldots, F_9) \prod_{i=1}^{9} p(F_i|A_i) \tag{1}$$

where S is the permutation selected above, A_i represents the i-th image block, and F_i forms an intermediate feature representation. Our aim is to make feature F_i have semantic attributes that can recognize the relative position between image blocks.

If only one Jigsaw puzzle was generated for each sample, t would be probable to learn only the information of absolute position, which will be irrelevant to our requirements. Hence, it is necessary to generate multiple Jigsaw puzzles for a sample. If a location list S = $(L_1, L_2, \ldots, L_9)$ is generated for each part of the configuration S, then $p(S|F_1, F_2, \ldots, F_9)$ can be written as:

$$p(L_1, L_2, \ldots, L_9|F_1, F_2, \ldots, F_9) = \prod_{i=1}^{9} p(L_i|F_i) \tag{2}$$

In this way, the position of each block is determined by the corresponding features.

2.4 Shortcuts Prevention

In case of using shortcuts while solving Jigsaw puzzles, a series of measures are made. In the process of randomly extracting from the image block with the size of 85×85, the average gap of 21 pixels is specially divided, which can prevent learning low-level information. As mentioned above, an image is divided into 9 image blocks, with a total of 362880 different segmentation methods. Some block methods are very similar to the original image, but what we need are some methods that Jigsaw puzzles permutation is quite different from the original image. Hence, Hamming distance is required. Hamming distance indicates the number of different characters in the corresponding position of two strings of the same length. According to the Hamming distance before and after the reshuffle, we select the first 100 permutations as the way to choose the puzzle.

2.5 Downstream Tasks

After the upstream task, the learned features are used for the pre-trained weight of the scene classification task on the SAR image dataset, and we apply the weight of the upstream task network to initialize all the convolutional layers of the downstream network. The convolution layer of the downstream task network is the same as that of the upstream task network, but the full connection layer is different. Hence, we choose to copy only the weights of the convolution layers. However, unlike the upstream task, the downstream task sets the stride of the first layer of convolution to 4, which conforms to the standard AlexNet structure. Then we turn to train the rest of the network to make scene classification for SAR image data.

3 Experiments

3.1 Dataset and Experiment Settings

The data used in this experiment are shown in Fig. 2. The dataset of the SAR scene contains 25 different classes, and each class has 400 samples [6]. They are shot in Rosenheim, Toronto, Java, Colorado, Beijing and Hong Kong airport, in which abundant scenes can be found, such as large areas of farmland and forest areas, water surfaces and residential areas with different densities. These 25 scenes are named C1 to C25 respectively. Specifically, the 25 types of scenes are wasteland, airport runway, 3 types of water area, agriculture, 4 types of architecture, sparse residence, 4 types of dense residence, skyscraper, 2 types of river, 2 types of road, farmland, forest, grassland residence, railway track and vegetation farmland mixture. The size of each sample is 200×200. In the task of the Jigsaw puzzle reassembly of the SAR image block, the training set and test set are divided according to the ratio of 7:3, with 7000 training samples and 3000 test samples.

All the experiments are implemented on the Pytorch 1.8.0. The interface is Python 3.8 and the platform is an Intel Xeon(R) CPU, and an NVIDIA GeForce RTX 2080 Ti under Ubuntu 18.04. The learning rate used in the upstream task is 0.01, and we set the training samples batch size and the test samples batch size to 64 and 32 respectively. The training epoch is 300. Additionally, the adopted attenuation way is to reduce the learning rate to 0.5 times the original one per 50 epochs.

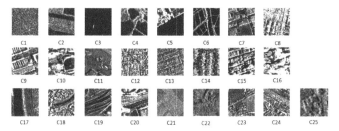

Fig. 2. SAR scene dataset used in our experiments. Each class is illustrated with one sample. C1 for wasteland; C2 for airport runway; C3, C4 and C5 for water area; C6 for agriculture; C7, C8, C9 and C10 for architecture; C11 for sparse residence; C12, C13, C14 and C15 for dense residence; C16 for skyscraper; C17 and C18 for river; C19 and C20 for road; C21 for farmland; C22 for forest; C23 for grassland residence; C24 for railway track; C25 for a mixture of vegetation and farmland.

3.2 Upstream Task Results

The upstream task is regarded as a sorting task to judge whether the correct sorting is found. By solving Jigsaw puzzles, the network learned how to recognize each image block as an object part and how to assemble it into the object, from which the network learns the feature that is beneficial for the downstream task. We train the upstream task following the same experimental setting described in Sect. 3.1. The accuracy of the upstream task is calculated in the following style: first, the index value of a permutation randomly selected from the pre-defined permutation set is obtained as the label. Then the image is scrambled according to this index value and the scrambled image blocks are fed into the network, obtaining a probability vector. Finally, the index value corresponding to the largest value in the probability vector is regarded as the predicted result and compared with the label to calculate the accuracy.

The experimental results are shown in Table 3.

Table 3. Training parameters of the upstream task.

Upstream tasks	Epoch	Training time	Training/Testing batch size	Accuracy
Jigsaw puzzles	300	10 h	64/32	72%

In the upstream task training, according to the number of training and test samples, we set the batch size of training and test to 64 and 32 respectively, and the initial learning rate is set to 0.01. It is found that the network converges after 300 epochs, and the accuracy of the upstream task is 72%.

3.3 Downstream Task Results

The goal of the downstream task is to fulfill SAR scene classification with labeled samples as few as possible. Hence, in the downstream task, a very small amount of samples is used to fine-tune the model. We select 1, 2 and 3 samples from each class to train the downstream scenes. The two samples in each class will include the situation of selecting one sample, and the three samples in each class will include the situation of selecting two samples, which constitutes incremental comparison settings to show the effect of choosing different samples on the experiment. As shown in Fig. 3, the downstream task is fine-tuned. Hence, we set the learning rate to 0.001 and verify the influence of different batch sizes on the experimental results. The test set of the upstream task is still considered as the selected test set, and we test whether it is classified into the corresponding scene class. Then it is compared with the method that does not take the weight obtained from the upstream task as the pre-trained weight, to verify the effectiveness of this experimental method. The results obtained are shown in Table 3.

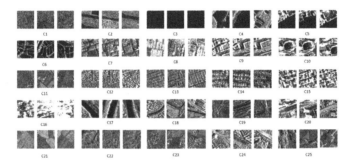

Fig. 3. The training samples for each class in downstream task.

Table 4. Experimental results of scene classification using 1 sample of each class for training in the downstream task.

Number of selected samples per class	Whether to use upstream task training weight	Training batch size	Classification accuracy
1	No	2	13.6%
1	No	4	12.6%
1	No	8	8.2%
1	No	16	7.5%
1	Yes	2	**25.0%**
1	Yes	4	17.3%
1	Yes	8	11.7%
1	Yes	16	10.8%

Table 5. Experimental results of scene classification using 2 samples of each class for training in the downstream task.

Number of selected samples per class	Whether to use upstream task training weight	Training batch size	Classification accuracy
2	No	2	14.7%
2	No	4	15.0%
2	No	8	10.7%
2	No	16	6.5%
2	Yes	2	**33.4%**
2	Yes	4	30.2%
2	Yes	8	18.4%
2	Yes	16	11.8%

Table 6. Experimental results of scene classification using 3 samples of each class for training in the downstream task.

Number of selected samples per class	Whether to use upstream task training weight	Training batch size	Classification accuracy
3	No	2	23.2%
3	No	4	23.2%
3	No	8	16.5%
3	No	16	10.1%
3	Yes	2	**38.1%**
3	Yes	4	37.8%
3	Yes	8	23.6%
3	Yes	16	12.8%

Table 4, 5 and 6 show the quantitative results of the different number of training samples, batch size and whether use the feature learned in the upstream task respectively. By comparing the results in Table 4, 5 and 6, it is obvious that the classification accuracy increases with the number of the sample, whether using the weights from the upstream task or not. This is also true for different batch size settings.

From each table, it can be observed that under the same parameter setting, the classification accuracy of the downstream task using weights learned from the upstream task is all higher than without it, which indicates the promotion of the Jigsaw puzzle task to the scene classification task. To be pronounced, the highest accuracy using the weights from the Jigsaw puzzle task of each table is higher than that acquired from the scratch training by over 10 points. This is a promising indicator to improve performance with related upstream tasks, instead of directly using lots of labeled samples in the task.

It can be noticed from Table 4, 5 and 6 that the performance decreases as the batch size increases. One possible explanation for this result is that the generalization of the model decreases with the batch size increasing, especially in the case of a few training samples. Specifically, the accuracy drops a few from 2 to 4, but a lot when the batch size is chosen as 8 and 16. Considering both accuracy and efficiency, picking 4 as the default batch size is a good choice for future research.

4   Conclusions

In this paper, a self-supervised learning framework consisting of Jigsaw puzzles sorting learning and scene classification is constructed to achieve SAR scene classification with few samples. By solving Jigsaw puzzles, the network learns feature which is suited for the downstream task. The experimental results show a notable improvement for SAR scene classification with an appropriate upstream task. What's more, the results obtained with few samples have a huge potential in real SAR applications. However, this is an initial research in this direction. Abundant experiments are still needed under more parameter settings and a larger dataset.

Acknowledgement. This work was supported in part by the National Natural Science Foundation of China under Grant 62171347, 61877066, 61771379, 62001355, 62101405; the Foundation for Innovative Research Groups of the National Natural Science Foundation of China under Grant 61621005; the fundamental Research Funds for the Central Universities under Grant XJS211904; the Key Research and Development Program in Shaanxi Province of China under Grant 2019ZDLGY0305 and 2021ZDLGY0208; the Science and Technology Program in Xi'an of China under Grant XA2020-RGZNTJ-0021; 111 Project.

References

1. Wang, H., Magagi, R., Goita, K.: Polarimetric decomposition for monitoring crop growth status. IEEE Geosci. Remote Sens. Lett. **13**(6), 870–874 (2016)
2. Del Frate, F., Latini, D., Scappiti, V.: On neural networks algorithms for oil spill detection when applied to C-and X-band SAR. In: 2017 IEEE International Geoscience and Remote Sensing Symposium (IGARSS), pp. 5249–5251. IEEE (2017)
3. Dumitru, C.O., Cui, S., Schwarz, G., et al.: Information content of very-high-resolution SAR images: semantics, geospatial context, and ontologies. IEEE J. Sel. Top. Appl. Earth Obs. Remote Sens. **8**(4), 1635–1650 (2014)
4. Chapelle, O., Haffner, P., Vapnik, V.N.: Support vector machines for histogram-based image classification. IEEE Trans. Neural Netw. **10**(5), 1055–1064 (1999)
5. McNairn, H., Kross, A., Lapen, D., et al.: Early season monitoring of corn and soybeans with TerraSAR-X and RADARSAT-2. Int. J. Appl. Earth Obs. Geoinf. **28**, 252–259 (2014)
6. Zhao, Z., Jia, M., Wang, L.: High-resolution SAR image classification via multiscale local Fisher patterns. IEEE Trans. Geosci. Remote Sens. **59**(12), 10161–10178 (2020)

7. Zhang, A., Yang, X., Fang, S., et al.: Region level SAR image classification using deep features and spatial constraints. ISPRS J. Photogramm. Remote Sens. **163**, 36–48 (2020)

8. Li, Y., Li, X., Sun, Q., et al.: SAR image classification using CNN embeddings and metric learning. IEEE Geosci. Remote Sens. Lett. **19**, 1–5 (2020)

9. Doersch, C., Gupta, A., Efros, A.A.: Unsupervised visual representation learning by context prediction. In: Proceedings of the IEEE International Conference on Computer Vision, pp. 1422–1430 (2015)

10. Noroozi, M., Favaro, P.: Unsupervised learning of visual representations by solving jigsaw puzzles. In: Leibe, B., Matas, J., Sebe, N., Welling, M. (eds.) Computer Vision – ECCV 2016: 14th European Conference, Amsterdam, The Netherlands, October 11–14, 2016, Proceedings, Part VI, pp. 69–84. Springer International Publishing, Cham (2016). https://doi.org/10.1007/978-3-319-46466-4_5

11. Richardson, J.T.E., Vecchi, T.: A jigsaw-puzzle imagery task for assessing active visuospatial processes in old and young people. Behav. Res. Meth. Instrum. Comput. **34**(1), 69–82 (2002)

12. Krizhevsky, A., Sutskever, I., Hinton, G.E.: ImageNet classification with deep convolutional neural networks. In: Advances in Neural Information Processing Systems, vol. 25 (2012)

YOLO-Head: An Input Adaptive Neural Network Preprocessor

Biao Hou, Shenxuan Zhou[✉], Xiaoyu Chen, Heng Jiang, and Hao Wang

Xidian University, Xi'an 710071, China
sxzhou@stu.xidian.edu.cn

Abstract. Over the past decade, object detectors have demonstrated remarkable performance in various applications, such as traffic monitoring, customer tracking, and surveillance. Although advanced lightweight models have been proved to have ultra real-time speed on GPU, in edge-based video analytics system, edge servers are usually embedded devices with NPU which support general neural network operators. When we implemented deep learning models on embedded devices, images usually need to be preprocessed to the network input size. This leads to the common target detectors not being end-to-end. Image preprocessing is not the key problem of real-time inferencing on devices with high-performance CPU, but the same algorithm will bring noticeable delay on embedded devices. To overcome this, we designed YOLO-Head, a module that can handle the input of arbitrarily size according to general neural network operators. Experiment results show that YOLO-Head achieves significant (60.89%) speed improvement when 1080p image zooms to 640×640. Furthermore, YOLOv5-S detector with adaptive head can effectively solve the delay problem due to the image resize. The frame rate improves to 35.2 FPS, approximately 6 times faster than the convectional method in video stream processing on RK3588.

Keywords: Video analytics · Deep neural networks · Object detection

1 Introduction

Video cameras are pervasive in today's society, with cities and organizations steadily increasing the size and reach of their deployments [1]. Key to video stream processing applications has been recent advances in deep learning which has obtained high accuracy in multiple scenes for object detection and recognition. In a typical real-time video analytics pipeline [2], a camera streams live video to cloud servers, which immediately run object detection models (e.g., YOLO [3]) to answer user queries about that video. Cloud-based video analytics requires a lot of computing resources and network resources. The end-to-end frame rate needs to be more than 30fps for real-time video streams in that case the network delay of information transmission can not be ignored.

Therefore, a large number of embedded devices on the edge side are added in edge-based video analytics paradigm [7]. They are deployed near mobile devices,

© IFIP International Federation for Information Processing 2022
Published by Springer Nature Switzerland AG 2022
Z. Shi et al. (Eds.): ICIS 2022, IFIP AICT 659, pp. 344–351, 2022.
https://doi.org/10.1007/978-3-031-14903-0_37

with small network delay. These devices are equipped with NPU instead of GPU, which execute neural operators quite efficiently as well. On the neural network arithmetic unit, most general neural network computing modules have been implemented, but special types of algorithms are difficult to implement such as image resize. On the other side, it is usually necessary for preprocessor to adjust the data size from image input to neural network [4]. It is mush slower than neural network computing modules.

Image scaling is usually accomplished by interpolations. In digital signal processing, it can be defined as the convolution of the continuous impulse response of a discrete image signal with a two-dimensional reconstructed filter. Continuous images can be reconstructed with appropriate window functions, e.g., rectangular windows(nearest neighbor interpolation), triangular functions(linear interpolation) [9]. The algorithm based on region mainly uses mean filter, which replaces the original pixel value with the average of all the pixels in the template(area interpolation). Although different scale algorithms employ different strategies, their speeds on ARM-based processors can not meet the real-time requirements as shown in Fig. 2.

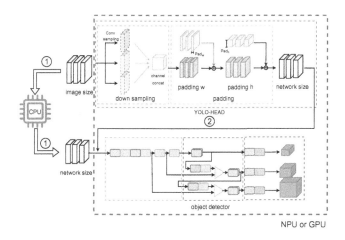

Fig. 1. In the popular target detection framework, it is usually necessary to use the interpolation algorithm in the CPU to scale the input image to the network input, as shown in way 1. In embedded devices, the relevant algorithms for scaling are quite time-consuming. We propose an adaptive head to complete data preprocessing making data flow always on NPU or GPU as shown in way 2.

One of the existing methods is to do two-dimensional image operation by designing special integrated circuits, while it is complicated and difficult to implement for ordinary developers [5,8]. From the perspective of software, we propose an algorithm instead of resize, which can be widely used in embedded development boards with NPU. We propose the adaptive head module solving the delay of its preprocessing, which is the key point to promote the efficiency of detector. Our contributions can be summarized as follows:

- **Convolution Sampling Unit.** We use convolution as adaptive down sampling unit, which has very excellent performance on NPU. With the complement unit composed of concat operation, arbitrarily scale can be completed. When the 1080p image is scaled to 640 × 640, the image preprocessing time is decreased to 60.89% by YOLO-Head.
- **Target Detector General Component.** YOLO-Head can be added to most target detectors to form an input adaptive model. Experiments on YOLOv5-S show that our proposed method improves video stream processing speed by approximately six times.

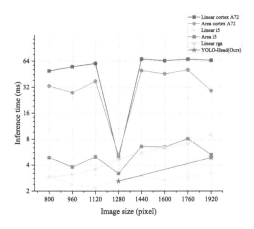

Fig. 2. Zoom the picture from image size to 640 × 640 pixels. The proposed YOLO-Head outperforms a range of state-of-the-art algorithms.

2   Method

2.1   YOLO-Head

Generally speaking, in the real-time video analytics pipelines, the image size in the video stream is fixed depends on cameras. With the development of photoelectric imaging, image size is generally more than 1080 × 1920 pixels. Due to the computing resources of devices, the input of deep learning network can not be as large as the video size. Therefore, it is necessary to resize the image to the network before inference. Figure 2 illustrates that the time required for this resize operation on personal computer (i5-6300HQ CPU) is less than 8ms. On high-performance processors resize algorithm is less affected by the origin size, but it will bring serious delay on embedded device. In particular, in some divisible sizes, different resize algorithms will be equivalent to certain algorithm.

According to the documentation of opencv [6], it is most precise to shrink the image using area interpolation, while in the case of magnifying cubic interpolation works best. Cubicis replaced by a slightly inferior linear algorithm because of its slow speed. In this paper, if there is no additional explanation, the resizing algorithm based on area interpolation is discussed.

The overall structure of YOLO-Head is shown in Fig. 1. It is equivalent to area interpolation and is designed to replace resize operation. Common operators such as conv(convolution) or pooling(averagepooling) can be used when down sampling data. Figure 3 is a convolution sampling operator to double the down sampling. Average pooling works the same as convolution sampling operator. Conv is selected as the down sampling unit in YOLO-Head, which is more efficient on RK3588. The lower sampling coefficient is:

$$scale = \min \left(\frac{net_w}{img_w}, \frac{net_h}{img_h} \right) \tag{1}$$

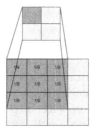

Fig. 3. Conv operator accomplish down sampling.

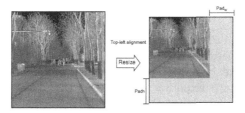

Fig. 4. Resize by aligning the upper left corner when img_w is not a multiple of net_w (or img_h is not a multiple of net_h).

In order to further reduce the computation of the model, the top-left edge alignment is adopted to handle the case where $1scale$ is not an integer, which has little impact on post-processing and is shown in Fig. 4. A compensation module is added to YOLO-Head to solve the problem of misalignment. The compensation values for height and width is

$$\begin{cases} pad_h = net_h - \frac{img_h}{scale} \\ pad_w = net_w - \frac{img_w}{scale} \end{cases} \tag{2}$$

After adding the adaptive head in front of the detector, the procedure of resizing the image to the network size will be omitted. Arbitrary images can be directly transmitted to the network. In addition, the implementation of resize algorithm on embedded devices may have slight differences, which may reduce the accuracy of model. The improved detector maintains the consistency of the algorithm on the inferencing side and training side.

2.2   Pipeline

Base Detector. The classic YOLOv5-S is selected as our default object detector. It inherits and carries forward YOLO series with several tricks, e.g., adaptive anchor, strong data argumentations, advanced network structure and outstanding loss function. Considering the handware implementation of NPU operator, we have modified the large step maxpooling operator, slice operator and activation function in Focus module. Max pooling layers with small steps in series instead of large steps are used because Max pooling with large steps on NPU takes a long time. The slice operator is also poorly implemented on some RKNN devices. We replaced it by a conv with a special weight distribution. The above two optimization strategies speed up without changing the runtime results. Since the convolution, Relu and BN layers can be combined on NPU devices, but special activation functions such as Silu are not supported, all activation functions are replaced with Relu. In addition, the data post-processing part of the model has serious quantification accuracy problems and has to be removed from the YOLO model.

Adaptive Head. During the translational deployment of the target detector, the input adaptive network designed by the input parameters of the task will added in front of the YOLO detector. Deployment details of YOLO-Head is depicted in Algorithm 1. Experiments show that the concat operator used in the adaptive head often runs on the CPU, which greatly increases the time consumed. Therefore, the specific deployment scheme is to use a simplified YOLO-Head which has no concat operations after image compensated to an integer multiple of the network input. Our strategy will not affect the results of YOLO-Head.

Train and Inference. The dataset, which is taken with the same camera, has the same picture size. According to Eqs. 1 and 2, our adaptive head is constructed and added to the YOLO detector. Since the weight data of adaptive network is constant, it will not affect the training results. In inferencing, our improved YOLOv5-S model can complete end-to-end feature extraction only by inputting source image. The real-time target prediction frames are obtained when data decoding and NMS are performed after feature results are transmitted to CPU.

Algorithm 1. Adaptive head deployment process

Input: A bitmap Im of size $Img_w \times Img_h$
Output: A bitmap Im_{resize} of size $Net_w \times Net_h$
    // *Calculate Construction parameters scale and (pad_h, pad_w)*
1: Update scale based on Eq. (1)
2: Update pad_h and pad_w based on Eq. (2)
    // *scaling in the original ratio*
3: **for** c in output_channels **do**
4:    sample_unit = Conv2d(input_c=1,output_c=1,kernal=scale)
5:    $Im_{resize}[c]$ = sample_unit($Im[c]$)
    // *two-dimensional padding*
6: $tmp_h = \frac{Img_h}{scale}$, $tmp_w = \frac{Img_w}{scale}$
7: **if** $pad_w! = 0$ **then**
8:    $padding = zeros_{1 \times 3 \times tmp_h \times pad_w}$
9:    concat(Im_{resize}, padding)
10: **if** $pad_h! = 0$ **then**
11:    $padding = zeros_{1 \times 3 \times Net_w \times pad_w}$
12:    concat(Im_{resize}, padding)

---

3 Experiments

3.1 Settings

Datasets. The experiment was carried out on our own infrared autopilot dataset including diverse urban outdoor scenes in Xi'an city. It has high frame rate(30 FPS) and high resolution(1080 × 1920 pixels) sensor data. The dataset is divided into two parts: training set and verification set. The verification set has 5 videos, with a total of 42378 frames.

Implementation Details. If not specified, we use YOLOv5-S as our default detector. The network input is 640 × 640 pixels while the picture size in the video stream is 1080 × 1920 pixels. We trained on 4 × 3090ti GPUs and got weight file. Because only RKNN model can be loaded on RK3588, we convert the weight file into RKNN model through onnx transition. In inferencing evaluation, we run on a single NPU of RK3588, including data post-processing and NMS time.

3.2 Evaluation for YOLO-Head

According to the deployment strategy of YOLO-Head in Algorithm 1, only the image size of an integer multiple of the network input size needs to be calculated during evaluation. The image of 1280 × 1280 pixels uses our input adaptive module resize to 640 × 640, which takes an average of 2.6ms, while the image of 1920 × 1920 pixels takes 4.9ms. 1920 × 1920 images use area interpolation on cortex A72 needs 29.1ms. The run time improvement comes from making full use of the parallel computing power of NPU and reduce the operation of CPU. Our method shows strong competitiveness on the embedded platform and solves the problem that the image preprocessing is time-consuming in the mobile terminal.

3.3   Application in Object Detector

The YOLOv5 source model is struggling when inferencing on RK3588. Table 1 shows after adopting the NPU optimization strategy, the modified YOLOv5 model has a slight loss in accuracy (reduced by 4.4%), but the running time of a single frame is reduced by 60.89%. Although the single frame operation result is acceptable, in real-time stream processing, image preprocessing and detection result post-processing bring serious delay.

Table 2 shows after using our adaptive input module, the FPS is increased from the original 5.78 frame/s to 37.59, which effectively reduces the delay caused by preprocessing. Our YOLO-Head can achieve the performance similar to that of RGA(a CPU-independent graphics acceleration engine RGA on RK3399/3588, with basic operations of 2D images). When there is no RGA on the general embedded device, our method can be used to replace it equivalently on NPU. When the error loss is allowed, YOLO-Head can be easily added before the trained model, which eliminates the step of retraining the deep learning model.

Table 1. YOLOv5-s single frame inference results on RK3588 (single core).

Model	Small stride	Slice	Relu	YOLO-Head	Inference time (ms)	AP
YOLOv5-S					165.31	87.6%
	✓	✓			64.65	87.1%
	✓	✓	✓		45.18	82.4%
	✓	✓	✓	✓	49.07	82.3%

Table 2. Real time video stream processing on RK3588 (single core).

SYSTEM	YOLO-Head	RGA (linear)	FPS	AP
YOLOv5-S (NPU modify)			5.78	82.4%
		✓	37.59	81.9%
	✓		35.20	82.3%

4   Conclusion

This paper presents an adaptive head module called YOLO-Head to handle the time-consuming problem of scaling on embedded devices. Our adaptive head is composed of general neural network operators, which is simple, fast and accurate. The idea can be widely applied to the deep learning model. Our initial experiments are encouraging and effectively solves the time delay problem of image preprocessing on embedded devices.

Acknowledgements. This work was supported in part by the National Natural Science Foundation of China under Grant 62171347, 61877066, 61771379, 62001355, 62101405; the Foundation for Innovative Research Groups of the National Natural Science Foundation of China under Grant 61621005; the Key Research and Development Program in Shaanxi Province of China under Grant 2019ZDLGY03-05 and 2021ZDLGY02-08; the Science and Technology Program in Xi'an of China under Grant XA2020-RGZNTJ-0021; 111 Project.

References

1. Li, Y., Padmanabhan, A., Zhao, P., Wang, Y., Xu, G., Ravi, N.: Reducto: on-camera filtering for resource-efficient real-time video analytics. In: Proceedings of the Annual Conference of the ACM Special Interest Group on Data Communication on the Applications, Technologies, Architectures, and Protocols for Computer Communication, pp. 359–376 (2020)
2. Can 30,000 Cameras Help Solve Chicago's Crime Problem? https://www.nytimes.com/2018/05/26/us/chicago-police-surveillance.html
3. Redmon, J., Farhadi, A.: YOLO9000: Better, Faster, Stronger. In: CVPR (2017)
4. Redmon, J., Farhadi, A: Yolov3: an incremental improvement. arXiv preprint arXiv:1804.02767 (2018)
5. Open source warehouse for acceleration engine RGA. https://github.com/rockchip-linux/linux-rga. Accessed 26 June 2021
6. OpenCV. Geometric Image Transformations. https://docs.opencv.org/4.x/d9/df8/tutorial_root.html. Accessed 10 May 2022
7. Chen, J., Ran, X.: Deep learning with edge computing: a review. Proc. IEEE **107**(8), 1655–1674 (2019)
8. Wang, P., Cao, Y., Ding, M., Zhang, Z., Qu, J.: A SoC collaborative accelerated design method of image scaling algorithm. J. Beijing Univ. Aeronaut. Astronaut. **45**(02), 333–339 (2019)
9. Huang, Y.: Research on Image Scaling Algorithms. HeFei University of Technology, Master (2010)

SR-YOLO: Small Objects Detection Based on Super Resolution

Biao Hou, Xiaoyu Chen[✉], Shenxuan Zhou, Heng Jiang, and Hao Wang

School of Artificial Intelligence, Xidian University, Xi'an 710071, China
15091892956@163.com

Abstract. Since the introduction of convolutional neural networks, object detection based on deep learning has made great progress and has been widely used in the industry. However, because the weak and small object contains too little information, the samples are rich in diversity, and there are different degrees of occlusion, the detection difficulty is too great, and the object detection has entered a bottleneck period of development. We firstly introduce a super-resolution network to solve the problem of small object pixel area being too small, and fuse the super-resolution generator with the object detection baseline model for collaborative training. In addition, in order to reinforce the weak feature of small objects, we design a convolution block based on the edge detection operator Sobel. Experiments show that proposed method achieves mAP50 improvement of 2.4% for all classes and 4.4% for the relatively weak pedestrian class on our dataset relative to the Yolov5s baseline model.

Keywords: Small object detection · Image super resolution · Infrared image

1 Introduction

Object detection, also known as object category detection or object classification detection, returns the category information and location information of the object of interest in the image. In the past two decades, it has been a research hotspot in the field of computer vision and digital image processing. During the two decades of development of object detection technology, various object detection architecture widely used in the industry have emerged. However, the most state-of-the-art object detection architecture are still a tough act to follow human eyes. The current object detection still faces many obstacles, among which the problem of poor performance of small object detection has not been completely solved.

In the object detection task, the small object contains too little RGB information due to its own definition, it contains too few discriminative features. The existence of the problem is also accompanied by dataset imbalance. As far as the COCO [1] dataset is concerned, only 51.82% of the pictures contain small

© IFIP International Federation for Information Processing 2022
Published by Springer Nature Switzerland AG 2022
Z. Shi et al. (Eds.): ICIS 2022, IFIP AICT 659, pp. 352–362, 2022.
https://doi.org/10.1007/978-3-031-14903-0_38

objects, and that is a serious image-level imbalance. Most of the current mainstream object detection architecture are anchor-based methods, but since the ground truth and anchor of small targets are very small, if there is a slight offset between the two, the IoU will become very low, resulting in the network being misjudged as a negative sample. In addition, there is a difficulty in small object detection that cannot be ignored: for some small object samples, there are different degrees of occlusion, blurring and incompleteness. Also taking the COCO dataset as an example, 41% of the annotations are small objects. In the case of, the problem of small object detection is still not alleviated, because most of the annotations in these small and difficult objects are difficult to be effectively utilized. Our work can be summarized as follows:

- **Super Resolution Generator.** In view of the low detection performance of small object due to their small pixel area, we introduce the generator component of the super-resolution network before the current detection of the backbone network. Unlike the general generative adversarial network, the parameters of the generator network we introduce update relies on the loss return of object detection.
- **Edge-oriented Sobel Block.** In order to strengthen the object edge information, a convolution block based on the Sobel edge extraction operator is designed.

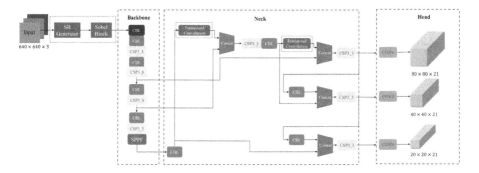

Fig. 1. Yolov5-Super Resolution Generator. On the basis of the original yolov5s model, the improvements we have made include: (1) Adding SR generator and Sobel block to the front end of the model. (2) Replace upsampling in the original model with transposed convolution.

2   Related Work

2.1   Object Detection

Object detection has also entered the period of deep learning. According to whether the algorithm needs to generate a pre-selection box, the object detection algorithm based on deep learning can be divided into one-stage detection algorithm and two-stage detection algorithm. Representative networks in one-stage detection algorithms include YOLO [2] series, SSD [3], and RetinaNet [4]. The basic idea of the YOLO series of object detection algorithms is to send the input image into the feature extraction network to obtain a feature map of S×S size, and divide the input image into S×S cells. Each grid uses logistic regression to predict B bounding boxes, outputting the location information of the bounding boxes and the probability information of the C categories. Among them, Yolov5 [5] is the latest network structure of the Yolo series.

Data augmentation is the simplest and most effective way to improve the performance of small object detection. From early distortion [6], rotation and scaling, to elastic deformation [7], random cropping [8] and translation [9] derived later, until now Horizontal flip used in Fast R-CNN [10], CutOut [11], MixUp [12], CutMix [13] and other methods used in YOLO. Mosaic data enhancement was further proposed in YOLOv4 [14] with reference to the CutMix data enhancement method, and the four pictures were spliced by random scaling, random cropping, and random arrangement. Yolov5 follows the Mosaic enhancement used by Yolov4. Multi-scale learning combining deep semantic features and shallow representation information solves the problem of small object detection to a certain extent. The feature pyramid proposed by Liu [3] et al. is currently the most widely used multi-scale network, and many variants of FPN have also appeared. Context learning is to model the coexistence relationship between objects and scenes and objects and objects, thereby improving the performance of small object detection. Generative adversarial learning [15] generates features that are equivalent to those of high-resolution targets from the feature map of low-resolution small targets, which improves the detection performance of low-resolution targets to a certain extent.In addition, Anchor-free abandons the anchor mechanism and converts the target detection task into the detection of key points, avoiding the small target detection problem caused by the small offset between the anchor and the ground truth.

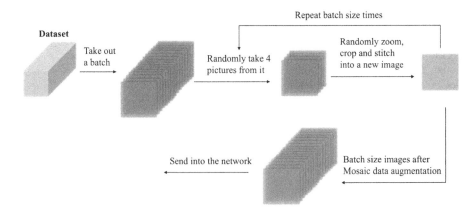

Fig. 2. Mosaic-4 data augmentation process

This paper further uses Mosaic-9 on the basis of Mosaic-4, randomly selects nine pictures in a training batch, randomly scales, randomly crops, and randomly arranges. Figure 2 illustrates the processing of mosaic enhancement. The difference between Mosaic-9 and Mosaic-4 is that Mosaic-9 uses nine images. This approach further expands the number of small objects in the data set, and alleviates the imbalance of the data set The problem.

2.2 Image Super Resolution

High-resolution images tend to contain greater pixel density, richer texture details, and higher reliability than low-resolution images. But usually limited by the limitations of the acquisition equipment and environment, it is impossible to obtain an ideal image with sharp edges and no blur. Image super-resolution reconstruction technology refers to the restoration of a given low-resolution image into a corresponding high-resolution image through a specific algorithm. It has a wide range of applications and research significance in many fields, such as image compression, medical imaging, remote sensing imaging and video perception, etc. According to time and effect, image super-resolution algorithms can be divided into two categories: traditional algorithms and deep learning algorithms. Traditional super-resolution reconstruction algorithms mainly rely on conventional digital image processing and other technologies. Dong et al. proposed SRCNN [16] (Super-Resolution Convulution Neural Network), the first application of deep learning technology to the field of image super-resolution. In 2017, Christian Ledig et al. proposed SRGAN [17] (Super-Resolution Generative Adversarial Networks), which defines a perceptual loss function and uses a generative adversarial network to reconstruct low-resolution images into high-resolution images. Based on the work of the above scholars, we believe that the generator in SRGAN has a structural advantage in image super-resolution, combining it with the object detection backbone network. Using the loss of object detection to update the weights of the generator, the goal is to allow the generator to generate high-resolution images that are more conducive to small object detection.

3 Method

3.1 Image Super Resolution Based on Generative Adversarial Networks

SRGAN consists of two parts: generator and discriminator. The generator is used to generate high-resolution images from low-resolution images, and the discriminator is used to compete with the generator, so that the generator can generate more realistic high-resolution images. In this paper, the generator structure in

SRGAN is integrated into the original Yolov5s model, which is different from the use of perceptual loss in SRGAN. The loss of Yolov5s is used to update the generator parameters, so that the high-resolution model generated by the generator is more suitable for the object detection task. Essentially alleviates the detection performance problem caused by more small object samples.

Figure 3 illustrates the network structure of the generator part of SRGAN, which is mainly composed of a deep residual module and a sub-pixel convolution module. The generator uses multiple deep residual modules to extract features from images, which ensures the stability of the generation network. Sub-pixel convolution, also known as pixel shuffle is different from upsampling and other methods, avoiding the introduction of too many artificial factors, and using the method of sample learning to enlarge the feature map.

3.2   Feature Extraction Backbone Considering Edge Information

The object information extracted by the feature extractor includes edge information, and the edge information occupies the main position in the feature information, and the human brain also mainly relies on the edge information when distinguishing objects. In this paper, the Sobel [19] edge detection operator is used to strengthen the edge information of the target, and the Sobel convolution is designed to fix the value of the convolution kernel to extract the edge information of the target.

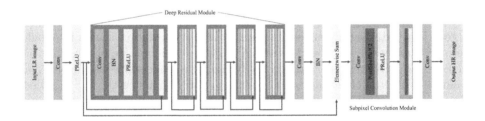

Fig. 3. Super resolution generator

Specifically, the input features are first subjected to 1×1 convolution for channel expansion, and then the output is sent to two Sobel convolution layers Sobel-x and Sobel-y with fixed weights in the vertical direction, respectively. Let D_x and D_y denote the convolution kernels used to extract the gradients of features in the x and y directions, respectively.

$$D_x = \begin{bmatrix} +1 & 0 & -1 \\ +2 & 0 & -2 \\ +1 & 0 & -1 \end{bmatrix}, D_y = \begin{bmatrix} +1 & +2 & +1 \\ 0 & 0 & 0 \\ -1 & -2 & -1 \end{bmatrix} \tag{1}$$

The input is finally summed with the output of the Sobel convolutional layer. The specific structure of the Sobel block is shown in Fig. 4.

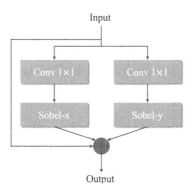

Fig. 4. Edge-oriented Sobel block

4 Experiment

4.1 Datasets

The infrared data set used in this paper was collected in the spring of 2022, and the infrared video data of Taibai South Road and Xifeng Road Section in Xi'an City, Shaanxi Province were collected from 3:00 p.m. to 5:00 p.m. The total duration is two hours, including 2342 images in the training set, 585 in the validation set, and 1000 in the test set, with an image size of 1920 × 1080. The objects in the dataset are labeled according to the YOLO format, and the labeled categories include pedestrians and vehicles. The specific data distribution is shown in Fig. 5. Figure 6 shows part of the dataset. It can be seen that in addition to the problem of class imbalance, the dataset also has a large number of weak and small objects.

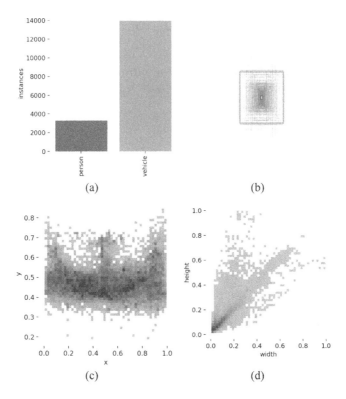

Fig. 5. Illustration of dataset distribution. (a) Shows that the dataset has a serious class imbalance problem. (b) Draws all the ground truth boxes. (c) and (d) Show the distribution of the center point coordinates and width and height of the real box of the dataset, respectively

Fig. 6. Part of the dataset

4.2   Experimental Environment and Training Settings

The experimental environment uses the Ubuntu20.04 operating system and a Nvidia GeForce RTX 3090 for computing, its video memory size is 24268MiB, the CPU configuration is Intel(R) Xeon(R) Silver 4216 CPU @ 2.10 GHz, the Pytorch version is 1.9.0, and the Python language environment is 3.7.11.

All experiments were trained for 100 epochs, batch-size is set to 32, the optimizer chooses SGD, the initial learning rate of the optimizer is 0.01. The learning rate in the model training phase is warmed up using Warmup, using one-dimensional linear interpolation to update the learning rate of each iteration, and the cosine annealing algorithm is used after the warmp-up stage to update the learning rate.

4.3   Evaluation Indicators

The indicators used to evaluate the model detection performance in target detection are: **AP** (Average precision),**Precision** and **Recall** and comprehensive evaluation index **F-Measure**.

Precision and Recall. Precision: The proportion of true targets among the targets detected by the model. Recall: The proportion of all real objects detected as positive. Precision-Recall Curve: The horizontal axis is the Recall, and the vertical axis is the Precision. The two variables are negatively correlated, that is, when the precision is larger, the Recall is smaller, and conversely, when the Recall is larger, the precision is lower. The more ideal the curve, the better the performance of the model and the larger the area enclosed by the abscissa and ordinate.

AP (Average Precision). Average precision refers to the area under the PR curve, which refers to the average precision for different recall rates. The higher the AP, the better the recognition performance of the model. mAP is the mean average precision. When the sample has multiple categories, the AP of each category is averaged. mAP measures the detection performance of the model on various samples of the dataset.

4.4   Analysis of Experimental Results

Tables 1 and 2 illustrate the detection performance of the baseline model and our model on the dataset, respectively. The results described in Table 1 are for the entire data set. It can be seen that the Sobel module can improve the precision of the model with almost no increase in computational cost. Unsurprisingly, the SR module has improved various indicators of the model. The validity of the Sobel module and the SR module can be demonstrated. As mentioned above, the dataset has severe class imbalance, and there are many weak objects in pedestrian samples. To verify the improvement of our method for weak and

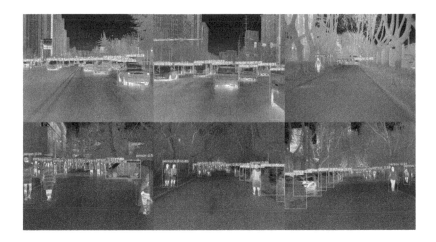

Fig. 7. Partial inference results

Table 1. Comparison of the validation results of our method and the baseline method

Method	Layers	Weight (M)	Presicion (%)	Recall (%)	mAP@.5 (%)	mAP@.5:.95 (%)
Baseline	213	6.69	86.6	79.1	86.2	53.2
Sobel	225	6.70 (↑ 0.01)	**88.3 (↑ 1.7)**	78.7 (↓ 0.4)	85.8 (↓ 0.4)	**53.4 (↑ 0.1)**
SR	257	7.37 (↑ 0.68)	**88.2 (↑ 1.6)**	**88.5 (↑ 9.4)**	**88.6 (↑ 2.4)**	**56 (↑ 2.8)**

Table 2. Comparison of the performance difference between our model and the baseline model in the detection of weak pedestrian objects

Method	Layers	Weight (M)	Presicion (%)	Recall (%)	AP@.5 (%)	AP@.5:.95 (%)
Baseline	213	6.69	80.9	67	76.5	36.8
SR+Sobel	257	7.37(↑ 0.68)	**83.7(↑ 2.8)**	**70.9(↑ 3.9)**	**80.9(↑ 4.4)**	**41.8(↑ 5)**

small object detection, Table 2 records the results of the two models that are only validated for the pedestrian category. Obviously, our model has achieved greater improvements in Precision, Recall, and mAP than the overall dataset relative to the baseline model, which shows that the performance improvement in Table 1 is mainly due to the performance improvement of the model for weak and small target detection.

5   Conclusion

In this paper, we propose a framework for small target detection: SR-YOLO, which combines the image super-resolution network SRGAN and the target detection baseline network Yolov5s, and uses the structural advantages of the super-resolution network generator to effectively improve the detection accuracy on self-collected dataset, especially in relatively weak categories.

Acknowledgements. This work was supported in part by the National Natural Science Foundation of China under Grant 62171347,61877066, 61771379,62001355,6210 1405; the Foundation for Innovative Research Groups of the National Natural Science Foundation of China under Grant 61621005; the Key Research and Development Program in Shaanxi Province of China under Grant 2019ZDLGY03-05 and 2021ZDLGY02-08; the Science and Technology Program in Xi'an of China under Grant XA2020-RGZNTJ-0021; 111 Project.

References

1. Lin, T.-Y., et al.: Microsoft COCO: common objects in context. In: Fleet, D., Pajdla, T., Schiele, B., Tuytelaars, T. (eds.) ECCV 2014. LNCS, vol. 8693, pp. 740–755. Springer, Cham (2014). https://doi.org/10.1007/978-3-319-10602-1_48
2. Redmon, J., Divvala, S., Girshick, R., Farhadi, A.: You only look once: unified, real-time object detection. In: Proceedings of the IEEE Conference on Computer Vision and Pattern Recognition, pp. 779–788 (2016)
3. Liu, W., et al.: SSD: single shot MultiBox detector. In: Leibe, B., Matas, J., Sebe, N., Welling, M. (eds.) ECCV 2016. LNCS, vol. 9905, pp. 21–37. Springer, Cham (2016). https://doi.org/10.1007/978-3-319-46448-0_2
4. Lin, T.-Y., Goyal, P., Girshick, R., He, K., Dollár, P.: Focal loss for dense object detection. In: Proceedings of the IEEE International Conference on Computer Vision, pp. 2980–2988 (2017)
5. Jocher, G., et al.: Ultralytics/yolov5: v6.0 - YOLOv5-P6 1280 Models, AWS, Supervisely and YouTube Integrations (2022)
6. Yaeger, L., Lyon, R., Webb, B.: Effective training of a neural network character classifier for word recognition. Adv. Neural Inf. Process. Syst. **9** (1996)
7. Simard, P.Y., Steinkraus, D., Platt, J.C., et al.: Best practices for convolutional neural networks applied to visual document analysis. In: ICDAR, vol. 3 (2003)
8. Krizhevsky, A., Sutskever, I., Hinton, G.E.: Imagenet classification with deep convolutional neural networks. Adv. Neural Inf. Process. Syst. **25** (2012)
9. Wan, L., Zeiler, M., Zhang, S., Le Cun, Y., Fergus, R.: Regularization of neural networks using dropconnect. In: International Conference on Machine Learning, pp. 1058–1066. In: PMLR (2013)
10. Girshick, R.: Fast R-CNN IEEE International Conference on Computer Vision, pp. 1440–1448. IEEE (2015)
11. DeVries, T., Taylor, G.W.: Improved regularization of convolutional neural networks with cutout. arXiv preprint arXiv:1708.04552 (2017)
12. Zhang, H., Cisse, M., Dauphin, Y.N., Lopez-Paz, D.: mixup: beyond empirical risk minimization. arXiv preprint arXiv:1710.09412 (2017)
13. Yun, S., Han, D., Oh, S.J., Chun, S., Choe, J., Yoo, Y.: Cutmix: regularization strategy to train strong classifiers with localizable features. In: Proceedings of the IEEE/CVF International Conference on Computer Vision, pp. 6023–6032 (2019)
14. Bochkovskiy, A., Wang, C.-Y., Mark Liao, H.-Y.: Yolov4: optimal speed and accuracy of object detection. arXiv preprint arXiv:2004.10934 (2020)
15. Goodfellow, I., et al.: Generative adversarial nets. Adv. Neural Inf. Process. Syst. **27** (2014)
16. Dong, C., Loy, C.C., He, K., Tang, X.: Image super-resolution using deep convolutional networks. IEEE Trans. Pattern Anal. Mach. Intell. **38**(2), 295–307 (2015)

17. Ledig, C., et al.: Photo-realistic single image super-resolution using a generative adversarial network. In: Proceedings of the IEEE Conference on Computer Vision and Pattern Recognition, pp. 4681–4690 (2017)
18. Neubeck, A., Van Gool, L.: Efficient non-maximum suppression. In: 18th International Conference on Pattern Recognition (ICPR'06), vol. 3, pp. 850–855. IEEE (2006)
19. Sobel, I.E.: Camera Models and Machine Perception. Stanford University (1970)

Multi Recursive Residual Dense Attention GAN for Perceptual Image Super Resolution

Linlin Yang[1], Hongying Liu[1(✉)], Yiming Li[1], Wenhao Zhou[1], Yuanyuan Liu[1], Xiaobiao Di[2], Lei Wang[2], and Chuanwen Li[2]

[1] Key Laboratory of Intelligent Perception and Image Understanding, School of Artificial Intelligence, Xidian University, Xi'an, China
hyliu@xidian.edu.cn
[2] China Petroleum Pipeline Telecom and Electricity Engineering, Co., Ltd., Langfang, China

Abstract. Single image super-resolution (SISR) has achieved great progress based on convolutional neural networks (CNNs) such as generative adversarial network (GAN). However, most deep learning architectures cannot utilize the hierarchical features in original low-resolution images, which may result in the loss of image details. To recover visually high-quality high-resolution images, we propose a novel Multi-recursive residual dense Attention Generative Adversarial Network (MAGAN). Our MAGAN enjoys the ability to learn more texture details and overcome the weakness of conventional GAN-based models, which easily generate redundant information. In particular, we design a new multi-recursive residual dense network as a module in our generator to take advantage of the information from hierarchical features. We also introduce a multi-attention mechanism to our MAGAN to capture more informative features. Moreover, we present a new convolutional block in our discriminator by utilizing switchable normalization and spectral normalization to stabilize the training and accelerate convergence. Experimental results on benchmark datasets indicate that MAGAN yields finer texture details and does not produce redundant information in comparison with existing methods.

Keywords: Image super-resolution · Generative adversarial networks · Multi-recursive residual dense network · Attention mechanism

1 Introduction

Single image super-resolution (SR) is a fundamental low-level vision task in computer vision, which aims to recover a high-resolution (HR) image from a single low-resolution (LR) one via SR methods. SR is also a research hotspot in computer vision, and recently attracts increasing attention in image restoration applications. Especially, SR has been popular in various applications [1] such as medical imaging, image generation, security, and surveillance systems. In fact, SR is an ill-posed inverse problem because there are a large number of solutions for restoration from LR images to HR images. To deal with this issue, a great number of SR methods have been proposed, and they mainly

© IFIP International Federation for Information Processing 2022
Published by Springer Nature Switzerland AG 2022
Z. Shi et al. (Eds.): ICIS 2022, IFIP AICT 659, pp. 363–377, 2022.
https://doi.org/10.1007/978-3-031-14903-0_39

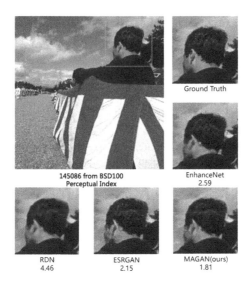

Fig. 1. Comparison of experimental results (i.e., Perceptual Index, PI) of the existing methods and our MAGAN method for image SR tasks with a scale factor of 4×. Note that a lower value of PI indicates better perceptual recovery quality.

can be categorized as the methods based on reconstruction [2], interpolation [3], and learning [4–6], respectively. Since the pioneering work, SRCNN [7], was proposed, many deep learning based methods such as convolutional deep neural networks (CNNs) have brought about great progress in SR tasks. A variety of architectures and training approaches have continually enhanced the performance of SR in terms of some evaluation metrics.

Deep learning based SR algorithms generally fall into the following two classes: one is based on CNNs by utilizing classical L1- or L2-norm regularization at pixel level as a minimization loss function term, which can usually lead to higher PSNR performance but may over-smooth since it lacks high-frequency details. Some typical methods include EDSR [8], SRResNet [9], RDN [10], and [11, 12]. The second category is the perceptual loss based approaches such as SRGAN [13], EnhanceNet [14], ESRGAN [15], and NatSR [16], which aim to make the SR result better accordant with human perception. In these methods, the generative adversarial network (GAN) [17] was introduced for SISR tasks. By using the alternating training between the discriminator and generator, GAN encourages the networks to tend to output results, which are visually more like real images. And they utilized perceptual loss as in [18] to optimize the SR model at a feature level. In [19], the semantic prior knowledge in images is further included to enhance the details of reconstructed texture. With these techniques, the perceptual loss based methods significantly improve the visual quality of the restored SR images, compared with those of the PSNR-oriented methods. However, the objective evaluation is still not satisfied to some extent, and the visual quality can be further improved.

To restore high-resolution images with more detailed textures, this paper proposes a novel Multi-recursive residual dense Attention GAN (MAGAN) for image SR tasks.

The comparison of the experimental results of existing methods and MAGAN is demonstrated in Fig. 1. It is clear that our MAGAN generates finer texture details and more realistic visual effects than other methods. We first construct a novel deep GAN, which also includes one discriminator and one generator, as shown in Fig. 2. We also design a new multi-recursive residual dense network (MRDN) for our generator to fully use hierarchical features from the original low-resolution image. Moreover, unlike the conventional GAN-based SR networks, as shown in Table 1, we present a new multi-attention mechanism for our discriminator to further discriminate refined features. Moreover, we present a new convolutional attention block, which consists of convolutional blocks (CBs) and an attention module, i.e., the convolutional block attention module (CBAM). To stabilize training and accelerate convergence, our CBs adopt spectral normalization and switchable normalization. In particular, our CBAM can capture more features by using both channel attention and spatial attention sub-modules. With such an architecture, the discriminator can learn to determine whether the restored image is more actual than the other, and the generator helps to restore more realistic texture details. To the best of our knowledge, it is the first GAN-based network that designs a multi-recursive structure and introduces a multi-attention mechanism to the discriminator.

The main contributions are summarized as follows:

– We propose a new deep GAN-based network (called MAGAN) to recover visually high-quality high-resolution images, which has a novel multi-recursive structure.
– We present the efficiency of the multi-recursive residual dense network, which function as the generator of our MAGAN, by extracting the hierarchical features from original LR images. We also introduce a multi-attention mechanism into our discriminator to extract more refined features.
– Finally, we design the new convolutional blocks for our discriminator, which applies both switchable normalization and spectral normalization to the proposed convolutional blocks. They can help to stabilize the training of the proposed network. Many experimental results show that MAGAN yields finer texture details than state-of-the-art methods.

2 Background

Generative adversarial network (GAN), which was proposed by [17], consists of a generator and a discriminator and has wide applications in a variety of areas, such as image generation, image to image translation, image completion, and image SR. Especially, SRGAN [13] was proposed for image SR, where both a discriminator and a generator were defined. One can optimize between them to solve the adversarial min-max problem in an alternating manner. The purpose of the generator is to yield a realistic image and try its best to fool the discriminator. In contrast, the discriminator aims to differentiate between the ground truth and the super-resolved images. Thus, the discriminator and the generator come into a game. With an alternating training way, the real images and the fake ones can finally follow a similar distribution statistically. [14] proposed the EnhanceNet, which also applied a GAN and introduced an additional local texture matching loss. Thus, EnhanceNet can reduce visually unpleasant artifacts. In the [15], the authors presented a perceptual loss that was posed on features before activation,

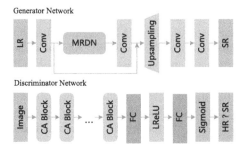

Fig. 2. The architecture of our MAGAN with its generator (top) and discriminator (bottom).

and relativistic GAN [20] was used in this work. As it is known, in GANs, the general discriminator can judge whether the input image is real and natural. In relativistic GAN [20], the discriminator attempts to calculate a probability indicating that a real image is relatively more realistic than a fake one.

The perceptual loss has been proposed by [18] and aims to make the SR result better accordant with human perception. Note that the perceptual loss can be computed by using high-level features extracted from pre-trained networks (e.g., VGG16 and VGG19) for the tasks of style transfer and SR. Previously, the perceptual loss function was defined on the activation layers of a deep pre-trained network, where the distance between two activated features requires to be minimized. Moreover, [21,22] proposed the contextual loss, which is based on natural image statistics and is used in training objective function. The algorithms in [21,22] can achieve better visual performance and perceptual image quality, but they are unable to yield superior results in terms of some objective evaluation criteria. There are other deep neural networks for image SR, for a more comprehensive review of those techniques, please refer to [1,23].

3   Proposed Methods

In this section, we design MAGAN, which mainly includes a new generator and a new discriminator, as shown in Fig. 2. Our MAGAN is expected to improve the overall perceptual quality for image SR tasks. The goal of SISR is to recover a SR image I^{SR} from a low-resolution input image I^{LR}. Note that I^{HR} denotes the high-resolution counterpart of a low-resolution image I^{LR}.

3.1   Our Multi-recursive Residual Dense Network in the Generator

In our MAGAN, we design a new multi-recursive residual dense network (MRDN) as the main module for the generator, as shown in Fig. 3. Our MRDN module combines the proposed multi-recursive residual network and dense connections. Considering the common observation that more network layers and connections can usually enhance real-world performance, our MRDN module is designed as deeper and more complex network. More specifically, as shown in Fig. 3, our MRDN module has a deep residual learning structure, where residual structures are used in different layers. To expand the

Table 1. Comparison of the architectures in these GAN-based methods. Here, Conv denotes convolution, BN is batch normalization, SpectN is spectral normalization, and SwitN is switchable normalization.

Methods	Generator	Discriminator
SRGAN [13]	Residual	Conv, BN
EnhanceNet [14]	Residual	Conv
ESRGAN [15]	Residual dense	Conv, BN
NatSR [16]	Residual dense	Conv, Maxpool
MAGAN (ours)	Residual dense, Learnable, Multi-recursive	Conv, Multi-attention, SpectN & SwitN

capacity of learning features, we use the dense block as the basic structure in our multi-recursive residual network, which mainly includes the multiple convolutional layers and the LeakyReLU activation function.

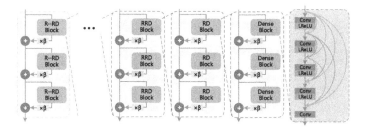

Fig. 3. The architecture of our proposed multi-recursive residual dense network (MRDN) used for the generator of MAGAN, where β is a learnable residual scaling parameter for each block, and $\oplus$ denotes element-wise addition.

Inspired by ReZero [24], we introduce a learnable parameter β into our MRDN module for modulating the non-trivial transformation of its each layer. Here, $F_{i,j}$ is defined as the output of the i-th cell in the j-th level of our MRDN module, where $i = 2, 3, ..., M$, and $j = 1, 2, ..., N$. Let (i, j) represent the i-th cell in the j-th level of our multi-recursive residual dense network, and $F_{(i-1),j}$ is the output of the $(i-1)$-th cell in the j-th level. The multi-recursive residual dense block can be expressed as follows:

$$F_{i,j} = F_{(i-1),j} + \beta \times H_{i,j}(F_{(i-1),j}), \tag{1}$$

where β is a learnable residual scaling parameter. $H_{i,j}()$ is the output of the i-th residual dense (RD) block in j-th level. And we set $\beta = 0$ at the beginning of training, i.e., initializing each layer to perform the identity operation.

In our GAN generator, the basic block is the proposed multi-recursive residual dense network, where most calculation operators were carried out in the feature space of low-resolution images. Our MAGAN with MRDN is shown in Fig. 2. Besides the residual learning within MRDN, we also utilize global residual learning to obtain the feature-maps before up-sampling between the convolutional layers. Then the up-sampling layers can up-scale I^{LR} to attain an initial I^{SR}. Followed by two layers of convolutional operations, the generator outputs I^{SR}.

Moreover, as shown in Table 1, the MRDN module in the generator of our MAGAN is different from those of ESRGAN [15] and NatSR [16]. Though these three methods all use residual dense networks, our MRDN has a recursive structure that can learn multiple levels of the features.

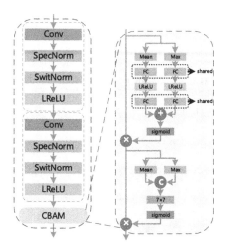

Fig. 4. The structure of the proposed convolutional attention (CA) block includes a sub-module of our convolutional blocks in the green dotted boxes and a convolutional block attention sub-module CBAM. (Color figure online)

3.2   Our CA Network in the Discriminator

To further improve the performance of the discriminator in common GANs, we propose a new CA block, as shown in Fig. 4, which includes a sub-module of convolutional blocks and an attention sub-module. The details of them are given below.

Our attention sub-module aims to capture the fine structures of the images, and we employ the Convolutional Block Attention Module (CBAM), as shown in Fig. 4. The CBAM is a general attention module for feed-forward CNNs, which was proposed in [25] and is widely used in classification and recognition tasks. It consists of both one channel attention sub-module and one spatial attention sub-module. As illustrated in the red dotted box, CBAM utilizes both channel (top) and spatial-wise (bottom) attention. Here, the channel attention sub-module uses both mean-pooling (also called average-pooling) and max-pooling operations with a network with one shared layer (called FC), which is the multi-layer perceptron with a hidden layer. The spatial attention sub-module is composed of mean-pooling, max-pooling, concatenation, and convolutional operations. Note that $\otimes$ and $\oplus$ denote element-wise multiplication and addition operations, $\copyright$ is the concatenation operation, and 7×7 is a convolution operation with a filter size of 7×7.

Suppose that the intermediate feature map is $\mathbf{F}_{\mathbf{imi}} \in \mathbb{R}^{C \times H \times W}$ as input, CBAM sequentially infers the attention map $\mathbf{A_C} \in \mathbb{R}^{C \times 1 \times 1}$ and the attention map $\mathbf{A_S} \in \mathbb{R}^{1 \times H \times W}$, along the two dimensions, channel and spatial. The outputs of the channel attention and spatial attention sub-modules are formulated as follows:

$$\begin{aligned} \mathbf{F}_{\mathbf{imt}} &= \mathbf{A_C}(\mathbf{F}_{\mathbf{imi}}) \otimes \mathbf{F}_{\mathbf{imi}}, \\ \mathbf{F}_{\mathbf{imo}} &= \mathbf{A_S}(\mathbf{F}_{\mathbf{imt}}) \otimes \mathbf{F}_{\mathbf{imt}}, \end{aligned} \tag{2}$$

where $\otimes$ is element-wise multiplication operation, and $\mathbf{F}_{\mathbf{imo}}$ denotes a final refined output. As shown in Fig. 4, our CBAM is a relatively lightweight module, and it is integrated into our attention convolutional module with negligible overheads, which is also end-to-end trainable.

Empirically, we find that adding the attention module to the discriminator of our MAGAN can attain more finer texture, while if the attention module is also added to the generator, this may cause severe texture blending. Since the attention module adopts pooling layers, it easily results in loss of location information. Therefore, we only apply the CBAM to the discriminator of MAGAN to improve SR performance. Thanks to the powerful ability to capture detailed information, relatively shallow neural networks (e.g., a multi-layer perceptron with one hidden layer) also have the ability to recover fine texture details.

Moreover, the proposed convolutional block is a basic one to construct the discriminator of our MAGAN. The detailed structure of our convolutional block is shown in the green dashed box in Fig. 4. Compared with the traditional convolutional structure, which uses batch normalization, our convolutional block is with both switchable normalization [26] and spectral normalization [27].

It is well known that normalization can stabilize the training in each iteration, improve SR performance and reduce computational cost in different PSNR-oriented tasks. However, the computational cost is greatly increased in many experiments, since it enhances the training time of each iteration. Thus, we borrow the idea of switchable normalization and spectral normalization to reduce the computational cost. Unlike the conventional GAN and SRGAN whose normalization is in its generator, we utilize the two types of normalization in our discriminator to stabilize and accelerate the training.

As GANs, our discriminator is also trained to discriminate whether real high-resolution images are more realistic than generated SR samples. Our discriminator contains several convolution layers, which have an increasing number of filters, starting from 64 filters in the first layer and then increasing by a factor of 2. Here strided convolutions are used to reduce the size and computation of each layer, and it doubles the number of map features. The resulting feature maps were followed by two dense layers and a sigmoid function to calculate the probability of image classification: HR or SR.

As it is indicated in the study [26], the performance of the network degrades when the batch size is one for most normalization, such as batch normalization. While the switchable normalization is not sensitive to the batch size. And it does not weaken the performance for small batch sizes compared with other normalizations. Moreover, the spectral normalization can constrain the Lipschitz constant of our discriminator by restricting the spectral norm of each layer. Compared with other normalization techniques, spectral normalization does not need an additional hyper-parameter tuning.

It is well-known that the conditioning of a generator in various GANs is an important factor affecting the real-world performance of GANs [28]. Therefore, the generator in GANs can benefit from spectral normalization. In fact, we also find empirically that spectral normalization in both our generator and discriminator can make our MAGAN possible to use fewer discriminator iterations to update per generator, which significantly reduces the computational cost during training. With a comprehensive trade-off, we apply normalization in the discriminator of our MAGAN to stabilize and accelerate the training.

3.3   Loss Functions

Similar to other GAN-based networks, we alternately optimize the generator and discriminator of the proposed MAGAN until our model converges. First, the adversarial loss function of our generator is

$$L_{ad} = -\mathbb{E}_{I^{HR}}[1 - \log(D(I^{HR}, I^{SR}))] - \mathbb{E}_{I^{SR}}[\log(D(I^{SR}, I^{HR}))], \qquad (3)$$

where $D(I^{HR}, I^{SR}) = \phi(H(I^{HR}) - \mathbb{E}_{I^{SR}}[H(I^{SR})])$, $\mathbb{E}_{I^{SR}}[\cdot]$ denotes average computation in the mini-batch for all fake images, $H(\cdot)$ is the output of discriminator, and ϕ denotes a sigmoid function.

The total loss function of the generator of our MAGAN is formulated as follows:

$$L = L_p + \gamma_1 L_{ad} + \gamma_2 L_1, \qquad (4)$$

where L_p denotes the perceptual loss used in [29], $L_1 = \|I^{SR} - I^{HR}\|_1$ represents the content loss, γ_1 and γ_2 are two parameters to balance these loss function terms.

For our discriminator, its loss function can be formulated as follows:

$$L_D = -\mathbb{E}_{I^{HR}}[\log(D(I^{HR}, I^{SR}))] - \mathbb{E}_{I^{SR}}[1 - \log(D(I^{SR}, I^{HR}))]. \qquad (5)$$

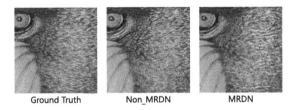

Ground Truth   Non_MRDN   MRDN

Fig. 5. The image SR visual results of our MAGAN without (middle, Non _ MRDN) and with (right) MRDN on the Baboon image.

4 Experiments and Analysis

In this section, we conduct many experiments for image SR tasks to verify the effectiveness of our MAGAN method.

4.1 Implementation Details

In all the experiments, the scaling factor is ×4 for the SR. In addition, we can downsample all the HR images to obtain LR images following [14,15], and the mini-batch size is set to 16. It is known that a larger receptive field can obtain more informative features from the image, and as in the work [15], we set the size of cropped high-resolution patches to 128×128.

Our training process of MAGAN includes the following two steps: pre-training and fine-tuning. The first step is pre-training, i.e., we train our model with the L1-norm regularized term. Specifically, an initial learning rate is set to 2×10^{-4}. And the pre-trained model was used as initialization to the generator for fine-tuning of our MAGAN. The generator is trained by using the weighted sum of the loss function from the generator and the perceptual loss with $\gamma_1 = 5 \times 10^{-3}$ and $\gamma_2 = 10^{-2}$. The learning rate here is 10^{-4}. Moreover, the discriminator is trained, where the LeakyReLU activation function [30] is used. We adopt eight convolutional layers with an increasing number of 3×3 filters. The size of the resulted feature maps is 512. We use the optimization algorithm, ADAM, to train our MAGAN. In addition, the generator and discriminator are alternately updated until they converge. Here, in the generator, we set $M = 4$ and $N = 3$. That is the basic recursive residual connection, which consists of 3 dense blocks, and we use 3 layers of recursive RD blocks considering the computational cost and effectiveness. Our MAGAN is implemented with the Pytorch framework (version 1.0) on a GPU with NVIDIA Titan Xp (12 GB memory).

4.2 Experimental Data

In the experiments, the images from the DIV2K dataset [31] are utilized for training our network, and this dataset mainly contains 800 RGB high-quality (2K resolution) images training for image restoration. Our MAGAN method was trained in the RGB channels, and the training dataset is augmented by using the widely used techniques, such as random flips. Some popular benchmark datasets including Set14 [32], BSD100 [33] and Urban100 [34] were used to evaluate the SR performance of our MAGAN and existing state-of-the-art (SOTA) methods. Note that the former two benchmark datasets consist of natural RGB images, and the Urban100 dataset contains RGB images about building structures.

4.3 Ablation Studies

In order to study the contributions of some components (e.g., MRDN, CBAM and pre-training) in our MAGAN, we conduct the following ablation studies.

MRDN. The MRDN structure is used to extract more detailed features for our network. We compare the results of MAGAN with and without MRDN, as shown in Fig. 5. Note that MAGAN without MRDN uses the residual-in-residual dense block (RRDB) proposed in [15] as the generator, as the RRDB structure is similar to our MRDN. The result shows that texture features become more complete and natural by using MRDN, and no obvious cracks appear at the corners of the eyes. This is because the multi-recursive residual learning structure can better retain the information of original images.

CBAM. In the experiment, we add the attention module (i.e., CBAM) to the generator and discriminator of MAGAN, respectively. In Fig. 6 (center), we can clearly observe that CBAM is used in the generator, there is more sharper and conspicuous feather edges than that CBAM is used in the discriminator (right), but its generated images are unreal. It is probably because the generator does not has more constraints on the images when it is with the CBAM module as the discriminator is not subjected to the attention module and can not determine whether the generated image is fake. The CBAM module is used in the discriminator, which enhances the discriminative ability of the discriminator and can improve the quality of the generated images.

Pre-training. It can be seen clearly from Fig. 7 (right) that the restored image of our pre-trained network is better than that of our network without pre-training in terms of detail texture discrimination. With a large number of experiments, we find that pre-training is helpful for the performance of most GAN-based models, especially in the case that the model is more complex.

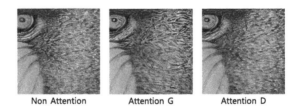

Non Attention   Attention G   Attention D

Fig. 6. Visual results of our MAGAN without (left, Non_Attention) and with CBAM applied in our generator (middle, Attention_G) or discriminator (right, Attention_D) on the Baboon image.

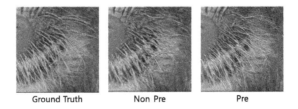

Ground Truth   Non Pre   Pre

Fig. 7. Visual results of our MAGAN without (middle, Non_Pre) and with (right, Pre) the use of pre-training on the Baboon image.

4.4   Experimental Results

The image SR results of our MAGAN are compared with both of the PSNR-oriented algorithms such as SRResNet [7], RDN [10], and GAN-based methods which are EnhanceNet [14] and ESRGAN [15]. The quantitative results of the SR images recovered by these methods are reported in Table 2. We adopt the Perceptual Index (PI) [29] as a measurement metric for comparison. PI is a relatively effective indicator of visual quality than the others. It can be seen from the table that our MAGAN has gained a relatively lower average perceptual index 2.89 than the popular PSNR-oriented methods and the other GAN-based methods on Set14. The PIs of SRResNet and the RDN are much larger than GAN-based methods. It is because these methods are not trained with perceptual index. All the results show that our MAGAN usually outperforms other methods in terms of perceptual index, especially on the Set14 and BSD100 datasets.

Table 2. Average perceptual index results of SR images with scaling factor ×4 on the three benchmark data sets. Note that the best results are shown in bold and the second-best results in italics.

Methods	SRResNet [7]	RDN [10]	EnhanceNet [14]	SRGAN [13]	ESRGAN [15]	NatSR [16]	MAGAN (ours)
Set14	4.96	5.25	3.01	3.09	2.93	3.11	**2.89**
Urban100	5.15	5.05	**3.47**	3.70	3.77	3.65	3.59
BSD100	5.34	5.24	2.92	2.55	2.48	2.78	**2.43**

The image SR results of a selected region of the image_089 from the Urban 100 dataset are shown in Fig. 8 (a). It can be seen that our MAGAN achieves the best visual result and its perceptual index are the lowest, i.e., 2.64. Compared with the traditional deep learning algorithms, SRResNet and RDN, which are optimized with classic L1- or L2-norm regularization, the GAN-based methods with perceptual loss can restore more detailed textures and gain a lower perceptual index. Moreover, our MAGAN yields much better results than the GAN-based methods such as EnhanceNet and ESRGAN. The result of EnhanceNet appears mixed textures and that of the ESRGAN represents blurry. The reason is probably that our MAGAN learns more detailed features with the proposed techniques: MRDN and CBAM, and therefore it generates perceptually superior results.

Furthermore, the image SR results of a selected region of the image_099 from the Urban 100 dataset are shown in Fig. 8 (b). All the results also indicate that our MAGAN achieves the best visual result and its perceptual index is 3.65. The original image has many grids as details. The images recovered by SRResNet and RDN, which are PSNR-oriented models, are blurred. Although the perceptual index of EnhanceNet is the lowest for this image, the visual result is inferior to those of MAGAN and ESRGAN. Since this image is a selected small region from image_099, the local result is probably not good. That may also result from the weakness of the metric of the perceptual index, which measures the global result of a recovered image but not locally. As indicated by the result of ESRGAN, for this image with fine texture details, the GAN based model easily generates redundant and nonexistent information resulting in a sharper effect so that the resulting images are different from the real images. On the contrary, our MAGAN performs well without generating redundant information.

Moreover, we present more representative results of all the methods for image SR tasks, as shown in Fig. 9. As there is no standard and effective metric for perceptual

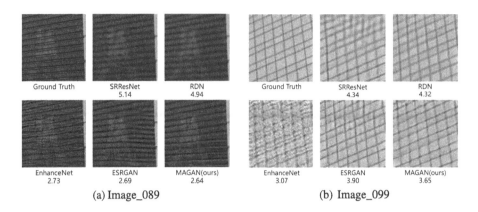

Fig. 8. Comparison of the image SR results of SRResNet [7], RDN [10], EnhanceNet [14], ESR-GAN [15] and MAGAN (ours). Among them, (a) and (b) are the SR results of Image_089 and Image_099, respectively.

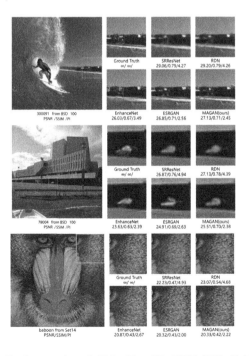

Fig. 9. Image SR qualitative results of SRResNet [7], RDN [10], EnhanceNet [14], ESR-GAN [15], and MAGAN (ours) for a scale factor of $4\times$.

quality evaluation, we show the three common measurements: PSNR, SSIM, and PI (perceptual index). It is clear that our MAGAN usually recovers better images than the other methods in terms of PI, and is much better than the perceptual-driven methods including EnhanceNet [14] and ESRGAN [15] in terms of PSNR, SSIM and PI.

It can be observed from these experimental results that our MAGAN method consistently outperforms other approaches in terms of both details and sharpness. For example, MAGAN produces better restored images (e.g., sharper, more natural baboon's whiskers and fur) than the PSNR-oriented methods (e.g., SRResNet), which tend to produce blurry results, and the GAN-based approaches, whose textures contain unpleasing noise and are unnatural. MAGAN can be capable of generating more detailed structures in buildings (see image_089), while other methods (including EnhanceNet and ESRGAN) either fail to add undesired textures or produce enough details. Moreover, existing GAN-based methods usually introduce unpleasant artifacts in their results. For instance, ESRGAN produces superfluous whiskers that do not exist as shown by the image baboon. Our MAGAN method can get rid of artifacts and also produces natural restored results.

5   Conclusion and Further Work

In this paper, we proposed MAGAN that performs consistently better in terms of perceptual quality than existing image SR methods. We also designed a novel architecture of a multi-level residual dense network for the generator in our MAGAN. Moreover, we introduced a multi-attention mechanism to our MAGAN by the CBAM, which can capture more detailed textures. In addition, we also improved our discriminator to stabilize the training by utilizing a new convolutional block, which applies both switchable normalization and spectral normalization. Experimental results confirmed the effectiveness of our MAGAN, and indicated the advantage of the proposed method: 1) MAGAN can restore visually high-quality images compared with existing state-of-the-art methods. 2) It can retain sharpness and yield fine textures for images as it utilizes the hierarchical features. 3) It does not generate unpleasant artifacts. In the future, more techniques such as the improved perceptual loss [35] and deformable convolution [36] will be investigated to generate more realistic images, and we will also apply the proposed network for video SR tasks [37–39].

Acknowledgements. This work was supported by the National Natural Science Foundation of China (Nos. 61976164, 61876221, 61876220), and Natural Science Basic Research Program of Shaanxi (Program No. 2022GY-061).

References

1. Yang, W., Zhang, X., Tian, Y., Wang, W., Xue, J., Liao, Q.: Deep learning for single image super-resolution: a brief review. IEEE Trans. Multimedia **21**(12), 3106–3121 (2019)
2. Zhang, K., Gao, X., Tao, D., Li, X.: Single image super-resolution with non-local means and steering kernel regression. IEEE Trans. Image Process. **21**(11), 4544–4556 (2012)
3. Zhang, L., Wu, X.: An edge-guided image interpolation algorithm via directional filtering and data fusion. IEEE Trans. Image Process. **15**(8), 2226–2238 (2006)

4. Hsu, J., Kuo, C., Chen, D.: Image super-resolution using capsule neural networks. IEEE Access **8**, 9751–9759 (2020)
5. Shi, Y., Li, S., Li, W., Liu, A.: Fast and lightweight image super-resolution based on dense residuals two-channel network. In: IEEE International Conference on Image Processing (ICIP) 2019, pp. 2826–2830 (2019)
6. Haris, M., Shakhnarovich, G., Ukita, N.: Deep back-projection networks for super-resolution. In: The IEEE Conference on Computer Vision and Pattern Recognition (CVPR), pp. 1664–1673 (2018)
7. Dong, C., Loy, C.C., He, K., Tang, X.: Learning a deep convolutional network for image super-resolution. In: Fleet, D., Pajdla, T., Schiele, B., Tuytelaars, T. (eds.) ECCV 2014. LNCS, vol. 8692, pp. 184–199. Springer, Cham (2014). https://doi.org/10.1007/978-3-319-10593-2_13
8. Lim, B., Son, S., Kim, H., Nah, S., Mu Lee, K.: Enhanced deep residual networks for single image super-resolution. In: The IEEE Conference on Computer Vision and Pattern Recognition (CVPR) Workshops, pp. 1132–1140 (2017)
9. Shi, W., et al.: Is the deconvolution layer the same as a convolutional layer? arXiv:1609.07009 (2016)
10. Zhang, Y., Tian, Y., Kong, Y., Zhong, B., Fu, Y.: Residual dense network for image super-resolution. In: The IEEE Conference on Computer Vision and Pattern Recognition (CVPR), pp. 2472–2481 (2018)
11. Hu, Y., Gao, X., Li, J., Huang, Y., Wang, H.: Single image super-resolution with multi-scale information cross-fusion network. Signal Process. **179**, 107831 (2021)
12. Chang, K., Li, M., Ding, P.L.K., Li, B.: Accurate single image super-resolution using multi-path wide-activated residual network. Signal Process. **172**, 107567 (2020)
13. Ledig, C., et al.: Photo-realistic single image super-resolution using a generative adversarial network. In: The IEEE Conference on Computer Vision and Pattern Recognition (CVPR), pp. 105–114 (2017)
14. Sajjadi, M.S.M., Scholkopf, B., Hirsch, M.: EnhanceNet: single image super-resolution through automated texture synthesis. In: The IEEE International Conference on Computer Vision (ICCV), pp. 4501–4510 (2017)
15. Wang, X., et al.: ESRGAN: enhanced super-resolution generative adversarial networks. In: Leal-Taixé, L., Roth, S. (eds.) ECCV 2018. LNCS, vol. 11133, pp. 63–79. Springer, Cham (2019). https://doi.org/10.1007/978-3-030-11021-5_5
16. Soh, J.W., Park, G.Y., Jo, J., Cho, N.I.: Natural and realistic single image super-resolution with explicit natural manifold discrimination. In: The IEEE Conference on Computer Vision and Pattern Recognition (CVPR) (2019)
17. Goodfellow, I., et al.: Generative adversarial nets. In: Ghahramani, Z., Welling, M., Cortes, C., Lawrence, N.D., Weinberger, K.Q. (eds.) Advances in Neural Information Processing Systems, vol. 27, pp. 2672–2680. Curran Associates Inc. (2014)
18. Johnson, J., Alahi, A., Fei-Fei, L.: Perceptual losses for real-time style transfer and super-resolution. In: Leibe, B., Matas, J., Sebe, N., Welling, M. (eds.) ECCV 2016. LNCS, vol. 9906, pp. 694–711. Springer, Cham (2016). https://doi.org/10.1007/978-3-319-46475-6_43
19. Wang, X., Yu, K., Dong, C., Change Loy, C.: Recovering realistic texture in image super-resolution by deep spatial feature transform. In: The IEEE Conference on Computer Vision and Pattern Recognition (CVPR), pp. 606–615 (2018)
20. Jolicoeur-Martineau, A.: The relativistic discriminator: a key element missing from standard GAN. In: International Conference on Learning Representations (2019)
21. Mechrez, R., Talmi, I., Zelnik-Manor, L.: The contextual loss for image transformation with non-aligned data. In: Ferrari, V., Hebert, M., Sminchisescu, C., Weiss, Y. (eds.) Computer Vision – ECCV 2018. LNCS, vol. 11218, pp. 800–815. Springer, Cham (2018). https://doi.org/10.1007/978-3-030-01264-9_47

22. Mechrez, R., Talmi, I., Shama, F., Zelnik-Manor, L.: Learning to maintain natural image statistics. arXiv: 1803.04626 (2018)
23. Wang, Z., Chen, J., Hoi, S.C.H.: Deep learning for image super-resolution: a survey. IEEE Trans. Pattern Anal. Mach. Intell. **43**, 3365–3387 (2020)
24. Bachlechner, T., Majumder, B.P., Mao, H.H., Cottrell, G.W., McAuley, J.: ReZero is all you need: Fast convergence at large depth. arXiv:2003.04887 (2020)
25. Woo, S., Park, J., Lee, J.-Y., Kweon, I.S.: CBAM: convolutional block attention module. In: Ferrari, V., Hebert, M., Sminchisescu, C., Weiss, Y. (eds.) ECCV 2018. LNCS, vol. 11211, pp. 3–19. Springer, Cham (2018). https://doi.org/10.1007/978-3-030-01234-2_1
26. Luo, P., Ren, J., Peng, Z., Zhang, R., Li, J.: Differentiable learning-to-normalize via switchable normalization. In: International Conference on Learning Representations (ICLR) (2019)
27. Miyato, T., Kataoka, T., Koyama, M., Yoshida, Y.: Spectral normalization for generative adversarial networks. In: International Conference on Learning Representations (ICLR) (2018)
28. Odena, A., et al.: Is generator conditioning causally related to GAN performance? In: Proceedings of the 35th International Conference on Machine Learning (ICML), pp. 3849–3858 (2018)
29. Blau, Y., Mechrez, R., Timofte, R., Michaeli, T., Zelnik-Manor, L.: The 2018 PIRM challenge on perceptual image super-resolution. In: Leal-Taixé, L., Roth, S. (eds.) ECCV 2018. LNCS, vol. 11133, pp. 334–355. Springer, Cham (2019). https://doi.org/10.1007/978-3-030-11021-5_21
30. Maas, A.L., Hannun, A.Y., Ng, A.Y.: Rectifier nonlinearities improve neural network acoustic models. In: Proceedings of the 30th International Conference on Machine Learning (ICML) (2013)
31. Agustsson, E., Timofte, R.: NTIRE 2017 challenge on single image super-resolution: dataset and study. In: IEEE Conference on Computer Vision and Pattern Recognition Workshops (CVPRW) 2017, pp. 1122–1131 (2017)
32. Zeyde, R., Elad, M., Protter, M.: On single image scale-up using sparse-representations. In: International Conference on Curves and Surfaces, pp. 711–730 (2012)
33. Martin, D., Fowlkes, C., Tal, D., Malik, J.: A database of human segmented natural images and its application to evaluating segmentation algorithms and measuring ecological statistics. In: Proceedings Eighth IEEE International Conference on Computer Vision. ICCV 2001, pp. 416–423 (2001)
34. Huang, J., Singh, A., Ahuja, N.: Single image super-resolution from transformed self-exemplars. In: IEEE Conference on Computer Vision and Pattern Recognition (CVPR) 2015, pp. 5197–5206 (2015)
35. Rad, M.S., Bozorgtabar, B., Marti, U.-V., Basler, M., Ekenel, H.K., Thiran, J.-P.: SROBB: targeted perceptual loss for single image super-resolution. In: The IEEE International Conference on Computer Vision (ICCV), 2019, pp. 2710–2719 (2019)
36. Zhu, X., Hu, H., Lin, S., Dai, J.: Deformable ConvNets V2: more deformable, better results. In: The IEEE Conference on Computer Vision and Pattern Recognition (CVPR), pp. 9300–9308 (2019)
37. Liu, H., Zhao, P., Ruan, Z., Shang, F., Liu, Y.: Large motion video super-resolution with dual subnet and multi-stage communicated upsampling. In: Proceedings of the Thirty-Fifth AAAI Conference on Artificial Intelligence (AAAI) (2021)
38. Liu, H., et al.: A single frame and multi-frame joint network for 360-degree panorama video super-resolution. arXiv Preprint arXiv:2008.10320 (2020)
39. Liu, H., Ruan, Z., Zhao, P., Shang, F., Yang, L., Liu, Y.: Video super resolution based on deep learning: a comprehensive survey. arXiv Preprint arXiv:2007.12928 (2022)

Relay-UNet: Reduce Semantic Gap for Glomerular Image Segmentation

Zhen Cao[✉], Chuanfeng Ma, Qian Wang, and Hongwei Zhang

School of Artificial Intelligence, Xidian University, Xi'an, Shaanxi, People's Republic of China
icaozhen@163.com

Abstract. With the increasing number of patients with chronic kidney disease (CDK), the workload of pathologists is heavy and the diagnostic efficiency is low. Therefore, the use of computer technology to assist the diagnosis of nephropathy becomes the trend of future development with a great application space. In recent years, UNet network has been widely used in medical image segmentation, and many improved algorithms have appeared. Most of existing methods focus on adding new modules or incorporating other design concepts on the basis of UNet, however, the structure of UNet network has not been fully analyzed. This paper points out two problems existing in UNet network: insufficient feature extraction in encoder interferes with the accuracy of image segmentation, and the fixed mode of skip connection in each layer leads to information redundancy in the network. To solve these problems, we improve the encoder and feature fusion method of UNet and named the new network as Relay-UNet. Experiment results show that under the condition of almost no change in consumption time, the Dice coefficient of Relay UNet on the glomerular dataset reaches 97.5%, and the training process is more stable than that of UNet.

Keywords: Glomerular image segmentation · Feature fusion · Skip connection

1 Introduction

CDK is a general term for a group of kidney diseases, also known as chronic nephrotic syndrome, which refers to the structural changes and functional disorders of chronic kidney caused by various reasons. According to the survey report of the world's authoritative medical journal the LANCET, by 2017, the number of patients with chronic kidney disease in the world had reached 697.5 million [1]. In the process of diagnosis and treatment of CDK patients, renal biopsy plays a very important role. Pathologists can judge the type and development stage of the disease by observing the morphological changes of glomeruli in tissue sections. However, in the traditional diagnostic methods, pathologists need to look for glomeruli in tissues and compare their morphological changes through long-term naked eye observation under a microscope. High-intensity and repetitive work will greatly reduce the diagnostic efficiency of pathologists. Therefore, if computer technology can be used to automatically and accurately mark the position of glomerulus,

© IFIP International Federation for Information Processing 2022
Published by Springer Nature Switzerland AG 2022
Z. Shi et al. (Eds.): ICIS 2022, IFIP AICT 659, pp. 378–385, 2022.
https://doi.org/10.1007/978-3-031-14903-0_40

accurately segment its outline and visually present it, the workload of pathologists will be greatly reduced.

At present, the common glomerular segmentation methods can be divided into edge-based segmentation algorithm, region-based segmentation algorithm and deep learning-based segmentation algorithm [2]. Edge-based segmentation algorithm uses the edge information of glomerulus in pathological slices to segment. If the gray value of a certain part of the slice image has obvious step change, it can be determined as the edge of glomerulus. The biggest disadvantage of this method is its weak anti-noise ability, especially in the case of high noise frequency, which may lead to false detection results. The region based segmentation algorithm divides the image into several different regions according to the similarity. However, after the kidney section is stained, the attribute values such as color and gray scale are similar among different tissue areas, so it is necessary to use the prior information of glomerular shape and position to achieve accurate segmentation.

In recent years, the deep learning model represented by UNet network has become a research hotspot, and achieved good results in various medical image segmentation tasks. These deep learning models make use of the powerful computing power of modern computers, and continuously extract and learn the feature information of images through convolution operations, so as to complete the target segmentation. After UNet was put forward, many researchers improved its structure and put forward new models, but most of the improvement methods were to add new modules or incorporate other design concepts on the basis of UNet. For example, LinkNet added residual operation in the encoder of the original UNet [3], and Attention-UNet added attention mechanism in the jumping connection process of the original UNet [4]. Although these methods can improve the segmentation performance of UNet, they do not fully consider some problems existing in the network itself. Considering that the setting of UNet network depth and feature fusion mode is not optimal, UNet++ embeds U-shaped structures with various depths into the network and designs a more flexible hopping connection mode [5]. However, this design also makes the network structure too complicated, and a large number of parameters increase the training time of the network.

To sum up, the main contributions of this paper are as follows:

The Problems of UNet are Pointed Out and Verified: Firstly, because of the small number of convolution layers in the encoder, the semantic difference between the two parts of feature fusion between codecs is large, which interferes with the accuracy of image segmentation; Secondly, the fixed mode that each layer of the network structure is connected by hopping leads to information redundancy in the network.

Relay-UNet is Proposed to Improve UNet: First, add a feature extraction module to the encoder to narrow the semantic gap with the decoder; Secondly, by adding a weighting factor in the process of feature image splicing, the constraint of the network on the jump connection can be slowed down, so that the network can decide which layer to fuse features on.

The Performance of Relay-UNet is Better than UNet: on the glomerular data set, the Dice coefficient of Relay-UNet reaches 97.5%, which is 1.5% higher than UNet.

2   Related Work

Because this paper is to improve UNet and increase its accuracy in glomerular segmentation. Therefore, in the following paragraphs, we briefly review some existing work in the field of glomerular segmentation and the basic structure of UNet.

2.1   Glomerular Image Segmentation

Glomerular Image Segmentation Based on Traditional Methods. Jiaxin Ma et al. proposed using Canny edge detection algorithm to extract the discontinuous edge of glomerulus [6]. After the noise is removed by labeling, the genetic algorithm is used to search the best repair segment, and these edges are connected together to form a complete glomerular contour. Jun Zhang et al. proposed a glomerular extraction method based on wavelet transform and watershed algorithm [7]. Firstly, the LOG filter is applied to the low-resolution image, which corresponds to the low-frequency sub-band after wavelet transform, so that rough edge information can be obtained. After eliminating noise, genetic algorithm is used to search the best fitting curve.

Glomerular Image Segmentation Based on Deep Learning Method. In 2019, Robin Liu et al. made use of the accurate positioning ability of Faster R-CNN and the powerful segmentation ability of U-Net [8], and realized the localization of glomerulus from the whole slice image, so that the segmentation only focused on the most relevant areas in the image. In 2020, Gloria Bueno et al. compared the pixel-level segmentation of UNet and SegNet [9]. In 2021, Yuan Liu et al. proposed a semantic segmentation method FEU-Net for pathological sections, which improved the accuracy of glomerular segmentation and achieved end-to-end segmentation [10]. FEU-Net uses EfficientNet after transfer learning as the encoder and UNet as the decoder.

2.2   UNet Structure

UNet is a full convolution segmentation network, which is mainly used for semantic segmentation of biomedical images. It inherits the idea of FCN, puts forward a completely symmetrical U-shaped encoding-decoding structure, and realizes the semantic fusion of different levels by using jump connection.

In UNet structure, if the two convolution operations of the same layer are regarded as a whole, which is called block and sorted in turn, then block1 and block9 are spliced, and so on. It can be found that the original image is only convolved twice in block1, and the semantic features of the image are not fully extracted. As the last part of the network, block9 contains rich semantic features after a large number of convolution operations. The original UNet structure directly splices the output feature mapping of block1 to block9, which may affect the accuracy of image segmentation due to the differences between the two parts and too much semantic information. The splicing of other layers also has the same problem.

In addition, the codec in each layer of UNet structure is connected by default, and four feature fusion is performed accordingly. However, the semantic information of the feature map output by the adjacent layers of the encoder is similar. Frequent feature fusion leads to information redundancy in the network and increases the risk of over fitting.

To sum up, there may be two problems in the feature fusion part of UNet structure: insufficient feature extraction in the coding part affects the segmentation result; The fixed mode of splicing each layer will make the information redundant in the network.

In order to verify the two questions, a control experiment was designed in this paper. Randomly delete some hopping connections in UNet network, and form five groups of different skip connection structures. Table 1 shows the grouping.

Table 1. Experimental grouping table

Group	Skip connection structure
L1	Delete all skip connections
L2	Keep the skip connection of the first layer
L3	Keep the skip connection between the second layer and the third layer
L4	Keep the skip connections of the second, third and fourth layers
L5	Keep all layers of skip connections

In addition to the number of layers including skip connections, all other parameters are fixed, and the network performance of these five groups of different network structures on the same data set is observed. Figure 1 shows the training results of each group of networks, from which it can be seen that: (1) the performance of network structure segmentation with all hopping connections is not optimal, and the performance of the network may be better after some hopping connections are removed, such as L4 and L5; (2) The addition of the first layer hop connection may cause the decline of network performance, such as L1 and L2. Therefore, the rationality of the two questions mentioned above can be verified.

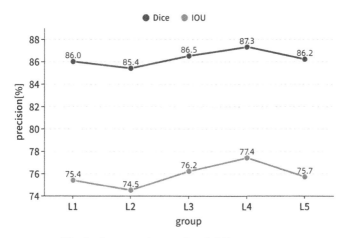

Fig. 1. Segmentation results of different groups

3 Methodology

3.1 Relay-UNet Structure

To solve the above two problems, this paper improves the encoder and feature fusion method of UNet, and calls the new network Relay-UNet. Figure 2 shows the concrete structure of the improved network, The pink background part is the original UNet network structure, and the blue background part is the newly added or improved structure.

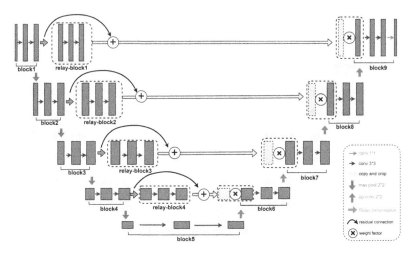

Fig. 2. Relay-UNet structure

3.2 Improved Method

Relay-UNet firstly improves UNet coding structure by adding four relay blocks, namely relay-block1 to relay-block4. As can be seen from Fig. 2 when UNet performs downsampling and feature graph dimension splicing, Relay-UNet divides into two branches. The first is down sampling, and continue the encoding operation; The other one is not directly spliced into the decoder of the same layer, but enters the relay-block block to continue convolution operations for many times, and its feature map is spliced into the decoding structure only after deeper semantic information is extracted. But at the same time, the addition of relay-block will also bring new problems. On the one hand, it is not certain that setting several convolutions in relay-block will make the network performance the best. If the number of convolutions is insufficient, the semantic level difference between the two sides of the jump connection is still too big to achieve the expected effect; If the convolution times are too many, the final output will lose low-level features, which will also decrease. On the other hand, the addition of relay-block makes the network structure more complicated, which may lead to over-fitting in network training and reduce its performance. Therefore, learn from Resnet's idea [11], add the residual structure, and add the output of relay-block to the result of the last convolution layer in front of it, as shown by the black arrow in the Fig. 2. In this way, the fitting of relay-block becomes the learning residual, which reduces the risk of over-fitting, and also enables the network itself to decide how to use the convolution operation in relay-block.

Another improvement of Relay-UNet is to improve the splicing method of feature graphs in jump connection. The original UNet directly splices the two feature maps. The Relay-UNet multiplies the two spliced parts by a weight factor α_i and β_i, respectively, so that $\alpha_i + \beta_i = 1$. The weight factor acts on each pixel of each channel of the feature map to reduce the overall value of the feature map, and then the dimension is spliced. Let $F \in R^{H \times W \times C}$ be the feature tensor to be spliced, where H, W, and C are the height, width, and channel dimensions of the feature tensor, then the formula for multiplying the ith channel of the tensor by the weight α_i is:

$$
\begin{aligned}
\mathbf{F}_i \otimes \alpha_i &= \begin{pmatrix} F_i^{1,1} & F_i^{1,2} & \cdots & F_i^{1,W} \\ F_i^{2,1} & F_i^{2,2} & \cdots & F_i^{2,W} \\ \vdots & \vdots & \ddots & \vdots \\ F_i^{H,1} & F_i^{H,2} & \cdots & F_i^{H,W} \end{pmatrix} \otimes \begin{pmatrix} \alpha_i & \alpha_i & \cdots & \alpha_i \\ \alpha_i & \alpha_i & \cdots & \alpha_i \\ \vdots & \vdots & \ddots & \vdots \\ \alpha_i & \alpha_i & \cdots & \alpha_i \end{pmatrix} \\
&= \begin{pmatrix} F_i^{1,1} \cdot \alpha_i & F_i^{1,2} \cdot \alpha_i & \cdots & F_i^{1,W} \cdot \alpha_i \\ F_i^{2,1} \cdot \alpha_i & F_i^{2,2} \cdot \alpha_i & \cdots & F_i^{2,W} \cdot \alpha_i \\ \vdots & \vdots & \ddots & \vdots \\ F_i^{H,1} \cdot \alpha_i & F_i^{H,2} \cdot \alpha_i & \cdots & F_i^{H,W} \cdot \alpha_i \end{pmatrix}
\end{aligned}
\tag{1}
$$

Figure 3 shows this process. When the features from the encoder are not needed in the decoder, the smaller α_i is, the larger β_i is; When the features from the encoder are needed in the decoder, the larger α_i is, the smaller β_i is, which realizes the effect of feature dilution by weighting.

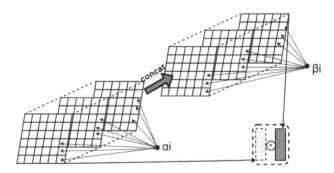

Fig. 3. Improved feature fusion method

4 Experiment and Result Analysis

4.1 Dataset

The data used in this experiment are 1250 kidney biopsy specimens with different staining from Shanxi Provincial People's hospital. After obtaining the slice samples, the biopsy microscope slides were digitized into WSIS using a digital slide scanner. 1000 glomerular images with good staining and structure were cut out from renal tissue sections as the data set of this experiment. The data is enhanced by cutting and rotating, expanded to 2500 pieces, and divided into training set and test set according to the ratio of 8:2.

4.2 Evaluating Metrics

In order to evaluate the network performance, this paper uses two evaluation indexes, namely IOU (intersection over union) and Dice (similarity coefficient).

IOU is the overlapping area between predicted segmentation and labels divided by the joint area between predicted segmentation and labels. The range of this indicator is 0–1, where 0 means no overlapping and 1 means complete overlapping segmentation; **Dice** coefficient is defined as twice the intersection divided by the sum of pixels, also known as F1 score. Similar to IOU, they all range from 0 to 1, where 1 indicates the maximum similarity between prediction and reality.

4.3 Training Process

Figure 4 shows the changes of Dice evaluation index in the process of UNet and Relay-UNet network training, respectively.

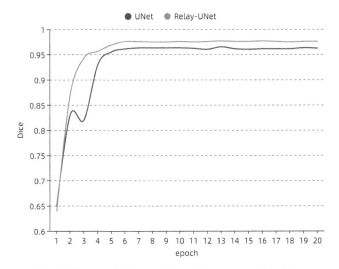

Fig. 4. Change of Dice coefficient during network training.

It can be seen from the Fig. 4 that after the Relay-UNet network converges, Dice reaches 0.975, which is greatly improved compared with UNet's 0.961, and it can be found that the training process is more stable. Therefore, the improved method in this paper has a good effect on improving the UNet segmentation effect.

5 Conclusion

In this paper, a glomerular image segmentation algorithm based on improved U-Net is proposed, named Relay-UNet. A feature extraction module relay-block is added to the encoder to reduce the semantic information, and the constraint of the network on the hop connection is slowed down by adding a weight factor in the process of splicing feature graphs. Experiments show that the proposed method has better segmentation performance than the traditional UNet, and its accuracy on glomerular data sets is improved by about 1.5%.

Acknowledgements. This work was supported in part by the China Postdoctoral Science Foundation under Grant 2019M663637, in part by the Natural Science Basic Research Program of Shaanxi under Program 2021JQ-201, and in part by the National Natural Science Foundation of China under Grant 62104176.

References

1. Rule, A.D., Bergstralh, E.J., Melton, L.J., et al.: Kidney stones and the risk for chronic kidney disease. Clin. J. Am. Soc. Nephrol. **4**(4), 804–811 (2009)
2. Yuheng, S., Hao, Y.: Image segmentation algorithms overview. arXiv preprint arXiv:1707. 02051 (2017)
3. Zhou, L., Zhang, C., Wu, M.: D-LinkNet: LinkNet with pretrained encoder and dilated convolution for high resolution satellite imagery road extraction. In: Proceedings of the IEEE Conference on Computer Vision and Pattern Recognition Workshops, pp. 182–186 (2018)
4. Oktay, O., Schlemper, J., Folgoc, L.L., et al.: Attention u-net: learning where to look for the pancreas. arXiv preprint arXiv:1804.03999 (2018)
5. Zhou, Z., Siddiquee, M.,Tajbakhsh, N., et al.: UNet++: a nested U-Net architecture for medical image segmentation (2018)
6. Ma, J., Zhang, J., Hu, J.: Glomerulus extraction by using genetic algorithm for edge patching. In: 2009 IEEE Congress on Evolutionary Computation, pp. 2474–2479. IEEE (2009)
7. Zhang, J., Fan, J.: Medical image segmentation based on wavelet transformation and watershed algorithm. In: 2006 IEEE International Conference on Information Acquisition, pp. 484–488. IEEE (2006)
8. Liu, R., Wang, L., He, J., et al.: Towards staining independent segmentation of glomerulus from histopathological images of kidney. bioRxiv **2019**, 821181 (2019)
9. Bueno, G., Fernandez-Carrobles, M.M., Gonzalez-Lopez, L., et al.: Glomerulosclerosis identification in whole slide images using semantic segmentation. Comput. Methods Prog. Biomed. **184**, 105273 (2020)
10. Liu, Y., Wang, J.: FEU-Net: glomeruli region segmentation network based on pseudo-labelling and channel attention mechanisms. In: International Conference on Image Processing and Intelligent Control (IPIC 2021). SPIE, vol. 11928, pp. 41–51 (2021)
11. He, K., Zhang, X., Ren, S., et al.: Deep residual learning for image recognition. In: Proceedings of the IEEE Conference on Computer Vision and Pattern Recognition, pp. 770–778 (2016)

Mobicfnet: A Lightweight Model for Cattle Face Recognition in Nature

Laituan Qiao, Yaojun Geng$^{(\boxtimes)}$, Yuxuan Zhang, Shuyin Zhang, and Chao Xu

College of Information Engineering, Northwest A&F University,
Yangling, Shaanxi, China
gengyaojun@nwsuaf.edu.cn

Abstract. In smart livestock, precision livestock systems require efficient and safe non-contact cattle identification methods in daily operation and management. In this paper, we focus on lightweight Convolutional Neural Network (CNN) based cattle face identification in natural background. Particularly, we first construct a fine-grained cattle recognition dataset with natural background. Then, we propose a lightweight CNN model MobiCFNet, containing a two-stage method that can realize one-shot cattle recognition. Finally, a series of experiments are conducted to validate the effectiveness of our proposed network.

Keywords: Cattle recognition · Lightweight Convolutional Neural Network · Cattle dataset

1 Introduction

Intelligent agriculture has become a better option for growing agricultural production, improving resource management, and saving labor costs in recent years [4]. Precision livestock and smart livestock are a significant aspects of intelligent agriculture that can realize intelligent management of animal farming, improve the quality of meat products and reduce the amount of labor [7]. Accurate identification of individual cattle in intelligent pasture management is an essential problem to be solved in food traceability [14], false insurance claims [9], vaccination [11], and disease prevention [5].

Research on traditional cattle identification methods, for example, ear tags, nameplates, and tattoos began in the 1960s [10]. However, these methods may cause permanent damage to cattle and reduce accuracy due to loss of flag (i.e., ear tags, nameplates, and tattoos) [2]. In the 1980s the emergence of radio frequency identification (RFID) technology improved the accuracy and enhanced the intelligence of identification, but also revealed high-cost and low-security weaknesses. With the rapid development of Deep Learning (DL) research, especially CNN, cattle identification methods based on DL alleviated mentioned problems existing in the previous recognition system [12].

At present, there are some difficulties in DL-methods based cattle identification research. Firstly the complex environment of the pasture adds uncertainty

© IFIP International Federation for Information Processing 2022
Published by Springer Nature Switzerland AG 2022
Z. Shi et al. (Eds.): ICIS 2022, IFIP AICT 659, pp. 386–394, 2022.
https://doi.org/10.1007/978-3-031-14903-0_41

to the collected images. Then, collecting a rich dataset is a labor-intensive and time-consuming task due to the limitation of pasture size and cattle population. Finally, the similarity in appearance between different cattle makes accurate identification difficult.

To settle these difficulties, we use a modified MobileNet V2 to complete the individual recognition of cattle based on cattle facial features. We introduce the Global Deep Convolutional (GDConv) layer that enables the network to extract cattle face features more fully. The introduction of Large Margin Cosine Loss (LMCL) makes the difference between classes increase and reduces the probability of model misjudgment. Our contribution could be summarized as follow: first, we construct a Qinchuan cattle and cows natural background dataset based on Northwest A&F University posture, containing 35000 images of 82 cattle. And then we propose a lightweight CNN called MobiCFNet and introduce a two-stage method that can realize one-shot cattle recognition. In the end, we compare conventional methods with our proposed methods on our dataset and show the effectiveness and robustness of our methods.

The rest of this paper is structured as follows: Sect. 2 introduces the work related to cattle recognition, Sect. 3 introduces the constructed dataset, Sect. 4 describe the proposed method to solve the problem of cattle face recognition, Sect. 5 summarizes the specific experimental results and discusses them, and Sect. 6 is the conclusion of this study.

2   Related Work

Cattle identification has become a global issue involving scientific management of postures, food safety, false claims insurance, and more.

Since the 21st century, computer vision-related methods have been gradually applied in cattle recognition. Authors in [1] proposed a cattle face representation model based on local binary pattern texture features and trained Thirty cattle's normalized gray face images separately. Experiments show that the LBP texture descriptor has good accuracy but low robustness.

In recent years, CNN has made a series of breakthroughs in computer vision, such as face recognition, target detection, and image classification. Authors in [8] proposed a CNN method to identify individual cattle, focusing on the pattern features of the cattle muzzle. In several test sets, the recognition accuracy of this method reaches 98.99%. The authors of [12] has designed a network framework that combines the advantages of CNN and Long Short-Term Memory to identify individual cattle. The dataset uses a fixed Angle rear view of the cattle. However, the dataset of the above two identification methods are not collected in natural scenes.

The continuous advancement of computer performance means that we can train CNN with larger dataset, thus significantly enhancing the recognition accuracy. Authors in [6] proposed a model of individual identification of dairy cows using CNN in the actual cattle farm environment. The model was trained using 60,000 trunk images of 30 cattle, and 90.55% of the 21,730 images tested were accurately identified. But this method is not applicable in pasture with a high number of cattle.

3   Fine-Grained Face Individual Recognition Dataset

In this section, we describe the workflow of constructing our Cattle Face Recognition Dataset.

The individual cattle breeds we identified are mainly Qinchuan cattle and dairy cows. The body of Qinchuan cattle is yellow and red, so it is challenging to identify the cattle from its body. However, Qinchuan cattle have more facial features compared with the body, including hair color, pattern, face shape, and other characteristics, as shown in Fig. 1. Therefore we choose to construct the individual recognition dataset of cattle face features and study the individual recognition based on cattle face features.

Fig. 1. The cattle face are diversified

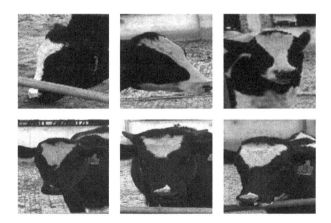

Fig. 2. Large intra-class differences and small inter-class differences in the dataset

We visit cattle farms several times to collect data in different weather conditions and at different periods. Abundant cattle front or side face images under different backgrounds were taken to ensure a more comprehensive background of images in the dataset and a more diverse angle of cattle face.

A dataset of 82 Qinchuan cattle and dairy cows with 35,000 cattle face images was constructed, which are RGB images of 224×224. Then, it was divided into the training set, verification set, and test set in a ratio of 7:2:1. We found that different images of the same cow differ greatly. The first row of Fig. 2 shows three different images of a specific cow, with significantly different posture, background, and angles. Meanwhile, images of different cows at the same angle may vary slightly. The second row of Fig. 2 shows three images of different cows, which are relatively similar in appearance from the same angle. The constructed dataset has significant differences within classes and slight differences between classes, which brings great challenges to the cattle recognition work.

In conclusion, we constructed a fine-grained cattle recognition dataset which consists of dairy cows and Qinchuan cattle face images with complex and diverse natural backgrounds that collect from various angles.

4   Proposed Method

This section describes our proposed cattle face identification network MobiCFNet. First, we introduce CNN and Lightweight CNN. Then, the Large Margin Cosine Loss (LMCL) in our work is described. Finally, we give the entire network architecture and describe the proposed feature dictionary based recognition method.

4.1   CNN and Lightweight CNN

Since AlexNet unexpectedly won the ImageNet competition in 2012, there has been a growing amount of innovative work in this area. In particular, ResNet, proposed by Kaiming He et al. in 2015, reduced the recognition error rate on the ImageNet dataset to 3.57% by introducing residual blocks and deepening the design of network layers.

However, the model structure of CNN becomes more complex to pursue high accuracy, which causes difficulty in transplantation to mobile devices or Internet of Things (IoT) devices. To this end, Google developed MobileNet series CNN models, which use deep separable convolution to decompose standard convolution into depthwise convolution and pointwise convolution to reduce computation and amount of parameters [3]. MobileNet V2 model adopts the Inverted Residuals structure, firstly elevates the features' dimension, then carries out convolution operation, and finally reduces the dimension. Besides, Linear Bottleneck is used instead of non-linear activation function to avoid information loss. Experiments show that the precision and portability of the model are well balanced [13].

4.2   Large Margin Cosine Loss

LMCL is a loss function that rethinks softmax loss from the view of cosine perspective, firstly proposed for face recognition in [15]. In the output layer of a CNN, we have

$$f_j = W_j^T x + B_j, \tag{1}$$

where W_j is the weight and B_j is the bias, set B_j to zero, we can derive that

$$f_j = W_j^T x = \|W_j\|\|x\| \cos \theta_j, \tag{2}$$

where θ_j is the angle between W_j and x. Face recognition is realized by cosine similarity between feature vectors. Set $\|x\|$ to s and $\|W_j\|$ to 1 as

$$L_{ns} = \frac{1}{N} \sum_i -\log \frac{e^{s \cos(\theta_{y_i,i})}}{\sum_j e^{s \cos(\theta_{j,i})}}. \tag{3}$$

In this way, LMCL forces classifier to learn separable features in angle space by normalizing feature vectors and removing radioactive variables. The second contribution of LMCL lies in the incorporation of cosine margin m into cosine formula as

$$L_{lmc} = \frac{1}{N} \sum_i -\log \frac{e^{s(\cos(\theta_{y_i,i})-m)}}{e^{s(\cos(\theta_{y_i,i})-m)} + \sum_{j \neq y_i} e^{s \cos(\theta_{j,i})}}, \tag{4}$$

which reduces cosine similarity between feature vectors of different classes, forcibly increases the distance between classes, and increases the accuracy of recognition.

LMCL is a classifier designed for human face recognition. In LMCL, maximizing the variance between classes and minimizing the variance within classes is adopted. Cattle face also contains rich feature information. The facial contour, facial features, and hair texture of cattle are significant characteristics in cattle face identification. So migrating LMCL to cattle face identification based on cattle face features still works.

4.3   MobiCFNet

We propose a lightweight CNN model for cattle face recognition called MobiCFNet. Figure 3 shows the architecture of MobiCFNet, we replace the last global average pooling layer and the fully connected layer of MobileNet V2 with GDConv layer and an LMCL classifier.

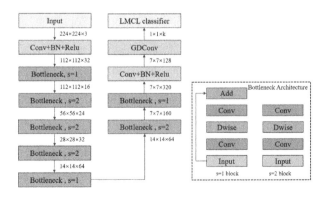

Fig. 3. MobiCFNet architecture

Compared with pooling layers, the advantage is that GDConv layer introduces attention mechanisms, which assign different regions in the input feature map with different importance. Therefore, GDConv layer contributes to extracting the features of essential regions in the image. The LMCL classifier in our work uses 128-dimensional features to distinguish 82 cattle in the dataset. Compared with traditional softmax loss, LMCL is more in line with the fine-grained classification tasks, forcing the interval between classes of the classifier to be greater than or equal to a certain hyperparameter m.

Based on MobiCFNet, we propose a flexible way of cattle individuals recognition, the workflow of which is plot in Fig. 4. First, a characteristic dictionary of cattle is constructed after training by combining feature vectors corresponding to 82 cattles in the dataset. The feature vector is the 128-dimensional output before LMCL classifier of MobiCFNet that use each cattle's face image with rich features as input. When we need to classify an image, we pass the image through the feature extraction network to get a 128-dimensional feature vector. Then, normalized inner product vector between the feature vector the feature of each cow in the dictionary and then the cow with the largest inner product result is selected as the predicted result.

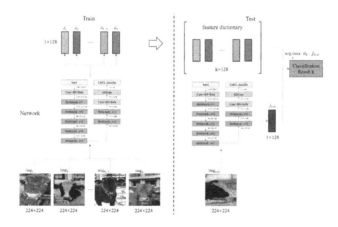

Fig. 4. Workflow of feature dictionary method in MobiCFNet

The principle is that LMCL migrates softmax to the angle space during network training and deliberately increases the interval between classes. The feature vectors of the same cattle image are clustered together in the hypersphere, and their normalized inner product results are close to 1. Besides, the most significant advantage of the feature dictionary construction method is that it enables the network to add or delete cattle after the training procedure while keeping the accuracy of cattle recognition at the same level. When we need to delete a cattle, we delete the characteristics of this cattle from the feature dictionary. If the data used in the training model is rich enough, we can assume that the network can robustly extract individual characteristics of cattle. Under this condition, we can easily add new cattle. We input a representative image of the new cattle through the feature extraction network and then add the feature to the feature dictionary. Deleting cattle from the trained model is simple. We only need to delete the corresponding feature in the feature dictionary.

5   Experiment

We accomplish experiments on the server with Tesla V100 GPU and Core i7 8-core CPU. We implement MobiCFNet using PaddlePaddle DL framework. We verify cattle recognition ability of MobiCFNet in two cases: traditional end-to-end method and feature dictionary method. We compare MobileNet V2 with other proposed MobiCFNet on our cattle recognition dataset. In order to improve the reliability of comparison, we set batch size as 64, learning rate as 0.001, optimizer as Adam, and epoch numbers as 500. In order to verify the practicality of MobiCFNet, we ported it to an Android device and verified the experimental results in the pasture.

Table 1. Accuracy and inference time on android device.

Network	Accuracy (%)	Inference time on android device
MobileNet V2 + softmax	84.57	28 ms
MobileNet V2 + LMCL	85.62	28 ms
MobiCFNet + softmax	86.38	24 ms
MobiCFNet + LMCL	87.44	24 ms

In the experiment, we take the cattle images as the input of MobiCFNet and connect the feature extraction network with the softmax classifier directly. In this case, 86.38% accuracy was achieved, which verified that MobiCFNet has strong feature extraction ability. In the feature dictionary experiment, the recognition accuracy of MobiCFNet reached 87.44%, performing better than MobileNet V2. Besides, we compare infer time of MobiCFNet on an Android device (Redmi K30 Pro) with MobileNet V2. All results are available in Table 1.

In conclusion, the MobiCFNet proposed in our work can achieve higher accuracy and faster infer time than MobileNet V2 in the classification task of cattle face identification. In particular, our method with feature dictionary can improve the recognition accuracy and easily add and delete cattle in the pasture, which meets the actual need in the pasture.

6   Conclusion and Future Scopes

In this paper, we construct a fine-grained cattle recognition dataset and propose a lightweight convolutional neural network named MobiCFNet. Our proposed method can solve the problem of large intra-class differences and small inter-class differences in the dataset that can robustly recognize individual cattle images from different angles. In addition, we proposed a recognition method based on feature dictionary in which cattle can be added and deleted after the network is training. Feature dictionary based cattle recognition meets the needs of pasture management. In the future, the proposed method can be combined with the target detection method to realize multi-cattle identification to realize end-to-end automatic pasture monitoring.

References

1. Cai, C., Li, J.: Cattle face recognition using local binary pattern descriptor. In: 2013 Asia-Pacific Signal and Information Processing Association Annual Summit and Conference, pp. 1–4. IEEE (2013)
2. Fosgate, G., Adesiyun, A., Hird, D.: Ear-tag retention and identification methods for extensively managed water buffalo (Bubalus bubalis) in Trinidad. Prev. Vet. Med. **73**(4), 287–296 (2006)
3. Howard, A.G., et al.: MobileNets: efficient convolutional neural networks for mobile vision applications. arXiv preprint arXiv:1704.04861 (2017)
4. Hu, X., Sun, L., Zhou, Y., Ruan, J.: Review of operational management in intelligent agriculture based on the internet of things. Front. Eng. Manage. **7**(3), 309–322 (2020)
5. Ismail, W.N., Hassan, M.M., Alsalamah, H.A., Fortino, G.: CNN-based health model for regular health factors analysis in internet-of-medical things environment. IEEE Access **8**, 52541–52549 (2020)
6. Kaixuan, Z., Dongjian, H.: Recognition of individual dairy cattle based on convolutional neural networks. Trans. Chin. Soc. Agric. Eng. **31**(5), 181–187 (2015)
7. Kim, W., Cho, Y.B., Lee, S.: Thermal sensor-based multiple object tracking for intelligent livestock breeding. IEEE Access **5**, 27453–27463 (2017)
8. Kumar, S., et al.: Deep learning framework for recognition of cattle using muzzle point image pattern. Measurement **116**, 1–17 (2018)
9. Kumar, S., Singh, S.K., Dutta, T., Gupta, H.P.: A fast cattle recognition system using smart devices. In: Proceedings of the 24th ACM International Conference on Multimedia, pp. 742–743 (2016)
10. Kumar, S., Singh, S.K., Singh, R., Singh, A.K.: Animal Biometrics. Springer, Singapore (2017). https://doi.org/10.1007/978-981-10-7956-6
11. Manoj, S., Rakshith, S., Kanchana, V.: Identification of cattle breed using the convolutional neural network. In: 2021 3rd International Conference on Signal Processing and Communication (ICPSC), pp. 503–507. IEEE (2021)
12. Qiao, Y., Su, D., Kong, H., Sukkarieh, S., Lomax, S., Clark, C.: Individual cattle identification using a deep learning based framework. IFAC-PapersOnLine **52**(30), 318–323 (2019)
13. Sandler, M., Howard, A., Zhu, M., Zhmoginov, A., Chen, L.C.: MobileNetV2: inverted residuals and linear bottlenecks. In: Proceedings of the IEEE Conference on Computer Vision and Pattern Recognition, pp. 4510–4520 (2018)

14. Tang, Q., et al.: Food traceability systems in China: the current status of and future perspectives on food supply chain databases, legal support, and technological research and support for food safety regulation. Biosci. Trends **9**(1), 7–15 (2015)

15. Wang, H., et al.: CosFace: large margin cosine loss for deep face recognition. In: Proceedings of the IEEE Conference on Computer Vision and Pattern Recognition, pp. 5265–5274 (2018)

Molecular Activity Prediction Based on Graph Attention Network

Xiaowei Cao, Tiwen Wang, Ruohui Cheng, and Jingyi Ding[✉]

Joint International Research Laboratory of Intelligent Perception and Computation,
International Research Center for Intelligent Perception and Computation,
School of Artificial Intelligence, Xidian University, Xi'an 710071, China
jyding@xidian.edu.cn

Abstract. Spatial convolutional models of Graph Neural Networks (GNNs) updates embeddings of nodes by the neighborhood aggregation, it has obvious advantages in reducing time complexity and improving accuracy. Therefore, it is a very important task to change the way of neighborhood aggregation to learn better node embeddings. Attention mechanisms are usually used to assign trainable weights to nodes in neighborhood aggregation, so that the node influence can also participate in the process of neighborhood aggregation. We propose the ATT-MLP model that combines attention mechanism and multi-layer perception(MLP), and applys node attention weights to graph pooling. Experiments on graph prediction show that our algorithm performs better than other baselines on commonly used datasets.

Keywords: Graph Neural Networks · Graph prediction · Attention mechanism · Neighborhood aggregation

1 Introduction

It takes a lot of time and money in drug research. Moreover, screening a large number of compounds is costly. High-throughput screening methods that show molecular activity in drug research from a large number of compounds are popular. By contrast, machine learning is expected to be used to predict the compound activity efficiently using known compound activity information as a training label. In molecular activity prediction, each atom of a molecular is considered as a node of a graph, and a bond is regarded as an edge of a graph. Based on this, neural networks can be used to perform feature extraction [16–18]. Graph convolutional neural network (GCN), which realizes the convolution on graph, is also used to complete such works naturally. Neural graph fingerprints (NGF) [16], GCN by Han et al. [17] and weave module [18] are often used for feature extraction of graph [4].

ⓒ IFIP International Federation for Information Processing 2022
Published by Springer Nature Switzerland AG 2022
Z. Shi et al. (Eds.): ICIS 2022, IFIP AICT 659, pp. 395–401, 2022.
https://doi.org/10.1007/978-3-031-14903-0_42

1.1   Graph Neural Networks

Graph is a kind of non-Euclidean data, which can represent nodes and the relationships (edges) between them [1]. Different from Euclidean data such as text and image, graph-structured data is irregular, so convolution operation cannot be used in graph datas directly.

In recent years, many researchers have used graph neural networks (GNNs) to process graph structure datas for graph classification [2,3,5,14]. GNNs have important applications in various domains, e.g., chemistry [7], bioinformatics [4, 5], social networks [8], and recommendation systems [9]. GNNs can iteratively update embeddings of nodes to generate a higher-level node representation, and map embeddings of nodes into a graph representation vector combining with readout operation to achieve end-to-end training [6].

The semi-supervised classification model in GCN applies the spectrum convolution classification method to node classification tasks [10]. After adding readout layer, the model can be applied to the graph classification tasks, the model will overfit if there are too many layers in the network. To solve this problem, some researchers use residual networks to construct deep graph neural networks, which can obtain good prediction accuracy, but the time complexity is high [11]. The spatial-convolution method of GCN uses multi-layer neighborhood aggregation to enhance the representation ability of node embeddings, which obtains more efficient graph representation vectors than the spectral convolution model after the readout layer. GIN proposes to use MLP to build the model and batchnorm layer to reduce the over-fitting problem. However, GIN does not consider the hidden information between nodes [8].

1.2   Attention Mechanism

Attention mechanism focuses on the most relevant part to make decisions and obtain more effective node embeddings by aggregating the effective information of neighborhood nodes. Attention mechanism can also process the input information of different scales and focus on the most important part of the input information. Therefore, it also has a good application in graph prediction. Velikovi proposed a graph attention network GAT, which use self-attentional layer to several key challenges of spectral-based graph neural networks simultaneously, and make model readily applicable to inductive as well as transductive problems [12]. DAGCN automatically learns the importance of neighbors at different hops using a novel attention graph convolution layer, and then employs a second attention component, a self-attention pooling layer, to generalize the graph representation from the various aspects of a matrix graph embedding [13]. Zhang propose cardinality preserved attention (GCT-GC) models that can be applied to any kind of attention mechanisms [15].

1.3   Motivation and Contribution

In this work, we add the attention mechanism into the process of hierarchical iteration to enhance the ability of mining node hidden information. We combine attention weights with the graph pooling process to reinforce the expression ability of the graph representation vector.

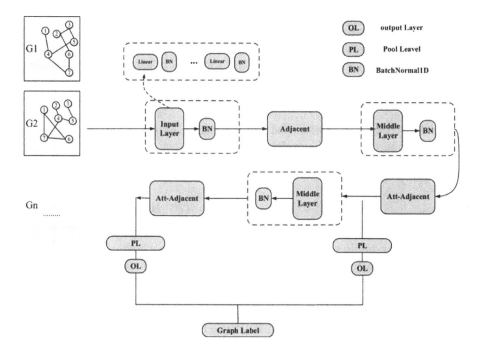

Fig. 1. The architecture of prediction model.

Contributions of this paper:

(1) A prediction algorithm is proposed to classify molecular graphs. An attention mechanism is added into the process of the neighborhood aggregation to obtain a better prediction performance.
(2) The attention adjacency matrix is combined with graph pooling to obtain a more representative graph representation vector.
(3) Experiment results demonstrate that the prediction accuracy of our algorithm is significantly improved without a significant increase in time complexity.

1.4   Organization

The rest of the paper is organized as follows: Sect. 2 describes the problem formulation. The experiments and analyses are provided in Sect. 3. Finally, Sect. 4 concludes the paper with some discussions and promising future work.

2   Method

2.1   The Overall Framework

We proposes ATT-MLP model by adding the attention mechanism to the process of hierarchical iteration and readout, As shown in Fig. 1, ATT-MLP model mainly includes three parts: the input layer, the middle layer, the graph pooling layer. Graph datas are input to the input layer. The attention mechanism needs enough rich node features, so the neighborhood matrix is used to aggregate node features after the input layer to obtain richer node features. The middle layer is MLP layers, a batchnormal layer after the MLP layers prevent over-fitting, the middle layer uses the attention adjacency matrix to aggregate node features, and all attention layers share parameters. Finally, we weight node embeddings by the attention adjacency matrix to obtain the graph representation vector in the graph pooling layer.

$$H^{(l+1)} = MLP^{(l+1)}(I + ATT)H^l \tag{1}$$

As shown in Eq. (1), ATT represents the attention adjacency matrix, which is obtained by adding the node attention vector. Input characteristic matrix $H^{(0)} = \{h_1^{(0)}, h_2^{(0)}, ..., h_N^{(0)}\}$, Where n represents the number of nodes, $h_v \in R^F$, h_v is the node representation vector, F is the number of node labels. $H^{(l)} = \{h_1^{(l)}, h_2^{(l)}, ..., h_N^{(l)}\}$ is obtained after the input characteristic matrix passes through the $l - th$ layer MLP.

Node update formulas of ATT-MLP algorithm are Eqs. (2) and (3). $att(h_v, h_u)$ is the attention coefficients computed by adding the node attention vector to measure the relation between v and u, a is the attention vector, W is the attention layer parameter, h_v, h_v are vector embeddings with edge connections, $||$ is the combination two vectors of Wh_v and Wh_u, h_v^l is the vector embedding of v in the $l - th$ layer, $\mu(v)$ is the neighborhood node set of node v.

$$h_v^l = MLP^{(l)}(h_v^{l-1} + \sum_{u \in \mu(v)} att(h_v, h_u)h_u^{(l-1)}) \tag{2}$$

$$att(h_v, h_u) = \frac{\exp(LeakyReLU(a^T[Wh_v||Wh_u]))}{\sum_{k \in \mu(v)} \exp(LeakyReLU(a^T[Wh_v||Wh_k]))} \tag{3}$$

3   Experiment

To verify the effectiveness of the proposed ATT-MLP algorithm, we compared it with six other algorithms. All algorithms are implemented on Windows operating system and are built on AMD Ryzen5 2600 and NVIDIA GeForce GTX 1070. We use 6 Common public datasets, as shown in Table 1: 4 bioinformatics datasets (MUTAG, PTC, PROTEINS, ENZYMES), 2 movie collaboration datasets (IMDB-B and IMDB-M), - means that the dataset has no node labels, which is uniformly set to 1 in experiments.

Table 1. Graph classification datasets

Dataset	Graph number	Classes	Node labels
MUTAG	188	2	7
PTC	344	2	19
PROTEINS	1112	2	4
ENZYMES	600	6	3
IMDB-B	1000	2	–
IMDB-M	1500	3	–

3.1 Experimental Setting

We compare our model (ATT-MLP algorithm) with several baselines: GCN [10], DGCNN [14], GAT [12], DAGCN [13], GIN [8], GCT-GC [15]. We set 3 layers of MLP and 32 hidden layers in ATT-MLP algorithm. We conduct 10-fold cross-validation and repeated the experiments for 10 times independently to obtain the mean value. Each model runs 200 epochs for each dataset. All models are trained with the Adam optimizer and the learning rate is dropped by a factor of 0.8 every 50 epochs with an initial learning rate of 0.01, dropout $\in \{0, 0.5\}$, batchsize $\in \{16, 64\}$ for all datasets, we use the same hyperparametric configuration in all models to get a fair conclusion (Table 2).

3.2 Experimental Result

Table 2. Classification accuracy on six datasets

Algorithm/Datasets	MUTAG	PTC	PROTEINS	ENZYMES	IMDB-B	IMDB-M
GCN	84.2 ± 5.9	59.1 ± 6.0	74.1 ± 3.1	28.8 ± 6.4	69.3 ± 4.4	49.7 ± 1.0
DGCNN	85.8 ± 7.9	58.6 ± 6.4	75.3 ± 2.4	49.8 ± 9.3	70.0 ± 3.8	47.8 ± 2.9
GAT	86.4 ± 5.7	59.7 ± 6.7	74.7 ± 3.0	30.2 ± 5.6	70.5 ± 4.7	43.5 ± 3.5
DAGCN	86.1 ± 6.1	61.8 ± 9.6	73.7 ± 4.3	40.1 ± 8.8	73.3 ± 2.7	48.3 ± 3.4
GIN	88.1 ± 7.6	64.6 ± 7.0	75.2 ± 2.8	32.5 ± 6.5	73.6 ± 5.3	49.8 ± 3.2
GCT-GC	90.4 ± 4.7	64.0 ± 7.3	76.9 ± 5.1	**59.0 ± 3.8**	67.8 ± 4.0	45.6 ± 4.3
ATT-MLP	**95.6 ± 4.8**	**74.1 ± 4.7**	**78.5 ± 4.1**	55.2 ± 5.7	**75.6 ± 4.6**	**51.5 ± 2.5**

Graph classification results are shown in Table 2. We highlight the best result of each dataset. We observe that ATT-MLP algorithm performs better than simple attention mechanisms and hierarchical methods. ATT-MLP algorithm significantly improves the classification accuracy on most datasets, attention mechanism redistributes node relationships according to node features, the more node labels in the datasets, the greater improvement of ATT-MLP algorithm, which i algorithms also the reason why the improvement effect is not obvious on the ENZYMES dataset.

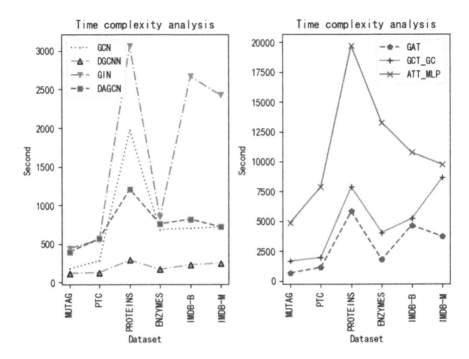

Fig. 2. Time complexity of different algorithms

As shown in Fig. 2, the line chart represents the running time of each algorithm on different datasets. ATT-MLP algorithm uses the attention mechanism in neighborhood aggregation. Moreover, the weighted sum of attention matrix is used for node features in graph pooling, so the time complexity of ATT-MLP algorithm is the highest.

4   Conclusion

We propose the method ATT-MLP which embedding the nodes by changing the way of neighborhood aggregation through an attention mechanism, and combine the attention adjacency matrix with graph pooling. ATT-MLP algorithm can re-learn the attention adjacency matrix between nodes based on the hierarchical model. Moreover, our proposed algorithm can mine the hidden information of nodes, and get more representative graph vector representation. Compared to other methods, ATT-MLP achieves competitive performance. However, this model has high time complexity. Learning attention weights more effectively and model parallelization to reduce time complexity are important research tasks in our next work.

References

1. Yanardag, P., Vishwanathan, S.: Deep graph kernels. In: KDD 2015: Proceedings of the Twenty-First ACM SigKDD International Conference on Knowledge, pp. 1365–1374 (2015)
2. Ma, Y., Wang, S.: Graph convolutional networks with EigenPooling. In: KDD 2019: Proceedings of the 25th ACM SIGKDD International Conference on Knowledge Discovery and Data Mining, pp. 723–731 (2019)
3. Li, S., Zhang, L.: MutagenPred-GCNNs: a graph convolutional neural network-based classification model for mutagenicity prediction with data-driven molecular fingerprints. Interdiscip. Sci. Comput. Life Sci. **13**, 25–33 (2021)
4. Ohue, M., Ii, R.: Molecular activity prediction using graph convolutional deep neural network considering distance on a molecular graph. In: Proceedings of the Twenty-First ACM SigKDD International Conference on Knowledge (2019)
5. Ying, Z., You, J., Morris, C., et al.: Hierarchical graph representation learning with differentiable pooling. In: Advances in Neural Information Processing Systems, vol. 31 (2018)
6. Zhang, M., Cui, Z., Neumann, M., et al.: An end-to-end deep learning architecture for graph classification. In: Thirty-Second AAAI Conference on Artificial Intelligence (2018)
7. Gilmer, J., Schoenholz, S.S., Riley, P.F., et al.: Neural message passing for quantum chemistry. In: International Conference on Machine Learning. PMLR, pp. 1263–1272 (2017)
8. Xu, K., Hu, W., Leskovec, J., et al.: How powerful are graph neural networks?. arXiv preprint arXiv:1810.00826 (2018)
9. Gao, C., Yao, Q., Jin, D., et al.: Efficient data-specific model search for collaborative filtering. In: Proceedings of the 27th ACM SIGKDD Conference on Knowledge Discovery & Data Mining, pp. 415–425 (2021)
10. Kipf, T.N., Welling, M.: Semi-supervised classification with graph convolutional networks. arXiv preprint arXiv:1609.02907 (2016)
11. Chen, L., Wu, L., Hong, R., et al.: Revisiting graph based collaborative filtering: a linear residual graph convolutional network approach. Proc. AAAI Conf. Artif. Intell. **34**(01), 27–34 (2020)
12. Veličković, P., Cucurull, G., Casanova, A., et al.: Graph attention networks. arXiv preprint arXiv:1710.10903 (2017)
13. Chen, F., Pan, S., Jiang, J., et al.: DAGCN: dual attention graph convolutional networks. In: 2019 International Joint Conference on Neural Networks (IJCNN), pp. 1–8. IEEE (2019)
14. Phan, A.V., Le Nguyen, M., Nguyen, Y.L.H., et al.: DGCNN: a convolutional neural network over large-scale labeled graphs. Neural Netw. **108**, 533–543 (2018)
15. Zhang, S., Xie, L.: Improving attention mechanism in graph neural networks via cardinality preservation (2019)
16. Duvenaud, D., Maclaurin, D., Aguilera-Iparraguirre, J., et al.: Convolutional networks on graphs for learning molecular fingerprints. In: International Conference on Neural Information Processing Systems. MIT Press (2015)
17. Han, A.T., Ramsundar, B., Pappu, A.S., et al.: Low data drug discovery with one-shot learning. ACS Central Sci. **3**(4), 283–293 (2016)
18. Kearnes, S., McCloskey, K., et al.: Molecular graph convolutions: moving beyond fingerprints. J. Comput.-Aided Mol. Des. **30**, 595–608 (2016)

Tracking Multi-objects with Anchor-Free Siamese Network

Bingyu Hui, Jie Feng$^{(\boxtimes)}$, Quanhe Yao, Jing Gu, and Licheng Jiao

Key Laboratory of Intelligent Perception and Image Understanding of Ministry of Education,
Xidian University, Xi'an 710071, China
353626620@qq.com

Abstract. Single object tracker based on siamese neural network have become one of the most popular frameworks in this field for its strong discrimination ability and high efficiency. However, when the task switch to multi-object tracking, the development of siamese-network based tracking methods is limited by the huge calculation cost comes from repeatedly feature extract and excessive predefined anchors. To solve these problems, we propose a siamese box adaptive multi-object tracking (SiamBAN-MOT) method with parallel detector and siamese tracker branch, which implementation in an anchor-free manner. Firstly, ResNet-50 is constructed to extract shared features of the current frame. Then, we design a siamese specific feature pyramid networks (S-FPN) to fuse the multi-scale features, which improves detection and tracking performance with the anchor-free architecture. To alleviate the duplicate feature extraction, RoI align is operated to extract all trajectories' template feature and search region feature in a single feature map at once. After that, anchor-free based Siamese tracking network outputs the tracking result of each trajectory according to its template and search region feature. Meanwhile, current frame's detection results are obtained from the detector for the target association. Finally, a simple novel IOU-matching scheme is designed to map the tracking results to the detection results so as to refine the tracking results and suppress the drifts caused by siamese tracking network. Through experimental verification, our method achieves competitive results on MOT17.

Keywords: Multi-object tracking · Siamese network · Anchor-free

1 Introduction

Multi-Object Tracking (MOT) is the problem of detecting object instances and then temporally associating them to form trajectories [1], which is a long-standing problem in the computer vision field. With the development of artificial intelligent society,

This work was supported in part by the National Natural Science Foundation of China under Grant 61871306, Grant 61836009, Grant 62172600, Grant 62077038, by the Innovation Capability Support Program of Shaanxi (Program No. 2021KJXX-08), by the Natural Science Basic Research Program of Shaanxi under Grant No. 2022JC-45 and 2022GY-065, and by the Fundamental Research Funds for the Central Universities under Grant JB211901.

© IFIP International Federation for Information Processing 2022
Published by Springer Nature Switzerland AG 2022
Z. Shi et al. (Eds.): ICIS 2022, IFIP AICT 659, pp. 402–408, 2022.
https://doi.org/10.1007/978-3-031-14903-0_43

object tracking is widely used in automatic driving, robotics, security monitoring and other fields. Multi-Object Tracking technology has experienced great progress since its emergence, however, this field still faces great challenges due to its stringent performance requirements for precise object detection and fine-grained classification of similar objects.

In earlier work [2, 3], MOT has been regarded as a objects-to-trajectories matching problem, most of the earlier works design their networks based on the Tracking-by-Detection (TBD) paradigm, that is, training the detector separately, modeling the motion model to predict each trajectory's position in current frame, and assigning the objects to the trajectories by the Hungarian algorithm or some other data association algorithms. Benefitting from the development of person re-identification, tracking network based on Re-ID has gradually become the mainstream. It is worth mentioning that Re-ID in object tracking task refers to a column vector of a particular dimension extracted from the object, and the category of the object depends on the data, rather than the characteristics of the person in person re-identification task. Some methods [3–9] try to solve tracking task by a separate detection model and a separate Re-ID feature extraction network: detection model detects objects firstly and then get the Re-ID features extracted from the detected bounding boxes' corresponding image patch. Finally, links the detection to one of the existing trajectories or creates a new trajectory according to their metrics defined on Re-ID features. In recent years, many methods [10–14] tend to make detection and tracking simultaneously in a common network for its outstanding performance benefited from end-to-end training network, defined as Joint Detection and Tracking (JDT) paradigm. In recent JDT methods, some methods [10, 11] design the network structure to extract detection results and Re-ID features at the same time, while others implement tracking [12–14] by unique tracking methods.

However, most Re-ID based methods' over-reliance on appearance feature also creates problems hard to solve. One problem is Re-ID feature of similar or occluded object is always indistinguishable at the common natural video scale, such as several people with same clothes or people whose body is blocked by obstacle. Another problem is that continuous information contained in the video is wasted in most Re-ID matching method.

Siamese neural network is widely used in Single-Object-Tracking (SOT) filed for its excellent discrimination of objects and online learning ability. Recently, *Shuai et al.* proposed a SiamMOT method [1] for multi-object tracking, which achieved start-of-the-art tracking performance in several public datasets. Nevertheless, due to the anchor-based single object tracking and detection network, during the matching process, each object needs to be re-modeled once, which brings huge time and computing resource cost.

To solve these problems, in this paper, we propose an anchor-free based Siamese network to realize multi-object tracking task, which can achieve both high accuracy and FPS. As show in Fig. 1, the proposed network consists of two parallel branch: anchor-free based one-stage detector branch and anchor-free based siamese tracker branch. No predefined anchor is required for the entire network, benefit from the specifically designed S-FPN, the detector directly predict the interest objects' global heatmap and objects' size information, during the tracking, Siamese-BAM tracker get the template feature of each trajectory and search region feature to regression the tracking result.

Finally, after a simple IOU match, tracker matches the objects with the trajectories and generates new trajectories.

The contributions of this work are described as follows:

– We propose an anchor-free based Siamese network for multi-object tracking, which can extract multi-trajectories' template and search region feature at once, enhanced the siamese architecture's inference speed.
– We design a S-FPN module to enhance the tracking and detection performance on anchor-free based network.
– The proposed tracking method can alleviate the object drift problem of siamese tracking network and improve the performance by simple IOU-matching.

2   SiamBAN-MOT

SiamBAN-MOT consists of detection branches and tracking branches. As show in Fig. 1. The detection branch is designed as an anchor-free one-stage detection network, with using ResNet-50 [16] as the backbone network to extract the image feature. And we design a S-FPN module to enhance the discrimination of feature. In the tracking branch, a multi-object tracker based on Siamese network is constructed, during the tracking, same as the Siamese RPN++ [17], templates of trajectories are used as convolution kernel to regression tracking results in current frame. Finally, after simple IOU matching, the objects and trajectories are matched. Unmatched objects will be assigned to a new trajectory.

In the next section we will introduce the details of our SiamBAN-MOT, both include the detector (Sect. 2.1) and tracker (Sect. 2.2).

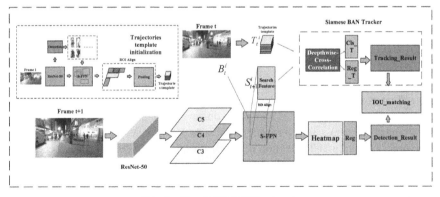

Fig. 1. SiamBAN-MOT network

2.1   Anchor-Free Network with Detector and S-FPN

With the excellent feature extraction performance of ResNet-50, we design an anchor-free basic network and used it for detection.

In detail, we extract the features of ResNet-50's convolutional layers 3, 4 and 5 (denote as C3, C4 and C5), and the stacked features is fed into the S-FPN module for multi-scale fusion (as show in Fig. 2). It is important to note that the SFPN is also designed for tracking branch's accurately regression, as template features' requirement of multi-scale enhancement. Then, computing with simple regression head and heatmap head and decoding the heatmap, we can get accurate detection results.

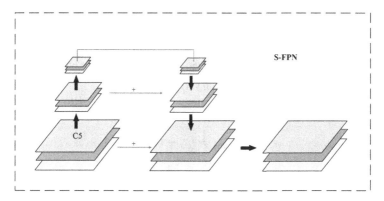

Fig. 2. S-FPN module

In addition, same as Siam-BAN [15], we set the stride to 1 in the conv4 and conv5 blocks in ReNet-50.

2.2   Siamese Tracker for Multi-object Tracking.

The input of tracking branch are template feature (defined as T_t^i, which represents the feature of the i-th trajectory sampled at frame t) and the search region feature (defined as S_{t+1}^i, which represents the feature cropped from a specific region of frame $t + 1$ feature, according to the ith trajectory's location in frame t). t represents the serial number of the image in the video and i represents the t-th trajectory in trajectories set.

Defining inference result of tracking in frame $t + 1$ as $\tilde{B}_{t+1}^i$ and inference result of detection in frame $t + 1$ as B_{t+1}^i, the bounding box in ground-truth as $\overline{B}_{t+1}^i$, Formally,

$$\tilde{B}_{t+1}^i = \Gamma\left(T_t^i, S_{t+1}^i, \theta\right) \tag{1}$$

where Γ represent the learnable Siamese tracker with parameters θ.

The strategy for calculating candidate regions of S_{t+1}^i is as follows: set the t-th trajectory's search region in frame $t + 1$ according to B_t^i by keeping the same geometric center of B_t^i and expanding region's width and height to α and β times that of B_t^i.

The final accurate tracking result can be obtained by simple IOU matching, which can both realize tracking motion suppression and object matching with existing trajectories.

2.3 Ground-Truth and Loss

During the training, we set detector's loss function as:

$$l_{det} = l_{heat} + l_{size} \tag{2}$$

where l_{heat} defined as:

$$l_{heat} = focal\_loss(heatmap, heatmap\_gt) \tag{3}$$

and the l_{size} defined as:

$$l_{size} = l1\_loss(size, size\_gt) \tag{4}$$

the *heatmap_gt* is got in the way mentioned in FairMOT [11]. And the *size* and $size_{gt}$ represent the width and height of B_{t+1}^i and $\overline{B}_{t+1}^i$.

As for tracker, we use the same strategy in SiamBAN [15] to take positive and negative samples and then we set tracker's loss function as:

$$l_{track} = l_{cls} + l_{reg} \tag{5}$$

where l_{cls} is the cross-entropy loss and l_{cls} is the IOU loss.

3 Experiment

Our SiamBAN-MOT is implemented in Pytorch on a single RTX 2080Ti 11GB GPU, it achieves the average running speed of 18 FPS on MOT17.

3.1 Datasets and Metrics

MOT17 [18] is one of the most popular datasets for multi-object tracking, which consists of both 7 videos in training set and test set, ranging from 7 to 90 s long. These videos contain various scene of crowd people indoor or outdoor streets. Following the [1], we only using MOTA (multiple object tracking accuracy), IDF (ID F1 score), and FPS to evaluate the tracker's tracking performance both in accuracy and inference speed.

3.2 Implementation Details

Network. We use a fixed ResNet-50 which set the kernel stride to 1 in the conv4 and conv5 blocks in ReNet-50 and keep the feature' size in different blocks by change the padding size. We set (α, β) to (3, 2) to get the search region.

Training. We jointly train the tracker and detection network end to end. SGD with momentum is used as optimizer. Setting learning rate of 0.05 and decrease it by factor 10 after 50% of the iterations, we set the batch size of 16 image pairs and weight decay of 10^{-4}.

Inference. We use a dynamic IOU threshold that is 0.5 while only one object can achieve this threshold, otherwise, match the object with the largest IOU value to the trajectory. We keep a trajectory active 30 frames since it disappears and expand the search region 2 times every 10 frames.

3.3 Experiment Results on MOT17

Finally, we compare our SiamBAN-MOT with several excellent models on MOT17 datasets with MOTA, IDF1 and FPS metrics.

Table 1. Results on MOT17 test set with public detection.

Method	MOTA	IDF1	FPS
SST	52.4	49.5	<3.9
CTracker	66.6	57.4	6.8
CenterTrack	67.8	64.7	17.5
SiamMOT	65.9	63.3	16
SiamBAN-MOT	64.8	60.9	18

4 Conclusion

In this report, we present an anchor-free based siamese network for multi-object-tracking. The purpose of this method is to replace the step of data association between frames by template matching, so that the existing object matching methods can be more learnable. However, due to the specific of the siamese-network-based method, it always achieves a low FPS performance in multiple object tracking comparing with Re-id based method. According to the results in Table 1, without using any tricks, our method declined in accuracy, but achieved better FPS performance than other methods. And there is still a great potential for our method because it is not optimized.

References

1. Shuai, B., Berneshawi, A., Li, X., et al.: SiamMOT: Siamese multi-object tracking. In: Proceedings of the IEEE/CVF Conference on Computer Vision and Pattern Recognition, pp. 12372–12382 (2021)
2. Bewley, A., Ge, Z., Ott, L., et al.: Simple online and realtime tracking. In: 2016 IEEE international conference on image processing (ICIP), pp. 3464–3468. IEEE (2016)
3. Wojke, N., Bewley, A., Paulus, D.: Simple online and realtime tracking with a deep association metric. In: 2017 IEEE International Conference on Image Processing (ICIP), pp. 3645–3649. IEEE (2017)
4. Mahmoudi, N., Ahadi, S.M., Rahmati, M.: Multi-target tracking using CNN-based features: CNNMTT. Multimedia Tools Appl. **78**(6), 7077–7096 (2019)
5. Zhou, Z., Xing, J., Zhang, M., Hu, W.: Online multi-target tracking with tensor-based high-order graph matching. In: 2018 24th International Conference on Pattern Recognition (ICPR), pp 1809–1814. IEEE (2018)
6. Fang, K., Xiang, Y., Li, X., Savarese, S.: Recurrent autoregressive networks for online multi-object tracking. In: WACV, pp. 466–475. IEEE (2018)

7. Bewley, A., Ge, Z., Ott, L., Ramos, F., Upcroft, B.: Simple online and realtime tracking. In: ICIP, pp. 3464–3468. IEEE (2016)
8. Chen, L., Ai, H., Zhuang, Z., Shang, C.: Real-time multiple people tracking with deeply learned candidate selection and person re-identification. In: 2018 IEEE International Conference on Multimedia and Expo (ICME), pp. 1–6. IEEE (2018a)
9. Yu, F., Li, W., Li, Q., Liu, Y., Shi, X., Yan, J.: POI: Multiple object tracking with high performance detection and appearance feature. In: Hua, G., Jégou, H. (eds.) ECCV 2016. LNCS, vol. 9914, pp. 36–42. Springer, Cham (2016). https://doi.org/10.1007/978-3-319-488 81-3_3
10. Wang, Z., Zheng, L., Liu, Y., et al.: Towards real-time multi-object tracking. In: Vedaldi, A., Bischof, H., Brox, T., Frahm, J.-M. (eds.) European Conference on Computer Vision, pp. 107–122. Springer, Cham (2020). https://doi.org/10.1007/978-3-030-58621-8_7
11. Zhang, Y., Wang, C., Wang, X., et al.: Fairmot: On the fairness of detection and re-identification in multiple object tracking. Int. J. Comput. Vision **129**(11), 3069–3087 (2021)
12. Zhou, X., Koltun, V., Krähenbühl, P.: Tracking objects as points. In: Vedaldi, A., Bischof, H., Brox, T., Frahm, J.-M. (eds.) ECCV 2020. LNCS, vol. 12349, pp. 474–490. Springer, Cham (2020). https://doi.org/10.1007/978-3-030-58548-8_28
13. Peng, J., et al.: Chained-tracker: chaining paired attentive regression results for end-to-end joint multiple-object detection and tracking. In: Vedaldi, A., Bischof, H., Brox, T., Frahm, J.-M. (eds.) ECCV 2020. LNCS, vol. 12349, pp. 145–161. Springer, Cham (2020). https://doi.org/10.1007/978-3-030-58548-8_9
14. Zheng, L., Tang, M., Chen, Y., et al.: Improving multiple object tracking with single object tracking. In: Proceedings of the IEEE/CVF Conference on Computer Vision and Pattern Recognition, pp. 2453–2462 (2021)
15. Chen, Z., Zhong, B., Li, G., et al.: Siamese box adaptive network for visual tracking. In: Proceedings of the IEEE/CVF Conference on Computer Vision and Pattern Recognition, pp. 6668–6677 (2020)
16. He, K., Zhang, X., Ren, S., et al.: Deep residual learning for image recognition. In: Proceedings of the IEEE Conference on Computer Vision and Pattern Recognition, pp. 770–778 (2016)
17. Li, B., Wu, W., Wang, Q., et al.: SiamRPN++: evolution of Siamese visual tracking with very deep networks. In: Proceedings of the IEEE/CVF Conference on Computer Vision and Pattern Recognition, pp. 4282–4291 (2019)
18. Milan, A., Leal-Taixe, L., Reid, I., Roth, S., Schindler, K.: Mot16: a benchmark for multi-object tracking. arXiv preprint arXiv:160300831 (2016)

Feature Learning and Change Feature Classification Based on Variational Auto-encoder for SAR Change Detection

Huan Chen[1]([✉]), Hongming Zhang[1], and Zhixi Feng[2]

[1] College of Information Engineering, North West A&F University, Yang Ling, Xianyang 712100, China
huanchen@nwafu.edu.cn
[2] School of Artificial Intelligence, Xidian University, Xi'an 710071, China

Abstract. As a special auto-encoder, variational auto-encoder (VAE) is not only known as a branch of generation model, but also plays an important role in image feature extraction. Since VAE can get Gaussian distribution with different parameters from different types of inputs or with approximately the same parameters from the same type of input, the latent variables have obvious differences between different categories. This paper put forward a supervised variational auto-encoder (SVAE) to study the representation ability for synthetic aperture radar change detection. Firstly, the difference image is obtained by log ratio method from two original images preprocessed. Then fuzzy c-means (FCM) clustering is used to analyze difference image with the aim of acquiring pseudo labels. As for the inputs of the SVAE, they are selected directly from two SAR images instead of sampling from difference image (DI). Having the inputs and pseudo labels, SAVE can learn latent Gaussian representations according to which SVAE can make a classification for change detection (CD). Experiments on four data set demonstrate that SVAE can obtain discriminative features for CD and outperforms some related approaches.

Keywords: Generation model · Variational auto-encoder · Change detection · Supervised variational auto-encoder · Representation ability

1 Introduction

Change detection (CD) is a meaningful process which refers to recognize changes by analyzing two or more images over the same area acquired at different times. It has been widely used in various applications, such as urban change analysis [1], agricultural survey [2], environmental monitoring [3], and hazard assessment [4]. Due to the coherent principle of SAR imaging system, there would generate some speckle noises, which makes it more difficult to detect changes than optical ones. It is essential to develop a robust SAR image change detection technique against the speckle noise.

Z. Shi et al. (Eds.): ICIS 2022, IFIP AICT 659, pp. 409–416, 2022.
https://doi.org/10.1007/978-3-031-14903-0_44

Generally, CD approaches are often comprised of three steps: (1) image preprocessing, (2) DI generation, and (3) unsupervised or supervised classification of the DI into changed and unchanged classes. Recently, deep learning has become a powerful tool in the field of feature learning. Inspired by the architectural depth of the brain, deep learning has the ability to transform the raw pixels into a higher feature space to capture the discrimination information, and has become a popular way for automatically classification. Geng Jie [5] developed a supervised contractive auto-encoder (SCAE) combined with FCM for SAR CD. Changed features were extracted from two original images and DI based on SCAE, which has been proved to optimize feature representations and enhance classification accuracies. Gong [6] applied a deep belief network (DBN) to SAR images CD without the generation of DI, where CD problem is transformed into a classical classification task. In our previous work [7], a fast unsupervised deep fusion framework based on SAE was proposed for SAR CD. However, DI was generated based on the extracted feature in this work, resulting in redundancy. In addition, unsupervised clustering analysis of DI may lead to low accuracy. However, as mentioned in [5], methods conducted on DI may lose useful information during the DI generation. If representative features are directly extracted from two original images and a more accurate classification model is utilized, there would be a considerable room to improve.

In this paper, supervised variational auto-encoder (SVAE) combined with FCM are developed for SAR CD. The SVAE consists of the encoder of a variational auto-encoders [8] (VAE) and a softmax layer following. The purpose of SVAE is to learn a latent variable which obeys Gaussian distribution and to classify it by the following softmax layer. Since VAE can get Gaussian distribution with different parameters from different types of inputs or with approximately the same parameters from the same type of inputs, the latent variables have obvious differences between different categories. Better results can be achieved in classification and retrieval tasks. To explore the representation ability of VAE in SAR CD, image pairs from two original image are fed to VAE and the learned latent variables are put into a softmax layer. In addition, the training of SVAE are guided by pseudo labels obtained by FCM. Once the SAVE training is done, all image pairs from the two raw image are fed into the learned SVAE, and the final change detection results can be acquired.

The rest of this paper is organized as follows: Sect. 2 describes the proposed method in details. The experimental results and the corresponding analysis are illustrated in Sect. 3. Finally, a conclusive remark on this study are summarized briefly in Sect. 4.

2　The Proposed Method

In this section, the proposed method is illustrated in detail. The general flowchart of the proposed framework is shown in Fig. 1. As we can see, given two coregistered SAR images, DI can be obtained by log ratio method, and then FCM is used to analyse DI in order to acquire the pseudo labels. After that, the corresponding neighborhood pixels of two SAR images are selected and transformed into vectors as the input of SVAE. Having the input and the corresponding pseudo labels, SVAE can be trained to learn the concept of changes and unchanges. At the testing stage, all samples from the two SAR images are fed into SVAE and the final change results can be obtained.

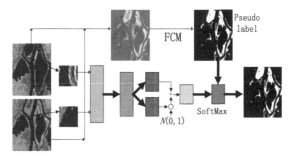

Fig. 1. Illustration of the architecture of SVAE. The green box is the first hidden layer and the blue box is the second hidden layer. The final red box is the latent variable constrained by a Gaussian variation (red box and purple box) (Color figure online).

2.1 Preprocessing and FCM

In order to obtain the pseudo labels, we first preprocess two SAR images by mean filter. This process can remove some speckle noises of SAR images. Next, log ratio method is used to acquire DI, and FCM is adopted to analyses DI in order to obtain pseudo labels. Specially, FCM is applied to detect changed and unchanged regions by clustering with high probability, and percent of changed and unchanged are used as pseudo labels. As for the input of SVAE, we flatten each pixel combined with its neighbor pixels of two SAR images and concatenate them into pixel vectors. Thus, pixel vectors and pseudo labels are fed into SVAE for training.

2.2 SVAE for Feature Learning and Classification

Unlike the traditional methods that analyze DI to obtain change results, we desire to learn the representation from two SAR images directly instead of DI, considering useful information would be lost during generating DI. Neighborhood pixel features of two SAR images are input into SVAE to extract effective representations due to the powerful ability of VAE. Traditional AE learn the representation of data by reconstructing the input. While the VAE adds a variation constraint to latent variable, which obeys a Gaussian distribution, and can generates a new sample through the decoder network by sampling from a Gaussian distribution. Thus, VAE not only compresses the input but also studies the distribution of data. The parameters of Gaussian distribution of the same type are approximately the same, while the input belongs to different types have quite different parameters of Gaussian distribution. So VAE can often achieve better results in classification and retrieval tasks [9].

Suppose the pixel vectors $s^i = [s_1^i, s_2^i]$, then in the encoding step, the vector s^i is transformed into hidden representation h by the following expression:

$$h = \tanh(W_1 \cdot s^i + b_1) \tag{1}$$

The mean and variance of the approximation Gaussian distribution is computed as:

$$\mu = W_2 \cdot h + b_2 \tag{2}$$

$$\sigma = W_3 \cdot h + b_3 \tag{3}$$

Then the final latent expression is:

$$z = \mu + \sigma \odot \varepsilon \tag{4}$$

As for the decoding step, the expression is as follows:

$$\widehat{h} = \tanh(W_4 \cdot z + b_4) \tag{5}$$

$$\widehat{s^i} = \tanh(W_5 \cdot \widehat{h} + b_5) \tag{6}$$

Then the last optimization can be written as:

$$L = \frac{1}{2}||\widehat{s^i} - s^i||^2 + \frac{1}{2}(-\log\sigma^2 + \mu^2 + \sigma^2 - 1) \tag{7}$$

After that, we can optimize the VAE with SGD or Adam. Once the VAE has been trained well, the decoder part is removed and the weightings/biases in the encoder are fixed. Then a softmax classifier is added on the top of encoder. At this moment, the pseudo labels of the corresponding pixel vectors are adopted to train the classifier and fine tune the whole SVAE network. At last, the final change detection results can be acquired directly by feeding all pixel vectors one by one.

3   Experimental Settings and Results Analysis

3.1   Data Description

To confirm the advantages of SVAE, extensive experiments have been performed on the following data sets:

(1) Ottawa: This data set contains a section (290350 pixels) of two SAR images (C-band and HH polarization) with 10-m resolution acquired in May and August 1997, respectively. They are over the city of Ottawa acquired by RADARSAT SAR sensor and provided by the Defence Research and Development Canada, Ottawa. The available ground truth (i.e., reference image) is shown in Fig. 2(c), and was created by integrating prior information and photointerpretation based on the input images Fig. 2(a) and (b). The two images present the areas where they were once afflicted with floods. The changed areas represent the affected areas. The experiment on Ottawa dataset is an instance of disaster evaluation.

(2) San Francisco: The second dataset, as shown in Fig. 3, is called the San Francisco dataset. It presents a section (256 256 pixels) of two SAR images acquired by the ERS-2 SAR sensor. The original images are 77497713 pixels. The images were captured in August 2003 and May 2004, respectively. The ground truth change map shown in Fig. 3 (c) is generated by integrating prior information with photo interpretation based on the input images in Fig. 3(a) and (b).

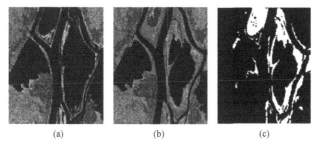

Fig. 2. Illustration of Ottawa data set. (a) Image acquired in July 1997. (b) Image acquired in August 1997. (c) Ground truth.

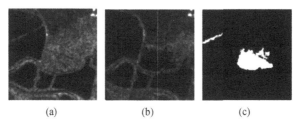

Fig. 3. Illustration of San Francisco dataset. (a) Image acquired in August 2003. (b) Image acquired in May 2004. (c) Ground-truth image.

3.2 General Information

Having change detection results, it is necessary to use some criteria to evaluate the results quantitatively. FP: This index is the number of pixels falsely classified as changed class. FN: This index is the number of pixels falsely classified as unchanged class. OE: The overall error. It is the sum of the FP and FN. KC: Kappa coefficient. It is used to evaluate the effect of the result in the domain of image segmentation. The higher the value of Kappa is, the better the segmentation result is. PCC: Percentage correct classification. It represents the proportion of observed agreement in Kappa. AA: The averaged accuracy, which represents the average percentage of correctly classified pixels for each class. In order to demonstrate the effectiveness of the proposed approach, principal component analysis (PCA), AE and Sparse AE (SpAE) are used to compare with our method. All methods, extracting discriminative features, are followed by FCM to generate the final change detection results.

3.3 Analysis of the Representation Ability

In this subsection, we evaluate the representation ability of SVAE based on Ottawa dataset. As a comparison, PCA, AE and SpAE are selected. We use the t-SNE [10] to visualize the latent representations learned by different methods. The visualization is shown in Fig. 4. It can be seen that the intra class separation distance in Fig. 4(d) is the minimum, while the intra class separation distance of PCA and AE in Fig. 4 (a) and (b)

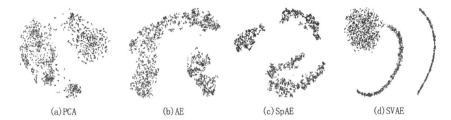

(a) PCA	(b) AE	(c) SpAE	(d) SVAE

Fig. 4. Latent representation visualization of different methods. (a) PCA. (b) AE. (c) SpAE. (d) SVAE.

are larger. This proofs that SVAE can learn better latent representations than PCA, AE and SpAE. The following comparison will also illustrate this point.

3.4   Results Comparison with Other Methods on Ottawa Data Set

The results of experiment on the Ottawa data set are shown in Fig. 5 and listed in Table 1. As shown in Fig. 5(a), it can be found that there exists many white noise spots in the change detection results obtained by PCA. Comparing with the PCA method, AE approach can gain a much better result, as shown in Fig. 5(b). Due to the additional constraint condition, SpAE can learn the useful information from the samples. As for the result of SVAE shown in Fig. 5(d), it looks most like the Ground truth. In addition, Table 1 also proof that SVAE can acquire better change detection results than other methods.

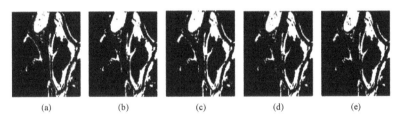

(a)	(b)	(c)	(d)	(e)

Fig. 5. Change detection results for Ottawa data set obtained by different methods. (a) PCA. (b) AE. (c) SpAE. (d) SVAE. (e) Ground truth.

Table 1. Results obtained by different methods on Ottawa data sets.

Method	FN	FP	OE	PCC (%)	KC	AA
PCA	694	2976	3670	96.38	0.87	96.09
AE	735	3006	3741	96.31	0.86	95.95
SpAE	**137**	2663	2800	97.24	0.9	98.01
SVAE	312	**1092**	**1404**	**98.61**	**0.94**	**98.38**

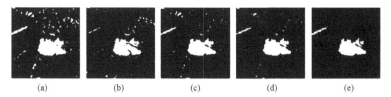

(a)   (b)   (c)   (d)   (e)

Fig. 6. Change detection results for San Francisco data set obtained by different methods. (a) PCA. (b) AE. (c) SpAE. (d) SVAE. (e) Ground truth.

Table 2. Results obtained by different methods on San Francisco data sets.

Method	FN	FP	OE	PCC (%)	KC	AA
PCA	**10**	2906	2916	95.55	0.73	97.5
AE	416	1400	1816	97.22	0.81	94.4
SpAE	68	1061	1129	98.27	0.88	98.4
SVAE	126	**744**	**870**	**98.67**	**0.91**	**98.04**

3.5 Results Comparison with Other Methods on San Francisco Set

The second experiment is carried on the San Francisco data set. The change detection results of different methods are shown in Fig. 6. It can be seen that there are so many isolated white noisy points in Fig. 6(a), which reflects higher FP in Table 2. Moreover, the FP values of AE and SpAE are smaller than that of PCA, this can also be seen from Fig. 6(b) and (c) where exist less white noisy points. Comparing with the other three methods, SVAE can obtain the best result as shown in Fig. 6(d). The FP, OE, PCC and KC values of SVAE in Table 2 are the best.

4 Conclusion

In this paper, SVAE combined with FCM are developed for SAR CD with the aim of studying the representation ability. SVAE can learn a latent variable which obeys Gaussian distribution and to classify it by the following softmax layer. What is more, SVAE can get Gaussian distribution with different parameters from different types of inputs or with approximately the same parameters from the same type of input, the latent variables have obvious differences between different categories. To explore the representation ability of SVAE in SAR CD, image pairs from two original image are fed to SVAE and the learned latent variables are put into a softmax layer. In addition, the training of SVAE are guided by pseudo labels obtained by FCM. Once the SAVE training is done, all image pairs from the two raw image are fed into the learned SVAE, and the final change detection results can be acquired. Experiments on two data set demonstrate that SVAE can obtain discriminative features for CD and outperforms some related approaches.

References

1. Ban, Y., Yousif, O.A.: Multitemporal spaceborne sar data for urban change detection in china. IEEE J. Sel. Top. Appl. Earth Obs. Remote Sens. **5**(4), 1087–1094 (2012)
2. Lv, P., Zhong, Y., Ji, Z., Jiao, H., Zhang, L.: Change detection based on a multifeature probabilistic ensemble conditional random field model for high spatial resolution remote sensing imagery. IEEE Geosci. Remote Sens. Lett. **13**(12), 1965–1969 (2017)
3. Mas, J.F.: Monitoring land-cover changes: a comparison of change detection techniques. Int. J. Remote Sens. **20**(1), 139–152 (1999)
4. Giustarini, L., Hostache, R., Matgen, P., Schumann, J.P., Bates, P.D., Mason, D.C.: A change detection approach to flood mapping in urban areas using TerraSAR-X. IEEE Trans. Geosci. Remote Sens. **51**(4), 2417–2430 (2013)
5. Jie, G., Wang, H., Fan, J., Ma, X.: Change detection of SAR images based on super vised contractive autoencoders and fuzzy clustering. In: International Workshop on Remote Sensing with Intelligent Processing, pp. 1–3. IEEE, Shanghai (2017)
6. Gong, M., Zhao, J., Liu, J., Miao, Q., Jiao, L.: Change detection in synthetic aperture radar images based on deep neural networks. IEEE Trans. Neural Netw. Learn. Syst. **27**(1), 125–138 (2017)
7. Chen, H., Jiao, L., Liang, M., Liu, F., Yang, S., Hou, B.: Fast unsupervised deep fusion network for change detection of multitemporal SAR images. Neurocomputing **332**, 56–70 (2019). https://doi.org/10.1016/j.neucom.2018.11.077
8. Kingma, D.P., Welling, M.: Auto-encoding variational bayes. arXiv.org (2014)
9. Fu, X., Wei, Y., Xu, F., Wang, T., Lu, Y., Li, J., Huang, J.Z.: Semi-supervised aspect-level sentiment classification model based on variational autoencoder. Knowl. Based Syst. **171**, 92 (2019)
10. van der Maaten, L., Hinton, G.: Visualizing data using t-SNE. J. Mach. Learn. Res. **9**(11), 2579–2605 (2008)

A Simple Structure for Building a Robust Model

Xiao Tan[✉], Jingbo Gao, and Ruolin Li

Xidian Hangzhou Institute of Technology, Hangzhou, Zhejiang, China
1203550038@qq.com
https://hz.xidian.edu.cn

Abstract. As deep learning applications, especially programs of computer vision, are increasingly deployed in our lives, we have to think more urgently about the security of these applications. One effective way to improve the security of deep learning models is to perform adversarial training, which allows the model to be compatible with samples that are deliberately created for use in attacking the model. Based on this, we propose a simple architecture to build a model with a certain degree of robustness, which improves the robustness of the trained network by adding an adversarial sample detection network for cooperative training. At the same time, we design a new data sampling strategy that incorporates multiple existing attacks, allowing the model to adapt to many different adversarial attacks with a single training. We conducted some experiments to test the effectiveness of this design based on Cifar10 dataset, and the results indicate that it has some degree of positive effect on the robustness of the model. Our code could be found at https://github.com/dowdyboy/simple_structure_for_robust_model.

Keywords: Robustness · Adversarial training · Deep learning

1 Introduction

Currently, applications using deep learning methods are gradually and widely used in our lives [1]. In many scenarios, deep learning algorithms and models must be secure. However, models trained by general deep learning methods are often very sensitive to the input data. Small changes in the input data can lead to large deviations in the model output, which makes it possible to spoof the model by falsifying data that is indistinguishable to the human eye. Such artificially created samples used to deceive the model are called adversarial samples [2]. To reduce the negative impact of such problems, there are two mainstream approaches, one is adversarial sample detection [3] and the other is training robust models [4].

Supported by AutoDL.

We carefully analyzed the existing methods [5] and found that the two solutions can be used not only in combination at the application level, but also in conjunction with each other at the training stage. Therefore, we propose a simple structure (Fig. 1), which improves the efficiency of robustness training through the intermediate results of adversarial sample detection. We also designed different adversarial sample detection networks and conducted experiments, and found some interesting results (Table 3).

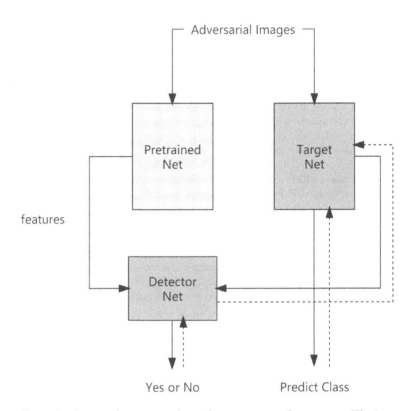

Fig. 1. Pretrained net and target net have the same network structure. The input samples are entered into these two networks separately and the intermediate feature maps of the network outputs are obtained. The two feature maps compute the differences in detector net and provide feedback and fine-tuning to the upstream network.

We tested our designed structure using the Cifar10 dataset [6] and found that our scheme can improve the robustness of the model to some extent compared to the common adversarial training method [4]. Also, because of the new data sampling strategy, the model is able to be more adaptable to more complex testing environments.

2   Related Work

Here, we will discuss those methods that are relevant to our schema and what they bring to our design.

2.1   Adversarial Attacks

Gaussian Noise. The simplest adversarial attack is to add Gaussian noise to the image [7]. These Gaussian noises, because they possess local randomness, can interfere with the pixel value distribution of the image.

FGSM. FGSM was proposed by Goodfellow et al. and is a classical algorithm in the field of adversarial samples [8]. The main reason for the vulnerability of neural networks to adversarial perturbations is their linear nature and, the linear behavior in high-dimensional spaces is sufficient to cause misclassification of samples.

BIM. The BIM algorithm [10] uses an iterative approach to search for perturbations at individual pixel points, rather than modifying all pixel points at once as a whole.

DeepFool. The DeepFool algorithm [11] adds less noise and takes less time to generate samples compared to the FGSM algorithm. It is based on the classification idea of hyperplane and can accurately calculate the perturbation value.

C&W. The C&W algorithm [12] is an optimization-based attack algorithm. It sets a special loss function to measure the difference between the input and the output.

NST. Neural Style Transfer is a way to perform style changes on images [13]. Since the texture of the image is modified during the transformation of the image, it can obviously be applied to generate adversarial samples as well.

2.2   Adversarial Defensive

Currently popular adversarial defense methods include model distillation [14] and adversarial training [4]. Model distillation uses a teacher model to guide the training of the student model, and the teacher model is a pre-trained model. When training is performed, the input data are first entered into the teacher model and the probability distribution of the output is obtained.

Adversarial training is a commonly used method to improve the robustness of models. It is to exploit the powerful expressive power of deep neural networks [15] to improve the robustness of the model by learning adversarial samples.

3   Methods

3.1   Structure Design

Adversarial training is an effective way to resist adversarial samples and improve model robustness. However, due to the large number of adversarial samples added to the training data, this leads to a longer convergence process of the training. Inspired by the design of the auxiliary head [17], our method also adopts a similar design as a way to improve the model convergence speed.

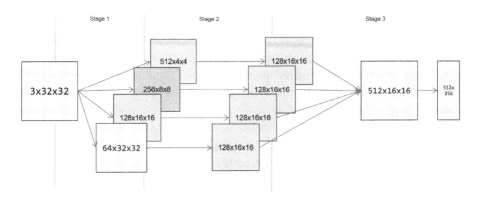

Fig. 2. The adversarial detection network receives the image input and goes through three stages of processing: in the first stage, the data is fed into the backbone network to obtain feature maps of different layers; in the second stage, data embedding is performed, and the feature maps are convolved or deconvoluted and outputted uniformly as feature maps of the same size and number of channels; in the third stage, all the feature maps are stitched and spread into the output that transformer can receive.

We designed a simple shallow Transformer [18] structure as an auxiliary network to perform the adversarial sample detection task. However, unlike a normal network model, its input is not the original data, but a feature map of the output of an intermediate layer of a network that has been pre-trained on a clean dataset. And, inspired by Vision in Transformer [19], we abandon the use of fully connected layers as embedding layers and use convolutional structures as embedding layers instead (Fig. 2). Since our input needs to fuse feature maps from different levels of the pre-trained network as input, we introduce deconvolution in our embedding layer [20]. After experiments, we found that fusing other levels of feature maps with a shallow feature map as the center can have better results.

Because the secondary and primary networks perform different classes of tasks, they cannot simply perform gradient returns and updates separately. For this case, our approach is to capture the output of a specific layer in the auxiliary network and then find the differential performance of the output features of the pre-trained network and the target network on the auxiliary network by using the Smooth L1 function [9] as part of the loss function. The final loss function consists of the categorical cross-entropy error and the L1 error (Eq. 1).

$$loss(X, Y, L) = \sum_{i=1}^{N} \alpha \times CrossEntropyLoss(X_i, L_i) + \beta \times SmoothL1Loss(X_i, Y_i)$$

$$(1)$$

3.2 Sampling Strategy

Classical sampling strategies for adversarial training tend to use a fixed ratio of adversarial samples as input [4], however, this approach may in some cases make the network overfit to the selected adversarial sample data [16]. We designed a more flexible sampling strategy. It uses a dynamic probability with a bounded range to determine the type of adversarial attack to which the sample belongs.

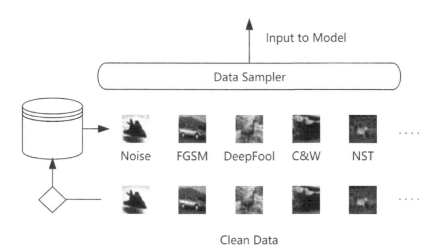

Fig. 3. The clean dataset is programmed in an offline manner to generate adversarial samples of all categories and stored in a database. The sampler samples the database according to the configured dynamic probability range and feeds the selected samples to the model.

In addition, we take the approach of generating adversarial samples offline (Fig. 3). Adversarial samples of all attack types are generated for each sample in the training dataset and stored in the database before starting training.

4   Experiments

For our proposed model architecture, we conducted a series of experiments. All of our experiments were run on a dual-card RTX A4000 mainframe. The experimental results show that our method is able to make the network model more robust compared to ordinary adversarial training (Table 2).

Table 1. Intensity of sample noise under different types of adversarial attacks.

Name:	Gaussian	FGSM	BIM	Deepfool	C&W	NST
Value:	0.1	0.005	0.001	0.1	0.005	0.1

We used the Cifar10 dataset [6] for our experiments. We randomly sampled 45,000 images from the original training set as our training set and the remaining 5,000 images as the test set.We generated datasets with adversarial sample ratios of 0.5, 0.75, and 0.25, the types of adversarial samples contain FGSM, DeepFool, etc., and they use the appropriate noise intensity (Table 1), respectively.

Table 2. Comparison of the prediction results of the ordinary model, the adversarial training model and our method, in terms of accuracy.

Structure	Adv. data ratio	Accuracy
Baseline	0.5	0.6778
Adv train	0.5	0.8464
Adv Train + Detector (ours)	0.5	**0.8688**

We chose ResNet34 [21] as our experimental network, and we modified the network model so that it can output all intermediate feature maps. We first performed training on a clean dataset and general adversarial training, after which we conducted experiments using our method on the same dataset (Table 1), and finally, we conducted some exploratory experiments for different parameter configurations of our method (Table 3). In addition, experiments were conducted on a single adversarial sample test set in order to more fully validate the expressiveness of the model (Table 4). The number of iterations in the training phase for all models is 150 epochs.

With the same adversarial sample ratio, our method has some improvement in accuracy over the general adversarial training (Table 2). Also, our method is more robust to each different type of adversarial attack (Table 4), which indicates that it does not have a significant bias on the performance improvement and is a more general method to improve the robustness of the model.

We also tried to configure different input types, adversarial sample ratios, and the number of self-attentive modules for the detection network (Table 3).

Table 3. Comparison of results on adversarial sample detection and classification for different input types, adversarial sample ratios, and number of self-attentive layers.

Input type	Adv. data ratio	SA layers	Detector accuracy	Classification accuracy
Low	0.5	4	0.734	0.8658
Low	0.75	4	0.8332	0.842
Low	0.75	8	0.8302	0.845
Low	0.5	2	0.735	0.8694
Low	0.75	2	0.8364	0.8416
Full	0.5	4	0.7538	0.8674
Full	0.75	4	0.8458	0.8406
Full	0.75	8	0.8492	0.8446
Full	0.5	2	0.7506	0.8688
Full	0.75	2	0.8536	0.8462

We find that embedding all level feature maps can improve the accuracy of the detection network compared to embedding only low level feature maps, but has no significant effect on the classification accuracy of the images.

Table 4. Prediction results of different structures on different types of adversarial sample datasets.

Structure	Clean	Gaussian	FGSM	BIM	Deepfool	C&W	NST
Baseline	0.9012	0.6616	0.307	0.1748	0.1984	0.1074	0.6236
Adv Train	0.8737	0.8282	0.751	0.7906	0.867	0.7736	0.836
Adv Train + Detector (ours)	**0.8916**	**0.8542**	**0.7834**	**0.8296**	**0.8884**	**0.8066**	**0.8592**

5   Conclusion

As the security and robustness of deep learning models are increasingly emphasized, adversarial attacks may gradually become a necessary factor to be considered for training models. An effective way to deal with adversarial attacks is to train the model adversarially, which enhances the performance and robustness of the model in a hostile environment by strengthening its adaptation to adversarial samples. Our proposed method adds a small adversarial sample detection network to the adversarial training by which some additional features of the data are extracted and used to improve the efficiency and performance of the adversarial training. In addition, we design a new offline data sampling strategy that incorporates a variety of adversarial attack types and has stronger randomness, allowing the trained model to be more adaptable to complex environments while improving the training efficiency to a certain extent.

References

1. Kuutti, S., Bowden, R., Jin, Y., Barber, P., Fallah, S.: A Survey of deep learning applications to autonomous vehicle control. IEEE Trans. Intell. Transp. Syst. **20**, 712–733 (2020)
2. Lust, J., Condurache, A.P.: A survey on assessing the generalization envelope of deep neural networks: predictive uncertainty, out-of-distribution and adversarial samples. arXiv:2008.09381 (2021)
3. Feinman, R., Curtin, R.R., Shintre, S., Gardner, A.B.: Detecting adversarial samples from artifacts. In: ICML (2017)
4. Qian, Z., Huang, K., Wang, Q.-F., Zhang, X.-Y.: A survey of robust adversarial training in pattern recognition: fundamental, theory, and methodologies. arXiv:2203.14046 (2022)
5. Scher, S., Trügler, A.: Robustness of machine learning models beyond adversarial attacks. arXiv:2204.10046 (2022)
6. Krizhevsky, A.: Learning Multiple Layers of Features from Tiny Images (2009)
7. Bogunovic, I., Scarlett, J., Jegelka, S., Cevher, V.: Adversarially robust optimization with Gaussian processes. arXiv:1810.10775 (2018)
8. Goodfellow, I.J., Shlens, J., Szegedy, C.: Explaining and harnessing adversarial examples. arXiv:1412.6572 (2014)
9. Xuan, H., Pless, R.: Dissecting the impact of different loss functions with gradient surgery. arXiv:2201.11307 (2022)
10. Kurakin, A., Goodfellow, I., Bengio, S.: Adversarial examples in the physical world. arXiv:1607.02533 (2016)
11. Moosavi-Dezfooli, S.-M., Fawzi, A., Frossard, P.: A simple and accurate method to fool deep neural networks. In: CVPR, DeepFool (2016)
12. Carlini, N., Wagner, D.: Towards evaluating the robustness of neural networks. IEEE (2017)
13. Li, Y., Wang, N., Liu, J., Hou, X.: Demystifying neural style transfer. In: IJCAI (2017)
14. Sau, B.B., Balasubramanian, V.N.: Deep model compression: distilling knowledge from noisy teachers. arXiv:1610.09650 (2016)
15. Sharir, O., Shashua, A., Carleo, G.: Neural tensor contractions and the expressive power of deep neural quantum states. arXiv:2103.10293 (2021)
16. Zhang, H., Chen, H., Song, Z., Boning, D., Dhillon, I.S., Hsieh, C.-J.: The limitations of adversarial training and the blind-spot attack. In: ICLR (2019)
17. Ye, J., Batra, D., Wijmans, E., Das, A.: Auxiliary tasks speed up learning PointGoal navigation. In: CoRL (2020)
18. Vaswani, A., et al.: Attention is all you need. arXiv:1706.03762 (2017)
19. Dosovitskiy, A., et al.: An image is worth 16×16 words: transformers for image recognition at scale. In: ICLR (2021)
20. Dumoulin, V., Visin, F.: A guide to convolution arithmetic for deep learning. arXiv:1603.07285 (2016)
21. He, K., Zhang, X., Ren, S., Sun, J.: Deep residual learning for image recognition. arXiv:1512.03385 (2015)

Wireless Sensor

An Adaptive Spatial Network for UAV Image Real-Time Semantic Segmentation

Qian Wu$^{(\boxtimes)}$, JiaYu Song , YanBo Luo, Hao Li, Qin Tian , Qi Wang, Jinglong Gao, and Zhuoran Jia

Institute of Information and Navigation, Air Force Engineering University, Xi'an 710038, Shaanxi, China
zhuangzaierhao@163.com

Abstract. Unmanned aerial vehicle (UAV) aerial image interpretation plays an important role in the military and civilian files. The latest semantic segmentation methods are based on deep learning with different structure to encoder spatial feature. However, they are larger networks which are not effective for UAV with limited resources. Thus, a real-time adaptive spatial structure semantic segmentation network, ASRNet, is proposed for UAV aerial image. Firstly, ASRNet is based on an encoder-decoder structure with a module called local structure feature descriptor in the middle. Secondly, the descriptor utilizes features at different abstraction levels from both the encoder and decoder to describe different target with higher spatial resolution adaptively. Lastly, the local structure feature descriptor enables a better gradient flow from deeper layers to shallower layers by adding short paths for the back-propagation. The experiments validate the effectiveness of the proposed method from the accuracy and computation time.

Keywords: UAV aerial image · Real-time semantic segmentation · Encoder-decoder · Adaptive feature descriptor

1 Introduction

With the development of UAV technology, image interpretation on the UAV platform is of increasing importance in the application of urban scene observation, reconnaissance and navigation [1,2]. Semantic segmentation is an essential task for the UAV image interpretation. Recently, the state-of-the-art semantic segmentation methods are based on deep neural network with multi-layer non-linear function, which maps the input image to the semantic label output [3]. Despite these advances of deep learning methods, it remains a challenging task for UAV image.

Supported by the Natural Science Basic Research Plan in ShaanXi Province of China under Grant 2022JQ-0344.

Z. Shi et al. (Eds.): ICIS 2022, IFIP AICT 659, pp. 427–438, 2022.
https://doi.org/10.1007/978-3-031-14903-0_46

Most aerial images obtained by UAV are with oblique views which have a much larger land coverage. The images in oblique view have very large spatial resolution variation across the entire image. As shown in Fig. 1, the semantic segmentation of a small car in the aerial image is better handled in higher resolution where finer details can be observed, such as wheels. For larger objects like roads and buildings, it is better to have more global context with low resolution to recognize the objects since their whole shapes can be observed for semantic segmentation. For the boundary between different objects, such as vegetation and road, the detailed local descriptor with high resolution should be adopted to distinguish different category. When designing the deep neural networks, there is usually a performance trade-off for objects in different scales.

Fig. 1. Example of images with different scales objects, the wheels in red is in small scale, the vegetation in green in large object, the boundary between vegetation and road is in small scale. (Color figure online)

1.1 Related Work

The end-to-end semantic segmentation of deep learning method is introduced by Long [4] with the seminal fully convolutional network (FCN). In order to handle the complex spatial structure with different resolution targets, various network structures have been designed.

1) Context-based models: To capture the contextual information at multiple scales, DeepLabV2 [6] and DeeplabV3 [7]] exploit multiple parallelatrous convolutions with different dilation rates, while PSPNet [9] performs multi-scale spatial pooling operations. Although these methods encode rich contextual information, they can not capture boundary details effectively due to strided convolution or pooling operations [8].

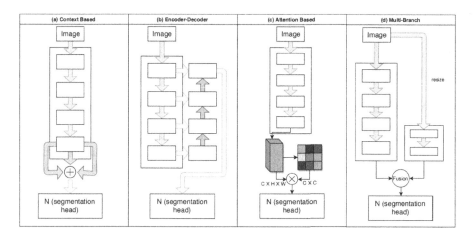

Fig. 2. Illustration of different semantic segmentation methods [20].

2) Encoder-decoder structure: Encoder extracts global contextual information and decoder recovers the spatial information. To meet the real-time requirements of CNN tasks in mobile devices, a lightweight network is proposed, named LEDNet, which adopts asymmetric encoder-decoder architecture. Encoder Network is a network similar to FCN, and the decoder is an attention pyramid [5]. Sun et al. augments the high-resolution representation by aggregating the (up-sampled) representations from all the parallel convolutions rather than only the representation from the high-resolution convolution [19]. However, implementation of dilated convolution at higher dilation rates is computationally intensive making them unsuitable for real-time applications.

3) Attention-based models: Attention mechanisms, which help networks to focus on relevant information and ignore the irrelevant information. Wang et al. [13] formalized self-attention by calculating the correlation matrix between each spatial point in the feature maps in video sequences. To capture contextual information, LEDnet [5], DaNet [12] and OCNet [14] apply a self-attention mechanism. PSANet [15] learns to aggregate contextual information for each individual position via a predicted attention map. Attention models, however, generally require expensive computation cost.

4) Multi-Branch models: The deeper branches extract the contextual information by enlarging receptive fields or shallower branches retain the spatial structure, which makes them suitable for run time efficient implementations [16,17]. However, they are mostly applicable to the relatively simpler datasets with fewer number of classes. On the other end, HRNet [18] proposed a model with fully connected links between output maps of different resolutions. However, without reduction of spatial dimensions of features, the computational overhead is very high and makes the model no longer feasible for real-time usage (Fig. 2).

Building on these observations, we propose a real-time general purpose semantic segmentation architecture that obtains deep features with high resolution resulting in improved accuracy and lower latency in a single branch encoder-decoder network.

1.2 Motivation

Semantic segmentation, which associates each pixel to the object class it belongs to, is a computationally expensive task in computer vision. Fast semantic segmentation is broadly applied to several real-time applications including autonomous driving, medical imaging and robotics. However, accurate CNN-based semantic segmentation requires larger neural networks which are therefore not suitable for UAV as they are cumbersome and require substantial resources.

Down-sampling operations, such as pooling and convolutions with stride greater than one, can help decrease the latency of deeper neural networks, however they result in decreased pixel-level accuracy due to the lower resolutions at deeper levels. Many recent approaches employ either encoder-decoder structure, a two or multi-branch architecture or dilated convolutions to recover spatial information. While these real-time architectures perform appropriately on simple datasets, their performance is sub-optimal for complex datasets possessing more variability in terms of classes, sizes, and shapes.

Thus, there is a significant interest in designing CNN architectures that can perform well on UAV datasets and, at the same time, are mobile enough to be of practical use in real-time applications of UAV aerial images.

1.3 Contributions

In this paper, A real-time adaptive spatial structure semantic segmentation network, ASRNet, is proposed that performs well on complex scenarios. ASRNet is based on an asymmetric encoder-decoder structure with a new module called local feature descriptor in the middle. The descriptor utilizes features at different abstraction levels from both the encoder and decoder to improve the feature refinement at a given level allowing the network to preserve deeper level features with higher spatial resolution. Furthermore, the descriptor enables a better gradient flow from deeper layers to shallower layers by adding short paths for the back-propagation. Since training an average deep learning model has a considerable carbon footprint, we reduce the training time by 60% with negligible effect on performance by applying progressive resizing for training.

The contributions are summarized as follows: We propose ASRNet as a real-time semantic segmentation architecture that obtains deep features with high resolution resulting in improved accuracy and lower latency in a single branch network. It performs competitively in complex environments. We introduce an adaptive local descriptor module to capture multiple levels of abstraction to help in boundary refinement of segments. Besides, progressive resizing technique is adopted during the training which leads to 60% reduction in training time and the environmental impact. We combat aliasing effect in label map on lower resolutions by employing a modified label relaxation.

The remainder of the paper is organized as following. In Sect. 2, the proposed adaptive spatial network for real-time semantic segmentation (ASRNet) is shown in detail. The analysis of parameters and the experimental results on one UAV image are described in Sect. 3 to validate the real-time and effectiveness. In the end, the conclusions and future work are drawn in Sect. 4.

2   Proposed Approach

ASRNet is based on a light-weight encoder-decoder structure for fast and efficient inference. It comprises of three components: an encoder which extracts high-level semantic features, a light asymmetric decoder, and an local feature descriptor which links different stages of encoder and decoder. The encoder decreases the resolution and increases the number of feature maps. The decoder reconstructs the lost spatial information. The local feature descriptor combines the information to preserve and refine the information between multiple levels.

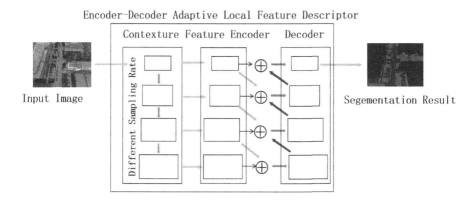

Fig. 3. Framework of the proposed ASRnet with the local feature descriptor "Encoder" and label relaxation: "Decoder".

2.1   Structure of ASRnet

ASRnet architecture is illustrated in Fig. 3. All the tensors have the same spatial resolution with the number of channels in the same row. Four level outputs are extracted from the encoder at different spatial resolutions $\frac{1}{4}$, $\frac{1}{8}$, $\frac{1}{16}$ and $\frac{1}{32}$ with 256, 512, 1024 and 2048 channels, respectively. The number of channels are reduced by a factor of four using 1×1 convolutions followed by batch norm and ReLU activation function at each level. These outputs are then passed through a decoder structure with descriptor in the middle. Finally, segmentation output is extracted from the largest resolution via 1×1 convolution to match the number of channels to segmentation categories. The object function of the three levels is as below:

$$x_s^a = D(T(x_{s-1}^a)) + T(x_s^e) + U(x_{s+1}^d) \tag{1}$$

where a, e, and d denote descriptor, encoder, and decoder respectively. Besides, s represents the spatial level in the semantic segmentation network. $D(\cdot)$ and $U(\cdot)$ are down-sampling and up-sampling functions. Down-sampling is carried out by convolution with stride 2 and up-sampling is carried out by de-convolution with stride 2 matching spatial resolution as well as the number of channels in the current level. $T(\cdot)$ is a transfer function that reduces the number of output channels from an encoder block and transfers them to the descriptor:

$$T(x_s^e) = \sigma(w_s^a \otimes x_s^e + b_s^a) \tag{2}$$

where w and b are the weight matrix and bias vector, $\otimes$ denotes the convolution operation, and σ is the activation function. The decoder contains a modified basic residual block, F, where we use shared weights within the block. The decoder function is as follows:

$$x_s^d = F(x_s^m; \omega_s^d) \tag{3}$$

2.2   Adaptive Local Feature Descriptor

Stepwise resizing is a commonly used technique to reduce training time for classification. The image size is small at the beginning of the training, and then gradually increased until the final stage of the training using the original image size. However, applying progressive resizing in semantic segmentation is more challenging because it needs to be applied to the image and its corresponding label mapping. Bilinear or bicubic interpolation cannot be applied to label maps because they exist in integer space, and these methods will result in floating point values for tags. Besides, nearest neighbor interpolation for resizing introduces noise into label maps near object boundaries due to aliasing. Thus, Inspired by Zhu et al. [9], an optimized variant of the label relaxation method named local feature descriptor is proposed, as shown in Fig. 4, in order to reduce the influence of boundary artifacts in the gradual adjustment of the label map adaptively.

In the cross entropy loss function, the negative logarithmic likelihood of soft-maximum probability is used for a given label. In contrast, label relaxation is a loss function where the negative logarithmic likelihood of soft-maximum probability for a given label as well as for adjacent pixel labels is maximized. This is established by taking the sum of the soft maximum probabilities mentioned earlier before applying negative log likelihood. We identify boundary pixels as those with multiple unique labels in the window centered around the kernel size K. The loss at a given boundary pixel is calculated as follows, where N is the boundary label set:

$$\mathcal{L} = -\log \sum_{C \in N} P(C) \tag{4}$$

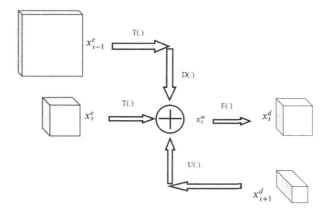

Fig. 4. Illustration of the local feature descriptor.

To apply label relaxation effectively, a hot label from the label map is created, followed by a max-pooling operation with Stride 1. This will effectively expand each single hot label channel and transform it into multi-hot labels along the boundary, thus realizing optimal selection of boundary pixels and their corresponding labels. Border pixels are usually in the minority. The loss function applies only to boundary pixels, and the normal cross entropy loss applies to the remaining pixels.

3   Experiments

The experiments are conducted on Urban Drone Dataset (UDD) [21] as the complex dataset. UDD are collected at Peking University, Huludao city, Henan University and Cangzhou city, which includes six categories: Vegetation, Building, Road, Vehicle, Roof and Other. All the results are with the average of 5 experiments.

The ASRnet are implemented based on PyTorch framework [22]. For training, a polynomial learning rate policy is employed where the initial learning rate is multiplied by $(1 - iter/totaliter)^{0.9}$ after each iteration. The learning rate is set to 1×10^{-3}. Momentum and weight decay coefficients are set to 0.9 and 1×10^{-4}, respectively.

The performance evaluation indexes used in this part are the ratio of pixels correctly classified named pixel accuracy (PA), the mean of PA named mean pixel accuracy (MPA) and the mean intersection over union (mIOU). These three indexes are computed with the following equations:

$$PA = \sum_{i=0}^{k} \frac{p_{ii}}{\sum} \sum_{i=0}^{k} \sum_{j=0}^{k} p_{ij} \tag{5}$$

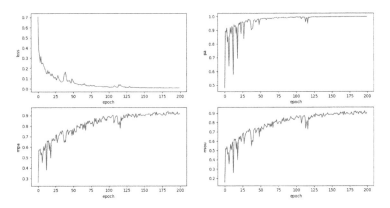

Fig. 5. Indexes of segmentation results of methods ASRnet, LEDnet, Segnet, Unet and DeeplabV3.

$$MPA = \frac{1}{k+1} \sum_{i=0}^{k} \frac{p_{ii}}{\sum_{i=0}^{k}} \sum_{j=0}^{k} p_{ij} \tag{6}$$

$$mIOU = \frac{1}{k+1} \sum_{i=0}^{k} \frac{p_{ii}}{\sum_{j=0}^{k} p_{ij} + \sum_{j=0}^{k} p_{ji} - p_{ii}} \tag{7}$$

First of all, the convergence of the algorithm is evaluated on the dataset UDD as shown in Fig. 5, four curves corresponding to the loss and three performance indexes are given. It can be seen that the loss is decreasing with each iteration, while the three performance indexes of PA MPA and mIOU are increasing with each iteration. The general trend shows that the proposed ASRnet can converge in a much faster time.

Two real-time semantic segmentation methods LEDnet [5], Unet [10] and two non real-time methods Segnet [19], DeeplabV3 [11] are compared with the proposed method to validate the effectiveness from the perspective of accuracy and time. These two methods are both based on encoder-decoder structure with different local feature descriptor. The segmentation result images are given in Fig. 6 for the compared methods. From the visual results in Fig. 7, it can be seen some pixels of road are classified wrongly which results from the illumination intensity in the first image. Because the detail local feature descriptor, the narrow road can be segmented from the background which can not be realized by the compared methods. Besides, in the last image there are great differences in shape and size of different object. ASRnet can segment the small cars more accurate than the compared methods due to the adapt local feature descriptor.

From the segmentation index values given in Fig. 7 with PA, MPA and mIOU of the compared methods. The index PA and mIOU of the proposed ASRnet is the best among the compared methods, higher almost 5% to 15%, as for the adaptive descriptor of local feature. A detailed descriptor is adopted for the boundary to improve the segmentation result with complex texture. While a larger local feature descriptor is adopted for the smooth region to reduce

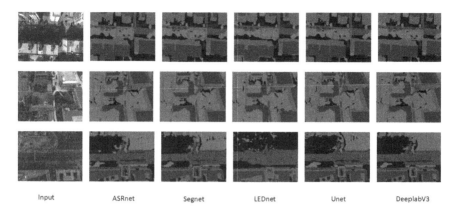

| Input | ASRnet | Segnet | LEDnet | Unet | DeeplabV3 |

Fig. 6. Segmentation results on data set UDD with different methods including: (a) is the aerial image of UAV; (b)–(f) are the segmentation results with methods ASRnet, LEDnet, Segnet, Unet and DeeplabV3, respectively.

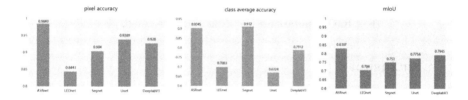

Fig. 7. Indexes of segmentation results of methods ASRnet, LEDnet, Segnet, Unet and DeeplabV3.

the computation complexity. Thus, it results into the improvement of overall accuracy value. Besides, the MPA value of the proposed method is similar to the best one of Segnet which results from the much more computation time.

As for the computation time, the results of the five compared methods are given in Fig. 8. It can be seen the time of real-time methods ASRnet, LEDnet and DeeplabV3 all are 3 times less than that of Segnet. Although the computation time of LEDnet is less than the proposed method, the segmentation accuracy value shown in Fig. 8 of LEDnet is much less than Segnet and ASRnet.

Therefore, by comparing the semantic segmentation networks designed for specific datasets, ASRnet is a real-time semantic segmentation model that performs competitively both on semantic segmentation results and computation time.

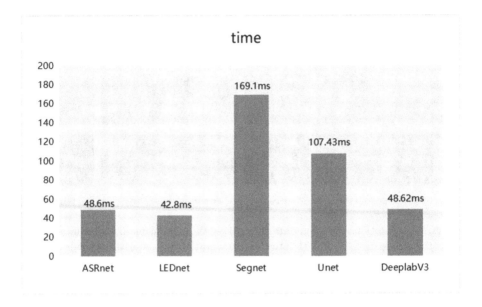

Fig. 8. Computation time of the compared methods.

4   Conclusion

In this paper, an adaptive spatial structure learning network is proposed for UAV aerial image semantic segmentation. It incorporates a local feature descriptor that aggregates features from different abstraction levels and coordinates with encoder-decoder framework. This model is conceptually simple yet effective to achieve efficient inference speed and accuracy on resource constrained devices UAV in complex environment. By employing an optimized progressive resizing training scheme, the training time on dataset UDD is less 3 times than the state-of-the-art non real-time method. Overall, the proposed ASRnet can generate semantic segmentation results in real-time and comparable accuracy. This optimal balance of speed and accuracy makes our model suitable for real-time applications of UAV aerial images where the environment is highly dynamic due to the presence of high variability in real world scenarios.

Acknowledgements. Thanks the open datasets UDD of UAV to validate the proposed semantic segmentation method.

References

1. Demir, I., Koperski, K., Lindenbaum, D., et al.: DeepGlobe 2018: A Challenge to Parse the Earth through Satellite Images. IEEE (2018). Author, F.: Article title. Journal **2**(5), 99–110 (2016)
2. Ivancsits, C., Lee, M.: Visual navigation system for small unmanned aerial vehicles. Sens. Rev. **33**(3), 267–291 (2013)

3. Ye, L., Vosselman, G., Xia, G.S., et al.: Bidirectional multi-scale attention networks for semantic segmentation of oblique UAV imagery (2021)
4. Long, J., Shelhamer, E., Darrell, T.: Fully convolutional networks for semantic segmentation. In: Proceedings of the IEEE Conference on Computer Vision and Pattern Recognition, pp. 3431–3440 (2015)
5. Wang, Y., Zhou, Q., Liu, J., et al.: Lednet: a lightweight encoder-decoder network for real-time semantic segmentation. In: IEEE International Conference on Image Processing, 25–28 Oct 2020
6. Chen, L.C., Papandreou, G., Kokkinos, I., et al.: Semantic image segmentation with deep convolutional nets and fully connected CRFs. Comput. Sci. **4**, 357–361 (2014)
7. Chen, L.C., Papandreou, G., Kokkinos, I., et al.: DeepLab: semantic image segmentation with deep convolutional nets, atrous convolution, and fully connected CRFs. IEEE Trans. Pattern Anal. Mach. Intell. **40**(4), 834–848 (2018)
8. Chen, L.-C., Zhu, Y., Papandreou, G., Schroff, F., Adam, H.: Encoder-decoder with atrous separable convolution for semantic image segmentation. In: Ferrari, V., Hebert, M., Sminchisescu, C., Weiss, Y. (eds.) ECCV 2018. LNCS, vol. 11211, pp. 833–851. Springer, Cham (2018). https://doi.org/10.1007/978-3-030-01234-2_49
9. Zhu, Y., Sapra, K., Reda, F.A., et al.: Improving semantic segmentation via video propagation and label relaxation (2018)
10. Ronneberger, O., Fischer, P., Brox, T.: U-Net: convolutional networks for biomedical image segmentation. In: Navab, N., Hornegger, J., Wells, W.M., Frangi, A.F. (eds.) MICCAI 2015. LNCS, vol. 9351, pp. 234–241. Springer, Cham (2015). https://doi.org/10.1007/978-3-319-24574-4_28
11. Chen, L.-C., Papandreou, G., Kokkinos, I., Murphy, K., Yuille, A.L.: Deeplab: semantic image segmentation with deep convolutional nets, atrous convolution, and fully connected CRFS. IEEE Trans. Pattern Anal. Mach. Intell. **40**(4), 834–848 (2017)
12. Fu, J., Liu, J., Wang, Y., et al.: Stacked deconvolutional network for semantic segmentation. IEEE Trans. Image Process. (2019)
13. Wang, X., Girshick, R., Gupta, A., et al.: Non-local neural networks. In: Proceedings of the IEEE Conference on Computer Vision and Pattern Recognition, pp. 7794–7803 (2018)
14. Yuan, Y., Huang, L., Guo, J., et al.: OCNet: object context for semantic segmentation. Int. J. Comput. Vis. 1–24 (2021)
15. Zhao, H., Zhang, Y., Liu, S., et al.: Psanet: point-wise spatial attention network for scene parsing. In: Proceedings of the European Conference on Computer Vision (ECCV), pp. 267–283 (2018)
16. Yu, C., Wang, J., Peng, C., Gao, C., Yu, G., Sang, N.: BiSeNet: bilateral segmentation network for real-time semantic segmentation. In: Ferrari, V., Hebert, M., Sminchisescu, C., Weiss, Y. (eds.) ECCV 2018. LNCS, vol. 11217, pp. 334–349. Springer, Cham (2018). https://doi.org/10.1007/978-3-030-01261-8_20
17. Zhao, H., Qi, X., Shen, X., et al.: ICNET for real-time semantic segmentation on high-resolution images. In: Proceedings of the European Conference on Computer Vision (ECCV), pp. 405–420 (2018)
18. Sun, K., Zhao, Y., Jiang, B., et al.: High-resolution representations for labeling pixels and regions (2019)
19. Badrinarayanan, V., Kendall, A., Cipolla, R.: Segnet: a deep convolutional encoder-decoder architecture for image segmentation. IEEE Trans. Pattern Anal. Mach. Intell. **39**(12), 2481–2495 (2017)

20. Arani, E., Marzban, S., Pata, A., et al.: RGPNet: a real-time general purpose semantic segmentation (2019)
21. Chen, Y., Wang, Y., Lu, P., Chen, Y., Wang, G.: Large-scale structure from motion with semantic constraints of aerial images. In: Lai, J.-H., et al. (eds.) PRCV 2018. LNCS, vol. 11256, pp. 347–359. Springer, Cham (2018). https://doi.org/10.1007/978-3-030-03398-9_30
22. Paszke, A., Gross, S., Chintala, S., et al.: Automatic differentiation in PyTorch. In: Conference and Workshop on Neural Information Processing Systems (NeurIPS) Workshop (2017)

Medical Artificial Intelligence

Knowledge Learning Without Forgetting for the Detection of Alzheimer's Disease

Ruotong Liu[1], Yue Yin[2], Jing Bai[1(✉)] [ID], and Xu Wang[1]

[1] Xidian University, Xi'an 710071, China
{rtliu1004,xuwangxd}@stu.xidian.edu.cn, baijing@mail.xidian.edu.cn
[2] The First Affiliated Hospital of Air Force Medical University, Xi'an 710071, China

Abstract. Alzheimer's disease (AD) is an extremely damaging, slow-progressing neurological disease that causes tremendous inconvenience to patients' lives. Numerous medical professionals have researched that timely diagnosis and early therapy of AD when it is in its early stages could slow down the progression of AD and even be cured. Therefore, early diagnosis of AD is in urgent need of significant advancement. Nevertheless, there are problems such as brain images with many similar features that are difficult to extract and classify, and insufficient data for training. In this paper, a transfer learning-based knowledge learning without forgetting method we proposed for AD detection, which can preserve the learned knowledge during the transfer process so that it will not be excessively forgotten and this method achieve promising outcomes. The classification accuracy of our method based on resnet50 and resnet18 on the ADNI dataset reached 96.15% and 96.39%, compared to training directly on resnet50 and resnet18, our method increased the classification accuracy by 2.16% and 3.61%, which achieved remarkable results and contributes greatly to the development of AD detection.

Keywords: Alzheimer's disease · Transfer learning · Convolutional neural network (CNN) · MRI · ADNI

1 Introduction

Alzheimer's disease (AD) is a slowly developing, irreversible neurological disease with unknown causes. It affects mainly the aged population. The symptoms of AD usually include memory impairment, executive dysfunction, and impaired cognitive behavior, etc. This disease dramatically influences the patient's normal life. A large number of medical researchers have found that there are three primary

This work was supported in part by the Key Research and Development Program of Shaanxi under Grant 2022GY-062, in part by the National Natural Science Foundation of China under Grant 61772401, and in part by the Science and Technology on Communication Information Security Control Laboratory. (R. Liu and Y. Yin — Contributed equally to this work.).

categories of the early AD: late mild cognitive impairment (LMCI), early mild cognitive impairment (EMCI) and subject memory concern (SMC) [1]. Therefore, how to efficiently and accurately detect AD disease has become a crucial challenge to be overcome. Currently, numerous scientists are trying to explore new features that may emerge in brain regions during the early stages of AD.

With the continuous development of artificial intelligence, deep learning has made significant achievements in the field of computer vision [2]. Accordingly, in recent years, an increasing number of researchers have attempted to use deep learning with its powerful feature extraction ability on the detection of AD [3–7].

However, the acquisition and collation of medical images is labor-intensive and time-consuming, therefore, inadequate data for training for training has become a problem which should be seriously concerned. On the basis of this problem, in particularly, transfer learning [8,9] have been widely utilized for AD detection. In further, [10,11] made enhancements to the fine-tuning department and achieved good results in image classification.

In this paper, we propose a knowledge learning without forgetting method that keeps as much of the knowledge learned in the pre-trained network as possible and ensures that knowledge would not inordinately be dissipated during the transfer learning. We are inspired by [10,11] and chiefly use transfer learning based on its promising performance in AD detection and cleverly integrate multiple losses which includes distillation loss, cross-entropy loss, and improved contrast loss used exclusively for self-supervision. We select Resnet as the pre-training network, use the Alzheimer's Dataset as the source domain, the classification results are obtained by training on the source domain with the pretrained network and then importing our target domain ADNI to the network with fine-tuned weights. We obtained 96.39% classification accuracy on ADNI for AD, MCI and NC. The improved transfer learning we proposed could perform well in the AD detection and greatly contribute to the early detection of AD.

2 Method

2.1 Transfer Learning for AD Detection

Our improved transfer learning method mainly contains two stages: In the first stage we take the Alzheimer's Dataset as the source domain and use Resnet as our backbone for pre-training. Second stage, we initialize the weights and reset the fc layer, then fine-tune the weights and apply them to the target domain ADNI for training to effectively classify the categories AD, MCI, and NC on MRI images. Two stages of transfer learning is shown in Fig. 1.

On the classification mission of the target domain ADNI dataset, we mainly categorize into one primary task and two auxiliary tasks. We input the target domain ADNI data into the network that has been pre-trained in the source domain, and the principal task is to fine-tune the pre-trained network to get the normal three-class output, doing cross-entropy loss and contrast cross-entropy loss with the normal labels. The four-class output obtained by the primary task

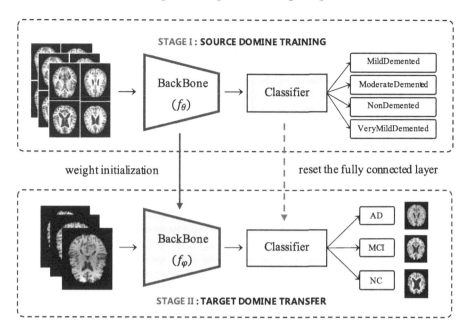

Fig. 1. Two stages of transfer learning for AD detection

then does distillation loss with the four-class source domain output of the auxiliary task 1. Additionally, another branch of the main task takes the classification results into a projection head and processes them for output, doing improved classification contrast loss with the projection head output in auxiliary task 2. The overview of knowledge learning without forgetting is shown in Fig. 2.

Based on this transfer learning architecture, we skillfully combine distillation loss, cross-entropy loss, and improved contrast loss to achieve preservation of learned knowledge from over forgetting, realize knowledge learning without forgetting.

2.2 Knowledge Learning without Forgetting

In the auxiliary task 1, the distillation loss is used to ensure that the response of the new data ADNI on the new model retains as much of the response of the old model as possible. First, the target domain ADNI is fed into the pretrained network, to extract its response at the last layer of the old model, which is the confidence $y^{'}$ of the new class of data over the old class. Afterwards, the new model is trained with transfer learning, which sets the classifier with the correct number of categories for the new class while introducing a new branch to generate the response with the new model on the classification by the old class. The distance class between $y^{'}$ and $y^{''}$ is measured with relative entropy, also known as KL loss, the formula is as follows:

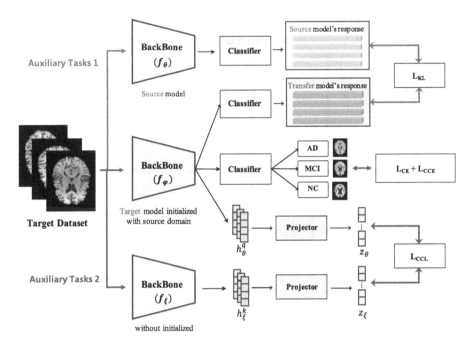

Fig. 2. Knowledge learning without forgetting method overview

$$L_{KL} = -\sum_{i=1}^{k} y'^{(i)} log y''^{(j)} \tag{1}$$

KL loss ensures that the knowledge already learned will not be easily lost after fine-tuning. It keeps the majority of information learned from the old model.

2.3   Transfer Based on Improved Contrastive Loss

Based on the utilization of the source domain network, we consider the optimal exploitation of the intrinsic structure of the target domain data, ADNI. Inspired by self-supervised learning that uses unlabeled samples for pre-training, we construct the internal structure between the target domain ADNI data by adopting a contrast learning approach. The loss of contrastive learning L_{self} is expressed as:

$$L_{self} = -log \frac{exp(q \cdot s_+/\tau)}{\sum_{i=0}^{K} exp(q \cdot s_i/\tau)} \tag{2}$$

q means the query sample, the positive key s_+ is the data-augmented positive sample, and s_i is the negative sample, and the contrast loss is to obtain the maximum value of similarity between the query q and the corresponding positive key s_+.

Based on this contrast learning approach, the improved contrastive loss are utilized in the main task and auxiliary task 2 separately. It contains contrastive cross-entropy loss L_{CCE} and improved classification contrast loss L_{CCL}.

In the main task, the target domain ADNI is entered into the fine-tuned network to obtain the classification results, which are applied to the corresponding labels with normal cross-entropy loss L_{CE} and contrast cross-entropy loss L_{CCE}.

We search for the most similar prediction to the ground truth of each instance by using the contrastive cross-entropy loss L_{CCE}. It permits better utilization of instance comparisons to exploit label information. It allows better use of the formula is as shown below:

$$L_{CCE} = -\sum_{i=1}^{N}\sum_{k=0}^{K} \amalg(h_k^k \in S_i)log\frac{exp(c_{y_i} \cdot h_i^q/\tau)}{\sum_{j=0}^{K}exp(c_{y_i} \cdot h_j^k/\tau)} \tag{3}$$

K is the candidate keys' size, h_k^k denotes samples generated by the key generating mechanism from the hidden key pool, S_i denotes the set of positive keys for example i, h_i^q denotes the features extracted by the neural network, c_{y_i} denotes the prediction result of the classifier.

In the auxiliary task 2, the strategy we used in consonance with the self-supervised approach is to export the target domain ADNI to the old model for extracting features, and input the extracted features to a projector, this projector maps the pre-trained representation h_i^q to the embedding space z_i^q. However, the implicit requirement of contrastive loss that each instance belongs to a separate class is not suitable for supervised classification tasks. Therefore, we use an improved classification contrast loss L_{CCL}, which takes other samples from the identical category to use as positive keys for query matching.

Like the format of L_{self}, the improved classification contrast loss L_{CCL} formula is as follows:

$$L_{CCL} = -\sum_{i=1}^{N}\sum_{k=0}^{K} \amalg(z_k^k \in S_i)log\frac{exp(z_i^q \cdot z_k^k/\tau)}{\sum_{j=0}^{K}exp(z_i^q \cdot z_j^k/\tau)} \tag{4}$$

The improved contrast learning loss allows for the full utilization of the inner structure of the learned knowledge in a category-consistent manner.

Consequently, our knowledge learning without forgetting method based on transfer learning can be expressed as:

$$L = L_{CE} + \alpha L_{KL} + \beta(L_{CCE} + L_{CCL}) \tag{5}$$

where α, β are hyperparameters, the value range of α, β are set to 0–1.

3   Experiments

3.1   Datasets

ADNI. This dataset is a publicly available dataset used specifically for the AD detection experiments. It mainly consists of three categories: AD, MCI and NC. In our experiments, the ADNI dataset is utilized as the target domain in transfer learning. The three classes of AD, MCI, and NC images in ADNI are shown in Fig. 3:

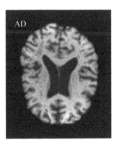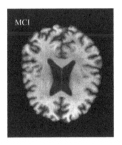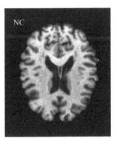

Fig. 3. The three classes of AD, MCI, and NC image in ADNI

Alzheimer's Dataset. This dataset is used exclusively in the Kaggle competition. It contains four classes of AD images: mild demented, moderate demented, non demented, very mild demented. In our experiments, this dataset is used as the source domain in transfer learning. The four classes images in Alzheimer's Dataset are shown in Fig. 4:

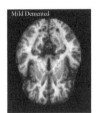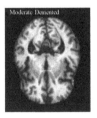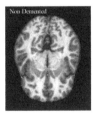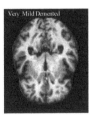

Fig. 4. The four classes images in Alzheimer's Dataset

In our experiment, we first process 3D MRI images into 2D slices before sending the data to the network for training. This pre-processed dataset procedure to some extent could solve the problem of insufficient medical images for training. Then we pre-train the weights in Resnet by using Alzheimer's Dataset, and after fine-tuning the weights, the ADNI is fed into the pre-training network for training to obtain the classification results.

3.2   Experimental Setting

In our experiments, we use the optimizer is SGD, the learning rate is set to 0.001, and we set the batch size to 32. The operating environment for our experiments is mainly as follows: Ubuntu 18.04, GPU 3090, CUDA 11.0, torch 1.7.1+, torchvision 0.8.2+, numpy 1.21.6, and python 3.8.

3.3   Experimental Results

We apply Alzheimer's Dataset as source domain for training, the ratio of the divided training set to the test set is 4:1. And we use ADNI as target domain for training, the ratio of the divided training set to the test set is 4:1, either. In the experiment, we found that by setting the learning rate to 0.001, the loss started to decay to 0.8 times of the original per 10 epochs. The classification accuracy on ADNI is shown in Table 1.

Table 1. Accuracy of classification on ADNI

Backbone	Method	25%	50%	75%	100%
Resnet50	train	65.69%	84.89%	91.71%	93.99%
	train_tsfr	67.37%	86.29%	93.29%	94.38%
	train_lwf	71.08%	87.39%	94.12%	95.08%
	train_con	72.53%	87.63%	94.71%	95.45%
	ours	**72.61%**	**87.76%**	**94.36%**	**96.15%**
Resnet18	train	65.23%	82.12%	90.75%	92.78%
	train_tsfr	66.91%	84.11%	91.47%	94.71%
	train_lwf	64.99%	85.48%	91.84%	94.95%
	train_con	66.30%	86.58%	92.46%	95.08%
	ours	**67.72%**	**87.06%**	**92.56%**	**96.39%**

In Table 1, 100%, 75%, 50%, 25% indicate the percentage of the data excluding the test data, train means direct training, train_tsfr means using transfer learning, train_lwf means using transfer learning with unforgetting loss, train_con means using transfer learning with improved contrast loss, ours means our method.

Our method enables to achieve 96.39% accuracy of classification on ADNI. In particular, the accuracy can be enhanced by 7% when only 25% of the data is used. The accuracy of classification results indicate that transfer training can lead to a significant improvement over direct training. And both transfer learning optimization strategies can bring increases compared to direct transfer learning.

In addition, the best accuracy results demonstrate the advanced and efficient performance of the better method we proposed to tranfer learning, and achieve a great integration of the two mentioned strategies.

4   Conclusion

In this paper, a transfer learning-based knowledge learning without forgetting method we proposed for the detection of AD, which could ensure that the knowledge acquired during pre-training is well maintained and does would not be excessively dissipated during the transfer process. Our substantial experimental results demonstrate that the method we proposed can work effectively in the detection of AD, with an accuracy of 96.15% and 96.39% in the classification of AD, MCI and NC on the ADNI dataset based on resnet50 and resnet18, compared to training directly on resnet50 and resnet18, our method increased the classification accuracy by 2.16% and 3.61%, and it enables to solve the problem of insufficient training data for AD detection.

In forthcoming studies, we intend to pursue our attempts to explore innovative methods on self-supervised learning to achieve greater performance that could be valuable for AD detection.

References

1. Kruthika, K., Maheshappa, H., Initiative, A.D.N., et al.: Multistage classifier-based approach for Alzheimer's disease prediction and retrieval. Inf. Med. Unlocked **14**, 34–42 (2019)
2. Yang, K., Mohammed, E.A.: A review of artificial intelligence technologies for early prediction of Alzheimer's disease. arXiv preprint arXiv:2101.01781 (2020)
3. Sarraf, S., Tofighi, G.: Classification of alzheimer's disease using FMRI data and deep learning convolutional neural networks. arXiv preprint arXiv:1603.08631 (2016)
4. Amin-Naji, M., Mahdavinataj, H., Aghagolzadeh, A.: Alzheimer's disease diagnosis from structural MRI using Siamese convolutional neural network. In: 2019 4th International Conference on Pattern Recognition and Image Analysis (IPRIA), pp. 75–79. IEEE (2019)
5. Fulton, L.V., Dolezel, D., Harrop, J., Yan, Y., Fulton, C.P.: Classification of Alzheimer's disease with and without imagery using gradient boosted machines and Resnet-50. Brain Sci. **9**(9), 212 (2019)
6. Liu, S., Yadav, C., Fernandez-Granda, C., Razavian, N.: On the design of convolutional neural networks for automatic detection of Alzheimer's disease. In: Machine Learning for Health Workshop, pp. 184–201. PMLR (2020)
7. Fedorov, A., et al.: On self-supervised multimodal representation learning: an application to Alzheimer's disease. In: 2021 IEEE 18th International Symposium on Biomedical Imaging (ISBI), pp. 1548–1552. IEEE (2021)
8. Ebrahimi, A., Luo, S., Chiong, R.: Introducing transfer learning to 3d Resnet-18 for Alzheimer's disease detection on MRI images. In: 2020 35th International Conference on Image and Vision Computing New Zealand (IVCNZ), pp. 1–6. IEEE (2020)
9. Shanmugam, J.V., Duraisamy, B., Simon, B.C., Bhaskaran, P.: Alzheimer's disease classification using pre-trained deep networks. Biomed. Signal Process. Control **71**, 103217 (2022)

10. Li, Z., Hoiem, D.: Learning without forgetting. IEEE Trans. Pattern Anal. Mach. Intell. **40**(12), 2935–2947 (2017)
11. Zhong, J., Wang, X., Kou, Z., Wang, J., Long, M.: Bi-tuning of pre-trained representations. arXiv preprint arXiv:2011.06182 (2020)

CA-ConvNext: Coordinate Attention on ConvNext for Early Alzheimer's Disease Classification

Weikang Jin[1], Yue Yin[2], Jing Bai[1(✉)](ID), and Haowei Zhen[1]

[1] Xidian University, Xi'an 710071, China
{weikang-jin,20061212353}@stu.xidian.cn, baijing@mail.xidian.edu.cn
[2] The First Affiliated Hospital of Air Force Medical University, Xi'an 710071, China

Abstract. Early diagnosis of Alzheimer's disease allows patients to receive early and effective treatment as a way to increase their chances of survival. We propose CA-ConvNeXt for Early Alzheimer's disease classification to solve the common MCI, AD, and NC classification problems. We employ the latest ConvNeXt network, which has a simpler topology and greater performance than ResNet and Swin Transformer. We effectively increase the model performance and reach 96% accuracy on the public ADNI dataset by adding Coordinate Attention to the ConvNeXt network.

Keywords: Early Alzheimer's disease · Coordinate attention · ConvNeXt

1 Introduction

Alzheimer's disease(AD), a type of dementia, is probably the most common neurological illness. Normal cognition(NC), moderate cognitive impairment(MCI), and Alzheimer's disease(AD) are the three basic stages. It is evident that AD is a progressive neurodegenerative disease [6], with results demonstrating that the transition cycle can last up to 20 years or longer. As a result, many patients are unable to detect the early indications of AD, and by the time the symptoms arise, the situation has already worsened. Furthermore, the effects of AD are permanent, and current medical treatments can only slow the progression of symptoms rather than cure the disease. AD kills brain cells over time, resulting in cognitive damage which including memory loss, inability to make decisions, and trouble communicating, all of which can get a massive effect on a patient's daily

This work was supported in part by the Key Research and Development Program of Shaanxi under Grant 2022GY-062 and 2020GXLH-Y-023, in part by the National Natural Science Foundation of China under Grant 61772401, and in part by the Science and Technology on Communication Information Security Control Laboratory. (W. Jin and Y. Yin — Contribute equally to this work.).

life. This could have a massive influence on the patient's daily life. The related medical costs are unaffordable for most families, and the treatment procedure might take a long time. Mental illness affects more than 50 million individuals worldwide, according to Alzheimer's Disease International (ADI). This number is forecast to rise to 152 million people [1]. However, with appropriate treatment, many people can survive this disease.

Over the years, researchers have worked to develop better computer-aided systems as a way to help doctors make better early diagnoses of patients. Early prediction of AD is the task of classifying different stages of neurodegeneration, mainly NC, MCI and AD. With the rise of machine learning, there has been a lot of research on early diagnosis of AD based on machine learning; Liu et al. [10] proposed a multi-template feature representation AD diagnosis method based on multi-view learning and support vector machines, and Lizarraga et al. [12] provided a web platform for AD diagnosis using SVM. Earlier traditional methods required specific preprocessing steps to extract image features by manual features, which were not only time consuming but also relied on the experience and repeated attempts of the technique. Therefore, deep learning methods, which have emerged in recent years, have become a good means to extract features automatically and efficiently.

For the early diagnosis of AD, the most commonly used deep learning method over the years is convolutional neural network (CNN), Habes et al. [9] proposed the use of CNN to classify AD and NC. M. Kavitha et al. [8] investigated a modified U-net-like architecture to AD, NC and MCI with remarkable results. M. Nguyenet et al. proposed an RNN network based method to diagnose AD [14]. M. Hon and N. M. Khan applied transfer learning to the diagnosis of AD [3].

Over the previous two years, with the successful application of transformer in the field of vision, a wave of transformer work has erupted. Its powerful performance once eclipsed CNN as the standard framework, which was even considered to replace CNN. Transformer was first applied to visual images with good results by Dosovitskiy et al. [2]. While Vit requires large dataset pre-training to have better results and requires high computing power. Touvron et al. Furthermore, several researchers have attempted to apply transformer to medical images, but due to a shortage of medical data sets, the results are not as good as expected. Sarraf et al. [15] first successfully applied transformer to the early diagnosis of AD and achieved good results, but this was due to their large amount of slice data. Matsoukas et al. [13] combined self-supervised and Deit together and found that in the case of self-supervised pre-training and large dataset, the transformer outperforms CNN.

However, due to complex strcture, transformer can present various problems in practical applications. Liu et al. [11] did a lot of experimental study to figure out why it outperforms CNN, and they came up with a pure CNN-based ConvNeXt network that not only outperforms the Swin Transformer but also keeps CNN's simplicity and efficiency. As a result, we are attempting to apply ConvNeXt to the early diagnosis of AD.

The attention mechanism can emphasize the part of interest in the network by autonomously learning a set of parameters. Hu et al. [5] proposed a channel attention SE-Net that adaptively adjusts the feature response between channels by feature rescaling. Woo et al. [16] proposed CBAM, which solves the problem that SE-Net does not incorporate spatial attention. Later, Hou et al. [4] proposed a more efficient Coordinate Attention(CA) that can better utilize the position information on channel.

We propose a CA-ConvNeXt with the following main contributions:

- The Convenext, which is built on CNN and has outperformed Swin Transformer, is used in this paper as a new benchmark in CNN structure. For the first time, the ConvNeXt network was employed on the ADNI data set, and its performance was excellent, according to the experiments' results.
- Adding CA mechanism to the ConvNeXt network makes full use of the position information in the channel direction and effectively improves the network performance.

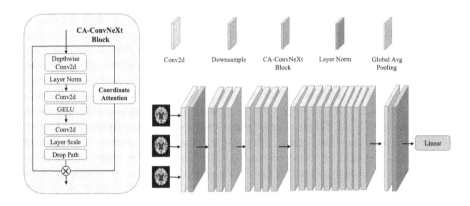

Fig. 1. Main framework of the proposed method.

2   Method

We adopt ConvNeXt as the main feature extraction framework and add CA as a module to the ConvNeXt block as a new line, and do a weighting with the normal ConvNeXt block as the output of the current block. Figure 1 shows our overall framework.

2.1   ConvNeXt

ConvNeXt's network architecture contains no structural or methodological innovations. It simply outperforms Swin Transformer in terms of performance and code complexity. This is mainly due to the effect of using Swin Transformer's strategy to train convolutional neural networks.

First, ConvNeXt takes ResNet50 as the benchmark model, Changing stage compute ratio, in the general ResNet50 network, the number of blocks stacked in four stages is (3,4,6,3), and the ratio is 1:1:2:1, but in Swin Transformer stage3 stacks a higher ratio of blocks. Therefore, ConvNeXt tries to modify the stacking number of ResNet50 from (3,4,6,3) to (3,3,9,3), and after this adjustment, the overall computation is about the same as Swin-T, and the accuracy rate is slightly improved. The original ResNet50 downsampling module is composed of a 7×7 convolutional layer with steps of 2 and a maximum pooling downsampling with a step of 2, and a width and height downsampling of four times. Then it was modified to Swin Transformer with a convolutional kernel of 4×4 with a step size of 4 to form a patchify, again with a width and height downsampling of four times, and no effect, but with a small improvement in accuracy.

Besides, ConvNeXt learns the ResNeXt group conv to increase performance. By grouping the channels of the input conv, group conv decreases computation. ConvNeXt is using each channel as a group, which becomes depthwise conv (dw conv). ConvNeXt adopts dw conv because it is quite comparable to Swin Transformer's local attention. To maintain flop consistency, the final ConvNeXt replaces the 3×3 conv in ResNet50 with a 3×3 dw conv and increases the base width of ResNet50 from 64 to 96. To emulate the transformer block's MLP module, ConvNeXt uses the inverted bottleneck from MobileNetV2, as the inverted bottleneck is very similar to the transformer block's MLP module, which also gives a small performance boost to ConvNeXt.

CNN networks after VGG use small convolutional kernels 3×3, while Swin-T uses a window size of 7×7, so to be consistent with Swin-T, ConvNeXt uses a large convolutional kernel of 7×7, which will increase Flops. to balance the computation, before this, ConvNeXt also moves the dw conv to the before this, to balance the computation, ConvNeXt also moves the dw conv to the top of the inverted bottleneck block. After this operation, the flops are about the same as before and the performance of the model unchanged.

Finally, some details were modified according to the Swin Transformer, replacing ReLU with GELU, using fewer activation functions and normalization layers, replacing the BN layer with an LN layer and adding a separate downsampling layer. Thus, based on these improvements, the final ConvNeXt is generated.

2.2   Coordinate Attention

Commonly used channel attention cannot save position information, and can only globally encode spatial information as channel information, and CA emerges to solve this problem. CA [4] is mainly divided into two parts: coordinate information embedding and CA generation. Figure 2 shows its structure.

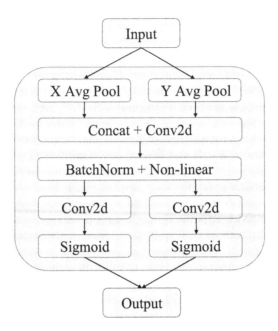

Fig. 2. Coordinate attention

To obtain the important position information of the **x** and **y** axes, the global pooling layer is first decomposed into two one-dimensional feature codes, one for the horizontal direction and one for the vertical direction, as detailed in the following equation:

$$m_c^h(h) = \frac{1}{W} \sum_{0 \le i < W} x_c(h, i) \tag{1}$$

$$m_c^w(w) = \frac{1}{H} \sum_{0 \le j < H} x_c(j, w) \tag{2}$$

This allows CA to capture accurate position information in a channel direction, and in order to have a more accurate position information representation for the above operation, the CA generation is designed.

$$\mathbf{K}^h = \sigma \left(F_h \left(\mathbf{f}^h \right) \right) \tag{3}$$

$$\mathbf{K}^w = \sigma \left(F_w \left(\mathbf{f}^w \right) \right) \tag{4}$$

The two feature maps generated in the previous step are F1 transformed with a 1×1 shared convolution to generate intermediate feature maps in the horizontal and vertical directions, and the module size is then controlled by the downsampling ratio. The intermediate feature map is split into two tensors and transform to the same number of channels as the input **x** with two 1×1 convolutions, respectively, to obtain $\mathbf{K}^h$ and $\mathbf{K}^w$, which are finally expanded to obtain the final CA module output $\mathbf{n}$.

$$n_c(i,j) = x_c(i,j) \times K_c^h(i) \times K_c^w(j) \tag{5}$$

3 Experiments and Results

3.1 Data Pretreatment

For the dataset we used the AD Neuroimaging Initiative (ADNI) database [7]. The downloaded 2032 samples were in NII format, which cannot be directly input into a two-dimensional network and have an obscure structure, so we pre-processed them. First, they were AC-PC corrected using the icbm152 template, and then linearly aligned and cranially separated using FSL. After preprocessing, the pathological structure of the brain map was more clearly defined. However, since it is still three-dimensional, we obtained coronal slices by fixing one of the axes. One NII subject can be sliced into 181 pieces, and we selected the middle-most one as a representative. This gave us a total of 2032 PNG images, including 1100 MCI, 321 AD and 611 NC.

3.2 Experimental Details

Our experiments were conducted on a dell workstation configured with 64 G of RAM, 3090 with 24 g of video memory, 24cores Intel(R) Xeon(R) Gold 6248R CPU, python version 3.8, and cuda 11.0, Ubuntu 18.04.

We divided ADNI datasets into training and validation set with 4:1 ratio. Baseline control experiments use ResNet50 and Swin Transformer as a way to verify the advantages of the ConvNeXt network on the ADNI dataset. In the ablation experiments, we choose to add CA to the framework of ConvNeXt and not to add CA, respectively, to derive the performance improvement of CA on the network.

In terms of experimental parameters, experiments use the imagenet pre-training weights officially released by the respective models. Batchsize is set to 32, optimizer is selected AdamW, learning rate is $5e^{-4}$, decay weight is $5e^{-2}$, loss function is selected cross-entropy loss function. Swin Transformer was fine-tuned for 90 epochs and the rest of the experiments were fine-tuned for 50 epochs, each experiment was done 5 times and averaged, and each experiment is done 5 times to take the average. We choose accuracy as the main evaluation index.

3.3 Experimental Result

According to the Table 1, the ConvNeXt network outperforms resnet50 and Swin Transformer on the ADNI dataset with only 2032 images, and its performance is good, 1.2% times better than resnet50 and 2.0 times better than Swin Transformer. Furthermore, adding CA improves the performance of ConvNeXt by

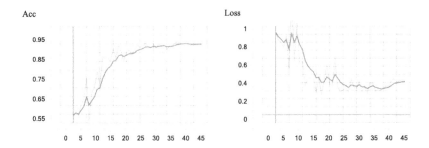

Fig. 3. Accuracy and loss in validation set of CA-ConvNeXt

Table 1. Accuracy on ADNI dataset

Dataset	Mothed	Accuracy
ADNI	ResNet50	93.8%
ADNI	Swin Transformer	94.3%
ADNI	ConvNeXt	95.3%
ADNI	CA-ConvNeXt	96.0%

0.7%, and the accuracy reaches 96%. We can see from the Fig. 3 that the CA-ConvNeXt our proposed, final losses have all converged, and the accuracy can no longer rise. Its demonstrating the effectiveness of coordinating attention on ConvNeXt.

4   Conclusions

In this paper, we proposed CA-ConvNeXt network is experimentally proven to be effective in classifying the three categories of AD, MCI, and NC on the publicly available ADNI dataset. This is also the first application of ConvNeXt network on AD early diagnosis classification. Based on the experiments we can conclude that ConvNeXt is able to have better performance than Resnet50 and Swin Transformer on ADNI, and the experimental results meet the expectation, and the performance is further improved with the addition of CA. As can be observed, our proposed network has a high level of performance.

References

1. Association, A., et al.: 2018 Alzheimer's disease facts and figures. Alzheimer's & Dementia **14**(3), 367–429 (2018)
2. Dosovitskiy, A., et al.: An image is worth 16x16 words: transformers for image recognition at scale. arXiv preprint arXiv:2010.11929 (2020)
3. Hon, M., Khan, N.M.: Towards Alzheimer's disease classification through transfer learning. In: 2017 IEEE International conference on bioinformatics and biomedicine (BIBM), pp. 1166–1169. IEEE (2017)

4. Hou, Q., Zhou, D., Feng, J.: Coordinate attention for efficient mobile network design. In: Proceedings of the IEEE/CVF Conference on Computer Vision and Pattern Recognition, pp. 13713–13722 (2021)
5. Hu, J., Shen, L., Sun, G.: Squeeze-and-excitation networks. In: Proceedings of the IEEE Conference on Computer Vision and Pattern Recognition, pp. 7132–7141 (2018)
6. Islam, J., Zhang, Y.: Brain MRI analysis for Alzheimer's disease diagnosis using an ensemble system of deep convolutional neural networks. Brain Informatics **5**(2), 1–14 (2018)
7. Jack, Jr, C.R., et al.: The Alzheimer's disease neuroimaging initiative (ADNI): MRI methods. J. Magnet. Resonan. Imaging: Off. J. Int. Soc. Magnet. Resonan. Med. **27**(4), 685–691 (2008)
8. Kavitha, M., Yudistira, N., Kurita, T.: Multi instance learning via deep CNN for multi-class recognition of Alzheimer's disease. In: 2019 IEEE 11th International Workshop on Computational Intelligence and Applications (IWCIA), pp. 89–94. IEEE (2019)
9. Li, H., Habes, M., Wolk, D.A., Fan, Y., Initiative, A.D.N., et al.: A deep learning model for early prediction of Alzheimer's disease dementia based on hippocampal magnetic resonance imaging data. Alzheimer's & Dementia **15**(8), 1059–1070 (2019)
10. Liu, F., Shen, C.: Learning deep convolutional features for MRI based Alzheimer's disease classification. arXiv preprint arXiv:1404.3366 (2014)
11. Liu, Z., Mao, H., Wu, C.Y., Feichtenhofer, C., Darrell, T., Xie, S.: A convnet for the 2020s. arXiv preprint arXiv:2201.03545 (2022)
12. Lizarraga, G., Cabrerizo, M., Duara, R., Rojas, N., Adjouadi, M., Loewenstein, D.: A web platform for data acquisition and analysis for Alzheimer's disease. In: SoutheastCon 2016, pp. 1–5. IEEE (2016)
13. Matsoukas, C., Haslum, J.F., Söderberg, M., Smith, K.: Is it time to replace CNNs with transformers for medical images? arXiv preprint arXiv:2108.09038 (2021)
14. Nguyen, M., Sun, N., Alexander, D.C., Feng, J., Yeo, B.T.: Modeling Alzheimer's disease progression using deep recurrent neural networks. In: 2018 International Workshop on Pattern Recognition in Neuroimaging (PRNI), pp. 1–4. IEEE (2018)
15. Sarraf, S., et al.: Ovitad: optimized vision transformer to predict various stages of Alzheimer's disease using resting-state FMRI and structural MRI data. bioRxiv (2021)
16. Woo, S., Park, J., Lee, J.Y., Kweon, I.S.: CBAM: Convolutional block attention module. In: Proceedings of the European Conference on Computer Vision (ECCV), pp. 3–19 (2018)

Data Augmentation Method on Pine Wilt Disease Recognition

Weibin Li[1,2], Bingzhen An[1,2(✉)], and Yuhui Kong[1,2]

[1] School of Artificial Intelligence, Xidian University, Xi'an 710075, China
weibinli@xidian.edu.cn, abz24423@163.com
[2] Beidou Space-Time Intelligence Research Center, Xidian University,
Xi'an 710075, China

Abstract. In recent years, deep learning has made a breakthrough in image recognition. However, it often requires a large amount of label data as the sample set. In most practical applications, the neural network is prone to over-fitting or weak generalization due to the lack of annotation data. This phenomenon is especially obvious in a small-scale data set. To solve this problem, pine wilt disease data is used as an example to adopt mirroring, flipping, adding noise, rotating, scaling, and other augmentation methods to enhance the amount of the image sets. It can not only increase sample diversity but also make the network more stable for training. In this paper, the effects of different amplification methods and training samples size on the Faster R-CNN and YOLOv3 models are tested, and its results show that scaling has the greatest impact on the two models for the reason that the two models are both sensitive to the size of sample images. The accuracy of Faster R-CNN starts to decline when the number of training sets is expanded to 60% of the new training samples, the accuracy of YOLOv3 starts to decline when the number of training sets is expanded to 75%.

Keywords: Data augmentation · Image recognition · Small-scale data sets · Pine wilt disease

1 Introduction

Recently, Pattern Recognition System based on CNN(Convolutional Neural Network) has made breakthrough advances in many tasks. Deep Learning often encounters over-fitting problems although it has shown outstanding performance in many aspects. The problems of over-fitting are mainly caused by three reasons: complex models, data noise, and limited training data. Most neural networks require a large number of parameters and sample data for training to

Supported by the organization the Key R & D projects in Shaanxi Province (No. 2021GY-102); National Natural Science Foundation of China No. 6217020827), the Key R & D projects in Xi'an (21RGZN0012), the Key R & D projects in Xianyang (2021ZDYF-GY-0031).

make these parameters work correctly. The data set is the basis of training deep learning models. The quantity, diversity, quality, and imbalance of the training data significantly affect the robustness and generalization of the deep learning model [1]. Data sources mainly include self-established datasets and existing public datasets. Creating a data set with enough samples is often a tough and time-consuming task. Particularly, some images are hard to obtain, such as agricultural and forestry pests and diseases, or medical images. Therefore, data augmentation is an effective way to artificially increase the training data, when the number of samples is insufficient or imbalanced.

Pine is one of the important tree species in China's forest resources, accounting for 70% of the artificial forest area [2]. However, in recent years, a large number of pine resources have been attacked by the invasive pest pine wilt disease, which has seriously endangered the utilization and sustainable development of forest resources. The disease mainly affects pine tree species and has two main routes of transmission: natural transmission (Monochamus alternatus) and human transmission [3,4]. Due to the difference in chlorophyll and water content between healthy pine trees and diseased pine trees, resin secretion, growth vigor, and needle color are important indicators for judging pine wilt disease.

Pine trees infected with pine wilt disease generally die especially in summer and autumn. The disease goes through three distinct stages of infection. In terms of the color of needles, dark green needles of healthy pine trees become yellow in the mildly damaged stage, yellow-brown in the moderately damaged stage, and red-brown in the severely damaged stage [5–7]. A pine tree with pine wilt disease can be identified by checking whether the pine tree has reddish brown or yellowish brown needles or the whole pine tree has withered, withered and drooped needles but does not fall off. Due to the insufficiency of available UAV images, the differences in background, illumination, and target size, as well as the differences in the number of samples at different stages of infection, lead to the imbalance in samples size. Due to the insufficiency of available UAV images, the differences in background, illumination, and target size, as well as the differences in the number of samples at different stages of infection, lead to the imbalance in samples size.

Data augmentation is an essential method to improve the training effect of CNN. There are a series of augmentation ways, including rotation, flip, scaling, translation, adding noise, and so on. Through the enhancement of training data, the network with stronger generalization ability can better adapt to the application scene. Data enhancement has been widely used in deep learning of plant pest images. For example, Deng [8] et al. enhanced the diseased pine tree samples through rotation, flipping, and comparison, and the AP (Average Precision) value of the model increased from 72.5% to 80.2%. Qin [9] et al. adopted multi-scale segmentation to improve the number and diversity of samples. However, few researchers pay attention to which enhancement strategy can effectively improve the accuracy of the model. Moreover, too many enhancement samples may lead to inadequate fitting. Therefore, it is necessary to select the optimal number of training samples for the enhanced data set.

This paper studies the impact of different data enhancement methods on the accuracy of the Faster R-CNN and YOLO models. By testing the influence of different training samples size on model results, the optimal training data set size is found.

2   Augmentations

Traditional data enhancement strategies are based on camera models and imaging principles. By using different enhancement methods, it can simulate the effects of the lens, focal length, and aperture on pictures in real scenes. For example, a fisheye lens will cause image deformation, but can obtain a wider scene in a smaller scene; Focal length will blur the background and affect the resolution of the picture; The aperture can affect the brightness and chroma of images. The fisheye effect can simulate the image shot by a fisheye lens. Scaling can simulate different focal length sizes and different shooting distances; Color transformation can simulate images under different aperture sizes and lighting; Translation and rotation can simulate different perspectives; Gaussian noise and salt-pepper noise can simulate the noise caused by camera sensors. The eight data enhancements used in this paper all rely on the UAV camera model, imaging principles, and changes in the external environment. Each augmentation technique is as follows(see Fig. 1) [10, 11]:

Flips: flip horizontally and vertically for each image in the training set.

Rotation: rotate each image in the training set randomly clockwise at the angle of from 0°to 360°;

Scaling: the training set image is linearly enlarged or reduced. The part of the enlarged image that exceeds the original image size needs to be cropped, and the part between the reduced image boundary and the original image is filled with a black background.

Color transform: modify image brightness, contrast, and saturation.

Nonlinear scaling: the training set images are enlarged or reduced according to different aspect ratios. That is, the aspect ratio of the scaling image is different from the original image.

Translation: each image in the training set is shifted 50 pixels along the horizontal axis and filled in with a black background.

Adding noise: noise refers to the random superposition of some isolated pixels or pixel blocks on the original image which can cause strong visual effects, to disrupt the observable information of the image. Gaussian noise and salt & pepper noise are respectively added to the images of the training set, and salt & pepper noise is distributed in each image as random white or black pixels.

Fisheye effect: simulate the fisheye lens effect on the training set.

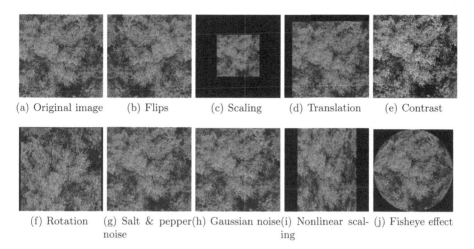

(a) Original image   (b) Flips   (c) Scaling   (d) Translation   (e) Contrast

(f) Rotation   (g) Salt & pepper (h) Gaussian noise (i) Nonlinear scal- (j) Fisheye effect
noise   ing

Fig. 1. Eight data augmentation methods

3 Materials and Methods

The UAV remote sensing image was collected by a visible-light camera mounted on Multi-rotor light UAV. The field plot is a pine wilt disease endemic area located in Xianhe Town, Hanbin District, Ankang City, Shaanxi Province, and its area is 0.0775 square kilometers. The dead trees of pine wilt disease are mainly divided into three types: yellow-brown needles moderately dead trees, red-brown needles severely dead trees, and white needles dead trees. The size of pine wilt disease images is 4000 * 3000. The full-sized images are cropped to 150 sub-images about 500 * 500 pixels. After cropping, sub-images are filtered to be used as the data set. We select 85 sub-images as the original data set for each augmentation technique. Among these samples, 60% are used for the training set, 20% for the validation set, and 20% for the testing set. Before training the models, we use eight augmentation strategies to generate eight new training sets. Each new training set consists of the original training sub-images and the new training sub-images enhanced by one of the above techniques. The annotation file of each sub-image is also transformed synchronously.

With the development of deep learning, object detection based on deep learning has been widely used because of its excellent performance. Faster R-CNN and YOLOv3 are the most classical algorithms in the field of object detection. As a classical two-stage model, Faster R-CNN mainly generates a series of candidate regions through the method of region proposal and then performs classification and position regression on extracted features of candidate regions, which is better in detection accuracy. YOLOv3 is a classic one-stage model based on regression, which directly extracts features from the network to predict the classification and position of objects. And its detection speed is fast. Different target sizes and the unbalanced number of pine wilt disease samples at different stages will lead to distortion or over-fitting in the identification process. In addition, the

Faster R-CNN and YOLOv3 models are easy to be ignored for small targets due to their low resolution and few features when detecting infected pine images. Therefore, more training samples are needed to learn data features and achieve higher accuracy. Data augmentation can make the model learn more invariance features through geometric transformation, thus improving the robustness of the models.

With the increase of the training data set, the detection performance of the model is improved gradually. In addition, the model may also go from over-fitting to under-fitting when increased to a certain extent. Therefore, To further analyze the impact of image data set size on the model and find the inflection point of different data-set sizes on model performance [12], we select 150 samples divided into a training set, validation set, and test set according to 6:2:2. The new data set is made with original training data and augmented data generated by the above augmentation techniques, which reach 1183 data. We randomly select 182, 364, 546, 728, 910, and 1183 data among them to form a dataset and train the Faster R-CNN and YOLOV3 models to obtain the corresponding AP curve. AP is the metric to measure the performance of object detectors like Faster R-CNN and YOLOV3. It is the average of the maximum precision at different recall values.

Before evaluating the model performance, for each augmentation method, we used the cross entropy(CE) function to compare the similarity between each image of orignal training set, D and corresponding image of post-augmented training set, D'. CE is a measure of the difference between two images. In this paper, the cross entropy mean value between D and D 'is used to quantify the augmentation

$$CE(p,q) = \sum p(i) \times \ln \frac{p(i)}{q(i)} + \sum q(i) \times \ln \frac{q(i)}{p(i)} \tag{1}$$

4   Results

The experimental operating platform is Ubuntu 20.04, Intel(R) Core(TM) i9-10900K CPU @ 3.70 GHz, NVIDIA Corporation Device 2208, based on Pytorch as a deep learning framework. We use eight augmented training sets to train Faster R-CNN and YOLOV3 networks. To evaluate the impact of different data augmentation methods and different numbers of training data sets on the identification of pine wilt diseased trees, the index AP is used to evaluate model performance. The increased range is userd to compare AP values before and after augmentation. The mean CE between the each augmented training set and the original data set is userd to analyzed the effect of each augmentation on the training result. It can be seen from Table 1 that the scaling augmentation method has the highest AP value and CE value for the two models. a higher cross entropy means that the image augmented by scale have the more abundant and varied images information, which enhancing the diversity of the samples.

Table 1. Influence of traditional image data augmentation techniques on Faster R-CNN and YOLOV3 models.

Augmentation type	CE	Faster R-CNN		YOLOV3	
		AP	Increase range	AP	Increase range
Original image		0.573	0	0.380	0
Saturation	0.0005	0.576	0.003	0.391	0.011
Flip	0.0006	0.721	0.148	0.504	0.124
Gaussian noise	0.0222	0.668	0.095	0.386	0.006
Salt & pepper noise	0.0395	0.720	0.147	0.416	0.036
Rotation	0.1615	0.630	0.057	0.498	0.118
Translation	0.1947	0.648	0.075	0.426	0.046
Contrast	0.2011	0.688	0.115	0.487	0.107
Brightness	0.2244	0.786	0.213	0.469	0.089
Fisheye effect	0.2444	0.777	0.204	0.410	0.03
Nonlinear scaling	0.3663	0.798	0.225	0.423	0.043
Scaling	0.6971	0.894	0.321	0.642	0.262

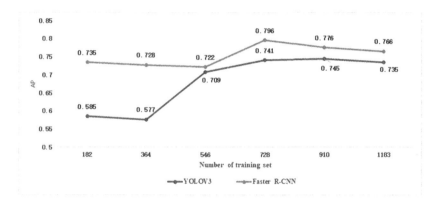

Fig. 2. Impacts of the growing number of datasets on the performance of YOLO3 and Faster R-CNN.

As can be seen from (see Fig. 2), the size of the training data set has a great influence on the detection capability of the models. With the increase in training set size, the detection performance of the model is improved gradually. However, when the data set grows to 60% of the new training samples, AP arrives at the maximum value and then begins to decline for the Faster R-CNN network. And for the YOLOV3 network, AP arrives at the maximum value when the data set increases to 75% of the new training samples.

5   Discussion and Conclusion

Traditional data augmentation techniques rely on rotation, translation, and other methods to fine-tune the existing data set and generate a large number of data sets slightly different from the original data set for model training. This technique can not only increase the number of training samples but also improve the robustness and the generalization ability of the model. In this paper, the optimal augmentation techniques and the optimal number of training samples for the identification of pine wilt disease were studied.

Looking at the results from Table 1, We can see that the cross entropy is proportional to the AP value of the Faster R-CNN model, in addition to Gaussian noise, Salt & pepper noise and flip. In other word, the new training set that has cross entropy about 0.6971-0.2444 (Scaling, Nonlinear scaling, Fisheye effect, Brightness) has AP value of 0.894-0.786. On the contrary, the cross entropy in 0.2011-0.1615 (Contrast, Translation, Rotation) corresponds to AP in 0.688-0.630. We notice that the Salt & pepper noise, Gaussian noise and flip has the low cross entropy about 0.0395, 0.0222 and 0.0006, but has the relatively high AP value about 0.720, 0.668 and 0.721. The same augmentation method has different gains for different networks, so it is necessary to find suitable augmentation strategies according to different network models.

Although the data augmentation technique solves the problem of insufficient samples in the data set, poor data quality and insufficient sample diversity tend to cause overfitting, which affects the classification performance of the deep learning algorithm. In recent years, with the rapid development and wide application of deep learning, data augmentation through Generative Adversarial Networks (GAN) [13] has become a common method at the present stage. It is a generative model proposed by Goodfellow et al. in 2014 and consisted of a generative network and a discriminant network. GAN can increase the number of training set samples, reduce overfitting and improve the recognition effect [14–16]. Jain et al. [17] used a Conditional Generative Adversarial Network (CGAN) to generate synthetic images of tomato leaves, to improve the detection accuracy of tomato diseases. However, it needs a large amount of training data as support, and when the model takes a long time to train, it may appear instability and other problems. So the next step, we will compare the traditional data augmentation method with the GAN augmentation method, and select the optimal augmentation technology and the number of training samples.

The quality of the image recognition algorithm is related to the quality and quantity of the dataset. However, due to the limitation of time cost and financial cost, the image data set obtained is insufficient, its quality is poor, and the sample distribution is unbalanced. This makes the task of image recognition difficult. To solve the above problems and reduce the over-fitting probability, this paper adopts image data augmentation technology to increase the number of training samples of the model. The main work of this paper is to introduce the existing traditional image data augmentation techniques and find the optimal augmentation method and the optimal data set size suitable for model training, which provides research ideas for researchers to optimize the dataset and improve the accuracy of the model by using the corresponding data augmentation method.

References

1. Feng, X., Shen, Y., Wang, D.: Overview of the development of image-based data enhancement methods. Comput. Sci. Appli. **11**, 370 (2021)
2. Fang, X.: Research on the application practice of unmanned aerial vehicle monitoring pine wilt disease. Econ. Tech. Cooperation Inf. (5), 1 (2021)
3. Jiang, M., et al.: The distribution, harm, and control countermeasures of pine wilt disease. Zhejiang Forest. Sci. Technol. **38**(6), 9 (2018)
4. Hunt, D.: Pine wilt disease: a worldwide threat to forest ecosystems. Nematology **11**(2), 315–316 (2009)
5. Zhang, S., et al.: Study on spectral characteristics and estimation model of masson pine damaged by pine wood nematode. Spectro. Spectral Anal. **39**(3), 8 (2019)
6. Kim, S.R., et al.: Hyperspectral analysis of pine wilt disease to determine an optimal detection index. Forests **9**(3), 115 (2018)
7. Vollenweider, P., Günthardt-Goerg, M.S.: Diagnosis of abiotic and biotic stress factors using the visible symptoms in foliage. Environ. Pollut. **140**(3), 562–571 (2006)
8. Deng, X., Tong, Z., Lan, Y., Huang, Z.: Detection and location of dead trees with pine wilt disease based on deep learning and uav remote sensing. AgriEngineering **2**(2), 294–307 (2020)
9. Qin, J., Wang, B., Wu, Y., Lu, Q., Zhu, H.: Identifying pine wood nematode disease using uav images and deep learning algorithms. Remote Sensing **13**(2), 162 (2021)
10. Hussain, Z., Gimenez, F., Yi, D., Rubin, D.: Differential data augmentation techniques for medical imaging classification tasks. In: AMIA Annual Symposium Proceedings, vol. 2017, p. 979. American Medical Informatics Association (2017)
11. Shorten, C., Khoshgoftaar, T.M.: A survey on image data augmentation for deep learning. J. Big Data **6**(1), 1–48 (2019)
12. Luo, Z., Yu, H., Zhang, Y.: Pine cone detection using boundary equilibrium generative adversarial networks and improved yolov3 model. Sensors **20**(16), 4430 (2020)
13. Goodfellow, I., et al.: Generative adversarial nets. In: Advances in neural Information Processing Systems, vol. 27 (2014)
14. Zhao, Y., et al.: Plant disease detection using generated leaves based on doublegan. IEEE/ACM Trans. Comput. Biol. Bioinf. **19**(3), 1817–1826 (2022). https://doi.org/10.1109/TCBB.2021.3056683
15. Cao, K., Wu, F., Qian, X., Yang, Z.: Gan-based uav aerial image reconstruction. Electron Technol. **32**(8), 5 (2019)
16. Hu, G., et al.: Detection of diseased pine trees in unmanned aerial vehicle images by using deep convolutional neural networks. In: Geocarto International, pp. 1–20 (2020)
17. Jain, S., Gour, M.: Tomato plant disease detection using transfer learning with c-gan synthetic images. Comput. Electron. Agric. **187**(2021), 106279 (2021)

Correction to: Weakly Supervised Whole Cardiac Segmentation via Attentional CNN

Erlei Zhang, Minghui Sima, Jun Wang, Jinye Peng, and Jinglei Li

Correction to:
Chapter "Weakly Supervised Whole Cardiac Segmentation
via Attentional CNN" in: Z. Shi et al. (Eds.):
Intelligence Science IV, **IFIP AICT 659,**
https://doi.org/10.1007/978-3-031-14903-0_9

In the originally published version of chapter 9, by error, the author Jinye Peng had been assigned affiliation no. "3" instead of "2". This has been corrected.

The updated original version of this chapter can be found at
https://doi.org/10.1007/978-3-031-14903-0_9

Author Index

Printed in the United States
by Baker & Taylor Publisher Services